COMPARING

The Ptolemaic and Seleucid empires are usually studied separately, or else included in broader examinations of the Hellenistic world. This book provides a systematic comparison of the roles of local elites and local populations in the construction, negotiation, and adaptation of political, economic, military, and ideological power within these states in formation. The two states, conceived as multiethnic empires, are sufficiently similar to make comparisons valid, while the process of comparison highlights and better explains differences. Regions that were successively incorporated into the Ptolemaic and the Seleucid state receive particular attention and are understood within the broader picture of the ruling strategies of both empires. The book focuses on forms of communication through coins, inscriptions, and visual culture; settlement policies and the relationship between local and immigrant populations; and the forms of collaboration with and resistance of local elites against immigrant populations and government institutions.

CHRISTELLE FISCHER-BOVET is Associate Professor in the Departments of Classics and History at the University of Southern California. She specializes in the social and cultural history of the Eastern Mediterranean from Alexander to the Romans, with a particular interest in Greco-Roman Egypt. Her book *Army and Society in Ptolemaic Egypt* (Cambridge, 2014) combines documentary evidence with social theory to examine the role of the army in Hellenistic Egypt.

SITTA VON REDEN is Professor of Ancient History at the University of Freiburg. She is a specialist in ancient Greek economic history, and her books include *Money in Ptolemaic Egypt: From the Macedonian Conquest to the End of the Third Century* BC (Cambridge, 2007) and *Money in Classical Antiquity* (Cambridge, 2010). In 2017 she won an Advanced Grant of the European Research Council for the Project 'Beyond the Silk Road: Exchange, Economic Development and Inter-Imperial Relationships in the Afro-Eurasian World Region (300 BCE–300 CE)'.

COMPARING THE PTOLEMAIC AND SELEUCID EMPIRES

Integration, Communication, and Resistance

EDITED BY

CHRISTELLE FISCHER-BOVET
University of Southern California

SITTA VON REDEN
University of Freiburg

CAMBRIDGE
UNIVERSITY PRESS

Shaftesbury Road, Cambridge CB2 8EA, United Kingdom

One Liberty Plaza, 20th Floor, New York, NY 10006, USA

477 Williamstown Road, Port Melbourne, VIC 3207, Australia

314–321, 3rd Floor, Plot 3, Splendor Forum, Jasola District Centre, New Delhi – 110025, India

103 Penang Road, #05–06/07, Visioncrest Commercial, Singapore 238467

Cambridge University Press is part of Cambridge University Press & Assessment, a department of the University of Cambridge.

We share the University's mission to contribute to society through the pursuit of education, learning and research at the highest international levels of excellence.

www.cambridge.org
Information on this title: www.cambridge.org/9781108749527

DOI: 10.1017/9781108782890

© Cambridge University Press & Assessment 2021

This publication is in copyright. Subject to statutory exception and to the provisions of relevant collective licensing agreements, no reproduction of any part may take place without the written permission of Cambridge University Press & Assessment.

First published 2021
First paperback edition 2023

A catalogue record for this publication is available from the British Library

Library of Congress Cataloging-in-Publication data
NAMES: Fischer-Bovet, Christelle, 1977– editor. | Reden, Sitta von, editor.
TITLE: Comparing the Ptolemaic and Seleucid empires : integration, communication, and resistance / edited by Christelle Fischer-Bovet, University of Southern California, and Sitta von Reden, Albert-Ludwigs-Universität Freiburg, Germany.
DESCRIPTION: Cambridge, United Kingdom ; New York : Cambridge University Press, 2021. | Includes bibliographical references and index.
IDENTIFIERS: LCCN 2021029017 | ISBN 9781108479257 (hardback) | ISBN 9781108749527 (paperback) | ISBN 9781108782890 (ebook)
SUBJECTS: LCSH: Egypt – History – 32–30 B.C. | Ptolemaic dynasty, 305 B.C.-30 B.C. | Seleucids – History. | BISAC: HISTORY / Ancient / General | HISTORY / Ancient / General
CLASSIFICATION: LCC DT92 .C66 2021 | DDC 932/.021–dc23
LC record available at https://lccn.loc.gov/2021029017

ISBN   978-1-108-47925-7   Hardback
ISBN   978-1-108-74952-7   Paperback

Cambridge University Press & Assessment has no responsibility for the persistence or accuracy of URLs for external or third-party internet websites referred to in this publication and does not guarantee that any content on such websites is, or will remain, accurate or appropriate.

Contents

List of Contributors	*page* vii
Preface	xiii
Note on Abbreviations	xiv
Introduction Christelle Fischer-Bovet and Sitta von Reden	1
PART I CITIES, SETTLEMENT AND INTEGRATION	15

1 Imperial *metropoleis* and Foundation Myths: Ptolemaic and Seleucid Capitals Compared 17
    1A Alexandria 18
    1B Seleucid Royal Cities 33
    Sitta von Reden and Rolf Strootman

2 Reassessing Hellenistic Settlement Policies: The Seleucid Far East, Ptolemaic Red Sea Basin and Egypt 48
    2A Reassessing Settlement Policies in the Hellenistic Far East 49
    2B Reassessing Ptolemaic Settlement Policies: Another Look at the *poleis* 64
    Rachel Mairs and Christelle Fischer-Bovet

3 The Integration of Indigenous Elites and the Development of *poleis* in the Ptolemaic and Seleucid Empires 86
    Philippe Clancier and Gilles Gorre

4 Contextualizing a Ptolemaic Solution: The Institution of the Ethnic *politeuma* 106
    Patrick Sänger

PART II COMMUNICATION AND EXCHANGE — 127

5 Imperial and Indigenous Temporalities in the Ptolemaic
   and Seleucid Dynasties: A Comparison of Times — 129
   5A The Seleucid Horizon and Indigenous Elites — 129
   5B Indigenous Elites and Ptolemaic Dynastic Time — 146
   Paul Kosmin and Ian Moyer

6 The Visual Representation of Ptolemaic and Seleucid Kings:
   A Comparative Approach to Portrait Concepts — 164
   Ralf von den Hoff

7 Monetary Policies, Coin Production, and Currency Supply
   in the Seleucid and Ptolemaic Empires — 191
   7A The Seleucid Empire — 192
   7B The Ptolemaic Empire — 210
   Panagiotis P. Iossif and Catharine C. Lorber

PART III COLLABORATION, CRISIS, AND RESISTANCE — 231

8 Legitimizing the Foreign King in the Ptolemaic
   and Seleucid Empires: The Role of Local Elites and Priests — 233
   8A The Egyptian Priests and the Ptolemaic King — 235
   8B The Babylonian Priests and the Seleucid King — 246
   Stefan Pfeiffer and Hilmar Klinkott

9 Antiochus III, Ptolemy IV, and Local Elites: Deal-Making
   Politics at Its Peak — 262
   9A The Greek Elites and the Crisis of the Ptolemaic Empire — 264
   9B The Greek Elites Before and During the Seleucid-Roman War — 284
   Boris Dreyer and François Gerardin

10 Regional Revolts in the Seleucid and Ptolemaic Empires — 301
   Sylvie Honigman and Anne-Emmanuelle Veïsse

Bibliography — 329
Index — 386

Contributors

PHILIPPE CLANCIER is HDR Lecturer at the Pantheon-Sorbonne University. His doctoral dissertation focuses on Babylonian libraries during the Hellenistic and Parthian periods. He is now working on the political history of Babylon during these periods as well as on the history of the Middle Euphrates in the Middle and Neo-Assyrian periods. He is also one of the epigraphists of the archaeological mission at Kunara in Iraqi Kurdistan.

BORIS DREYER is Professor of Ancient History at the University of Erlangen-Nuremberg. His doctoral dissertation focuses on the democracy of Athens in late Classical and Hellenistic periods, while his Habilitation explores the development of the internal system of the Roman Republic in the early second century BC. He was fellow at the Center for Hellenic Studies in Washington, DC, and Fellow at the Institute for Advanced Study. He is also cooperating with several Turkish excavations (Magnesia, Metropolis, Nikaia) and specializes in epigraphy, Roman administration, especially in Asia Minor, and on the Germanic–Roman frontier conflicts.

CHRISTELLE FISCHER-BOVET is Associate Professor of Classics and History at the University of Southern California. She specializes in the social and cultural history of the eastern Mediterranean from Alexander the Great to the Romans, with a special interest in Greco-Roman Egypt. Her book *Army and Society in Ptolemaic Egypt* (2014) combines documentary evidence with social theory to examine the role of the army in Hellenistic Egypt. She has also published several articles exploring state formation and ethnic interaction, for instance "Social Unrest and Ethnic Coexistence in Ptolemaic Egypt and the Seleucid Empire" (*Past and Present* 229, 2015).

FRANÇOIS GERARDIN is a postdoctoral assistant at the University of Basel. His first book, which comes out of his doctoral dissertation, is currently under review. In it, he uses ancient documents (mostly papyri and inscriptions) to elucidate the importance of cities for state formation in Egypt and western Asia in the Hellenistic period.

GILLES GORRE is Lecturer at the University of Rennes and specializes in the relationship between temples and the Hellenistic political authority. His work examines the integration of local elites in the Hellenistic states both through the strategies adopted by local elites towards the Crown and through the royal policy put in place to ensure control of the territory. He is the author of *Les relations du clergé égyptien et des Lagides*, Studia Hellenistica 45 (2009).

SYLVIE HONIGMAN is Professor of Ancient History at Tel Aviv University. She is the author of *Tales of High Priests and Taxes: The Books of the Maccabees and the Judean Rebellion Against Antiochus IV* (2014) and of several articles on the Maccabean revolt.

PANAGIOTIS P. IOSSIF is Professor of Ancient and Medieval Numismatics at the Radboud University, Nijmegen, and Deputy Director of the Belgian School of Archaeology at Athens. His research focuses on Hellenistic numismatics, economy and statistical models using hoard evidence and excavation finds, fields in which he has extensively published. He is also interested in new approaches of coin iconography and recently co-edited three volumes: *TYPOI. Greek and Roman Coins Seen through Their Images. Noble Issuers, Humble Users* (2018), *Greek Iconographies*, Pharos 26.1 (2018) and *Charon's Obol: the end of a myth?*, JAN 9 (2019).

HILMAR KLINKOTT is Professor of Ancient History at the University of Kiel. His main fields of research are the history and administration of the Achaemenid, Ptolemaic and Seleucid empires, as well as the late Roman Republic. His publications include *Der Satrap, ein achaimenidischer Amtsträger* (2002) and several articles, such as "Alexandria – Polis ohne Metoiken? Möglichkeiten sozialer Mobilität bei alexandrinischen Politen," in L.-M. Günther, *Migration und Bürgerrecht in der hellenistischen Welt* (2012); "Parther – Pest – Pandora-Mythos: Katastrophen und ihre Bedeutung in der Regierungszeit Marc Aurels," in V. Grieb, *Marc Aurel – Wege zu seiner Herrschaft* (2017), and with N. Kramer "Zwischen Assur und Athen. Altorientalisches in den Historien Herodots," *SpielRäume der Antike* 4 (2017).

PAUL J. KOSMIN is Philip J. King Professor of Ancient History at Harvard University. He is the author of *The Land of the Elephant Kings: Space,*

Territory and Ideology in the Seleucid Empire (2014) and *Time and Its Adversaries in the Seleucid Empire* (2018) and co-editor (with Andrea Berlin) of *Spear-Won Land: Sardis from the King's Peace to the Peace of Apamea* (2019) and *The Middle Maccabees: Archaeology, History, and the Rise of the Hasmonean Kingdom* (2021). His work examines, broadly, the relationship between ancient empires and systems of knowledge and practice, and the interaction between the Greek world and its Near Eastern neighbors.

CATHARINE C. LORBER is an independent scholar specializing in ancient numismatics, particularly the coinages of the Seleucid and Ptolemaic dynasties. Her interests also include political and economic history, iconography, and ruler cult. She is a coauthor of the standard reference on Seleucid coinage, *Seleucid Coins: A Comprehensive Catalogue* (Part I 2002, Part II 2008). She has written a similar work on Ptolemaic coinage. *Coinage of the Ptolemaic Empire*, Part I: *Ptolemy I through Ptolemy IV* appeared in 2018. Part II, covering the rest of the dynasty, is in press.

RACHEL MAIRS is Professor of Classics and Middle Eastern Studies at the University of Reading. Her research focuses on questions of ethnicity and multilingualism in Hellenistic Egypt and Central Asia. She has also published on the colonial history of archaeology in the Middle East. Her publications include *The Hellenistic Far East: Archaeology, Language and Identity in Greek Central Asia* (2014), *Archaeologists, Tourists, Interpreters* (with Maya Muratov, 2015) and *From Khartoum to Jerusalem: The Dragoman Solomon Negima and His Clients* (2016).

IAN MOYER is Associate Professor in the Department of History at the University of Michigan in Ann Arbor. His interests include the ancient history and modern historiography of cross-cultural interaction, magic and religion, and the politics of race and ethnicity in classical receptions. He is the author of *Egypt and the Limits of Hellenism* (Cambridge, 2011), co-editor (with Celia Schultz) of a special issue of *Archiv für Religionsgeschichte* on "The Religious Life of Things" (2016) and co-editor (with Adam Lecznar and Heidi Morse) of *Classicisms in the Black Atlantic* (2020).

STEFAN PFEIFFER is Professor of Ancient History at the University of Halle-Wittenberg since 2013. His areas of specialization are the history of Greco-Roman Egypt, ruler cult in antiquity and Judaism in Alexandria. He has, among other aspects, published books on multilingual texts from Egypt (the Decree of Canopus and the victory stela of C.

Cornelius Gallus). Furthermore, he has published a study-book on Greek and Latin epigraphical records from Egypt (2015) and a general overview on the Ptolemaic Empire (2017).

PATRICK SÄNGER is Professor of Ancient History at the University of Münster. His main interests are the administrative, legal and social history of the eastern Mediterranean, especially of Egypt from the Hellenistic to the Late Antique period. He has also worked on the editing of documentary papyri and of Ephesian inscriptions. His most recent book examines a particular Ptolemaic form of organization called *politeuma* (2019).

ROLF STROOTMAN is Associate Professor of History at the University of Utrecht. His research focuses on imperialism, court culture and cultural interactions in the Achaemenid and Seleucid empires. He is the author of *Courts and Elites in the Hellenistic Empires* (2017) and *The Birdcage of the Muses: Patronage of the Arts and Sciences at the Ptolemaic Imperial Court* (2017), and co-editor of the volumes *Persianism in Antiquity* (2017), *Feasting and Polis Institutions* (2018) and *Empires of the Sea: Maritime Empires in World History* (2019).

ANNE-EMMANUELLE VEÏSSE is Professor of Ancient Greek History at the University of Paris Est Marne la Vallée. Her research focuses on the political and social history of Hellenistic Egypt. She is the author of *Les « révoltes égyptiennes ». Recherches sur les troubles intérieurs en Égypte du règne de Ptolémée III à la conquête romaine* (2004) and the co-editor of *Identité ethnique et culture matérielle dans le monde grec* (2014), *L'armée en Égypte aux époques perse, ptolémaïque et romaine* (2014) and *L'identification des personnes dans les mondes grecs* (2019).

RALF VON DEN HOFF is Professor of Classical Archaeology at the University of Freiburg. His research interests include the visual culture of ancient Greece and Rome and ruler representation in antiquity. Among his recent publications are *Divus Augustus. Der erste römische Kaiser und seine Welt* (together with M. Zimmermann and W. Stroh, 2014) and "Ruler Portraits and Ruler Cult in the Pergamon Gymnasion", in Mania and Trümper (eds.), *Development of Gymnasia and Graeco-Roman Cityscapes* (2018).

SITTA VON REDEN is Professor of Ancient History at the University of Freiburg. Her academic interest focuses on the economic history of

Classical Greece and the Hellenistic empires. She is author of *Money in Ptolemaic Egypt* (2007) and *Antike Wirtschaft* (2015). Currently she has an interdisciplinary research project on the economic history of ancient Eurasian empires and their inter-imperial relationships. The first volume of this collaborative project has appeared as *Handbook of Ancient Afro-Eurasian Economies (300 BCE– 300 CE)*, vol. 1 (2019).

Preface

We have the pleasant task of expressing our gratitude to several people who supported this project. We wish to thank all contributors for their collaborative effort and their willingness to communicate and cooperate intensely, in some cases over long distances. We also thank the respondents, Dorothy Thompson (Cambridge), Christopher Tuplin (Liverpool) and John Ma (Columbia) who encouraged us to explore further ideas and made helpful suggestions for the revision of the papers, as well as the anonymous reviewers and Michael Sharp at Cambridge University Press. We also wish to thank Boris Chrubasik (Toronto), Peter Eich (Freiburg), Ole Johannsen (Freiburg) and Benjamin Wieland (Freiburg) for contributing stimulating papers to the conference preceding this book yet not converting their talks to chapters in this volume. We are indebted to several funding bodies who generously contributed to the funding of the conference, in particular the Alexander von Humboldt Foundation, the Humanismus Heute Foundation Baden-Württemberg and the Deutsche Forschungsgemeinschaft and the American Friends of the Alexander von Humboldt Foundation. Finally, special thanks to Clara Hillebrecht, Stephan Neitmann, Alison Weaverdyck and Deirdre Klokow who helped to prepare the manuscript for publication.

Note on Abbreviations

We refer to editions of papyri and ostraca according to the abbreviations used in the *Checklist of Editions of Greek, Latin, Demotic and Coptic Papyri, Ostraca and Tablets*, available online at papyri.info. Abbreviations of epigraphic corpora generally follow the list of the *Supplementum Epigraphicum Graecum*, and C. Lorber, *Catalogue of Ptolemaic Coins. Part 1: Ptolemy I to IV* (New York, 2018) serves as the reference for numismatic abbreviations. Unless specific comments from editors are mentioned, editions of all such texts and coins are not included in the bibliography. For ancient authors we follow the abbreviations used in the *Oxford Classical Dictionary*, 4th edition. Finally, Greek names and proper names are given Latinate forms for well-known historical figures and places but a more authentic transliteration for lesser-known people and places.

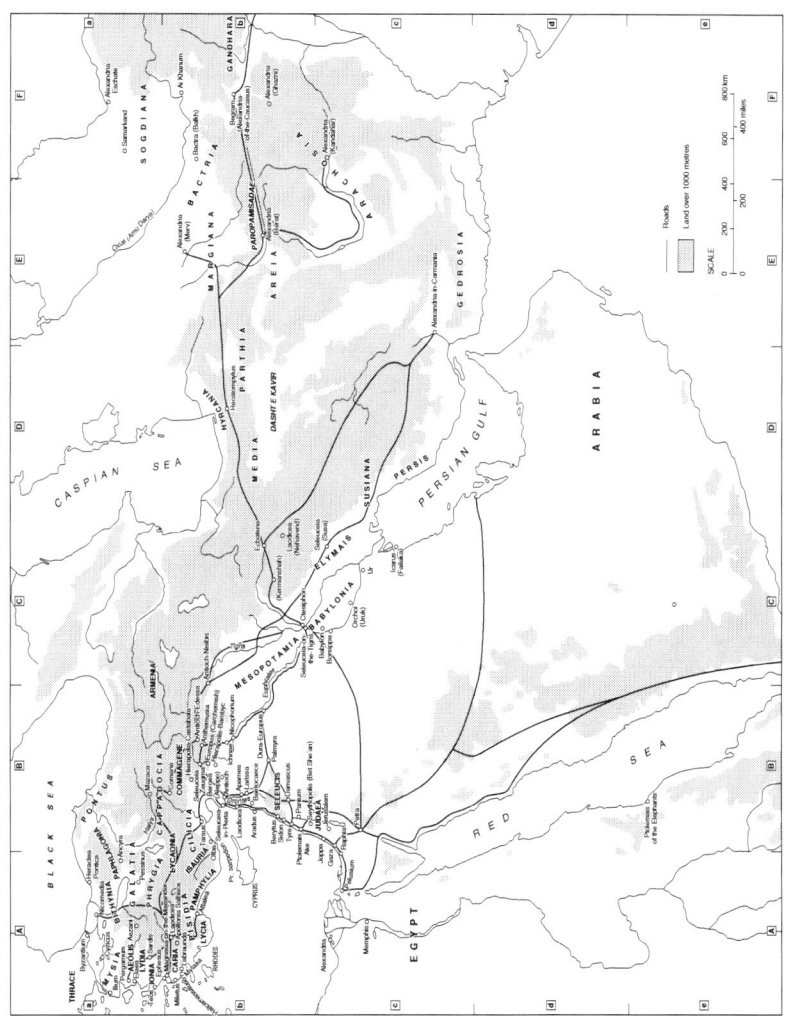

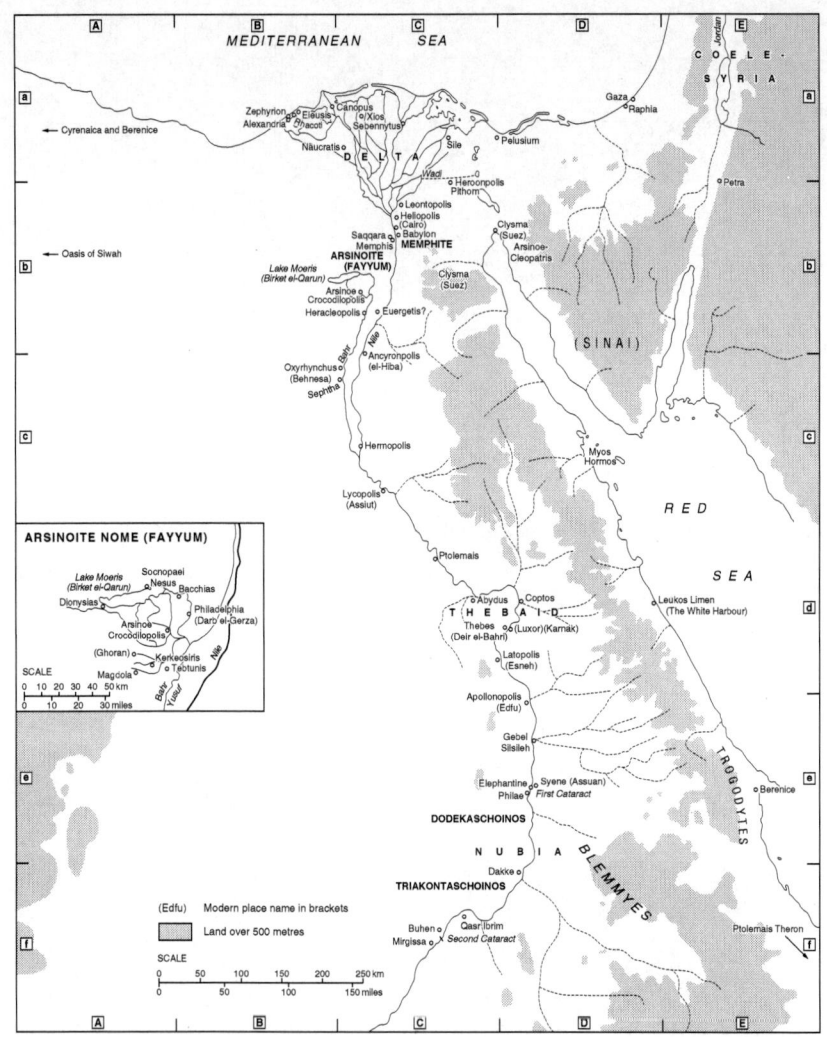

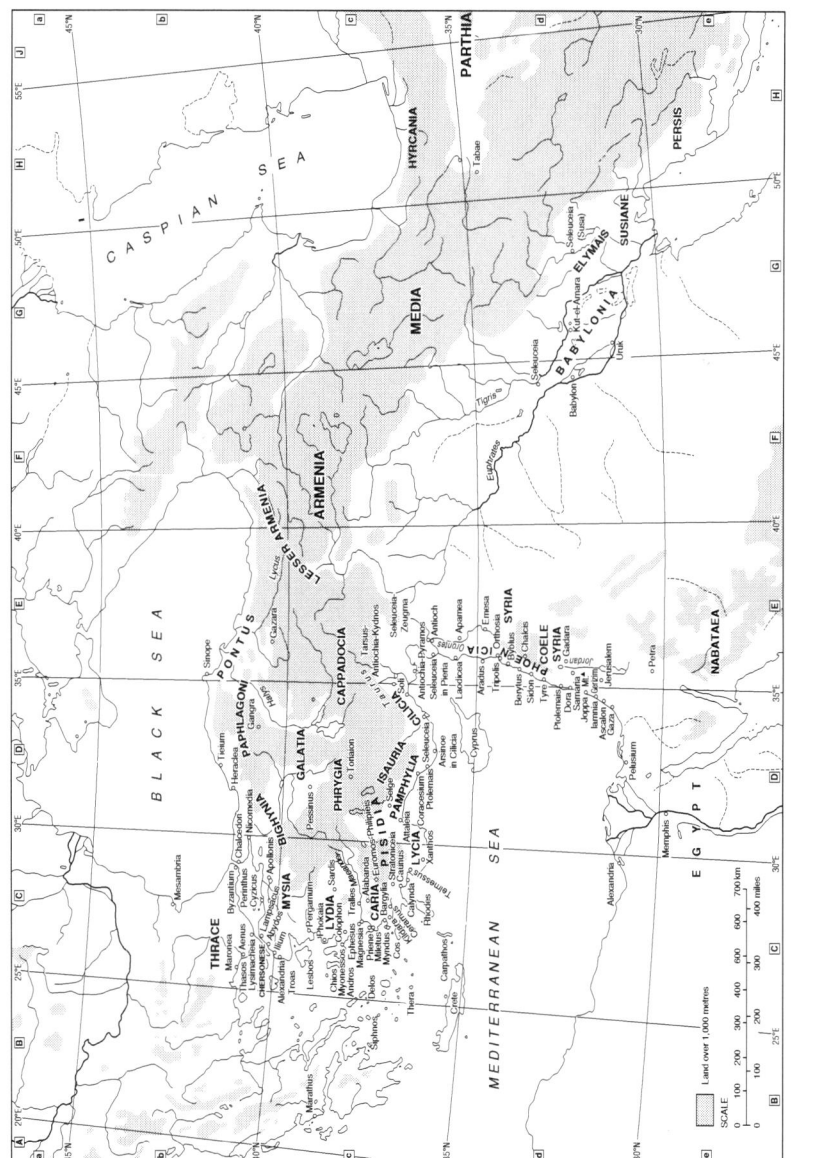

Introduction

Christelle Fischer-Bovet and Sitta von Reden

1 Comparing the Ptolemaic and Seleucid Empires

The Ptolemaic and Seleucid empires are usually studied separately, or otherwise included in broader examinations of the Hellenistic World. This book proposes a more dynamic comparison, with a particular, though not exclusive focus on the interaction of the royal centers with local populations and elites. Both political entities are approached as multiethnic empires whose resemblance and entanglement are sufficient to make comparisons meaningful. In the process of comparing them, differences and connections become more salient and better explained. We aim to explore the different structural capacities for, and levels of, integration that were either aspired to or achieved by the kings and populations of each empire.

The volume contributes to at least three wider issues that concern both scholars and broader audiences. First, it reorients the traditional focus of the so-called classical world from its centers in Greece and Rome to its outer reaches in Asia and Africa; second, it is anchored in the comparative history of empires by paying particular attention to the multiple social, economic, and epistemic entanglement of social and ethnic groups in the course of imperial change; and third, it engages with the increasing awareness of, and anxieties about cultural globalization and transfers. The interaction between different ethnic and socioeconomic groups, as well as local elites as mediators between centers of power and peripheries, is crucial factor in such mutual cultural exchanges.

The chapters compare the two largest political formations in the Hellenistic period after Alexander's conquest of the Persian empire. They explore difference, similarity, and purposeful imitation and interaction, especially as they present themselves in forms of exchange and ritual communication, taxation, and administration, as well as settlement and territorial policies. This introduction offers a frame for focusing our comparison, setting out empire as an analytical tool for understanding the role of local elites within them, and delineating lines of research along which the chapters evolve. "Local elites," however, simply serve as an umbrella term, since they are rarely homogenous groups and variously consist of particular ethnic or religious groups, military or priestly personnel, civic officials or *poleis* benefactors, or even vassal/client kings. The chronological survey in Section 3 of this introduction narrates imperial development in territorial terms, a perspective that will be challenged and moderated in the following chapters. Yet it helps to suggest that comparison close in time and space is a fertile ground for investigating imperial communication, and the nature of interaction and competition beyond their territorial expansion. As the following chapters will show, the two largest political entities deriving from Alexander's conquest were 'false twins' among the Hellenistic polities; they look similar but at the same time were quite different.

2 States and Empires

While the Ptolemaic and Seleucid empires can safely be regarded as political entities or polities, their status as empires is more controversial.[1] The Ptolemaic polity is sometimes considered as an expansive maritime empire[2] and sometimes as a state with a maritime empire, as Roger Bagnall's classic book title *The Administration of the Ptolemaic Possessions Outside Egypt* (1976) suggests.[3] The weak and ailing polity of the Seleucids, in contrast, was long regarded as not deserving the term 'state' or 'empire' at all.[4] This was challenged most influentially by Pierre Briant who in many publications from the 1990s onwards pointed to the elements of political cohesion the Seleucids took over from the Persians.[5] However, as the Persian empire conquered by Alexander was divided between several Successors, many scholars are still reluctant to call any of the Successor polities 'empires.'[6] Instead, both are generally referred to as kingdoms, which comes closest to the term *basileia* that the Greco-Macedonian rulers gave to their realms.[7]

---

[1] Doyle (1986); Hurlet (2008) on 'polities' as an umbrella term for empires, states, city-states, and other forms of government different from tribes; see also Tilly (1992).
[2] Strootman (2014a) and (2019b). [3] Followed more recently by Meadows (2012).
[4] Tarn (1951) [1938]; Will et al. (1993) 447–9.
[5] E.g. Briant (1990); (2002) [1996], now collected in translation in (2017); also Sherwin-White and Kuhrt (1993); Strootman (2014a and 2014b).
[6] Capdetrey (2008) 59. [7] Von Reden (2019) 40.

Over the past thirty years, the concept of empire has spurred numerous studies and debates over imperial structures, their development, and transformation, in order to show the difference between imperial and nation states: above all their different territoriality and boundaries, their different governance structures, and integration politics.[8] Although the concept of 'empire' is not uncontroversial – depending on what scholars associate with it,[9] and which historical empire they regard as most typical –[10] we regard an approach to the Hellenistic states as empires helpful. Both debates and individual historical and archaeological studies have sharpened our perspective on problems that are strongly related to this approach, such as a focus on zones that are regarded as peripheral to the center, forms of interaction between central governments and local populations, the impact of (imperial) memories on social and normative behavior, multiethnicity and transcultural forms of communication, as well as the processes that *make* a state in contrast to its institutional and constitutional frame. In contrast to nation states, empires are defined more loosely as multiethnic political entities, formed by conquest or nonviolent imperial takeover, held together by a fiscal military regime, some legitimizing ideology, and several forms of interaction between politically dominant centers and sometimes distant peripheries.[11] Despite their relatively loose control of imperial regions and populations, empires develop – like more tightly integrated states – a certain degree of institutional stability through administrative and material infrastructures, protection, access to adjudication, and sometimes coinage.[12] From these stabilities, not only the core regions and centers but also peripheries and local polities benefit.[13] Yet the integrative capacities of empires are weaker than those of nation states. Because of their fluid, multiethnic composition and local autonomies, empires rely on particular social networks, legitimacy structures, and integration

---

[8] Classically Doyle (1986), and comparative investigations in e.g. Alcock et al. (2001); Hurlet (2008); Burbank and Cooper (2010); Cline and Graham (2011); Bang and Bayly (2011); Gehler and Rollinger (2014a); Düring and Stek (2018); and Ando and Richardson (2017), despite their hesitation to adopt the concept of empire.

[9] Imperial nostalgia, admiration for their stability, and admiration of the success of individual emperors, on the one hand, weakness of governance and rather contiguous governmental knowledge, on the other; Ando (2017).

[10] The Roman empire as a 'worthy' predecessor of Western empires in contrast to the Assyrian, Achaemenid, and Byzantine empires which have been seen through a more critical Biblical lens, see Düring and Stek (2018).

[11] Doyle (1986); Allsen (2011); Gehler and Rollinger (2014b).

[12] Allsen (2011); Thoneman (2013).

[13] L. Doyle (2014 a and b); on stability and duration of empires, see also Scheidel (2013) 30.

mechanisms.[14] The more that imperial governments can adapt to new circumstances and to renegotiate relationships with local elites, the longer their influence is likely to last.

Central to the concept of 'empire' is the variety of processes that developed to access regions, their resources, and the social hierarchies that controlled them.[15] We therefore pay particular attention to the strategies of local control, local responses to these strategies, and the structural capacities of the Ptolemaic and Seleucid imperial states to change and modify them.[16] The relationship between core and local elites is so essential to the nature of premodern empires that some time ago Liverani already called empires networks of communication rather than spreads of land.[17] Particular to the Hellenistic empires is their respective claims to universal rule, their common cultural and political background, their continuous competition among each other, and the development of peripheries that in the course of the Hellenistic period formed into politically independent but still culturally connected polities.[18]

3 The Ptolemaic and Seleucid Empires across Space and Time

The Ptolemaic and Seleucid polities were competitive and entangled empires that shared a common chronological frame. The following survey of the development of the Ptolemaic and Seleucid polities shows that their politics were intertwined from the start, but that they rapidly moved into the realm of competitive imperial politics.[19] A first period, from 323 to c. 220 BCE (**Period A**), is marked by the establishment and organization of each imperial space (see Maps 1, 2, and 3).[20] Both Ptolemy and Seleucus first were satraps, that is, governors of a region of the Persian empire conquered by Alexander: Egypt in 323 BCE and Babylonia in 320 BCE respectively when the Successors met at Triparadeisus. Already by 310 BCE, after the murder of Alexander's son and legitimate heir Alexander IV, they had expanded their territorial power beyond the cores. They received legitimacy to their imperial claims in 306/5 BCE by adopting the title of king as other Successors did. The defeat of Antigonus and Demetrius at

---

[14] Barkey (2008); Burbank and Cooper (2010); Mann (1986).   [15] Monson (2015) 170.
[16] Ando (2017).
[17] Liverani (1988); Ristvet (2015) for network empires; for the implications of network empires on mapping, Smith (2005).
[18] Strootman (2014 a and b).   [19] Hauben and Meus 2014; von Reden (2019).
[20] Longer overview in Fischer-Bovet (2020); detailed historical studies in Hölbl (2001); Huß (2001); Sherwin-White and Kuhrt (1993); Ma (1999).

Issus in 301 BCE suppressed their main common rivals but marked a new level of rivalry between their own expanding empires. Ptolemy had not sent troops to the battle of Issus. Instead, he invaded Syria and Phoenicia in the southern part of the Levant adjacent to Egypt. Though Seleucus may have consented to the Ptolemaic appropriation of the region at first, it became contested territory, leading to no less than six wars over the course of a century. By about 250 BCE, both empires had reached their maximum imperial consolidation, though the Seleucids had already lost the kingdom of Bactria to a local usurper in 255 BCE. The Ptolemies controlled territories all along the Eastern Mediterranean from Cyrenaica to Southern Anatolia, Cyprus, and Thrace (with a few cities in Crete, mainland Greece, and the Aegean), as well as Lower Nubia. The Seleucids' imperial power extended from Anatolia and Northern Syria to Central Asia.

Period B from c. 220 to c. 160 BCE saw intensive warfare between the two empires, starting with the temporary conquest of Syria and Phoenicia by Antiochus III during the Fourth Syrian War (219–217 BCE) and the victory (or rather confirmation of *status quo*) of Ptolemy IV who recuperated the lost territories in the battle of Raphia. The Fifth Syrian War (202–195 BCE) ended with the definitive loss of these territories to the Seleucids, who now faced a new rival in Asia Minor, Rome. During the Sixth Syrian War (170–168 BCE) Antiochus IV temporarily invaded Egypt, only to withdraw after an ultimatum was set by the Roman Popilius Laenas.[21] This period is also marked by important reforms that led to the Ptolemies and Seleucids gaining more direct control of their territories, however reduced they were in number and size. The repression of concomitant internal revolts was successful in the case of the Great Revolt in Egypt, but not so in the case of the Maccabean Revolt in Judea.

Period C from c. 160 to 30 BCE is characterized by extended dynastic conflicts and external pressure from the Romans in the West and the Parthians in the East. By 129 BCE, the Seleucid polity was reduced to the territory of Northern Syria before becoming a Roman province in 63 BCE. In 94 BCE, Rome had seized Cyrenaica according to the will of Ptolemy Apion and took Cyprus in 58 BCE, reducing Egypt to its core state. But soon after, thanks to her remarkable alliances with Julius Caesar and Marc Antony, Cleopatra VII was able to recoup the empire of her forefathers, though at the cost of Egyptian autonomy. After the final defeat of

---

[21] Mittag (2006); Feyel and Graslin (2014).

Cleopatra and Antony at Actium in 31 BCE, Egypt became a Roman province in 30 BCE.

To be sure, the Ptolemaic and Seleucid empires were different in territorial extension and morphology. Yet despite these differences, models of center–periphery relationships, though much debated, can be applied usefully.[22] As Motyl suggests, it does not matter whether empires are geographically contiguous or discontinuous, that is, whether they have overseas possessions or a more tightly organized territorial texture.[23] Both our cases are different from any of these imperial types, which have developed largely in response to the European colonial period. Macedonia, the point of origin of the core elite, was not the core state of any of the empires. Nor was Greece, the symbolic center of all Hellenistic empires. The capitals or royal cities within the core states (arguably Egypt and Babylonia) had physical and social infrastructures close to Greco-Macedonian cultural and political forms.[24] And yet, both were built close to the old royal cities of Memphis and Babylon. In the vast Seleucid empire, further royal centers were erected in Syria under Seleucus I (Antioch, Laodiceia, Apameia, and Seleucia-Pieria), while Ptolemy I founded Ptolemais Hermiou as a political outpost of the Alexandrian administration in the Thebaid. These urban similarities, and simultaneous important differences of the geographies of power, lead us to the study's main areas of investigation.

In a comparative volume on the Hellenistic local elites, Dreyer, Mittag, and their contributors showed that local factions in favor of and against royal power emerged within the local elites of Judea and of the Greek city-states, while there seem to have been fewer tensions or open revolts in Egypt and Babylonia.[25] How can this be explained? Thanks to the rapid advance in Seleucid and Ptolemaic studies during the past three decades, it is now possible to provide balanced and nuanced comparative answers to this and similar questions. Local archaeological and textual sources offer unprecedented opportunities for investigating the interactions between the centers of power and local elites and populations. The nature of the sources, though very different for each empire, still favors top-down approaches, and the voice of ordinary people is hard to grasp independently of their representation in elite forms of expression. Even so, and for this very reason, the role of local elites as mediators between core and

---

[22] E.g. Wallerstein (1974); cf. (2004) 11–12; Doyle (1986) 130; Motyl (1997) 20; Osterhammel (2001) 209–15; Scheidel (2013) 28; Gehler and Rollinger (2014b) 20.
[23] Motyl (2001) 4.   [24] Weber (2007).   [25] Dreyer and Mittag (2011).

peripheries can be demonstrated, and thus the ways in which they participated in the formation and transformation of the Ptolemaic and Seleucid empires.

4 The Structure of This Book

The three parts of the book reflect three complementary lines of research that assess and compare the nature and level of integration, communication, and resistance within each empire. The first part explores capitals and settlement policies: their effects on and responses to relationships and tensions between immigrants and local populations, as well as between local populations and rulers. Each type of settlement may have had different effects on integration and inspired different responses and feelings of belonging to a Ptolemaic or Seleucid culture as well as their wider imperial universe. Particular emphasis is given to the foundation of new capitals, as preserved in textual and visual evidence, and to settlements of different kinds of peripheries, such as Bactria, the Red Sea basin, and Lower Nubia. We also ask why new semiautonomous administrative units called *politeumata* emerged under the Ptolemies, and what we can learn from them about the status of immigrant soldiers in the later Hellenistic period. The second part examines forms of communication and exchange, both between the two empires, and between imperial centers and local elites. We look at media as diverse as portrait sculpture, calendars, coins, and inscriptions. Given the different forms of communication considered, very different kinds of exchange stand out. They range from intense local engagement (Kosmin and Moyer) to a relative absence of local involvement in some areas of governance, such as coinage (Lorber and Iossif). Moreover, the relationship between rulers and local elites in regions undergoing transition deserves particular attention. The third part looks at forms of active reassertion of cooperation and violent resistance of local elites in moments of political crisis. It explores when and why elite brokerage, especially that by priestly elites, failed.

As the Ptolemaic and Seleucid empires were part of a connected imperial history and because their study has different historiographical traditions going back even to antiquity (Kosmin and Moyer in this volume), the comparative endeavor of this volume is sensitive to both the historical entanglement and historiographical discrepancies of these empires. We have preferred an open dialogue in which the coauthors or single authors of each chapter have chosen an approach and focus that they regard as suitable to their evidence, sociopolitical contexts, and historiographical discourse.

Some readers may miss a one-by-one comparison of specific phenomena, yet we follow the classical formulation of McMichael, stating that the "goal is not to develop invariant hypotheses via comparison of more or less uniform 'cases,' but to give substance to a historical process (a whole) through comparison of its parts."[26] Clancier and Gorre, as well as von den Hoff, have attempted direct comparison of very specific phenomena, while Sänger explains why some developments were apparently unique to one imperial context. We hope that by this approach we avoid superimposing comparability artificially, while at the same time drawing attention to the historical and historiographical complexities that comparison entails.

Von Reden and Strootman (Chapter 1: *Imperial* metropoleis *and Foundation Myths: Ptolemaic and Seleucid Capitals Compared*) deal with two different types of capital formation. In the case of Egypt, Alexandria was by far the most important royal city in Egypt, rivalled only by the "second city" (Strab. 17.1.32) of Memphis that became a religious center instead. Urban centers in the imperial possessions outside of Egypt never conflicted with the centrality of Alexandria. The Seleucids, by contrast, took over a much more heterogeneous, mobile and, at the same time (paradoxically) more connected empire with a tradition of several royal cities already established. Identifying a political center is more problematic there, as Strootman argues, but governance was "a network of ever-shifting, personalized relationships between interest groups and powerful individuals based on reciprocal transactions." There was particular need here to establish a symbolical political center that was Seleucia-Pieria first, but moved to Antioch by the time of Antiochus IV. Both von Reden and Strootman observe, however, that it was above all imperial competition, and to a lesser extent local discourse, that shaped the vision of Ptolemaic and Seleucid capitals. Looking at foundation myths as a guide to the symbolic construction of Ptolemaic and Seleucid capitals, they observe a deeply entangled discourse. The Seleucid and Ptolemaic courts and populations constantly reacted to each other as well as to Rome in an antagonistic interaction that manifested itself in many other forms than war alone.

The foundation of *poleis* beyond the capital cities, as well as the alteration and renaming of settlements, are explored as marks of imperialism by Mairs and Fischer-Bovet (Chapter 2, *Reassessing Hellenistic Settlement Policies: The Seleucid Far East, Ptolemaic Red Sea Basin and Egypt*). Rather than presenting an exhaustive survey of the (re)foundations

---

[26] McMichael (1990) 386.

throughout both empires, the authors emphasize the methodological issues faced by historians of identifying and assessing new settlements – Mairs by focusing on the historiography and archaeology of the early Seleucid Far East, and Fischer-Bovet by offering a typology of Ptolemaic settlements. Seleucid settlements in Bactria can only be understood as a continuation of Alexander's settlement policy. Their strong military character shows the early Seleucid interest in Central Asia and is not representative of the Seleucid empire as a whole. The Ptolemaic empire was also connected through a network of either new or transformed settlements, whose type and variety were adapted to each region, and actively shaped by their local populations. The existing urban and administrative networks in Egypt, moreover, did not create the need for new *poleis* – and complementary explanation to the question raised by Clancier and Gorre in Chapter 3 – but the new and altered settlements reflect the Ptolemaic strategy of combining Greek and Egyptian elements.

Clancier and Gorre focus on Babylon and Egypt (Chapter 3, *The Integration of Indigenous Elites and the Development of* poleis *in the Ptolemaic and Seleucid Empires*) and offer a systematic comparison of the role of the local elites in the temple administration within the Seleucid and Ptolemaic governmental structures. While in both regions temples were the centers of public life before the Macedonian conquest, the traditional religious role of the king offered to the Ptolemies in Egyptian temples granted them a unique position that was not paralleled by the Seleucids in Babylonia. Moreover, the authors emphasize that the temple's elite was representative of the local elite in Egypt, but that this was not the case in Babylonia. Therefore, these different traditions, notably the conception of the Egyptian king as a high priest superior to all the other priests, may explain why the administrative functions of the temples in Egypt, as well as the priestly elites, were largely integrated into the state structures of power, and why this did not happen in Babylonia. There, Seleucid kings could not play this role through the existing temple institutions and instead founded *poleis* as tools of governance of local communities.

Part I ends with an individual chapter (Chapter 4: *Contextualizing a Ptolemaic Solution: The Institution of the Ethnic* politeuma) since this particular type of political organization is attested in Egypt and Cyrenaica only. Sänger examines the question of precisely why *politeumata* are not found in other Hellenistic kingdoms. He argues that they were a specific response to the internal and external conflicts faced by the Ptolemies during the second century BCE. By offering the opportunity of founding a *politeuma*, the Ptolemies tightened the loyalty of ethnic groups settling or settled in Egypt while attracting new immigrants. The core members of a *politeuma* belonged to the army as mercenaries and would identify with a given ethnic group. After their settlement, they formed an 'ethnic community' sharing a temple and a quarter of the urban space. Sänger suggests, furthermore, that since *poleis* in the Greek constitutional sense played a limited role in Egypt (see the previous chapters), constitutional terms connected to the Greek *polis* were applied freely, thus allowing derivatives such as the *politeuma* to develop. The apparent specificity of Ptolemaic *politeumata* emerges as just a particular case of binding soldiers to urban spaces and attracting them as identity groups. These show altered ruling strategies when compared with the Ptolemaic *cleruchies* and army organization of the third century BCE.

Kosmin and Moyer (Chapter 5: *Imperial and Indigenous Temporalities in the Ptolemaic and Seleucid Dynasties: A Comparison of Times*) compare different temporal regimes developed by the Seleucid and Ptolemaic dynasties. Kosmin suggests that the Seleucids created a new "historical field" when Seleucus proclaimed a new epoch of Babylonian history and called the year of his conquest of Babylon year 1. The third-century Babylonian historian and priest Berossus takes over the concept of temporal rupture. Despite writing a history of pre-Seleucid Babylonia in Greek, he situates himself in the new world of the Seleucids, acknowledging a preexisting world that was distinct from Seleucus's royal period. In Egypt, by contrast, the Ptolemies continued reckoning with traditional regnal years, showing their subordination to traditional uses of historical time. But there were changes, too. Greek regnal years started with the anniversary of the new king's accession rather than with the first day of Thoth. From the time of Ptolemy II onwards, oaths were sworn by the divinized members of the Ptolemaic dynasty rather than the reigning pharaoh. And Demotic dating formulae begin to use the eponymous priests of the royal cult. Moyer argues that all of this established the Ptolemaic dynasty as a unit and a method of structuring time in its own way. Manetho, like Berossus, took over dynastic history, creating thirty dynasties up to the Macedonian conquest, and formed a complete temporal unit ending with the Nectanebids. The Ptolemies thus created a *Neue Zeit*, too, although the Seleucids were more revolutionary. What is more, in both empires the representatives of local elites and populations participated in shaping the new politics of time.

Von den Hoff (Chapter 6: *The Visual Representation of Ptolemaic and Seleucid Kings. A Comparative Approach to Portrait Concepts*) looks at what he calls a "system of visual communication" in the Seleucid and Ptolemaic empires. He focuses on "portrait concepts" by which he refers to the double process of inventing an ideological image of the king's public body, on the one hand, and maintaining the conventions of particular visual media, the interests of the composer, and the expectations of the recipients, on the other. The portrait concept thus encapsulates communication and exchange before it reaches the eyes of the viewer. Considering a wide range of portraits across several media, he identifies three periods that can be distinguished in terms of their visual systems of communication. Between 323 and 280 BCE, the initial fifty years of **Period A** marked by the Wars of Succession, there was close entanglement between Ptolemaic and Seleucid portrait concepts. They drifted apart in the subsequent period (c. 280–160 BCE) due to dynamically changing local challenges. In the final period (160/40 to late second century, part of **Period C**), there was a renaissance of earlier types of portraiture. Von den Hoff does not venture into the question of the indigenous responses to royal portrait concepts, but his emphasis on imperial entanglement in the first period, diversification in the second, and historicizing endeavors in the final period raises questions about the local background to which the visual representation of the kings responded.

Iossif and Lorber (Chapter 7: *Monetary Policies, Coin Production, and Coin Supply in the Seleucid and Ptolemaic Empires*) concentrate on a medium that was closely related to central government structures, though they detect some possibilities of local (civic) involvement in the design of coinages. Seleucid coin policy was much more heterogeneous than the closed monetary system of the Ptolemies, thus providing better opportunities for establishing patterns of change and transformation.[27] This is important to note, as is the fact that Antioch superseded Seleucia-Tigris as the most important mint in the second century (see above Strootman). Iossif shows iconographic responses to local events to which von den Hoff's material only alludes. Moreover, Iossif draws important conclusions from local control marks: they displayed continuity and stability in local bureaucracies in times of political upheaval and change. This observation coincides with the remarkable fact, already noted some time ago, of Syria and Phoenicia remaining part of the Ptolemaic monetary zone even after falling under Seleucid control. Lorber, looking at Ptolemaic coin policy, shows a much more patterned development, related to the particular attention the Ptolemies paid to the metal supply and to fiscal cycles. Despite

---

[27] Le Rider and de Callataÿ (2006).

regional differences in Egypt, Cyrenaica, Cyprus, and Asia Minor, and despite significant change from the second century onwards, the coin policies of the Ptolemies thus reflect regularities in state control. In the second century, the contrast between Seleucid and Ptolemaic monetary policies converged, whereby the region of Syria and Phoenicia played an important part. In western Asia Minor, where there were strong traditions of local political cohesion, there are some indications that mint authority was shared between central and local governments. Continuities in local practice under different royal control emphasize the importance of local conditions shaping government responses. This supports their conclusion that, on the whole, the Seleucid and Ptolemaic dynasties adopted two different approaches to similar problems.

The last three chapters investigate the multifaceted relationship between the local elites at different levels of the power hierarchy and the king. They all focus on different moments and types of crises in order to assess and explain the level of collaboration and resistance of the local elites, be they priestly groups or individuals, cities or regions.

Pfeiffer and Klinkott's chapter (Chapter 8: *Legitimizing the Foreign King in the Ptolemaic and Seleucid Empires: The Role of Local Elites and Priests*) takes the same sort of negotiation that occurred between kings and priests in Egyptian and in Babylonia as a starting point because in both places their temples fulfilled similar economic, social, and religious roles. While the Ptolemies were integrated into the religious rituals from the time of Ptolemy I on, this also implied that they were responsible for maintaining stability within Egypt. Pfeiffer's aim is thus to assess how the king negotiated situations where his legitimacy was at risk, such as Nile failures and subsequent famines or social unrest. Focusing on the synodal (trilingual) decrees, especially the Canopus decree, Pfeiffer shows how Ptolemy in Egyptian documents acts perfectly according to Egyptian royal ideology, emphasizing that only the priests had sufficient knowledge of it to conceive such a narrative. He demonstrates, though, that this was not the doing of a homogenous priestly group, but mainly of the Memphite priests. Turning to Seleucid Babylonia, Klinkott examines different moments of interaction between kings and priests, such as temple rituals performed by Alexander and the Seleucid temple-rebuilding program. He sheds light on the process of negotiations that took place between the Seleucid kings and the priests, who possibly gathered in a synod, and on the adoption of older Babylonian traditions by the Macedonian kings. While Pfeiffer and Klinkott essentially focus on the early

Hellenistic period (**Period A**), the next chapter moves forward to the late third and early second century.

In *Antiochus III, Ptolemy IV, and the Local Elites: Deal-Making Politics at Its Peak* (Chapter 9) Dreyer and Gerardin compare forms of political cooperation between the king, the Greek (or hellenized) elites at the center and those at the peripheries during two wars of Antiochus III (222–187 BCE). They argue that these elites were a destabilizing factor in the structure of Ptolemaic and Seleucid imperial power. Their networks of communication were strong, becoming even more valuable, but also more fragile when war was threatening in a period of change (**Period B**). Gerardin shows how the communication with the ruler could be compromised, especially in the case of the young Ptolemy V, and how Antiochus was able to gain the support of elite and civic members, using some of the same strategies the Ptolemies had developed, such as court titles and royal priesthoods. Dreyer demonstrates that the political elites on all levels gained influence during the rivalry between Antiochus and Rome in Asia Minor because both based their influence on the rhetoric of the "freedom of the Greeks." But the Romans did so more effectively by altering the rules of this diplomatic game. In both cases, the influence of civic and supra-civic elite networks of communication was far more detrimental to the territorial power of both empires than so-called 'ethnic' or 'nationalist' revolts, an argument that resonates with the final chapter.

Honigman and Veïsse (Chapter 10: *Regional Revolts in the Seleucid and Ptolemaic Empires*), compare the two best-documented revolts, the Great Revolt of the Thebaid (206–186 BCE) and the Maccabean Revolt (starting in the 160s). Both took place in a period of important social, economic, and political change (**Period B**). Though the events preceding each revolt differ markedly (the founding of a *polis* in Jerusalem, for example, has no counterpart in the Thebaid), the authors emphasize multiple interconnected internal and external factors – including political miscalculations and expensive wars discussed in Chapter 9. They demonstrate well that it was not domination itself, but the *way* it was played out at a given moment that triggered revolts, especially a tighter royal control over land and taxation. Their remarks about using sources of a rather different nature for comparing the two imperial settings echo cautions raised throughout the volume. Still, a systematic examination of the causes of the revolts, of the ideological discourses that framed the events, of the reaction of the central government, and their aftermaths helps to identify different strategies applied by the different regimes in different regions. Honigman and Veïsse show how history and memories of the past, in addition to the structure of the territory, made indirect rule of Judea conceivable for both Seleucid kings and the locals, while it was unthinkable, both for the Ptolemies and the so-called rebels, in the case of the Thebaid.

PART I

Cities, Settlement and Integration

CHAPTER I

Imperial metropoleis *and Foundation Myths*
Ptolemaic and Seleucid Capitals Compared

Sitta von Reden and Rolf Strootman

Common Introduction

In the two parts of this chapter, we investigate the ways in which major royal cities of the Ptolemaic and Seleucid realms were constructed as capitals of imperial states. In particular, we discuss how the foundation stories of these cities reflect conflicts and integration politics, which the creation of imperial *metropoleis* involved and which these stories aimed to control. Against the common assumption that the capitals of the Ptolemaic and Seleucid empires were culturally and politically uncontested, we will suggest that both Ptolemaic and Seleucid royal cities were constantly positioned and re-positioned vis-à-vis other royal or imperial cities that expressed, or had expressed in the past, similar claims. In the foundation myths of royal cities, we observe both competition and accommodation: competition and accommodation, that is, across the imperial zones of the Seleucid and Ptolemaic kings, between Memphis and Alexandria, as well as between Alexandria and Rome.

With our focus on the discourses behind the descriptions of royal cities and their foundation stories, we try to move away from kings and emperors as the sole makers of royal and imperial capitals. Ancient authors constructed cities as having been planned by their founders and first kings for their future destiny. Every founder and subsequent king had materialized in stone a normative idea of how the city was to be. As royal cities were thus the tangible signs of imperial visions, their designs also reflected different possibilities of imperial authority vis-à-vis different elites and populations. The literary resonances of the imperial cities, the stories of their foundation, the praise of their beauty, as much as lamentations about their decay, were reactions to changing structures of legitimacy spreading within and beyond the edges of empire.

Our analysis is as much a comparative study as it is one of entanglement. Alexandria, Seleucia and Antioch formed as capitals in dialogue with each other as well as with other cosmopolitan cities, notably Athens, Pergamum and Rome. The images that poets, historians and visitors created were informed by shared visions of what it meant to be a world city. Yet through a shared and recognizable imagery some features unique to Ptolemaic and to Seleucid cities will stand out.

1A ALEXANDRIA

Sitta von Reden

1 Introduction

The *Bellum Alexandrinum*, transmitted to us in the corpus of Julius Caesar's writings, has preserved a remarkable description of Alexandria:

> Practically the whole of Alexandria is undermined with subterranean conduits running from the Nile, by which water is conducted into private houses, which water gradually settles down and becomes clear. This is normally used by the owners of mansions and their households; for what the Nile brings down is so muddy and turbid that it gives rise to many different diseases. The common people, however, are forced to be content with the latter, because there is not a single spring in the whole city.[1]
> (Ps.-Caes. *B. Alex.* 5)

This sketch of the city, focusing on its subterranean structures and unequal water supply, stands out against much more typical descriptions of Alexandria as the most beautiful, populous and prosperous city in the whole world.[2] Take the almost contemporary account of Diodorus, who visited Alexandria in 59 BCE:

> He [Alexander] laid out the site and traced the streets skilfully and ordered that the city should be called Alexandria after him. It was conveniently situated near the harbour of Pharos, and by selecting the right angle of the streets, Alexander made the city breathe with etesian winds so that, as those blow across a great expanse of the sea, they cool the air of the town; and so, he provided its inhabitants with a moderate climate and good health . . . The city in general has grown so much in later times that many reckon it to be

---

[1] Translations are, with minor adaptations, taken from the Loeb Classical Library, unless stated otherwise.
[2] See also Vitr. 2.4; Strab. 17.1.8–10 and 12–13; Plut. *Alex.* 26.3–7; Arr. *An.* 3.1.5; Am. Marc. 22.16.7, and below.

the first city of the civilized world, and it is certainly far ahead of all the rest in elegance and extent and riches and luxury. (Diod. 17.52.1–5)

Both Diodorus's and Pseudo-Caesar's descriptions were written against the background of another great imperial city: Rome.[3] While Diodorus left it to the reader to decide whether Alexandria was the first city of the *oikoumene*, he authenticated its size, wealth and elegance by his own observation. The *Bellum Alexandrinum*, too, invited its readers to comparisons with Rome. While Rome was well furnished with aqueducts, conducting spring water for everyone to enjoy, Alexandria's water supply mirrored the disruption of a city that had fallen into social, political and urban decay. And just as Alexandria's dirty water supply reflected a polluted city, the technically ingenuous strategy in the Alexandrian war reflected the demise of an empire that was famous for its patronage of science.[4]

Egypt invited its visitors, poets and ethnographers to cultural self-reflection. In its presumed otherness, it served as a trajectory for reflections about the cultural and geographical order of the world, cultural asymmetries and power struggles.[5] Alexandria occupied a paradoxical space in these reflections. As the city 'by Egypt' (*pros Aigyptō*, Strab. 5.1.7; *Romance* 1.34.6), it had a place and no place in Egypt.[6] Alexander had founded a city that was both Egyptian and non-Egyptian, Greek and non-Greek. Its uncertain cultural location was suggested by stories about its controversial initial siting. Both Plutarch and Curtius report that Alexander had an ideal place for the city in mind, but Homer suggested another location, the island of Pharos, just off the Egyptian coast. But this place was not appropriate, as the island was too small for the future size of the city (Plut. *Alex*. 26; Curt. 4.8.2). Alexander then built a coastal town with a maritime harbour linked to the island of Pharos by a shallow, quite against the ideas of preceding pharaohs who in the same place had stationed guards to ward off traders, as Strabo tells us (Strab. 17.1.6). Like the archetypal Greek founder (*Od*. 6.8–10), Alexander had surrounded

---

[3] For the literary responses to Rome in the late Republic and early Empire, see Edwards (1996). Direct dialogue between Alexandria and Rome can also be found in Suetonius's famous remark that Augustus 'rendered into marble a city of bricks not yet suitable for the grandeur of an imperial city' (*neque pro maiestate imperii ornata*, Aug. 29.1); see further below; and de Polignac (2005); Nawotka (2017) 26.
[4] Ps.-Caes. *B. Alex*. 5–6; Vasunia (2001) 278; Moyer (2011a) 10.
[5] Classically, Hartog (1988); also Vasunia (2001); Cartledge (2002); Pfeiffer (2005); Moyer (2011a) 1–41 for review and latest discussion.
[6] Vasunia (2001) 268–72, following Selden (1998); Savvopoulos (2010) for a changing discourse on Egyptian otherness.

Alexandria with city walls, distributed the land and endowed the city with an *agora* and temples.[7] Yet as if Alexandria was not just a Greek *apoikia*, the Egyptian name for Alexandria, Rhakotis (*r'qd*), was always remembered so as to emphasize that Alexandria was not just a Greek capital but had been an Egyptian village surrounded by pasture and animals.[8] The Alexandrians, moreover, were not Greek immigrants, as one might expect from a Greek colony, but Egyptians who had formerly lived in the surrounding villages (Curt. 4.8.5; cf. Ps.-Call. *Alexander Romance* 1.32.2–3). Alexander also had built not just Greek temples, but one for Isis as well, the most important Egyptian goddess (Arr. *Anab.* 3.1.5).[9] From the very beginning, Alexandria's cultural tensions were built into the city, just as its foundation prefigured its future size and greatness, and the rivalries that surrounded its growth.

The narratives of urban foundations wrote into space relationships and conflicts that gave meaning to an arbitrary assemblage of people, buildings and physical structures. Cities were founded by conquerors and colonizers, but they were written and rewritten by other people – their inhabitants and visitors, poets, ethnographers and enemies. These filled the cities with meanings reaching beyond their physical space. In fact, all that is known about ancient Alexandria today are ideas of the city, couched in seemingly accurate descriptions of monuments, street plans and infrastructures. Together they form a discourse over the question of what it meant to be an imperial capital.

In this part of the chapter, I explore some aspects of this discourse by looking at various texts that preserve Alexandria's foundation stories.[10] It is my contention that these stories offer access to the imperial aspirations of the city and the attempts of local elites and populations to participate in or to contest these aspirations. The task is a daunting one, as the details of Alexandria's foundation stories shifted with the shifting rhetoric of the texts within which they were told. All these texts were written or survive in a form that was fixed under the Roman empire. To ascertain layers that date back to Hellenistic times, or to disentangle the different voices that contributed to a changing discourse, is hardly possible. The chronological markers for identifying layers are purely contextual, supplemented by the suggestions of scholars that have studied these texts critically.[11]

---

[7] Arr. *An.* 3.1.5; Curt. 4.8.6; *Romance* 1.31.7.
[8] Nawotka (2017) 99 with discussion of the origin of the name Rhakotis.
[9] Selden (1998) with further details for Alexandria's untypical nature as a Greek foundation.
[10] The most important foundation stories are those in Diod. 17.52; Strab. 17.1.6; Curt. 4.8.1–2; Vitr. 2, pr. 3–4; Plut. *Alex.* 26.4–10; Arr. *An.* 3.1.5–2.2; Just. 9.11.13; *Alexander Romance* 1.31–32. For a comprehensive collection of passages, Nawotka (2017) 97.
[11] This holds true especially for the *Alexander Romance*, surviving mainly in three different medieval manuscripts composed in different sociocultural milieus over a period of 600 years. I follow

This part of the chapter therefore must adopt a broader focus than its second part. Alexandria continued to compete with Rome as a world *metropolis* long after the Hellenistic kings had been concerned with establishing their capitals in competition with each other (see below, part B). In the first section, I will start with three third-century BCE representations of Alexandria, whose ideological purposes can with certainty be related to the Ptolemaic court. Here we can grasp the imperial claims of the Ptolemies and the ways in which Alexandria was constructed as the centre of a universal empire vis-à-vis other such centres. In the second part, I shall discuss the foundation story of Alexandria as it has come down to us in the *Alexander Romance*. Some of its details had clearly developed further in Roman times, but others – strongly responding to Memphis – make sense against a Ptolemaic background only. In the third part, I shall turn to a text that preserves a story about Alexandria's second foundation, this time as a prosperous city that had escaped its early destruction under Ptolemy I. It tells about the origin of Serapis, who had travelled to Alexandria to rescue the city. Tacitus's version of the story had further developed in Roman times, as Memphis and the Ptolemies served as no more than elements of an imperial memory. Yet together, these stories show the lasting debates over the formation of *metropoleis*, just as they echo the voices that participated in the work that was necessary to establish, maintain and contest their status.

2 Alexandria as a Space of Empire

The Grand Procession of Ptolemy II, famously described by Callixeinus of Rhodes in the final decades of the third century BCE, has frequently been analysed as an early celebration of the Ptolemaic dynasty, its power and aspirations to universal empire.[12] Central to the procession was the pageant of Dionysus, the conqueror-god with whom the Ptolemies most strongly identified (197e–202a). It contained the god's triumphal return from India and associated his life and achievements with those of Alexander, the

---

Stoneman's (1991) introduction to the Penguin translation where he suggests that (a) the stories of the *Romance* developed in an Alexandrian context, (b) most of its stories were circulating already in the first 100 years after Alexander's death, and (c) it emerged in a transcultural exchange of Greek, Egyptian, Jewish and Persian narrative and literary traditions (10–15). Nawotka's argument that the Greek ms A of the *Romance* was written by a single author, Pseudo-Callisthenes, does not concern us here. On the dating of the *Romance*, see also Fraser (1972) I 677–8 and (1996) 205–11; Jouanno (2002) esp. 68–82; Stephens (2003) 64–5 with notes.

[12] Athen. 5.197e–203d with Rice 1983; Strootman 2014a; 2014b; Blanshard 2007 for its connection with Alexander and the Ptolemies.

founder of Alexandria. For the Ptolemies, the train offered the opportunity to present in public their collection of animals brought to Alexandria from all over the world (Thrace in the North, Ethiopia in the South, India in the East and Greece in the symbolic centre). Indian prisoners of war and a caravan of camels carrying the East's most precious commodities were on display: frankincense, myrrh, saffron, cinnamon, iris and other spices. Universal empire was captured geographically and temporally by the procession in its suggested identification of Dionysus, Alexander, the divinized Ptolemies and the imports of the living king.[13] The parade across the streets of Alexandria absorbed into the city the empire that stretched the very edges of the world.

Alexandrian court literature, too, constructed the city as a universe of people and commodities that were absorbed into the city through commerce and conquest. While in Perikles's funeral oration to the Athenians in 430 BCE, the commodities that came from all over the world had appeared as symbols of imperial power (Thuc. 2.38.2), in the case of Alexandria both the inhabitants and commodities came from everywhere. This is how visitors described the city, and this is how the city was staged in Theocritus's *Adoniazusai* (*Idyll* 15), composed under the patronage of Ptolemy II.[14] Theocritus himself was born in Syracuse but lived most of his life in Cos and Alexandria. In his *Encomium to Ptolemy* (*Idyll* 17), he called his patron lord over Syria, Phoenicia, Caria, Cilicia, Arabia, Ethiopia, the Cyclades and ruler of 11,333 cities (77–92).[15] Yet more than in the *Encomion*, Alexandria is made a space of the empire in the *Adoniazusae*. The *Idyll* connects inside and outside, the domestic household and the streets, the streets and the palace, as well as the enclosure of Alexandria and its imperial outreach. Praxinoa and her girlfriend Gorgo, two women from Syracuse, in their house bewail the long and busy roads of Alexandria, where one no longer could find one's own home (1–6, 40–55). Conquest and empire are immediately called into this space by the cavalry and '*chlamys*-wearing soldiers' who are among the many who congested the roads (6 and 45–50). The woolen *chlamydeis* of the soldiers, possibly by then, but certainly a generation later becoming a metaphor for the shape of Alexandria as well as the *oikoumene* (see further below), at an instance created a link between the streets, the empire and the feast for Adonis in which precious textiles formed an essential part. The chatter of the cocky

---

[13] Rice 1983 87–97 for the origins of the animals.
[14] For the influx of goods and people, see above and P.Oxy. II 2332, 61–2. The following interpretation owes much to the helpful articles by Whitehouse (1995) and Selden (1998).
[15] Strootman (2014a) 14–15 for further passages and discussion.

women about rouge (dye) and bath salt (natron; 8–10; 15–20) alluded to the weaving industry that Ptolemy II had encouraged. It also alluded to the Milesian sheep that Ptolemy had imported to the Fayum where their particularly fine wool was woven into precious fabric (P.Cair.Zen. 59430).

The high price of Praxinoa's dress and the women's domestic embroidering business (37–8) carry over to the 'looms of Samos and Miletus' which produced the tapestries for Adonis, whose feast the women are about to attend (126–7, cf. 66–71). The emphasis on textiles, their market price, their presence in the household, streets and palace, as well as their connection to faraway Samos and Miletus rendered textiles of various quality and function an image of colourful Alexandria as a political, commercial and ritual centre. Moreover, the domestic wool industry, the market for textiles and the Milesian/Samian tapestries and blankets in the royal palace together were a potent image of imperial success. Samos had fallen to Ptolemy II soon after the death of Lysimachus in 281 BCE, and Miletus had been detached from Seleucid influence at the beginning of Antiochus I's reign. Both these cities and the commodities and wool-bearing animals for which they were famous encapsulated the extent of the empire, just as the references to Cyprus (100–1) and Syria (114) referred to its inner radius contested by the Seleucids.[16]

Ptolemaic imperial ambitions extended even further in the next generation. Ptolemy III advanced as far as Babylonia (App. Syr. 65; BM 34428), and the Adulis *stele* made him conqueror of all Asia as far as Bactria, by then the end of the known world.[17] This was the time when Eratosthenes was a member of the Alexandrian *mouseion* and library. We can speculate that the polymath's interest in the world's circumference and geography was inspired not least by Ptolemy's recent conquest of this world. As Kosmin has argued, Alexandria was the point of reference for Eratosthenes's astronomical observations, and the distance between Syene and Alexandria gave him the clue for the globe's circumference.[18] This circumference was a multiplier of the distance between the southernmost edge of Egypt and Alexandria, just as Alexandria was the place where the circumference

---

[16] Memphis, too, was perhaps involved in this textile imagery, for Memphis had developed a sizeable textile industry in Ptolemaic times (Thompson [1988] 46–75). Both Apollonius, the *dioiketes* of Ptolemy II, and Zenon, the manager of his *doreiai*, had recognized its potential and established a large textile firm in the Memphite *nome*.
[17] OGIS 54 with Strootman 2014d.
[18] BNJ 241 F 16 = Athen. 7.276 a–c with Kosmin (2017) 85–6; Dicaearchus of Messana and Aristarchus of Samos, Eratosthenes's predecessors, had used the distance from Syene to Lysimmachea in Seleucid territory for the same measurement.

eventually could be calculated.[19] The Ptolemaic state, its administrative principles and the shape of Alexandria also provided the mental models for the world's geography. Here it is that the *chlamys* first appears as a metaphor for the shape of the world,[20] and just as Alexandria's Hippodamian street plan cut the city into a grid, Eratosthenes cut the *oikoumene* into perpendicular axes. Kosmin suggests Alexandria was a microcosm of Eratosthenes's geographical concept.[21] What is more, the distances and shapes (*sphragides*) into which Eratosthenes divided the world were guided by a Ptolemaic urban geography. Places like Athens, Massilia, Rhodes, Alexandria and Ptolemais played an important part. Yet within Asia, Eratosthenes silenced exactly this urban geography that the Seleucids had developed. Instead of using contemporary city names like Antioch, Laodikeia, Apamea, Seleucia-Tigris or Seleucia-Eulaeus for distances and cartographic units, he reactivated Persian geography with Babylon, Susa and (abandoned) Persepolis as Asia's most representative urban markers.[22]

While Alexandrian court literature and science conjured up a Ptolemaic world order, they also propagated a hierarchy of belonging within its core. Praxinoa and her girlfriend in *Idyll* 15 are not just babbling nonsense in a foreign accent, as a bystander complains. On the contrary, their Dorian dialect reveals that they are from Syracuse, descendants from Corinth, the city of Bellerophon, and therefore Peloponnesians (90–5). The outburst of words linking Doric dialect to Syracuse, Syracuse to Corinth and Corinth to the Peloponnese in this passage rendered Syracuse not just another place in the cosmopolitan mix of origins of the Alexandrian population. Rather, it gave Syracuse (also the birthplace of Theocritus), Corinth and the Peloponnese a particular place in a hierarchical order of descent. The singer in the *Adoniazusae* is explicitly referred to as the daughter of a woman from Argos, the place from which the Argead dynasty traced its origin. In contrast, the man pushing and pulling the women and complaining about their accents is an anonymous *xenos* of no clear origin (89). The insistence on ethnic belonging well fitted with the fact that the Ptolemies maintained their Doric dialect.[23] Very few members of the Alexandrian elite, moreover, called themselves Alexandrians under the first

---

[19] The choice of these two southernmost and northernmost markers had further implications, which Kosmin *ibid*. discusses.
[20] Zimmermann (2002); and Kosmin (2017) with Strab. 2.5.6 (BNJ 241.F30); 2.5.9 (F34); 2.5.14 (F53); 2.5.18; 11.11.7 using 'chlamys-shaped' for the *oikoumene*. For the city of Alexandria being chlamys-shaped, Strab. 17.1.8; Plin. NH 5.11.62; Plut. Alex. 26.5; Diod. 17.52.3.
[21] Kosmin (2017) 90–1.
[22] Kosmin (2017) 91–4 with BNJ 241 F83 and F62 (= Strab. 2.1.23, 25 and 36).
[23] Clarysse (1998), also for the following two observations.

Ptolemies. Throughout the third century, Greek immigrants maintained their native *ethnicon* and chose epichoric first names for their children. To judge from Theocritus and other Alexandrian writers, ethnic diversity was deliberately preserved as a mirror of imperial relationships and hierarchies that made up the city.[24]

3 Cooperation, Competition and Foundation Myths

A great range of imperial relationships and hierarchies were woven into the fabric of Alexandrian foundation stories. The most extensive, and in some respects earliest, account of the foundation of Alexandria can be found in the *Alexander Romance*. Unfortunately, this source is also the most difficult text to pin down chronologically and in ideological origin.[25] It is a multilayered text of which the first Greek manuscript, known as manuscript A, dates to the third century CE. This manuscript was derived from an earlier hypothetical text, *recensio* α, of which large portions seem to date back to the early Hellenistic period.[26] Because of its simple style and fanciful composition, the *Romance* is regarded as a popular text, based on various literary genres and traditions, and transmitted in a non-official Greco-Egyptian context.[27]

In the *Romance*'s attempt to develop images of belonging and legitimacy that transcended the political divisions between Alexandria and Memphis, it created a truly transcultural text in which separate cultural identities were given a 'shared prominence and value'.[28] But the *Romance* reached far beyond an inner-Egyptian agenda. In its juxtaposition of the creation of the city and Alexander's discovery of the temple of Serapis, it connected the foundation of the city to the foundation of the empire.[29] The *Romance* extensively comments on the size of Alexandria. This was one of the distinguishing characteristics of a world *metropolis*. It was a measurable sign of power and one by which Alexandria could be measured against

---

[24] Stephens (2003) 243.   [25] See above n. 11.
[26] Stoneman (1991) 14. Several passages of the description of Alexandria, especially the debate on its size, the centrality given to Serapis and his assimilation to the chthonic god Aion Plutonius in the foundation myth, as well as some of its buildings must, for contextual reasons, be regarded as belonging to the Roman period; see Nawotka (2017) 97; de Polignac (2005); Jouanno (2002) 77, and below.
[27] Stephens (2003) 67; Jasnow (1997); and Huß (1994) 129–33 who draws out the satirical and therefore oppositional tendencies of the Nectanebo story in the *Romance*. Fraser (1972) I 680–1, by contrast, regards the Nectanebo story as propaganda deliberately circulated by the Egyptian priesthood to legitimate Alexander's claim to the throne of Egypt; also Jouanno (2002) 80–2.
[28] Stephens (2003) 72.   [29] De Polignac (2005) 309.

other imperial cities. Diodorus reckoned Alexandria to be the first city in the world, Strabo commented on the size and population of Memphis as being exceptionally large but second (*deuteron*) to that of Alexandria (Strab. 17.1.32), and for Tacitus the Ptolemaic Serapeion was symbolic of the future size of the city (see below, Section 3). In the *Romance*, Alexandria's circumference takes some prominence:

> Alexander marked out the plan of a city, stretching in length from the place called Pandysia as far as the Heracleotic mouth of the Nile, and in width from the sanctuary of Bendis to little Hormoupolis (it is called Hormoupolis, not Hermopolis, because everyone who sails down the Nile puts in there). These were the dimensions of the city Alexander laid out, so that up to this day it is called 'territory of the Alexandrians'. (1.31.5, trans. Stoneman)

However, Cleomenes of Naucratis and Nomocrates of Rhodes warned Alexander not to build such a large a city:

> You will be unable to find people to fill the city, they said, and if you do fill it, the ships will be unable to transport sufficient food to feed them . . . Small cities [*mikropoliteiai*] are harmonious in debate and take council together [*eusymbouleutoi eisi*] to their mutual advantage; but if you make this city as you have sketched it, those who live there will always be at odds with one another, because the population is so huge. (1.31.6, trans. Stoneman)

The passage recalled other statements which emphasized that Alexandria was difficult to supply, difficult to fill with people (Curt. 4.8.1) and difficult to keep at peace (Strab. 17.1.12/Polyb. 34.14.6). But most importantly, it commented on the Aristotelian discussion about the relationship between size and prosperity for an ideal *polis*. Moderate size of territory and moderate numbers of citizens were the preconditions for a *polis* to be stable and thrive.[30] In some phrases the passage in the *Romance* picks up literally on Aristotelian formulations.[31] As de Polignac suggests, Aristotle was the common source for a flourishing discourse of what made a city great. In Aelius Aristides's *Encomion on Rome* (*Or.* 26; 144 CE), there are equally explicit references to Aristotle's discussion.[32] Via their common referent the two texts were related to each other and formed part of an intertextual

---

[30] Arist. *Pol.* 1223 b1–5 with 1326b28–34 and 1327a2–4; on size and self-sufficiency see esp. 1261b12–5; on the negative consequences of too large a city 1326b2–24. Size and prosperity formed a harmonious balance that varied according to the power and prosperity of each city. Alexander's being the pupil of Aristotle is strongly emphasized in the *Romance*, rendering Alexander's world empire Aristotle's prophecy, *Romance* 1.16.7.

[31] De Polignac (2005) 330–4 for the comparison; and esp. Arist. *Pol.* 1326a.   [32] Ibid.

competitive discourse about what made a large city great. It is therefore significant that Serapis in the *Romance* prophesized that Alexandria was to become the centre of the world forever, just as the fame of Alexander as a god was to become eternal:

> By my command you shall subdue while young
> all the races of the barbarians [and then
> dying and not dying you will come to me].[33]
> This city you will found will be the apple of the world's eye.
> As the years and the ages go by, it will grow
> in greatness, and it will be adorned
> with numerous temples, magnificent sanctuaries,
> exceeding all in beauty, size and number.
> Everyone who comes to dwell in it
> will forget the land that bore him.
> I myself shall be its protector.   (1.33.11, trans. Stoneman)

Rome, unlike Alexandria, was not a *polis* with clear boundaries. As Aelius Aristides put it, Rome rose to heaven and spread all over Italy (Aristid. *Or.* 26.63). But like the *polis* Alexandria, it was equipped with an *acropolis* and an *agora* which the entire *oikoumene* shared (*Or.* 26.60–1). Just like Alexandria (and Athens) its supplies came from everywhere (*Or.* 26.11–3; *Romance* 33.10; Thuc. 2.38.2) and both cities spread their benefits around the world. In the *Romance*, the latter is elaborated by the story of the birds picking up the seeds with which Alexandria's perimeter had been sketched out. This was the omen that Alexandria would feed the world and her inhabitants reach everywhere (32. 5).

While Alexandria's size, population and wealth positioned the city as 'the first' in an imperial hierarchy, other passages in the *Romance* placed Alexandria vis-à-vis Egyptian Memphis. Thus, for example, in honouring Serapis Alexander follows Sesonchis, the former ruler of the world (33.6).[34] An even more powerful symbol of Alexandrian–Memphite connections are the snakes that have crept into several scenes of the *Romance*. Snakes were quite ubiquitous signs of divine interference in both the Egyptian and Greek religious universe, as Ogdon has well shown.[35] But in this context they seem to refer more specifically to the syncretistic assimilation of the Greek *agathoi daimones* with the Egyptian serpent god Shai (Greek Psais), the god of good fate:

---

[33] Not part of MS A, according to Stoneman (1991) ad loc.
[34] For Alexander's assimilation with the semi-legendary pharaoh Sesonchis, Jouanno (2002) 65–6.
[35] Ogdon (2014); cf. (2009).

> When the foundations for most of the city had been laid and measured, Alexander inscribed five letters: ΑΒΓΔΕ. A for 'Alexander'; B for *basileus*, 'king'; Γ for *genos*, 'descendant'; Δ for *dios*, 'Zeus'; and E for *ektisen*, 'founded an incomparable city'. Beasts of burden and mules helped with the work. As the gate of the sanctuary [*heroon*] was being put in place, a large and ancient tablet of stone, inscribed with many letters, fell out of it; and after it came a large number of snakes, which crept away into the doorways of the houses that had already been built. Nowadays the doorkeepers reverence these snakes, as friendly spirits [*agathoi daimones*] when they come into their houses– for they are not venomous – and they place garlands on their working animals and give them a rest day. Alexander was still in the city when it and the sanctuary were being built, in the month of Tybi [. . .]. For this reason, the Alexandrians still even now keep the custom of celebrating a festival on the twenty-fifth day of Tybi. (1.32. 6–7, trans. Stoneman)

Snake imagery plays an important role in other places of the *Romance*.[36] Most prominently, a snake appears in the birth story of Alexander who in the *Romance* is sired by the last pharaoh of Egypt, Nectanebo. Nectanebo, spending his later years as a prophet at Philip's court, falls in love with his wife Olympias, while her husband is absent on campaign. When he becomes desperate to make love with her, he tricks her to let him into her bedchamber by his own prophecy that she will make love to the god Ammon, who will appear to her as a snake (1.4–6). Disguising himself as a snake and thus being accepted by the queen to make with her, Olympias becomes pregnant with Alexander. And it is again in the form of a snake that Nectanebo turns up during a feast upon Philip's return, lovingly curling up on Olympias's legs, hissing and frightening away the bystanders (1.10).

The story skilfully interweaves Alexander's divine origin with some Greco-Egyptian descent. At the surface, it was problematic to make Alexander both the offspring of Zeus-Ammon and the last Egyptian pharaoh, as Egyptian political mythology required. Yet the mythologies merged.[37] As Susan Stephens suggests, each father contributed a necessary piece to Alexander's complex mythology. 'By virtue of the one father (Nectanebo) Alexander is really Egyptian, or Greco-Egyptian on the human and political level; by virtue of the other (Ammon) he is really divine on the mythical and ceremonial level.'[38]

---

[36] Ogden (2009).
[37] For the connections between the Greek interpretation of the oracle given to Alexander at Siwa, and the oracle as an election oracle for a non-Egyptian pharaoh, see Pfeiffer (2014a) esp. 99–103.
[38] Stephens (2003) 72.

Alexander's Greco-Egyptian descent played a crucial part in Alexandria's foundation myth. It is as the son of Nectanebo that Alexander addresses the Memphites. There was an inscription on the base of an anonymous statue, stating that this king had fled from Egypt but would return as a young man and vanquish the Persians (1.34.2). Alexander recognizes this monument as Nectanebo's and the inscription as a prophecy of his own future deeds (cf. 1.3.6). Thus, the Macedonian conquest transforms into the return of the native king.[39] Alexander immediately plans to found the new capital, and the foundation is firmly approved by the Memphites. In a perfect connection between conquest, administration and benefaction, Alexander proposes to build Alexandria with the tribute the Memphites had formerly rendered to Darius and now paid to him. But he announces that he will not store these tributes in his treasury but spend them on 'your city of Alexandria which lies before Egypt and which will be the capital of the whole world' (Ἀλεξάνδρειαν τὴν πρὸς Αἰγύπτῳ μητρόπολιν οὖσαν τῆς οἰκουμένης, 1.34.6).

The *Alexander Romance* mapped out the city, its location, monuments and deities as a space that reflected the city's status as a *metropolis* eternal, both for Egypt and the whole world. Yet Alexandria was not quite a centre but an extraterritorial space *pros Aigyptō*. The location of the city indicated its 'in-between status', a status that also shifted according to the different ideological needs it had to satisfy.[40] The *Romance* moulded Alexandria's inherent tensions into a coherent narrative. Much of this narrative received its final elaboration in the Roman period. Yet carrying with it the sediment of past centuries, it allows us to identify Alexandria's foundation story as a competitive space in which over centuries the legitimacy of the city as a controversial capital of Egypt and *metropolis* of the inhabited world was negotiated.

3 Founding a Capital through the Cult of Serapis

Tacitus happens to transmit another foundation story of Alexandria.[41] This story does not deal with Alexandria's foundation in the course of the Macedonian conquest, but its second foundation as a prosperous city under the Ptolemies. This story shifted the role of the god Serapis from being prophet of Alexandria's greatness before its foundation to that of

---

[39] Ibid. [40] See above and Vasunia (2001) 270; and Seldon (1998) 299–300.
[41] Versions of the story also in Plut. *De Is. et Osir.* 28; and Clem. Alex. *Protr.* 4.48; Fraser (1972) I 246–51, with notes, and Fraser (1960); (1967).

making it great when the first Ptolemy was king.⁴² Tacitus takes the opportunity to belittle the god who made Alexandria great, for nothing was known to the Romans about his origin:

> The origin of this God Serapis has not yet been made generally known by our writers. The Egyptian priests give this account: While Ptolemy, the first Macedonian king who consolidated the power of Egypt, was setting up in the newly built city of Alexandria walls, temples, and religious rites, there appeared to him in his sleep a youth of singular beauty and more than human stature, who warned the king to send his most trusted friends to Pontus and fetch his statue from that country. This, he said, would bring prosperity to the kingdom, and great and famous would be the city which received it. (Tac. *Hist.* 4.83.1–3, trans. Brodribb with minor adaptations)

The story continues with Ptolemy investigating the meaning of the vision among the Egyptian priests. But they know nothing about Pontus. So, he turns to Timotheus, a member of the distinguished Eleusinian *genos* of the Eumolpids, who ran the Alexandrian mysteries at the time. Timotheus knew about a temple of Jupiter Dis in Sinope where the god was sitting next to Proserpina. This was the god to be fetched. Ptolemy, however, neglected the dream and left the statue where it was. But when the god became more insistent, threatening the king with death and destruction of his kingdom, he sent a mission to Scydrothemis, the Scythian king of Sinope, to ask for the statue. Yet the Sinopians did not want to give up the statue, as they were jealous of Egypt. Three years passed and, after more threatening signs, the statue embarked on a ship by itself, making its way to Egypt, miraculously, within two days. Tacitus comments on the strangeness of this detail, but also mentions other versions of the story:

> The story becomes at this point more marvellous and relates that the God of his own embarked on board the fleet, which had been brought close to shore, and miraculously, vast as was the extent of the sea, arrived at Alexandria on the third day. A temple, befitting the size of the city, was erected in a place called Rhakotis, where there had stood a shrine consecrated in old times to Serapis and Isis. Such is the most popular account of the origin and introduction of the God Serapis. I am aware indeed that there are some who say that he was brought from Seleucia, a city of Syria, in the reign of Ptolemy III., while others assert that it was the act of the same king, but that the place from which he was brought was Memphis, once a famous city. (*Hist.* 4.84. 4–6, trans. Brodribb with minor adaptations)

---

⁴² For this history Fraser (1960); (1967); and Sabottka (2008) for the archaeology of the Alexandrian Serapeion.

The statue of Jupiter Dis, identified with Pluto, Osiris and Serapis,[43] brought the predicted prosperity and fame to Alexandria, and the Ptolemaic empire. The country would have collapsed, the city would have been destroyed and the king killed, had the statue not arrived. As the statue was vital for Alexandria's future destiny, it is not surprising that writers elaborated on its origin. First, it is the Ptolemies rather than Alexander to whom the second foundation was attributed. This situated the origins of Alexandrian fame in the Ptolemaic period rather than the time of its political foundation in which Alexander and his connections to Serapis played the most important part.[44] Then, it is the Egyptian priests who told the story of Sinopian Serapis, and it is they to whom Ptolemy turned first when seeking advice. This acknowledged some complicity between the Ptolemies and the priests in preparing the ground for Alexandria's greatness. But the priests were not able to comply. They lacked the broader knowledge of the wider world of which Ptolemy and Alexandria were part. Ptolemy then turned to the Athenian Timotheus who was in charge of the Alexandrian mysteries, as Tacitus explicitly states. This makes the Athenian Eumolpids, rather than the Egyptian priests, the prophets of Alexandria's future fame.[45] The prominence of Timotheus in the story contrasted Athenian and Egyptian pre-eminence in the field of learning.[46] It might be of interest that Plutarch and Clement of Alexandria have both the Athenian Timotheus and the Egyptian Manetho identify the statue upon its arrival.[47]

The most important aspect of the story is the origin of the statue. It was a matter of controversy, as Tacitus points out, in which conflicting claims to the second foundation of Alexandria were negotiated.[48] Tacitus is fully aware of this fact, without deciding the matter. Fraser, and most other scholars, suggest that Serapis was called 'Sinopian' because the Memphite Serapeion was located in a region called *Sinopion* in Greek.[49] Here lived Osir-Apis whom the Greeks had worshipped long before the Ptolemies

---

[43] Pfeiffer (2008) on these identifications.   [44] Fraser (1967) 25–6 for discussion.
[45] Fraser (1972) I 251 suggests that Timotheus could be attributed a similar role in advising Soter in religious matters as Demetrius had in legal and constitutional matters.
[46] E.g. Vasunia (2001) 216–30; Stephens (2003) 33; and Hölbl (1994) 28, who draws out the rivalry of Alexandria and Memphis as an important reason for establishing the *mouseion* in Alexandria under Ptolemy I.
[47] See above, n. 39; and Bergmann (2010) 117.
[48] The *Alexander Romance* calls Serapis the 'Sinopean' and the Serapeion 'Sinopeion' several times, e.g. *Romance* 1.3.4; 34.5.
[49] Fraser (1972) I 246–59; cf. (1960) 36 with notes; Thompson (1988) 116; Huß (1994) 242, both following Fraser.

arrived.⁵⁰ The Pontic connection had crept into the story because of the coincidence of the toponyms. The Memphite origin of the cult statue, real or mistaken, is strikingly suggestive in a story that so obviously established credentials for the development of Alexandria as a prosperous city. Seleucia, too, was remembered to have claimed a part in it. This detail is likely to have entered the story when Ptolemy III had conquered Seleucia-Pieria in 241 BCE, an opportune moment for statues to be brought back to where they belonged.

If we consider the discursive nature of foundation stories, more than just an etymological confusion evicted Memphis from its role as original home of the Alexandrian god. The lack of Memphite participation (the priests fail to know the place) and the passiveness of Ptolemy (who keeps neglecting the dream) are striking. It looks as if their parts were deliberately erased from Alexandria's most important story. Subsequently, it could plausibly be told that the god came by itself from beyond the borders of the realm he was to inhabit. Sinope was far away from Egypt, and their king, Scydrothemis, a Scythian *barbaros*. The speedy journey of just two days from the northern regions to Alexandria added an additional miracle to the story. Sinope, moreover, was a commercial centre with numerous trade connections. This introduced commercial rather than political competition into the story, just as the Sinopians are said to have been just jealous of Egypt.

It is impossible to date the different layers of Tacitus's story, especially as it so obviously conflates elements that contributed to the story over time. It is important to note its Roman overtones. It is only in the Roman period that Serapis is attested to have become the most important god of Alexandria.⁵¹ It is also truly Tacitean to favour Pontic Sinope as the statue's origin and to pass over Memphis and Seleucia which were no longer very meaningful rivals of Alexandria at his time. Nevertheless, it is unlikely that the tale of Serapis's arrival originated in the Roman period. Both the emphasis on Soter as recipient of the god and the suggestion of Seleucia and Memphis as alternative places of the god's origins suggest a third-century background from which rival versions emerged in a competitive process of myth-making.

Through his account of the origins of Serapis, Tacitus, too, not only transmitted but also transformed ideas about Alexandria as a world city. As he emphasized, the Alexandrians rather superstitiously venerated their city god, whereas to him, the Roman, the origins of that god were rather unknown and no Roman writer had cared to write about the matter. In

⁵⁰ Hölbl (1994) 5 and 93 with UPZ I 1.   ⁵¹ Fraser (1972) I 259.

the deliberate distancing of Rome and Alexandria, the confrontation of Alexandria's local perception and perceptions from outside, Tacitus's story remains a perfect reflection of the continuous paradoxes of Alexandria as a world *metropolis*. As the capital of Egypt, a grand commercial hub, and centre of imperial memories, it was both local and global, both past and present, both locked into its local paradigms and entangled with an imperial world.

2B SELEUCID ROYAL CITIES
Rolf Strootman

1 Introduction

Our approach to Ptolemaic and Seleucid capitals is as much comparative as it is about entanglements. Comparing the imperial trajectories followed by the two rival dynasties should be more than merely the identification of distinctions and similarities. Significant commonalities can be connected with actual interactions between the empires, whereas noticeable differences can often be explained from specific peculiarities of the empires. There is now a broader tendency in premodern empire studies to consider empires in their entangled relationships, and to look at processes of interimperial exchange rather than to study specific imperial polities in isolation.[52] As Sanjay Subrahmanyam put it in the second volume of his *Explorations in Connected History* (2009) – a work that takes issue with national histories and the self-imposed restrictions of modern area studies – 'there were also larger spaces of shared culture *that transcended imperial frontiers*, and enabled scribes, poets, artillerymen, physicians, and even artisans to move across the frontiers demarcated by latter-day "area studies."'[53] It is my contention that in a world dominated by empires, the forms and directions of 'global' exchanges were determined more often than not by the dynamics of interimperial interactions.

An underlying notion of my dissertation on Hellenistic royal courts was the idea that the connected development of the Ptolemaic and Seleucid empires was brought about most of all by competition.[54] Between 274 and

---

[52] See e.g. Lieven (2000); Faroqhi (2004); Canepa (2009); Dale (2010); Barkey (2011); and for the importance of writing connected imperial histories in general Darwin (2007) 47–101.
[53] Subrahmanyam (2009) 11, with emphasis added; for a successful implementation of a similar principle, see Flood (2009).
[54] Strootman (2007) 26–30, using Charles Tilly's model of competitive state formation in early modern Europe (Tilly 1992); see also Strootman (2014b).

168 BCE, the two powers fought six major wars, followed by another three smaller ones in the later second century.[55] The six major wars are known as the Syrian Wars – a misleading designation because it suggests that they were fought over the possession of (Coele) Syria. The stakes in fact were profoundly higher. They were fought over no less a prize than imperial supremacy in the eastern Mediterranean. Military activity extended from the Aegean to Babylonia and southern Egypt. Like the previous Diadoch Wars, these were 'global' conflicts, and around them revolved most of the other military conflicts that made the Hellenistic period such a relatively violent episode in ancient history.[56] Because the Syrian Wars were conflicts between dynasties, not between nations or 'states', people, goods, and ideas travelled freely across the alleged borders of the empires, whose respective zones of imperial hegemony often overlapped.[57]

In this context of competitive development, three factors structurally enhanced similarities, notably in terms of imperial ideology, dynastic identity and court culture: (1) the Macedonian identity promulgated by the two imperial families; (2) intermarriage and diplomatic contacts between the two dynasties; and (3) a reliance on the same social group for the recruitment of their principal agents of empire: the so-called *philoi*, who overwhelmingly belonged to elite families of Aegean *poleis*.[58] All of this amounted to a culture of interaction rather than segregation. Imperial elites were continually reacting to each other, adopting new military, institutional and aulic practices and responding to each other's ideological claims. The royal court was the essential venue where representatives of the dynasties (envoys, royal women) met and interacted.

2 The Capital of the Seleucid Empire

Analysing Seleucid capital formation raises the question of which city should be considered the Seleucid capital. For where we are well-informed how Alexandria was developed as a Mediterranean imperial centre by Ptolemy I and especially Ptolemy II, the identification of the

---

[55] See Grainger (2010) for a comprehensive narrative of prolonged Seleucid–Ptolemaic warfare until the end of the second century BCE.
[56] Including, perhaps, Roman warfare in the Aegean between 200 and 168 (Eckstein [2008]).
[57] Strootman (in press).
[58] Strootman (2007) 19. On the Aegean origins of Ptolemaic and Seleucid *philoi*, see Strootman (2014a) 126–31, with further references. Of course, there were also various non-Greek courtiers and other powerful men associated with the Ptolemaic and Seleucid households; they, however, were rarely *philoi*. Also see Gerardin and Dreyer, Chapter 9 of this volume, on Ptolemaic commanders and local elite members switching sides during the Fourth Syrian War.

Seleucid capital remains controversial. Most of all, Seleucia-Tigris and Antioch-Orontes have been the prime candidates. It has been assumed that Seleucia-Tigris, founded between 311 and 300 BCE,[59] was the Seleucid capital in the early reign of Seleucus I, but that the capital later was transferred to Antioch.[60] The alleged westward shift of the Seleucid attention is often seen as a major cause of decline because it led to the relative neglect of the important regions of Babylonia, Iran and Bactria. This view is no longer widely accepted.[61] Hardly ever, however, is the question asked what a 'capital' precisely is. It is simply assumed that the Seleucid empire had one.[62] But if we define a 'capital' as 'the seat of government',[63] it is clear why the Seleucid capital is a mirage. An institutionalized, impersonal 'government' did not exist in the empire, which was essentially a network of ever-shifting, personalized relationships between interest groups and powerful individuals based on reciprocal transactions.[64] The ancient sources do not reveal a formal separation of 'state' administration and dynastic household. The only office holders who were not court officials were military commanders, and they, too, were attached to the dynasty by means of ritualized friendship or (fictive) kinship. With kingship being personal and military in nature, Seleucid courts were essentially itinerant and royal sovereignty resided with the king, his co-ruler or consort, but also his higher-ranking representatives.[65] Precisely because the empire had a mobile core, there were many residences: cities such as Sardis, Antioch, Seleucia-Tigris, Babylon, Susa, Ecbatana, Merw, Bactra,

---

[59] Held (2002) 221 with n. 16. However, no royal coins were struck at Seleucia before 300 BCE (Kritt [1997]).

[60] E.g. Invernizzi (1993) 230, 'Seleucus [I] certainly thought of his city on the Tigris as the centre of Asia, the capital, the seat of the royal power, as the political and economic centre of his empire. [...] Founded only a few years later, Antioch at the end replaced Seleucia-Tigris as the royal seat and became the actual capital of the Seleucids.' So also Seyrig (1970); Marinoni (1972). Honigman (1923/1924) argued that the capital was transferred to Seleucia-Pieria, because the tomb of Seleucus I Nicator, the Nikatoreion, was located there.

[61] See for Babylonia Kuhrt (1987); and Sherwin-White (1987), and for the importance of Iranian lands for the Seleucids Sherwin-White and Kuhrt (1993); Strootman (2011); Plischke (2014).

[62] E.g. Will (1990) argues that Antioch cannot have been the capital before the reign of Antiochus IV; cf. Held (2002), claiming that it was Seleucus II who made Antioch the Seleucid residence following the loss of Seleucia-Pieria.

[63] *Merriam-Webster Collegiate Dictionary* (Springfield, MA, 2006) ad loc.; *The Cambridge English Dictionary* defines a capital as 'a city that is the centre of government of a country or smaller political area' (dictionary.cambridge.org).

[64] For the Hellenistic empires as network polities, see Strootman (2014a); the notion of the Seleucid empire as a 'transactional' enterprise was explored by Ma (1999).

[65] Sherwin-White and Kuhrt (1993); Held (2002); Kosmin (2014a); Strootman (2014a). Cf. Cohen (1983) on the need to control roads as a major rationale behind Seleucid city foundations.

and perhaps Ai Khanoum, some of which doubled as provincial centres when a governor (*stratēgos*) or viceroy representing the king was present.[66]

According to two of our best sources – Polybius and Babylonian Chronicles – the Seleucids had a concept of 'royal city', or 'seat of sovereignty'. Two of these have been attested: Seleucia-Tigris in Babylonia and Seleucia-Pieria in northern Syria.[67] The similarity of the names may not be coincidental as both cities were founded by and named after the empire's founder, Seleucus I Nicator.

What does the designation 'Royal City' signify? Seleucus I Nicator was buried in Seleucia-Pieria.[68] For this reason, and because Seleucia-Pieria was an important Levantine port and a hub of long-distance land and sea routes, the city bears some similarity to early Ptolemaic Alexandria, the burial place of Alexander. Like Alexandria, Seleucia was a geographical and symbolical centre of an imagined world empire that never gave up its claims to the Aegean (including Greece). While the Ptolemies kept the memory of Alexander alive – at least in his capacity as the deified founder of Alexandria – the Seleucids, by contrast, radically erased Alexander from their ideology after 305 BCE. They let *their* imperial Golden Age begin with Seleucus, whose becoming king in Babylonia was retrospectively presented as a new beginning of time.[69] As in the Ptolemaic empire, it probably was the second ruler of the dynasty, Antiochus I, who laid the foundation for the unifying imperial ideology. Seleucia-Pieria, however, never developed into a city as grand as Alexandria because it fell into enemy hands in 246 BCE and did not regain its prominence after the city was recaptured in 219 (though it is in connection to this event that we first hear of Seleucia as a 'Royal City').[70]

---

[66] Viceroys (men whose power extended over several satrapies) have been attested for Asia Minor (Antiochus Hierax in 245; Achaeus in 223 [Polyb. 4.48.10; cf. 5.40.7]; Zeuxis [Liv. 37.45.5; Amyzon 43; OGIS 235; SEG 37, 1010]) and the Upper Satrapies (Antiochus I in his capacity as co-ruler; Antiochus II in 266/5 (?); Molon in 226 [Polyb. 5.40.7]; and Cleomenes in 148 [L. Robert in *Gnomon* 30 (1963) 76]).

[67] Seleucia-Tigris: BCHP 11 and 12; Seleucia-Pieria: Polyb. 5.58.4 (ἀρχηγέτιν οὖσαν καὶ σχεδὸν ὡς εἰπεῖν ἑστίαν ὑπάρχουσαν τῆς αὐτῶν δυναστείας).

[68] App. *Syr.* 63; Malalas 8.204 ed. Dindorf.

[69] Strootman (2014c); (2008). Also see Kosmin in this volume. The continuation of the throne name 'Ptolemaios' as well as the imagery of the first Ptolemaia described by Callixeinus (see below) suggests that the Ptolemies from the reign of Ptolemy II promulgated a similar ideology of 'imperial time' (Hazzard [2000], 18–46; Strootman [2014a], 254–61), though without taking the step of removing Alexander from their representation, at least not initially.

[70] See above.

The presence of a royal palace, owned by the dynasty and separated from the rest of the city on its own 'sacred' royal space,[71] is attested for several cities.[72] This does not necessarily make a 'Royal City'. There were (pre-Hellenistic) royal palaces in Babylon, and Seleucid kings are known to have stayed in that city.[73] Babylonian sources, however, emphatically distinguish their own city from the nearby 'Royal City', Seleucia-Tigris.[74] The difference apparently was that in Seleucia some kind of royal sovereignty was supposed to reside even in the king's absence as the Babylonian texts describe Seleucia as the base of the royal governor of Babylonia,[75] a presence that is corroborated by the large number of 'official' bullae found in the city's so-called Archives Building (or Administrative Building).[76] A possible additional meaning of the term 'Royal City' is that these were locations where pivotal rituals of royalty such as inaugurations could take place.

Antioch, the supposed 'capital' of the Seleucid empire of most older literature, in fact was elevated to the status of, mutatis mutandis, a Royal City only in the reign of Antiochus IV, continuing a large-scale process of imperial reorganization initiated by his father, Antiochus III.[77] The first attestation of a Seleucid king residing in Antioch is in Polybius (5.43.4), who reports a ritual of royal inauguration taking place there, namely the bestowment of the title of *basilissa* on Laodice, Antiochus III's Pontic bride, in 221 BCE. This suggests that already Antiochus III was developing Antioch as a symbolic centre of empire.

---

[71] Held (2002) 246, outlining a pattern of separation and pointing out similarities between the urban landscapes of Alexandria and Seleucia-Tigris (p. 235); note, however, that the identification of the palace district in Seleucia is uncertain (Coqueugniot [2015]). For the use of elevations and religious architecture to demarcate 'royal space' see Strootman (2014a) 88–90.

[72] On the variety of Seleucid palaces see Nielsen (1994); Held (2002); Strootman (2007) 66–74.

[73] See recently Madreiter (2016).

[74] See e.g. BCHP 11 ('Ptolemy III Chronicle', 246/5 BCE) ll. 12–14: 'troops / in great numbers, who were clad in iron panoply, from Seleucia, the Royal City (*Si-lu-ki-'-a* URU LUGAL-*ú-tú*), / which is on the Euphrates [sic], arrived at Babylon' (trans. Finkel/Van der Spek).

[75] See BCHP 12 ('Seleucus III Chronicle', 2224/3 BCE) = Grayson (1975) 283–4, no. 13b, l. 14' rev., mentioning a 'satrap of the land' (sc. Akkad/Babylonia) stationed at Seleucia, 'the city of kingship' (l. 13' rev.); cf. Sherwin-White (1983b) 267–8; van der Spek (1985). A '*stratēgos* of Akkad' is mentioned in BCHP 15 'Gold Theft Chronicle' (162/1 BCE), l. 8 obv.; though he is not associated with Seleucia, he is represented in Babylon by a lower-ranked commander or *epistatēs* (cf. l. 2 obv.).

[76] Only Greek and Babylonian deities appear on the c. 25,000 clay sealings found there; see Invernizzi et al. (2004). On the administrative function of the building see now Coqueugniot (2015).

[77] Strab. 16.2.4. The city is usually known as Antioch-Orontes, though its earliest recorded full name is Antioch-Daphne, cf. Cohen (2006) 80–93. On Antiochus IV's building activities in Antioch, see Downey (1961) 55–63; Mittag (2006) 145–9. Both father and son presumably developed the area partially with the intention to reestablish Seleucid dominance in Asia Minor and the Aegean (to which Antioch was directly connected by land and sea routes); on these ambitions of Antiochus IV see Strootman (2019a).

3 Seleucid Foundation Myths

Only for the cities belonging to the so-called Syrian Tetrapolis – Antioch, Seleucia-Pieria, Apamea, Laodicia-on-the-Sea – have foundation myths been preserved. For these myths we are mainly dependent on late Roman authors: Libanius and most of all Malalas. There are good reasons, however, to assume that the core of the stories recorded by these authors is historical, as they are corroborated by sources from the Hellenistic period (Polybius, Diodorus, Strabo). Moreover, both Libanius and Malalas draw upon Pausanias of Antioch, who worked in the first century CE.[78] Also the similarities with the Alexandrian foundation myth suggest a Hellenistic origin. I would suggest therefore that in their first form they came into existence either shortly after the cities' foundation under Seleucus I and Antiochus I, or in the reigns of Antiochus III and IV.

The most conspicuous of several recurrent themes is that of divine guidance: an eagle snatches away the sacrificial meat that Seleucus is offering to Zeus while asking for an oracle as to where to found a new city.[79] This also happens in the Alexandrian foundation myth in the *Alexander Romance*. There Alexander is led to an abandoned temple of Serapis, whose cult was supposed to be older than the existing Egyptian cults elsewhere in the landscape. This trope of rediscovery is pervasive in the Seleucid tales too: Seleucus and his men find altars that have been established by Perseus or Heracles, built upon ground that had become sacred because epiphanies of Zeus (and in one case Apollo) took place there. To quote one example:

> On the 23rd day of the month of Xanthicus, Seleucus went up to Mount Casius in order to sacrifice to Zeus Casius. After completing the sacrifice and cutting the meat, Seleucus prayed (to be shown) where to found a city. Suddenly an eagle snatched the meat from the sacrifice and took it away to the old city. Following behind with his augurs, Seleucus found that the meat had been dropped near the sea below the old city, in the place called the trading-station of Pieria. Immediately he constructed walls and built the foundations of a city, which he called Seleucia after his own name.[80]

Together, these tales suggest a divine plan consisting of three successive acts of creation. First, Zeus frees the place of primordial Chaos to make civilized Order possible. Zeus does so, for instance, when he battles the

---

[78] Garstad (2011) 669.
[79] On these foundation myths see now most extensively Ogden (2017) 99–173, which was not yet available while writing this chapter was conceived.
[80] Malalas 8 p. 199 ed. Dindorf; transl. Smith.

serpentine Chaos monster Typhon, thrusting thunderbolts at him from Mount Casius (near the later Seleucia) and forcing him underground to become the snake-like river Orontes.[81] Or by turning primordial Giants to stone – still to be seen today in the form of certain rock pillars in the Orontes Valley.[82] Much later one of his sons, Perseus or Heracles, founded a sanctuary at the spot where Zeus had earlier manifested himself. The foundation of an altar (i.e. a sanctuary) is the basic prerequisite for the establishment of a human community. Then finally, Seleucus, guided by Zeus, rediscovers the ancient sanctuary and founds a city there as a third and final act of creation. One does not have to be a structuralist to recognize a suggestion of a divine plan in these recurrent attempts to inscribe Seleucus into a drawn-out mythical narrative.

The myths explaining that the sanctuaries at the core of migrant settlements are not founded but *found* are charter myths that turn migration into homecoming and enable settlers to claim the land as originally theirs. Greek myths such as the story of Apollo and Daphne are inscribed in the Syrian landscape, often on pre-existing sacred sites – such as is most certainly the case with the peak sanctuary on the top of Mount Casius and very probably the sacred grove Daphne. But more may be going on here than just 'colonial appropriation': the translation of local cults into Greek cults also facilitates the interaction between various groups of colonists and local populations.[83] An interesting example of this procedure is the Syrian version of the myth of Io, which directly responds to the Ptolemaic version of that myth. This myth contains another recurring trope, that of the presentation of indigenous populations as the descendants of earlier Greek migrants.

Malalas reports that when Seleucus was looking for a site to found Seleucia, he discovered near the mouth of the Orontes 'a small city situated on the mountain, which had been founded by Syros son of Agenor'.[84] Syros is the name-giver of the land of Syria. More intriguing is the figure of Agenor, the mythical founder of kingship in Syria, and a grandson of Zeus and Io. Agenor is the central figure in a web of connections that link Syria and Phoenicia to Egypt and Europe, as we will see. From Strabo we know that Seleucus discovered an ancient settlement on Mount Silpius, the *acropolis* of Antioch. This place was said to have been founded by settlers

---

[81] Strab. 16.2.7; Malalas 8.200: '[Seleucus] laid the foundations of the city at the bottom of the valley opposite the mountain, by the great river called Dragon which was renamed Orontes, where there was a village called Bottius, opposite Iopolis.'
[82] Malalas 8.202.   [83] Strootman (forthcoming).   [84] Malalas 8, p. 199 ed. Dindorf.

from Argos, who called it Iopolis.[85] Pausanias of Antioch recounts an earlier discovery, set in the mythical past, in which the protagonist is the Argive hero Perseus:

> Perseus, after ruling the Persian land for many years, learning that Iopolitans from Argos were living in the Syrian land, came to them in Syria at Mount Silpius, as to his own relatives. These same Argive Iopolitans recognized him because he too was descended from the race of the Argives. Rejoicing, they hymned him.[86]

Perseus appears in his capacity of progenitor of the Persians. At this occasion, Perseus introduced a cult for Zeus Keraunios on Mount Silpius which was rediscovered by Seleucus:

> [Seleucus] returned rejoicing to Iopolis and after three days he celebrated a festival there for Zeus Keraunios, in the temple which had been established by Perseus, the son of Picus and Danae, on Mount Silpius, where Iopolis is situated. He performed the sacrifice on the first day of the month of Artemisios.[87]

Syrian foundation mythology associated Seleucus with Heracles and Perseus, making the king appear as a culture hero too. Perseus and Heracles are connected to each other by kinship. Most of the myths referred to by Libanius, Pausanias and Malalas belong to the mythological circle of Argos, home city of both Perseus and Heracles. To an even earlier generation of mythic antecedents belongs the Argive princess Io, who allegedly was revered as the eponymous 'national' deity of the Iopolitans living on Mount Silpius.

The reference to Io is noteworthy. In pre-Hellenistic Greece, this originally Argive myth was connected to Egypt, and after the Macedonian conquest of Egypt, Io is best known as a prominent figure in early Ptolemaic imperial myth-making.[88] This presumably developed at

---

[85] Strab. 16.2.5, claiming that several towns along the Orontes were founded by the Argive *hērōs* Triptolemus and his companions, who had come to Syria in search of Io; cf. Lib., *Or.* 11.91; Malalas 8.201.

[86] Pausanias of Antioch *FHG* IV F9 *ap.* Malalas, *Chron.* p. 37 ed. Dindorf; see Garstad (2011), 677. App. *Syr.* 57 mentions a foundation of Seleucus I in NW Syria named Heraia after the principal Argive deity, Hera (who was associated with both Io and Heracles); the location of this town is unknown.

[87] Malalas 8, p. 199 ed. Dindorf. On Perseus as a Seleucid dynastic model and his role in the mythology of Antioch see Ogden (2011) 155–7. Note that the Spring Equinox of 1 Artemisios (March/April) is the first day of the Macedonian New Year, which was synchronized in Hellenistic times with the last day of the Babylonian Akītu Festival (1 Nisannu): yet another indication of the connectedness of foundation myth and creation myth.

[88] The Hellenistic-period version of the myth has been best preserved in Apollod. 3.1.1; cf. Moschos 277; Diod. 5.78.1; Luc. *Dial. Marin.* 15; and *De Dea Syria* 4; Ov. *Met.* 2.836; and Ovid *Fasti* 5.603; Hyg. *Fab.* 178. From the third century BCE, Io was equated to Isis and credited with the

the court of Ptolemy II Philadelphus, and its intended audience was not the population of Egypt, but people from the Aegean, who were acquainted with these tales. Io and Zeus were the ancestors of Aegyptus, the eponymous first king of Egypt who fled to Argos after losing his throne to his treacherous twin brother, Danaus; by claiming descent from Aegyptus via Temenus, first King of the Macedonians, Philadelphus could present his father, Ptolemy I Soter, as Aegyptus's legitimate heir returning to Egypt to reclaim his ancestral realm.[89] This view was promoted most of all by the court poet Callimachus.[90] The Seleucids likely responded to the Ptolemaic appropriation of the Io myth.

In explaining the meaning of the Io myth for the Ptolemies, conventional scholarship has looked first of all for underlying Egyptian deities and pharaonic ideology – an exercise that all too often leads to the rather meaningless conclusion that such stories 'legitimized' Ptolemaic rule in Egypt. Another way of looking at these stories is to see them as the product of antagonistic exchanges between the entangled Ptolemaic and Seleucid courts. In contrast to the Ptolemaic version, the Argive myths of Seleucid Syria do not stress Egypt as Io's principal destination. Instead, they seem to aim at linking Europe to Asia by developing Io's connections to Syria. For just as Io came to Egypt in the form of a cow, so too did she arrive in Syria (to where she later was said to have returned in human shape). Her descendent Agenor, the son of Poseidon and Libya, later settled in the Levant where he fathered Syrus and Phoenix, the eponymous kings of Syria and Phoenicia.[91] Moreover, as father or grandfather of the maiden Europa and of Kadmos, Agenor linked Asia to Europe.[92] Being specifically associated with Seleucia and the cult on Mount Casius, Agenor, and the story of Zeus's abduction of his child Europa to Crete, also provided a mythical rationalization for the Hellenistic-period association of the cult of Hadad-Ba'al-Zeus Casius with the newly introduced cult of Zeus Cretagenes in Syria; this cult may have been a focus for identity formation, perhaps for settlers from Crete or for so-called 'Cretan' soldiers.[93]

---

establishment of the cult of Apis (Diod. 1.24.8; Apollod. 2.1.4; Hyg. *Fab.* 145.1; Luc. *Dial. Deor.* 3; cf. Hdt. 2.41); cf. Rutherford (2011).

[89] For a full discussion of Io's Egyptian connections see Kampakoglou (2016).
[90] Harder (2012) 400–1; Stephens (2015) 155; cf. Stephens (2003) 8–9.
[91] Apollod. 2.1; cf. Hdt. 2.145.1.
[92] The name of Europa's father is alternatively given as Agenor, the first king of the Phoenicians, or as Phoenix, Agenor's son and name-giver of Phoenicia.
[93] An altar of Zeus Cretagenes allegedly was discovered at the founding of Antioch (Mastrocinque [2002]). Note the well-known appearance of Zeus in the form of a bull; the Ugaritic storm god Hadad, whose sanctuary was on Mount Casius in the Late Bronze Age, was commonly depicted on

Thus both Seleucids and Ptolemies used Argive mythology to claim sovereign rights upon a variety of lands and peoples, including Egypt and Syria, remodelling these myths to suit their own respective aims and in reaction to the other's modifications of these myths.[94] Where the better preserved Ptolemaic material focused on links between Egypt and Europe (e.g. by foregrounding the myth of Aegyptus and Danaus), the Seleucids emphasized links between Asia and Europe by developing Io's connections to Syria and by foregrounding the figure of Agenor. The version of the Io myth promoted by the Ptolemaic court has been understood from the Ptolemies' broader strategy of framing the eastern Mediterranean as a coherent world of interconnected coasts under Ptolemaic hegemony.[95] But Seleucid imperial propaganda had much the same message. The Seleucid court upheld the conventional Greek view that Egypt is part of Asia (over which as 'Kings of Asia' they claimed imperial hegemony), while the Ptolemies from their maritime perspective maintained that Asia was essentially an interior continent to which Syria and other countries by the sea did not belong (for these lands, of course, were rightfully within the Ptolemaic sphere of influence).[96] Through the appropriation and adaptation of the myth of Io and especially her descendants, the Seleucids claimed possession of the Levant in opposition to the Ptolemies, who claimed the same thing using the same myth. Thus, Seleucid imperial cities of northern Syria, like Ptolemaic Alexandria (see above), were at once local and global, both locked into local 'traditions' and entangled with a wider world of competing empires.

Another illuminating example is provided by the sacred grove and oracle at Daphne (present-day Harbiye in Turkey), which was dedicated to the Seleucid tutelary deities Apollo and Artemis and in 166 was the scene of grand festivities organized by Antiochus IV (see below). In Seleucid times, the valley was identified as the place where the virgin Daphne had been touched by Apollo and was transformed into a laurel tree. Laurels descendant from her covered the area, as they still do today. This epiphany myth

---

reliefs while standing on a bull with a lightning bolt in his right hand; Hadad also is often represented with bull's horns, and the later Syrian deities Anat and Ba'al were sometimes worshipped in the shape of bovines (Lipiński [2000] 632). Any connection of course must at present remain provisional, but at least this shows that Io's bovine form *could* also have had other associations than with Apis or Isis-Hathor.

[94] That identity myths in particular are malleable is apparent here, e.g. from the fact that Io's father has been alternatively recorded as Inachus, Argus and Iasus, see inter alios Paus. 2.16.1; 3.18.13; Apollod. 2.1.3; Ov. *Met.* 1.583–5; Schol. on Eur., *Or.* (932).

[95] Stephens (2003) 171–237; Acosta-Hughes and Stephens (2012) 148–203; Strootman (2017) 115–34.

[96] Primo (2009); cf. e.g. Polyb. 5.67; 1 Macc. 11.13; and Strab. 11.9.2.

connected Daphne to Delphi. It was moreover said that Daphne's sacred spring, called Castalia, was fed by Delphi's sacred fountain Castalia through an underground river that ran all the way from Delphi to Syria, allowing Apollo of Delphi to pronounce oracles near Antioch as well.[97]

But that is not all. A second foundation myth was created according to which the culture hero Heracles had planted cypresses at Daphne and established a cult of Zeus there. Finally, Seleucus came around to discover the old altar built by Heracles and make it the heart of his settlement policy on the Upper Orontes, planting more cypresses.[98] Again we have a foundation myth in three parts. The first is set in the time of creation or shortly thereafter when Apollo's divine power descended on the grove and made it sacred for all times. A second tale is set at the temporal intersection of myth and history, when Heracles created a sanctuary and thereby laid the foundation for human habitation. And a final one is set in the present when Seleucus established settlements in the area. And here again, it may be surmised that a local cult was appropriated to make this sanctuary into a neutral 'middle ground' to accommodate both newcomers and local inhabitants and stimulate the emergence of a communal identity for the population of Antioch.[99]

4 The Daphne Festival (ca. 165 BC): The Imperial Court as Cosmopolis

If the Seleucid empire had a mobile core – in none of the 'Royal Cities' and various residences has monumental architecture been attested of the kind that adorned Alexandria – then it is the court where we should look for the Seleucid universalistic 'answers' to the Ptolemies' imperial cosmopolis Alexandria. Elite integration in the Seleucid empire was the sum of political, social and cultural factors working together to create a sense of imperial commonwealth. The umbrella ideology to bind together elites of various cultural backgrounds and belonging to a variety of types of polities (*poleis*, tribes, kingdoms) was the idea that the world was somehow a unity under a single imperial ruler: the Seleucid (great) king. This universalism followed from the empire's nature as an expansionist state based on conquest. It was also a heritage of previous Near Eastern empires – a heritage from which the Seleucids could not deviate, especially not in the

---

[97] For the sources see Downey (1961) 364, n. 217; cf. Queyrel (1990).
[98] Malalas 8, p. 204, ed. Dindorf.   [99] Strootman (forthcoming).

face of rival Ptolemaic claims to universal dominance.[100] Rivalry between the empires is particularly clear from a certain competition over the use of the title 'Great King', a title that Ptolemaic kings seem to have used specifically as an expression of victory over the Seleucids and subsequent claims to Seleucid 'Asia'.[101]

The famous festival celebrated at Daphne by Antiochus IV in the late summer of 166 capitalized upon Daphne's connection with the Greek world. The festival with its elaborate procession was connected with Antiochus's return from his second Egyptian campaign.[102] The main 'audience', however, were the *poleis* of the Aegean.[103] Of importance for the present argument is the construction of the festival terrain as a microcosm of empire, not unlike the way the Ptolemies had made Alexandria into an imperial microcosm in the third century BCE:

> [Antiochus] brought together at his festival the most distinguished men from virtually the whole world [*oikoumene*], adorned all parts of his palace [*basileion*] in magnificent fashion, and having assembled in one spot, and, as it were, put on a stage [*skene*] his entire monarchy [*basileia*], left them [*sc.* the Romans] ignorant of nothing that concerned him. In putting on these lavish games and this stupendous festival Antiochus outdid all earlier rivals.[104]

Polybius (30.25.1) adds that Antiochus 'sent out envoys and sacred embassies to the cities to announce the games', and that the Greeks 'were very eager to visit Antioch'.

This is how imperial festivals function, and how coronations and other great events of the court work: they are prepared and announced well in advance and meant to attract to the imperial centre representatives of (potential) subsidiary polities such as cities, temples or kingdoms. The Grand Procession of Ptolemy Philadelphus during the Ptolemaia in Alexandria about a century earlier had basically the same function, as it presented the riches of Egypt and Africa and Arabia, and the Ptolemaic empire's universalistic claims, with Dionysiac imagery centre stage, to civic elites in the Aegean, which was the main arena for Seleucid–Ptolemaic

---

[100] For the universalistic nature of Hellenistic imperialism, see Strootman (2007) *passim*; (2010); (2014b); and (2014d); also see Bang (2012); and Kosmin (2014a) on the creation of real and symbolic borders.
[101] Strootman (2010).
[102] See Polyb. 30.26.9 = Ath. V 195f: 'All the above display and outlay was provided for by the robberies he had appropriated in Egypt when he broke his treaty with king Philometor, who was then only a child, and partly by contributions by his *philoi*. He had also sacrilegiously despoiled most of the temples.'
[103] Strootman (2019a).   [104] Diod. 31.16.1.

rivalry. Though they took place about a century apart, both processions reflect imperial rivalry between Seleucids and Ptolemies.

We already saw that Diodorus uses the word *oikoumene* to describe the radius of the Daphne Festival. Universalistic imagery was a noticeable element in the procession at Daphne, which included images of Earth and Heaven, Night and Day, and Dawn and Noon.[105] Among the troops partaking in the procession were units from various parts of the world, including Thracians, Galatians, Mysians and Iranians. The various 'ethnic' units in the procession at Daphne may have had symbolic meaning as well; they presented Antiochus as a ruler of all nations and reanimated the dynasty's claims to Asia Minor and Thrace as Seleucid *doriktētos chōra*.[106]

There is, moreover, the probable association of the king with Dionysus. Such an association is best known from the Ptolemaic context: most of all, the Dionysiac imagery in the Grand Procession of Ptolemy Philadelphus had associated the advent of the victorious king with Dionysus's triumphant return from India.[107] Dionysiac imagery at Daphne included the king's disorganizing behaviour, the presence of 800 ivory tusks as votive offerings,[108] and chariots drawn by elephants. Dionysus featured on Seleucid coinage since the reign of Seleucus IV (187–175 BCE), who struck bronze coins at Ecbatana showing Dionysus on the obverse and an Indian elephant on the reverse.[109]

In the Hellenistic period, Dionysus became a powerful symbol of kingship: as the conqueror of Asia, Dionysus was a victorious god and a saviour whose arrival in the west signalled the beginning of a golden age of plenitude and good fortune.[110] There may be a link with the enigmatic

---

[105] Polyb. 30.25.16.   [106] Strootman (2007) 313; Iossif (2011c) 136–43.
[107] The Dionysiac procession of Ptolemy II is described in detail by Callixeinus of Rhodes, *FGrHist* 627 F 2 *ap*. Ath. 5.196a–203b. The association of Dionysus with India was not an exclusively Ptolemaic idea, as we find it also around 300 with Megasthenes, *viz.*, in a Seleucid context (Strab. 15.1.6); on Megasthenes and Seleucid myth-making, see Kosmin (2013).
[108] Polyb. 30.25.12.
[109] *SC* II nos. 1353–6. Antiochus IV used images of elephants on his bronze coinage too (*SC* II nos. 1554 f.), as did some of his successors: Demetrius I (*SC* II nos. 1646; 1745), Alexander I (*SC* II nos. 1791; 1872; 1876), and Antiochus VI (*SC* II no. 2243). The image of triumphant Dionysus was known in Greece already in the pre-Hellenistic period (see e.g. Hdt. 2.146); but it was only after the death of Alexander that he became associated with India, and elephants became part of Dionysiac processions, first of all in early Ptolemaic Alexandria (Goukowsky [1981]). Antiochus IV was the first Seleucid to portray himself wearing an elephant scalp: *SC* II no. 1533: Susa. Elephant scalps are later also worn by Demetrius I (SC II no. 1696: Seleucia-Tigris), Demetrius II (SC II no. 1989: Seleucia-Tigris) and finally Alexander II (*SC* II no. 2234: Antioch).
[110] Tondriau (1953); Versnel (1970) 250–3; Heinen (1983). On Golden Age imagery in Hellenistic royal ideology and representation see Alföldi (1977); Préaux (1978) 201–38; Strootman (2014c).

inscription OGIS 253, dated to 167/6 but of unknown provenance, in which Antiochus IV is hailed as the 'Savior of Asia'.[111] A promise of liberation and peace was thus conveyed at Daphne by a king who already in 172/3 had styled himself *Theos Epiphanes* and in *c.* 169/8 had adopted, in addition, the epithet *Nikephoros*, bringer of victory, to commemorate his Egyptian campaigns.[112] Interestingly, the image of Dionysus as the king-like conqueror of Asia had originally been developed at the Ptolemaic court in relation to Alexander. This image was then adopted by the Seleucids, too.

Common Conclusion

Imperial capitals do not come into existence naturally. They have to be constructed symbolically as well as practically. Even the Ptolemies had to reckon with pre-existing administrative and religious centres (most of all Memphis). These needed not to be replaced, but integrated. To create an imperial centre, a place's status not only had to be expressed in monumental space and architecture. Moreover, rituals were needed that put the empire and the empire's power and splendour on display. It most of all had to be communicated. Court poetry and philosophy were important for the spread of imperial ideologies. Myths and reports about spectacular ritual and ceremonial too could do the trick to create the idea of a new imperial or even global centre. Empires claim to exist for all eternity. To ingrain the establishment of an imperial centre permanently in the minds of future generations, these capitals were presented as having always been there – hence the references to a pre-cultural and prehistorical past, the discovery of primordial sanctuaries in the footsteps of gods and culture heroes creating order.

In this joint chapter, rather than looking for differences, we have emphasized similarities. The Ptolemaic and Seleucid empires are, to a high degree, entangled systems, partly employing as their main imperial elites the same social groups: representatives of civic elites in the Aegean *poleis*. Differences are mainly visible in core regions where direct control

---

[111] OGIS 253: Βασιλεύοντος Ἀντιόχου θ[εοῦ Ἐπιφανοῦς τοῦ] | σωτῆρος τῆς Ἀσίας καὶ κτίσ[του καὶ εὐεργέτου] | τῆς πόλεως, ἔτους σμ' καὶ [ρ' ἐν τῶι συντελουμένωι] | ἀγῶνι Χαριστηρίοις ὑπὸ [- - - - - - - - - - - - -] | ἀπιόντος Ὑπερβερεταίου· (ll. 1–5; emendations Dittenberger).

[112] Mørkholm (1963) 37 and 72; cf. Mittag (2006) 118–19.

was possible: the Nile Valley, Babylonia, Lydia or Bactria, but not where the empires competed, met and clashed, such as the Levant and the Aegean. Ptolemaic–Seleucid rivalry was not just a matter of war. The Seleucid and Ptolemaic courts constantly reacted to each other in antagonistic exchanges of many forms.

CHAPTER 2

Reassessing Hellenistic Settlement Policies
The Seleucid Far East, Ptolemaic Red Sea Basin and Egypt

Rachel Mairs and Christelle Fischer-Bovet

Common Introduction

The implementation of new settlements and settlers, the physical alteration of existing settlements and the renaming of settlements are traditional tools of colonization and can be considered as marks of imperialism when they form a network of communication that serves to project and maintain a political power. Settlers – whether voluntary or forced – could be recruited locally or from distant cities and regions. The early Hellenistic period, between the late fourth and the mid-third century, was a period of large-scale migration: perhaps up to 200,000 migrants (men, women, children) from the Greek world settled in Egypt and possibly twice as many migrants settled in Asia.[1] The establishment of new settlements by the Macedonian kings outside the Greek world has generated modern reflections on colonization in the ancient world. Drawing on postcolonial studies but going beyond them, current scholarship on the Hellenistic world takes into consideration multiple power relations and examines the complex processes of interaction, the appeal of certain cultural elements (in multiple directions) and the modes of integration that developed between the different populations.

Ideally, for comparing Seleucid and Ptolemaic settlement policies, we would need to assess the composition of the settlements (military vs. civilian, Greek vs. non-Greek, single vs. multiple ethnic origin), their size and number, and the policies developed to attract migrants and/or to control them, as well as the choice of location, the strategic purpose(s) of settlements and their stability. But the sources are limited: on the one hand, ancient authors often wrote long after the fact; on the other hand, there are only a small number of contemporary documentary texts and of well-excavated sites. It remains difficult to distinguish the new settlements

[1] Fischer-Bovet (2011); Scheidel (2004) 24–5.

in the archaeological record or to connect them to textual evidence. Because of the vast territories covered by the two empires under discussion, this chapter focuses on areas outside the existing spheres of Greek settlement. First, the Far East (Bactria and Central Asia) under Alexander and the early Seleucids; then the Red Sea basin under Ptolemy II and Ptolemy III and Upper Egypt/Lower Nubia under Ptolemy VI to Ptolemy IX. Settlements in other regions of these empires are not systematically examined in this volume, except for the foundations of capitals such as Alexandria and Antioch (see von Reden and Strootman) and the creation of *poleis* in Babylonia in the second century BC and of *politeumata* (see Clancier and Gorre as well as Sänger in this volume). Whenever possible, this chapter addresses the questions of the composition of the settlement and its type, whether new foundations, fictitious 'new' foundations in or near existing sites, or simple renamed settlements, best conceptualized on a spectrum rather than as clear-cut categories. While Mairs offers a historiographical typology of settlements in the Hellenistic Far East, Fischer-Bovet proposes a typology of Ptolemaic settlements.

A REASSESSING SETTLEMENT POLICIES IN THE HELLENISTIC FAR EAST

Rachel Mairs

1 Introduction

Homer Hasenpflug Dubs (1892–1969) is one of the least likely contributors to the study of Classical city foundations. In 1957, he published a short book with the provocative title *A Roman City in Ancient China*. At the time, he held the Chair of Chinese at the University of Oxford and had led a peripatetic life as the child of American missionary parents in China, as student and later post-holder at a number of American universities and living and studying in China for an extended period. He was an award-winning scholar, respected colleague (in China, Europe and America) and fondly remembered teacher.[2] But he was not immune to lapses in scholarly judgement.

Dubs's collaborator, named in the text but not on the title page of the book, was Sir William Woodthorpe Tarn (1869–1957), in one of his final

---

[2] Goodrich (1970).

scholarly contributions. The book's argument centres around a former city in present-day Gansu province called Liqian, which was also one of the words used in Chinese for the Roman empire. Dubs proposes an etymological derivation from 'Alexandria' and explains the extension of this term by the Chinese to the Roman empire as a whole through an anecdote about some Parthian jugglers.[3] After M. Licinius Crassus's defeat by Parthian forces at the Battle of Carrhae in 53 BC, so the Dubs–Tarn hypothesis goes, Roman prisoners were taken east to Margiana. This transfer is indeed historically attested. Pliny describes how 'it was to this place [Antioch in Margiana] that Orodes conducted those of the Romans who had survived the defeat of Crassus' (*Natural History*, 6.18). Horace uses the theme of the Roman soldiers' exile in Central Asia to make a point about civilization versus barbarity, and the moral decline of Rome:

> Didn't Crassus' soldiers live in vile marriage with barbarian wives, and (because of our Senate and its perverse ways!) grow old, in the service of their hostile fathers. (*Odes* 3.5.5, trans. A. S. Kline)

Dubs relates this exile of Roman soldiers to Central Asia to an episode in an eleventh-century AD Chinese account of a campaign in 36 BC against the Xiongnu leader Zhizhi Chanyu.[4] The account mentions a 'fish-scale' military formation used by soldiers defending a city. 'It was not the sort of thing any nomadic people, such as the Huns [i.e. the Xiongnu], could have achieved', in Dubs's view. 'Nomads and barbarians, like the Gauls, rushed to battle in a confused mass. A well-patterned array in battle can be achieved only by men long trained as professional soldiers.'[5] Dubs first thought of a Greek phalanx, but Tarn thought this unlikely and proposed a Roman *testudo*, pointing out to Dubs that 'there were Roman soldiers within walking distance of Jzh-jzh's town.'[6] The geographical distance from the possible Roman soldiers in Margiana is in fact around five hundred miles, and the chronological distance seventeen years. Even Roman soldiers captured as young men must by this date have been well past their prime. Nor is any plausible reason provided as to how and why these Romans would have moved from Margiana to Xiongnu territory.

'The presence of Romans at Jzh-jzh's town', Dubs continues, 'is confirmed by the double wooden palisade which the Chinese found outside the city wall.'[7] As with the fish-scale formation, Tarn rejects a Greek origin

---

[3] The ingenious, although dubious, chain of argumentation may be followed at Dubs (1957) 3.
[4] The work in question is the *Zizhi Tongjian*; see Yap (2009).   [5] Dubs (1957) 12.
[6] Dubs (1957) 13.   [7] Dubs (1957) 14.

and proposes a Roman one. Dubs concludes that 'Jzh-jzh undoubtedly had Roman engineering assistance in building his town.' His narrative has the surviving Romans leave their new homes in Margiana willingly with the Chinese, to be settled in a new foundation to guard the Chinese frontier. On this city's political organization, Dubs concludes:

> We know nothing except that there continued to exist the city of Li-jien in the west of China. We are not told that it was organized as a *colonia*. The number of Romans was probably too small and a constitution could not have been secured from the *Senatus*. It was, however, probably organized on a Roman model. Its people had not surrendered to the Chinese, but were freemen and consequently would not be expected in every way to submit to Chinese practices. The Chinese government generally left its people alone, as far as practicable, as long as they kept the peace, paid the taxes, and rendered due military service. The Chinese almost surely gave these Romans a centrally appointed Chief or Magistrate to oversee the city and county. That they married Chinese women may be taken for granted, since the city continued to exist for centuries. Whether or not some sort of *colonia* was effected, the place did constitute a Roman settlement and in that sense may be called a Roman colony.[8]

Initial reviews of the Dubs–Tarn hypothesis were sceptical.[9] Occasional sensationalist popular media interest in the question of 'Romans in China' still erupts. The theme was adopted for the 2015 Jackie Chan film *Tian Jiang Xiong Shi / Dragon Blade*. Elaborately argued but exceedingly dubious 'explanations' of assumed foreign, Greco-Roman presence at Zhizhi's city abound online, and even occasionally in academic journals.[10] In 2007, a study in the *Journal of Human Genetics* debunked the idea of any Roman paternal genetic contribution to the population of Liqian.[11]

My point is not to poke fun at long-dead eminent scholars who do not deserve to be so unkindly mocked. Rather, it is that scholarly expectations about what a colonial settlement should *look like* can lead us down some weird and wonderful rabbit holes. With the Far East of the Hellenistic world as my case study, I shall explore the archaeological signature of settlement under Alexander and the early Seleucids. Traces on the ground can be compared and contrasted with written sources. We find both cases where settlements mentioned by historians have left no identifiable Greek material signature, and settlements with material culture demonstrating

---

[8] Dubs (1957) 22–3.
[9] See, for example, Samuel Lieberman in *Classical Philology* 53, 1958, 210–11, and Germaine Faider-Feytmans in *L'antiquité classique* 26, 1957, 507, who found the connections 'extrêmement ténu'.
[10] Matthew (2011). [11] Zhou et al. (2007).

connections to the Greek world which are not mentioned in extant histories. Fischer-Bovet, in Chapter 2B, has proposed a typology of Ptolemaic settlements. I can offer only a historiographical typology of settlements in the Hellenistic Far East – from those where passing mentions offer up temptations to historians such as Dubs and Tarn, to those where historical evidence of Greek presence is also accompanied by recognizably 'Greek' material culture.

Misguided though his conclusions may be, Dubs does identify some important areas where we might look for evidence of Greek colonial presence. There may be historical evidence of population movements, as in Pliny's description of the removal of Crassus's soldiers to Margiana. Material culture offers a potential signature of colonization, but here we must be careful and critical in our analysis. Although he offers only literary testimony on material culture, Dubs treats the form of fortifications at the city of Zhizhi as indicative of a particular cultural tradition. Toponyms, too, may be significant. Liqian may not be an 'Alexandria', but there are plenty of sites whose names are less ambiguous. Forms of behaviour and social organization (such as Roman military discipline) may also indicate the presence of immigrant populations. Dubs, furthermore, highlights some key research questions in approaching ancient colonial foundations: military versus civilian composition, ethnic interaction, interethnic marriage, and forced versus free migration. Dubs is wrong not because he went looking for the wrong things, but because he thought he had found them.

2 The Early Hellenistic Settlement of Central Asia: Historical and Archaeological Evidence

In the final volume of his series on the Hellenistic settlements, *From Armenia and Mesopotamia to Bactria and India*, the late Getzel Cohen noted that where our sources do provide information on Seleucid settlement in the 'Far East' of the Hellenistic world, their focus is on dynasts rather than the settlements themselves.[12] The number of such references, moreover, is small, because the number of settlements is also comparatively small, and their duration short, in turn, because of the 'short and tenuous nature of Seleucid rule there'.[13] What evidence, then, do we have to work with in exploring early Seleucid settlements in the region? At one end of the spectrum are brief mentions of the names of settlements by much later writers. Strabo, for example, notes three settlements in Aria, of which we

---

[12] Cohen (2013) 9.   [13] Cohen (2013) 40.

know practically nothing more – not that that has stopped scholars from attempting to identify them:

> The length of Aria is about two thousand stadia, and the breadth of the plain about three hundred. Its cities are Artakoana and Alexandreia, and Achaïa, all named after their founders. The land is exceedingly productive of wine, which keeps good for three generations in vessels not smeared with pitch.[14]

Artakoana, as an existing city, does not concern us here (Arr. *Anab.* 3.25.6; Curt. 6.6.25–33). The namesakes of the other two cities are Alexander himself, and most probably Achaios, son of Seleucus I. We cannot, and should not, do much more with this information. Strabo is writing at a long chronological and geographical distance; and knowing Alexander's penchant for renaming existing cities after himself, we cannot even be sure that these are three separate places.

Other references are more dubious still. Isidorus of Charax is the source for an Alexandria or Alexandropolis in Sakastene, and a Demetrias and an Alexandria in Arachosia (*Parthian Stations* 18 and 19).[15] I shall return to the latter below.

These are the examples where we should refrain from excessive speculation. Where do we have more scope? We usually have better potential to look at settlements which fall into one or both of two categories: they are mentioned by the Alexander historians and/or they have been subject to archaeological excavation. I refer specifically to the Alexander historians, because there are so few references in any Greek or Roman histories to what happened in this region after Alexander, and because Seleucid control over the region comes down only to the mid third century BC. There are five I should like to consider, going by their modern names for reasons that will become apparent: Merv, Kandahar, Begram, Samarkand and Ai Khanoum. Ancient names I shall discuss include Alexandria Oxeiana, Alexandria in the (Central Asian) Caucasus, Alexandria in Arachosia, Eukratideia, and Alexandria or Antioch in Margiana.

2.1 Merv

Merv, around 35 kilometres to the east of present-day Mary in Turkmenistan, is an excellent example of a city where our Greco-Roman historical evidence of early Hellenistic settlement is at odds with the

---

[14] Strab. 11.10.1; (the same cannot be said of Central Asian wine today); see Cohen (2013) 225.
[15] Cohen (2013) 244, 272.

archaeological picture.[16] The sources, as is typical for Central Asia, are much later. Merv is not mentioned by Arrian. Curtius, with a certain geographical vagueness, describes Alexander's progress towards 'the city of Margiana'. The city itself is neglected in favour of describing Alexander's new settlements in the vicinity:

> Round about it six sites were chosen for founding towns, two facing south and four east; they were distant from one another only a moderate space, so that they might be able to aid one another without seeking help from a distance. All these were situated on high hills. At that time they served as curbs upon the conquered nations; to-day, forgetful of their origin, they serve those over whom they once ruled. (Curt. 7.10.15–16)

Curtius's testimony is inaccurate – the region around Merv has no hills – but it is notable that he does not claim that Alexander founded a new city in Margiana, only smaller settlements, nor that he introduced the name 'Alexandria'. His narrative of the degeneration and decline of the Greek colonies in Central Asia is a theme to which I shall return.

Pliny, in contrast to Curtius, does claim that Alexander founded an 'Alexandria' in Margiana, which was then 'destroyed by barbarians'. Later:

> Antiochos son of Seleukos re-established a city on the same site, intersected by the river Murghab, which is canalized into Lake Zotha; he had preferred that the city should be named after himself. Its circuit measures seventy stades. This is the place to which the Roman prisoners taken in the disaster of Crassus were brought by Orodes. (Plin. *HN* 6.18)

This is the same passage cited by Dubs to explain alleged Roman presence in China.

Strabo, likewise, identifies Antiochus I as the founder of a city at Merv: 'Margiana is similar to this country [Aria], although its plain is surrounded by deserts. Admiring its fertility, Antiochos Soter enclosed a circuit of fifteen hundred stadia with a wall and founded a city, Antiocheia' (Strab. 11.10.2).

Merv is less a single archaeological site than a landscape in which several successive cities were established. The Achaemenid period site is Erk-kala, a raised citadel. The Hellenistic-period site, Gyaur-kala, represents a significant accretion to this pre-existing settlement, multiplying it several times in size.[17] To date, there has been comparatively little archaeological exploration of Gyaur-kala; the adjacent Sasanian and Islamic period cities

---

[16] For résumés of the evidence on Merv and Margiana, see Cohen (2013) 245–50; and Coloru (2013b).
[17] On its fortifications, see Zavyalov (2007).

are better documented. Strabo's 'Wall of Antiochus' cannot be identified for certain because of the difficulties in dating mud brick constructions. Bader, Gaibov and Koshelenko argue that it is represented by a pre-Islamic wall relatively close to the oasis, and not by any of the fortifications further from the city.[18] The evidence of field survey and satellite imagery appears to support the theory that there was a general constriction in the area of settled and irrigated land around the oasis in the Hellenistic period, but this stands in contrast to a picture from historical sources in which the urban settlements and agricultural wealth of the region are stressed.[19] Given the problems in dating archaeological remains, and, indeed, artefacts and ceramics, from the region, it must be accepted that much about the extent and nature of the occupation of Margiana in the Hellenistic period remains to be determined.[20] But what is at any rate clear is that the early Hellenistic presence, and any deliberate Seleucid colonization, at Merv represented an addition to an earlier, well-established settlement.

2.2 Kandahar

There is both historical and archaeological evidence for early Hellenistic settlement at Kandahar, in southern Afghanistan, but the evidence that this was ever an 'Alexandria' is less secure. There is no indication of any Seleucid eponymous foundation (or refoundation) in Arachosia. An 'Alexandria in Arachosia', although commonly assumed to have existed, is difficult to identify securely in the ancient sources.[21] There is no city with this name in the accounts of the Alexander historians. Isidorus of Charax mentions an Alexandropolis or Alexandria as the 'metropolis of Arachosia' (*Parthian Stations*, 19). He describes the city as 'Greek' although what he means by this is not clear. The only name given for the principal city of Arachosia by earlier writers is that of the region itself.[22] Pliny refers to a 'city of the Arachosians' and later states that Arachosia, its river and city bear the same name (Plin. *HN* 61, 92). Strabo refers to 'the city Arachotoi' (Strab. 11.8.9). It is tempting to impose this name 'Alexandria' on earlier cities of Arachosia not so named by Strabo and Pliny, but 'if that equation does not hold, there is no peg available in the literary wardrobe on which to

---

[18] Bader et al. (1998).   [19] Callieri (1996).
[20] See Koshelenko et al. (1996) on changing settlement patterns in the Merv Oasis over the *longue durée*; Salvatori (2008) for a regional picture.
[21] Cohen (2013) 255–60.
[22] On Arachosia in the Hellenistic period, see Bernard (2005); Mairs (2011); and Mairs (2014b) 102–17.

hang an Alexandria of Arachosia founded by Alexander.'²³ In neither case are any details given of its history in the early Hellenistic period, or of the interest Alexander or the early Seleucids took in it.

Archaeological excavations at Old Kandahar were carried out between 1974 and 1978.²⁴ Old Kandahar is the name used for the site of Shahr-i-Kuhna, a large ruin field 3 km to the west of the modern city, which was abandoned in 1738. Because of constraints of time and resources, excavations were restricted to half a dozen or so individual areas within the much larger site.

Little or no material among the ceramics and small finds is overtly 'Greek' in the sense of representing direct connections with the Greek world to the west, although excavators found a few sherds of pottery which were probable imports. The initial reports cautiously argue that, while the ceramic and numismatic records reveal connections with other sites in the wider region, both inside and outside nominal Greek control, it is equally important to emphasize the extent to which Old Kandahar did not undergo any revolutionary change in material culture with the transition from Achaemenid, to Seleucid, to Mauryan, to Greco-Bactrian rule.

It is the later epigraphic record that presents the best evidence, albeit indirect, that Kandahar was the site of an early Hellenistic settlement. Arachosia passed from Seleucid to Mauryan control in 303 BC, under the terms of a treaty between Seleucus and Chandragupta. Assuming that no settlement under the Seleucid aegis took place after this date, then any Greek presence in Mauryan Kandahar must be the legacy of an early Hellenistic (Alexandrian or Seleucid) settlement. Three Greek inscriptions may be securely provenanced to Old Kandahar, and another is likely to come from the site.²⁵ Two of these inscriptions, edicts of the Mauryan emperor Aśoka, date from the mid third century BC. Another, a brief and cryptic inscription – with the letters 'Alex . . . ' followed by what must be the most unfortunate lacuna in the epigraphic record of the Hellenistic Far East – may be a couple of decades earlier. The inscription of Sophytos son of Naratos is probably somewhat later in the third century, and the editors state that it came from Kandahar.²⁶ It makes allusions to Greek culture and the arts. The later presence of the Greek language and culture at Kandahar therefore suggests an earlier Greek settlement of sufficient size and longevity for Greek inscriptions to continue to have been produced.

---

²³ Fraser (1996) 133.
²⁴ Whitehouse (1978); McNicoll (1978); Helms (1979); and Helms (1982), with fuller publication in McNicoll and Ball (1996); and Helms (1997).
²⁵ Rougemont (2012) nos. 81–4.   ²⁶ Bernard et al. (2004); Mairs (2014b) 106–17.

2.3 Begram

In contrast to the case of Kandahar, an 'Alexandria of the Caucasus' (i.e. the Hindu Kush) is well attested in ancient authors.[27] Some basic information is also given on the process by which the settlement was established, and its success or otherwise in weathering its early years.

Arrian (*Anab.* 3.28.4) recounts that Alexander founded a city named Alexandria near 'Mount Caucasus'. He appointed a Persian named Proexes as satrap of the region, and his Companion Neiloxenos son of Satyros as *episkopos* of the troops there. This practice of appointing, or confirming, a Persian or Iranian satrap was followed by Alexander elsewhere in the east, notably in the case of his father-in-law Oxyartes. On his return from Bactria, however, Alexander dismissed the city's governor (who goes unnamed, but is presumably Proexes) 'because he thought he was not ruling well' (4.22.4–5). He made one Tyriaspes satrap instead; he is not otherwise known, but bears an Iranian name. Another companion, Nikanor, was appointed 'to put the city in order'. At the same time, the city was given a new injection of population, with the settlement of soldiers who were unfit for service, and some *perioikoi*.

Curtius (7.3.23) claims that the city was founded at the foot of the mountain where Prometheus had, according to legend, been chained. He does not mention Arrian's two-stage settlement of the site, and states that the colony was composed of demobilized soldiers and seven thousand *Caucasii*. The city's inhabitants, he says, call it Alexandria.

Diodorus (17.83.1–2) mentions not only that Alexander founded a city called Alexandria in a pass in the Caucasus, but also that he established satellite cities, each around a day's march from Alexandria. He offers figures different to Arrian: seven thousand *barbaroi*, three thousand camp followers and volunteers from among the mercenaries. Pliny (*HN* 6.62) makes reference to an *Alexandri oppidum* below the Caucasus.

There is an intuitive identification to be made between the ancient historians' Alexandria in (or below) the Caucasus and the archaeological site of Begram.[28] Begram lies around 60 km north of modern Kabul, at a strategic river junction. There are no securely identified Hellenistic period remains; almost all of the excavated material comes from the Kushan-period city.[29] Most scholarly attention has been devoted to the cache of luxury items, imports from the Mediterranean, South Asia and

---

[27] Cohen (2013) 263–9. [28] See, inter alia, Bernard (1982).
[29] Hackin (1939); Hackin (1954); Ghirshman (1946).

China, found in two rooms in the area named by the excavators the 'New Royal City'. Fascinating though this material is for looking at the later connections of Begram to the Greco-Roman world,[30] it has little or no bearing on the existence and nature of any early Hellenistic settlement at the site itself. A fortified citadel – the Burj-e-Abdullah – 600 m to the north of the 'New Royal City', at the river junction itself, may be the best candidate, but no work has as yet been undertaken to confirm this.

2.4 Marakanda / Samarkand

Arrian and Curtius give the by-now familiar résumé of Alexander's foundation activities at Marakanda.[31] Arrian states that Alexander passed through Marakanda, 'the capital of the land of the Sogdianians', en route to the river Tanais (3.30.6). On his return, Arrian says that 'he sent Hephaistion away to plant colonies in the cities of Sogdiana' (*Anab.* 4.16). Curtius mentions the city's substantial fortifications (a city wall of seventy stadia and an inner walled citadel) and states that Alexander left a garrison of 1,000 men there, while ravaging neighbouring settlements (*Curt.* 7.6.10). No author claims that Alexander either established a new settlement at Marakanda or gave the city a new name.

The relevant archaeological site is Afrasiab, a tell within the present-day city of Samarkand.[32] There is evidence for two phases of Hellenistic occupation: one early Hellenistic (Alexander to early Seleucid) and a Greco-Bactrian reconquest in the mid second century BC. These phases coincide with the intensification of fortifications, and a small but noticeable Greek influence on the ceramic record.[33] A large public building and grain storage facility of the Hellenistic period have been excavated,[34] as well as craft production areas, but the residential areas of the Hellenistic period have proven difficult to locate.[35] A small number of low-denomination bronze coins have been found at Afrasiab with the legend 'of King Antiochos', evidence of an early Seleucid mint in the region, most probably of the period of Antiochus I.[36]

2.5 Ai Khanoum and Unlocated Hellenistic Foundations

The most extensive archaeological remains of the early Hellenistic period in Central Asia are those of Ai Khanoum, which makes it all the more

---

[30] Mairs (2012).   [31] Cohen (2013) 279–82.   [32] Bernard (1996).
[33] Chichkina (1986); Rapin and Isamiddinov (1994).
[34] Grenet and Isamiddinov (2001) 239–41; Baratin (2010).
[35] Bernard, et al. (1992) 292–4; Bernard, et al. (1996).   [36] Gorin (2014).

frustrating that there is little or no secure literary evidence for the city's name and early history. As I have argued elsewhere, it is probable that there was Achaemenid-period settlement at the site or in the vicinity.[37] That the city had some kind of foundation narrative may be seen in the presence of a founder's shrine within the city walls, containing the famous inscription of Delphic maxims.[38] The city underwent renovations throughout its life, notably a major phase of construction in the early second century BC, which makes it difficult to discern much about the city's early Hellenistic history, including whether it was an Alexandrian or a Seleucid foundation.

Attempts to identify the ancient name of Ai Khanoum in extant sources tend to focus on two candidates: Alexandria Oxeiana and Eukratideia.[39] An Alexandria Oxeiana is mentioned only by Ptolemy (*Geography* 6.12.5–6). Ptolemy also mentions a Eukratideia (6.11.8), which Strabo (11.11.2) says was named after its ruler. The king in question is the Greco-Bactrian king Eukratides, known from other Greco-Roman literary sources[40] and from his coinage. Alexandria Oxeiana has also been identified with other sites,[41] but its equation with Ai Khanoum or any other site must remain speculation.[42]

3 The Character of the Early Hellenistic Settlement

As may be seen from the preceding discussion, the Alexander historians are the best available source of information on the early Hellenistic settlement of Central Asia – a deeply unsatisfactory situation. What both the historical and archaeological evidence reveal is an Alexandrian settlement policy which prioritized the garrisoning and concentration of local populations into existing cities, often accompanied with the construction of fortifications. All settlements had a strong military component, often soldiers described as no longer fit for active service. The archaeological signature of such settlements is naturally a weak one. Cities such as Samarkand and Merv had been and continued to be regional centres of population and administration. Any Greco-Macedonian mark on the archaeological record is more subtle: shifts in intensity of agricultural exploitation, construction or renovations of fortifications; the appearance of new forms in the ceramic record. Only in a very small number of cases were Central Asian 'Alexandrias' entirely

---

[37] Mairs (2014c).   [38] Mairs (2015).   [39] Cohen (2013) 273.   [40] Karttunen (1999–2000).
[41] Such as Kamypr-tepe: Rtweladse (2009).   [42] Fraser (1996) 153–6.

new foundations, and where this was the case, they were vulnerable to outside attack and misgovernment.[43]

In his rapid progress through the region, Alexander had little time to consolidate the new foundations. Three weeks were spent at Alexandria Eschate to construct its walls, and all the buildings were completed seventeen days later (Arr. *Anab.* 4.4.1; Curt. 7.6.26). The historical sources give very little information on the foundation of Alexandria in the Caucasus, but it seems to have been ill-equipped to survive and develop as a settlement. When Alexander passed by it again, on his way to India, wholesale reorganization was necessary: the inefficient governor was dismissed, more settlers were provided from the local area and from among the troops, and a new city governor and satrap were appointed. Clearly the settlement had declined once the Macedonian army had gone. It was only because it happened to be on Alexander's route to India that some attempt was made to arrest and reverse this decline. It must therefore be assumed that the same hasty foundation led to similarly incohesive and poorly managed settlements elsewhere, but that most of these were essentially left to fall apart.

It should also be noted that not all demobilized troops were necessarily settled in the country on a permanent basis. Before crossing the Oxus, Alexander had sent home a mixed group of Macedonians too old for active service and mutinous Thessalians (Arr. *Anab.* 3.29.5; Curt. 7.5.27). Other troops may have been only temporarily garrisoned in one place to convalesce. Those of the Companion cavalry who were left in Zariaspa (Bactra) because of ill health, for example, were later capable of launching a counter-attack against Spitamenes's raid into Bactria (Arr. *Anab.* 4.16.6).

In all, the picture which emerges of the Greek settlements in Central Asia at the time of Alexander's departure for India is not a strong one. The settlements had a difficult birth and remained vulnerable to local uprisings, nomadic incursions or simply inefficient government. A force of 3,500 cavalry and 10,000 infantry was left in Bactria under Amyntas (the figures are Arrian's, Arr. *Anab.* 4.22.3; see also Curt. 8.2.14), but the Greek settlements and garrisons were spread out over a large area, and it is difficult to escape the conclusion that this force, despite its size, must have been dismally ineffective at securing the wider region against both external and internal (Greek and Central Asian) threats. Most detrimental to the settlements' survival beyond their early years were two major settler revolts:[44]

---

[43] Alexandria Eschate: Holt (1988) 54–9.   [44] Holt (1988) 70–87; Iliakis (2013).

What the Greek troops, left behind as settlers in the remote areas of Central Asia during the campaign, thought of their situation may be judged from the fact that once news of Alexander's death reached them they immediately packed their bags and began that journey home that soon ended in disaster.[45]

4 Seleucid Settlement in the Region

The settlement of the East continued under the first Seleucids. Little detail is available on Seleucus I's rapid conquest of the Iranian Plateau and the Upper Satrapies – Justin (*Epit.* 15.4.10–12) takes him practically straight from victory in Babylon to victory in Bactria – but the evidence suggests a largely peaceful transition of power, conducted through diplomacy with the various satraps. This was the same policy as had earlier been followed by Antigonus, and the continuity both in personnel and in the type of policy successfully implemented for dealing with this personnel is striking: Sibyrtios, for example, continued as satrap of Arachosia throughout the period in question.[46]

Central Asia was strategically important, and when Seleucus I appointed his son Antiochus as co-regent, it was with special responsibility for that region. Seleucus sent out fresh reserves of colonists, refounded cities and established royal mints.[47] Demodamas of Miletus was dispatched to campaign across the Jaxartes, where he set up an altar to Apollo of Didyma (Plin. *HN* 6.49; it is unclear whether this took place under Antiochus's co-regency in the East or earlier during the period of Seleucus's initial conquests). The archaeological evidence of continuing occupation, with no significant interruptions throughout the third century at many archaeological sites, demands that the old view of Seleucid disinterest in Central Asia be substantially revised.

The growing autonomy of Diodotid Bactria during the course of the third century will undoubtedly have affected Greek colonization. Without Seleucid state intervention in the process, settlement by incoming Greeks from the Mediterranean world will inevitably have become a matter of individual initiative. What motivation or incentive might a Greek have had for settling in the East? Bactria had urban centres, agricultural potential, important trade routes and mineral resources, and would therefore have

---

[45] Fraser (1996) 185. [46] Sherwin-White and Kuhrt (1993) 12.
[47] App. *Syr.* 57, gives an exaggerated account of Seleucus's foundations; on Seleucid royal mints in Bactria under Antiochus I, in addition to the new evidence from Samarkand, see Bernard (1985); Abdullaev et al. (2004).

held certain attractions for settlers. Communication between Central Asia and the Mediterranean could be a laborious and lengthy process, but transport links were reasonably efficient and well maintained under the Seleucids, just as they had been under the Achaemenids, and the later rise of Parthia did not greatly disrupt long-distance contact and trade.[48] The presence of commodities imported from the Greek Mediterranean, and even dramatic and philosophical works on papyrus, at Ai Khanoum attest regular, if small-scale, contact between the Hellenistic Far East and the Mediterranean world well into the second century.[49]

None of this, however, is enough to suggest that the Hellenistic Far East attracted Greek settlers on any great scale after the first military settlements. The region had much to offer an émigré Greek seeking to advance himself socially or economically, but in the early Hellenistic period it was up against some extraordinarily strong competition. Alexandria in Egypt, with its greater proximity to Greece and court patronage of the arts and sciences, could attract large numbers of prominent intellectuals. A Greek mercenary, too, could offer his services to several Hellenistic states which were easier to reach, and most probably offered better pay.

All these factors suggest that the nucleus of Bactria's Greek population was formed by the early settlers, under Alexander and the first Seleucids, and that subsequent migration from the western Greek world had only a limited impact. In *The Greeks in Bactria and India*, the second edition of which appeared a few years before his collaboration with Dubs, Tarn wrote that 'when in the middle of the third century BC Bactria began to break loose from the Seleucid empire there were obviously many Greeks settled in the country, but it is not clear how they got there.'[50] It is by now fairly clear how the Greeks got there, but the mechanisms and policies of early Seleucid settlement in the region remain obscure.

The place where we can best see the impact of the Seleucid involvement in Central Asia is in fact in a Greek city, not a Central Asian one. Apama, wife of Seleucus I, was the daughter of the Sogdian Spitamenes (Arr. *Anab.* 7.4.6). She was the mother of Antiochus I and also of Achaios, both of whom, as was discussed above, were claimed by Strabo to have had eponymous foundations in Aria (11.10.1). She was the object of an honorific decree by the *boule* and *demos* of Miletus in 299/8 BC (I.Didyma 480). In the same year, a decree was made in honour of her son Antiochus (I.Didyma 479).

---

[48] Gardin (1985); Mairs (2014a).   [49] Lerner (2003).   [50] Tarn (1951 [1938]) 72.

The proposals to honour Apama and Antiochus came from Demodamas of Miletus, because of mother and son's benefactions towards the temple of Apollo at Didyma but also – most importantly in the context of the present discussion – because 'Queen Apama has previously displayed all goodwill and zeal for those of the Milesians who served in the army with King Seleukos' (I.Didyma 480, trans. Austin (2001) No. 51).

The decrees are evidence of the support of a queen of Central Asian origin for Milesian troops under Demodamas in the very late fourth century or very early third century BC. The Central Asian–Milesian connection becomes clearer in the following decades. In the 290s and 280s, under both Seleucus and Antiochus, Demodamas served as commander in Bactria and Sogdiana. He campaigned beyond the river Tanais, where he set up altars to Apollo of Didyma.[51] The date of Apama's death is not known. In around 292 BC, her son Antiochus was appointed co-regent and took responsibility for the lands east of the Euphrates: the Iranian Plateau and Central Asia (App. *Syr.* 62). We should not jump to conclusions about the roles of Apama and Antiochus as intercultural mediators between Central Asia and Macedonia.[52] It may be deduced from the evidence, however, that both played an important role in consolidating Seleucid power in Central Asia, and in benefactions to commanders, troops and their city of origin.

The decrees in honour of Apama and Antiochus are, frustratingly, our strongest and most direct pieces of evidence for the military deployments and networks of patronage that supported early Seleucid settlement in Central Asia.

5 Conclusions

The criteria by which Dubs aims to identify foreign settlement in China – place names, historical evidence of population movement and suggestive material culture – are useful in approaching early Hellenistic settlement in Central Asia, even though we must analyse these pieces of potential evidence in a very different way. There are also questions which, although they are difficult to explore with the evidence in hand, must be borne in mind, notably that of the ethnic composition of settlements.[53] The settlements of the Hellenistic Far East cannot be taken as representative of the

---

[51] Plin. *HN* 6.49; on the campaigns of Demodamas, see Kosmin (2014b) 61–7.
[52] Mairs (2011); on an earlier Central Asian-Milesian connection, see Mairs (2013).
[53] Olbrycht (2011); Coloru (2013a).

Seleucid empire as a whole. Their distinguishing features are their military nature, the haste with which they were established by an army on campaign, and their almost exclusive concentration in well-established and important urban centres.

B REASSESSING PTOLEMAIC SETTLEMENT POLICIES: ANOTHER LOOK AT THE *POLEIS*

Christelle Fischer-Bovet

1 Introduction

For a long time, the view was that the Ptolemies were not active in creating *poleis* settlements, especially in comparison to their rivals the Seleucids, because as traditional Greek *poleis* they only developed Alexandria and founded Ptolemais in Upper Egypt.[54] The whole interpretative framework was that of rulers with few imperial ambitions and little interest in founding cities. In the most recent study devoted to Ptolemaic settlements in 2006 – in fact, the only monograph entirely devoted to this topic – Mueller has shown that the Ptolemies were quite active in developing all types of new settlements, pushing further the analyses of Cohen and Heinen in the 1980s and 1990s.[55] The Ptolemies were not only actively founding cities outside Egypt but also other types of settlements in Egypt and beyond. They had what we can call a settlement policy whose main principle was the same as that of the Seleucids, Mueller argues: new settlements were founded in regions with low density of settlement, and their natures varied according to the ecology – or landscape – of each region.

As in the Seleucid case, we are dependent on the accounts of later authors which are to be taken with caution, but at times epigraphic and papyrological sources shed a more detailed light on these settlements. Until recently, Ptolemaic sites in Egypt had rarely been the subject of proper archaeological excavations or excavated at all; but in the last two decades the situation has dramatically changed, notably with the works of Arnold and the Swiss and German team on Elephantine; Sidebotham at Berenike on the Red Sea; Davoli, Marouard, and Müller on urbanization; and

---

[54] Heinen (1997) 351–2; I thank Bérangère Redon and Dorothy Thompson for commenting on earlier drafts, and the contributors of this volume for their comments.
[55] Mueller (2006a) 2–6; Cohen (1983); Heinen (1997). For the second century BC, see Gerardin (2018).

Boussac and Redon on baths.⁵⁶ These have opened up new avenues to assess, in combination with textual sources, the impact of Macedonian rule on the landscape and urbanization, on continuities and adaptations, and the participation of the local populations in this process.

The purposes of Chapter 2B are threefold. First, it aims to characterize early Ptolemaic settlement as a counterpart to Mairs's examination of Hellenistic and early Seleucid settlements, yet the focus is not historiographical here. Instead, a typology of settlements is proposed to show the variety of Ptolemaic imprint on the territory beyond the foundations of Greek *poleis* (Section 2). In common with Mairs's Chapter 2A, it explores areas outside the existing spheres of Greek settlement to examine how different groups, including local elites and populations, participated in shaping new settlements. It focuses on urban settlements in Egypt and the Red Sea basin that resembled *poleis* but were not city states with political institutions as in the sphere of Greek settlements, or as in Ptolemais in Upper Egypt, called here 'political *poleis*' (Section 3). The Red Sea area, along which the Ptolemies developed settlements, is especially informative since the contemporary Egyptian account has been preserved for two new dynastic settlements, both of which are called *poleis* by Strabo two and a half centuries later. The second aim of this study is to compare new settlements from the third century with the *poleis* founded in Egypt and Lower Nubia in the second century and to show that Ptolemaic settlement policies did not disappear but remained similar to earlier ones even if their frequency was far lower (Section 4). Finally, by exploring alterations to existing settlements, a third aim is to suggest that urbanization (and architecture) had an impact on how the local population in Egypt came to conceptualize, symbolically, their *nome* capitals as *poleis*. This does not imply that the *nome* capitals developed the institutions of a Greek *polis* like Naucratis, but that part of their populations mimicked some aspects (including lifestyle), as may be seen already in the third century (Section 3) and later in second-century Elephantine and first-century Thebes (Section 5).

2 Typology

The variety of settlements attested in literary, documentary, and archaeological sources can be best conceptualized along three axes representing (1)

---

⁵⁶ Arnold et al. (2014); Sidebotham (2011); Davoli (2011); Marouard (2008); Müller (2010); Boussac et al. (2009); and Redon (2019).

the number of inhabitants, (2) the level of material change and name change (i.e. metonomasy), and (3) their political, military, and economic statuses and functions, what Davoli calls the juridical point of view.[57] On this model, the first axis represents the number of inhabitants in a settlement. On the second axis, existing settlements that are renamed, generally with a dynastic name, represent the lower level of change, although the lack of the archaeological context often prevents us from verifying the extent of material alterations or the complete absence of such.[58] Then come the renamed settlements for which new settlers and/or new constructions, some being culturally Greek, e.g. *agora*, *stoa*, baths, grid-plan, are attested. Mueller calls these 'mixed foundations', but both types have also been labelled 'fictitious "new" foundations' in the relevant literature.[59] The highest level of change is assumed to be that found in new foundations. These almost always bore a dynastic name that lay stress on them as the products of royal decisions; these are therefore known by historians as dynastic foundations. Such foundations were sometimes built on or very close to a previous settlement.[60] All three types are to be understood as ideal types, while in practice it remains difficult to disentangle new from mixed foundations and mixed from renamed foundations, and it would therefore be more accurate to conceptualize these settlements on a spectrum. Assuming that dynastic names suggest a high level of involvement and change, Mueller uses these as indicators for the frequency and volume of Ptolemaic settlement.[61]

The third axis represents the political, military, and economic status and functions of a settlement and is partly related to the number of inhabitants. The Greek terms *epoikion* designated a farmstead or hamlet, *phrourion* a fortress and *kome* a village; the latter two could function as a trading station or harbour, as could larger urban settlements (in Egypt often *nome* capitals) and *poleis*. In hieroglyphic and demotic Egyptian *tmy* (or *dmy*) could designate a *nome* capital, a large town, a harbour town or a village, while the old term *n(i)w.t* was used in hieroglyphic texts for a *nome* capital or an urban settlement.[62] In any type of settlements, military settlers called *cleruchs* could be granted land (*kleroi*) and sometimes also a billet or dwelling (*stathmos*).[63] Yet soldiers could also be stationed in these

---

[57] Davoli (2011) 69–70.　[58] E.g. Davoli (2011) 70.　[59] Mueller (2006a) 79, Table 2.2.
[60] Mueller (2006a) 79, Table 2.2.
[61] Mueller (2006a) 3 notes that dynastic settlements do not appear fundamentally different from other new settlements, but this is to be tested by current and future excavations.
[62] On the polysemy of the term, see Agut-Labordère (2013); on *n(i)w.t*, see Section 5.2.
[63] For Egypt, see Scheuble-Reiter (2012) and Fischer-Bovet (2014b) 238–78.

settlements without land allotments, simply as mercenaries (professional soldiers). As stressed by Mueller, each region is different, so settlements should be compared within their own 'ecological-system': for instance, a *polis* in Cilicia could have fewer inhabitants (and be smaller) than a village in Egypt.[64] Davoli insists that Egypt was an urban society from its beginning, and envisions, from an urbanistic and architectural point of view, three levels of settlements in Egypt: villages, towns, and cities (including *nome* capitals), acknowledging that from a juridical point of view such cities were not political Greek *poleis*.[65] Changes occurring in these cities in Egypt during the Hellenistic period – they are mostly *nome* capitals sometimes called *metropoleis* in the papyri – transformed them, it is argued below, into what could be called 'Greco-Egyptian *poleis*'.[66]

3 Character of Early Ptolemaic Settlements (III c. BC)

3.1 Foundations of New poleis

Even if Alexandria was founded by Alexander, who received a cult as founder (*ktistes*), Ptolemy I was the one who developed Alexandria, and he founded Ptolemais Hermiou in Upper Egypt, of which he was the *ktistes*.[67] With Naucratis, these formed the three political *poleis* of Egypt in the third century. Outside Egypt, Ptolemy put some constraints on the *polis* of Cyrene by restoring its constitution.[68] Because of Ptolemy I's early involvement in this region, Mueller argues that he also founded Ptolemais-near-Barca in Cyrenaica; this is plausible but cannot be ascertained.[69] Most of the *poleis* foundations or refoundations throughout the Ptolemaic territories were initiated by Ptolemy II and III (see Map 1, Map 2, and Map 3).[70]

Southern Anatolia offers a good example of Ptolemaic activities in founding political *poleis* in regions where they were rare and/or the density of settlement was lower. These *poleis* could therefore play the role of strong nodes in the network of Ptolemaic power. Both the Ptolemies and Seleucids were particularly active there: Ptolemy II and

---

[64] Mueller (2006a) 83–4.
[65] Davoli (2011) 69–70; for instance, in his survey of thirty-seven city state cultures, Hansen (2006) strangely omits Egypt and starts with Mesopotamia.
[66] The term *polis* is already attested in four papyri from the third-century Arsinoite nome, while P.Rev. refers to all *metropoleis* of Egypt: P.Cair.Isid 84 (264–257 BC), P.Rev. §48, l. 16 frag. 4 (259/8 BC), P. Tebt. III.1 703 (210 BC) and SB XX 14404 (225–221 BC).
[67] Howe (2014).   [68] SEG 9, 1 and SEG 18, 726 = Austin (2006) no. 29.
[69] Mueller (2006a) 114–16, esp. 143–6.   [70] Mueller (2006a) 142–3 on uncertain dating.

Ptolemy III founded or refounded eight *poleis* with a dynastic name, and the Seleucids before and after them nine.[71] These settlements provided military control but also access to economic resources, human and natural, and the possibility to increase tax revenues. Discussion of *poleis* foundations in the Ptolemaic empire is dominated by the foundation of Arsinoe in Cilicia, named after the sister-wife of Ptolemy II (Map 3).[72] Mentioned on an inscription that has been analysed in detail, it suffices here to underscore five elements that shed light on the character of early Hellenistic settlements, the last one typical of the creation of a Ptolemaic culture.[73] Firstly, the location was chosen because it was a strategic place (*topos epikairos*, l. 22). Secondly, the founder, Aetos, was a *strategos* (here with the meaning of 'high military commander') who belonged to what Ma has termed the 'supra-polis players'.[74] Thirdly, the foundation required expelling 'the Barbarians that were encroaching' on the land, probably local Cilician villagers.[75] Fourthly, the foundation process was long, because Ptolemy II lost control over the area and Ptolemy III regained it probably in the 230s. Aetos's son Thraseas, *strategos* of Cilicia (here with the meaning of 'governor'), continued the foundation process when his help was needed regarding a dispute over the territories. Finally, in addition to the usual civic institutions, the cult of the Brother-Sister Gods (*Theoi Adelphoi*) was to be central not only to the city of Arsinoe but also to that of Nagidos.[76]

When compared to the Seleucids, the first point to be made is that the Ptolemaic settlement policies also started early on. There was competition between the different kings to offer appealing settlement opportunities, especially to soldiers. If one could establish the total number of *polis* foundations for each empire in the third century, the Seleucids would probably lead, but this would not take into consideration the geographical particularities of each region, the size of their territories and the extension of non-*polis* settlements. Furthermore, political *poleis* were complemented by a network of non-*polis* settlements, which are slowly being uncovered through archaeological excavation or survey, such as the fortress of Meyddancikale in Cilicia, discovered in the 1980s, that shows how the

---

[71] Fischer-Bovet (forthcoming).   [72] SEG 29, 1426.
[73] Habicht and Jones (1989); Chaniotis (1993); Petzl (2002) with corrections.
[74] On Aetos' family, especially Ptolemaios son of Thraseas, see Gerardin in this volume; Peremans and Van 't Dack (1950–81) vol. II/VIII 1828; Habicht and Jones (1989) 337–45; Sosin (1997).
[75] See Habicht and Jones (1989) 324 on l. 23–4.
[76] On this cult, see Caneva (2016) 129–78, esp. 167–8; Meadows (2013) 29–31 on this cult and other eponym (re)foundations.

Ptolemies projected their control beyond the coastal areas.[77] Thus, to have an overall picture of the settlement policies of a particular regime, we also need to consider settlements that were not political *poleis*.

3.2 Foundation of Non-polis Settlements in Egypt

The Ptolemies thought beyond the settlement of political *poleis* by creating trading posts, fortresses, villages, towns, or harbours, whether as new or mixed foundations. This is especially true in Egypt, where Ptolemy I started settling *cleruchs*, notably in the Fayyum area that was expanding through land reclamation (Map 2).[78] Many new settlements in Egypt were villages and some did not bear a dynastic name. In the Fayyum, eighteen new villages bore dynastic names such as Ptolemais, Arsinoe, and Berenike.[79] Names generally are significant. Dionysias, for instance, came from the god's name or from a *deme* in Alexandria and was called 'The New Village' (*P3-tmy-n-m3y*) in Demotic, while the names Arabon Kome, Syron Kome, and Thrakon Kome reflected the origin of a large number of settlers, probably many soldiers and policemen among them.[80] Inhabitants of new villages were, however, a mix of Egyptian and foreigners, civilians and soldiers, and so were those of existing villages with new settlers.[81] Only rarely in the papyrological sources can we see clusters, such as the Judaeans in Trikomia, who populated one area of the village, but there is no evidence of ghettoization.[82]

In terms of settlement layout, Philadelphia, on the estate granted by Ptolemy II to his finance minister (*dioiketes*) Apollonios, was even planned according to the Hippodamian grid used for *polis* foundations, but this was exceptional for a village.[83] Yet the fact that Philadelphia's main orientation following the canal rather than any theoretical orientation, as outlined in Vitruvius, rather hints at adaptation to the landscape.[84] Dionysias also had

---

[77] The low level of *polis* foundations in Syria and Phoenicia noted by Gerardin in this volume in comparison to Seleucid settlements should also be explored from this perspective.
[78] Mueller (2006a) 149–51 and Crawford (1971) 55.   [79] Clarysse (1991b) 77.
[80] Clarysse (2007) 70, 75, 78–9; on Dionysias, see P.Sorb. IV 152, l. 3 and Chaufray and Wackenier (2016).
[81] Clarysse (1991b) 71.
[82] *Ioudaios* is translated by 'Judaean' rather than 'Jew', since at that time immigrants from Judaea represented an ethnic group and not all came from a homogeneous religious background; see Honigman (2016) 29; Mueller (2006a) 136–8; Clarysse and Thompson (2006) 147–8.
[83] Marouard (2017); Clarysse and Vandorpe (1995); see e.g. P.Cair.Zen. II 59168 = SB 3, 6806 and Pfeiffer (2008) 403–4; there is no evidence that Apollonios founded Philadelphia (he would be the only non-military founder).
[84] Davoli (2001) 73–4.

an orthogonal pattern with roads parallel to the canal, and the temple and its dromos were inserted into the grid.[85] Even if these two settlements were usually called 'villages', their size and the monumentality of their temples place them, from an urbanistic (and architectural) point of view, into the (small) town category, such as Soknopaiou Nesos, Tebtunis, and Karanis in the Fayyum.[86]

3.3 Alteration of Settlements and the Term polis in Egypt

Both foreigners and Egyptians settled in existing settlements that could be physically altered and sometimes received a Greek name that was not a translation of their Egyptian names.[87] Some settlements continued to grow organically with no organized structure in relationship to the main temple and its *dromos*, as in the case of Tebtunis: these are known as 'cellular constructions'.[88] Often the temple was founded or refounded, as again in Tebtunis where Ptolemy I refounded the main temple.[89] Many new or expanded villages and urban settlements developed with streets parallel and perpendicular to the *dromos*, which archaeologists called hybrid or mixed style, emphasizing adaptation rather than imposition. This is found at Narmouthis, but in many cases only a limited area of the town plan is known.[90] *Agorai* used as marketplaces are known from texts but have not been archaeologically identified; it has, however, been suggested that in Tebtunis there was a marketplace on either side of the dromos already in the Ptolemaic period.[91] In Hermopolis, a Greek-style temple was dedicated to Ptolemy III, and there are hints of modification to the city's layout.[92] Sometimes new types of buildings appeared, such as Greek baths, a mark of new cultural habits then adapted by local inhabitants; thus, as stressed by Redon, overall Ptolemaic settlements were 'hybrid settlements'.[93] Greek architecture and the choice of building materials (e.g. mud bricks) were adapted to the local environment, proof that, whoever they were, the architects were familiar with the milieu. Influences occurred in both directions, for instance, houses with two to four stories were inherited from the pre-Ptolemaic tower-houses.[94] Such cultural changes

---

[85] Davoli (2011) 74; Hippodamian grid possibly attested at Kom Talit, see Kirby and Rathbone (1996).
[86] Davoli (2011) 70.   [87] Clarysse (1991b) 70.
[88] Müller (2010) 231 speaks of a typical Pharaonic agglutinating cityscape.
[89] Marouard (2012) 128.   [90] Davoli (2011) 70, Fig. II; Müller (2010); Redon (2019).
[91] Davoli (2011) 80–1.   [92] I.Herm.Magn. 1; Gorre (2021).
[93] E.g. baths in Taposiris Magna, see Fournet and Redon (2006) and full catalogue in Fournet et al. (2013); Redon (2019); on village *gymnasia* in the Fayyum, see Fischer-Bovet (2014b) 280–90.
[94] Redon (2019); Marouard (2014).

and hybridity are known in particular for some *nome* capitals. The *nome* capital of the Fayyum, Shedet in Egyptian, was named Crocodilopolis in Greek, while in Demotic it was usually called *Ḥw.t-Sbk*, the temple of Sobek.[95] Because of its status and function, Crocodilopolis accumulated, beside an Egyptian temple of Sobek, all the administrative infrastructures and some new types of buildings, such as a *gymnasium* (not yet archaeologically attested), which was privately founded, several Greek-style collective baths, and even a theater built by a Ptolemy.[96] With 3,500 inhabitants and 288 hectares in the mid third century, what has become a Greco-Egyptian urban settlement was larger than many 'political' cities of the Greek world and as large as Seleucia-Pieria.[97] It was, in fact, sometimes simply called *polis* in tax lists and in other papyrological documents.[98] At first, such a designation seems anodyne, since no less than ten meanings have been recorded for *polis* in the papyri by Cadell. These can be grouped into four main categories: (1) political Greek city states, (2) rarely city quarters (Neapolis in Alexandria), (3) some villages, especially in the Fayyum, and (4) *nome* capitals.[99] The first two categories require no explanation, while regarding the third category, many Fayyumic villages were in fact named after *nome* capitals, such as Aphroditopolis or Hermopolis.[100] Philadelphia, known as a village (κώμη), was sometimes called *polis*.[101] Yet this is not really surprising in view of its generally unique character. Finally, following Herodotus, the Ptolemaic administration either transliterated the names of *nome* capitals into Greek (e.g. Sebennytos) or translated them, adding *polis* to the name of the patron god (e.g. Hermopolis).[102] Perhaps the fact that many had harbours and were economic centres also reminded the Greeks of some aspects of typical coastal *poleis*.[103] The usage of the term *polis* spread despite the nome capital's lack of institutions specific to Greek city states (i.e. an assembly, a council, magistrates, and courts) and their lack of political autonomy – but that was the case too for some *poleis* in the Greek world.[104]

---

[95] In contrast, the expression *tmy-Sbk*, the village of Sobek, is a general epithet common among villages of the Arsinoite *nome* but is not the name of one single village; see de Cenival (1984) 32–3 and e.g. P.Chic.Haw. 4, p. 25, where it is the epithet of Hawara; for *Ḥw.t-Sbk*, see P.Dime II, p. 76 with Lippert and Schentuleit (2005) 74. I thank Marie-Pierre Chaufray for these references.
[96] Fournet and Redon (2010) 57; Davoli (2011) 71–2.
[97] For comparison with other dynastic foundations, see Mueller (2006a) 90, table 3.2, 208, no. 7.
[98] P.Count. 1, l. 32; 12, l. 77–8.   [99] Cadell (1984) 240–6.   [100] Clarysse (2007) 74.
[101] Cadell (1984) 241 and notes 70–1 with references.   [102] Clarysse (2007) 74.
[103] Hansen (2006) 134 contrasts typical *poleis* with market and harbour to Seleucid inland *poleis*.
[104] Heinen (1997) 352; Heinen (2000) 128–9; Hansen (2006) 132–3 points out that from the mid second century BC on, almost all *poleis* of the Greek world had become dependent states, but in contrast they still had their typical institutions.

3.4 Dynastic Settlements in the Red Sea Basin

New settlements in the Red Sea basin were founded under Ptolemy II as a network of harbours and fortresses to transport his captured war elephants; at the same time he could benefit from the ivory trade and claim control over this region.[105] The settlements received the same dynastic names as *polis* foundations in the Mediterranean; Arsinoe was the most common name for harbour cities throughout the Mediterranean – a sign of a consistent policy.[106] When more than two centuries later Strabo enumerates the new foundations of Arsinoe – later renamed Kleopatris and today Suez – at the end of the new Ptolemaic canal between the Nile and the Red Sea, of Philotera (near Myos Hormos), of the nearby Arsinoe and finally of Berenike Troglodytika, he calls them all *poleis*.[107] In fact, he describes most urban sites as *poleis*, referring to the urbanistic (and architectural) but non-political meaning of the term. In Egypt, for instance, he calls Memphis, Syene, and Elephantine *poleis* and Thebes a *metropolis*.[108] In contrast, Philae is called a 'settlement' (*katoikia*) and Abydos a 'small settlement' (*katoikia mikra*), while he notes that Abydos used to be a large city (*polis megale*).[109] Often he uses the more general term κτίσμα, meaning 'foundation', for smaller settlements, such as fortresses or hunting stations – Ptolemais Theron, for instance, today in the Sudan – but sometimes he concentrates on the foundation process of a settlement that he otherwise calls a *polis* – as in the case of Philotera, designated the (*ktisma*) of Satyros.[110] Unsurprisingly, as noted by Mairs, Strabo is not completely consistent, bringing in his own perspective and not offering any systematic terminology.[111]

The hieroglyphic stele of Pithom offers another perspective, that of the Egyptian priestly elite that partook in two foundations.[112] Written by the priests of Atum in Tjekou (i.e. Heroonpolis, modern Tell el-Maskhuta) about one hundred kilometres north of Suez, this narrates the foundation of two harbours, Arsinoe and Ptolemais. The priests state that they performed the inaugural rituals for the temple of the late queen Arsinoe II in Arsinoe and took care of the erection of the statues of the *Adelphoi Theoi*, that is the queen and Ptolemy II. The document sheds light on several

---

[105] Burstein (2008).   [106] Cohen (1995) 329–30.
[107] Strab. 16.4.5, 17.1.25; Cohen (2006) 305–43.   [108] Strab. 17.1.32; 17.1.46; 17.1.48.
[109] Strab. 17.1.48 and 17.1.42.
[110] E.g. Strab. 16.4.7–8 for Ptolemais, *ktisma* of Eumedes, and for the *phrourion* of Souchos.
[111] Cohen (2006) 322–4 on Strabo's sometimes confused or erroneous account.
[112] New edition and commentary in Thiers (2007); English translation in Mueller (2006a) 192–9; comparison with Strabo in Mueller (2006b).

aspects of the foundation process. First, the temple of Arsinoe was an Egyptian temple, as emphasized by Thiers; thus Egyptian priests accomplished the central element of this dynastic foundation.[113] In contrast, Strabo does not mention the temple but only the *polis* and other *poleis* not recorded in the Pithom stele.[114] Secondly, the most economic way to explain why the priests of Heroonpolis mention the foundation of Arsinoe is that some settlers must have come from Heroonpolis (just as settlers in Arsinoe in Cilicia came from nearby Nagidos). Thirdly, building and/or dedicating temples to members of the royal family was an essential element of Ptolemaic settlement policies throughout their territories. This was also the case in Arsinoe in Cilicia and, perhaps, as we will see, foundations and refoundations of Egyptian temples by the Ptolemies can also be understood in a similar way.

The second new foundation mentioned in the Pithom stele was Ptolemais Theron (Ptolemais-of-the-Hunt), probably also because some of its settlers came from Heroonpolis. The process of foundation was a careful balance of disruption and negotiation. The text on the stele does not give the name of the founder and reconstructs the story in a positive way, with the priests promoting the royal ideology of asserting authority over the land as a sort of civilizing process.[115] Interestingly, Strabo is more explicit about the local disruption brought by empires but also about negotiation with the locals (as we saw in Cilicia).[116] He reports how Eumedes was a skilful negotiator, since he first tricked the local inhabitants by building a ditch and wall around the area and, when they opposed to it, he was able to gain their friendship with a speech.[117] Arsinoe and Ptolemais Theron were each described as a *dmy* in hieroglyphic Egyptian, probably in reference to their function as harbours and their imprint on the land as towns or villages. Ptolemais was never conceived as a political *polis* and with the decline of elephant hunts probably remained a fortified village or fortress. Strabo calls it a *ktisma* and Pliny an *oppidum*, in contrast to Berenike Troglodytika which is an *urbs*.[118]

As Berenike Troglodytika, Arsinoe-Suez is also called a *polis* by Strabo, so these may have been thought of as cities (according to Davoli's architectural terminology) that functioned as administrative centres for their respective areas. Yet they were not Greek political *poleis* from a juridical point of view and might rather be coined

---

[113] Thiers (2007) 124, commentary to lines 21–3.   [114] Strab. 16.4.5.
[115] Mueller (2006a) 198, l. 24 and Appendix.   [116] SEG 39, 1426 l. 23.
[117] Strab. 16.4.7. On craftsmen attached to these expeditions, see I.Paneion 9bis.
[118] Strab. 16.4.7; Plin. *HN* 2.183–4; Thiers (2007) 147.

Greco-Egyptian *poleis*/cities.[119] The exact location of Arsinoe has not yet been established, but archaeological research of the last twenty years in Berenike has shown that it was the most important of the network of harbours along the Red Sea coast, with perhaps 5,000 to 10,000 inhabitants, mostly Egyptians.[120] Excavation in recent years has revealed a large third-century defensive complex in the western, Ptolemaic area of the town and a rectangular rock-cut shaft that was perhaps an underground installation for collecting water.[121] The city developed in the second century, when the so-called Serapis temple was built in an area where some sort of orthogonal planning is perhaps to be dated to the Ptolemaic period; miniature temple doors found in the Ptolemaic industrial area suggest that Egyptian religious traditions were present in the town.[122]

3.5 Urban Settlements and Greco-Egyptian Cities

As in the case of the foundation of Arsinoe in Cilicia, the role of the local populations is attested in the examples discussed above. Many of the new and altered settlements presented a hybrid Greco-Egyptian style. The development of public buildings already started reflecting multidirectional changes in the lifestyle; collective baths were adopted and adapted by the locals, and Egyptian temples remained central to the settlements, their gods sharing their shrines with the divinized Ptolemies. The material distinction between a settlement that was a political *polis*, as experienced or imagined by immigrants to Egypt and by their descendants, and an urban settlement in Egypt with administrative, religious, and economic structures was becoming fuzzy, even if these structures were often built in Egypt in mud bricks rather than in stones.[123] Moreover, more than a third of the immigrants were Macedonians, or even Thessalians, and had not previously lived in Greek political *poleis*.[124]

---

[119] Mueller (2006a) 203, nos. 22 and 27 indicates a status of *polis*, but this term is only found in Strabo, which is problematic, as discussed above.
[120] Cohen (2006) 308–10, 320–5; Sidebotham (2011) 21–53, 58; on forts between Berenike and the Nile valley, see Sidebotham and Gates-Foster (2019).
[121] Woźniak and Rądkowska (2014). I thank François Gerardin for this reference. See also Zych et al. (2016) 322–6 and 339.
[122] Sidebotham (2011) 58; Sidebotham (2014) 614, 619; SB 2039 = I.Pan 70 (Ptolemy VIII).
[123] For Davoli (2011) 89–90 the use of cheaper material would explain why these structures are attested papyrologically but not archaeologically.
[124] Fischer-Bovet (2011) 142–3.

In the new Egyptian context, the meaning of the term *polis* was adapted when used for existing *nome* capitals and for new settlements: in other words, the urbanistic and architectural aspects were taking over the political and juridical meaning. With a network of urban settlements in Egypt resembling Greek *poleis*, the Ptolemies did not need to found political *poleis* beyond the three existing *poleis*, and did it only in the case of the new *polis* of Euergetis discussed below.

4 Foundation of *poleis* by Boethos in Second-Century Egypt and Lower Nubia

Under Ptolemy IV Philopator and Ptolemy V Epiphanes, no new settlements seem to have been established outside Egypt, and only two villages were named Philopator after Ptolemy IV in the Fayyum.[125] This slowing down of settlement policies can be explained by the end of immigration to Egypt and disrupted times due to the Fifth Syrian War and the Great Revolt.[126] Then under Ptolemy VI Philometor and Ptolemy VIII Euergetes II a 'renaissance' appears: for instance, Arsinoe-Suez was renamed as Kleopatris and Crocodilopolis changed into Ptolemais Euergetis.[127] The foundations of three new *poleis*, one in Egypt and two in Lower Nubia, are to be understood within the context of military reforms following the Great Revolt as well as the invasion by Antiochus IV and the revolt of Dionysios-Petosiris in the 160s. New garrisons and military camps were established or reinforced, especially in Heracleopolis, the gate to the Nile valley, and in Upper Egypt and Lower Nubia, manned with soldiers of Egyptian and Greco-Egyptian descent.[128] The foundations are one more indication of the reorganization of the Ptolemaic territories after the Fifth Syrian War and the Great Revolt, despite dynastic conflicts. On the basis of textual evidence only – since the exact locations of the three *poleis* have not been identified – it is argued below that the foundation process and purposes did not differ from those of the preceding century, even if on a smaller scale, and that the role of the local Egyptian population was central. A comprehensive analysis of these foundations is to be published by Gerardin, while the publication of papyri concerning Boethos, the

---

[125] Mueller (2006a) 142; nos. 80–1.
[126] See also Mueller (2006a) 59; on the revolts, see Veïsse in this volume, Veïsse (2004); McGing (1997).
[127] Mueller (2006a) 61, 203, 205, 208, nos. 22 and 67.
[128] Vandorpe (1995) 233; Vandorpe (2014), Kruse (2011); Thompson (2011b) 21; Fischer-Bovet (2014a) 247–9.

central figure of the settlement policies of the mid second century BC, is in preparation.[129]

The single mention of two of these 'foundations' comes from a dedication to the king (Ptolemy VI), his family and the gods of the first cataract dated to 152–145 BC, in which Boethos, *archisomatophylax* and *strategos* (i.e. a high military officer and official, and an important figure at the court), is honoured as the founder (*ktistes*) of the *poleis* of Philometoris and Kleopatra.[130] These *poleis* are said to be located in the Triakontaschoinos, that is the Ptolemaic province of Lower Nubia which had been reconquered by Ptolemy VI.[131] Those who decided to celebrate annually the royal annual festivals as well as Boethos's birthday according to the royal law were the priests in Elephantine of the local gods and of the dynastic cults, gathered together as members of an association (*synodos*), as was the main initiator of the dedication, Herodes, garrison commander of Syene also in charge of the upper territories, that is, part of Lower Nubia.[132] Some sort of responsibility on their part for the establishment of the royal cult in the two so-called *poleis* could explain the specific mention of the *poleis*, but nothing can be confirmed without some archaeological context. It has been proposed that these *poleis* were refoundations of Buhen, Dakke, Qasr Ibrim, or Mirgissa or even perhaps no more than the fortification wall around a temple in Debod; these were probably military settlements rather than political *poleis*, according to Dietze.[133] In any case, these refoundations demonstrate that Ptolemy VI aimed to reconstruct a military network, and perhaps an administrative one too, in the newly re-controlled province and to consolidate his power through the royal cult – implied by the choice of dynastic names – in new or existing temples.

Boethos remained a central figure under Ptolemy VIII, so his role was clearly not perceived as a threat, despite the king's rivalry with his late brother Ptolemy VI. He held the highest court title of kinsman (*suggenes*) and was *epistrategos* and *strategos* of the Thebaid. In 133/2 BCE, Boethos

---

[129] Gerardin (2018); see the forthcoming editions of papyri from the Kölner collection on Euergetis by Armoni, petitions to Boethos at the Beinecke library at Yale University by Duttenhöfer and some Trier papyri by Kramer.

[130] On Boethos, Mooren (1975) no. 053; Kramer (1997); Heinen (1997); and Heinen (2000).

[131] The Triakontaschoinos, i.e. 30 *schoinoi* (= 300 km) laid between the first and second cataracts, the northern part of which was the Dodekaschoinos. Locher (1999) 230–56; Eide et al. (1994–2000) 588–9, 611–12; Rose (2012); Mueller (2006a) 162 suggests a reconquest by Ptolemy VI rather than Ptolemy V.

[132] I.ThSy. 302 = OGIS I 111 (152–145 BC, Satis island), Heinen (1996); different interpretation in Heilporn (1990).

[133] Dietze (1994) 105–7; Mueller (2006a) 160–5, esp. 164, note 73 with map and bibliography; Heinen (2000) 139 n. 28, 147.

founded a third town, named Euergetis after the epithet of Ptolemy VIII, Cleopatra II and Cleopatra III's as *Theoi Euergetai* (Benefactor Gods). For a long time its location was debated, but unpublished papyri indicate that this city was established in the Heracleopolite *nome* and even contained some of the institutions expected for a political *polis*, such as the *prytaneis*.[134] Two papyri with the same text (a draft and a copy) already provided information on the practicalities of the city foundation and its architectures:[135] a *stathmos* of 4.6 by 9 m (i.e. a lodging, a term normally used for a soldier's billet) was measured out by Paniskos, the *stathmodotes* (responsible for assigning quarters), next to a rectangular *agora* for the innkeeper Tanoupis, daughter of Tpheophis, a woman of Egyptian descent. Tanoupis did not have to pay taxes or fees but could only transfer her property to family members or to people 'among those in the city registered in the army'. This indicates that some settlers did not belong to the army but that her family did, and that tax exemptions were granted to the military milieu. Finally, the town contained typical Greek architectural structures such as the rectangular *agora* but also a *stoa*, so it seems that the town was planned according to a Hippodamian grid pattern.

Similarities between the foundation of Euergetis and third-century *poleis* foundations are evident. Firstly, the founder of Euergetis was also a high military officer and all were non-royal *ktistai*; they received orders from the king but seem to have had a certain freedom of action.[136] Boethos received extremely high honours as recorded in the dedication by the priests in Elephantine, and shared a status that must have been similar to the third-century *ktistai*, who were still mentioned by Strabo two centuries later.[137] Secondly, the location of Euergetis in the Heracleopolite *nome* was also militarily strategic: there was no doubt a garrison since soldiers registered in the new city. Thirdly, besides the military component, economic purposes and, in the unpublished papyri, the aim to create some civic structures appear. Though not all the typical institutions may be attested (yet?), there was an understanding in Egypt of what a real political *polis* could be, as well as of an adapted version. Finally, there was a strong participation of the local population in shaping the *polis* as settlers, in this case Egyptians and

---

[134] I thank Charikleia Armoni and François Gerardin for their personal communications, see e.g. P.Köln inv. 20956a, 20957+20956b and 20973 a+b+c+ 20971; for the *prytaneis*, see P.Köln inv. 20971.
[135] A draft (SB 24 15973 = P.Trier S 135–3) and a copy (SB 24 15974 = P.Trier S 135–3), see Kramer (1997) and Heinen (1997); Mueller (2006a) 134–5 with translation.
[136] See also Heinen (2000) 148–50.
[137] Strab. 16.4.5 and 7 is short on details on Satyros regarding Philotera on the Red Sea or on Eumedes for Ptolemais Theron.

Greco-Egyptians. Whether it was a successful undertaking remains unclear.

5 Symbolic *poleis* in Elephantine and Thebes

5.1 The Symbolic Refoundation of Elephantine?

When read against the context of second-century foundations and refoundations, the correspondence between the king – first Ptolemy VIII, then his son Ptolemy IX – and the priests of Khnum in Elephantine takes on another dimension. The text, carefully engraved on a stele in 115 BC, records the rulers' *philanthropa* towards the priests, that is, the donation of the island of Pso as temple land as well as 200 *artabas* of wheat annually, which are presented as royal benefactions while in fact the donation was, according to Diezte, the resolution of a legal case.[138] The first section of the text narrates the royal visit and rituals that took place to celebrate the *philanthropa*, the first lines written in larger characters as a sort of title and ending with the mention of Elephantine as the newly founded *polis* (*n]eoktiston polin* in l. 4) possibly repeated on line 11 (*ekt[ismenêi polei]*).[139] The new edition of this highly damaged text by Piejko has many gratuitous restitutions, but the minimal restitutions of these two lines, already suggested by Mahaffy, Strack, and Dittenberger, are worth at least taking into consideration, since the alternative is problematic.[140] Indeed, Wilcken and some followers, including Bernand, preferred the restitution 'built by the gods' (*[th]eoktiston*) in line 4, firstly because Herodotus and Strabo called Elephantine a *polis*, which for them means that Elephantine could not be 'newly founded', and secondly because there is no archaeological evidence for such a foundation (or indeed refoundation).[141] But the use of the term *polis* by Greek authors is not a sufficient argument for reconstructing the status of an ancient settlement,

---

[138] OGIS I 168 = SB V 8883 = I.ThSy. 244 = re-edition in Piejko (1992), thoroughly analysed in Dietze (1995) esp. 183.

[139] l. 4 [... εἰς τὴν ν]εόκτιστον πόλιν Ἐλεφαντίνην πρῶ[τον μὲν ...] and l. 11 ...]ων εὐωγηθεὶς ἐπὶ τοῦ Ἡραίου τῆι τε ἐκτ[ισμένηι πόλει ....] in Piejko (1992) 5–6; see SB 24, 15973, l. 3 and 15974, l. 3 and the unpublished P.Köln inv. 20969+20973, l. 7–9.

[140] Critique of Piejko (1992) by Dietze (1995) 183–4; SEG 42, 1556 offers no comments at all for this reason; Piejko offers no commentary for these two restitutions; (ἐκτ[ισμένηι) is attested in the papyri concerning the *polis* of Euergetis, yet it is clearly a new foundation there; I thank Cathy Lorber for this reference.

[141] θ]εόκτιστον: Marshall (1916) 199; Bernand (1989) 203 with Hdt. 2. 9, 17, 18, 28, 29, 30, 69, 175 and Strab. 17.1.48; Rubensohn followed Wilcken because he found no archaeological support for the foundation, see Houroth et al. (1909) 16.

as shown in Mairs's chapter and in the present study, and in any case Strabo's text post-dates the possible refoundation.

Renaming still occurred in the late second century, such as the *nome* capital of the Arsinoite which became Ptolemais Euergetis in 116 BC, but there is not even a dynastic renaming in Elephantine. However, three sets of elements suggest that a sort of symbolic refoundation may have occurred. Firstly, the royal visit of Ptolemy IX in the region and his donations to the temple of Khnum denote a particular interest of the king in Elephantine at the beginning of his reign, while several other political and ritual actions on his part, such as perhaps the inauguration of the temple of Kalabsha in the Dodekaschoinos, can be associated with his visit to the first cataract region.[142] Elephantine was traditionally considered as the capital of the first *nome* of Upper Egypt, though possibly Ombo (c. 50 km north) may have had this function instead. By the middle of 135 BC, as Locher has shown, it is certain that there were two *nomes* (Peri Elephantine and Ombite), though it is not clear whether Elephantine or Ombo was the capital until 88–80 BC, when Elephantine is attested as the capital of the 'Peri Elephantine and Philae' *nome*.[143] Dietze has argued that Ptolemy VI and Ptolemy VIII favoured Philae and Kom Ombo over Elephantine because temple-building seems to have reached a smaller scale there, and Török has made a similar argument on the basis of the donation of the Dodekaschoinos to Isis of Philae in 157 BC.[144] Whether or not this was the case, the *philanthropa* reported on the stele of 115 BC suggest that Elephantine was still or again in favour and that it was (possibly again) the capital, and the term *polis* used in this inscription could support such an interpretation.

Secondly, on the ideological or symbolic level, the priests of Khnum and the land they received may be conceived of as forms of symbolic *boule* and *chora*, respectively. Such terms were not used here, but the vocabulary of the *polis* had already been borrowed for translating Egyptian realities at least from the time of the trilingual Canopus decree (238 BC), where in each Egyptian temple five priests were chosen annually in each of the five priestly tribes (*phylai*) as 'priest councillors' (*bouleutai hiereis*).[145] For Moyer, the Egyptian priests at Canopus were creatively and actively

---

[142] On Kalabsha, see de Meulenaere (1961); Winnicki (1996) suggests that he came to celebrate a victory over the Nubians after a possible expedition in Lower Nubia; Clarysse (2000b) 32–3 seems to accept other events that scholars associated with the visit of 115 BC but warns us against the reliability of hieroglyphic texts in view of their ritual/fictive functions.
[143] Locher (1999) 15–57, esp. 281–5. [144] Dietze (2000) 79; Török (2009) 400–1.
[145] OGIS I 56, l. 30–1; trilingual texts and commentary in Pfeiffer (2004) 109–21, esp. 117–19.

portraying themselves as a Greek political body.¹⁴⁶ Thirdly, the legal ethnic label 'Elephanteus' is attested in two papyri dated to shortly after the king's visit. The first one identifies two such individuals within a long list of mummies in a contract about transfers of revenues from tombs, while the second one is a receipt for the *akrodrua* tax.¹⁴⁷ This label and the term *polis* in line 4 of the stele are no proof of the existence of a civic body but rather of the administrative and religious importance of Elephantine within the hierarchy and network of settlements from both the king's and the local point of view.

Finally, some physical changes are expected in a refounded settlement, yet these might be minimal on this small island dominated by the temple of Khnum. Ptolemy VI and Ptolemy VIII actively decorated the temple and added a *pronaos*.¹⁴⁸ Some architectural fragments suggest that there were one or several Hellenistic buildings within the *temenos* of the temple of Khnum (dated to Ptolemy VIII and the later Roman period).¹⁴⁹ Possible change in the function of a nearby house – from group festival activities to a domestic structure – could be one more hint of change.¹⁵⁰ The symbolic refoundation, if such there was, need not imply Greek-style building, but there are fragments of decoration with the cartouche of Ptolemy IX in both Elephantine and Syene resembling material dated to Ptolemy VI and perhaps suggesting that Ptolemy IX continued the work of his predecessors.¹⁵¹ This points to temple-building as another facet of the settlement policies of the Ptolemies. It is well attested in Upper Egypt under Ptolemy VI and Ptolemy VIII, with soldiers involved in the process, and can be understood as one of the means to recontrol regions where large groups could not be settled.¹⁵² The symbolic refoundation of the *polis* of Elephantine would belong to the same process.

5.2 *Diospolis* Megale *(Thebes) under Cleopatra VII*

The term *polis* in Upper Egypt was also used for Thebes. The first-century Greco-Demotic bilingual inscription that honours Callimachus, responsible for the finances of the Peri-Theban *nome* and *strategos*, grants him the title of 'Savior of the *polis*' and offers a different perspective on the large *nome* capital, often perceived by modern historians

---

¹⁴⁶ Moyer (2011b) 121–4.
¹⁴⁷ UPZ II 180 (113 BC) col. 43, l. 1 and 3 and p. 173; BGU XX 2848, l. 6.
¹⁴⁸ Bagnall and Rathbone (2004) 239; Manning (2012). ¹⁴⁹ Raue et al. (2007) 9–13.
¹⁵⁰ Berlin (2013). ¹⁵¹ Raue et al. (2008) 17 and Kopp et al. (2011) 16.
¹⁵² Fischer-Bovet (2014b) 329–62.

mainly as the center of a series of Egyptian revolts.[153] Its Greek name, Diospolis *(Megale)*, '(the great) city of Zeus', was a translation of *n(i)w. t-Imn*, 'city of Amun', *n(i)w.t* being the term used for *nome* capitals and religious capital cities in the New Kingdom and still used in Ptolemaic hieroglyphic archaizing texts for *nome* capitals, and even other urban settlements.[154] After the Great Revolt, some changes connected to the military reforms mentioned earlier occurred in the urban setting of this city. A new garrison was established around that time and a *gymnasium* is mentioned six times in our documentation from the 170s onwards.[155] Clarysse has argued that the high number of names formed on Hermes and Heracles attested in Thebes suggests the integration of new families in the *gymnasium*.[156] Even in Diospolis, a more integrated local elite of Greek, Egyptian, and Greco-Egyptian origins developed, as illustrated by the Alexandrian family of the *strategos* Plato, who married an Egyptian woman and whose son Plato, a royal official with police and judicial functions, was also prophet of Amun and received oracles from the god.[157] The newly discovered baths located in front of the temple of Amun, organized according to the Classical Greek traditions (two *tholoi*) but also with Egyptian adaptations (private tubs), complement the picture of demographic but also urbanistic and architectural changes that occurred around that time, though the baths were abandoned around 150–120 BC.[158] Already in the second century, Diospolis showed the mark of what we defined earlier as a Greco-Egyptian *polis*.

The decisions to honour Callimachus were voted (*edoxe*) around 39 BC by the priests of the Great Diospolis *Megale*, of Amonrasonther the Great God, by the Elders (*presbyteroi*) and all the others (l. 2–3). Among his many benefactions Callimachus took great care after its destruction of the city of Thebes, called *polis* throughout the text, and saved the priests and the population during a famine thanks to the help he received from an oracle of

---

[153] I. Prose 46 = OGIS 1.194 = SEG 24, 1217 (c. 39 BC, Thebes); Heinen (2006); Pfeiffer (2015) no. 40; no edition of the Demotic text exists since the stone is almost illegible; the publication announced by Farid (1993) 49 was never published; Blasius (2001) on Callimachus and his homonymic ancestors.

[154] Vandorpe (1995) 211–12; Moreno García (2011) 3; for instance, the hieroglyphic term is used on the statue of Plato, official and priest in Thebes, and on the statue of a Tanite *nome-strategos* from his hometown Sile, see Gorre (2009a) nos. 24 and 84.

[155] Winnicki (2001); Clarysse (1995) 7 n. 17. [156] Clarysse (1995).

[157] Coulon (2001) and Gorre (2009a) no. 24.

[158] Dated to the late third or more probably to the early second century BC; Redon and Faucher (2015); Boraik et al. (2013) 47–8; on baths in Egypt, see Boussac et al. (2009); on Greek-style construction near or within Egyptian temple precincts, see Gorre (2021).

the god Amun in front of the population on the terrace of the temple, where the stele was to be erected. He received high honours, such as the title of 'Savior of the *polis*' and the public celebration of his birthday every year, a day that was named after him (l. 29). Boethos and Callimachus are in fact the only non-royal individuals to receive such honours in Egypt: perhaps such yearly celebrations gave the illusion that Callimachus was a sort of symbolic refounder of Diospolis.

Finally, the details about the erection of three statues (*eikonas*, l. 28) for Callimachus shed light on the identities of those who voted the honours. While Dittenberger initially considered the Elders and the others as priests too, Hutmacher and Heinen have proposed taking them as evidence for a council and a *demos*, since the term *polis* is so prominent.[159] The statement that one statue, in hard stone, was to be erected by the priests and two by the *polis*, one in bronze and the other in stone, in my opinion confirms the view that not all the voters were priests – though some of the Elders were perhaps also priests and the others may have formed a symbolic *demos*. The Theban population, at least its upper strata, seems to have organized itself into bodies that partly mimicked political *poleis*, yet adapted the overall structure by giving the first place to the Egyptian priesthood. Even if from a juridical point of view Thebes was not a political *polis*, its local population could behave similarly in some realms, such as granting honours to benefactors and using the typical formulas of decrees issued by Greek *poleis*, as the priests at Canopus mentioned above. This was also the case, for instance, in the inscription of the *politeuma* of the Idumeans and of the Idumeans of the *polis* (l. 3, i.e. Memphis), honouring the *strategos* Dorion in 113/2 BC and conceiving themselves symbolically as a *polis* (l. 24).[160] Privileged groups among the population of Egypt had adopted and adapted to their own context the tool of negotiations of the Greek political cities such as the form and content of Greek honorific decrees and voting bodies partly imitating those of Greek *poleis*. As late as the 30s, the emphasis on Diospolis *Megale* as being a *polis*, even if only symbolically, was a convenient political tool for both parties: for the ruler, to strengthen the administrative, military, and religious network through which to project political power; and for the local elites, to reaffirm their role within it.

---

[159] Heinen (2006) esp. 31–5; Hutmacher (1965).
[160] SB V 8929 = OGIS II 737 (112/11 BC) with Thompson (1984) and Gorre (2009a) 263–9; on the *politeumata*, see Sänger in this volume.

6 Concluding Remarks

The Early Ptolemies practiced active settlement policies beyond Egypt. Many foundations were near the sea and some were refoundations or renamings of settlements, but there was also a reasonable number of real foundations and inland settlements. These *poleis* served to build the administrative, military, economic, and religious structure of the empire, complemented by non-*polis* settlements. The Ptolemaic settlement policies within Egypt implied the foundation or refoundation of villages and urban settlements that were not political *poleis* and the establishment of foreign settlers in existing settlements. As there was no status of citizen or the legal system attached to the latter, it may have facilitated, probably unexpectedly, the interaction between the new and old local elites and populations perhaps more than in regions of the Seleucid empire such as Syria, Babylonia, Persia, and Susiana with their numerous *polis* foundations.[161] The Far East, with the absence of *polis*-like settlements, may more resemble Egypt in some respects.

When in the second century BC, Seleucus IV and Antiochus IV actively founded and refounded cities, the Ptolemies also reorganized their now smaller territories in order to control them better, though the existing urban and administrative network did not require the foundation of new political *poleis* in Egypt. This is one of the reasons why in Egypt there was no 'poliadization', an argument which may complement the analysis offered by Clancier and Gorre in this volume, in contrast to the Seleucid empire. This neologism refers to both the creation of civic institutions and the diffusion of a civic model from an urbanistic, architectural and social point of view.[162] In Egypt only the second aspect of it partially occurred in some settlements. The only exception, besides two so-called *poleis* founded in Lower Nubia whose exact nature remains unknown, seems to be the city of Euergetis, which displayed – at least partially – the institutions expected of a political *polis*. Yet this was founded through similar mechanisms and had similar functions as foundations of the third century, with perhaps even more participation on the part of the local Egyptian population.

In fact, the Ptolemaic administration certainly did not reject the idea of founding *poleis* but the concept of *polis* was rather adapted to the Egyptian context, conceptualized here as a 'Greco-Egyptian *polis*', by founding city harbours on the Red Sea coast and by slowly altering the physicality of the

---

[161] See maps 8 and 9 in Kosmin (2014a) 184–5.
[162] On 'poliadization' as a French neologism, see Couvenhes and Heller (2006) 17.

existing *nome* capitals, as they gathered administrative buildings and functions including new buildings belonging to the Greek cultural sphere. All these settlements came to bear a combination of Greek or Egyptian elements typical of Ptolemaic culture, while the *nome* capitals were sometimes called *metropoleis* in the papyri.[163] From a bottom-up perspective, the Greek term *polis* was commonly used for the *nome* capitals by the Greek speakers in Egypt, while the lack of political autonomy does not seem to have been felt at odds in the Egyptian context. Several examples have shown that local elites and populations were active in shaping the new settlements and altering existing ones. The Ptolemaic local elites, and sometimes broader groups in the population, had also become used to participating in social bodies that committed themselves as a group to decisions, often socio-religious associations that sometimes included priests (as in the inscription honouring Boethos), sometimes members of the *gymnasium*. Those who granted honours to Callimachus, or even the priests in the Pithom stele, illustrate well the essence of the new 'Greco-Egyptian *poleis*' that developed under the Ptolemies.

Common Conclusion

Our two case study regions – Ptolemaic Egypt with the Red Sea basin and Central Asia – complement one another, even if both the historical sources at our disposal and the historical processes by which settlements were created are different in each case. In neither case do we have contemporary historical accounts which would aid our analysis (except for the Pithom stele): the authors who transmit information on the topic wrote long after the fact. Nor is the available archaeological material as comprehensive as we would like. Settlements in both Egypt and Central Asia have only rarely been subject to the kind of extensive excavation which would reveal their evolution over time.

The greatest contrast between the two regions is in the chronological span over which Greek settlement was imposed (a long process in Egypt, a much shorter one in Central Asia) and in the civilian versus military nature of the settlement. In Central Asia, the short period of settlement for which we have evidence relates to military garrisons and settlements of demobilized soldiers founded by Alexander the Great and his immediate successors. In Egypt and the Red Sea basin, in contrast, Ptolemaic

---

[163] The term is attested in about twenty Ptolemaic papyri, slightly more often from the second century on, especially in the Heracleopolite *nome*.

settlement was not exclusively military. Our sources hint at the role and presence of civilian local settlers. On the Red Sea, harbours were a priority, not only for bringing in war elephants and ivory but also for long-distance trade.

The diversity of our sources and the origins of the settlers themselves is greater in Egypt than in Central Asia. In Egypt, we have sources in the Egyptian language, and can access the voices of Egyptian participants in the settlement process. Settlements in Egypt and the Red Sea basin ran the gamut from political *poleis* to smaller villages, with various types of organization.

These differences have led the two authors of this section, Mairs and Fischer-Bovet, to explore different, yet complementary aspects of the settlement policies of the Seleucid and Ptolemaic empires. Mairs's Chapter 2A provides an up-to-date characterization of Hellenistic and early Seleucid settlement in the Far East and a methodological and historiographic perspective. These methodological remarks should be kept in mind when looking at the Ptolemies. Even though more Ptolemaic sources are available, the caveats remain and the study of the Ptolemies belongs to the same historiographic context. Fischer-Bovet's Chapter 2B aims to reconstruct how the local elites and population participated in shaping new settlements and in altering existing ones. By piecing together how these two groups of people conceptualized their own settlements within a constructed hierarchy of settlements, it shows how the concept of *polis* was reinvented, or at least adapted, within the Egyptian context. This may only suggest how much (more) we are missing – in the Seleucid case but also in the Ptolemaic case – about the participants in the process of founding new settlements and altering those that already existed.

CHAPTER 3

The Integration of Indigenous Elites and the Development of poleis *in the Ptolemaic and Seleucid Empires*

Philippe Clancier and Gilles Gorre

1 Introduction

When Alexander the Great entered Babylon at the end of October 331, Babylonia had not possessed an autonomous monarchy since 539. The Persian rulers who controlled the region had not really played the ancient role of a Babylonian king.[1] The political traditions of Southern Mesopotamia had vanished during the two centuries preceding Macedonian conquest. The situation in Egypt was different. After the first Persian occupation (526–404)[2], Egypt was independent, and the last Egyptian Pharaoh had only just been removed by the Persian king Artaxerxes III at the beginning of the fourth century. Moreover, Ptolemy ruled a former kingdom with a unified culture, while Achaemenid kings and then Seleucid ones built an imperial structure over many regions with numerous different traditions. And so, when the Ptolemies and the Seleucids established local administrative structures they integrated the long historical heritage of their kingdoms as well as different ways of thinking about the basic levels of the administration in Egypt and Babylonia.

Babylonia, a small part of the Seleucid empire, had a long tradition of having each town led by the first high-ranking men. These persons may have varied from time to time, but one of them could have also been the head of the main local temple. So, for more than a millennium before the Hellenistic period, temple staff had been deeply involved in the political direction of the big cities of Babylonia, such as Sippar, Babylon, Borsippa

---

[1] Tolini (2012).
[2] Agut-Labordère (2016) 326: 'The Persian authorities diverted a large part of the wealth of the temples and monitored closely the financial staff of the Great temples.'

and Uruk.³ However, the fact that the temple administration may have led the town was a pragmatic solution and not an expression of any kind of city-temple.⁴ During the Neo-Babylonian period, two situations existed in Babylonia: first, in small or medium-size towns, the temple administration led the town; second, in the biggest towns such as Babylon, Borsippa or Uruk, a *šakin ṭēmi*, a governor, was designated by the king to do the job.

In 539 the Persian king, Cyrus, conquered Babylonia. The royal power was almost no longer interested in sustaining the temple economy and played no more part in one of the most important activities of restoring sanctuary buildings. Moreover, after the rule of Cambyses ended in 522, the Achaemenids did not continue to fulfil the cultic obligations of the Babylonian kings. In these respects, Persian rule in Babylonia represented a major transformation compared with the preceding periods. Even though the administrative system had remained largely unchanged until the reign of Xerxes, many alterations occurred with the revolts of 484, involving a large part of the local elites working for the temples. Indeed, Xerxes punished these temples' elites by closing some sanctuaries such as the Ebabbar of Sippar and the Eanna of Uruk, destroying cults that had lasted for millennia.⁵ In other towns, he imposed huge changes in the administration of temples such as the elimination of the position of high administrator in the Esagil, the temple of Bēl-Marduk in Babylon. He went as far as to destroy cultic buildings such as the tower of Babel, the Etemenanki.⁶

These actions had a direct impact on written sources which became far less abundant afterwards. Because of this so-called 'end of archives' phenomenon, it is more difficult to study the local organisation of temples and cities. We have to wait until the very late Achaemenid period to again have a substantial amount of archival material for studying local temples, especially for Babylon. For instance, the Esagil temple administration was at this time divided between the temple scribes and the *bēl piqnēti*, representatives of the professional assemblies of the temple. A royal

---

³ See, for example, the case of Sippar during the Neo-Babylonian period in Bongenaar (1997), esp. 22–3, for the judicial competencies of the *šatammu*, the high administrator of the Ebabbar, the main temple of Sippar.
⁴ The situation may vary and, for example, in Sippar, during the second millennium, the high administrator of the local temple was sometimes at the head of the city, sometimes it was the chief of the merchants, depending on the importance of the commercial activities of the town, and sometimes a *rabiānum*, a mayor.
⁵ See for the revolts and their consequences Waerzeggers (2003–4).
⁶ For the destructions of cultic buildings in Babylonia after the revolts of the beginning of Xerxes's reign, see George (2010).

controller, with the designation *qīpu* or *paqdu*, was still in place.[7] Under Darius III, the office of high administrator of the Esagil reappeared in Babylon. The lack of written evidence means that it is not possible to say why or even exactly when these modifications occurred. More generally, the cuneiform sources are mainly concentrated in two towns during the late Achaemenid and Hellenistic periods: Babylon and Uruk. There are still other archives or tablets from other cities (Borsippa, Kuta, Nippur, Ur and Larsa, for instance).[8]

In contrast with Babylonia, in pre-Hellenistic Egypt there was a separation between the head of the administrative district and the head of the temple's administration.[9] From the sixth century BC, the Egyptian state witnessed increased centralisation and the development of a proper royal administration, notably in fiscal matters, that was distinct from the local priestly administration.[10] Since the time of the Nectanebids (fourth century BC), royal scribes had been appointed in some temples as accounting officers. Their first duty was to control the royal subsidies and in so doing they also controlled the temple's internal administration. However, royal control was far from being complete. Firstly, we do not know if royal scribes were appointed systematically in all temples. Secondly, the representative of the inner administration of the temples, the *lesonis*, was elected by the local priesthood. The *lesonis* still maintained a prominent place, especially when he was also nominated as royal scribe.

As in Babylonia, the subsidies allocated to Egyptian temples were substantially cut down under the Achaemenids.[11] At the same time, state control over the temples was reduced compared to the last Egyptian dynasties, particularly the very last one, the Nectanebids (Thirtieth dynasty). The temples gained more autonomy during the troubled period of the end of the fourth century BC due to the disorder caused by the collapse of central authority.[12] This relative independence was only temporary and ended with the establishment of the Ptolemaic dynasty.

---

[7] This kind of royal intervention inside the temples for better controlling them or to break the local notabilities was also a practice of the Neo-Babylonian king who already suppressed this function of *šatammu* in the main temple of Uruk, the Eanna of the goddess Ištar. For the temple organisation of the late Achaemenid period, see Hackl (2018).

[8] For the sources of this period, see Oelsner (1986).

[9] In Egypt, the *nome* was the administrative unit, while in Babylonia it was the town.

[10] Agut-Labordère and Gorre (2014).

[11] At least during the first well-documented period, see Agut-Labordère (2021). Due to the lack of sources, it is more difficult to reconstitute the policy towards the temple during the second domination; between the Nectanebids and the Argeads, however, several clues show that the period was difficult for the country in general and for the temples in particular; see Chauveau (2017).

[12] Gorre (2009a) 495–6.

Turning to Babylonia during the Hellenistic times, we can see two distinct periods of administrative control. The first began with the conquest of Babylon by Alexander and, after the Wars of the Diadochi, the situation stabilised during the early part of Seleucid rule. During this time Babylonia was a satrapy, divided between different cities, some being *poleis*, some not. The city was thus the basic level of the country's administrative division. The non-*poleis* cities, which were administrative entities mostly equal to the *poleis*, were held by a local nobility linked to the temples of the old Sumero-Akkadian religion. This situation mainly characterised the third century and the beginning of the second in Babylon and Uruk.[13] The second period, during the reigns of Antiochus III, Seleucus IV and Antiochus IV, is characterised by the administrative reforms that changed Babylon into a city politically organised as a Greek one, a *polis* – a process we will call here 'poliadisation'.[14] It is most likely that the same process occurred in Uruk.[15]

Explaining this major evolution is difficult. There is no equivalent of these types of reforms in Egypt. However, rather than examine a chronology of the creation of *poleis*, we can study the integration of the temple staff in the Ptolemaic state through the chronology of synodal decrees, one of the most famous types of Ptolemaic documents. Three periods can be distinguished.[16] First, in the 260s, local synods were summoned by the Ptolemies in the context of the introduction of their dynastic cult in Egyptian temples and the promises of royal donations. Second, from Ptolemy III's rule to 196, there were two types of synods gathering the priests coming from the Egyptian temples of the first three categories: annual synods summoned in Alexandria and extraordinary synods for particular occasions such as the victory of Raphia in 217 BC. And third, from 196 to 182 or perhaps to the middle of second century, only extraordinary synods are known of, mostly in the context of crises. It seems curious that no synodal decree has been recorded after the middle of the second century, since the crises did not stop. Gorre and Véïsse have recently explained the end of the synodal decrees by arguing that they were not needed anymore due to the integration of the temple's staff by the Ptolemies, without poliadisation.

The chapter first analyses the political, economic and religious roles of priestly elites and temples during the first part of the Hellenistic period and

---

[13] Data for other Babylonian cities are very scarce.
[14] This process is described in Clancier (2017).   [15] Clancier and Monerie (2014) 220–3.
[16] Gorre-Véïsse (2020).

then examines the different kinds of local administrative reforms in Egypt and Babylonia at the end of the third and during the second centuries. It proposes a tentative explanation of why the Ptolemies and the Seleucids adopted different solutions to control the temples and the big old cities.

2 Temples during the Early Hellenistic Period

2.1 Local Elite, Temples and Local Administration

Between the entry of Alexander the Great in Babylon and the beginning of the Seleucid era, the political position of the Babylonian sanctuaries evolved from what may have been close to total submission under the Achaemenids to a kind of autonomy under the first Seleucids. Indeed, in Babylon from Alexander onwards many references are made to the *šatammu*, the administrator of Esagil, leading the Assembly of the Babylonians (i.e., the assembly of the temple staff), which was at the head of the town.[17] The reason for that is surely because, as in earlier periods, the temple assembly remained the best organised administrative structure in the city following the departure of the Persian administration with Mazaios. Furthermore, the Esagil complex remained physically imposing, still dominating the areas of Eridu and Šuanna in the inner city of Babylon.

This administrative situation was also attested in the largest city of the South: Uruk. Here Anu-uballiṭ-Nikarchos, descendant of Aḫ'utu, an important family clan in Uruk, held the title of *šaknu*, or 'governor' of Uruk. Nikarchos was also head of the Rēš temple, the main Urukean temple, in the middle of the third century.[18] But the best example of an administrator of the sanctuaries leading the town is Anu-uballiṭ-Kephalôn.[19] Also a descendant of Aḫ'utu, he bore two different titles: 'chief of the officers of Uruk' (*rab ša rēš āli ša Uruk*) and 'administrator of the temples of Uruk' (*šatammu*).[20] Even if the same person led the city and the temple through the temple assembly, a distinction was formally made between civil and religious responsibilities. The political domination of the temple administration over the city allowed Nikarchos and Kephalon to restore and regularly expand their sanctuaries.

---

[17] For the organisation of the Esagil, see, for instance, van der Spek (2000); and (2006) with previous bibliography.
[18] Monerie (2014) 154–5.   [19] Monerie (2014) 146–7.
[20] This last title is only attested in the tablet AO 6498 from the Louvre and published in Clancier and Monerie (2014) 236–7.

In Egypt, the beginning of the Hellenistic era was characterised by a return to the policies of the last Egyptian dynasties. The heritage of these dynasties provided the Ptolemies with a template for their own policy of control of the Egyptian temples. As far as we can say it seems that the Babylonian temple administration (which *de facto* formed the political elite of Babylonian towns) was composed of families all from the old priestly staff, well educated in Sumero-Akkadian culture. It is also likely that it was difficult for a person external to this small group to be able to integrate into the temple assembly and therefore the political power structure of these cities. Therefore Greeks, Iranians, Jews and other foreigners may have been essentially excluded from political decisions concerning the town.[21] In contrast, almost all the elites involved in the local affairs could find a place in the Egyptian temples. This situation arose firstly because the population was far more homogenous than in Babylonia. Secondly, according to Egyptian tradition, the most prominent local families were involved in the life of the local sanctuary. In other words, the local elite and the temple's elite were formally mostly the same except for the leaders of some few communities such as the Judaeans.[22] Thirdly, the numerous examples of Greek graffiti in Egyptian temples and the very cosmopolitan crowd settled in the Serapeum of Memphis, at least since the second century,[23] suggest that unlike Babylonian temples, Egyptian priestly elites were relatively open to the outside world, and notably to foreigners.

2.2 *Kings and Temples*

Yet in both kingdoms the king and his administration aimed to control the local communities. This control took various forms partly depending on the relationship between kingship and temples. Unlike the Babylonian situation during the Hellenistic period, cultic duties represented a fundamental part of the role played by the Egyptian king. The pharaoh was part of the divine world, the sole intercessor between mankind and the gods and so, technically speaking, the sole priest of the country. The members of the local priesthood in the temples were only deputies of the

---

[21] Clancier (2017) 80–1.
[22] Judeans and others such as the Idumeans were organised in a *politeuma* since Ptolemy VI. On this subject, see the chapter of Sänger in this volume.
[23] Legras (2011). Earlier multi-ethnic populations in Memphite, such as the Hellomemphites and Caromemphites, may suggest that it was already true in the third century and explain the interest of the Ptolemaic dynasty for this temple and its cults that already constituted a common religious interest for both Greeks and Egyptians; see Section 3.1.

king.²⁴ Moreover, the Ptolemies could even create new deities and install them in Egyptian temples on an equal footing with local gods. This is exactly what happened with the dynastic cult and the introduction of princesses and queens such as Philotera, Arsinoe and Berenice as goddesses in Egyptian temples besides the local gods as *synnaoi theoi*. The Ptolemies were far more involved in Egyptian temples than the Seleucids were in Babylonian temples, being the highest religious authority due to their pharaonic status. This particular aspect of Egyptian royal ideology had been reasserted in late dynastic times, resulting in increased pharaonic control of temples' economic assets. The Ptolemies upheld this doctrine. Indeed, this traditional status of the king in Egyptian temples certainly helped the Ptolemies tighten royal administrative control.

The Seleucids' Neo-Babylonian heritage gave them no such status because cultic activities were the responsibility of the Babylonian priests. When the king took part, it was not as a god or as a priest but as man in debt to the gods, especially Bēl-Marduk, for having been chosen as king.²⁵ The main cultic duty of the Babylonian king, after making regular sacrifices, was to be present during the New Year festival when his kingship was confirmed by the *Šešgallu*, the high priest of the Esagil temple. As far as we know, the Seleucids did not normally participate in this ceremony. One well-known exception is Antiochus III who probably did so just before coming to Elam where he died.²⁶ But as the temples were at the same time the political centres of the Babylonian cities and held great economic power, the royal administration needed to keep a close control of their activities.

The Ptolemies had a much easier task in their efforts to exert influence over temple administrators. According to J. Quaegebeur, Egyptian temples can be defined as 'centre[s] of the public life' not only from the point of view of the local community but also for the royal administration.²⁷ This was already true during the last Egyptian dynasties. However, the Ptolemaic period is characterised by an increasing weakening of the temples' administration that benefitted the royal authority. K. Vandorpe has shown that at the end of the third century, royal scribes replaced the families of temple scribes who had traditionally collected the taxes. Through this new way of collecting the harvest tax, temple granaries

---

[24] Gorre and Honigman (2013) 107–10; and (2014) 308–10.
[25] Linssen (2004) esp. 127 for the ruler cult as an illustration of the ambiguous place of the king in the Babylonian religious practices.
[26] This is reported in the astronomical diary AD 2, -187A. See Del Monte (1997) 66–8.
[27] Quaegebeur (1979) 716.

became royal granaries.²⁸ Probably in conjunction with this reform, temple lands themselves became subject to this tax.²⁹ The same picture is true for notarial activity, where temple scribes were replaced by *agoranomoi*. Moreover, the temples were used not only as administrative centres but also as garrisons.³⁰

This was not true in the main Babylonian cities, where the Seleucids inherited the separated royal and temple administrations of the previous Neo-Babylonian and Achaemenid regimes. Indeed, royal local administrative structures such as the *chreophylakion* and the *basilikon* were located outside the temples.³¹ So the Babylonian case is rather different than the Egyptian one even if, at the beginning of our story, it has many parallels. Indeed, as we already stated, under the Neo-Babylonian kings the temple authorities were sometimes at the head of the cities and sometimes not. In any case, the kings wanted to have significant control over their activities. For this reason, they designated officials, sometimes from the royal court itself, to be part of the temple administration. They oversaw all the economic, administrative or judicial activities of the temples. The title of these officials varied over time but was mostly *qīpu*, *bēl piqitti* or *paqdu*.³²

In the Hellenistic period the function of this trusted person, the *paqdu*, remained, but he was drawn from quite different origins. Again, the two best attested examples are from Uruk and Babylon. In Uruk, the *paqdu*, the controller of the temple for the king, was no longer from the royal entourage but from the temple staff itself. We can illustrate this point with the example of the Ah'utu clan which was at the head of the Rēš temple administration in Uruk. Anu-balassu-iqbi³³ was at the same time 'chief of the officers of Uruk', which means the leader of the city, and *paqdu*, who was the trusted man of the king to control the temple. So, he was at the same time the controller and the person to be controlled. He gave his responsibilities of 'chief of the officers of Uruk' to one of his sons, the same Anu-uballiṭ Kephalon whom we mentioned earlier; and the

---

²⁸ Vandorpe (2000a); and (2000b).   ²⁹ Vandorpe (2005).
³⁰ Dietze (2000); Fischer-Bovet (2014b) 340–2.
³¹ However, in Babylon it is most likely that the Juniper Garden was an open area where different administrative and erudite activities took place. In Uruk, and maybe in Kutha, the temples had permanent employees whose role was to establish legal documents on leather or papyrus in Greek (i.e. the *paradeixis* in Kutha, the *graphē* in Uruk, for instance). These employees, the *sepīru*, could have been in charge of the legal documents produced not only for the temple but also for inhabitants of Uruk. The activities of the *chreophylax* are attested by seals' impressions. See Doty (1977) 308–29; and Messina (2005) for the links between the Urukean fiscal administration and the one of Seleucid-on-the-Tigris.
³² For the *paqdu* in Hellenistic time, see Boiy (2004) 209–10.   ³³ Monerie (2014) 82–4.

charge of 'controller' to another son called Anu-belšunu and then to another one named Timokrates.³⁴ So in Uruk, the royal control of the temple was transferred from inside its walls to be put at the head of administrative structures such as the *chreophylakion* or the *bīt šarri* that was the *basilikon*.

In the city of Babylon, the extant documentation is less detailed but indicates the existence of a *paqdu* there as well. One of them is known from a small group of administrative texts and he is listed along with the main administrative elements of the Esagil temple:³⁵

> Letter of Marduk-šumu-iddin, the temple administrator of Esangil, father of Bel-re'ušunu, the *šatammu* of Esangil, Belšunu, the *paqdu* of Nikanor, and the Babylonians of the temple assembly of Esangil, to Muranu, the son of Bel-bullissu (...)

Here we are under Antiochus II (261–246), and Belšunu has been named the *paqdu* of Nikanor. The information on this Nikanor is scanty and he is known only in this context, but J. Monerie has proposed giving him the title of *epi tôn hierôn*, the high priest in charge of the financial supervising of the sanctuaries of a satrapy.³⁶ If he is right, the *paqdu* (called *episkopos* in Nippur) was under Nikanor's authority. But in any case, no external royal agent was in the temples as a *paqdu*. This surely limited the effectiveness of royal control.

In Egypt, royal control seems to have been far more extensive. Macedonian kings manifested their concern to increase the 'honours' offered to the gods by granting temples regular royal subsidies.³⁷ However, in exchange, the Ptolemies expected to increase their financial control over the temples in line with the principle of reciprocity. The Ptolemies systemised the degree of control initiated by the Nectanebids on a larger scale and in line with the policies of the last Egyptian kings.³⁸ The introduction of the Ptolemaic dynastic cult of Arsinoe in the temples and the relative reform of the *apomoira* to finance it offered Ptolemy II the chance to tighten his grip on the internal priestly administration, as did the regular payment of the *syntaxeis* to the temples as grant subsidies for the daily cult at the end of the third century or at the beginning of the second century³⁹

The subordination of the temples to the royal financial administration was reinforced by the 'agent of Pharaoh', the Greek *epistates tôn hierôn*.⁴⁰

---

[34] Monerie (2014) 172–3.   [35] Jursa (2006) 156 and 191–2.   [36] Monerie (2014) 153.
[37] There is no evidence for Babylonia.   [38] Agut-Labordère and Gorre (2014).
[39] Clarysse and Vandorpe (1998).   [40] See Monson (2012) 216–18.

This man was the local representative of the royal fiscal administration. He acted as a member of the royal administration in the temple and, as such, he had authority over the *lesonis*, the representative of the internal administration of the temple. The powers of the 'agent of pharaoh' were far more extensive than the powers of the royal scribes appointed by the Nectanebids. Another form of royal control is known from the example of the *praktor Milon* in the temple of Edfu at the end of the third century. This man was sent directly by the central fiscal administration on a short-term assignment due to financial wrongdoing committed by the *lesonis*.[41]

In short, not only was the temple administration supervised by the agent of the pharaoh, a local representative of the royal administration, but the temples could also be subjected to occasional royal inspection. Not content with prompting the creation of new temple personnel to manage the royal subsidies, the Ptolemies intervened in the appointment of the head of the major temples. Therefore, it appears that there was a tighter royal control over the temple in Egypt than in Babylonia. According to us, the differences that we have identified between Babylonia and Egypt explain why there was a poliadisation in one case and not in the other.[42] There were two types of temples headed by two elite groups who played different roles in their respective society: in Babylon, the priestly elite was not representative of the local elite, whereas in Egypt the temple's elite was representative of the local elite. Finally, the two Hellenistic rulers possessed different degrees of freedom of action when it came to controlling temples. All these factors led to two types of evolution.

3   A New Administrative Deal: Two Kinds of Evolution

3.1   Poliadisation in Babylonia

In Babylonia, the main reform of the Hellenistic period took place at the beginning of the second century from the reign of Antiochus III to Antiochus IV. Babylon was refunded as a *polis*, a Greek city.[43] The Esagil temple remained a major local religious institution but lost its political and judicial responsibilities to the new civic structure of the *polis*.[44] As Sciandra has demonstrated, there is no evidence for a dual leadership of the city after

---

[41] Clarysse (2003) 17–27.
[42] On 'poliadisation' as a French neologism, see Couvenhes and Heller (2006) 17.
[43] Clancier (2017).
[44] For a discussion of the extension of this new political organisation inside Babylon, see the opposite point of view of van der Spek (2005); and Sciandra (2012).

Antiochus IV. It is probable that most – if not all – the 'Babylonians,' that is the members of the Assembly of Esagil, became citizens of the new *polis*, although we have no firm attestation of that. In any case the changes were huge for the local political life. Indeed, the *epistates*, called *pāhāt Bābili* in Akkadian,[45] was now the head of the city and the citizens gathered in new assemblies in the theatre.[46]

If the *polis* of Babylon is attested with certainty, there are some clues that a *polis* was also founded at Uruk. Indeed, through administrative and economic tablets it is possible to see some changes inside and outside the main sanctuaries of the city.[47] First, a new assembly appeared for the first time in 185 under Seleucus IV. Simply named the 'assembly of Uruk,' it acted from that date on beside the temple authorities on economic matters concerning the sanctuaries of the city. In the same years the 'assembly of the temples of Uruk' also appeared, a separate entity from the assembly of the whole city as well as the *kiništu ša Bīt Rēš*, the 'assembly of the Rēš temple'. Afterwards, the 'chief of the officers of Uruk,' still attested in 168, became just 'chief of the town officers of the sanctuaries' sometime in the following decade.[48] This new title indicated only responsibilities inside the sanctuaries. For instance, the '*paqdu* of Uruk' disappeared for the '*paqdu* of the sanctuaries' (*paqdu ša bīt ilāni*) from the reign of Seleucus IV onwards.[49]

3.2 The Egyptian Temples and the Royal Administration

This kind of reform was not necessary in Egypt. As previously noted, the royal military and fiscal administration was located in the Egyptian temples. The temples' internal administration survived until the end of the Ptolemaic period and was formally distinct from the civil and military administration. But from the end of the second century BC on, royal administration and the temple administration were both headed by local royal representatives, at least in the southern part of Egypt, as the local *strategoi* were also the high priests of all the temples of their administrative districts.[50] It is quite the opposite situation from the previously quoted example of Uruk in the third century BC where the head of the temple administration was also the head of the civil administration.

---

[45] Boiy (2004) 204–6 and more specifically on this title see Muccioli (2016), esp. 173–5.
[46] van der Spek (2001). The theatre was situated in the city quarter of Ālu-eššu in the northern part of the inner city.
[47] Clancier and Monerie (2014) 220–3.   [48] *OECT* IX 62 in McEwan (1982).
[49] Clancier and Monerie (2014) 221 with bibliography.   [50] De Meulenaere (1959).

From this perspective, one document published in 2009 by Christophe Thiers[51] is particularly interesting. It is the *Heracleion stela* found near Alexandria, dated to 118 BC. This document looked like a synodal decree but this similarity in form must not mislead us. It is a completely different sort of document for two reasons. Firstly, since the Alexandria decree of 243, the men summoned by the king were the intendants of the temples. These men, like the *lesoneis*, were the representatives of the internal administration of the temples and as such cannot be conflated with royal officers. On the contrary, in the *Heracleion stela*, according to Christophe Thiers, the men who discussed the matters of the temples were royal officers. Secondly, the text of the *Heracleion stela* focuses only on matters related to the temple as is usual in synodal decrees. However, the context of the meeting and the identity of its members indicate that the agenda was far more important. Christophe Thiers proposes connecting this meeting with the great amnesty decree of Ptolemy VIII, Cleopatra II and Cleopatra III of 118 BC.[52] This decree consisted of a vast programme of reorganisation for the country after a period of civil war. And, of course, the question of the temples was only one part of this decree and not the main subject. It is a major difference to the synods of the third and second century BC. That the royal officer discussed questions regarding the temples as only one issue among many other state matters shows that, at least by 118 BC, the Ptolemies succeeded in completely assimilating the temple's staff amongst royal officers without poliadisation.

4 Reforms of the Local Administration

One way to reform the local administration in Egypt and Babylonia was for the king to directly intervene in the organisation of the local elites. If this was a long-lasting tradition in Egypt, it seems to have been less true in Hellenistic Babylonia before Antiochus IV in the second century. However, the reign of Antiochus IV proved to be a turning point when the king played a central role on the reorganisation of the temple staff.

4.1 Changes to High-Ranking Temple Staff

It seems that the main reforms of the political structure of Babylon were undertaken from 169 onwards. In this process, Antiochus IV intervened directly in the administrative structure of the Esagil temple. The

---

[51] Thiers (2009).   [52] P.Tebt. I 5.

Astronomical Diary (-168 A) states that the *šatammu* was replaced by his brother on a royal order:[53]

> This month, the 6, a Babylonian, a jeweller, brother of the *šatammu* of Esagila who in his stead *p[erformed]* the administrative duties (^{lú}šà.tam$^{ú\text{-}tú}$), was entrusted with the office of *zazakku* by a message (^{kuš}ši-piš-tú) of the king.[54]

From 169 on, the *zazakku*[55] worked in place of the *šatammu* until at least its last attestation in the first two months of 163.[56] The *zazakku* was a trustee of the king in charge of the financial control of temples. So, it seems that king Antiochus IV wanted to exert greater control over the Esagil, its staff and its resources. During the same period, from 169 onwards, the Esagil sanctuary seems to have lost its judicial privileges.[57]

Egypt can offer a parallel for the appointment of a new temple head for the purpose of increased royal control of the temples' finance and staff. The Egyptian example is, contrary to the Babylonian case, a long-term institution. In the set of reforms carried out by Ptolemy II Philadelphos in the 260s, the introduction of the royal cult in the Egyptian temples, the distribution of the tax of the *apomoira* to the temples, and the assignment to the same family of both the office of the high priest of Ptah in Memphis and the office of 'director of all the prophets of the gods and goddesses of Lower and Upper Egypt' were interconnected. The high priest of Ptah enjoyed both cultic and administrative powers and had, at least nominally, primacy over all Egyptian high priests and acted as a delegate of the king-pharaoh.[58]

The high priest appointed by Ptolemy II was the first of a priestly dynasty which ended only with the Romans. However, the function of high priest was not totally hereditary, and a member of this family had to be confirmed by the Crown for each generation of new high priest. So, even if the power of the high priest of Ptah increased during the third century, this family was utterly subordinate to the Crown.

Such a dependency on the Crown can also be seen in Uruk. In 169 at the latest, the Ahʾutu clan in charge of the sanctuaries and the city was replaced as the head of the sanctuaries by the Hunzu clan.[59] We could find no

---

[53] Del Monte (1997) 78–9. Here, we are in autumn of 169, and it is the first attestation of the *zazakku* as well as the fact that the *šatammu* had been replaced for a time.
[54] Astronomical diary AD 2 No. -168 A, r. 12'-13'.
[55] For the *zazakku* see Dandamayev (1994); Joannès (1994); and MacGinnis (1996).
[56] AD 3 No. -163 C$_2$, r. 17–18.   [57] Clancier (2017) 73–6.   [58] Gorre (2009a) 605–22.
[59] Clancier and Monerie (2014) 221–2.

apparent internal reason for this evolution, and so we may deduce that the king intervened directly in Uruk as he did in Babylon. So, if there is no definitive argument demonstrating the foundation of Uruk as a new *polis*, the situation presents many parallels with Babylon. We can see that these reforms were undertaken in two phases. First during the poliadisation of Babylon and perhaps also Uruk, which was undertaken at the beginning of the second century but before Antiochus IV, it seems that the temples remained important political and judicial centres. The reforms that took place under Antiochus IV in Babylon and probably in Uruk, however, ended the political and judicial activities of the temples. It appears that in this process the king made changes at the head of these institutions. The change from one clan to another at the head of the temple of Uruk could imply that the Seleucid kings played with internal priesthood rivalries. But no evidence exists on this matter.

In Egypt, the Ptolemies may have played off the rivalry between the priesthood of Ptah in Memphis and the priesthood of Amon in Thebes.[60] According to their royal pharaonic titles and their choice for the construction sites in the temples, the first Macedonian kings seemed to have given the first role to Amon. However, from the start, this royal favour did not really benefit the family of the High Priest of Amon who was just secondarily involved in the Macedonian construction projects inside the temple of the god[61]. Under Ptolemy II, the revival of the function of high priest of Ptah clearly changed the power relationship between the temple of Amon and the temple of Ptah. In addition, the prominent status of Ptah in the Pharaonic titles of the Ptolemies from Ptolemy III onwards, and the connection between the bull Apis, the hypostasis of Ptah, and Serapis the new dynastic god, clearly marked the importance of the cults of Memphis.[62]

Besides the establishment of the primacy of the high priest of Ptah, the Ptolemies used their right to nominate the personnel of the temples in another way. An interesting example is the case of the Theban priest Amasis, known from the biographical inscription of his statue. He belonged to a secondary rank family of the Theban priesthood. However, he was responsible for the construction of the main monument built by Ptolemy III in Thebes, the so-called Euergetes gate.[63] Although it is not clearly stated, the biographical inscription contained some hints of

---

[60] Gorre (2009a) 504–6. [61] Ladynin (2014). [62] Legras (2014).
[63] According to Quaegebeur (1989) 111, n. 122 followed by Gorre (2009a) 72, n. 184. However, Mekis (2016) 389–90 has recently proposed to date the monument from the last Egyptian dynasty with three major arguments. Firstly, on p. 389, he postulated that the cult of Nectanebo II indicates a date

a royal assignment in surviving evidence; it seems likely that, due to the nature of the construction site, he owed his appointment to a royal nomination. Here is the more interesting excerpt according to the translation of the first editor of the document:[64]

> I went to the Royal Residence, I sailed to Hermopolis, a royal order being with me. I bent my arms to the prophet and their priests. I did good to their citizens. The reward was that I arrived at Thebes as an honoured one.

Even if the purpose of his assignment is not clear, it appeared that it was entirely due to the royal nomination. It has been suggested that the royal order was a *prostagma*.

This order explains his authority in the sanctuaries, which is expressed by the title of 'ruler of the temples of the Hermopolite'.[65] This is not a common title; however, it indicates an extended power over the temple, since usually the title of ruler is applied to the pharaoh. Moreover, Amasis had authority over all the temples of the Hermopolite district. As a 'ruler of the temples' Amasis should not be confused with the elected administrator from the local priesthood of each temple, the local *lesoneis*. Nonetheless, considering his royal appointment and the large scale of his jurisdiction, it seems likely that he had authority over the local *lesoneis*. His Egyptian title is not the usual one for translating the Greek *epistates tôn hierôn*, and Amasis seems more comparable to the *praktor* Milon previously quoted (see supra 1.2). The figure of Amasis seems to have no equivalent in Babylonia, illustrating the different abilities of the Seleucids and the Ptolemies to interfere in matters regarding the temples.

4.2 Royal Interventionism in Babylonia and Egypt

In Babylonia, the main period of royal interventionism took place in the second century when the Seleucid kings transformed into *poleis* (or 'poliadised') some old towns of Babylonia. But the question is: why change a political system if it was efficient? We have no definitive answer to this question, but we can propose different elements from former examples and new contexts.

---

prior to the Macedonian conquest, quoting Gorre (2009b), which, on the contrary, underlined the maintenance of this cult during the Ptolemaic period. Secondly, according to Mekis, the royal appointment and the mission accomplished in the temples of Hermopolis are not imaginable under the Ptolemies because these kings did not meddle with the temples' life. According to us, the evidence precisely shows that the Ptolemies interfered in the administration of the Egyptian temples.

[64] Fairman (1934).   [65] *ḥq3* for 'ruler'.

The former elements consist of the past examples of the different reforms made by the king to better control the sanctuaries and the town that the sanctuaries led. Under Nebuchadnezzar II (604–562), many reforms occurred in the big temple of Eanna in Uruk. The king eliminated the function of high administrator, which therefore meant that his representative, the *qīpu*, was at the head of the sanctuary. Nebuchadnezzar may have done this to be ensure the participation of the temple in his numerous building and military activities. The Persian kings dismissed numerous temple administrations because the elite that constituted them revolted against the new domination.[66] And so we could ask if the Seleucid kings of the beginning of the second century were still happy with the local elite of the town leading the temple administration. We saw that even the *paqdu*, normally the man of the king, was part of the local elite. It is possible that this system was no longer useful but was exceedingly difficult to transform. So maybe the best way was to exchange it for a more understandable and flexible organisation of a *polis*.

In Egypt, on the other hand, the permeability of the temples to the royal administration rendered the establishment of *poleis* unnecessary. This is the top-down explanation.

4.3 The Local Interest

We must also focus on a bottom-up explanation. We have stated that Egyptian temples were widely open to any members of the local elite. It seems that this was no longer the case in Babylonia. Indeed, if any high-ranking individuals were able to integrate into the temple administration during the Neo-Babylonian and Achaemenid periods, even this limited integration became impossible in the Hellenistic period. The temple administration and the royal administration were two different entities, the first being at the head of the town, even if controlled by the king. So, to be part of the political elite of the town one had to belong to a priestly family. But the population of Babylonia was cosmopolitan, and we may wonder if the Greeks, the Iranians, the Jews, the Arabs and other groups, who formed the population of Babylon and Uruk but were not part of the priesthood families, wanted to have a political role in their town. It is quite possible that the Seleucid kings were reacting to a demand coming from the inhabitants themselves.

---

[66] Waerzeggers (2003–4).

In Egypt there are many pieces of evidence which demonstrate that the Egyptian temples completely integrated the Greek or Hellenised elite who were mostly royal civil or military officers. We can quote three examples. Let us start by papyrological evidence combined with archaeology: a papyrus from the beginning of the first century states that the Great Hermaion in Hermopolis, meaning the *temenos* of the Egyptian god Thot (identified as Hermes), is now known as the *phrourion* of the king. This meant that the Hermaion was now the military and administrative centre. Even if the elites who ruled the temple at this time are not known, it is quite likely that royal officers were amongst those who administrated the *phrourion*. The excavation of the site of Hermopolis showed indeed a major transformation of the *temenos* of Hermopolis: perhaps since the reign of Ptolemy III, in the second part of the third century BC, it was reorganised with the piercing of a new street, probably the 'dromos of Hermes' of the previously quoted papyrus, which became the new axial line of the *temenos*. Subsequently to the disuse of the pharaonic axial line, a part of the sacred enclosure in mud brick of the XXXth dynasty and several old pharaonic buildings were dismantled, and their materials reused for this *dromos* of Hermes. Moreover, despite the name of *dromos*, the nature of this route differs from a traditional Egyptian *dromos*: it was not an extension of the sacred space in the urban area but contrariwise a public street in a space previously cut off of the profane world according to the traditional pharaonic organisation of a *temenos*.[67]

These archaeological and papyrological evidences can be completed by prosopographical data. In the middle of the second century, we find in the sanctuaries of the first cataract Herodes, who, among other titles, was *Pergamenon, tôn diadochôn* and *phrourarchos*. He is a good example of a local military high officer who claimed his Greek identity, who was connected to the royal court by his aulic title and who, nonetheless, was priest in the local temples.[68] Later in the first century BC, these same temples were headed by Eraton, *strategos* and *archiereus* of Philae.[69] The case of Eraton is not an isolated one, but, on the contrary, reflects the integration of royal elite at the higher level of the Egyptian temples. This permeability of the Egyptian temples to the Ptolemaic administration explains why it was possible for the local royal representatives to integrate into the temples[70] and consequently there was no need of poliadisation. Moreover, Egypt has a tradition of direct control of the territory by the

---

[67] Gorre (2021). [68] Gorre (2009a) no. 1. [69] Gorre (2009a) no. 2.
[70] We are not discussing here the cases where Crown representatives are recruited from temple staff.

royal administration: the creation of *poleis* would have led to the creation of an intermediate, which was not in the interest of the Ptolemies. On the contrary, in Babylonia the Seleucids' interventions in the temples were limited by the temples' autonomy and status of the king. This religious framework, along with the fact that the temples' elite were not representative of the local elite, explain the need for poliadisation.

5 Conclusion

In Babylonia, it is still difficult to explain why the temple administration lost its power. It is, however, most likely that it was to benefit some of inhabitants which had been, until then, left out of the temple administration and so excluded from positions of political power in the towns. For the king, it was a way to reform the local administration. In former periods he would have put a governor at the head of the town. Now he had another political structure to better reinforce his control: the *polis* with the nomination of the *epistates* as its leader. But in any case, this does not mean that the old priestly elite was left out of the new structure. On the contrary, it is probable that this old elite was assimilated into the new citizenship.

Poliadisations were clearly not necessary in Egypt due to the ability of the temples to integrate the new elite and the king's ability to interfere in the administration of the temples. When the royal power decided to tighten its authority over temples, this had different consequences in Babylonia and in Egypt. If in Babylonia the temples that were deprived of their administrative role were henceforth converted to a new institution like the theatre, in Egypt, the contrary happened. The temples kept their position as the centres of the public life, as the renaming of the *temenos* of Thot as the *phrourion* of the king shows. In these circumstances, the elite who headed the temple was also at the head of society precisely because they integrated the service of the Crown, which was, in Ptolemaic times, the best way to increase their social status.[71]

If we return to the chronology of the synodal decrees invoked in the introduction, we can now understand why these decrees disappeared. It has been recently suggested that the disappearance of the synodal decrees resulted from the disappearance of the synods themselves.[72] If the Ptolemies stopped summoning national synods it was because the kings

---

[71] Thompson (1988) 113: 'the absorption of Egyptians who were also priests into the upper ranks of the Ptolemaic army may have proved an effective means of integrating native institutions within the new Ptolemaic state.'

[72] Gorre-Veïsse (2020).

simply ceased to need them: there was complete integration of the temple elite with their royal administration. It is this integration that seems to be a central factor that could explain the absence of poliadisation in Egypt.

APPENDIX

Tabulation of the main changes in Babylonia and Egypt

	Babylonia	Egypt
260s		• Introduction of the Ptolemaic dynastic cult in the temples • Fundraising of the temples through the *apomoira* • Appointment of the founding high priest of the Ptolemaic-era line of Ptah pontiffs as privileged interlocutor of the king and first religious authority of the country
243 BC		• First (?) national synod
End third c.		• Replacement of temple scribes by royal scribes for the levying of taxes in kind on wheat in the Thebaid (it took place earlier in the rest of the country)
180 or 160 BC		• End of the royal convocation of priests in synod
180s	• *ca.* 187: under Antiochus III Babylon became a *polis* (or under Antiochus IV, *ca.* 172) • *ca.* 191–185: Uruk became a *polis* (?). • 185: first attestation of the assembly of Uruk	
160s	• Babylon, 169: the *šatammu* of Esagila is replaced by his brother with the title of *zazakku* • Babylon, after 169: end of the judicial responsibilities of Esagila • Uruk, 168: the title 'chief of the officers of Uruk' (*rab ša rēš āli ša Uruk*) borne by the	

(cont.)

	Babylonia	Egypt
	administrator of the temples is attested for the last time	
	• Uruk, after 168: the temples administrator bore the title 'Chief of the town officers of the temples' (*rab ša rēš āli ša bīt ilāni*). The temple assembly is named 'Assembly of the temple of Uruk' (*kiništu ša bīt ilāni ša Uruk*)	
Since 141 BC	• 141: Parthian conquest of Babylonia. No change in the political organisation of Babylon	
Since 125 BC		• The temples of the Thebaid are under the control of the local *strategoi*

CHAPTER 4

Contextualizing a Ptolemaic Solution
The Institution of the Ethnic politeuma*

Patrick Sänger

1 Introduction

There existed under the Ptolemaic kings of Egypt an institution, or association, called a *politeuma*, or 'polity'. Usually, the word *politeuma* is related to Greek city states or *poleis*. In this context *politeuma* can mean 'political act', 'government', 'citizenry', 'polity' or 'state' or, as a technical term, refer to the body of citizens who had political rights.[1] The Ptolemies seem to have adopted the word *politeuma* and transferred it to a specific form of association which was apparently destined for organized groups of persons living within an urban area and named after an ethnic designation. Indeed, this particular word usage occurs only on the territory of the Ptolemaic empire.[2] In Hellenistic Egypt, *politeumata* of Cilicians, Cretans (both in the Arsinoite nome?), Boeotians (in Xois in the Delta) and one of Idumaeans (in Memphis) are attested.[3] We come across all these *politeumata* in the second or first century.[4] In Roman times we encounter a *politeuma* of Phrygians at the end of the first century, whose location in Egypt is unknown, and in the year 120 CE, a *politeuma* of Lycians which existed in Alexandria.[5]

---

* The present text contains single passages of my articles (2015a); (2015c); and (2016b); on the topic taken up in the Sections 3 and 4 see also Sänger (2019) 191–6; 198–206. I thank Christelle Fischer-Bovet for her comments and Robert Kugler for his help with the English style.
[1] On the meaning of the word see, e.g., Ruppel (1927); Biscardi (1984); Zuckerman (1985–1988) 174; Lüderitz (1994) 183; Förster and Sänger (2014) 157–64; Sänger (2016d).
[2] On the evidence for *politeumata* see most recently Sänger (2014) 53–5; and (2016a) 28–32.
[3] Boeotians: SEG II 871 = SB III 6664; Cretans: P.Tebt. I 32 = W.Chr. 448; Idumaeans: OGIS 737 = Milne (1905) 18–9 no. 33027 = SB V 8929 = A. Bernand (1992) no. 25; on the identification of the Idumaean *politeuma* see Thompson (1984); and Thompson (2012) 93–6; Cilicians: SB IV 7270 = SEG VIII 573 = É. Bernand (1975) no. 15 = id. (1992) no. 22.
[4] The testimony for the Cilician *politeuma* mentioned above could also be dated to the third century. É. Bernand (1992) 65 no. 22 summarized the various dating suggestions (from the third to the first century) and favoured, following Mooren (1975) 173, no. 281, a dating to the first century; this was recently also suggested by Sänger (2015b).
[5] Phrygians: IG XIV 701 = OGIS 658 = SB V 7875 = IGR I 458 = Kayser (1994) no. 74; on the provenance of the inscription see also Huß (2011) 299 with further bibliographical references in

In 2001 the papyrus archive of the Jewish *politeuma* of Heracleopolis (the capital of the Heracleopolite *nome*) was published as P.Polit.Iud.[6] It provides the first definite documentary attestation of a Jewish *politeuma* in the Hellenistic period.[7] The only other Jewish *politeuma* that is known so far was located in Berenice in the Cyrenaica and appears in two inscriptions dated to Roman, not Ptolemaic, times.[8] It is in fact the only *politeuma* that is securely attested outside of Egypt.[9] P.Polit.Iud. consists of twenty papyri texts in Greek dated between 144/3 and 133/2. These documents suggest that the Jewish *politeuma* of Heracleopolis actually governed its own district of the city. It was probably this district where the Jews belonging to the *politeuma* were concentrated. There the officials of the Jewish *politeuma*, the *archons*, under a higher official called the *politarch*, seemed to act (at least in judicial matters) like state functionaries. Like Ptolemaic officials, the officials of the *politeuma* were approached by means of petitions, ordinarily in private legal disputes between Jews, but sometimes also in disputes between Jews and non-Jews. The petitioners appear always to be members of the *politeuma* or Jewish non-members. What they expected of the archons was judgment of cases and the enforcement of legal claims by virtue of the archons' official position. The procedure followed the same patterns as the judicial procedure of the Ptolemaic administration, in which officials dispensed justice by virtue of their position as magistrates.[10]

---

n. 232; Lycians: SB III 6025 = V 8757 = IGR I 1078 = SEG II 848 = A. Bernand (1992) no. 61 = Kayser (1994) no. 24.

[6] On the Jewish *politeuma* of Heracleopolis see, in general, Cowey and Maresch (2001), P.Polit.Iud. 1–34; Falivene (2002); Honigman (2002); Kasher (2002); Maresch and Cowey (2003); Cowey (2004); Kruse (2008); (2010); (2015a); Arzt-Grabner (2012); Sänger (2016b).

[7] Against Ritter (2011), who rejects the commonly accepted existence of a Jewish *politeuma* in Heracleopolis, see Sänger (2014) 54, n. 7; and (2016a) 29, n. 10.

[8] CIG III 5362 = SEG XVI 931 = Lüderitz (1983) no. 70 (Augustan period?); and CIG III 5361 = Lüderitz (1983) no. 71 (24/25 CE).

[9] Outside Egypt, three ethnic *politeumata* are also attested for Sidon (now in Lebanon) at the end of the third century, when it was still under Ptolemaic control (see Sänger 2014, 61–6; and 2016a, 38–3). For these Sidonian *politeumata*, see Macridy-Bey (1904) 549: stele A; 551: stele 2; 551–2: stele 3. A *politeuma* is also mentioned in stele 8 (553–4); however, the name of the city from which the members of this *politeuma* came is lost. The Sidonian *politeumata*, consisting of persons from the three cities of Kaunus (in Caria), Termessus Minor near Oinoanda, and Pinara (both in Lycia) – situated in the south of Asia Minor – thus differ from the *politeumata* in Egypt because they are associated with a home city rather than a region. The Sidonian *politeumata* could lend some support to the hypothesis that the origin of the form of organization in question lay in the third century (see below Section 3). However, because it is uncertain whether the term *politeuma* in Sidon referred to the Ptolemaic institution or was simply used in its common meaning of 'citizenry of a *polis*' (see Sänger 2019, 229–239), these ethnic *politeumata* will be excluded from the present study.

[10] On the character of the jurisdiction of the Jewish *politeuma* in Heracleopolis see most recently Sänger (2016c).

The Jewish *politeuma* was located in the harbour district of Heracleopolis. The area was about a mile removed from the town centre and located on the Bahr Yusuf, the western branch of the Nile. A fortress had been built there in the 150s, shortly before the *politeuma* is attested. Thus, a substantial part of the membership of the Jewish *politeuma* of Heracleopolis could have consisted of Jewish soldiers residing near their military base.

There is no reason to regard the Jewish *politeuma* of Heracleopolis as unique, or distinct from the *politeumata* of other ethnic groups. For we now know that Jews in general did not form a separate class of the population for legal or tax purposes but were classified among the ethnic category of *Hellenes* or Greeks,[11] and so, whether they were authentically Greek or not, were all the other groups we know were constituted as *politeumata* in Hellenistic Egypt: Boeotians, Cilicians, Cretans, Idumaeans, Lycians and Phrygians (these *Hellenes* were exempt from the obol tax: a very modest fiscal privilege).[12] The Jewish *politeuma* of Heracleopolis should not, therefore, be considered a special case.[13] Rather, it should be our working hypothesis that all the *politeumata* in the territory ruled by the Ptolemies held the same position in the Ptolemaic state.[14]

But how can this position be characterized? The following will shed light on this issue by adopting an administrative, political and social perspective. As we will see, the institution of the *politeuma* appears to be a unique, well thought-out, though hybrid political tool to advance, at an administrative level, the social status of persons the Ptolemaic government regarded as desirable. Furthermore, it will be argued that the establishment of the Ptolemaic *politeumata* was of ideological, strategic and sociopolitical significance – all the more since they can be regarded as a response to domestic and foreign conflicts the Ptolemies had to cope with in the second century.

2   The Character of the Institution of the *politeuma*: Administrative and Social Issues

The documents in P.Polit.Iud. seem to indicate that a *politeuma* was an administrative unit based on a (semi-autonomous) community and its

---

[11] See Mélèze Modrzejewski (1983) 265–6; Clarysse and Thompson (2006) 147–8.
[12] On the category of *Hellenes* see, in general, Mélèze Modrzejewski (1983); Thompson (2001); Clarysse and Thompson (2006) 138–47; 154–7. Although Egyptians could become members of this group, too, as a result of their occupation, see Thompson (2001) 310–2; and Clarysse and Thompson (2006) 142–5), the term *Hellen* ("Ἕλλην), in practice, mostly denoted an 'immigrant' or a 'foreign settler' who was to be distinguished from 'native Egyptians' (*Aigyptioi*); see Bagnall (2006) 3; Clarysse and Thompson (2006) 142–3; 155.
[13] See Honigman (2003); Kruse (2008); (2010); Thompson (2011a) 109–13; (2011b) 21–2.
[14] See Sänger (2016a) 38.

territorial base.[15] Accordingly, the judicial competences of the officials of the Jewish *politeuma* of Heracleopolis illuminated by the papyri were due to their public position as officials of an administrative unit – their *politeuma*.[16] Therefore, by means of a *politeuma* a community that was concentrated in a certain urban district was integrated into the Ptolemaic administrative structure and obtained public sanction – that public and territorial-based character set the association called *politeuma* apart from an ordinary association or club. Because of this character, state authorization was certainly required to constitute a *politeuma*,[17] whereas the emergence of communities or associations *per se* was not (or could not be) controlled. The fact that there are no indications that the Ptolemies tried to control the establishment of associations raises doubt as to whether they were ever interested in, or capable of, systematic monitoring or control of the groups formed by their subjects.[18]

Although a *politeuma* may physically have looked like a self-contained settlement within a larger urban area, it has not been proven that the members of a *politeuma* formed a body of second-class citizens in comparison to the citizens of a Greek *polis*. Given the present state of evidence, an ethnic *politeuma* should therefore be ranked, on a constitutional level, among associations and not be defined as a small-scale, second-class *polis*.[19] That members of the Jewish *politeuma* of Heracleopolis could call themselves *politai*[20] ('citizens') does not provide clear-cut evidence for their belonging to any sort of *polis*: *polites* is a vague and flexible term, being, for instance, a common term adopted by Jews to designate their membership in the *politeia* of Moses, as is already attested in the Septuagint.[21] What we are dealing with are, therefore, groups in which being a member was *primarily* significant for an individual's social life.

The information on the Jewish *politeuma* of Heracleopolis also confirms that ethnic *politeumata* are linked to military groups.[22] This approach was

---

[15] See Sänger (2016a) 35–8; 44; (2016b); Kruse (2010) 95; 97; 99–100.
[16] Similarly, Honigman (2003) 94–5.
[17] See Launey (1949–50) 1077; 1079; Cowey (2004) 30; Kruse (2008) 172; (2010) 98; Sänger (2016b).
[18] See San Nicolò (1915) 10; (1927) 299–300 about state authorization.   [19] See Sänger (2016b).
[20] P.Polit.Iud. 1.18.
[21] See Strathmann (1990) 525. For the use of the word in the context of the Jewish *politeuma* in Heracleopolis cf. Cowey and Maresch, P.Polit.Iud. 22–3, 38; Honigman (2002) 253–4; (2009) 126, n. 18; Ameling (2003) 98. There is no proof that *polites* was used as a (technical) designation for a member of a *politeuma*, contrary to Cowey (2004) 33–4; Kasher (1985) (for instance) 30; 127; 130, n. 71; 192–4 (disputed by Zuckerman [1985–1988] 184; Mélèze Modrzejewski [1997] 82; Lüderitz [1994] 194–5); Kasher (2002) 266–8; (2008) 115–7; 124–5; Capponi (2007) 141–2.
[22] For previous approaches see Launey (1949–50) 1077; Honigman (2003) 67; Thompson (2011a) 109–13; (2011b) 21–2 with further references in n. 47.

already suggested by the Boeotian *politeuma* whose priest was the Boeotian Kaphisodoros, who also held the office of a *strategos* (the highest *nome* official).[23] His *politeuma* apparently consisted of a group of soldiers and a group of civilians.[24] In the case of the Cilician *politeuma*, we encounter Arrhenides, a high-ranking military officer of *machairophoroi* (a troop of professional soldiers, literally 'saber-bearers'), who was probably of Cilician origin and acted as a benefactor of the community concerned.[25] As regards the Idumaean *politeuma*, it was Dorion, son of an Egyptian priest family, who was honoured by the Idumaeans, and he held the office of a *strategos* and simultaneously was a priest of *machairophoroi*.[26] Given the position of both the benefactor of the Cilician *politeuma* and the honouree of the Idumaean *politeuma*, it is natural to assume that some members of these *politeumata* served as *machairophoroi*. As far as the Cretan *politeuma* is concerned, we are informed that two representatives of the community were involved in the administrative processing of the promotion of a member of the *politeuma* to a higher rank within the military hierarchy. Furthermore, an inscription that dates from the year 112/11 or 76/75 refers to a *politeuma* of soldiers of unspecified ethnicity stationed in Alexandria.[27] This *politeuma* is an exceptional case because its members are not described in terms of their origins in a foreign geographical region, but by their profession. But that oddity aside, this Alexandrian *politeuma* of soldiers supports the theory that the *politeumata* had a military background.

What about the internal administration and the religious identity of the *politeumata*? Although they represented administrative units, this does not mean that all *politeumata* were organized identically: to be sure, a council of archons, which presided over the Jewish *politeumata* of Heracleopolis and Berenice, is well known from Jewish associations or synagogue communities.[28] But non-Jewish ethnic *politeumata* seem to have employed different officials which are well-known from the context of common associations sharing religious, professional, social and/or economic

---

[23] Person and rank: See Peremans, Van 't Dack, De Meulenaere and Ijsewijn, Pros.Ptol. III 5167; Launey (1949–50) 1067; Bengtson (1952) 52–5; Mooren (1977) 20–1, 36, 97–102.
[24] See Zuckerman (1985–8) 175; Thompson (2011a) 110.
[25] Person and rank: Peremans and Van 't Dack, Pros.Ptol. II 4338; Launey (1949–50) 1068; É. Bernand (1992) no. 22.1; Mooren (1975) 173–4; (1977) 172–3, 214.
[26] Person and rank: Peremans and Van 't Dack, Pros.Ptol. I 248 (with Mooren and Swinnen, Pros. Ptol. VIII) = Peremans and Van 't Dack, Pros.Ptol. II 2113b (with Mooren and Swinnen, Pros.Ptol. VIII) = Peremans, Van 't Dack, De Meulenaere and Ijsewijn, Pros.Ptol. III 5519, 6337 (with Clarysse, Pros.Ptol. IX); Thompson (1984) 1070–11; (2012) 105–6; Gorre (2007) 242–5; Fischer-Bovet (2014b) 291–2; 353.
[27] SEG XX 499.   [28] See Claußen (2002) 273–8; Stökl Ben Ezra (2009) 291.

activities. In the case of the *politeuma* of soldiers stationed in Alexandria, one encounters a *prostates* (president) and a *grammateus* ('scribe'); as we have already seen, for the Boeotian *politeuma* a priest (*hiereus*) is attested. Furthermore, we are informed that the Boeotian, Cilician and Idumaean *politeumata* each had its own sanctuary or temple district; it can, therefore, be assumed that in the Cilician and Idumaean *politeumata*, like in the Boeotian *politeuma*, a priest presided over the cult of each group. In the case of the Boeotians and the Idumaeans, it is unquestionable that their religious identities were strongly connected to the homelands to which their respective ethnic designations alluded: the Boeotians worshiped Zeus Basileus, a particularly Boeotian aspect of Zeus,[29] and the Idumaeans Apollo (as their sanctuary, called an Apollonieion, reveals), who is to be identified with Qos, the main god of the Idumaeans before they converted to Judaism.[30] The cult of the Cilicians is less specifically directed at a homeland god but has at least a strong Greek connotation: it is devoted to Zeus and Athena. In the case of the Jewish *politeuma* of Heracleopolis, Jewish belief becomes apparent in the petitions addressed to the archons, and the titles of these officials may suggest that behind the *politeuma* is hidden a synagogue community.

Given the fact that *politeumata* formed cult associations that carried on the rites of the 'homeland' indicated by their ethnic designation and had their own administration, which – if the Jewish *politeuma* of Heracleopolis is anything to go by – seems to have a territorial character (a feature which, by the way, fits the most common Greek sense of the word *politeuma*), they cannot be categorized merely as 'ethnic networks' or 'ethnic associations', but should be regarded as 'ethnic communities' according to the terminology of social science.[31] Furthermore, the location of the *politeumata* and their connection with military groups suggest that these communities were the outcome of mercenary groups. This approach, which is also supported by the ethnic designations the *politeumata* bore – and we will return to this aspect shortly – is based on the fact that the Ptolemies recruited full-time mercenary soldiers to use in war, but who also functioned in peacetime to

---

[29] See Launey (1949–50) 954–5; 1067.
[30] See Rapaport (1969) 73; Thompson (1984) 1071; (2012) 92–3.
[31] For this definition see Smith (1986) 22–31; Delanty and Kumar (2006) 171–2; Eriksen (2010) 48–53 based on Handelman (1977). See also Sänger (2015d) 232–4 and Thompson (2011a) 108–9 summarizing her view of features by which members of an ethnic group can be identified: 'Whereas many of these factors [ethnic designation, language, nomenclature, a person's appearance, cultural practices, occupation] serve to identify individuals rather than communities, in the case of the last four features – temples, the existence of ethnic quarters, of ethnic leaders and local responsibility for some degree of legal control – we have features which may define communities.'

garrison strategically important points.³² A significant proportion of such military bases were in larger or urban settlements.³³ Therefore, it is fair to assume that the *politeumata* were rooted in ethnically defined mercenaries whose units had been stationed – as far as we can see – in *nome* capitals, where most of these professional soldiers lived in the same neighborhood and probably in the vicinity of their garrison.³⁴

These ethnic *politeumata* were well integrated into the power structures of Ptolemaic society. Analysis of their social relations illuminates vertical networks between the *politeumata* on the one hand and members of the ruling class on the other hand. In this respect, the *politeumata* can be distinguished from the – epigraphically attested – ethnic *koina* on Cyprus representing associations or assemblies of mercenaries or professional soldiers of the same origin who merely met or gathered in order to honour high officials, predominantly the governor of the island, but sometimes also other dignitaries.³⁵ In contrast, the epigraphic evidence on the *politeumata* indicates close relationships that existed between them and members of the Ptolemaic elite. The latter to some extent played a dual role:³⁶ on the one hand, they were, such as Kaphisodoros and probably Arrhenides, members or, perhaps as Dorion, sympathizers of the respective *politeuma*; on the other hand, they held court titles and were high-ranking representatives of Ptolemaic central authority, who probably had direct access to the king and his closest advisors or, at least, were able to initiate such contacts because of their position. The papyrus that attests the Cretan *politeuma* could show that the network character of the *politeumata* cannot be underestimated. It reveals the case of Asklepiades who belonged to the 500 men who are said to have reinforced the Cretan *politeuma* and, thus, will have become its members. Asklepiades was counted among the military status group of *Makedones* and seems to have been promoted – after his attachment to the

---

³² See Scheuble (2009) 214–5; Fischer-Bovet (2014b) 261–3; 269–79.
³³ The roots of this system lay in late Pharaonic times and can be traced back to the seventh century; see Fischer-Bovet (2014b) 18–37.
³⁴ The *politeumata* are without doubt the best example for a process described by Thompson (2011a) 112–3: 'Local ethnic communities in the Ptolemaic period often derived in origin from military groups; [but] in their developed form they were total communities, consisting of far more than just the military.'
³⁵ The word *koinon* can refer to associations or assemblies; see Poland (1909) 164–5; Rzepka (2002) 227–34; Oetjen (2014) 148–9. On the ethnic *koina* on Cyprus, cf. Bagnall (1976) 56–7 and Appendix B; Launey (1949–50) 1032–4; San Nicolò (1913) 198–200. Cf. also below n. 75.
³⁶ Cf. also Fischer-Bovet (2014b) 294–5.

politeuma – immediately or fairly rapidly from an *ephodos* (a local paramilitary police officer serving on active duty and thus, although owing a *kleros*, not to be equated with an ordinary *cleruch* representing a reservist regular) to a *katoikos*, a member of the *cleruchic* cavalry. However, whether this advancement happened because the representatives of the Cretan *politeuma* additionally held a function in the royal administration – which is not known to us – and thereby had good relations with military authorities must remain open. Nor can we obtain certainty whether it was just due to the negotiation skills of Kaphisodoros, Arrhenides and Dorion that the ethnic or military community, whose members they were or to which they were bound for professional reasons, was defined as *politeuma*. An alternative explanation could be that the institution of the *politeuma*, because of its specific profile, opened up promising career opportunities to some of its members culminating in assuming the highest military and administrative offices or because of its cultic activities generated group dynamics that attracted external dignitaries, as in the case of Dorion. Overall, there is no doubt that a *politeuma* provided its members with plenty of opportunities to strengthen and advance their social networks which could lay the basis for the enhancement of one's social position.

3 The Political Intention behind the *politeumata*: Reflections on the Time of Their Foundation and Their Ideological, Strategic and Sociopolitical Significance

Before we turn to the political intention behind the establishment of the *politeumata*, some general remarks concerning the recruitment policy of the Ptolemaic army are needed. In this context we first must differentiate between two different kinds of Ptolemaic soldiers: the military settlers or *cleruchs* – reservist regulars who served only when called up (this could also happen at peacetime for garrison duties) – representing the regular army and the mercenaries or professional soldiers. Statistical analyses of ethnic designations show that, at least in the third century, both groups were recruited mainly from outside Egypt. Apparently the Ptolemies even tried – as far as they could – to channel recruitment from certain extra-Egyptian regions into the two different military 'job profiles': *cleruchs* were mainly recruited from Macedonia, mainland Greece, and Thrace – regions that were not or, as Thrace under Ptolemy III, were partially controlled by the Ptolemies – and mercenaries or professional soldiers in regions where they had possessions or influence, as in Asia Minor, Crete, and the Levant.³⁷ From the second century onwards, the Ptolemies slightly altered their recruitment policy: mercenaries or soldiers receiving pay were primarily recruited locally and, therefore, within Egypt, and also the recruitment practice regarding *cleruchs* was subject to changes insofar as now men from the Egyptian milieu were increasingly included into the higher ranks of the system of the *cleruchy* which previously had been reserved for immigrant soldiers and their descendants.³⁸

Although the patterns of recruitment may imply that most of the *politeumata* go back to the third century, because afterwards the Ptolemies lost their large extra-Egyptian possessions in Asia Minor and the Levant (regions which are concretely reflected in the *politeumata* of Cilicians, Idumaeans, Jews and Lycians), the evidence must lead to the conclusion that this institution was of growing importance only for the following two centuries of Ptolemaic rule: we should be aware of the fact that the earliest secured attestation of a *politeuma* falls into the reign of Ptolemy VI (180–145);³⁹ thus, there is no actual testimony for a *politeuma* dated to the third century, nor for that matter, for the date of foundation of any of the *politeumata* in Egypt. Therefore, it would be reasonable to assume that at least some (if not all) of them were founded in the second or first century.

It is not only important to notice that nothing excludes the foundation of *politeumata* in Egypt after the third century. We should moreover consider the possibility that some communities, upon which the *politeumata* were based, had their roots in migrations that took place in the second (or even first) century. For there is some evidence suggesting that even after the territory of the Ptolemaic kingdom had been reduced to Egypt, Cyprus and the Cyrenaica, the Ptolemies were still eager and able to recruit soldiers from other regions.⁴⁰ From lands once Ptolemaic but now

---

[37] *Cleruchs*: Bagnall (1984); Scheuble-Reiter (2012) 18–23; 114–8; Stefanou (2013). Mercenaries: Bagnall (1984) 16; Stefanou (2013) 127–31.

[38] *Cleruchs*: Fischer-Bovet (2014b) 216–21; Scheuble-Reiter (2012) 138–9. Mercenaries: Fischer-Bovet (2014b) 119; 262; 269; 273–9; 293; cf. Scheuble (2009) 220, n. 47.

[39] This has led to the widespread assumption that the form of organization in question was introduced by this king: see Launey (1949–50) 1077; Honigman (2003) 67; Thompson (2011b) 21–2 with further bibliographical references at n. 47; cf. also Fischer-Bovet (2014b) 293–4.

[40] Until the reign of Ptolemy VI Philometor (180–145) active Ptolemaic policy in the Aegean is attested, and until his reign Ptolemaic garrisons were kept in Itanus (north-eastern Crete), Methana (Eastern Peloponnese on the Saronic Gulf), and on the Aegean island of Thera; see Buraselis (2011); Winter (2011); Scheuble-Reiter (2012) 117–8; Fischer-Bovet (2014b) 168–9. All these outposts could have assisted recruitment in the surrounding areas. The Ptolemies also employed trusted recruitment officers (*xenologoi*) to hire soldiers outside Egypt (Polyb. 5.63.8–9; 15.25.16–18).

under hostile control, powerful political refugees and their existing forces or retainers were natural recruits, a fact illustrated by the Ptolemaic reception of the Judaean Onias, member of the Oniad family.[41] Political confusion in Judaea, a consequence of the revolt of the Maccabees, drove Onias – accompanied by fellow Jews – to Egypt, and he was allowed by Ptolemy VI to found a Jewish temple and form a military colony in Leontopolis (south-east of the Nile Delta).[42] The start of construction can, depending on our interpretation of Josephus, be dated between 164 and 150.[43] Some years later, Idumaeans possibly took refuge in Egypt after Idumea had been captured and annexed by the Jewish leader John Hyrcanus in ca. 125.[44] In short, even in a period of declining Ptolemaic power, there is no reason to think the influx of outside soldiers into Egypt ever came to an abrupt end. It rather continued to a lesser degree even in an altered geopolitical context.[45] Therefore, although the Ptolemies started to recruit professional soldiers primarily within Egypt at the turn of the second century,[46] they seem also to have tried as far as possible to maintain the recruitment patterns they used in the third century when the kingdom ruled the sea and had far-flung possessions – a sign of some continuity and stability.

This last aspect is all the more important for explaining why the institution of the *politeuma* appears after the third century and not earlier. For the ideological, strategic and sociopolitical significance of the *politeumata* becomes apparent when considering their establishment as

---

Stefanou (2013) 118–20 concluded (p. 120) 'that individual Macedonians might render their services to the Ptolemies, regardless of Ptolemaic relations with the Antigonids', and see pp. 120–1 for Ptolemaic recruitment of prisoners of war and renegades.

[41] The Oniads were the descendants of Zadok, high priest under Solomon, whose ancestors had held the office of high priest at Jerusalem since Onias I (ca. 320–280). It is still not possible to determine with certainty whether Onias should be identified with Onias III or his son, though the second possibility is slightly preferred in the literature: see Kasher (1985) 132–5, for the controversy, but who leaves open whether Onias III or IV is meant. Parente (1994) argued for Onias III, as did (with more or less conviction); Taylor (1998) 298–310; and Ameling (2008) 118–9. Mélèze Modrzejewski (1997) 124–5 identifies Onias with Onias IV, an identification also preferred by Gruen (1997) 47–57 (n. 26 cites older literature for this position); Capponi (2007) 42–53; Nadig (2011) 188–94.

[42] See Joseph. *BJ* 1.33; 7.427; *AJ* 13.65–66.

[43] See Capponi (2007) 59; Nadig (2011) 188; 191–3; see also Gruen (1997) 69–70 pointing to 159–152, when the office of high priest was vacant. As to whether the military colony of Onias was organized as a *politeuma*, which seems likely, see Sänger (2015a).

[44] See Rapaport (1969) 78–9; 81–2; Thompson (1984) 1071–2; (2012) 79–80; Honigman (2003) 66 n. 22; 83–4.

[45] See Fischer-Bovet (2014b) 293: 'Indeed, the reorganization of the army during the period of crisis (Period B) [ca. 220 and ca. 160] favored the use of professional soldiers in garrisons. Even if recruitment was mainly internal to Egypt, foreigners were also hired at times.'

[46] See the preceding n. and Fischer-Bovet (2014b) 269–71; 273–9.

a multifaceted reaction to the changing political conditions the Ptolemaic kingdom had to face from the very start of the second century (and which also prompted the Ptolemies to alter their recruitment policy). In this respect, it is probably no coincidence that it is during the reign of Ptolemy VI we encounter an ethnic *politeuma* for the first time because in the first half of the second century the Ptolemaic kingdom was seriously tested, both in terms of foreign policy and domestic policies: as was already indicated, Ptolemy V had lost all Ptolemaic outer possessions in Asia Minor and Coele-Syria in the 190s. Although a few years later his reign saw the end of the great twenty-year-long revolt of the Thebaid in 186 (see Honigman and Veïsse in this volume), Egypt continued to be affected by several domestic political crises under his successor Ptolemy VI. In 169 and 168 the Seleucids invaded Lower Egypt and soon after (ca. 165) the revolt of Dionsyius Petosarapis started near Alexandria and obviously spread through the Heracleopolite *nome* in Middle Egypt.[47] At roughly the same time another uprising broke out in the Thebaid or Upper Egypt.[48] Finally, Egypt was burdened by the dispute between Ptolemy VI and Ptolemy VIII because the latter, although his authority had been limited to the Cyrenaica in 164/3, continued to pose a significant threat to his older brother's rule over Egypt in the 150s.

Despite the weak position of the Ptolemaic kingdom from the second century onwards, the ideological principles of categorizing the population of Egypt in the third century, when the Ptolemaic kingdom ruled the sea and had far-flung possessions, remained largely the same over the subsequent period: Persons who were assigned to the population categories of *Hellenes* and *Makedones* still held a privileged position within Ptolemaic society,[49] and therefore the ideological significance of the *politeumata* may not be underestimated. By referring to regions that once represented outlying possessions, or, at least, to areas which did not belong to the remaining parts of the Ptolemic kingdom, they perhaps attempted to allude to continuing glory and power in the second and first centuries. Furthermore, there could have been a political message behind the fact that

---

[47] See McGing (1997) 293.
[48] See Hölbl (1994) 157–8. On the Egyptian revolts in Ptolemaic Egypt see, in general, McGing (1997); Veïsse (2004).
[49] On the continued use of the categories 'Greeks' (*Hellenes*) and 'Egyptians' in the administrative language see P.Tebt. I 5 = C.Ord.Ptol. 53.207–210 (118) with Mélèze Modrzejewski (1983) 255; Thompson (2001) 302–3. On the tax-*Hellenes* see in particular Huß (2011) 247–8 making reference to BGU XIV 2429.13 (Heracl., after 94 or 61 [?]). For the second-century military designation *Makedon* which (like the term *Perses*) probably denoted a status group within the army see Thompson (2001) 306; Vandorpe (2008); Fischer-Bovet (2014b) 177–91.

the *politeumata* were set up as 'Greek' focal points at strategic locations, especially in Lower and Middle Egypt and, therefore, close to the Mediterranean and the connecting route to Palestine, the only land bridge to the Levant and the Greek core areas – a political message that was possibly directed against the archenemies of the Ptolemies, the Seleucids, who themselves (just like the Antigonids and Attalids) never seem to have decided to utilize such kind of association in their realm (which will be discussed in more detail below). Thus, the foundation of the *politeumata* might be understood as a mixture of diplomatic and military strategy.

Another facet of this institution is related to its sociopolitical significance. In order to approach this aspect, it is once again useful to turn to the organization of the Ptolemaic army. Here, it is important to notice that the distribution of the Ptolemaic soldiers in two different military occupational groups (i.e. *cleruchs* and mercenaries) is also reflected in the strategies employed to retain these immigrants in Egypt. On the one hand, *cleruchs*, who were *a priori* intended for long-term employment, were granted *kleroi*, plots of land, for cultivation. On the other hand, there were the *politeumata*. They appear in the second century and – because their number seems to have been limited – probably bear witness to the selective promotion of certain ethnic communities which were of particular importance for the Ptolemaic government and originated in contingents of mercenaries or professional soldiers. By incorporating communities of valuable mercenary warriors into the administrative structure of Ptolemaic Egypt, the *politeumata* reflect strong efforts also to keep professional soldiers on the long term. Thus, this institution can be regarded as the urban counterpart of the *cleruchic* settlements that were created with land grants: both testify to how the Ptolemies tried to strengthen the ties between them and their army.[50]

In general, the institution of the *politeuma* enabled the Ptolemies, at an administrative and sociopolitical level, to have a direct influence on the structures of a major (and already mentioned) component of the Ptolemaic defensive concept: the garrison towns located at strategically important sites.[51] In the Nile Valley this defensive concept was rooted in

---

[50] See also Thompson (1984) 1074–5; (2011a) 109–13; (2011b) 21–2 who argued that *politeumata* should be treated as an expression of military and related immigration policies the Ptolemies pursued in the middle of the second century as an alternative to granting land to military immigrants as they did in the previous century. However, it has to be stressed that settlements of *cleruchs* are (to a lesser extent) also attested for the second and first centuries; see Scheuble-Reiter (2012) 23–4; Fischer-Bovet (2014b) 204–6. Therefore, it should be made clear that the institution of the *politeuma* could indeed be regarded as an alternative to the granting of *kleroi* but not as a substitution for this kind of military policy.

[51] See Scheuble (2009) 214–5; Fischer-Bovet (2014b) 18–37 (on the origins); 261–3; 269–79 (with the map on p. xxiii); cf. Griffith (1935) 131–5; Van 't Dack (1977) 91–2.

pre-Hellenistic times, but it also finds parallels in the Antigonid, Attalid and Seleucid kingdoms. Perhaps, garrison crews and their surroundings came especially into focus in the first half of the second century because the years of domestic and foreign political crises have made necessary a renovation and, where appropriate, expansion of these military bases. A good example for the increased security measures that appear to have been carried out in second-century Egypt is provided by the case of the *nome* capital of Heracleopolis, which in the 150s saw the construction of the already mentioned fortress in the harbour district (where the Jewish *politeuma* was located) and the renovation of a further fortress in the actual town.[52] These initiatives are likely to be interpreted as an immediate governmental response to the tense political situation during the reign of Ptolemy VI.[53] This situation had obviously prompted the Ptolemaic authorities to strengthen the cordon of fortresses in the Heracleopolite *nome* in order to improve the military defense of Middle Egypt, at the entrance to the economically important Arsinoite *nome*.[54] In this region as well as in Lower Egypt such security measures were supported insofar as some garrison towns became locations of *politeumata* and, thus, centres of attraction for groups with the same ethnic and military affiliation. It is noteworthy that different patterns of Ptolemaic military policy seem to appear in more southern regions of Egypt: according to the evidence from Akoris (Hermopolite *nome*), Krokodilopolis and Pathyris (both to the south of Thebes), the new garrisons that were established in these villages in the second century (after the revolt of the Thebaid) were made up of locally recruited soldiers coming from a Greco-Egyptian or Egyptian milieu.[55]

4   The Ptolemaic Ruling Strategy in Context: A Structural Comparison with Other Hellenistic Kingdoms

Given the uniqueness and peculiarity of the phenomenon under investigation, the questions may arise: why was an association like the *politeuma* a suitable institution for Ptolemaic administration? Why was it limited to the Ptolemaic kingdom? To answer these questions, we have to take one factor into consideration, which is decisive for understanding the structure of the administrative and army organization of Ptolemaic Egypt, and to

---

[52] See P.Berl.Zill. 1–2 (prov. unknown, 156/5).   [53] See Kruse (2010) 100; (2011) 264–7.
[54] On the cordon of fortresses in the Heracleopolite *nome* see Cowey Maresch and Barnes, P.Phrur. Diosk. 8–9; Kruse (2011) 262.
[55] See Vandorpe (2008); Fischer-Bovet (2014b) 187–91; 269–71; 273–9 (with the map on p. xxiii).

put it into a comparative context: the Ptolemies' attitude towards the institution of the *polis*. With regard to the Ptolemaic core territory, the Nile Valley, it is a well-known feature of Ptolemaic ruling strategy that, firstly, the *nome* capitals were not constituted as *poleis* in order to 'hellenize' the traditional *nome* administration of Egypt and, secondly, there were no obvious intentions of founding new *poleis* beside the already existing Greek cities of Alexandria and Naukratis. For the late fourth and the third centuries, we indeed know of only one foundation: Ptolemais Hermeiou in Upper Egypt. At a first glance, these tendencies stand in sharp contrast to Seleucid rule which was generally characterized by the foundation of numerous *poleis*. However, we should by no means overestimate this fundamental difference in Hellenistic urban policies because the Seleucids did not tend to found new *poleis* in already urbanized and densely populated territories, as, for example, in the Persian heartland.[56] A comparable and particularly well-documented example of this ruling practice is offered by the highly urbanized region of Asia Minor under Seleucid and Attalid control where we observe predominantly refoundations of already existing cities (Greco-Macedonian military settlements, indigenous cities); *poleis* that were completely new foundations which were based on the settlement of Greco-Macedonian colonists are clearly in the minority in Hellenistic Asia Minor.[57] Therefore, the fact that the Nile Valley by no means required structural support for administrative development might explain the Ptolemaic reluctance to found new *poleis* in Egypt in terms of a pragmatic decision (while the lack of refoundations remains noticeable). This reluctance is, indeed, only partially symptomatic of the way the Ptolemies ruled their kingdom because until the second half of the third century, the first three Lagids (re)founded some cities outside of Egypt in the Cyrenaica, on the western coast of the Red Sea and in southern Anatolia; in the Aegean area, Ptolemaic political and economic presence is also attested by several already existing settlements (villages, cities) temporarily bearing Ptolemaic dynastic names.[58] In this context we should also mention Ptolemy VI and Ptolemy VIII who both entrusted Boethos, a high-ranking official with the epithet *ktistes* or 'founder', with

---

[56] On the settlement policies of the Seleucids and the Ptolemies, see the chapter by Mairs and Fischer-Bovet in this volume.

[57] For the situation in the Persian heartland and Asia Minor see Aperghis (2004) 90–2; 95–6; Mileta (2009); Daubner (2011); Fischer-Bovet (2014b) 296–7.

[58] See Heinen (1997) 350–4; Winter (2011); Laronde (1987) 405–6 (focussing on the Cyrenaica). On the Ptolemaic settlement policy see, in general, Mueller (2006a). With regard to southern Anatolia, Fischer-Bovet (forthcoming) discusses how the Ptolemies and the Seleucids (re)founded a similar number of cities and had similar policies.

city foundations in the Nile Valley, first Philometoris and Kleopatra in the Triakontaschoinus (Lower Nubia) and then Euergetis, which unpublished papyri locate in the Heracleopolite.[59] These activities are remarkable because they took place in a period when there seem to have also been efforts to establish *politeumata*. The foundation of Philometoris, Kleopatra and Euergetis was probably, as the *politeumata*, a security-motivated response to the great revolt of the Thebaid and/or to other domestic and foreign political crises that threatened the Ptolemaic kingdom in the first half of the second century: the geographic position of Philometoris and Kleopatra, though not precisely identified, suggests that these cities were intended to be military outposts, and in Euergetis a large part of the population demonstrably seems to have been employed as soldiers.[60]

The *poleis* located in Egypt were certainly of considerable strategic importance, but it is also obvious that because of their small number the role they played in securing or defending the Nile Valley and the significance they might have had for the Ptolemaic regime as reservoirs of Greco-Macedonian manpower should not be overestimated. These considerations point to a fundamental difference between Hellenistic Egypt (without taking into account Ptolemaic possessions outside of Egypt) on the one hand and the Antigonid, Attalid and Seleucid kingdoms on the other hand, where Greek cities played a crucial part in ensuring strategic control over territories. Since the Ptolemies saw no reason to secure their rule over Egypt by systematically (re)founding numerous *poleis* – and, thus, did not remodel the traditional *nome* administration of Egypt – there was only one military concept that was able to prevent them from being forced to entrust almost all internal and external security duties to soldiers of a standing army and spend considerable sums of money for maintaining them: the institutionalization of an army of reservists composed of *cleruchs*. From a pragmatic point of view such a step – once again – seems reasonable given the fact that granting land to *cleruchs* was more cost saving for the Ptolemies than founding *poleis*, which would have caused a loss of taxable land.[61] Furthermore, the settlement of *cleruchs* (in newly founded or

---

[59] For Philometoris and Kleopatra see the inscription OGIS I 111 = Bernand (1989) no. 302 = É. Bernand (1992) no. 14 which comes from the southern border zone of Egypt and is dated to the reign of Ptolemy VI, for Euergetis SB XXIV 15973 (prov. unknown, 132) and 15974 (prov. unknown, 129); see also Thompson (2011a) 103 with n. 8. On Boethus and his city foundations see Kramer (1997); Heinen (1997) and Fischer-Bovet in this volume with bibliography.

[60] See the papyrus SB XXIV 15974.9–10 (prov. unknown, 132) which is related to the foundation of Euergetis: οἷς . . . τῶν ἐν τῆι πόλει ἐν στρατείᾳ φερομένων (see also SB XXIV 15973, 6 the draft of the text, of which SB XXIV 15974.9–10 is the copy); Heinen (1997) 361–2.

[61] See Fischer-Bovet (2014b) 298.

already existing villages or, occasionally, in *nome* capitals)[62] also reduced the costs of the land forces,[63] because there was no need to regularly maintain a large standing army beside the reservists, which was a welcome compensation for the costly Ptolemaic fleet.[64] Finally, *cleruchs* could be used to cultivate land, and this is true for the most important *cleruchic* settlements which were located in the Arsinoite *nome*: probably already during the reign of the first Ptolemaic king, Ptolemy I Soter (305–293), and certainly under his successor Ptolemy II Philadelphus (285–246), this region was drained and resettled, and the *cleruchs* were key figures in this land reclamation.[65]

Another positive side effect of institutionalizing a force of reservist regulars was that the Ptolemies could provide soldiers coming to Egypt to serve them with unique living conditions. In contrast, the military importance of the *cleruchy* in the kingdoms of the Seleucids, Antigonids and Attalids was probably relatively limited, but our sources are scarcer, too. Like the Seleucid army, the forces of the Antigonids and Attalids in peacetime were predominately composed of units of active soldiers stationed in garrisons.[66] Therefore the army organization of these kingdoms – administratively shaped and strategically secured by numerous *poleis* – was not fundamentally based on the vast deployment of reservist regulars. Furthermore, the Seleucid, Antigonid and Attalid *cleruchy* lacked a homogeneous military character. To be sure, there were the *paroikoi*, *cleruchs* who were obliged to serve in the fortress of Rhamnous in northeast Attica on a regular basis; they can be traced back to Macedonian soldiers settled by Antigonus Gonatas and probably remained in service after Athens had been freed from Antigonid domination.[67] However, apart from that, the intention behind the Seleucid, Antigonid and Attalid *cleruchy* seems to have been simply to settle or resettle civilians or former soldiers (whereby the latter group of new settlers, of course, should enhance the military potential of the respective site). Accordingly, it has been argued that outside the Ptolemaic kingdom, owners of *kleroi* cannot be limited to reservists; thus, contrary to the Ptolemaic system, the ownership of a *kleros* does not appear to have implied an obligation to perform

---

[62] On the settlement of the *cleruchs* see Scheuble-Reiter (2012) 27–32; on the residence of the *cleruchs* in the villages see Scheuble-Reiter (2012) 33–8; Fischer-Bovet (2014b) 239–42.
[63] Cf. also Scheuble-Reiter (2012) 40.   [64] See above n. 61.
[65] See Crawford (1971) 55; Mueller (2006a) 149–51; Fischer-Bovet (2014b) 201.
[66] For the character of the Seleucid army see below, n. 68; for the Antigonid army Launey (1949–1950) 56–7 and the hints given by Oetjen (2014) 93 with n. 227; for the Attalid army Daubner (2011) 56 with n. 55.
[67] See Oetjen (2014) 76–92.

military service.⁶⁸ From this perspective, a *cleruchic* system whose only purpose was to provide the basic organizational structure of a force of reservists (and policemen) which, moreover, formed the regular part of the royal army (and security forces), can be regarded as a particularity of Ptolemaic ruling practice. Perhaps, such a peculiarity was intended to create a distinctive feature that clearly set the Ptolemaic regime apart from other Hellenistic kingdoms, and particularly in the third century – when the Ptolemaic kingdom reached the peak of its power – it was arguably aimed at luring recruits from the Greek heartlands to Egypt.⁶⁹

As we have seen, the difference between the administrative organization of Ptolemaic Egypt, based on *nomes*, and the *polis* structures, upon which the Antigonid, Attalid and Seleucid kingdoms were built, seems to have led to (or required) different forms of army organization. Based on a comparison between the Ptolemaic and Seleucid army, it has recently been argued that the different character of their organization affected their capability of stimulating social processes. In this respect, it has been convincingly pointed out that, because of the limited number of *poleis* in Hellenistic Egypt and the strong presence of Greek *cleruchs* in the Egyptian *chora* (where they could, indifferently, live close to each other, or have Egyptian neighbours),⁷⁰ the Ptolemaic army and its organization – especially, due to the tendency towards mixed marriages –⁷¹ turned into an 'engine of interaction'⁷² among various population groups of different origin in the second century. It has been further noted that for several reasons the Seleucid army most probably did not initiate such manifold processes of social interaction: on the one hand, because of 'the limited presence of Greco-Macedonian soldiers outside the structures of the city-states',⁷³ on the other hand, because the regular forces of the Seleucid army were not composed of reservists but of active soldiers who served on military campaigns or garrisoned strategically significant points. Since

---

⁶⁸ For discussion of the *katoikiai* which are, different from older scholarship, not any more regarded as 'military or veteran colonies' and as basis of Seleucid (and Attalid) military policy see Cohen (1991); Aperghis (2004) 194–7; 201; Capdetrey (2007) 158–66; Sekunda (2007) 334–5; Daubner (2011); Fischer-Bovet (2013); (2014a) 82; 297; Oetjen (2014) 82.

⁶⁹ On this recruitment practice see also the preceding section.

⁷⁰ See Clarysse (1998) 1–2; Clarysse and Thompson (2006) 151; Scheuble-Reiter (2012) 27–32; Fischer-Bovet (2014b) 247.

⁷¹ On the mixed marriages within the milieu of the *cleruchs* see Fischer-Bovet (2014b) 247–50; Scheuble-Reiter (2012) 140.

⁷² Fischer-Bovet (2014b) 297.

⁷³ See the preceding note. With regard to Syria, Andrade (2013) 39–48; 66; 105–6 pointed to the closed character of Greek cities and settlements under Seleucid rule.

the Seleucid forces had the same character as the Antigonid and Attalid ones,[74] the social impact of their armies may be regarded as equally limited.

The minor importance that *polis* structures had for the administration of Hellenistic Egypt is not only a decisive feature for understanding the character of the Ptolemaic *cleruchic* system but it can also likely be regarded as a key factor for enabling a smooth implementation of the institution of the *politeuma*. For, as the administration of Egypt was fundamentally built on the traditional *nome* system, the inclusion of administrative units like the *politeumata* into the existing structures generally did not generate tensions which could have occurred with old-established *poleis*. Accordingly, it seemed appropriate to attach *politeumata* to *nome* capitals which, from a Greek perspective, did not hold the legal status of *poleis*. If *politeumata* are also attested in *poleis* which were, like Alexandria, either founded by Alexander the Great or, like Berenice in the Cyrenaica, refounded on Ptolemaic initiative, this may suggest that the Ptolemies did not intend to use the *politeumata* as a means for intervening in old, established *polis* structures.[75]

But was it not somewhat odd to detach the word *politeuma* from its original meaning and use it to designate a hybrid (city-like) form of organization? In the case of the Ptolemaic kingdom such a reinterpretation came as no surprise, because in Egypt a *polis*-related terminology was occasionally adopted in an official context (in papyri and inscriptions) to refer to abstract or social features apart from its original legal meaning: the term *polis* did not need to indicate that the so-called town had a Greek constitution – it was rather a common designation for *nome* capitals and some villages –[76], a *polites* could be a member of an ethnic *politeuma*,[77] and *sympoliteumomenoi* a description for persons belonging to an association or sharing a ceremonial act.[78]

---

[74] See above n. 66 and 68.
[75] See also Kruse (2015) 295–6. Similarly Thompson (1984) 1073–4 with regard to the cities of Cyprus; though for her, consideration of *poleis* was limited insofar as the *politeumata* on Cyprus were designated as *koina*, 'thereby avoiding confusion with the *politeumata* of the more traditional type on the island.' However, because the character of these *koina* is uncertain (see above n. 35), Thompson's view is questionable.
[76] For a definition of the use of the word *polis* in Ptolemaic Egypt see, e.g., Heinen (1997) 352 and Fischer-Bovet in this volume.
[77] P.Polit.Iud.1.18; see Sänger (2016b).
[78] SEG II 871 = SB III 6664 (*sympoliteumomenoi* of the *politeuma* of Beotians); SB V 8066 = Bernand (1999) no. 6, 1–5 (78): *sympoliteumomenoi* of the cult association of the *Apollonia(s)tai* (see Sänger [2015c] 250–1); OGIS I 143 = SEG XIII 554, 4–6 (Salamis, ca. 116); OGIS I 145 = SEG XIII 579, 3–5 (Palaipaphos, 123–118): *sympoliteumomenoi* of ethnic *koina* on Cyprus (on the character of these *koina* see above section 2 with n. 35); SB I 1106, 4–6 with Van 't Dack (1984) (Sebennytus in the Nile Delta; after third cent.): *sympoliteumomenoi* of a *gymnasion*.

These semantic shifts or linguistic hybridizations seem, once again, to be a consequence of the almost entirely lacking *polis* structures in Egypt so that the reinterpretation of Greek legal terms seemed to be less problematic than in regions dominated by old, established *poleis*. The minor role polis structures played for the administrative organization of the Ptolemies' core territory is also indicated by the fact that the government does not seem to have been granted specific privileges to citizens of *poleis*. This stands at least in contrast to the situation observable in Roman Egypt where citizens of *poleis* (as well as some Egyptian priests) were defined as the most privileged population group of non-Roman citizens or *peregrini* because they were (like the Roman citizens) exempted from the Roman poll tax (*laographia*) by the provincial administration.[79] In Ptolemaic Egypt, the group of *polis* citizens was apparently not granted a comparable tax relief, which would have meant exemption from the Ptolemaic salt tax.[80] But even if citizens of *poleis* had been exempted from paying the salt tax, this would not have represented an exclusive privilege, because they would have enjoyed such a tax exemption alongside persons categorised by the Ptolemaic fiscal administration as 'teachers', 'athletic trainers', and 'artists (*technitai*) of Dionysus' (i.e., actors).[81] Thus, the Ptolemaic authorities do not seem to have particularly singled out the status of *polis* citizens among other subjects or to have established them at the top of a social pyramid whose formation would have rested upon the distinction between citizenship and non-citizenship status. Indeed, apart from indicating membership in the citizenry of Alexandria, Naukratis or Ptolemais Hermeiou – which, of course, served as one marker of social and legal affiliation – the inhabitants of Ptolemaic Egypt were, as already indicated, divided into several occupational and ethnic (or pseudo-ethnic) categories: for instance, teachers, farmers, *Hellenes*, Persians and so on, all of which were called *ethne* ('ethnic groups', the plural form of the word *ethnos*).[82] These designations represented official categories that were of legal and fiscal relevance.[83]

The Ptolemaic ruling principles with regard to the institution of the *polis* and its citizens may explain why the Ptolemies could smoothly create and

---

[79] See, e.g., Bowman and Rathbone (1992) 112–4; 116; Heilporn (2009) 77–81.
[80] See Clarysse and Thompson (2006) 44; 88–9.   [81] See Clarysse and Thompson (2006) 125–38.
[82] This word usage appears in tax lists. In Ptolemaic rulings (P.Hamb. II 168.10 [mid third cent.]; BGU XIV 2367.12 [late third cent.]) the occupational category was called *genos*. In this context, *ethnos* and *genos* were probably interchangeable terms for 'occupation'; see Mélèze Modrzejewski (1983) 256, n. 72; Clarysse and Thompson (2006) 146–7, n. 115; Thompson (2001) 305; 308–9.
[83] On this *communis opinio* see, e.g., Mélèze Modrzejewski (1983); Thompson (2001); Clarysse and Thompson (2006) and, focusing on the Jewish population, Mélèze Modrzejewski (1997) 73–83; Honigman (1997) 62–5; 89–90; (2003) 67–96.

use an institution like the *politeuma* in order to reach their ideological, strategic and sociopolitical goals (which were dealt with in the preceding section). Perhaps they also intended to provide an alternative to, though not a substitution for,[84] the *cleruchic* system in the second century and, thus, to also offer to their mercenaries or professional soldiers an opportunity for social organization which set this regime apart from the other Hellenistic realms. However, despite the specific characteristics of the *politeumata* – and after the preceding discussion, this perhaps appears to be paradoxical – they were only partially emblematic of the differences between the ruling practice of the Ptolemies and that of the Antigonids, Attalids and Seleucids because this institution intended to promote urban communities associated with active military service. Thus, the *politeumata* did not follow the lines of the Ptolemaic settlement policy and army organization which were represented by the third-century *cleruchic* system in Egypt. Yet, the *politeumata* were emblematic of the Ptolemaic support to local structures despite the centralist bureaucracy of the regime.[85]

5 Conclusion

The *politeumata* are emblematic of a time when the Ptolemies struggled for internal and external power and promoted ethnic communities connected to the military in order to secure their support. In the wake of the crisis-torn first half of the second century – possibly because of a growing need for security – the establishment of *politeumata* could bind the respective ethnic communities more closely to their places of employment or hometowns. To achieve this, the Ptolemaic regime offered an administrative or public status to ethnic communities within the framework of the institution of the *politeuma* in order to strengthen, at least in Lower and Middle Egypt, the relationship of these groups with their place of residence in Egypt. This shows that the Ptolemies aimed to remain an attractive country of residence, where persons useful to the regime would cluster and be available when needed – probably mainly for military purposes. Furthermore, through the establishment of *politeumata*, the Ptolemies used ethnicity for ideological reasons probably in link with domestic and foreign political developments and strategic considerations. The intention of the Ptolemies was probably to issue a signal about their settlement policy and to continue to attract immigrants from foreign cities or regions. Additionally, by the institution of the *politeuma*, the Ptolemaic regime

---

[84] See above n. 50.   [85] On this polarity of Ptolemaic ruling practice, see Manning (2003b) 235–6.

also strengthened the social networks of the respective members and, in some individual cases, probably also encouraged career advancement.

Thus, the *politeumata* illuminate an aspect of Ptolemaic policy where administrative and social status were negotiated to meet the political and ideological goals of the regime. Administrative and social status as well as ethnic belonging functioned as desirable objectives converging into a specific kind of association that could give its members the impression of forming a small, ethnically based *polis* community. The target group of the Ptolemaic *politeuma* policy were not *cleruchs*. Rather, they were mercenaries or professional soldiers who performed (active) military service in central towns and, if applicable, in local fortresses. This was a considerable departure from the principles of Ptolemaic military policy in the third century, and certainly a response to the strength of the Seleucid empire in the first half of the second century and the internal weakness of the Ptolemaic kingdom.

Finally, this analysis showed that the differences between the character of the Ptolemaic kingdom and that of other Hellenistic kingdoms – with regard to administration, army organization and their impact on social processes – are related to different uses of similar ruling strategies: foundation of *poleis*, application of the *cleruchic* system, deployment of mercenaries or professional soldiers. These elements were adapted to different geographic, economic and structural conditions in the respective regions under control, and (as was possibly the case with the Ptolemies) shaped by competitive thinking. This consideration should also include the institution of the *politeuma*, which seems to witness the efforts taken by the Ptolemies to shed a good light on their administrative, military and social policies. In this sense, the *politeuma* was a complementary measure to the Ptolemaic *cleruchic* system.

PART II

Communication and Exchange

CHAPTER 5

Imperial and Indigenous Temporalities in the Ptolemaic and Seleucid Dynasties
A Comparison of Times

Paul Kosmin and Ian Moyer

Common Introduction

We open our comparison with a simple observation: textbooks for ancient Near Eastern history tend to conclude their narratives with the arrival or death of Alexander the Great, whereas textbooks for ancient Egyptian history typically continue into late antiquity, right up to the death of Theodosius.[1] It is tempting and necessary to challenge such periodizations on each side; indeed, that has been a project of much post–Second World War Hellenistic scholarship. Yet the chronological frames of these textbooks – the reproductive distillations of our respective fields' arguments and reflexes[2] – in fact respond, however indirectly, to a very real distinction in perceived historical continuity between the Seleucid and Ptolemaic empires, their ideological systems, and the indigenous experience of these imperial historicities.

IA   THE SELEUCID HORIZON AND INDIGENOUS ELITES

Paul Kosmin

1   Introduction

To reconstruct something as inwardly apprehended and conceptually nebulous as a temporal experience would require an accumulation of evidence and a mode of analysis far beyond the scope of this

---

[1] Compare, e.g., Marc van der Mieroop, *A History of the Ancient Near East, ca. 3000–323* BC (Oxford, 2007) and Amélie Kuhrt, *The Ancient Near East c. 3000–330* BCE (London, 1997) with Marc van der Mieroop, *A History of Ancient Egypt c. 3400* BC–AD *395* (Oxford, 2011) and Ian Shaw, *The Oxford History of Ancient Egypt c. 7000* BC–AD *395* (Oxford, 2004). Note that both explicitly state the significant continuities after Alexander's conquests.
[2] On the use of textbooks and syllabi for disciplinary modeling, see Smail (2005).

chapter.³ So here I will focus on one particular phenomenon – the extent to which the Seleucid empire was considered by its rulers and subjects to have opened a discrete historical period.

Let me lay out my claim as bluntly as possible: the developed Seleucid empire delimited for itself a closed temporal field, a fairly coherent boundary of relevance and recollection before which it did not reach. This temporal field, generated at court, propagated throughout the empire, and re-enunciated by subject communities, took as the limit point of appropriate historical reference the return of Seleucus I Nicator to Babylon in 312/1 BCE or, as prologue, this founder king's early life. Such a 'Seleucid horizon', as I will term it, generated an enclosed and self-referencing imperial temporality and constructed for itself a recursively linked past and future. I will try to limn this Seleucid horizon in three ways, moving from the most explicit to the least, before exploring its impact on two works of indigenous historiography from Babylonia.

2 A New Beginning

By far the most important formalization of this imperial horizon was the Seleucid Era (SE) dating system. This innovative technology was a transcendent, linear, and irreversible numbering system for dating calendar years, of the kind we use today (2021 CE). Following a certain amount of chronographic experimentation, it was employed by Seleucus I Nicator from his self-coronation in 305 BCE, with its 'epoch', or first year, retrospectively set at autumn 312 BCE, according to the Macedonian calendar, and spring 311 BCE, according to the Babylonian. Seleucid Era years descended serially, paratactically, and without break from this beginning. As no new Seleucid monarch restarted the count, durational time according to the Seleucid Era was simply a number that got bigger and bigger.

This annual dating was deployed systematically across the imperial landscape, as much in personal or local affairs as in the imperially directed procedures of royal communications, coin minting, fiscality, authorized trade, and so forth. Many thousands of Seleucid Era year-dates survive from across the under-explored imperial landscape; presumably, tens or hundreds of thousands remain to be discovered. Tim Edensor has recently explored how media, state institutions, sporting events, and so forth function in our contemporary societies to domesticate, coordinate, and

---

³ This has subsequently been attempted in Kosmin 2018, with which much of this material overlaps.

embed a coherent sense of national standard times.[4] Similarly, I would suggest that such a pervasive display of automated Seleucid Era year numbers, stamped or inscribed on quotidian and public objects, must have carried the count deep into private spaces and personal thoughts, generating an intuitive, 'second-nature' sense of temporal location.

In contrast to both the regnal dating system employed in Ptolemaic Egypt (and most Hellenistic kingdoms), which started again at a Year 1 with every coronation, and the eponymous dating systems of city-states and federations, which were as directionless as a metronome, the Seleucid year count fixed a single, historical 'Big Bang' to which all later years referred. Everything dated in this way – tombstones, seal rings, horoscopes, tetradrachms, letters, and so forth – had an immediately legible temporal depth with reference to this 1 SE, a horizon reaffirmed at every use. BSE, Before the Seleucid Era, was unthinkable in its own terms. While the existence of a prior, pre-Seleucid world was in no way doubted, it could not be as easily grasped by the same temporal understanding, just as if we employed Common Era dating without any Before the Common Era enumeration. So, for the central provinces of the Seleucid empire at the very least, we have a political landscape scattered with tens of thousands of Seleucid Era dates, all of which acted like temporal milestones, counting the durational distance from the singular epoch of imperial time.

If accumulating numbers established a discrete temporal field with unsurpassed clarity, we can also see its more complicated expression in political myth and ruler cult. Already from the early third century BCE, Apollo was being claimed as Seleucus I's biological father.[5] Whatever else was achieved by this conceit, it functioned to uproot Seleucus: whether believed or not, the tale worked to transcend Seleucus's Macedonian background and paternity with the heavenly and universal Apollo. In contrast to the extended genealogies of the Ptolemaic and Antigonid houses, Seleucid kingship descended directly from heaven. Similarly, the official cult of royal ancestors introduced at a state level by Antiochus III and attested in its civic form across the empire did not reach back before Seleucus I.[6] These cults of divine ancestors, into which the reigning monarch was sometimes incorporated, honored an ordered succession of god-kings. A priest-list from Seleucia-in-Pieria, dating to the reign of Seleucus IV, names a certain [- -]ogenes, son of Artemon, as priest of 'Seleucus (I) Zeus Nicator and Antiochus (I) Apollo

---

[4] Edensor (2006). [5] See *IErythrai* 205 ll.74–6, with Kosmin (2014b) 178–80.
[6] *Contra* Rostovtzeff (1935) 62–5.

Soter and Antiochus (II) Theos and Seleucus (II) Callinicus and Seleucus (III) Soter and Antiochus (the Son) and Antiochus (III) Megas'. A famous civic decree from Antioch-in-Persis, by the Persian Gulf, gives an eponymous dating by Heraclitus, son of Zoes, priest of Seleucus (I) Nicator, Antiochus (I) Soter, Antiochus (II) Theos, Seleucus (II) Callinicus, Seleucus (III), the reigning Antiochus (III) and his son Antiochus.[7] These cults, which incorporated local elites as their agents, established a unified king-list of cult recipients. These functioned as timelines, opening with Seleucus I, and omitting all predecessors, pretenders, or regents. They offered a kind of authorized historical review in religious mode that reasserted the imperial time horizon.

This exclusively intra-dynastic focus can also be seen in the historiographic output of the Seleucid court. The evidence is undeniably scanty, but no Seleucid court histories of either Alexander the Great or Asia's pre-Hellenistic past are known – an obvious contrast with the Ptolemaic house.[8] Instead, from when they first begin to appear in the latter half of the third century BCE, Seleucid court historians appear to have fixed their gaze resolutely within the Seleucid horizon, narrating the origins of the dynasty, the heroism of its earlier kings, and, thereby, the precedents for current restoration. So, in the court of Antiochus III, Simonides of Magnesia-by-Sipylus composed an epic poem about Antiochus I's victory over the Galatians, perhaps in the famed Elephant Battle described in Lucian's *Zeuxis*.[9] Hegesianax of Alexandria Troas, also a trusted *philos* and ambassador to the Romans,[10] wrote of the crossing of the Galatians from Europe in the aftermath of Seleucus I's death.[11] This Galatian invasion was narrated in thirteen books by Demetrius of Byzantium, who went on to compose, perhaps in continuation, a history *On Antiochus and Ptolemy and Their Settlement of Libya*, presumably dealing with the First Syrian War;[12] while we know nothing more of Demetrius, his historical focus suggests a Seleucid affiliation.[13] Mnesiptolemus, another historian associated with Antiochus III,[14] incorporated into his *Histories* a personal autopsy of king

---

[7] OGIS 245.
[8] The Alexander historian Aristos of Salamis (BNJ 143) is likely a late Hellenistic writer, not the lover of Antiochus II (Ath. 10.438d), *contra* Meißner (1992) 465.
[9] BNJ 163 T1 = Suda *s.v.* Σιμωνίδης· Μάγνης <ἀπὸ> Σιπύλου; with Primo (2009) 87–8.
[10] BNJ 45 T3 = Ath. 4.155a–b; T4a = Polyb.18.47.14; T4b = Polyb. 18.49.2–18.50.3; T5 = Liv. 34.57.1–6; see Olshausen (1974) 191–2.
[11] BNJ 45 F3 = Strabo 13.1.27, possibly in the context of Hegesianax' *Troica*.
[12] BNJ 162 T1 = Diog. Laert. 5.83.   [13] Primo (2009) 104–5.
[14] BNJ 164 T1 = Ath. 15.53.697d: Μνησιπτολέμου ... ποτε τοῦ ἱστοριογράφου τοῦ παρὰ Ἀντιόχῳ τῷ προσαγορευθέντι Μεγάλῳ πλεῖστον ἰσχύσαντος υἱὸν γενέσθαι Σέλευκον.

Seleucus II's or III's drinking habits, indicating an earlier presence at court.[15] A certain Protagorides of Cyzicus described the extravagant down-river voyage of a king Antiochus, probably Antiochus IV Epiphanes during the Sixth Syrian War, and the great festivities at Daphne near Antioch.[16] An otherwise unknown Timochares treated, in his *On Antiochus*, the defensive topography of Jerusalem. Together with the work's title, his exaggerations of the city's size (40 *stades* in circumference) and natural situation – 'it is difficult to conquer [δυσάλωτον], since it is surrounded on all sides by precipitous ravines [πάντοθεν ἀπορρῶξι περικλειομένην φάραγξι]' – indicate an encomiastic biography of either Antiochus IV, who plundered the Judean capital, or, more likely, Antiochus VII, who besieged it.[17] Additionally, the surviving fragments of official city-foundation narratives, centered entirely on the potent image of the *roi bâtisseur*, seem to have omitted all pre-Seleucid precedent.[18]

This intra-dynastic focus was shared by the monarchs themselves, whose own language of precedent was almost exclusively restricted to the ruling dynasty. Of the many examples of such 'auto-historiography,' that is, of the king and his court engaged in a contemplation of their dynastic past, here are two representative examples from the fairly thickly attested interactions with the empire's Jews. In a famous letter preserved by Josephus, Antiochus III proclaimed his wish to transfer two thousand Babylonian and Mesopotamian Jewish families to the troubled regions of Lydia and Phrygia. For, Antiochus writes, 'I am persuaded [πέπεισμαι]' that the Jews would make loyal guardians of Seleucid interests because 'I know that they have had the testimony of my ancestors to their trustworthiness and eagerness to do as they are asked [μαρτυρουμένους δ' αὐτοὺς ὑπὸ τῶν προγόνων εἰς πίστιν οἶδα καὶ προθυμίαν εἰς ἃ παρακαλοῦνται].'[19] Almost a century later, when Jewish piety had turned against the empire, dynastic history was again invoked: Diodorus Siculus, ultimately drawing on a Seleucid historian, reports that the friends of Antiochus VII Sidetes, who was conducting a siege of Jerusalem in 134 BCE, 'reminded him of the hatred felt by his ancestors toward this people [ὑπέμνησαν δὲ αὐτὸν καὶ περὶ τοῦ προγενομένου μίσους τοῖς προγόνοις πρὸς τοῦτο τὸ ἔθνος]' and

---

[15] BNJ 164 F1 = Ath. 10.42.432b–c, with the commentary of Michel Cottier, *contra* Primo (2009) 90. A Delian proxeny decree (BNJ 164 T3 = *IG* XI.4 697) for 'the historian Mnesiptolemus' may indicate political importance at the Seleucid court.
[16] BNJ 853 F3 = Ath. 3.98.124d–f, with Primo (2009) 106.
[17] BNJ 165 F1 = Euseb. *Chron.* 9.35 p. 452; see Bar-Kochva (2010) 458–68.
[18] See Kosmin (2014a) 211–8; and von Reden and Strootman in this volume.
[19] Joseph. *AJ* 12.150; the authenticity of this letter has been much discussed: see, e.g., Cohen (1995) 212–3 and Marcus (1943) 473–81, 494–6.

'related in detail [διεξιόντες]' Antiochus IV's persecution in order to encourage its repetition.[20] The historical lessons contradict, but the temporal domain of historical learning is identical.

This has been a brief survey; presumably, the break from the past was also visible in less obviously delineated phenomena, such as the use of Greek in administration or the extensive program of Seleucid colonization. Taken together, I would suggest that the Seleucid horizon, this sense of discontinuity from the pre-Seleucid past, was both easily felt and deliberately evoked. Theirs was a period grounded only in itself, a dynastic here-and-now, walled off from past regimes, and absorbed in its own reflection. As we shall see, the Ptolemies' sense of their own dynastic time presents a strong contrast in its dialog with past pharaonic temporalities.

3 Distance and Totality

The second half of this chapter will suggest that the Seleucid horizon created the conditions for new attitudes to the pre-conquest world. For the historiographical writings produced by the Seleucids' indigenous subjects show two interrelated characteristics: first, a historical dissociation – that is, the sense of the pre-Hellenistic past as having been superseded and the present as owing little to it; and second, the totalization and objectification of this lost world – that is, the sense that this closed past has a graspable unity and completeness of its own, distinct from the series of events that constituted it. Two works from Hellenistic Babylonia – the *Babyloniaca* of Berossus and the *Uruk List of Kings and Sages* – make good case studies of this new historical positioning. In their structure, content, and authorial persona they thematize the closural effects of Seleucid time.

The *Babyloniaca* was a three-book account of Babylonian culture and civilization, written in Greek in the third century BCE by the Babylonian priest Berossus/Bēl-reʾušunu ('The Lord is their shepherd'). While the *Babyloniaca* has not itself survived, its context and texture are fairly reliably known from a first-century BCE epitome by Alexander Polyhistor that was extensively cited by Josephus, Abydenus, Eusebius, and Syncellus.

Berossus opened his *Babyloniaca* by establishing his own temporal location. His proemial comments, at the beginning of book one, indicated, first, that he was in some sense contemporary with the coming of Alexander the Great – the Greek κατ' Ἀλέξανδρον γεγονώς can indicate either his birth or his adulthood at the Conquest – and, second, that he dedicated his

[20] Diod. 34–35.1.3–4.

three-book history to a king Antiochus.[21] This Antiochus is identified either as the third ruler after Alexander the Great,[22] in which case, with some wriggling, Antiochus I Soter, or as the third ruler after Seleucus I Nicator,[23] in which case, with equal wriggling, Antiochus II Theos. While most scholars have preferred the earlier king, it is at least suggestive that, during the reign of Antiochus II, the šatammu, or high-priest, of Babylon's Esagil temple, and so the most senior indigenous official in the city, was a certain Bēl-re'ušunu.[24] In either scenario, Berossus's introductory comments chose to closely situate his biography and literary product within the Macedonian conquest and the subsequent Seleucid regime: he is of the new world.

Given his explicit self-positioning with reference to the Greco-Macedonian imperial environment, it is all the more significant that Berossus's history ran, as a continuous and unbroken narrative, from the beginnings of organized life up to the conquests of Alexander the Great;[25] and then it stopped. Depending on the date of dedication (Soter or Theos), this left a textual no-man's-land between the closing-point of Berossus's history and the Seleucid context of its composition of between five and nine decades – approximately the duration of the entire Neo-Babylonian dynasty. As far as we can tell, Berossus's contemporary world had no place within his history. His textual content came to a close at the Seleucid horizon and reproduced its logics. It is noteworthy that a text of close comparison and possible influence, the *Indica* of Megasthenes, a Seleucid-affiliated early third-century BCE three-book ethnographic history of Gangetic India, ran from the primordial cultural heroism of the god Dionysus up to and including the contemporary Mauryan state, beyond the boundaries of the Seleucid empire, to which Megasthenes had been dispatched as Seleucus I's envoy: whereas Chandragupta Maurya's peer kingdom is the

---

[21] BNJ 680 T1 = Eusebius (Armenius), *Chron.* p. 6, 14 (Karst), T2 = Tatian, *Oratio ad Graecos* 36.
[22] BNJ 680 T2 = Tatian, *Oratio ad Graecos* 36.
[23] Variant reading: τῷ μετὰ Σέλευκον τρίτῳ (Eusebius).
[24] Attested on cuneiform administrative documents from 258 to 253 BCE; see van der Spek (2000) 439. The Antiochus II date has recently been supported by Bach (2013) 157–62.
[25] Abydenus BNJ 685 F7 = Euseb. *Chron.* (Arm.), p. 25, 26–26 K: 'Thus do the Chaldeans regard the kings of their land, from Alorus up to Alexander; they do not themselves pay any attention to Ninus or Semiramis.' Further, according to Abydenus BNJ 685 F1a = Eusebius (Arm.), *Chronographia* p. 19, 18–25 K and F1b = Euseb. *Praep. Evang.* 9.41.6, reproducing Berossus's account, the wall of Babylon, first constructed by Bel, 'lasted up to the rule of the Macedonians [τὸ μέχρι τῆς Μακεδονίων ἀρχῆς διαμεῖναν];' Burstein (1978) 17 n. 23 places this statement in the *Babyloniaca*'s first book. Diod. 2.31.9, with Boncquet (1987) 191–2, on Chaldean astronomical record-keeping 'from earliest times until the crossing of Alexander to Asia'; see below.

culmination of the logics of Indian history,[26] Antiochus's imperial formation stands beyond Babylon's.

The overriding impression given by Berossus the author and his text the *Babyloniaca* is of externality: the Seleucid present is an observation point for gazing back upon and evaluating all the formations that have preceded it. Even the autoethnography of Babylonia's landscape at the opening of book one – a description of the region's productive and infertile soils, its grains, fruits, and roots, together with glosses for Greek readers – displays a remarkable capacity for distance and disembeddedness; its self-description is entirely without parallel in any cuneiform text.[27] More fundamentally, Berossus's project constituted an unprecedented unification into a single, coherent, linked-up narrative account of Mesopotamian myths, dynastic histories, local cultural practices, and other elements of scribal science and local lore. This emptying of the cuneiform drawers, their ordering by chronology, and the translation of their contents comes close to a universal library or total history of pre-Seleucid Babylonia: 'the totality of the past ... meant something in and of itself, distinct from the series of discrete events that constituted the histor[y].'[28] The *Babyloniaca* achieved this unity and completeness of its history in two ways: first, it emphasized the sealed totality of knowledge; second, it established a single, coherent timeline.

In his first book, Berossus reported that a certain Oannes, the earliest of Babylonia's culture-heroes (Akkadian *apkallū*), squelched out of the Persian Gulf to educate humanity in all that constituted an ordered existence:

> In Babylon there was a great crowd of men, who had settled in Chaldea. They lived without order like wild animals [ζῆν δὲ αὐτοὺς ἀτάκτως ὥσπερ τὰ θηρία]. In the first year [ἐν δὲ τῷ πρώτῳ ἐνιαυτῷ] there appeared out of the Erythraean Sea, at the place bordering Babylonia [κατὰ τὸν ὁμοροῦντα τόπον τῇ Βαβυλωνίᾳ], a sentient creature by the name Oannes ... having a body entirely like a fish, but underneath his head another head which had grown under the head of the fish, and feet similarly of a man which had grown out from the tail of the fish; it possessed a human voice, and the image of him is preserved even now [τὴν δὲ εἰκόνα αὐτοῦ ἔτι καὶ νῦν διαφυλάσσεσθαι]. [Berossus] says that this creature passed the days with the humans, not taking any food, but giving to the humans knowledge of

---

[26] See Kosmin (2014a) 37–53.
[27] On the implication of an uninformed, external audience in Greek local historiography, reframing the esoteric as exoteric, see Tober (2017).
[28] Dillery (2015) 352.

writing and learning and crafts of all sorts; and he was teaching also the founding of cities, the building of temples, the introduction of laws and geometry; he was revealing planting and the harvesting of crops, and in sum all the matters that pertain to the amelioration of life he was handing over to men [παραδιδόναι τοῖς ἀνθρώποις]. From that time, nothing more in addition has been discovered [ἀπὸ δὲ τοῦ χρόνου ἐκείνου οὐδὲν ἄλλο περισσὸν εὑρεθῆναι].[29]

Berossus goes on to describe how Oannes, after civilizing humanity, then composed and handed over a written account of creation.

And Oannes wrote about origins and government [τὸν δὲ Ὠάννην περὶ γενεᾶς καὶ πολιτείας γράψαι] and handed over this account to mankind [καὶ παραδοῦναι τόνδε τὸν λόγον τοῖς ἀνθρώποις]. 'There was a time,' he says, 'when all was darkness and water [γενέσθαι φησὶ χρόνον, ἐν ᾧ τὸ πᾶν σκότος καὶ ὕδωρ εἶναι].'[30]

Berossus then reproduces, in the embedded voice of Oannes, a subtly reworked version of the *Enūma eliš*, the great myth of Marduk's victory over the chaotic Tiamat and the cosmogonic shaping of the world from her carcass.

This inaugural moment of Babylonian civilization was also its completion – since Oannes, humanity has discovered nothing. To Berossus's evident argument for Babylonian cultural primacy, presumably directed as much toward other Near Eastern populations as to the youthful Greeks and Macedonians, he has added the claim of a singular, momentous, and unchanging cultural package. As expressed by Stanley Burstein, 'the beginning of history was also its end since everything thereafter could only be, and quite explicitly was, preservation, exegesis and application of that initial revelation to life.'[31] While a sense of antediluvian 'classic' texts certainly existed earlier than the Seleucids, such an all-embracing model of civilizational, textual origins and subsequent historical stasis is not found outside Berossus.

This textual totality appears once more in Berossus's retelling of the deluge myth in book two. The god Cronus, visiting the flood hero Xisouthros in a dream to warn of the impending cataclysm, charged him to bury 'the beginnings, middles, and endings of all writings' (γραμμάτων πάντων ἀρχὰς καὶ μέσα καὶ τελευτὰς) in the city of Sippar and then to construct his ark. After the deluge, when the flood waters had withdrawn

---

[29] BNJ 680 F1b = Syncellus, *Chron.* 3–4, translation after Dillery (2015) 74. F1a = Eusebius (Armenius), *Chronographia* 16–26 A.
[30] BNJ 680 F1b = Syncellus, *Chron.*, 5–6.   [31] Burstein (1978) 7.

and the survivors dared to disembark their ark, now stranded in the Armenian mountains, a voice from heaven instructed them to return to Babylon, to excavate the writings deposited at Sippar, and to pass them on to mankind (εἶπέ τε αὐτοῖς, ὅτι ἐλεύσονται πάλιν εἰς Βαβυλῶνα, καί ὡς εἴμαρται αὐτοῖς, ἐκ Σι[σ]πάρων ἀνελομένοις τὰ γράμματα διαδοῦναι τοῖς ἀνθρώποις).[32] That Sippar, city of the sun-god Šamaš, escaped the cataclysm is already found in the early first-millennium *Erra Epic*;[33] but the preservation there of all writings is otherwise unattested.[34] The *Babyloniaca*, therefore, transforms the ancient flood myth into an iteration of the original, total revelation, a now human-directed repetition of Oannes's wisdom from the waters.[35]

It is tempting to detect in these two episodes an internal model for Berossus's own project: that what the merman-sage had imparted to the first of men and the flood survivors to the postdiluvian world, Berossus is now directing to the Macedonian king.[36] If so, this third revelation projects a periodizing distinction, a closure and a new beginning, quite as profound as the flood and requiring a similar operation of cultural salvage. Indeed, Johannes Haubold has brilliantly suggested that Berossus's phrase for the completeness of the rescued knowledge – 'the beginnings, middles, and endings of all writings' – precisely maps the tripartite division and totalizing embrace of his own *Babyloniaca*: from cosmogony and civilizational foundations in book one, through a postdiluvian line of kings in book two, to the succession of territorial empires up to Alexander in book three; needless to say, 'endings' (τελευτάς) implies completion, the closure of the textual archive.[37]

Secondly, the *Babyloniaca* established a single, foundational timeline in which myths were embedded, empires sequenced, and events related to one another. Babylonia's historical beginning is established in book one, at the opening of the civilizational narrative. As we have seen, in the passage cited above, Berossus started his historical account with, not the creation of the world, but the appearance and cultural heroism of the fish-man Oannes. The *Babyloniaca*'s account of the world's genesis is

---

[32] BNJ 680 F4a = Eusebius (Arm.), *Chronographia* 10.17–12.16 Karst, F4b = Syncellus p. 53, 19.
[33] *Erra Epic* 4.50: 'As for Sippar, the primeval city, through which the Lord of the countries did not let the deluge pass because she was the darling of his eyes' (šá^{uru}si-par uru ṣa-a-ti šá^{d}en kur.kur ina a-qar pa-ni-šu abu-bu la uš-bi-'u-šu).
[34] Berossus may be punning on the city's meaning in Aramaic, where the verbal root *spr* is used for writing and scribal recording of all kinds; see Knobloch (1985).
[35] Dillery (2015) 256; Lang (2013) 54; Haubold (2013a) 156–60.
[36] See Dillery (2015) 70; Lang (2013) 54; Kosmin (2013) 210–11.
[37] Haubold (2013a) 160. The 'closed archive' formulation is from Haubold (2013a) 156.

only then delivered to the now civilized and literate humans by Oannes as an embedded, retrospective, written text. This exegetical orientation to earliest history, that is, the scribal quotation of an already existing textual canon, is crucial to the chronological shaping and historical positioning of Berossus's entire work; it is as distinctive as Hellenistic rewritings of the Hebrew Bible that open, not with the Genesis account, but with the giving of the Torah at Sinai and Moses's retrospective reading of the written record of creation.[38] Berossus dates this Oannes episode – cultural-heroism and recital of creation – 'in the first year' (ἐν δὲ τῷ πρώτῳ ἐνιαυτῷ). Except for its geographic-ethnographic elements, the narrative of book one is entirely devoted to this Babylonian year.[39] Such a numericalized opening of time has no precedent or background in the extant cuneiform record;[40] as far as we can tell, no first year or month or day had ever been marked or discussed. Rather, we can discern behind Berossus's dated beginning an echo of the Seleucid Era epoch. Berossus's Year 1 is both subsequent to the uncountable *illud tempus* of the created but unordered world[41] and immediately anterior to the creation of kingship. As John Dillery has emphasized, Oannes's appearance is not assigned to the regnal date 'Year 1 of king Alorus,' the first antediluvian ruler in Berossus's king-list: ordered government had not yet been revealed, so there was no throne for Alorus to ascend.[42] Instead, it is a freestanding, absolute time-marker, a directional origin for all subsequent narrative, establishing the foundational point of a linear, forward-moving temporality. It is, in essence, the epoch of Babylonian history. In these respects, it corresponds to 1 SE (312/1 BCE), which both acknowledged a preexisting world and was distinct from Seleucus I's subsequent self-coronation in 305/4 BCE.

Berossus's account descends vertically in a continuous line from the transcendent Year 1 of Babylonian civilization to the Macedonian

---

[38] *Jubilees* 1–2, where Moses, on the peak of Mt. Sinai to receive the tablets, copies down the direct speech of the angel of the presence, as recited from celestial documents.

[39] Dillery (2015) 72: 'In terms of his own scale, then, Berossus spent about as much time on the first year or so of human history as he spent on the next 432,000 years.'

[40] See the discussion in Dillery (2015) 77–8. Note that a Late Babylonian text, BM 74329, the so-called Theogony of Dunnu, uniquely provides day and month dates for each stage of its divine succession myth (e.g., Obv. 20: *i-na* ⁱᵗⁱ*kislimi* (gan.gan.è) ud.16.kám en-*ta ù* lugal-*ta il-qú-*[*ú*], 'In the month Chislev, on the 16th day, he took the overlordship for himself'); Lambert and Walcot (1965) propose that the reference is cultic not historical, i.e., that the dates refer to events in the city of Dunnu's festive calendar.

[41] On *illud tempus*, see Eliade (1969) *passim*.

[42] Dillery (2015) 75–7, *contra* Burstein (1978) 13 n. 6.

conquest. His second book generates a chronographic backbone from king Alorus to king Nabonassar, counting years either by the regnal lengths of successive kings or by coherent, often dynastic, and somewhat era-like groupings. So, Berossus calculated the total chronological periods of the ten antediluvian monarchs, from Alorus to Xisouthros, as 432,000 years; then, after the flood, the next eighty-three kings from Xisouthros to the Gutians ('Medes'), eight Gutian rulers, forty-nine Chaldean kings, nine Arabian kings, and forty-five Assyrian kings, totaling something more than 34,592 years (only some numbers are extant and none can be trusted).[43] The third book continues the count, from the Neo-Assyrian Sennacherib and through the Neo-Babylonian and Achaemenid dynasties, again as individual monarchic reigns or grouped into periods.[44]

All historical episodes or *logoi* are subordinated to the directional time frame in which they are anchored; the *Babyloniaca* takes its structure and meaning not from a Herodotus-like accumulation and juxtaposition of episodic narratives but from this underlying, unbroken, and now complete temporal axis.[45] This chronologizing, this repeated totting up of dates for Babylonia's deep history, was recognized by Berossus's readers as a distinctive characteristic of his work: for Josephus, Berossus 'catalogs the descendants of Noah (i.e., Xisouthros) and appends their dates' (τοὺς ἀπὸ Νώχου καταλέγων καὶ τοὺς χρόνους αὐτοῖς προστιθείς);[46] for Eusebius, 'in [his books] he narrates the counting of the eras.'[47] Accordingly, Berossus provided for Babylonia an uncomplicated, linear chronology from Oannes's original revelation to the coming of Alexander. Indeed, the 'total duration' of Babylonian clay records, as given in several classical sources, likely derives from this Berossean sum. According to Diodorus Siculus, for example, '[the Chaldeans] count up [καταριθμοῦσιν] that it has been 473,000 years from when they began to make their observations of the stars in early times [ἀφ' ὅτου τὸ παλαιὸν ἤρξαντο τῶν ἄστρων τὰς παρατηρήσεις ποιεῖσθαι] until Alexander's crossing over into Asia [εἰς τὴν Ἀλεξάνδρου διάβασιν].'[48]

---

[43] On the chronological problems of reconciling the surviving fragments with cuneiform data, see Burstein (1978) 33–5.
[44] Both forms are attested: BNJ 680 F7c, F9a, F10.
[45] On Herodotus' temporal space taking its shape from the flow of *logoi*, see, e.g., Schiffman (2011) 38–47.
[46] BNJ 680 T3 = Joseph. *Ap.* 1.131. [47] BNJ 680 F1a.
[48] Diod. 2.31.9. Alternative totals, from highest to lowest: BNJ 680 F16b = Plin. *HN* 7.193 (490,000 years); Julius Africanus F15 (ed. Walraff) (480,000 years); Cic. *Div.* 1.36, 2.97 (470,000 years) Chaeremon BNJ 618 F7 = Michael Psellos, Πρὸς τοὺς ἐρωτήσαντας πόσα τῶν φιλοσοφουμένων λόγων 443–4 (more than 400,000 years). Berossus is accepted as the common source for these

Pre-Hellenistic Babylon appears as an objectified, closed, and numericalized unit.[49]

There is, of course, much more to say on this extraordinary text. But to sum up: Berossus's *Babyloniaca* is a repeated drama of textual loss, historical closure, and scribal responsibility, of which it must be the culmination and end. At each stage, a temporal rupture has prompted the sealing and historiographical packaging of distinct *spatia historica*: fish-man Oannes for prehistoric, timeless creation; the flood survivors for antediluvian wisdom; Berossus for the postdiluvian kings and, indeed, for all that preceded. Each re-presentation of the Babylonian world involved a distancing from it. Berossus's external positioning extends even to the *Babyloniaca*'s form. The history was not inscribed in Akkadian on clay tablets – the medium of his source texts that, as Berossus himself was aware, could survive cataclysm, biblioclasm, and the passing of millennia.[50] Instead, the *Babyloniaca* was composed on papyrus or parchment and in Greek – the prestige and power language of rulers who arrived on stage only after the curtain had come down. As Svetlana Boym has observed, some things can only be written in a foreign language: 'they are not lost in translation, but conceived through it.'[51]

We find this powerful sense of a deep historical continuity and its Seleucid supersession even in Akkadian cuneiform. Our second case study, the so-called 'Uruk List of Kings and Sages,' presents another perspective on such dissociation.[52] The tablet in question was inscribed by the lamentation-priest, Anu-bēlšunu ('Anu is their Lord'), in 165 BCE, during the reign of

---

figures. Diodorus's textual frames – the origins of astronomy and Alexander's conquest – are precisely the boundaries of Berossus's history, from Oannes's cultural teachings to the fall of the Achaemenids; see Eck (2003) 161; and Boncquet (1987) 191–2. On Cicero, see Wardle (2006) 202; and van der Horst (2002) 164–5. Note that Julius Africanus seems to have known Berossus in some form (F34 τοῦ δὴ Ναβουχοδονόσορ μνημονεύει Βηρωσσὸς ὁ Βαβυλώνιος).

[49] For comparison, note that, according to Hecataeus of Abdera, the Egyptian priests computed 23,000 years from the reign of Helios to Alexander's crossing (BNJ 264 F25 = Diod. 1.21.6 οἱ δ' ἱερεῖς τῶν Αἰγυπτίων τὸν χρόνον ἀπὸ τῆς Ἡλίου βασιλείας συλλογιζόμενοι μέχρι τῆς Ἀλεξάνδρου διαβάσεως εἰς τὴν Ἀσίαν φασὶν ὑπάρχειν ἐτῶν μάλιστά πως δισμυρίων καὶ τρισχιλίων), and the third-century Samian historian Duris counted one thousand years from the capture of Troy to Alexander's invasion of Asia (BNJ 76 F41a = Clement, *Stromateis* 1.21.139.4 ἀπὸ Τροίας ἁλώσεως ἐπὶ τὴν Ἀλεξάνδρου εἰς Ἀσίαν διάβασιν ἔτη χίλια); Burkert (1995) 143 detects here chiliastic speculation.

[50] Note that Burstein (1978) 13 n. 3 considers Chaeremon's observation (BNJ 618 F7 = Michael Psellos, Πρὸς τοὺς ἐρωτήσαντας πόσα τῶν φιλοσοφουμένων λόγων 443–4), that astronomical wisdom 'was inscribed on baked tablets so that neither would fire take them away nor overflowing water ruin them' (ἐν ὀπταῖς πλίνθοις ταῦτα ἐγγράψασθαι, ἵνα μήτε πῦρ αὐτῶν ἅπτοιτο μήτε ὕδωρ ἐπικλύσαν λυμαίνοι), to derive from Berossus.

[51] Boym (2001) 307.

[52] *Ed. pr.* van Dijk (1962) 44–52, with suggested emendations in van Dijk (1963) 217; Klotchkoff (1982); and Lenzi (2008).

Antiochus IV. It was excavated from the Bīt Rēš, the vast Hellenistic sanctuary complex of Anu, god of the sky, in the southern Babylonian city of Uruk.⁵³ The tablet must be reproduced in full, as part of its force is visual:

OBV. 1: [In the ti]me of king Ayalu, U'an was sage (*apkallu*).
[In the ti]me of king Alalgar, U'anduga was sage.
[In the time of] king Ameluana, Enmeduga was sage.
[In the time of] king Amegalana, Enmegala was sage.
[In the time of] king Enmeušumgalana, Enmebuluga was sage.
[In the time of] king Dumuzi, the shepherd, Anenlilda was sage.
[In the time of] king Enmeduranki, Utu'abzu was sage.

8 [After the flood,] in the time of king Enmerkar, Nungalpirigal was sage, [whom Ištar] brought down from heaven to Eana. [He made] the bronze lyre, [whose . . .] (were) lapis lazuli, according to the technique of Ninagal. The lyre was placed before Anu [. . .,] the dwelling of (his) personal god.

12 [In the time of king Gilgam]esh, Sîn-lēqi-unninni was scholar (*ummânu*).
[In the time of king Ibb]i-Sîn, Kabti-ili-Marduk was scholar.
[In the time of king Išbi]-Erra, Sidu, also known as Enlil-ibni, was scholar.
[In the time of king Abi-e]šuḫ, Gimil-Gula and Taqīš-Gula were scholars.
[In the time of king . . .,] Esagil-kīn-apli was scholar.

REV. 1 [In the time of] king Adad-apla-iddina, Esagil-kīn-ubba was scholar.
[In the time of] king Nebuchadnezzar, Esagil-kīn-ubba was scholar.
[In the time of] king Esarhaddon, Aba-Enlil-dari was scholar, whom the Arameans call Aḥiqar.

5 [. . .]Nikarchos.

6 Tablet of Anu-bēlšunu, son of Nidintu-Anu, descendant of Sîn-lēqi-unninni, the lamentation-priest of Anu and Antu, an Urukean. By his own hand.
Uruk, 10th Iyyar, 147 (SE), king Antiochus. The one who reveres Anu will not carry it off.

The tablet comprises a historical review, organized into three sections. The first part, lines 1 to 7 of its obverse side, lists in chronological order the names of seven antediluvian kings, each paired with a fishman sage (*apkallu*). As has long been recognized, this accords with Berossus' presentation of primordial history in the first book of his *Babyloniaca* – the tablet's first yoke-team of king Ayalu and *apkallu* U'anu is identical to king Alarus and fishman Oannes.⁵⁴ A double line, incised across the full

---

⁵³ On Hellenistic Uruk and its Bīt Rēš, see, e.g., Baker (2014); and (2013) 56–61; and Röllig (1991).
⁵⁴ See, e.g., Dillery (2015) 66–72; Ristvet (2015) 192; Tuplin (2013) 183; see also Reiner (1961) 9–10.

breadth of the tablet's obverse, represents the great deluge. The second section, from line 8 of the obverse side to line 4 of the reverse side, continues its double-list of kings and scholar-advisers, from Enmerkar (Berossus's Evexios)⁵⁵ until the Neo-Assyrian king Esarhaddon.⁵⁶ As we shall see, line 5 of the reverse side concludes the historical review in the third century BCE by breaking its pattern. Finally, following another incised line, the colophon provides Anu-bēlšunu's name, genealogy, and place and date of inscription.

The double-list incorporates a chronologically ordered selection of southern Babylonian rulers, spaced at intervals of several centuries – Enmerkar and Gilgamesh, the legendary, third-millennium BCE hero-kings of first-dynasty Uruk;⁵⁷ Ibbi-Sîn and Išbi-Erra, respectively the last ruler of the Ur-III empire and founder of the Isin dynasty, in the early second millennium BCE; Abi-ešuḫ of the first dynasty of Babylon in the seventeenth century BCE; Adad-apla-iddina and Nebuchadnezzar I, both of the late second-millennium BCE fourth dynasty of Babylon; and Esarhaddon, the seventh-century BCE successor of Sennacherib.⁵⁸ The sages and scholars, *apkallū* and *ummânū*, are known from first-millennium BCE library catalogs, tablet colophons, and various kinds of scribal listings as authors of epics, incantation series, medical works, and so forth.⁵⁹ This tablet, synchronizing each celebrated ruler with his learned adviser, constructs an idealized image of a stable, millennia-long union of Mesopotamian political leadership and indigenous intellectual authority. It is a model that emerges at the first origins of civilization and continues after the flood, through military conquests, and over dynastic transitions.

This double review, unprecedented in its historical systematization and implicit claims, bears the imprint of the Seleucid temporal regime. Anu-bēlšunu's repetitive catalog patterns a millennia-long paradigm of Babylonian history in order to demonstrate, in the final line, its Hellenistic undoing. The tablet, advancing several centuries from Esarhaddon, names as the tenth postdiluvian entry (reverse line 5)

---

⁵⁵ BNJ 680 F5a = Euseb. (Arm.), *Chron*. p. 12, 13–17, 18.
⁵⁶ Note that the exceptionally long entry for Enmerkar and his *apkallu* (not *ummânu*) Nungalpirigal seems to provide an aetiological myth for certain cult objects at Uruk; see Lenzi (2008) 161. There are slight traces of a ruled line beneath this entry.
⁵⁷ On the mythological foundations of this dynasty, see, e.g., Woods (2012).
⁵⁸ Note that Uruk had been well treated by the Neo-Assyrian kings, who sponsored its Ishtar cult and renovated the Eanna temple; see, e.g., Krul (2014) 16; and Clancier and Monerie (2014) 208, n. 105.
⁵⁹ See, e.g., Lambert (1962).

a certain Nikarchos (¹*ni-q(a)-qu-ru-sú!-ú*).⁶⁰ It is all but certain that this Nikarchos was a late contemporary of Berossus and the mid-third-century BCE *šaknu*, or governor, of Uruk, called at birth Anu-uballiṭ.⁶¹ From Anu-uballiṭ's foundation inscription at the Bīt Rēš, Uruk's main sanctuary, which he reconstructed and rededicated in Nisannu 68 SE (244 BCE), we learn that he had been awarded a Greek name by the Seleucid king, possibly Antiochus I, probably Antiochus II: the temple's dedicatory cylinder gives his full title as 'Anu-uballiṭ, son of Anu-iqṣur, descendant of Aḫ'utu, *šaknu* of Uruk, whom Antiochus, king of lands, assigned as his other name Nikarchos [*ša* ¹*an-ti-'-i-ku-su* lugal kur.kur^meš ¹*ni-qí-qa-ar-qu-su* mu-*šú ša-nu-ú iš-kun-nu*].'⁶² Like Joseph at Pharaoh's court or Daniel and his companions in Nebuchadnezzar's Babylon,⁶³ by a kind of linguistic baptism this local Urukean representative has been redesignated with a cognomen derived from the ruler's prestige tongue.⁶⁴

Anu-bēlšunu had opened his list of kings and sages at world's first light with the pair Ayalu/Alarus and U'an/Oannes; he closed it with, not the Seleucid king and a Babylonian scholar, but Uruk's governor at the time of his birth. Nikarchos's entry represents a distinct rupture from all that had come before. He stands alone, unpaired with a list-mate. He is attributed no title, neither 'king' (*šarru*) nor 'sage' (*ummânu*). He is represented only by his Greek name, an award of the Seleucid monarch. Moreover, in contrast to the *šaknu*'s own practice, his birth-name, the fine Babylonian theophoric Anu-uballiṭ ('Anu causes to live'), is simply omitted. Indeed, alone of every word and name in the tablet, Nikarchos is meaningless cuneiform.⁶⁵ The entry's inscribed line-length falls far short of all the others, creating at the list's conclusion, as in the English translation, a visual and logical emptiness. Moreover, the line lacks the regnal dating formula (*ina tarṣi*, 'in the time of') employed in all the previous entries. Nikarchos is without explicit chronographic marking – perhaps his tenure as city-governor could date itself; perhaps the Seleucid Era system,

---

⁶⁰ This is preceded by the broken sign [*-i*]*š* indicating, in all likelihood, an adverb. Restoration is difficult: Klotchkoff (1982) 153 suggested *paniš*, 'before' ('Before Nikarchos'), Lenzi (2008) 141, n. 12 *ediš*, 'alone' ('(But) Nikarchos is alone').
⁶¹ See Clancier and Gorre in this volume.
⁶² *YOS* 1.52 ll.1–3. The rendering of Nikarchos into cuneiform was enormously varied: *ni-iq-ar-ku-su*, *ni-iq-ar-qu-ra*, *ni-iq-ar-qu-su*, *ni-iq-ar-qu-ú-su*, *ni-iq-ar-ra-su*, *ni-iq-ár-ra-su*, *ni-i-qí-ar-qu-su*, *ni-iq-qar-su*, and *ni-qí-ar-qu-su*; see Monerie (2014) 40, 72–3, 154–5; and Lenzi (2008) 163 n. 91.
⁶³ Exodus 4:45; Daniel 1:7.
⁶⁴ For the phenomenon of double names in Seleucid Babylonia, see Monerie (2014); and Sherwin-White (1983a) 214–18; for the biblical parallels, see Newsom (2014) 46–7.
⁶⁵ Hallo (1963) 175–6 suggests that the names of the antediluvian *apkallû* encode the incipits of cuneiform literary series.

employed by Anu-bēlšunu in his colophon, is recognized as a distinct, non-regnal temporal order. Whatever the tablet's mood and purpose – nostalgia[66] or an appeal for scribal recognition[67] or the construction of an intellectual genealogy –[68] the tenth and final postdiluvian entry shows the disintegration of its historical system.

The Uruk List of Kings and Sages is situated within the age-old Mesopotamian scribal tradition of *Listenwissenschaft*, 'list-thinking,' that 'takes as its prime intellectual activity the production and reflection on lists, catalogs, and classifications, which progresses by establishing precedents, by observing patterns, similarities, and conjunctions, by noting repetitions.'[69] These Babylonian scribal catalogs are pointed. They yield propositions. As Alan Lenzi has observed, 'the culmination of an Akkadian list occurs in its final line where matters are summarized or its *telos* obtained.'[70] The Uruk List of Kings and Sages characterizes several millennia of southern Babylonian history and then, in its closing, seals them off. The Seleucid present of Anu-bēlšunu is sundered from this totalized past by a linguistic, chronographic, and structural distinction.[71] Despite being written in cuneiform and by a scribe claiming an honorable, antique genealogy, its periodization is as effective and final as Berossus's exterior positioning and use of Greek.

So, we have arrived back at the textbook periodization of Near Eastern history with which we opened. The Seleucid world is fenced off from a closed history that has run its course. These writings by Seleucid subjects – of which there are many more – reproduced their past in a manner in which they could take full possession of it. It is as if their contemporary, Seleucid situation were a point of Archimedes in time: the Seleucid horizon's break with the past was not only the structural limit of these works but also, in some sense, generative of them.[72] It is a historiographical perspective that accords with certain modern reflections on the writing or contemplation of history that have emphasized its basis in temporal interruption, in the differentiation of past from present. It is argued that,

---

[66] Klotchkoff (1982) 154. [67] Lenzi (2008) 164–5.
[68] Krul (2014) 67–9; Beaulieu (2000) 11; van Dijk (1962) 50.
[69] Smith (1982) 47; see also Van de Mieroop (2016) 219–24; and Neusner (1990).
[70] Lenzi (2008) 162, *contra* what Eco (2009) 81 characterizes as 'the *etcetera* of the list.'
[71] See, also, the similar conclusion of Krul (2014) 69: 'By placing Nikarchos alone at the end, the List of Kings and Sages expresses the notion that the relationship between rulers and advisors was different under Seleucid rule than it had been throughout history.' *Pace* Stevens (2016) 74–7, who sees in the Uruk List of Kings and Sages an integration of the Seleucid regime.
[72] De Certeau (1988) 4: 'Breakage is therefore the postulate of interpretation (which is constructed as of the present time) and its object (divisions organizing representations that must be interpreted).'

since the physical time that we perceive spontaneously does not have a historical character, its unrolling must be halted for historicity to be possible: history must treat the past as unitary, factual, and finished.[73] Accordingly, the objectification, even incarceration, of the past that we see in these Hellenistic indigenous histories inscribes as the fundamental characteristic of this past time its absence.[74] '*Was* is not *is*.'

Accordingly, I would suggest that the Seleucid temporal regime, with its strong distinction from the pre-Seleucid past, had the capacity to generate a system of two ages. Indigenous total histories, like our two case studies, could consolidate this horizon from the other side. These periods were correlative: where one began, the other stopped. Of course, this was by no means the only mode of indigenous thinking about durational time and local pasts within the Seleucid empire, but it may go some way to explaining the emergence of the periodization of time, the distinction between discrete historical ages, as a central concern of historical and religious thought in the Hellenistic east.

2B INDIGENOUS ELITES AND PTOLEMAIC DYNASTIC TIME
Ian Moyer

1 Introduction

Paul Kosmin's analysis of the Seleucid Era illuminates a blunt politics of time: this was historical periodization as a sovereign decision and a claim on the now.[75] The Seleucid Era not only marked a historical rupture, it constituted that rupture by creating a 'Seleucid horizon' and propagating a new universal age cut off from a distantiated and objectified past. In some respects, the Seleucid Era was the kind of modernity defined by Reinhard Koselleck.[76] This *Neuzeit* was a *Neue Zeit*, a 'new temporality,' in which a sense of rupture entailed the perception of a gap between experience of the past and expectations in the present and of the future. This era not only cut itself off from prior times, but its cumulative counting of years eschewed the cyclical patterns of regnal years and temporalized historicity

---

[73] See, e.g., Mosès (1994) 117; and Collingwood (1946) 233.   [74] See Fasolt (2004) 4–20.
[75] Davis (2008) critiques the modern politics of periodization in which the hegemonic distinction between the modern and the medieval entails a distinction between religion and secularism, between feudalism and democratic politics, and thus plays the role of a sovereign decision in the political theology of the modern state. In contrast to the effacement and naturalization of these distinctions in the modern construction of the past, the Seleucid horizon was much more open.
[76] See, for example, Koselleck (2004) 9–25.

in an open-ended continuum from the foundational moment of Seleucus I Nicator's return to Babylon to an unspecified future that was nevertheless grounded in intra-dynastic self-referentiality. Both those at court and subject communities responded to and rearticulated that new temporality, through the quotidian practices of the new time regulation, and through self-reflective intellectual productions – histories of their time and of a different time now past. It is in the latter especially that we can trace the engagement of indigenous elites with the construction of a new age. In the comparative frame of this collection, my goal will be to consider parallel phenomena in the Ptolemaic kingdom. Was there a Ptolemaic *Neue Zeit*, and in what ways did indigenous elites participate in the construction and contestation of that *Neue Zeit*?

For the Ptolemies, the 'facts on the ground' of Egyptian historicity and temporality were less manifold and varied than those in the Seleucid empire, with its extensive patchwork of cultural and social geography inherited from the Achaemenid empire and its antecedent states and traditions. In the case of Mesopotamia, on which Paul Kosmin focused, the past was also, as evident in the work of Berossos, a deep sedimentation of successive sovereignties. Ptolemaic antecedents could rival the temporal depth of Mesopotamia, but the pharaonic past was, with some interruptions, a homogeneous pharaonic continuum. Egypt did have a variety of temporalities encoded in local myths, histories and festival calendars, but its cities and *nomes* shared common time frames in the agricultural rhythms of the Nile Valley, the solar civic calendar, and especially in Egyptian kingship traditions and their patterns of historicity. These well-known patterns include the pharaoh's embodiment of key mythical roles in the Osirian cycle, his repeated performance of traditional pharaonic activities, but also his place in the linear sequence of unique past pharaohs, their deeds, and their material memorials that stretched back to the time when the gods ruled Egypt. These formed, in varying degrees across the social strata – but especially among indigenous elites – a context of past experience from which to look toward a horizon of expectations.[77] In official representations and memorializations of the past, however, it was continuity that was deliberately projected as a matter of pharaonic theology. Erik Hornung's concept of *Geschichte als Fest*, best understood as ritual re-enactment rather than 'celebration,' is still a useful encapsulation of this tendency, even if its pharaonic focus risks

---

[77] Koselleck (2004) 255–75.

obscuring other modes of historicity.[78] In as much as there was an official, collective Egyptian historicity, it was not unlike the historicity of other monarchic states and societies. The pharaonic Egyptian *Geschichte als Fest*, for example, shares qualities with Marshall Sahlins's 'heroic history,' including the 'positional succession' through which a current ruler re-enacts and embodies past pharaonic rulers and actions.[79] As a significant body of scholarship has shown, the Ptolemaic dynasty and the court at Alexandria, in a broad array of Egypt-facing representations that were produced in dialog with indigenous elites, assimilated to pharaonic precedents, whether in epigraphical praise of royal deeds or in visual representations of typical pharaonic action in temple sculpture. On this considerable evidence, together with a broad recognition of the Ptolemaic maintenance of fundamental structures from past regimes, historians of Ptolemaic Egypt have for several decades now stressed the continuities between the Ptolemies and the pharaohs.[80]

In looking for commensurable elements in the comparison of Seleucid and Ptolemaic historicities and temporalities and the roles of indigenous elites in their construction, a different perspective emerges: a shift in focus from king to dynasty, from the repetitive succession of pharaohs and generations embodied, for example, in the king-list, to the 'dynasty' as a unit of Ptolemaic Egyptian historicity and temporality, and to an examination not only of continuities with past concepts, but also innovations. My goal is to sketch out the spectrum of relations that indigenous elites in the Ptolemaic kingdom had to official dynastic temporality, whether sustaining it in religious and ceremonial acts and in day-to-day documentary practices, offering equivocal translations of Ptolemaic dynastic time into indigenous terms, or in occasional moments of overt discursive or practical resistance. My basic contention is that although less radical than in the Seleucid case and drawing on pre-existing traditions to a greater

---

[78] On this Egyptian notion of history as cyclical royal ritual and performance, see Hornung (1966) which – it is important to remember – was originally a comparative pair of essays on Egyptian and Aztec historicity. See also the English translation of the Egyptian half of the original pair, 'History as Celebration,' in Hornung (1992) 147–64. See Schneider (2014) for an excellent critique of the predominance of Hornung's idea in approaching the broader question of whether or not 'the Egyptians had history.'

[79] Sahlins (1985) 36–54.

[80] On the 'two faces' of Ptolemaic kingship, see Peremans (1987); Clarysse (1991a); Koenen (1993). For a general overview of the Ptolemaic adoption of pharaonic precedents and ideology, see Hölbl (2001) 77–90. Perhaps a culmination of this trend is the title of a recent history of Ptolemaic Egypt (Manning 2010): *The Last Pharaohs*.

degree, Ptolemaic dynastic time did establish a rupture with the past and was indeed a *neue Zeit*, and this new time was both constructed and contested by indigenous elites. In what follows, I shall begin with documentary practice before turning to historiographic and prophetic responses.

2 Marking Dynastic Time: The Dating Formula in Documentary Practice

Unlike the innovative Seleucid Era, the official time of Ptolemaic documents was reckoned with a traditional regnal year count. On the face of it, this shows continuity with prior traditions and so relatively slight demands for accommodation made on indigenous elites and populations, but there are some well-known minor discrepancies. In the transitions from one king to another, the Greek regnal year ran from the anniversary of the earlier king's accession to the new king's accession, while the Egyptian regnal year was fixed to the first day of the month of Thoth (I Akhet), with part years belonging to the succeeding king. Egyptian scribes adhered to the Egyptian regnal year count with the result that there were at times discrepancies in the beginnings and ends of years and reigns.[81] There also came to be two independent calendars in operation in Egypt –[82] the Macedonian lunar calendar and the Egyptian solar civil calendar – at least until the reign of Ptolemy VI, when the Macedonian months were assimilated to the Egyptian calendar. As the late Chris Bennett showed, attempts to synchronize the two in documents were often only rough estimates outside of Alexandria. Bennett also showed that the reformed calendar of the Canopus decree was, in fact, used at times, albeit only in Alexandria or in documents with a close connection to the court, before fading away in the reign of Ptolemy IV. So, to varying degrees, in the third and early second centuries, Alexandria and the *chora* were, in at least a technical sense, different documentary chronotopes.[83]

These little discrepancies had a more significant counterpart in the way that dynastic time was marked off. To return to regnal years: the Greek

---

[81] For detailed information on the features of Ptolemaic chronology discussed below, see Samuel (1962); Bennett (2011); and for a detailed discussion of the Macedonian and Egyptian calendars under Ptolemy I Soter, see Bennett (2018).

[82] Under Ptolemy II, a Ptolemaic fiscal year was also introduced, with a year that started around the beginning of the Egyptian month of Mecheir. This was not, however, an independent calendrical system, but, as argued by Bennett (2018) 58–60, based initially on the Macedonian regnal year and reckoned in relation to the existing calendars.

[83] Bennett (2011); (2018), 53–4.

years of Ptolemy Soter were backdated so that they included his years as satrap and began immediately after the reign of Alexander the Great, erasing the reigns of Philip Arrhidaios and Alexander IV – Alexander's nominal successors in the Argead dynasty. The Egyptian regnal year count, however, was not backdated and included the Argead successors as independent rulers, so there was an eighteen-year discrepancy between Greek and Egyptian year counts. This was not only a difference in recordkeeping; it was consistent with the distinctive way that the Ptolemaic dynastic cult was eventually translated into the spaces and practices of Egyptian temples. The dynastic cult at Alexandria was attached to the cult of Alexander, who was entombed there as founder (*ktistes*) of the city, thus emphasizing the Ptolemies' personal connection with the great conqueror and claims of kinship with the Argead house. The process of forming this dynastic cult began in year 14 of Ptolemy II (272/1) with the inclusion of the *Theoi Adelphoi* in the cult of Alexander, and, with gradual additions, took its full dynastic shape fifty-seven years later with the retroactive inclusion of the *Theoi Soteres* (in year 8 of Ptolemy IV / 215/14).[84] On the other hand, the dynastic cult in the Egyptian temples, to which I will return shortly, did not include Alexander or Ptolemy I Soter. The starting point of Ptolemaic dynastic time, in short, was not the clearly established 'Year 1' of the Seleucid Era. Egyptian and Greek reckonings of Ptolemaic time agreed neither in the identity of its first ruler, nor in the count of his regnal years.

Despite these discrepancies, the Alexandrian version of the dynasty, as expressed in the title of the eponymous priest, did find a place in the scribal practice and time-reckoning of indigenous elites. It was incorporated into authoritative formal documents in Demotic, such as notary contracts (*sḫ-*contracts),[85] in which the regnal year date was usually supplemented with the name of the eponymous priest of Alexander and the Ptolemies. This eponymous priest was introduced in Greek documents from ca. 290 (year 34 of Ptolemy I Soter), at first cited only as the priest of Alexander, and then, from 272/1 BCE, as priest of Alexander and the *Theoi Adelphoi*. The Demotic documents began to include these eponymous titles in 265/4 BCE (year 21 of Ptolemy II Philadelphus) and also began to include double dates in the Macedonian and Egyptian calendars. The timing of these changes in Demotic documentary practice is suggestive: they came just a few years after the inclusion of the *Theoi Adelphoi* in the cult of Alexander, and shortly after Ptolemy the Son became coregent (268/7

---

[84] Winter (1978); Quaegebeur (1989); Lanciers (1991); Koenen (1993); Minas-Nerpel (2000).
[85] For a brief description of the characteristics of *sḫ*-contracts, see Depauw (1997) 123–4.

BCE).⁸⁶ In other words, the move to include the eponymous priest in the dating formulae of Demotic documents occurred at just the moment when dynastic continuity was being addressed through a coregency (even if Ptolemy the Son later lost his position in 259/8). It was also in the late 270s and early 260s BCE that Ptolemaic royal oaths began to appear in an innovative form. In contrast to earlier pharaonic antecedents, they were sworn not only by the reigning pharaoh, but also by the divinized members of the dynasty.⁸⁷ The motives for all these innovations and reforms of traditional practice must often be inferred, but it is clear that in a relatively brief period in the middle of the reign of Ptolemy II Philadelphus there developed a coherent emphasis on the Ptolemaic dynasty as a unit⁸⁸ and on dynastic time in official reckoning, alongside the traditional pattern of regnal years of an individual pharaoh. Though this was an innovation relative to prior practice in Egypt and an effort to construct a new temporality, there remains a significant contrast with the Seleucid era, which dated from the initiation of continuous Seleucid kingship upon the return to Babylon in 311 BCE.⁸⁹ What was distinctive in the Ptolemaic case, especially in the use of eponymous priests in Demotic dating formulae, was not the assertion of an absolute timescale relative to an event that constituted the sovereignty of state, but emphasis on the dynastic succession of a self-contained lineage distinct from others in the Egyptian past. As we shall see, this development was contemporary with Manetho's synthesis of Egyptian

---

⁸⁶ In three Demotic documents dating to years 20 and 21 of Ptolemy II (265–264 BCE), the *kanephoros* of Arsinoe II is included in the dating formula without the priest of Alexander. The use of this priestess of Arsinoe II for eponymous dating may have become accepted practice in Demotic documents slightly before the priest of Alexander. For discussion, see Minas-Nerpel (2000) 96–7; Caneva (2016), 170. On Ptolemy the Son, see Huß (1998).

⁸⁷ The earliest attestations are a Greek papyrus (*BGU* VI 1257) dated 270–258 BCE and a Demotic papyrus (*P. dem. Testi Botti*, pp. 38–41), dated 265/4 BCE. See Minas-Nerpel (2000) 163–71; Caneva (2016), 154–5, 225–31. There may be other foundational moments connected with this period as well, though their interpretation is disputed. Hazzard has argued that a new dynastic era was inaugurated in 262 BCE with the celebration of the Ptolemaia, the grand procession of Ptolemy Philadelphus at Alexandria, and the inauguration of the era of Soter, which, he argues was the basis of historical chronology in the *Marmor Parium* (see Hazzard [2000] 3–46 and 161–7). As Chaniotis points out, there is no explicit connection to an era of Soter in the *Marmor Parium* (see *SEG* 53 871), and Lorber (2007a) has argued that the Ptolemaic era coinage emerged on Ptolemaic Cyprus and in a military rather than dynastic context.

⁸⁸ On the broader context of the construction of the dynasty, see now Caneva (2016).

⁸⁹ Although there appears to have been an era system in use on Ptolemaic Cyprus and in Ptolemaic holdings in Phoenicia and Coele Syria, there is no evidence of its use in Egypt – and its connection to the Ptolemaic dynasty is unclear. See n. 13 above. In Alexandrian scholarly circles, moreover, there is no clear evidence of the development of a Ptolemaic era system. Eratosthenes, for example, used an era system keyed to various significant events and synchronisms between Greek dating systems from the Trojan War to the death of Alexander. See Möller (2005).

historical records and principles in a way that also brought the dynasty to the fore as a unit that structured past time.

The Ptolemaic system of eponymous dating was an innovation and a recognition of a *neue Zeit* in another, clearer way. This supplement to the regnal year, unprecedented in Egyptian practice, was a form of time-reckoning centered on a particular place: Alexandria, or, in some Demotic documents from Upper Egypt dated to 215 BCE and after, the Greek *polis* of Ptolemaïs Hermiou.[90] Both of these dating formulae evoked common patterns of time-reckoning in the city-states of the Greek world. Those indigenous scribes who composed *sḫ*-contracts, in which they acted as notaries representing the priests of a temple in warranting a document, were incorporating an official temporality from Alexandria and Ptolemaïs, and the wider world of Greek city-states, into an Egyptian documentary genre that originated in the Saïte period. In this way, indigenous scribes sustained and affirmed the official time of the dynasty and its seat in Alexandria (or Ptolemaïs). Egyptian elites also used the eponymous dating formula, along with double dates in the Macedonian and Egyptian calendars, in the sacerdotal decrees, including the Demotic and Hieroglyphic versions. These were composed in the Hellenistic genre of the honorific decree, and through eponymous dating and other formal features they framed communication between the Ptolemies and the indigenous elites as taking place in the imagined chronotope of a *polis*: at a quasi-civic assembly of priests directing praise to their *basileus*-pharaoh.[91]

To sum up briefly: the dating formula in documentary practice attests to the well-known linguistic and cultural duality of the Ptolemaic state, but it was not just a matter of separate cultural continuities. There were innovations that defined a new era. Local elites who composed documents maintained the traditional regnal year count, but also – particularly in those documents that relied on and sustained the authoritative backing of the state – incorporated references to the new time standard that celebrated the Ptolemaic dynasty and its seat(s) of power. We can hypothesize that this was, at least in formal terms, and in the domain of official practice, a *neue Zeit*, and that indigenous elites played a role in the creation of this new temporality.

3 Visualizing Ptolemaic Time: Dynastic Lists in the Temples

One visible, material result of the introduction of the Egyptian dynastic cult was that local elites arranged the depiction of sequences of Ptolemaic

---

[90] Minas-Nerpel (2000) 114–16.   [91] Clarysse (2000a) 48–50; see also Moyer (2011b) 117–25.

rulers in the decorative and epigraphic programs of Egyptian temples, a phenomenon very well studied by Martina Minas-Nerpel.[92] In these lists and reliefs, they rendered visible the structure of the Egyptian version of the dynastic cult. Indigenous elites translated the dynastic cult from the *polis* into the temple on their own terms, which is not to say that this was a grudging acknowledgement of the dynasty –[93] only that they did not follow the Alexandrian conception of dynastic continuity and cultic co-presence with Alexander: the *ktistes* and his satrap were not part of their vision of the dynasty or its divine antecedents. Instead, the dynasty began with Ptolemy II Philadelphus, and its members were *synnaoi theoi* with the Egyptian gods. The Egyptian lists, therefore, separated the dynastic era of the Ptolemies from Alexander and the Argead dynasty in both historical and cultic terms. In addition, however, the lists in the temples also separated the Ptolemaic dynasty from Egypt's pharaonic past. These lists of names were most frequently arranged in symmetrical patterns on door frames and posts or columns on either side of the central axis of the temple. They were in the public areas of the temple and so visible not only to the priests who entered the inner, more restricted spaces of the temple, but also to others who might visit the temple to observe and take part in festivals or in the more quotidian activities that took place in these areas. For example, an inscription on the post of the doorway into the east tower of the first pylon of the Isis temple at Philae, completed under Ptolemy VI, mentions the king and Cleopatra II together with a sequential list of their predecessors from the *Theoi Adelphoi* (*nṯr.wy sn.wy*; i.e. Ptolemy II and Arsinoe II) to the *Theoi Epiphaneis* (*nṯr.wy pr.wy*; i.e. Ptolemy V and Cleopatra I).[94] On the façade of the Ptolemaic pronaos of the temple of Montu at El-Tod was engraved a scene of Ptolemy VIII and Cleopatra II making offerings to their divine predecessors in the dynasty, beginning as usual with Ptolemy II and ending with Ptolemy VI and the short-lived Ptolemy Eupator. This latter is an especially striking example of a scene of dynastic cult that is also a visual dynastic list.[95] The representation of a succession of kings' names in a temple context had antecedents in Egypt, especially in famous examples from the New Kingdom, such as the lists of Seti I and Rameses II at Abydus. These were visible and accessible as models in the Late Period (as suggested by nearby graffiti), but the Ptolemaic dynastic lists are

---

[92] Minas-Nerpel (2000).   [93] Quaegebeur (1989); cf. Winter (1978).
[94] Minas-Nerpel (2000) 6–7, pl. 3.
[95] Minas-Nerpel (2000) 24–5, pl. 17; on the scenes of Ptolemies offering worship to dynastic ancestors, see also 62–4, and the earlier discussion in Quaegebeur (1989) 99–101.

constructed quite differently. As Minas-Nerpel has pointed out,[96] they restricted themselves to members of the Ptolemaic dynasty and did not make a connection, as in the Rameside lists, with the succession of prior kings going back all the way to the first pharaoh, Menes. The Ptolemies were isolated from other historical kings.

Circumstantial evidence suggests that this may have been part of a change in the orientation of the dynasty: as Gilles Gorre has pointed out in his article on Nectanebo the Falcon and the Ptolemaic dynasty (Gorre 2009), the cult of Nectanebo II was a prestigious religious duty in the hands of prominent Egyptian priests connected with the Ptolemaic dynasty, but the evidence for such priesthoods seems to disappear just when the cult of the Ptolemaic dynasty is established in Egyptian temples. Cults of royal statues, including ones from the pharaonic past, were continued, but there does not seem to have been an explicit connection made between the sequence of the Ptolemies and prior kings such as the Nectanebids.

The isolation of the Ptolemaic dynasty from pharaonic predecessors, and installation in the temples as *synnaoi theoi*, in effect short-circuited another variant of the king-list tradition that stretched back in time beyond Menes to the succession of Egyptian gods, a tradition embodied in the Turin King-List and Manetho's *Aegyptiaca*, to which I turn next.

4 Manetho's *Aegyptiaca* and the *Turin List*

So far, I have used 'dynasty' as if it were a self-evident term, but the use of the Greek word δυναστεία to mean a sequence of rulers with a common origin appears to be a Hellenistic development. Elsewhere, it has the more general meaning of power, lordship, and domination. The earliest attestations of the term in its genealogical sense are to be found in the fragments of the Egyptian priest and historian Manetho, and it is possible that this was his coinage.[97] The objectification of a particular royal descent group as a temporal and political concept was certainly not alien to either Greek or

---

[96] Minas-Nerpel (2000) 74–9 (esp. 77), 176.
[97] *LSJ vid. sub* δυναστεία; Verbrugghe and Wickersham (1996) 98. Though Greek historians prior to and contemporary with Manetho refer to royal descent groups, they do not use the term δυναστεία to describe them; Herodotus, for example, tends to use the name of the descent group (e.g. Mermnads or Heraklids). The use of the English term in the current sense is, according to the *Oxford English Dictionary*, first attested in John Capgrave's *Abbreuiacion of chronicles* (1464), on p. 22 of the 1983 Early English Texts edition, referring to Egyptian Dynasties and perhaps Manetho. The term also appears in Sir Walter Raleigh, *The History of the World* (1614) 1.1.ii. §2. 237. This usage is ultimately derived from Manetho via Eusebius and others.

Egyptian ways of representing the past, but Manetho appears to have brought the concept of 'dynasty' into greater focus by structuring his *Aegyptiaca* not just as a sequence of kings, but as a sequence of dynasties. The nature of Manetho's work has been much discussed and debated in relation to both his intellectual and political context,[98] but here it should be enough to note that he was an Egyptian priest connected with the Ptolemaic court and that he likely completed his work sometime after ca. 256 BCE, possibly as late as the reign of Ptolemy III.[99] In other words, not long after the introduction of the eponymous priests into Demotic documents, and at about the time when the dynastic cult was introduced into the Egyptian temples – all of which, as I have been arguing, contributed to the creation of a new Ptolemaic dynastic time separated from the past.

As Kim Ryholt has shown,[100] the greater part of Manetho's dynastic divisions in his first two books can be traced back to the same tradition represented by the Nineteenth-Dynasty text known as the *Turin List*. On the other hand, Manetho did also innovate by further subdividing some of the groupings present in the Turin List. Although familial relations are explicit or implicit in most dynasties in Manetho, almost all of the dynasties are also identified with a particular city, to the extent we can tell from the epitomes of Africanus and Eusebius preserved in Syncellus (BNJ 609 F2). The exceptions are those identified with a foreign ethnic, such as the Hyksos, Ethiopians and Persians.[101] Only one group of kings in the *Turin*

---

[98] Verbrugghe and Wickersham (1996) 84–141; see also now Moyer (2011a), and Dillery (2015), who mischaracterizes my interpretation of Manetho's counter-discursive strategy of presenting an Egyptian sense of history to the Ptolemaic court as 'nationalist' (see esp. pp. xvi–xvii). Dillery is careless to claim that I am ignorant of the relationship between Manetho, Berossus and their common circumstances (Dillery [2015] xiv–xv): 'as seems to be a matter lost on Moyer there is surely a major point of significance in the fact that the two histories – the *Babyloniaca* of Berossus and the *Aegyptiaca* of Manetho – were written at almost exactly the same time, in almost identical circumstances, and with very similar results.' In fact, I refer to that relationship in the work Dillery critiques (Dillery [2015] 98, n. 51; 100, n. 59; 105, n. 73) and I subsequently published an article on the relationship between the two (Moyer [2013]). Dillery was aware of this article (Dillery [2015] xvii, n. 34), and yet apparently was unwilling to give credit for discussing the very evidence and ideas that he cites against me. Compare, for example, Dillery (2015), 215–22 with Moyer (2013); and Dillery (2015) xv with Moyer (2013) xiv–xv.

[99] For discussions of Manetho's dates, see Dillery (2015) 85–7; Moyer (2011a) 213–15.

[100] Ryholt (2004) 146.

[101] Manetho connects neither the Ethiopians nor the Persians with Memphis, although both governed from that capital. The Hyksos have both an ethnic designation and a city, since they 'founded a town in the Sethroite nome' (the *nome* is in some versions noted incorrectly as 'Saïte'; BNJ 609 F2, F3b, F7). The town was called Avaris (BNJ 609 F8). The peripheral location of this city and its non-Egyptian associations make this reference somewhat ambiguous. The kings of Dynasties 22 and 23, who are connected with Bubastis and Tanis, seem to have been recognized by Manetho as Egyptian, despite their Libyan background, perhaps because they did not come to power through a decisive military invasion.

List is identified with a place: the group corresponding to the Twelfth Dynasty are kings of the residence *Ỉt-t3wy*.[102] So, although not unprecedented in Egyptian tradition, Manetho emphatically linked dynasty with place in a way that resonated with the contemporary emergence of a dynastic temporality centered on Greek cities.

Another innovation that is perhaps so familiar that it sometimes goes unnoticed is that Manetho numbered his dynasties, ending with the Nectanebids, the Thirtieth Dynasty.[103] The number 30 has a range of associations that suggest authority or canonicity.[104] Thirty appears to have been a canonical number of precepts or chapters in wisdom texts, such as the *Teachings of Amenemope*.[105] The Egyptian grand jury, and the tribunal of the gods who judged between Horus and Seth were known as the 'Council of the Thirty.'[106] More important for our purposes is the fact that 30 was the number of days in an Egyptian month and the number of years of rule celebrated at a pharaoh's *ḥb-sd* (jubilee festival).[107] Manetho's 30 dynasties, therefore, suggest a complete temporal unit. If so, subsequent time was a new, undefined era, and a line was drawn under past historical time. Whether the new era was like the past, or different, was left open, but with the closure of a canon of dynasties and kings Manetho surely posed the question of the future and how to define the horizon of expectations of the Ptolemaic dynasty.[108]

---

[102] It is also possible that the kings of Dynasty 11 in the Turin Canon were also identified with their royal residence (Ryholt [2004] 141, 143). The mention of dynastic capitals is among the innovations relative to the Turin List credited to Manetho by Ryholt (2004) 87. Dillery is incorrect, however, in stating that the Turin List has no dynastic capitals (cf. Dillery [2015] loc. cit.), and probably also incorrect in stating that Manetho was unique in including chronicle notices in the text. There is one fragmentary remark preserved in relation to king Huni (Ryholt [2004] 145) that could derive from either a chronicle or some other Egyptian source.

[103] For the evidence showing that Manetho's *Aegyptiaca* ended with the Thirtieth Dynasty and not the spurious Thirty-First Dynasty added in some fragments and testimonia, see Ryholt (2004) 93–4.

[104] Moyer (2011a) 139; (2013).

[105] British Museum EA 10474, translated in Lichtheim (1976), 146–66. See also *O. Medin. Madi* I 27 (Shirun-Grumach [1980], 45–6, pl. 9).

[106] *Admonitions of Ipuwer* (P. Leiden 344 6, 10); *Book of the Dead* 125; *P. Chester Beatty* I recto 3, 9.

[107] Note also that in the *Prophecy of the Lamb* (P. Vindob. D 10 000), the lamb predicts that he will return as the *uraeus* on the head of the king, after the Medes and Greeks, thus ushering in an era of prosperity after 900 years; Zauzich has suggested the symbolic qualities this number: 900 = 30 × 30 (30 ḥb-sd/jubilee periods of 30 years). Note that the text as it appears in Syncellus has 990 years, but this is probably corrupt and should be read 900. See Hoffmann (2000) 173, n. 5; Zauzich (1983) 10, n. 9; Koenen (1984) 10–11.

[108] I have argued elsewhere (Moyer [2011a] 139–41) that the closure of Manetho's king-list history, together with narrative patterns of dissolution and restoration, were an invitation to the Ptolemaic court to consider their sense of history and prospective action in relation to a pharaonic Egyptian historicity.

5 Prophetic Responses to Ptolemaic Dynastic Temporality

As Reinhart Koselleck argued, 'the more a particular time is experienced as a new temporality, ... the more that demands made of the future increase.'[109] Koselleck was setting modernity's notions of progressive advance and its foreshortened expectations of imminent utopian change against an older apocalyptic temporality in which such change was only going to come in a repeatedly deferred Hereafter.[110] For historians of antiquity, apocalyptic temporality looks somewhat different: it is not a past background but an emergent phenomenon, and some of its roots can be found among the responses of indigenous elites to the Seleucid Era with its open futurity, as Paul Kosmin has argued elsewhere. Did the *neue Zeit* of the Ptolemaic dynasty, shaped in part by indigenous elites, result in corresponding reorientations of the relationships between past, present, and future?

The text known as the *Demotic Chronicle* offers an indigenous perspective on this question, though one that is filled with interpretive difficulties.[111] Nevertheless, I would like to point to a few signs that the authors of this highly learned and esoteric text, who were roughly contemporary with Manetho,[112] were engaged in the construction of the Ptolemaic *neue Zeit* and its horizon of expectations. The text consists of a series of oracular pronouncements together with exegetical comments that, in many cases, connect the prophecies to historical rulers and events that are both in the past and in the future relative to the dramatic date of the text: the coregency of Nectanebo I and Tachos, not long before the rule of Nectanebo II, the last pharaoh of Dynasty 30. The historical references in the text run from the reign of Amyrtaios (404–399 BCE) to Greek rule over Egypt, while the prospective parts of the text predict the coming of a man from Heracleopolis who will be an ideal ruler for Egypt.[113] Like the *Aegyptiaca*, the *Demotic Chronicle* marks a boundary at the end of the Nectanebids. From the dramatic date of the text forward, time takes on the less precise quality of prophetic futurity. Although further *ex eventu* predictions are made to accord with past time, there are no references to specific historical rulers, only the rule of Persians and Greeks. The boundary point is the end of the Nectanebid dynasty (Dynasty 30), but the

---

[109] Koselleck (2004) 3.   [110] Koselleck (2004) 13–17.
[111] For a translation and discussion of the text, see Felber (2002); see also the overview in Quack (2009) 181–5.
[112] Felber (2002) 68 argues for a date in the reign of Ptolemy III.
[113] For discussion of the complex temporal structure of the *Demotic Chronicle*, see Moyer (2011a) 128–35.

prophetic lemmata through which that end is 'predicted' are also the ends of temporal units – indeed, the end of the dynasty is identified with a coincidence between festivals of the lunar cycle and of the solar calendar:

Col. II/8:

pꜣ wrše mte n Py II pr.t– ḏ pꜣ mnk̲ pꜣ dm r ḥ(.t) pꜣy ir=w sḥn.t̲=f (n) II pr.t– ḏ iir-ir tꜣ wꜥb.t ḫpr n-im=f

The *wrše* festival takes place in Pe in the second month of winter (Mecheir). That is: the end of the family,[114] according to what was ordered in the second month of winter, since that is the month in which the 'purification' takes place.

Col. II/9:

ḫpr wrše pꜣ mnk̲ n pꜣ ꜣbd pꜣy

It happens that the *wrše* festival is the end of the month.

Col. II/10:

ḥꜣ.t nbty Tpꜣy ꜣbd III pr.t– ḏ ḥꜣt ir ḥry nt ir pꜣ nt ir ḥry iir=f ꜣbd III pr.t pꜣy ḫpr nbty ḥꜣ.t ꜣbd pꜣy

The beginning of the Nebty-festival is in the third month of winter (Phamenoth). That is: the beginning of the rule, of the one who will rule, is the third month of winter. It happens that the Nebty-festival is the beginning of this month.

The new moon festival (*wrše*),[115] at the end of the month of Mecheir, is followed by the Nebty-festival (the day of the new moon's first visibility) at the beginning of the subsequent month (Phamenoth). In the solar calendar, this marks the halfway point of the year (the end of the sixth month and the beginning of the seventh). The reign of the future ruler is said to begin at that point.

Later in the text, when the coming of the 'man of Heracleopolis' (*Pa-Ḥw.t-nsw.t*) is predicted (II/23–III/17), he is also said to assume the crown in Phamenoth (*III pr.t–* III/10). As I mentioned, the temporal structure of the future-oriented part of the text is less clear than the neatly ordered section dealing with the last seven Egyptian rulers, but there are two possibilities for interpreting the beginning of the new era of the 'man

---

[114] Felber (2002) 76–7 suggests that the word *ḏm* could be translated not only as 'family' but as 'Dynastie.'

[115] The interpretation of this part of the text as *wrše* (new moon festival) is due to J. Quack (see Felber 2002, 77).

from Heracleopolis' in reference to the month of Phamenoth. The first possibility is that the author considered it to begin in the reign of Nectanebo II, or at its end, when Thoth is said to go to Heracleopolis and to conduct an inquiry there. This new era would therefore encompass the post-Nectanebid tribulations and the rule of the Persians and the Greeks as a long prelude. Alternatively, the new era could begin with a new annual cycle after the post-Nectanebid period, and the tribulations would occur in that intervening time. Either way, there is a decisive break at the end of the Nectanebid dynasty, and the subsequent sections of the text appear to outline both troubles under the Persians as well as improved conditions under the Greeks, who will 'rule Egypt for a long time' (VI/20), so the text cannot be taken as anti-Greek.[116] Heinz Felber, moreover, has argued that the man from Heracleopolis is none other than Ptolemy I Soter. Despite some circumstantial and symbolic arguments in favor of this position, there are still considerable doubts about whether the 'man from Heracleopolis' comes after the Macedonian Dynasty, or after the Greeks more generally (including the Ptolemies).

The critical passage for Felber is in chapter 8 (II/19–II/21), where a sequence of three rulers are predicted in the exegesis of a series of oracular statements regarding three *phylai* of priests who carry out in turn the actions of approaching the bolt of a shrine, sliding it open, and opening the shrine before the *uraeus*. There are, however, no clear indications in the text as to when exactly the three kings corresponding to the three bolts are to be placed. The only clue is that the people will rejoice over the third one and that he will become king in the foreign lands. Felber has interpreted the three kings as Alexander III, Philip Arrhidaios and Alexander IV, but another trio is also possible: Nectanebo I, Teos, Nectanebo II. The latter could be the one who became king in (ḫn) the foreign lands, since Nectanebo II was on campaign with Teos in Phoenicia and Syria when he was called to the throne by a revolt against Tachos.[117] This interpretation has the further advantage that it recognizes the three rulers of Dynasty 30 as a unit (as in Manetho's *Aegyptiaca*).

The most telling factor against interpreting the Heracleopolitan ruler as the founder of the Ptolemaic dynasty is the very fact of his association with Heracleopolis, and a consistent emphasis on Upper Egypt as the source from which the new era of benevolent rule will spring.[118] The new era

---

[116] On this point, see Johnson (1984).
[117] Kienitz (1953) 97–8; the sources for this sequence of events are Plut. *Ages.* 37; Diod. 15.92.
[118] See also Quack (2009) 185–6.

begins with an investigation into 'what happened in Memphis' (II/5) before Thoth turns to Heryshef and to Heracleopolis. In the oracles addressed to Nectanebo I in V/21–VI/12, there is a consistent theme of shift in power from lower Egypt to Upper Egypt: it is the *uraeus* associated with the white crown of Upper Egypt that is healthy, while the red crown of Lower Egypt has clouding in its eye (V/21–3). The goddess Mut is the medicine for this affliction, but she flees to Amun, a Theban divinity (VI,1–2), And finally, the youth (or servant) is hungry, but the craftsman (high priest) of Memphis can only provide chaff (VI,10–12). All this suggests that the benevolent ruler to come was not connected with the Ptolemaic dynasty, which had a close relationship with the high priests of Memphis.[119] In relation to the dynastic chronotope of official Ptolemaic historicity – Alexandria and its eponymous priests and dynastic cult – the 'horizon of expectation' in the *Demotic Chronicle*, as a response to the Ptolemaic *neue Zeit*, was both temporal and spatial, and it looked beyond the Ptolemaic present to a future king and a new seat of power.[120]

As I have suggested in this very brief overview, indigenous Egyptian elites played a range of roles in constructing, translating and contesting the new temporality of the Ptolemaic dynasty and also in evaluating whether this was a time of redemption from recent misfortunes, a time that raised expectations of better days, or a time from which Egypt was to be redeemed into a new era and a return to such traditional dynastic seats as Memphis or Heracleopolis. The evidence for these roles is scattered across documentary texts, temple inscriptions, histories, and prophecies but collectively suggests that, along with helping to capture for the Ptolemaic dynasty traditional Egyptian rhetoric and practices of state authority (as Stefan Pfeiffer has shown in this volume), indigenous elites also contributed to creating new frameworks of authority, including the dynastic temporality of the kingdom. This dynastic *neue Zeit*, for all its reuse of past traditions and symbols, was also presented as historically self-contained and separate from the sequence of kings and dynasties in a canonical Egyptian past. Though less radical than the Seleucid Era and more heterogeneous in its manifestations, the

---

[119] Thompson (1990).
[120] An even stronger case for the spatial dimension of post-Ptolemaic aspirations can be found in a later prophetic text: the *Oracle of the Potter*. This text is much more overtly hostile to Alexandria, and the overthrow of the 'Typhonian' Greeks is presented as the displacement of Agathos Daimon and Knephis from Alexandria to Memphis where the king from the sun will arise, ushering in the new era. P.Oxy. 2332.50–52; see Koenen (1968) 204–7; Koenen (2002); English translation in Burstein (1985) 136–9.

Ptolemaic dynasty did mark a break with past time, and a different orientation toward a future or perhaps a future past.

A final example may serve to illustrate this last point. Shortly after the rebel Haronnophris (*Ḥr-wn-nfr*) assumed the title of pharaoh and established his palace at Thebes in 215, he 'egyptianized' the chancellery, as evident in the fictive model letter re-published by Depauw (Cairo 38258), in which an archaizing title, 'scribe of the directive' (*sḫ n pꜣ wḫꜣ*), was introduced.[121] The new documentary regime also, of course, included a new regnal year count and an abandonment of the eponymous priests of Alexandria. Perhaps even more intriguing is the peculiarity, first pointed out by Pestman,[122] that the only plausible reconstruction of the regnal years of the two-member dynasty at Thebes requires that the years of Haronnophris continue on to those of Chaonnophris (that is, year 6 of the former is followed by year 7 of the latter). Unless they are the same person, the new dynasty, beloved of Amonrasonter of Thebes (rather than Ptah of Memphis), established a continual year count from one pharaoh to the next. Together with the aspirations to cyclical Osirian dynastic renewal encoded in the names 'Horus-Onnophris' and 'Onnophris lives,' this represents an effort to establish a new dynastic time to rival and supplant the dynastic time of the Ptolemies – perhaps even a new era.[123] In this latter case, and in the examples of prophetic texts, it appears that the co-option of indigenous elites into the project of constructing a new Ptolemaic dynastic temporality resulted in creative recalibrations of official temporality that at times evaded or resisted the control of the regime itself. Perhaps it is even possible that in instituting a continuous year count, the Theban pharaohs adapted to their own purposes the new temporal modality of the Seleucid Era or one of the many other eras that it seemed to have spawned.

Common Conclusion

At the outset of our comparative contribution, Paul Kosmin pointed out the different weight that Alexander has as an epochal figure in standard histories of antiquity in the Near East and in Egypt. Histories of the Near

---

[121] Depauw (2006).   [122] Pestman (1995) 130–1.
[123] According to Bennett (2011), the Philae II decree of 186 BCE appears to have used the assimilated calendar. In that text, contrary to prior practice, the Egyptian and the Macedonian months are equated: the same day number (3 or 9) is given for Peritios and the Egyptian month Mesore. Though this decree was passed in Alexandria, the Macedonian calendar appears to have been harmonized with the Egyptian calendar. Since this decree commemorates the end of the Theban rebellion, one possible explanation is that this was a symbolic harmonization of time between Alexandria and the *chora*.

East appear to reflect a rough scholarly consensus around rupture, while ancient Egyptian histories, even if they recognize the advent of a new period within Egyptian history, are more likely to emphasize continuity and then to proceed until Rome, Christianity, Byzantium, or Islam provide another turning point.[124] All these dividing lines have been open to productive debate, but they are nevertheless broadly emblematic of differences in the two fields and in the underlying historical evidence on which each has constructed its (meta)narratives. As our joint essays have argued, the creation of a linear, irreversible, totalizing temporality in the Seleucid Era dating system and in various historical works marked a more decisive break than did the disjointed, overlapping constellations of documentary, cultic, and historiographic practices through which immigrant and indigenous elites negotiated a new Ptolemaic dynastic temporality. In marking their respective new ages, the Seleucid state was the more revolutionary, while the Ptolemaic state was the more traditional. And while Seleucids and Ptolemies both made familial and/or paradigmatic claims on the legacy of Alexander, the role of the great conqueror in constructing the temporalities of each state was more variable than modern periodizations often suggest. Here we have multiple disjunctures in the marking of eras: the disjunctures between modern historical periodizations and ancient ones and between the different ways that ancient subjects, including indigenous elites in the Seleucid and Ptolemaic kingdoms, perceived and constructed ruptures in time.

That some ancients did so at all challenges a recurrent insistence on modernist exceptionalism and casts some light on the politics of temporality. One of the most influential statements on the emergence of modernity not only as a new era, but also as a new sense of time – both *Neuzeit* and *neue Zeit* – comes in Reinhard Koselleck's profound meditation on Albrecht Altdorfer's *Alexanderschlacht*, the masterful painting of the battle of Issus commissioned in 1528 by William IV of Bavaria. For Koselleck, the painting represents the epochal moment of Hellenism but also heralds the beginning of the Early Modern period (*Frühe Neuzeit*) with its nascent humanism. Between Altdorfer's anachronistic representations of Persians as Turks and Alexander as Maximilian, and Friedrich Schlegel's observations on the painting 300 years later, Koselleck traces the transformation from an early modern sensibility that could collapse all times into one

---

[124] Though it is true that more recent general histories of ancient Egypt (Shaw [2003]; and Van de Mieroop [2011]) tend to go to the Roman period, there are other approaches. Grimal (1992), e.g., takes his history up to Alexander.

plane, to a temporalized, multiplanar modern historicity in which the divide between these times and those was felt much more acutely. At the end of the essay, however, Koselleck gestures to the complexities of what E. Bloch called 'nonsynchronism' or 'noncontemporaneity' (*Ungleichzeitigkeit*)[125] by observing that the *Alexanderschlacht*, in a *revanchement* of the premodern, was seized by Napoleon, who styled himself as a new Alexander and married the daughter of the last Holy Roman Emperor. At the dawn of classical modernity, not everyone was always living in the same time. For some the future was in the past, just as for Bloch, writing in 1932, the 'fairy tale of the good old days' was a powerful attraction for those in Germany who felt out of step with the present. This is also the politically charged temporality of the 'again' in the slogan 'Make America Great Again.' Temporalization and especially the construction of temporal difference were and are double-edged swords and fields for political maneuver.

Such constructions of temporal difference are, of course, not the exclusive province of modernity.[126] In the aftermath of Alexander, there were not only the varied material, cultural, and political conditions of continuity and discontinuity that the textbook periodizations suggest, but also the varied and contested conditions of temporality, objectified and subjective, that we have explored in this joint contribution. In both the Seleucid and the Ptolemaic cases, indigenous elites played significant roles in the politics of time, both in carrying forward received legacies and in facilitating and resisting dynastic efforts to renovate or recalibrate official temporalities in the service of state power. These roles ranged from constructing histories of other times to resisting official temporalities through prophecies of futures past. The snapshots of evidence we have considered suggest that even if the *Neuzeit* of Hellenism[127] was heterogeneous and filled with contradictions and non-synchronisms, a new temporal landscape of political maneuver and retreat had developed, in which new eras emerged and were contested.

---

[125] Bloch (1977) [originally published 1935 in *Erbschaft dieser Zeit*].
[126] Davis (2008) esp. chapter 4.
[127] For numerous historians of the Hellenistic period, from the nineteenth century to the present, the Hellenistic period has appeared as an analog to modernity. This goes back at least to Droysen (1877–8) 3.27–8. See, e.g., the brief discussion in Momigliano (1970) 152.

CHAPTER 6

The Visual Representation of Ptolemaic and Seleucid Kings
A Comparative Approach to Portrait Concepts
Ralf von den Hoff

1 Introduction

The portraits of the Seleucid and Ptolemaic kings have been widely studied. Yet most studies either focus on each dynasty separately[1] or are limited to single and group portraits in either sculpture, coinage, or other genres.[2] On the other hand, diachronic and comparative analyses of Hellenistic royal portraiture as a system of visual representation[3] are highly instructive on three levels. First, identifying and comparing traditions, transformations, and periodical booms of specific portrait iconographies offer a way of approaching the history of royal portraiture. Second, a comparative analysis of the portraiture helps us to identify relationships, competition, and mutual responses between empires. And third, it makes us recognize salient aspects of royal representation as well as their variation.[4]

A comparative approach to the *visual* representation of Hellenistic kings is a particularly suitable guide to royal ideologies, as royal portraits were widely disseminated and played an important role in the communication between kings, subordinates, and other recipients.[5] A detailed comparative

---

[1] Ptolemies: Kyrieleis (1975); Ashton (2001); Stanwick (2002); Queyrel (2002); (2009); for the coinage: Svoronos (1904); Mørkholm (1991) 63–70; 101–11; 183–4; Lorber (2012b); Lorber (2014a); Casagrande-Kim (2014); Lorber (2018). Seleucids: Fleischer (1991b); Fleischer (1991a); Meyer (2000); for the coinage: Mørkholm (1991) 71–6; 113–27; 177–9; Houghton et al. (2002); Houghton et al. (2008); Houghton (2012).

[2] Cf. for example: Divine attributes: Svenson (1995); further studies see below, n. 51. Diadem: Lichtenberger et al. (2012); Haake (2014). Double/jugate portraits: Platz-Horster (1997); Svenson (1995) 123–7; Martin (2012a) 398–400. *Imitatio Alexandri*: Bohm (1989); Kovacs (2015); Kovacs (2017). Statuettes: Laubscher (1985); (1988); (1991); (1992); Thomas (2002); Rabe (2010).

[3] Comparative studies: Smith (1988) 112; (1991) 206–7; Fleischer (1996); Smith (1996); Fleischer (2002); Kyrieleis (2005); Kovacs (2017); for more than portraits cf. Panagopoulou (2005–6).

[4] Fleischer (1996); cf. also Fleischer (1991a).   [5] Ma (2010); Ma (2013b).

analysis of the total of Seleucid and Ptolemaic portraiture in different media would allow us to explain in detail the communication between kings, elites, and cities within and between each empire. Yet such an investigation goes beyond the present study, as it requires a better understanding of the history, conventions, rules, and usages of each of the different portrait media, which so far is lacking.[6] The following chapter will therefore not attempt to systemize how different media worked together/influenced each other and how visual communication by means of portraiture worked in practice. Instead, I will address Greek male portrait concepts rather than individual portraits, media, or communication practices. I also have to refrain from explaining indigenous portrait concepts particularly in Egypt, which do not touch the question of Ptolemaic–Seleucid relations and are a topic of their own.

Indeed, what I shall call a 'portrait concept' helps to focus a comparative analysis of royal representation in portraiture. There is no need to mention that portraits were artificial and purposeful media of representation.[7] The physical likeness of a portrait to the sitter did not play a significant role, although it was a possible choice. We have departed radically from the idea that a portrait gives us a photographic reproduction of the appearance of a person. Thus, the portrait of Ptolemy I shown in fig. 6.1 does not represent the king's real physical appearance let alone sickness.[8] Rather, it refers to the imagination of the king's 'public body', associated as this was to more general royal ideology. Hence also the individuality of the first Ptolemaic and Seleucid portraits (fig. 6.1 and 6.2) was an ideological factor.[9] The term 'portrait concept' stands for the different components of a visual design tying together portraits of a single king, a royal family, or more than one dynasty over a period of time, be this in the round, on coinage or in another visual media.[10] 'Portrait concept' describes a typical combination of qualities and notions commonly represented in these portraits. It includes the typological, iconographical, physiognomic, and mimetic traditions and conventions, with particular emphasis on the citation of other portraits, their relationships to, and differences from, other contemporary portraiture. Individuality can be part of a portrait concept, but equally we find allusions to the divinity of a king, his physical presence, formulae of energy, and so on.[11] The following

---

[6] Smith (1988) 9–31; Müller (2009); Griesbach (2014); cf. also Sheedy (2007).
[7] Hölscher (1971); Fittschen (1988) 2–5; Smith (1988) 1; Stewart (1993); Dillon (2006); von den Hoff and Schultz (2007) 1–9; Jaeggi (2008); Keesling (2017); cf. now Vorster (2017); Ma (2017).
[8] Cf. only Coe (1987). [9] Cf. Smith (1988) 73–4; 90; 111–12.
[10] The term has been used, for example, by Bartman (2007) 311.
[11] Cf. Fleischer (1991a); Fleischer (1996) 39.

discussion thus does not aim at describing particular political messages related to individual kings, to certain coin issues or at explaining portraits historically. Rather, it sketches the *visual* notions and features separating and entangling the portraiture of the Seleucid and Ptolemaic dynasties as records of ideology and concepts of kingship.[12]

2.1 Portrait Concepts among the First Ptolemaic and Seleucid Kings

The first portraits of Seleucid and Ptolemaic kings emerged in the late fourth and early third centuries BC. In Egypt, the bust of Ptolemy I (366/305–293/2 BC) appeared on silver coins already during his lifetime (Fig. 6.1).[13] The first similar portraits preserved in the round were possibly produced slightly later.[14] In the Seleucid empire, we are less sure about the first coin portraits of Seleucus I (358/305–281 BC).

Possibly already around 300 BC, Seleucus I (or Alexander the Great?) appeared on silver issues from Susa with a helmet and bull's horn.[15] His definite appearance on coins started posthumously after 281 BC.[16] As far as images in the round are concerned, a Roman bronze copy of a portrait of Seleucus I was found in Herculaneum (Fig. 6.2).[17] A now lost inscription attests a statue of the "king" Seleucus I made by Lysippos, one of Alexander's favored artists, having been transferred to Rome.[18] We cannot be certain whether the bronze head is a copy of this statue. Judging from the diadem, the original portrait was produced after 306/5 BC. The stylistic similarities to works of Lysippos are striking, but his period of activity as

---

[12] The questions of the identification of portraits are not touched upon here.
[13] Kyrieleis (1975) 4–6 pl. 1b; Smith (1988) 13; 74; 90 pl. 75, 1–2; Mørkholm (1991) 65–7; 69 nos. 96–8, 100–1, 122; Lorber (2011); Lorber (2012b) 211–14; Lorber (2014a) 114–17; Lorber (2018) 55–6 fig. 1.7; 270–2 nos. 91–105 pl. 7–8; for the chronology Lorber (2005); Lorber (2012a); Lorber (2014a); Lorber (2018) 28–9.
[14] See the marble head in Copenhagen, Ny Carlsberg Glyptotek Inv. 2300: Kyrieleis (1975) 11–12; 165–6 A3 pl. 4–5; Smith (1988) 164 no. 47 pl. 34, 4–6, and the marble face fragment in Paris, Musée du Louvre Inv. Ma 849: Kyrieleis (1975) 165 A1 pl. 2; Smith (1988) 164 no. 46 pl. 34, 1–3.
[15] Smith (1988) 45; 60 pl. 74, 4; Fleischer (1991b) 5–7 pl. 57b; Mørkholm (1991) 72–3 nos. 139–40; Stewart (1993) 314–17 figs. 114; 116; Houghton et al. (2002) 6; 71–3 nos. 173–6; 76–8 nos. 195–9; Kovacs (2017) 272–3.
[16] Smith (1988) 74 pl. 76, 1–2; Mørkholm (1991) 116; 122; 128 nos. 354A–B; 388–9; 408; Fleischer (1991b) 6–10 pl. 1, c–f; 2a; Houghton et al. (2002) 114; 120–2 nos. 309–13; 123 no. 318; Houghton (2012).
[17] Naples, Museo Archaeologico Nazionale Inv. 5590: Lauter (1987) 67–70 pl. 7–8; Smith (1988) 73–4; 159 no. 21 pl. 16; Fleischer (1991b) 15–17 pl. 7–10; von den Hoff (2007) 55 fig. 41; La Rocca (2011) 154 no. 2.18 (M. R. Perrella); Kansteiner et al. (2014) 353.
[18] *IG* XIV 1206; Moreno (1974) 123–31 fig. 41; Lauter (1987) 67–70; Kansteiner et al. (2014) 352–3 no. 2208.

Fig. 6.1 Ptolemy I. Tetradrachm from Alexandria. Berlin, Staatliche Museen/ SMPK– Münzkabinett. Photograph: Staatliche Museen Berlin/SMPK

Fig. 6.2 Seleucus I. Roman copy after original from the school of Lysippus, 305/0 BC. Naples, Museo Archaeologico Nazionale Inv. 5590. Photograph: Deutsches Archäologisches Institut, D-DAI-ROM-83.1861

a sculptor started in 370 BC and thus can hardly be stretched down to 306 BC. The portrait might be an early work of one of his disciples.[19]

Turning to the portrait concepts of Ptolemy I and Seleucus I, the similarities are striking. On coinage, in both cases royal portraits replace the gods and heroes that had so far regularly been found on coins of Alexander's lifetime, and on posthumous coins of Alexander as well.[20] The diadem as the new royal attribute explicitly underlines each king's status as *basileus*.[21] Furthermore, while individual but typologically bound portraits existed already in the fifth century BC, both kings look rather lifelike due to their prominent chins and expressive facial features, which follow a new, early Hellenistic portrait style.[22] But even though they were mature men when the portraits were designed, their clean-shaven chins followed a Greek concept of youth, which had already been applied to Alexander portraits. After Alexander, this iconography was adopted in civic portraiture. In around 300 BC, it had already lost its significance as a reference to age, while the shaven chin became a common male fashion to which the elderly kings might have signed up.[23] It is worth pointing out that, at least on the coins, the advanced age of Ptolemy and Seleucus is alluded to by deep lines in the face and a receding hairline. Moreover, the hair is clearly not very long. The typical signs of Alexander's portraits – a youthful *physis* and long hair – are notably missing, as is the *anastole*, the fountain-like hair raising above the forehead. The bronze portrait of Seleucus shows an abundance of hair, but without referring typologically to Alexander's coiffure.[24] This is even more notable, as direct imitations of Alexander's portraits and *anastole* can be observed in portraits during the late fourth and early third century, but not in royal portraiture.[25]

On Ptolemaic coins (fig. 6.1), the aegis of Zeus introduced divine attributes to the portrait of a living king.[26] This conceptual phenomenon can also be

---

[19] Plin. *HN* 34, 86, testifies another portrait of Seleucus I made by Aristodemos, a disciple of Lysippos, cf. Kansteiner et al. (2014) 593–4 no. 2467. A further portrait of Seleucus, made by Bryaxis (Plin. *HN* 34, 73), more likely was sculpted before 306, due to the artist's lifetime.
[20] Kroll (2007); Alexander on posthumous coins: Lorber (2018) 46–56.   [21] See above, n. 2.
[22] Cf. already Smith (1988) 73–4; 90; 111–12; Fleischer (1991b) 120; Fleischer (1996) 30–1 ("Zeitgesicht"); Fleischer (2002) 61; von den Hoff (2007) 55; von den Hoff (2009) 51.
[23] Beardlessness: Smith (1988) 46; von den Hoff (2007) 55; cf. also Schmidt (2007).
[24] "Allusions to Alexander's type," as Casagrande-Kim (2014) 62 argues, are not evident. Alexander's *anastole*: Hölscher (1971) 25–31; Smith (1988) 47–8; Stewart (1993) 42–3; 76–8; 169–71; Reinsberg (2004) 324–6; Kovacs (2017) 61–145.
[25] Stewart (1993) 165–6; von den Hoff (1994) 51 with n. 99; von den Hoff (2013b) 85–6.
[26] Svenson (1995) 5–12; Lorber (2011); Kyrieleis (2015) 21–2; Lorber (2018) 56–7, but cf. her skepticism concerning the reference to Zeus: Lorber (2018) 238 n. 438.

observed in some coins of Seleucus with a bull's horn, but such divine attributes are not necessarily related to actual cult practice.[27] Hence, the images of the *diadochs* Ptolemy I and Seleucus I appear as energetic and fashionable. Their naturalistic physiognomies made them 'real-life kings,'[28] which somehow contrasted the rare iconographic signs of superhuman qualities. In portraiture, the first *diadochs* were mature, real-life generals and kings. At least in their visual representation, neither an *imitatio Alexandri* – rather a distance to his images – nor any clear divine or cult status – in contrast to metaphorically ascribed godlike qualities – were on the agenda.

2.2 The Third Century after Ptolemy I and Seleucus I

After the first generation of kings, the Ptolemaic and Seleucid portraiture moved in different directions. In Egypt, the portrait of Ptolemy I remained unchanged during the next centuries. Like a 'frozen type' the bust of the founder of the dynasty was regularly struck on coins and reproduced in the round, changing only slightly in detail.[29] As Lorber has demonstrated, portraits of reigning kings only rarely appeared on official coinage, as, for example, on special issues and in newly acquired territories.[30] She also argues that some of the portraits of Ptolemy I adopted features of the reigning kings and vice versa.[31] Such physiognomic assimilations (*Bildnisangleichung*), incidentally, can also be found in the portraiture of Hellenistic philosophers, relating them to specific intellectual schools.[32] Later, such assimilation of portraits became a common visual strategy of legitimation in ruler images.[33] The merging of Ptolemy Soter's portrait with that of later Ptolemies can thus be seen as an attempt to emphasize the

---

[27] The semantic of divine attributes in Hellenistic royal portraiture is still controversial; see below, n. 51. Portraits of kings with bull's horn: Smith (1988) 40–1; Fleischer (1991b) 6–8; 73–4; Svenson (1995) 33–5; 40–6; 118–21; Bergmann (1998) 24 n. 80; Thomas (2002) 16–21; Houghton et al. (2002) 114; Iossif and Lorber (2009) 132; Kovacs (2017) 230–1; 272–6; see above, n. 15.

[28] von den Hoff (2007) 54–5.

[29] Kyrieleis (1975) 4; Mørkholm (1991) 65; 101–2; 106; 108; 101 nos. 284; 291–3; 314–15; 328; Fleischer (2002) 65–7; von Reden (2007) 56; Picard (2012); Lorber (2012b); Lorber (2014a) 118; Lorber (2016a) 81 ("frozen type"); von den Hoff and Azoulay (2017) 191–2 figs. 58–60; Lorber (2018) 311–49 nos. 276–306; 370; 373–4; 377; 379; 382; 413–82 pl. 20–37; 393–413 nos. 732; 749–50; 755–58; 803 pl. 56–62; 435–52 nos. 899–901; 903; 911–14 pl. 70–71 and further examples;. For portraits in the round, cf. above n. 14 with further later examples in Kyrieleis (1975).

[30] Lorber (2014a) 120–32; Lorber (2016a) 79; Lorber (2018) 120; 171.

[31] Thus in terms of *Bildnisangleichung* already Fleischer (2002) 65–7 figs. 12–21; Lorber (2016a); cf. Sheedy (2007) 15.

[32] Smith (1991) 33–7; von den Hoff (1994) 59–62; 78–84; 122–8; Zanker (1995) 113–20.

[33] Maßner (1982); Maschek (2004); Fittschen (2010) 236–41; La Rocca (2011) 247–51 (K. Fittschen).

dynastic continuity between the present king and Ptolemy I as founder of the dynasty.[34] His portrait developed into a blueprint of later Ptolemaic portraiture, assuring stability, reliability and consistency of the dynasty. The fact that all kings after Ptolemy I carried the name Ptolemy points to the same dynastic reconnection.

On the Seleucid side, we find a different picture. The portraits of Seleucus I on coins ended during the reign of his son Antiochus I Soter (324/281–261 BC). Henceforth the Seleucids struck coins with the portrait of the actual king. Apparently, the image of the ruling king was of higher importance than tradition and continuity. Thus, visual legitimation was regularly renewed, and iconographic innovation was the rule. Already the portrait of Antiochus I (324/281–261 BC) presented a new concept (fig. 6.3)[35]: typical for his image was a regular, though sometimes curly hairline above the forehead. This was in contrast to his father's portrait and even increased the antithesis to the Alexander image. Some individual characteristics and features of old age remained visible, but we observe an altogether less aged appearance that also lacked the signs of energy.[36] In contrast to the *diadochs*, this was a concept of a quiet king, distant from the real world. The same concept can be detected in the portraits of Antiochus II (286/261–246 BC), Antiochus I's son, and Seleucus II Kallinikos Pogon (265/246–226 BC), the son of Antiochus II. Witness the regular hairline above the forehead and the calm face.[37] Father, son, and grandson were represented in a similar manner, underlining dynastic continuity within

---

[34] In local Egyptian sanctuaries, statues of the Ptolemies in Egyptian dress and iconography, though sometimes with Greek hair above the forehead, were set up regularly; see Ashton (2001); Stanwick (2002), and above n. 1.

[35] Smith (1988) 74 pl. 76, 3; Mørkholm (1991) 113; 116; 118–19; 122–3 nos. 330; 360; 371–3; 390; Fleischer (1991b) 19–22; 120–1 pl. 11c–f; 12a–b; Houghton et al. (2002) 115; 125 nos. 324–8; 126 no. 331; 127 no. 335; 135 no. 360; 139–40 nos. 378–80; 147 nos. 409–10; 151–4 nos. 426–39. For coins with similar portraits of Antiochus I issued after his death: Mørkholm (1991) 113–14; 123 nos. 335–6; 344; 394; Houghton et al. (2002) 173–4 nos. 481–2; 175 nos. 484–5; 192 no. 540 and further examples.

[36] Fleischer (1991b) 121 and Smith (1988) 112 already observed the younger, less expressive portrait concept of Antiochus I, even though some more expressive portraits of him were still issued. Despite this, Smith (1996) 203 called the Seleucid portrait concept energetic and dynamic, which Fleischer (1991b) 121, n. 830 questioned for the period before 200 BC.

[37] Smith (1988) pl. 76, 4; Mørkholm (1991) 113, 123 nos. 331–3; 395; Fleischer (1991b) 23–8; 121 ("energy no longer stressed") pl. 12 e–f; 14 a–b. Antiochus II: Houghton et al. (2002) 169; 174 no. 483; 176 nos. 487–8; 185 no. 519; 199 nos. 561–4; 200 nos. 570–1. Seleucus II: Houghton at al. (2002) 232–3; 237–42 nos. 643–56; 247 nos. 671–2; 253 nos. 687–90; 274–5 nos. 762–4 and further examples. Cf. the portraits of Seleucus III (243/226–223 BC) with more dynamic hair above the forehead: Mørkholm (1991) 114 nos. 337–8; Fleischer (1991b) 29–30 pl. 16 a–b; Houghton et al. (2002) 328; 331–4 nos. 315–21 and further examples.

Fig. 6.3 Antiochus I. Tetradrachm from Seleukeia. Wien, Kunsthistorisches Museum: Münzkabinett Inv. GR 20304. Photograph: © Kunsthistorisches Museum Wien

a period of about sixty years, yet without iconographic reference to the first king.[38] Divine attributes rarely appear.[39]

There was subtle variation in the Ptolemaic empire, too. On coinage, Ptolemy II Philadelphos (309/283–246 BC) was rarely depicted on his own as exceptionally on coins from southern Asia Minor during Philadelphos's lifetime (fig. 6.4). His portrait adorned mainly posthumous coinage.[40] In contrast to Ptolemy I, moreover, his hair arrangement over the forehead was more regular, the signs of energy were reduced, and his appearance less aged.[41] In this, it resembled the portraits of the Seleucid kings after Seleucus I (fig. 6.3) and suggests a change in both empires after around 280. The interest was less in age, energy and individuality, but rather in the serenity of a royal portrait not subject to age.[42] Yet Ptolemaic portraiture also took its own way. This can best be observed on the gold *mnaieia* and *pentekontadrachma* issued by Ptolemy II, depicting him and his wife Arsinoe II (309–268 BC?) as *adelphoi* (fig. 6.5).[43] The portraits of their

---

[38] Fleischer (1991b) 121.
[39] Mørkholm (1991) 124 no. 397; Fleischer (1991b) 21–2 pl. 12c–d; Svenson (1995) 161 no. 178–9 pl. 27; Thomas (2002) 17 pl. 7, 4; Houghton et al. (2002) 177 no. 492; 293–4; 393 no. 850; 308 nos. 871–2; 309–14 nos. 874–86; cf. also Svenson (1995) 58–61.
[40] Kyrieleis (1975) 17–24 pl. 8–15; 16, 4–5; Queyrel (2009); Lorber (2012b) 214–16; Lorber (2014a) 120–1; Lorber (2018) 333–5 nos. 400–6 pl. 31–2; for reidentifications of some of his portraits, originally identified as Ptolemy III, cf. Davesne (1999); (2005). Earlier, particularly the coinage of Tarsos (Fig. 6.4) during his lifetime had been taken to represent Ptolemy III: Kyrieleis (1975) 26–7 pl. 16, 4–5; Mørkholm (1991) 108 no. 312; see now Lorber (2014a) 120 figs. 7–8; Lorber (2018) 120–1 fig. 2.3. For the jugate portraits together with Arsinoe II on gold *mnaieia* see below.
[41] Fleischer (1991b) 121 ("Beruhigung und Erstarrung").
[42] Nevertheless, Smith (1996) 203–4, pointed to differences; see above n. 36.
[43] *Mnaieia*: Kyrieleis (1975) 17–8; 153–4 pl. 8, 1–3; Smith (1988) 91 pl. 75, 3–4; Mørkholm (1991) 103–4 nos. 297–8; von Reden (2007) 50–2; Cavagna (2008); Müller (2009) 353–64; Fulińska (2010) 75–6; Weber (2011) 84–8; Lorber (2012b) 215; Olivier and Lorber (2013); Lorber (2014a) 140–2; Lorber

Fig. 6.4 Ptolemy II. Tetradrachm from Tarsus. New York, American Numismatic Society Inv. 1944.100.77202. Photograph: © American Numismatic Society

Fig. 6.5 Ptolemy II and Arsinoe II. Gold Oktodrachm (*mnaieion*) from Alexandria. Berlin, Staatliche Museen/SMPK– Münzkabinett. Photograph: Münzkabinett, Staatliche Museen Berlin/SMPK

parents (*theoi*) fill the reverse. The invention of the double-portrait schema, the jugate images, followed Greek models of depicting siblings in this way, demonstrating *homonoia* as in the case of the Dioscuri.[44] Like the double cornucopia (*dikeras*), the jugate image expressed the Ptolemaic idea of unity between the sibling rulers and their parents.[45] The idea of royal couples was still unknown to the Seleucid royal iconography of this period. Within the Ptolemaic concept of unity and dynastic continuity, expressed in the jugate portraits and the obverse-reverse combination of images, it is not astonishing that we find physiognomic resemblances

(2018) 106–10; 116 fig. 2.1; 317–21 nos. 307–19 pl. 22–3; cf. Casagrande-Kim (2014) 63–4, who understands the portraits as a "scene of apotheosis," without any iconographic evidence. Cf. now Caneva (2016) 163–73 (thanks to T. Wild for this information).

[44] Jugate portraits: above n. 2 and n. 43, below n. 92; cf. Lorber (2018) 122–4.

[45] Kyrieleis (1975) 153–4. *Dikeras*: von Reden (2007) 53; Müller (2009) 373–9; Lorber (2012b) 215; Lorber (2015b); Lorber (2018) 125–7.

between the queens Berenice and Arsinoe on both sides of the coins. In contrast, except for the large eyes, similarities between the two male Ptolemies are not on display: both represent different ideals, expressed by both their physiognomy and hairstyle.[46] The serene Ptolemy II supplements the energetic image of his father but does not replicate the same ideal. Another feature separates Ptolemy II not only from his father but also from the comparably calm and quiet image of the new Seleucid kings: Ptolemy II has a fuller and more rounded face. This has been related convincingly to the concept of *tryphe*, of wealth and abundance, of which the cornucopia on Ptolemaic coins is also an expression.[47] In Egypt, the king's new physiognomy as a symbol of abundance and wealth thus was complemented by the notions of dynastic continuity, harmony, unity, and prosperity of the royal couple.

In the period after Ptolemy II, dynastic continuity became even more strongly articulated. *Tryphe* became a feature also of the portraits of Ptolemy III Euergetes (284/246–222 BC).[48] This shows once again that the stout physiognomy was neither a naturalistic feature nor an individual sign of individual kings, but a programmatic ideal. Again, the portrait of Ptolemy III is calm and bare of energy and mimic motion. However, the unnaturally big eyes – particularly evident on the posthumous *mnaieia* – relate this portrait to Ptolemy II, suggesting that a new concept dominated Ptolemaic portraiture from the time of the second Ptolemy: the serene and wealthy king lacking mimic tension; it appears like an icon bearing signs of remoteness from the real world.[49] If Kyrieleis's identifications, together with the recent reidentifications of the portraits of Ptolemy II and III in the round, hold true,[50] the same features can be identified in statues and statuettes. Again, coin portraits and portraits in the round would have taken the same path. On gold coins showing Ptolemy III, the abundance of divine attributes, including, for the first time in royal portraiture, the

---

[46] It has been argued that the "coins highlight ... the physical similarities between the various members of the family," Thonemann (2015) 151; cf. also Casagrande-Kim (2014) 64, which is not the case in this comprehensive sense, cf. Müller (2009) 359–60 with n. 1296.

[47] *Tryphe* as an element of portrait concepts: Kyrieleis (1975) 163–4; Kyrieleis (2005) 241–2; cf. Heinen (1983); Müller (2009) 159–72; Lorber (2018) 106.

[48] Kyrieleis (1975) 28–30; 156 pl. 17, 1–4; Smith (1988) 91 pl. 75, 9; Mørkholm (1991) 108–9 no. 316; Svenson (1995) 71–3; 164–5; Smith (1996) 203 fig. 6.2; Johnson (1999); Queyrel (2002) 6–13; Lorber (2011); Olivier and Lorber (2013); Lorber (2014a) 147–8; Lorber (2018) 152–82 fig. 6.3.1–3; 174–5 (*tryphe*); 399–413 nos. 751–4; 759–62; 766–76; 779–86; 792–802 pl. 57–62; posthumous gold issues: Lorber (2018) 206–7; 238–41; 431–42 nos. 887–90; 904–5; 915–6 pl. 69–71; see above n. 40, below n. 50 and n. 52.

[49] Smith (1988) 91; 112; Kyrieleis (2005) 238.

[50] Kyrieleis (1975) 20–4; 31–42; Queyrel (2002); (2009); La Rocca (2011) 173 no. 2.33 (F. Smith); for reidentifications and problems of identification see above n. 40 and already Smith (1988) 150.

radiate crown, further enhanced the notion of remoteness and combined divine qualities of Helios, Poseidon and Zeus.[51] Statuettes could add further divine or heroic attributes and forms of action, as had already been the case in statuettes of Ptolemy II.[52]

Comparing Ptolemaic and Seleucid royal portraits of the middle of the third century BC, it appears that serenity, wealth and luxury as well as divine qualities and distance were typical features of the Ptolemaic portrait. The Seleucids, in contrast, appear less distanced, do not emphasize wealth and prosperity in similar ways, and are rarely related visually to the realm of the gods. Yet the calm Ptolemaic faces are not in complete contrast to contemporary quiet Seleucids and suggest serenity and distance from the real world as common ideals in this period.[53]

The Ptolemaic ideal of *tryphe* did not remain limited to Ptolemaic portrait representation. It also spread to other portraits in different regions of the Mediterranean. In Asia Minor, around 270/60, the Pergamene ruler Philetairos adopted the *tryphe* ideal for his portraits after (and due to?) his separation from the Seleucid empire – even though complemented by features of dynamic energy.[54] On Cyprus, private portraits in the round also followed this ideal during the third and second centuries BC.[55] Around 250 BC, the honorific statue of the comic poet Poseidippos from Kassandreia adopted the ideal of a corpulent face.[56] Hence, the demonstration of wealth and luxury was an important factor in early Hellenistic portraiture and not confined to royal representation.

Another novelty can be observed in the Ptolemaic visual representation from the third century onwards. For the first time in the history of Greek portraiture, we find portraits of the same person on coins and in the round

---

[51] The semantic of divine attributes as visual signs of godlike qualities can be taken for granted, even though they were not proofs of divine status and cult, cf. only Smith (1988) 38–45 ("godlike power," "evocation of superhuman powers"); Svenson (1995) 182 ("Visualisierung von göttlichen Kräften"); 185 ("keineswegs nur eindeutig"; "allegorisch"; "vielschichtig"); Bergmann (1998) 26–7; 29–32; 60 (metaphoric signs of qualities); Johnson (1999) (association to gods, not assimilation); Thomas (2002) 61 ("Vergöttlichungen"); Thomas (2004); Kyrieleis (2005) 238–9 (pantheistic conception); Lorber (2018) 172–6. For the radiate crown see below n. 77.

[52] Statuettes of Ptolemy II/III: Kyrieleis (1975) 166 B1–B2 pl. 8, 5–6; 9; 10, 1–3; Laubscher (1988); Laubscher (1991); Smith (1996) 203–4 fig. 6.1; Cheshire (2009); Lorber (2014b) 210–12; cf. also Thomas (2002) with further bibliography.

[53] Fleischer (1996) 31.

[54] Smith (1988) 74–5; Brown (1995) 36–7; for the coin portraits cf. Westermark (1961).

[55] Connelly (1988); Karageorghis (2000) 246–53.

[56] Fittschen (1992); Zanker (1995) 134–9; La Rocca (2011) 192 no. 2.47 (R. Di Cesare).

being not only similar in their facial appearance and physiognomy, but in distinct motifs of the coiffure as well.[57] In this sense, a portrait head in the Louvre, possibly Ptolemy II, is strikingly similar to coin portraits of the same king from Tarsos (fig. 6.4). Witness the characteristic pincer-like arrangement of two curls of hair above the right temple.[58] This could happen only if the artists had the same model before their eyes. The fact that the portraits of Ptolemy I on coinage and in reliefs also resemble each other even in small details of the hair dress suggests an intentional dissemination of a portrait model.[59] Later, in the early second century, two portraits of Ptolemy VI Philopator (186/180–164 BC), one from Aegina and the other from Alexandria, are evidence of an almost copied model of a royal portrait in the round, showing identical arrangements of the hair curls above the forehead.[60] The hair scheme of another portrait head of the same king in Alexandria (fig. 6.11) again is very similar, though not identical.[61] It seems that the portraits of the kings of Egypt were the first to be spread by models. We do not know whether the royal court promoted their spread. But it is obvious that at least some customers cared for detailed resemblance of their royal portraits with official images of the Ptolemaic kings and wanted such portraits to be made visible.[62] Otherwise one cannot explain the identical features of coin portraits and portraits in the round, and between sculpted portraits respectively. It must remain an open question whether coin portraits were the guiding medium of this dissemination.[63]

2.3 Seleucid and Ptolemaic Portrait Concepts from the Late Third Century BC Onwards

Let us return to the Seleucid empire. Here the next step was the portraiture of Antiochus III (242/223–187 BC), son of Seleucus II, whose portrait

---

[57] Queyrel (2009); von den Hoff and Azoulay (2017) 171–4; cf. Smith (1988) 27–31; Sheedy (2007) 13.

[58] Queyrel (2009); von den Hoff and Azoulay (2017) 142–3 fig. 46; for the reidentification of these coin portraits see above n. 40.

[59] Smith (1988) 28; Fleischer (2002) 65–7; von den Hoff and Azoulay (2017) 191–3. For the coinage with typologically identical portraits of Ptolemy I in the third and second century BC cf. also above n. 29.

[60] Kyrieleis (1975) 59–60; 174 nos. F 1–2 pl. 47–8; 49, 1; Stanwick (2002) 57; 71; 107–8 nos. B 6; B 7 figs. 52–5; already discussed by Smith (1988) 93; 170 nos. 71–2 pl. 46, 2–4; Smith (1996) 205–7; cf. Smith (1991) 208–9 fig. 238; Palagia (2013) 157–8 fig. 9.10; von den Hoff and Azoulay (2017) 173–4 figs. 48–9; Kovacs (2017) 178–9.

[61] Alexandria, Musée Musée Gréco-Romain Inv. 24092 (Fig. 6.11): Kyrieleis (1975) 174 no. F 3 pl. 49, 2; 50–1; Smith (1988) 166 no. 55 pl. 38, 1–2; Smith (1991) 208 fig. 237; Smith (1996) 205–6 fig. 6.3.

[62] Smith (1996) 208; cf. von den Hoff and Azoulay (2017) 173–4.   [63] Sheedy (2007) 13–5.

concept changed within his own reign. It started, like Seleucus II's portraits, immediately after 223 (fig. 6.6).[64] In the last decade of the third century, however, that image changed.[65] This is most obvious on coins, but it is not limited to the numismatic evidence alone. We have also a Roman marble copy, now in Paris, of the king's portrait created about 205/200 BC (fig. 6.7).[66]

The thick *strophion* around the head is not the conventional royal diadem, but a Greek sign of receiving a cult or of some other heroic or priestly function.[67] As on the coins, Antiochus's appearance in the round is aged, even ascetic. The gaunt cheeks and the angular forehead add to the impression of this portrait being deliberately naturalistic and authentic. This is in striking contrast to the timeless serenity of the earlier Ptolemies and to his own two predecessors. Yet the former idea of the energetic *diadoch* did not come back: The portrait bears no signs of energy, even though it owns a slight mimic tension due to the contracted brows. The turn of the head is calm, and the mouth is closed. The mimic concentration as well as the designation of age is still far from contemporary, much more radically naturalistic portraits such as the aged and tense image of the stoic philosopher Chrysippos.[68] But it resembles civic portraits, as the one of the comic poet Menandros, set up around 290 in Athens.[69] In the Seleucid empire after around 210/200, therefore, a new royal image appeared: instead of the calm, quiet kings of the mid third century, the concept of an individually aged, experienced, and almost civic king circulated.[70]

Seleucus IV (281/187–175 BC), son of Antiochus III, continued the portrait concept of his father; his name *philopator* additionally emphasized the close

---

[64] Smith (1988) pl. 76, 7; Mørkholm (1991) 114–15; 118; 126 nos. 340; 343; 348; 363–4; 406; Fleischer (1991b) 31–3 ("Jugendlicher Typ 1") pl. 16 c–e; Houghton et al. (2002) 357–60 type AI and AII; 366; 390 nos. 1025–6; 393–4 nos. 1035–37; 395–6 nos. 1041–2 and further examples. Cf. also the coins with similar posthumous portraits of Seleucus III (?): Mørkholm (1991) 125–6 nos. 400–1.

[65] Smith (1988) 81–2 pl. 76, 8–9; Mørkholm (1991) 114–16 nos. 339; 345–6; 357–8; Fleischer (1991b) 33–4 ("Asketischer Typ 2") pl. 17a–d; Houghton et al. (2002) 357–60 type D and E; 366; 384 nos. 1007–9; 420 nos. 1106–7 and further examples.

[66] Paris, Musée du Louvre Inv. Ma 1204: Smith (1988) 81–2; 161 no. 30 pl. 24, 1–3; Fleischer (1991b) 99–102, 141–2 pl. 56 (not Antiochus III); von den Hoff (1994) 107 with n. 198; La Rocca (2011) 142 no. 2.6. (M. R. Perrella).

[67] *Strophion*: Krug (1968); Martin (2012b); von den Hoff (2017) 285; cf. Plut. *Arist.* 5, 7; *Arat.* 53, 6.

[68] Chrysippos: von den Hoff (1994) 96–111; Zanker (1995) 98–102; La Rocca (2011) 158 no. 2.21 (S. Millozzi).

[69] Menandros: Fittschen (1991); Zanker (1995) 80–5; Schmidt (2007); cf. now Palagia (2005).

[70] Cf. Fleischer (1991b) 122.

Fig. 6.6 Antiochus III (early portrait concept). Tetradrachm from Asia Minor. Wien, Kunsthistorisches Museum: Münzkabinett Inv. GR 20379. Photograph: © Kunsthistorisches Museum Wien

Fig. 6.7 Antiochus III (later portrait concept). Roman copy after original around 205/0 BC. Paris, Musée du Louvre Inv. Ma 1209. Photograph: © Réunion des Musées Nationaux RMN-Grand Palais (Musée du Louvre) / Les frères Chuzeville

relationship.⁷¹ The father's portrait was also guiding for his successor Antiochus IV (215/175–164 BC), Seleucus's younger brother.⁷² Antiochus IV was further depicted in an original Greek marble head now in Berlin (fig. 6.8), which belonged to a statuette, possibly a votive used in the ruler cult.⁷³ As on the coins, the calm habit of the angular face resembles Antiochus III, but the son appears to be younger; his mouth is open, demonstrating a certain active presence, without regaining Seleucus I's energy. The profile view reveals physiognomic features similar to his father, making Antiochus IV also visually a successor and son; but he looks less ascetic than Antiochus III. Furthermore, Antiochus IV's portrait has lost all signs of tension. The hair is short but now rather curly. As in Egypt a few decades earlier, a dynastic claim ruled royal portraiture from Antiochos III onwards. We can clearly relate this to the rivalry among the royal family and hence to more precarious legitimacy. Nevertheless, Antiochus's sons followed a model of less facial expression and a more juvenile appearance than their father.

Change occurred once again when Antiochus IV became *Theos Epiphanes* around 173/2 BC. On coins, the king now was rejuvenated, and the portrait's hair became fuller and curlier.⁷⁴ Above the forehead, we see a fountain-like hair motive. This hairdo appears in different versions, but without doubt, this is a reminder of Alexander's well-known *anastole*, even though it was not an exact imitation. It is visible best on coins from Antiochia after 173 BC (fig. 6.9).⁷⁵ Hence, for the first time in Seleucid portraiture, a conceptual *imitatio Alexandri* can be observed around 170 BC. This was the expression of a new concept of legitimacy, relating back to a visual Alexander code.⁷⁶ I can only

---

[71] Smith (1988) 81–2 pl. 76, 10; Fleischer (1991b) 41; 122 pl. 20a–d; Houghton et al. (2008) 4; 11–12 nos. 1306–9; 13–5 nos. 1313–14; 20–3 nos. 1326–9; 28–9 nos. 1344–5. Antiochus, son of Seleucus IV and adopted son of Antiochus IV, appeared together with his mother Laodice on coins (*mnaieia*) around 175 BC: Fleischer (1991b) 42–3 pl. 21b; Houghton et al. (2008) 35–6; 38 no. 1368. In this case – in contrast to the earlier Lagid couples on *mnaieia* (above n. 43–6) – the heads of mother and son are physiognomicaly assimilated, as Catherine Krier has observed in her Freiburg University master thesis in 2016.

[72] Mørkholm (1963); Smith (1988) 113 pl. 76, 11; Fleischer (1991b) 44–5 pl. 21c–d; 22d; Mørkholm (1991) 177 no. 629; Fleischer (2002) 61; Houghton et al. (2008) 46; 55 no. 1376; 63 no. 1385; 89 nos. 1472–4; Kovacs (2017) 496.

[73] Berlin, Antikensammlung SMPK Inv. 1975.5: Kyrieleis (1980); Smith (1988) 162 no. 36 pl. 27, 3–5; Fleischer (1991b) 52–3 pl. 24–7; Smith (1991) 224 fig. 236; von den Hoff (2013a).

[74] Mørkholm (1963) 58; Mørkholm (1991) 177 no. 630–1; Fleischer (1991b) 44–5; 123 pl. 21e–f; Houghton et al. (2008) 46; 55 no. 1377; 63–4 no. 1396–7, 1400; Fleischer (2002) 62; Iossif and Lorber (2009); Günther (2011) 106; Kovacs (2017) 496–502; cf. also Mittag (2006) 128–39.

[75] Fleischer (1991b) 49 pl. 22e; Houghton et al. (2008) 63–6 nos. 1396–7.

[76] This phenomenon has now been studied extensively by Kovacs (2017). Earlier *anastole* portraits in coinage adopting Alexander's coiffure are isolated cases: Fleischer (1991b) 21–2 pl. 12 c–d; Kovacs (2017) 483–8, see above n. 39 (Antiochus I); Mørkholm (1991) 120–1 nos. 374; 383; Dumke (2012); von den Hoff (2013b) 86–9 fig. 6.6; Kovacs (2017) 534–9 (Diodotus I); Lorber (2018) 240 nos. 904–5

Visual Representation of Ptolemaic and Seleucid Kings 179

Fig. 6.8 Antiochus IV (early portrait concept). Marble portrait bust, around 175/60 BC. Berlin, Staatliche Museen/SMPK– Antikensammlung Inv. 1975.5. Photograph: © Antikensammlung, Staatliche Museen zu Berlin/SMPK, Ingrid Geske

Fig. 6.9 Antiochus IV (later portrait concept). Tetradrachm. Photograph: Wikimedia Commons / Classical Numismatic Group, Inc. http://www.cngcoins.com

mention here in passing that at that time, and with Antiochus IV, the radiate crown, an attribute of Helios formerly used in the Ptolemaic portraiture, was introduced into Seleucid royal iconography. The star above the forehead or at the ends of the diadem appeared as an attribute of the helpfully appearing Dioscuri.[77] We see that changes in the nature of the reign, as witnessed also by the new name *Theos Epiphanes*, generated new needs for demonstrating legitimacy. It came with a new dynastic concept, the adoption of the Alexander code, a more juvenile appearance and new divine attributes, partly adapted from the Ptolemies.

Antiochus V (173/164–162 BC) had been shown as a child during the reign of Antiochus IV. But soon after the beginning of his own reign, a full-haired portrait, quite similar to the image of his father, appeared on coins in order to underline continuity of the Seleucid rule.[78]

In Egypt, there was no parallel. The contemporaries of Antiochus III, Ptolemy IV Philopator (245/222–204 BC) and Ptolemy V Epiphanes (210/204–180 BC) who, too, was a child when ascending the throne, issued coins which visually emphasized continuity with the serene, distanced, and wealthy images of their fathers. The gold coinage with Ptolemy III's divinely overloaded, radiated portrait was issued under Ptolemy IV, while the portraits of Ptolemy IV himself – some also gold *mnaieia* – adopted the *tryphe* ideal.[79] After 205, coins with the portrait of Ptolemy V were struck with the big eyes of his forefather, on *mnaieia* sometimes also with radiate crown and a spear presenting the boy as defender of Egypt.[80]

(posthumous Ptolemy III). Earlier cases include, as Martin Kovacs reminds me, portrait coins of Demetrius Poliorketes from Sikyon (291/90 BC): Newell (1927) 145 nos. 159, 314, and coins of Lysimachus, which, as Achim Lichtenberger and Dieter Salzmann suggested (even though this could be disputed), do not represent Alexander, but Lysimachus, Lichtenberger et al. (2008); cf. Kovacs (2017) 218 n. 324.

[77] Radiate crown: Mørkholm (1991) 177 no. 631; Fleischer (1991b) 45 pl. 22a–b; Svenson (1995) 19–23; 281–4 no. 275 pl. 11; Bergmann (1998) 58–66; Thomas (2002) 18; Mittag (2006) 130–6; Houghton et al. (2008) 108–10; Iossif and Lorber (2012); cf. Kyrieleis (2015) 20; Lorber (2018) 241–3; below n. 100. Stars and Dioscuri: Kyrieleis (1986); Fleischer (1991b) 46 pl. 21f; 22d; Svenson (1995) 24–6; Thomas (2002) 18; Mittag (2006) 130–6; Houghton et al. (2008) 89 nos. 1472–3; Kyrieleis (2015) 20–1; Lorber (2018) 180–2. For 'celestial' attributes in Antiochus IV's portraiture cf. also Iossif and Lorber (2009).

[78] Fleischer (1991b) 54–5; 123 pl. 28c–f; Fleischer (2002) 62–3; Houghton et al. (2008) 128; 133–9.

[79] Ptolemy III: see above n. 48. Ptolemy IV: Kyrieleis (1975) 42–51 pl. 30; Smith (1988) pl. 75, 10; Mørkholm (1991) 110 no. 321; Lorber (2012b) 218–20; Lorber (2014a) 127–8; 148–9; for the chronology cf. Lorber (2014a) 128; Kyrieleis (2015) 34 with n. 85; Lorber (2018) 243–5 fig. 4.6; 433–45 nos. 894; 902; 907; 909; 917–19; 921–5; 929 pl. 69–72.

[80] Ptolemy V: Svoronos (1904) 206 no. 1249; 208–9 nos. 1254, 1257–8, 1260; 1262–4; 211 no. 1271; 212 nos. 1274–5; 1277 pl. 41, 4–5; 41, 15–19; 41, 23–5; 42, 3; 42, 6–7; 42, 9–20 and further examples; Kyrieleis (1975) 52 pl. 40; 40, 4; Smith (1988) 92–3 pl. 75, 11; Mørkholm (1991) 109–10 nos. 319–20; 323; 324–5; 329; Kyrieleis (2005) 240; Mittag (2006) 134–5; Lorber (2012b) 220–2; Lorber (2014a)

This issue was complemented by reissues of the *theoi adelphoi* oktodrachms.[81] By contrast, looking at portrait sculpture in the round, a more dynamic and young ideal of the king was expressed in a portrait of Ptolemy IV, now in the Louvre (fig. 6.10), which was part of a cult-statue group of the king, his wife Arsinoe III, and Serapis.[82] The differing portrait concepts of the same king in different media show the importance of media differentiation when looking at royal portrait representation. It seems that some of the Ptolemaic royal portraits around 200 broke with the dynastic portrait tradition of *tryphe* and wealth, switching to a more energetic,

Fig. 6.10 Ptolemy IV. Marble portrait head, around 200 BC. Paris, Musée du Louvre Inv. Ma 3168. Photograph : © Réunion des Musées Nationaux RMN-Grand Palais (Musée du Louvre) / Hervé Lewandowski

128–30; 149–51; Kyrieleis (2015) 34. For chronology and identification cf. Lorber (2014a) 129; Kyrieleis (2015) 34 with n. 85.

[81] Svoronos (1904) 206 nos. 1247–8 pl. 41, 1–3; Mørkholm (1991) 110 nos. 327–8; Lorber (2014a) 151.
[82] Paris, Musée du Louvre Inv. Ma 3168 (Ptolemy IV) + Alexandria, Museum Inv. 3908 (Arsinoe III) + Alexandria, Museum Inv. 3912 (Serapis): Kyrieleis (1975) 46–7; 108–9; 171; 182–3 no. D 3; L 5 pl. 34–5; 95–6; 97, 1–2; Wildung and Grimm (1979) nos. 113–14; Kyrieleis (1980); Smith (1988) 92; 165 no. 51 pl. 36.

Fig. 6.11 Ptolemy VI. Marble portrait head, middle of the second century BC. Alexandria, Musée Gréco-Romain Inv. 24092. Photograph: Deutsches Archäologisches Institut, D-DAI-KAI-F-12677

youthful royal image, reminding us of comparable changes later in the portraits of the Seleucids in around 170.

In Egypt, political circumstances different from those in the Seleucid empire gave rise to specific changes. Ptolemy VI Philometor (186/180–145 BC), son of his predecessor Ptolemy V, also was a small child when he became king. He remained under the authority of his mother, hence possibly his epithet Philometor.[83] Coins with his portrait as an adult appear only in the later years of his reign after his mother's death around 170/163.[84] These images adopted Seleucid models. This was possibly due to his mother's Seleucid origin. Here we can observe an explicit connection between Ptolemaic and Seleucid portrait concepts. Even

---

[83] Cf. Smith (1988) 93 pl. 75, 15–16; Lorber (2014a) 152.
[84] Svoronos (1904) 244 no. 1486 pl. 48, 19–20; Kyrieleis (1975) 58–9 pl. 46, 1–4; Smith (1988) 93 pl. 75, 12–3; Lorber (2012b) 222–4; Lorber (2014a) 133–4; cf. Stanwick (2002) 71 for Ptolemy VI's "mature portrait type"; for the later date cf. Lorber (2014a) 133–4.

though Ptolemy's hair looks fuller, his profile and rather gaunt physiognomy go back to the portraits of his grandfather on his mother's side, Antiochus III, and to Antiochus's successors.[85] On the other hand, Ptolemy's portraits in the round present him with a rather curly hairdo; they highlight youth and pathos, witness the marble head from Alexandria (fig. 6.11).[86] These portraits follow the concept which already started to gain importance in the sculpted portraits of Ptolemy IV (fig. 6.10) and which became visible in the coin portraits of Antiochus IV. Hence, despite different circumstances in each empire, and despite differing concepts in the coinage and in sculpture within the Ptolemaic sphere of influence, we can observe a common trend in royal iconographies in both empires, bridging the differences between the Seleucids and Ptolemies in the first half of the second century BC. This was most likely due to closer dynastic relationships between the royal families in the two empires, but other dynamics might also have been at play.

In Egypt, the iconographies of Ptolemy V and VI were an interlude. Ptolemy VIII Euergetes (180/145–116 BC) followed his brother Ptolemy VI on the throne. He came back to the visual *tryphe* ideology – hence his nickname *physkon*, 'potbelly', due to his real or pretended obesity.[87] Both his coin portraits and his rare portraits in the round underline the importance of this notion in Ptolemaic portrait representation. For the following Ptolemies, the identification of their portraiture is still under discussion, so I will refrain from drawing further lines of comparison.[88]

Let us come back to the Seleucid empire after Antiochus V's death in 162. His successor was Demetrius I Soter (ca. 180/162–150 BC), the oldest son of Seleucus IV and grandson of Antiochus III. In his case, family lineage was not enough to visually legitimize his rule: Demetrius's coin portraits (fig. 6.12) show no signs of relationship to the images of his father and grandfather.[89] Rather, after ca. 155 BC, we find a new concept, building on an idea already present in a less radical manner under Antiochus IV (cf. fig. 6.9). We not only observe a slight resemblance with the youthful Alexander, as in the case of Antiochus IV; we also find an obvious Alexander *anastole* above the forehead, as in some of the late Antiochus

---

[85] Smith (1988) 93, argues in favor of differences to Seleucid portraits. [86] See above n. 60–1.
[87] Svoronos (1904) 249 no. 1507 pl. 52, 7–8; Kyrieleis (1975) 63–4 pl. 52–3; Smith (1988) 93–4 pl. 75, 17; Smith (1996) 207–8; Stanwick (2002) 71–3; Nadig (2007); Lorber (2012b) 225–6; Lorber (2014a) 134–5; Kyrieleis (2015) 35–6; cf. particularly the Brussels diorite head: Kyrieleis (1975) 64; 174 no. G 2 pl. 52, 4; 53; Smith (1988) 93; 170 no. 73 pl. 47; Stanwick (2002) 112 no. C 1 figs. 79–80.
[88] Kyrieleis (1975) 64–78; Smith (1988) 95–7; Lorber (2014a) 135–6; Kyrieleis (2015) 37–44.
[89] Smith (1988) pl. 76, 12; Fleischer (1991b) 56–7 pl. 29a; c–e; Fleischer (2002) 63; Houghton et al. (2008) 154; 159–67 nos. 1609–28; 168–72 nos. 1633–43 and further examples; Kovacs (2017) 502–6.

Fig. 6.12 Demetrios I Soter. Drachm. Photograph: Wikimedia Commons

IV coins, as well as long strands of hair on the neck.⁹⁰ This combination of features imitated the early Macedonian king's portraits, for example on the tetradrachms coined originally by Lysimachus and being still in use in the second century BC.⁹¹ Demetrius is the first Hellenistic king who, after more than 150 years, not only imitated formally Alexander's *anastole*, but adopted even more elements of the visual 'Alexander-code.'

At the same time, the double-portrait schema was used to present Demetrius with his wife Laodice.⁹² This can be taken as a new focus on *homonoia* and direct family ties in the Seleucid dynasty. The double-portrait schema is well known from the Ptolemaic *mnaieia* and images of the Dioscuri (see above).⁹³ It had already been adopted in the Seleucid realm for the first time to present the young son of Seleucus IV with his mother Laodice.⁹⁴ It was a potent image even before family ties to the Ptolemies had been established.

The following usurper Alexander I Balas (150–145 BC) claimed to be a son of Antiochus IV. Thus, the resemblances with the portrait concept of Antiochus's later reign can be well explained.⁹⁵ Following

---

⁹⁰ See particularly the tetradrachms after 155/4 BC: Fleischer (1991b) 57 pl. 29d; Fleischer (2002) 63 fig. 6.9; Houghton et al. (2008) 160 no. 1611; 165 nos. 1625–6; 170–2 nos. 1641–3; 174 no. 1652.
⁹¹ Mørkholm (1991) 81; 145; 147 nos. 178–9; 181–2; 490–3; 499–500.
⁹² Jugate portraits of Demetrius and Laodice: Fleischer (1991b) 58; Houghton et al. (2008) 184 nos. 1686–9; 185 no. 1691; Martin (2012a) 403.
⁹³ For further Ptolemaic references in Demetrius I's coinage: Lorber (2015b) 181–3.
⁹⁴ See above n. 71.
⁹⁵ Smith (1988) pl. 76, 13; Fleischer (1991b) 60–3 pl. 31c–e; Fleischer (2002) 63–4; Houghton et al. (2008) 211–12; 217–24 nos. 1776–87 and further examples.

up Demetrius's representation, the double-portrait (jugate) scheme was used again, showing the newly married couple of Alexander I Balas and his Ptolemaic wife Cleopatra Thea.[96] These images once again stress the family concept of Ptolemaic origin, especially with the wife in the foremost position and including attributes like a *kalathos*, cornucopia or *dikeras* on other issues. Also, in this case, the Alexander card was played out but in a new manner. Sometimes Balas is represented with the well-known *anastole*. Some of his bronze coins from Apameia show a portrait wearing a lion skin and with curly hair above the forehead, although this is only vaguely visible.[97] The lion skin, an attribute of Heracles, related the portrait to the well-known Heracles issues of Alexander, struck for a long time also posthumously. In the second century BC, in rare cases, these Heracles issues were taken as portraits of the great Macedonian king.[98] Hence, Alexander I Balas was assimilated to the Heracles-like Alexander,[99] and his name added to this relationship. Other coins present him with a radiate crown, thus adopting a divine attribute previously used in the coin iconographies of the Ptolemies and Antiochus IV.[100]

From this time on, Alexander the Great never completely lost relevance in the Seleucid royal iconography. While Diodotus (142/1–138/7 BC) adopted Tryphon as one of his regal names not related to Alexander, his image did only partially relate to the Ptolemaic concept of *tryphe* (fig. 6.13).[101] Names do not necessarily determine portrait concepts. Rather, Diodotus, who was another usurper not born directly into the Seleucid family, again adopted the hair style of Alexander the Great, already used by Antiochus IV, Demetrius I and Alexander I Balas, in order to testify his legitimacy.[102] His hair is even curlier and longer than in the case of Alexander I Balas, and the *anastole* more dynamic.

---

[96] Houghton (1988); Mørkholm (1991) 177–8 no. 635; Houghton et al. (2008) 211–12; 243 no. 1841; 249–50 nos. 1860–1; 244 nos. 1843–6; Martin (2012b) 399 n. 26 fig. 6.4.
[97] Houghton et al. (2008) 212; 226 no. 1795; 230 no. 1805; Kovacs (2017) 507–10; cf. Fleischer (1991b) 61 pl. 31f; Svenson (1995) 252 no. 194 pl. 50; Thomas (2002) 19; for the lion skin as royal attribute: Svenson (1995) 100–3.
[98] Stewart (1993) 432 fig. 121; Fleischer (2002) 68 fig. 22; Dahmen (2007) 18; 120–1 pl. 9; von den Hoff (2013b) 88–9 fig. 6.9.
[99] Houghton et al. (2008) 212; cf. Bohm (1989) 111–13 with n. 55.
[100] Fleischer (1991b) 61 pl. 31g; Svenson (1995) 286 no. 283 pl. 11; Thomas (2002) 19; Houghton et al. (2008) 228 no. 1799; 247 no. 1854; cf. Lorber (2015b) 183, for Ptolemaic relations.
[101] Smith (1988) pl. 76, 17; Bohm (1989) 120–7 pl. 7; Fleischer (1991b) 68–9 pl. 37c–d; Fleischer (2002) 68–9 fig. 24; Houghton et al. (2008) 336–7; 341–7 no. 2030 and further examples.
[102] Fleischer (1996) 29; Kovacs (2017) 511–18.

Fig. 6.13 Diodotos Tryphon. Tetradrachm from Antiochia. Berlin, Staatliche Museen/SMPK– Münzkabinett. Photograph: Münzkabinett, Staatliche Museen Berlin/SMPK

Fig. 6.14 Alexander II Zabinas. Bronze coin from Antiochia. New York, American Numismatic Society Inv. 1948.19.2388. Photograph: © American Numismatic Society

Alexander the Great also played a role in the portraiture of later Seleucid kings, even though they now were related politically to the Ptolemies. Alexander II Zabinas (129/8–123 BC) was proclaimed Seleucid king by Ptolemy VIII around 129 BC. His portrait followed the conventional Seleucid concept of the calm, young king with a regular hairline and without Alexander's *anastole*.¹⁰³ On the other hand, his name brought back the relationship to Alexander. On coin issues, showing exactly the same regular hairline as his other portraits do, he even adopted the Alexander-Heracles attribute of the lion skin, as Alexander I Balas had already done (fig. 6.14).¹⁰⁴ Thus a not-Alexander-like portrait head and coiffure were combined with an Alexander-related heroic attribute. The vocabulary and syntax of the *imitatio Alexandri* was complex – and each visual term could point to a slightly different direction, be it the more heroic Heracles-Alexander-semantic or the notion of the dynamic king. Alexander II is also shown wearing the radiate crown, introduced earlier on Seleucid and Ptolemaic coins.¹⁰⁵

In the Seleucid empire, during the more unsettled late second century, divine attributes, which had been present in Ptolemaic iconography long before, became more popular in royal representation. The Seleucids were obviously looking for persuasive new visual means of creating legitimacy.¹⁰⁶ Usurpation became one reason for looking back to the remote past and taking Alexander as well as his role as Heracles as a model. But the name and ideological reference to Alexander alone never were sufficient to result in Alexander-like portraits, witness Ptolemy X Alexander I (110–88 BC) whose portraits do not show any link to the great Macedonian king.¹⁰⁷

3 Conclusion

In summary, we can periodize royal portrait concepts between the late fourth and late second century. The first phase is limited to the first generation of kings, that is, the *diadochs* Ptolemy I and Seleucus I. Change occurred around 280 BC, when the second generation took

---

¹⁰³ Bohm (1989) 127–9; Fleischer (1991b) 75 pl. 43a–f; Houghton et al. (2008) 442–3; 447–64.
¹⁰⁴ Fleischer (1991b) 75 pl. 43c; Svenson (1995) 252 no. 195 pl. 50; Thomas (2002) 20; Houghton et al. (2008) 454 no. 2231; Kovacs (2017) 517–18; see above n. 97. Even the elephant's headdress reappears now, cf. Fleischer (1991b) 75 pl. 43d; Houghton et al. (2008) 456 no. 2234, as already for Alexander in the earliest Ptolemaic coinage and in portraits of Demetrius II, cf. Fleischer (1991b) 65 pl. 33-4; Svenson (1995) 106–12; Houghton et al. (2008) 311 no. 1989; Lorber (2012c); Kyrieleis (2015) 23–4; Kovacs (2017) 517.
¹⁰⁵ See above n. 48 and n. 77.
¹⁰⁶ For later Seleucid kings after Antiochus VIII: Fleischer (1991b) 82–90; Fleischer (1996) 36 ("*tryphe-kings*"); Kovacs (2017) 518–20; cf. Houghton et al. (2008) 521–612.
¹⁰⁷ Kyrieleis (2015) 38; cf. Bohm (1989) 134–45 with pl. 9, 1, who recognizes the *anastole* in Ptolemy X's portraits, even though the hair does not show clear similarities with Alexander's portraiture. The portraits of Mithridates VI of Pontos are a further, different case of non-dynastic, but ideological *imitatio Alexandri*: Kovacs (2017) 520–34.

over imperial rule. Another break can be observed around the end of the third century BC with Antiochus III and Ptolemy IV. From this time on, portrait concepts developed in more flexible ways. However, particular long-term fashions, or lines of tradition, are hard to detect. Possibly, this is due to the dynamically changing challenges within each empire, new mutual relations and disruptive alliances. Starting around 160/140 BC, further changes and new disparities can be observed, including in particular the renaissance of older models of royal representation.

As far as the portrait concepts are concerned, the idea of a mature, 'real-life' king who received his visual legitimation due to signs of energy, activity, and presence dominated the portraits of the *diadochs* in both empires. But astonishingly, this concept of the energetic ruler never came back afterwards, and it seems to have been a concept visually directed against the Alexander ideal from the beginning. After around 280 BC, it was replaced by the idea of a serene and more distant ruler and became the guiding idea of the following decades. In Egypt, the *tryphe* concept of wealth and luxury was also developed during this period. Late in the third and early in the second century, the concept of an aged and experienced king gained dominance in the Seleucid empire, while the idea of a young and dynamic ruler accompanied by some retrospective *tryphe* imagery characterized the portraits of the Ptolemaic kings.

A more juvenile appearance including adoptions of Alexander motifs characterized Seleucid portraiture around 170 BC. In Egypt, in the middle of the second century, the ideal of *tryphe* came back with Ptolemy VIII, while in the Seleucid portraiture, after ca. 170 BC, retrospect visual assimilations to the model of Alexander the Great and/or his Heracles relations received more attention. It appears that Alexander references as important factors of royal visual legitimation were used occasionally since the third century BC but came to be applied systematically to royal portraiture only some 150 years after the Macedonian's death. Alexander here became relevant the more complex and competitive the problem of succession became. In Ptolemaic portraiture, by contrast, Alexander never played a conceptual role.

Entanglements and relations between Seleucid and Ptolemaic royal portraiture can be observed in different ways and in specific periods. In the third century, quite similar concepts were dominant in both empires, but not without particular preferences like, for example, the Ptolemaic *tryphe* ideal. Between ca. 170 and 150/40, Seleucid portrait concepts were transferred to the Ptolemaic royal representation, while in the same period the jugate portraits of wife/mother and king, originally a Ptolemaic invention, were adopted in Seleucid representations.

The dynastic idea gained importance in the Ptolemaic and Seleucid royal representation in different intensity and with different visual strategies. In Egypt, Ptolemy I's coin portraits diachronically underlined the reference to the founder of the dynasty, as did reissues of coins with portraits of earlier kings under Ptolemy IV and V, while the *homonoia* motif of the jugate portraits of mother/wife and king underlined family relations as a factor of legitimacy. In the Seleucid empire, long-time dynastic continuity was far less a factor of royal portraiture. Yet during the third century, in both the Ptolemaic and the Seleucid realms, the assimilation of the portraits of actual kings to their forefathers (*Bildnisangleichung*) was a visual sign of dynastic relations. This strategy also played a role in the iconography of the sons of Antiochus III, while Antiochus IV in his later images distanced himself from this model. At this time, it is apparent that names like Alexander did not automatically result in associated portrait concepts. Furthermore, neither references to royal predecessors by name nor direct descent necessarily appear explicitly in portrait concepts. Rather, the strategies of adopting older models and assimilating portraits to the image of another king were guided by their own purpose. They formed additional strategies of legitimacy, possibly complementing other strategies of representation.

Finally, the interest in communicating imperial ideologies by disseminating official portrait models resulted in new strategies of the reproduction of images. This is particularly evident in the Ptolemaic kingdom where, from the early third century onwards, the portrait of Ptolemy I was reproduced on coins over a long period, while replica series of royal portraits in the round appear first during the reign of Ptolemy VI. We cannot say, unfortunately, if this happened due to court intervention. Be that as it may, this laid the foundation for the spread of centrally designed portrait models which in the Roman empire became a predominant factor of ruler representation. Comparable strategies of portrait dissemination cannot be observed in the Seleucid empire, pointing to a less centralized concept of kingship.

Acknowledgments

Thanks go to Tobias Wild for supporting the editing of this paper and to Sitta von Reden for correcting my English. The Freiburg University Collaborative Research Centre (SFB) 948 'Helden – Heroisierung – Heroismen', founded by the German Research Foundation (DFG), allowed me to continue my research on Hellenistic ruler portraits. Martin Kovacs, who was a postdoc in this centre, submitted a groundbreaking study of the iconography of Alexander the Great and the visual *imitatio Alexandri* as a Habilitationsschrift at Freiburg University in 2017 (Kovacs 2017), which is now in press. More than I could express in the footnotes, I owe much to his expertise. Any errors, of course, remain my own responsibility.

CHAPTER 7

Monetary Policies, Coin Production, and Currency Supply in the Seleucid and Ptolemaic Empires

Panagiotis P. Iossif and Catharine C. Lorber

Common Introduction

Some differences between Seleucid and Ptolemaic monetary policies have already received considerable scholarly attention.[1] Foremost among these are the contrast between the closure of the Ptolemaic currency zone and Seleucid adherence to the international Attic weight standard, the continuing circulation of Attic-weight coinage of Alexander the Great and the *diadochoi* in Seleucid territory, the openness of the Seleucid economy to foreign coinage of Attic weight, and the relatively minor proportion of specifically Seleucid currency in this mix.[2] This can give the impression that Seleucid monetary policy embraced the principle of laissez-faire whereas Lagid policy was protectionist or mercantilist. But this impression is valid only for the third century and a bit beyond. Some of these factors dramatically changed in the second century, and certain Seleucid kings innovated in their monetary policies.

A second major point of contrast is the higher valuation of gold in the Ptolemaic empire and the importance of gold in the Lagid currency system, whereas it ceased to be a regular part of the Seleucid currency system after the reign of Seleucus II and thereafter was employed only occasionally for emergency issues and issues of prestige. The third significant contrast involves the role of bronze coinage. In the Seleucid system it always functioned as small change, but in the Ptolemaic empire it largely replaced precious metal coinage for approximately a century, and in Egypt it served as a quasi-independent standard of value during the second and first centuries.

Because of the exceptionally large number of Seleucid mints and the current state of the research, the Seleucid section (Chapter 7A) cannot aspire to provide a complete overview of imperial finance over the history

[1] Le Rider and Callataÿ (2006). [2] Iossif (2015) for quantitative analysis of the last point.

of the dynasty. Instead, it treats several discrete topics relating to the management of coin production and currency supply, with a special focus on changes that occurred in the second century in the western part of the empire. Among these was the emergence of Antiochia-Orontes as the principal mint of the empire, surpassing Seleucia-Tigris, the most productive Seleucid mint of the third century.[3]

The Ptolemaic section (Chapter 7B) traces policies relating to coin production and currency supply, chronologically and by province, into the early first century. It thus provides a general impression of Lagid imperial finance and its evolution over time.

1A THE SELEUCID EMPIRE
Panagiotis P. Iossif&Catharine C. Lorber

1 Mints, Coordination, and Purposes of the Coinage

Both the Seleucids and the Ptolemies produced coinage at multiple centers even if the remarkably high number of mints producing Seleucid coins cannot be compared to the more discreet number of Ptolemaic mints. The locations of the major Lagid mints are known, thanks to the frequent use of mint marks outside of Egypt. Seleucid numismatists, like students of the coinage of Alexander the Great, are faced with multiple series of related coins, of which the longest and most abundant have been attributed, more or less plausibly, to the major cities of each satrapy or region.[4] The Seleucid model assumes multiple mints in regions dominated by the Greek *polis* system (western Asia Minor and Cilicia) and one major mint per satrapy farther east.

To some extent the mint attributions can be confirmed through archaeology. Although silver circulated widely, bronze tended to stay close to home. Thus, the bronze coins found in archaeological excavations may be products of a local mint.[5] In cases like Antiochia-Orontes, where the bronze coinage shares controls with the precious metal coinage, the excavated bronzes anchor the precious metal coinage as well.[6] Similar control links between bronze and silver assure the attributions to Seleucia-Tigris

---

[3] Iossif (2014b) 36–7.
[4] Largely still influenced by attributions proposed by Newell (1938); and (1941).
[5] Iossif (2016) calculated an average distance of less than 500 km between the production center and the find spots of Seleucid bronzes.
[6] Waage (1952).

and Susa,[7] at least for the third-century material. In the second century, Seleucia and Susa often minted unmarked bronzes, so the attribution of precious metal coins depends on continuities within the silver series. Other mints are more problematic. For example, the major Seleucid mint of Bactria was traditionally assumed to be Bactra; but finds from excavations at Ai Khanoum led American numismatists to reattribute coinage from Bactra to Ai Khanoum.[8] Bactrian specialists objected,[9] and the question remains open pending publication of the coin finds from excavations at Bactra. For a second example, Nisibis is known to have struck quasi-municipal bronze coinage under Antiochus IV, but the attribution of third-century silver and bronze coinage to this mint is speculative.[10] Other attributions rest on arguments that range from plausible to tenuous. Furthermore, numerous unattributed coin series seem to attest the operation of lesser or ephemeral mints, but their locations can be determined only roughly, if at all. In short, our understanding of the network of Seleucid mints is less secure than we could wish.

Beginning at a certain point in the reign of Antiochus I, one consistent policy can be observed at virtually all mints: they issued precious metal coins bearing the portrait of the reigning king paired with a designated dynastic or personal reverse type.[11] There can be little doubt that the iconographic instructions emanated from the court. An exception occurred under Antiochus II, however, when a small group of mints in western Asia Minor adopted distinctive reverse types, a weary Heracles for their tetradrachms and a standing Athena Nicephorus for the gold, perhaps reflecting the formation of a defensive league centered on Phocaea.[12] Regrettably, we have no further information whether the initiative for this coordinated change arose locally, or it was directed by the royal administration. Beginning under Antiochus IV, the policy concerning reverse types bifurcated: western mints often employed reverse types personal to the reigning king, while eastern mints retained the dynastic type of Apollo seated on the *omphalos*.[13]

Bronze iconography varied from mint to mint, indicating a degree of local control, but we cannot say whether this control was exercised solely by royal authorities, or civic officials had a voice in some decisions.[14] One

---

[7] Le Rider (1998); Le Rider (1965). [8] Kritt (1996), followed by Houghton and Lorber in *SC*.
[9] Bopearachchi (1999); (2004). [10] Newell (1941) 56–8; Mørkholm (1963) 44–5.
[11] On the reverse types of the Seleucids, see Iossif (2011) and (2011a).
[12] Macdonald (1907) 155–9. [13] See Iossif and Lorber (2009) 129–30.
[14] Iossif (2014b) argued for the case of Seleucia-Tigris that the types on both precious metal coinages and bronzes (as well as for seals) were dictated by targeted groups and different audiences for each medium.

early and exceptional attempt at standardizing bronze typology occurred late in the reign of Seleucus I, when the paired types of a profile head of Medusa and a rushing bull appeared at mints from Sardes to Ecbatana and Bactra/Ai Khanoum.[15] The techniques of flan production as well as the weights and diameters of the various bronze denominations also differed from mint to mint. This is much in contrast with practice in the Lagid empire, at least in the third century, where bronze production techniques were standardized at all major mints.[16]

The preponderance of non-Seleucid precious metal coinage throughout the empire[17] invites us to assume that the Seleucid issues were struck for specific purposes, presumably to make state payments in contexts where it was important to emphasize the identity of the royal paymaster. Foremost among these would be military pay (most likely exceeding by far any other expenditure),[18] construction projects associated with city foundations and refoundations, cults, temple activities, and monetary benefactions to subject or allied cities.[19] The pay of royal officials was probably also rendered in Seleucid specie. Many Seleucid bronze coins feature military types or symbols, and these indicate that bronze currency as well as silver played a role in military finance, probably mainly as provision money (*siteresion*).[20] This function compelled a certain degree of monetization in eastern markets that were unaccustomed to the use of fiduciary coinage.[21] But nothing allows us to assume that monetization per se was a goal of Seleucid monetary policy and indeed it appears likely that rural areas remained largely outside the monetary economy.[22]

---

[15] *SC* nos. 8; 21–4; 151–3; 191–3; 224–5; 290. Iossif (2012) 47–70 defined the rushing bull as a sacrificial animal.

[16] Wolf (2013).

[17] Iossif (2015) 249 estimated the ratio of Seleucid to non-Seleucid coins in SHD ("Seleucid Hoard Database") for the third century at 1 to 5. This ratio changed for the second century (see table 6).

[18] Duncan-Jones (1994) 45. See von Reden (2010) 12–5 for a more nuanced approach to expenditures by ancient states.

[19] See I.Iasos 4 where the donation by Queen Laodike of 196 BC clearly stipulates that the payment of the dowries for the daughters of the poor citizens of the city should be made in "Antiochean drachms" (*Antiocheoi drachmai*). Of course, it cannot be excluded that here the "Antiochean drachms" were a reference to the Attic-weight standard and not to the types of the coins.

[20] Cf. Iossif (2016) for the use of small bronzes as garrison payments based on analysis of the SED ("Seleucid Excavation Database").

[21] See the reaction of the Babylonians when Antiochus I introduced bronze coinage in the area for the first time in their history: *Astronomical Diary* of 274 BC.

[22] *Contra* Aperghis (2004) where it is assumed that the monetization of the economy becomes the goal of the kings. In *SED*, the percentage of bronzes coming from settlements considered as "rural" or "small cities" is very low: only 183 bronzes come from rural settlements and small cities out of 6,320 bronzes recorded, i.e. a mere 2.9 percent.

The vast majority of Seleucid coins have been recovered from within the empire. But the presence of early Seleucid tetradrachms and gold staters in twenty-six Greek hoards,[23] usually in small numbers, indicates that they circulated in the Greek homeland. Perhaps they were originally introduced through diplomatic activity, though they could also have entered Greece as the pay of returning mercenaries. (Few can be associated with the Greek campaign of Antiochus III.) On the other hand, a similar sprinkling of Seleucid precious metal coins in thirty-five hoards from Macedonia, Thrace, the Balkans, and the Black Sea region[24] most likely resulted at least in part from Seleucid military operations in these regions.[25] Even more clearly, the discovery in excavations at Cabyle of numerous Sardian bronzes of Antiochus II[26] shows that an important purpose of coinage was to finance Seleucid imperial expansion and further illustrates how a single mint could be tasked with providing the necessary resources for campaigns in far distant areas. Requirements in precious metal would normally need to be spread among several mints and treasuries. The Parthian campaign of Seleucus II, as traced solely through the growth of his campaign beard, entailed contributions in silver and/or bronze money from Nisibis, Susa, Ecbatana, an unidentified, probably eastern mint, and an unidentified mint in Mesopotamia.[27] Several new, ephemeral, or itinerant silver mints in Mesopotamia or Commagene, identifiable only in the reign of Seleucus II, surely shared in the burden of campaign finance.

2   Control Systems

Early Seleucid and Ptolemaic coinage are both characterized by control systems that rely heavily on monograms, sometimes appearing in groups, sometimes supplemented by symbols. The monograms are thought, for good reason, to abbreviate personal names. The most common assumption is that the control system was internal to the mint, identifying the moneyers responsible for production of the coins in order to deter malfeasance or, should it occur, to enable punishment of the guilty party or parties.[28] But another interpretation has been offered for at least some Seleucid controls, namely that the monograms served administrative purposes by identifying

---

[23] *SC* I/2, 125–7.   [24] *SC* I/2, 128–30.
[25] See now Iossif (2017) for the western-oriented movement of coins produced under Antiochus III.
[26] Draganov (1993).
[27] *SC* nos. 749–50; 759; Ad179; Ad181; 788; 795–8; 822–4; Ad189; 685–6 = SC Ad161–Ad162 (reattributed to Mesopotamia). On this and other Seleucid campaign beards, see Lorber and Iossif (2009).
[28] See, e.g., Newell (1938) 20–2.

the official who ordered the coinage to be struck and in some cases also the intended recipient of the coinage.[29] It is argued in the Ptolemaic section (Chapter 7B) that the controls of the Syro-Phoenician precious metal coinage struck between 261/0 and 242/1 probably also served administrative purposes.

Symbols are especially common on Seleucid coins emanating from Hellespontine Thrace, western Asia Minor, and Cilicia. They are presumed to be mint marks, often alluding to the types of civic coins once issued by these *poleis*. Their deeper significance is uncertain, as is also the case with civic mint marks on Ptolemaic coins. Possibly the mints were entirely under royal control and the symbols were merely a concession to civic pride. Possibly the mint marks indicate that the *polis* itself struck the coinage on behalf of the king, or that minting responsibilities were shared between royal and civic officials, or that the city supplied the bullion as part of its fiscal obligation to the crown.

We can observe a shift in the control system of Antiochia-Orontes. Under Seleucus IV the mint developed a new paradigm involving a primary control (symbol or monogram) that appeared with a secondary control selected from a repertory of letters and monograms that remained relatively stable from one issue to the next. Antiochus IV, Antiochus V, and Demetrius I in his early years reverted to a simpler system, generally dispensing with the primary control and displaying a single monogram only; but the underlying repertory of letters and monograms remained large (twelve for the tetradrachms of Antiochus IV, more than twenty for those of Demetrius I). In 155/4, when Demetrius began to date his silver coinage, he also added a fixed primary control, in effect reviving the pattern of Seleucus IV. This system of primary and secondary controls remained in place under most subsequent rulers, and until the arrival of Antiochus VII the repertory of secondary controls carried over from one reign to the next almost intact. We hypothesize that the fixed primary control represented a high-ranking supervisor and the secondary controls represented a corps of lesser officials who oversaw the actual production process. It appears that the Antiochia mint came to rely on a large staff of these overseers who alternated frequently in their duty, presumably to prevent collusion with the rank-and-file mint workers. This complicated system of marking the coins contrasts sharply with the simplicity of the contemporary Ptolemaic system, which relied on dates and mint marks, no doubt backed up by written records.

---

[29] Aperghis (2010).

The control system of the Antiochia mint in the second century, seemingly a technical topic, in fact allows us to draw a significant historical conclusion. Mint professionals normally retained their positions despite violent changes of regime.[30] The same was probably true for other state employees and officials at a similar level in the bureaucracy. Administrative stability was possible amid the remarkable political instability of this troubled period, and it probably had much to do with the survival of the Seleucid kingdom despite its travails.

The contrasting control systems of second-century Antiochia and the Ptolemies could perhaps serve as indicators of different interpretations of royal authority by each dynasty. For the Ptolemies, the simple reference to the regnal date and a mint mark (coupled with the generic and impersonal royal title and name) was enough to guarantee the royal character of the coinage; the Seleucids had to go through conspicuous controls representing various levels of the administration to achieve the same result. The former seems to refer to a centralized model where the *basileion* (i.e. the king and his court) was sufficient as the sole guarantor of the royal document with financial magistrates playing a minor role in the process of issuing coins. The latter involves a more decentralized state where the link between king/court and administrative officials was to be renewed and confirmed ad hoc, a sine qua non situation for conferring legal status to a coin. In fact, it could be argued that the process of producing coins reflects the general administrative models adopted by the two dynasties. This interpretation is offered with reservations, because we understand that in practice both empires employed similar hierarchies of communication in which royal orders were passed down through the levels of the bureaucracy, attested for the Ptolemies principally by papyrological documents and for the Seleucids by inscriptions.

3 The Special Case of Seleucid Coele Syria and Phoenicia in the Second Century

The hoard record reveals that silver coinage of Attic weight did not circulate in the core of Seleucid Coele Syria and Phoenicia.[31] Seleucid preservation of the closed monetary zone inherited from the Ptolemies is examined in the Ptolemaic section (Chapter 7B). Here we shall consider the provision of Seleucid money within the province.

[30] Schwei (2016).   [31] Le Rider (1995).

When Antiochus III occupied Ptolemaic Syria and Phoenicia in 198, he made no effort to appropriate the existing precious metal coinage by reminting it or even countermarking it with some symbol of his authority. However, he immediately inaugurated a bronze coinage at Tyre which employed reverse types of local significance; it was issued annually in his name and remained in regular production under his successors. Antiochus III may also have opened a bronze mint at Ptolemais which struck crude imitations of a small bronze denomination of Antiochia. Remnants of bronze military issues struck during his invasion probably also remained in circulation.[32] As Seleucid silver of Attic weight did not enter the closed monetary zone, the currency supply comprised Ptolemaic silver tetradrachms and explicitly Seleucid bronzes of low value. From 195 the tax revenues of the province were divided between Antiochus III and Ptolemy V (Joseph. *AJ* 12.155), and after the marriage of Ptolemy V and Cleopatra I the money taxes on the cities went to Ptolemy (Joseph. *AJ* 12.169), making it likely that Antiochus's share consisted of the taxes in kind on agricultural land and produce. We can only wonder how state payments were handled. Were they made in Ptolemaic silver, despite the possibly confusing message to recipients concerning their paymaster? Were they rendered in Seleucid bronze and/or in kind, or was there some system of credit giving access to Seleucid silver outside the province? We simply do not know.

Seleucus IV struck a single issue of Attic-weight tetradrachms at Ptolemais. Apparently, they were not intended for use within the province; they occur in mixed hoards (i.e. in hoards found beyond the borders of the closed monetary zone). Antiochus IV enlarged the production of Attic-weight tetradrachms at Ptolemais, employing thirteen obverse dies between c. 170 and 164.[33] At an average output of 20,000 tetradrachms per die,[34] these thirteen obverse dies imply the coining of 260,000 tetradrachms. This is dwarfed by the contemporary output of Antiochia (see Chapter 7 A.6 below), yet it is enough to surprise us that no trace of this coinage survives in the immediate region. The hoard record indicates that these coins circulated in the empire at large; they are found as far west as Pamphylia or Cilicia and are well dispersed in the Upper Satrapies.[35] To

---

[32] Houghton and Lorber (2002).   [33] Mørkholm (1963) 45–50; 52–3; Voulgaridis (2000).
[34] Callataÿ (2011) 9; 12–3; 23.
[35] Trebizond, 1970; Ordu (*CH* IX, 530); 2 in Pamphylia, or perhaps Cilicia, 2000; 2 in North Syria or Cilicia Pedias, 1994; 5 in Qal'at el Moudiq (Apamea region); 30 in Ma'aret en-Numan (*CH* IX, 511); Aleppo, 1931 (*IGCH* 1546); 15 in Syria, 1990 (*CH* VIII, 434); 2 in Babylon, 1900 (*IGCH* 1774); 2 in Baghdad environs (*IGCH* 1778); Susa excavations, 1933–1934 (*IGCH* 1804); 3 in Susiana, 1958–1959 (*IGCH* 1805); 4 in Susiana, 1965? (*IGCH* 1806); Hamadan, 1977; Media, 1923 (*IGCH* 1813); 3 in Kabala (*IGCH* 1737).

explain this volume of minting and the dispersion of the coinage, we hypothesize that military units of diverse origin were present in the closed monetary zone after the Sixth Syrian War; that they received their pay in the form of Attic-weight tetradrachms of Ptolemais which they could not spend locally;[36] and that they repatriated these earnings upon their discharge or after participation in the final eastern campaign of Antiochus IV.

The major numismatic innovation of Antiochus IV in Coele Syria and Phoenicia was the creation of new bronze coinages issued in the names of seven Phoenician cities (sometimes jointly with the king) and bearing royal portraits on the obverse. Important series were struck at Byblus, Laodicea in Canaan (Berytus), Sidon, Tyre, Antiochia in Ptolemais (Ptolemais), and Ascalon, with a single issue at Tripolis. Byblus, Berytus, Sidon, and Tyre inscribed their ethnics in Phoenician, sometimes with epithets recalling their past glories and the rivalry between Sidon and Tyre. These coinages were part of a larger program of quasi-municipal bronze currencies launched in 169/8 and involving nineteen cities in all, from Cilicia to Mesopotamia.[37] The use of previously unattested dynastic names by several of these cities indicates that the quasi-municipal bronze coinage was associated with a program of city refoundation.[38] This might lead us to assume that these coinages were conceived as a new civic institution at a time when the crown was promoting the spread of traditional Greek *polis* institutions in the eastern cities.[39] In the view of Otto Mørkholm, the blended character of the quasi-municipal coinages was intended to make the cities "active partners in the inner regeneration of [the] kingdom," but he also described the coinage more concretely as providing a new revenue stream to the cities, a share in the profits that flowed from minting fiduciary coinage.[40] For Laurent Capdetrey, the refoundations and quasi-municipal coinages were evidence that the Cilician and Syrian cities had received a new, cosmetic form of semiautonomy as one aspect of a restructuring of the empire after the loss of Asia Minor.[41]

The strong expressions of cultural and civic identity on the quasi-municipal coins of Byblus, Berytus, Sidon, and Tyre have no counterparts on quasi-municipal coins of Cilician, Syrian, or Mesopotamian cities.

---

[36] Mørkholm (1963) 53, also associated the Ptolemais tetradrachms with the Sixth Syrian War and Syrian operations against the Maccabean rebels, but he was unaware of the closed monetary zone.
[37] Mørkholm (1965).
[38] Besides Berytus and Ptolemais, Tarsus was refounded as Antiochia-Cydnus, Adana as Antiochia-Sarus, Mopsus as Seleucia-Pyramus, Edessa as Antiochia-Callirrhoe, and Nisibis as Antiochia-Mygdonia.
[39] Capdetrey (2007) 218–20.   [40] Mørkholm (1965) 67; Mørkholm (1984) 101.
[41] Capdetrey (2007) 213–4.

Oliver Hoover interpreted the Phoenician portion of the program in the context of negotiated power relations between the king and the cities and concluded that the use of Phoenician script was a concession granted on account of their importance to the Seleucid navy.[42] Capdetrey also assumed concessions, perhaps obtained through revolt, and excluded a simple model of Greek *polis* institutions in favor of increasing royal intervention in the institutions and finances of the cities of Phoenicia and Coele Syria.[43] Capdetrey noted in passing that an increasingly assertive Jewish identity may have influenced the concessions to the Phoenician cities.[44] Indeed, it is probably no coincidence that the conspicuous Phoenician legends made their appearance at the time of Antiochus's first attack on Jerusalem, and they may reflect deliberate favoritism by the crown. Ethnic tensions must have been rising since the advent of Tobiad tax farming on behalf of Ptolemy V, for Joseph son of Tobias was harshly discriminatory in his methods of collecting taxes (Joseph. *AJ* 12.182, 183, 200). After the outbreak of the Maccabean Revolt in 167, the gentiles supported the Seleucid king and took revenge on the Judahites, and the revolt soon devolved into an ethnic war (1 Macc. 3.10, 3.24–6, 3.41, 5.1–23, 5.28–44).

Andrew Meadows emphasized the top-down character of the quasi-municipal coinages, as implied by the imposition of royal types, but conceded some local control at the level of execution.[45] One of the present authors (Iossif) has challenged the idea that coining rights were a benefaction, floating the suggestion that the quasi-municipal coinages represented an imposition which compelled the cities to share in the king's financial burdens in the aftermath of the Sixth Syrian War.[46] Specifically, the cities were probably obliged to provide *sitarchia* (*siteresion, sitonion*) to troops operating or stationed nearby. The Ptolemaic precedents in Syria and Phoenicia for coinage as a form of *phoros* or *syntaxis* involved silver (see Chapter 7B). This fact would seem to imply that the exactions of Antiochus IV were lighter than those of the Ptolemaic kings.

Returning to the question of currency supply, it is striking that Antiochus IV had an ambitious program of reforms which affected some aspects of his currency, yet he did not provide a specifically Seleucid silver coinage suitable for circulation in the closed currency zone. Under Antiochus V Ptolemais produced a few more tetradrachms of Attic weight and alongside them the earliest Seleucid silver coins of Ptolemaic weight.

---

[42] Hoover (2004) 489–90.   [43] Capdetrey (2007) 220–1.   [44] Capdetrey (2007) 220.
[45] Meadows (2001) 59–60.   [46] Iossif (2014a) 79.

That experiment was institutionalized by Alexander I Balas, a pretender backed by Ptolemy VI. He inaugurated a new silver coinage in 151/0, the first year of his reign. Like the prototypes of Antiochus V, this coinage combined Seleucid and Ptolemaic characteristics. It was struck in Alexander's name and bore his portrait, but it conformed to the Ptolemaic weight standard and featured the Lagid eagle on the reverse. Four mints were involved: Laodicea in Phoenicia (Berytus),[47] Sidon, Tyre,[48] and Ptolemais. Each identified its coinage with a mint mark and each issued coins on an annual basis. These Seleucid eagles remained in production into the reigns of Antiochus VIII and Antiochus IX, with certain changes to the system caused by the political instability of the period, the most important being the disappearance of Berytus (destroyed by Tryphon), the addition of Ascalon as an initially minor mint, and the exit of Tyre after its grant of autonomy in 125. The Seleucid eagles conform to a model that could indicate that they represented annual tax payments by the cities, a model that dates back to the Syro-Phoenician precious metal coinage of Ptolemy II and Ptolemy III.[49]

One particular aspect may argue in favor of the implication of local elites in a shared effort of issuing coins. The die study of Seleucid eagles from Tyre demonstrated the extremely long life of a series of monograms, some of them repeated for long periods well beyond the life scope of a single individual. These monograms were interpreted as marks of elites and/or corporations involved in the regular, annual issues of the city.[50] If this interpretation is correct, then, together with Antiochus IV's quasi-municipal coinages, we have a strong indication of a royal policy aiming at integrating elites in the administrative, economic, and numismatic function of the empire.

The mints of Sidon, Tyre, and Ptolemais supplemented their Seleucid eagles with occasional emissions of Attic-weight silver employing the standard types of each reign (sometimes with minor variations). The denomination minted was usually the tetradrachm, but Tyre occasionally struck drachms. Like the Seleucid eagles the Attic-weight coins were identified by mint marks and dated according to the Seleucid era; but like other Attic-weight currency, they did not circulate in the closed monetary zone. These issues were extremely infrequent under Alexander I and Demetrius II but were produced annually under Antiochus VII and still frequent in the joint reign of Cleopatra Thea and Antiochus VIII and

[47] Sawaya (2005). [48] Iossif (2011b) for Sidon and Tyre. [49] Iossif (2104a) 71–2.
[50] Iossif (2011b) 217; Iossif (2014a) 72.

in the early sole reign of the latter. By the reigns of Antiochus VIII and IX, the Attic-weight issues of Sidon outnumbered the eagles – a sign that the eagles were becoming obsolete – and the issues of Ptolemais, of both varieties, were no longer identified by mint marks, another indication that the old system was unraveling.

But what was that system as it pertained to the Attic-weight silver of Sidon, Tyre, and Ptolemais? The mint marks and dates hint that these coins were part of the fiscal cycle, but we know of no process that involved occasional levies of taxes in one jurisdiction for delivery to another jurisdiction. The irregular pattern of their production further hints that the policies were personal to individual rulers. For only one king is it possible to suggest a hypothesis. The Attic-weight issues fall near the beginning of the two reigns of Demetrius II: 146/5 at Tyre, 145/4 at Sidon, 128/7 at Sidon, Tyre (where the issue involved drachms as well as tetradrachms), and Ptolemais. This pattern could reflect the belated production of coins to pay promised accession donatives at locations outside Phoenicia. The expedient could have been adopted because the Phoenician cities had reserves of silver that were lacking at the places where the donatives were to be distributed, which would further imply that there were no mint facilities in those locations.

4 Dating

After absorbing Ptolemaic Syria and Phoenicia, where the practice of dating coinage was well established though not invariant, the Seleucid kings adopted a policy of selectively dating a part of their coinage. There is a single and highly anomalous earlier example of a dated coin from the reign of Antiochus I, emanating from the principal mint of Bactria.[51] A unique silver tetradrachm with the portrait of Antiochus I and the Apollo on omphalos reverse type bears the supplementary inscription ETEI N MHNOΣ ΞA. The first part of the inscription reads year 50, and the latter part clearly alludes to the month Xandikos of the Macedonian calendar (equivalent to late February–March of the Julian calendar). No other Seleucid coin is dated with such precision, bearing also the name of a month in its inscription. We cannot know whether this date had some special significance, since no special event is known for 262/1 BC. An association with the celebration of Xandika (or Xanthika), a purification of the Macedonian army at the beginning of the campaign season by

---

[51] *SC* no. Ad104.

sacrificing a dog, cannot be excluded. As argued by different scholars, this celebration was known in both Thessaly and Macedonia.[52]

Dated Seleucid coinages of the second and first centuries were a phenomenon of the western empire almost exclusively. While the dating practices of Ptolemaic mints appear relatively systematic, dated Seleucid coinages present irregular patterns which are in some cases difficult to interpret.

In 198, the year of his conquest of Phoenicia and Palestine, Antiochus III inaugurated a dated bronze coinage at Tyre which was issued on an annual basis thereafter. The numismatic reform of Antiochus IV in 169/8 extended the practice of dating to Antiochia, Tripolis, and Ascalon; it was limited to the new class of bronze coins termed quasi-municipal (see above), and at Antiochia and Tripolis only single dated issues were struck, in 169/8 and 166/5, respectively.[53] Under Alexander I Balas isolated emissions of quasi-municipal bronzes were struck at Seleucia-Pieria in 151/0, at Apamea-Orontes in 150/49, and at Cyrrhestica in 149/8,[54] while more regular series of dated quasi-municipal bronzes commenced at Eupatria, Byblus, Laodicea-Berytus, and Ascalon, and slightly later (under Demetrius II) at Gaza.

In 158 SE (155/4 BC) Demetrius I instituted the policy of dating his Antiochene precious metal coinage. Curiously, in the same year Ptolemy VI inaugurated the long-lived series of dated tetradrachms at Alexandria. But the Alexandrian tetradrachms were differentiated only by their dates, whereas the Antiochene coins also bore two monogrammatic controls (see Section 2 above for this practice). Exceptionally, the practice of dating was extended to Ecbatana in 152/1, the penultimate year of Demetrius's reign. A silver drachm of superior style was dated, but the date was omitted from a companion tetradrachm that shared its portrait style and one of two signatory moneyers.[55] The Antiochene practice of dating precious metal issues continued under Alexander I, the first reign of Demetrius II, and Antiochus VI (who also applied it at his first capital, Apameia), until it was abolished by the usurper Tryphon after 144/3, in an effort to extirpate the Seleucid era along with the dynasty it commemorated. Balas also struck a dated silver tetradrachm at Seleucia-Pieria in 147/6, while under

---

[52] Chrysostomou (1993–4); Hatzopoulos (1997) 356; Trümpy (1997) 227.

[53] Tripolis produced one other dated quasi-municipal bronze issue, in 164/3, *SC* no. 1577.

[54] *SC* nos. 1799; 1803; 1809–10. Balas also struck a posthumous royal bronze coinage in the name of Antiochus IV, his purported father, in 151/0, probably at Apamea, *SC* no. 1883; Mørkholm (1984).

[55] *SC* no. 1737.3, drachm signed by Theo [...] and Philip [...]; *SC* 1730.1, tetradrachm signed by Philip [...] and Dion [...].

Demetrius II dated silver or bronze issues or series were emitted by numerous unidentifiable mints in Cilicia, northern Syria, and perhaps even Phoenicia.[56] Antiochus VII dated silver issues in his first year at Seleucia-Pieria (probably) and Antiochia,[57] but soon abandoned the practice even as he innovated by dating his Antiochene bronzes. He opened a new mint at Damascus which produced regular annual issues of dated tetradrachms and probably also dated bronzes. After his capture of Seleucia-Tigris from Phraates II in late summer of 130, Antiochus Euergetes replicated the practice of Antiochia, issuing undated silver while dating his bronzes. Other noteworthy dated issues of Antiochus VII are bronzes bearing the lily of Judea, struck at Jerusalem and dated to the years 132/1 and 131/0, and an unattributed gold stater with triumphal types and the epithet Megas (great), dated 134/3, several years before his initially successful Parthian campaign.[58] The practice of dating Antiochene bronzes (but not precious metal) was revived in the early years of Alexander II Zabinas and remained in force until 110/9, after which it was finally abandoned for good. The motive for dating bronze coinage remains unclear, but we cannot exclude an association with payments of the army during this period of continual military struggles among different kings and usurpers.[59]

It was suggested above that precious metal coin series with mint marks and annual dates could be related to the fiscal cycle. This hypothesis could also apply to dated precious metal series without mint marks, such as the coinage of Damascus and (at times) Antiochia. There was no absolute need to advertise the origin of coinage through mint marks because it was marked by controls whose significance was surely recorded in official archives. But if essential public information was indeed recorded in archives, it was also not strictly necessary to record the date of issue directly onto the coinage. This could explain why many coinages are undated, and why dating practices changed or were sometimes inconsistent.

We wish to suggest another possible explanation for the dating of Seleucid precious metal coinage. Demetrius I introduced the practice of dating the Antiochene precious metal coinage, and this may be related to

---

[56] *SC* no. 1798, 1899–1900; 1902–3; 1905; 1919–22; 1923A; 1929–30; 1933; 1935–6A; 1942–3; 1972.

[57] Lorber (2016c) 39–40. Antiochus Euergetes also struck a dated tetradrachm in his second regnal year at a mint tentatively identified as a workshop of Tarsus, *SC* no. 2053.1.

[58] *SC* nos. 2123.2–3; 2134. Less noteworthy dated issues of Antiochus VII include *SC* 2053.1; 2074; and 2075.

[59] We could only hypothesize (in an extremely cautious way) that this practice could be a possible way to keep track of their expenditures.

another of his innovations, the reminting of older silver coinage (see below). The dates were perhaps intended to ensure an orderly withdrawal of older coin issues in the future, much like the process documented for Egypt in the latter second century. It is not clear why Demetrius's son Antiochus VII dispensed with dating his Antiochene silver when he opted to date his Antiochene bronzes.

5 Recoining and the Monetary Mix

Recoining was a regular feature of Ptolemaic monetary policy. Episodes of recoining accompanied the weight reductions of Ptolemy I and the reforms of Ptolemy II. The introduction of new bronze series in Egypt often entailed the disappearance of older bronze coinage, and at least one papyrus alludes to retention of demonetized bronze coins in a royal bank.[60] Furthermore, the Ptolemaic section (see Chapter 7B.2.1) identifies a pattern in Egyptian silver hoards, which suggests that by the late second century only relatively recent coinage remained in circulation, implying that the coinage of the preceding reigns served as a source of bullion for new emissions.

Recoining was less frequent in the Seleucid empire, and it seems to have served two distinct policy goals. It could be used for political purposes, to obliterate the memory of a usurper or dynastic rival.[61] Recoining was also a method of managing the silver supply, as in the Ptolemaic empire. Some specialists have posited a constant replacement of the Seleucid silver currency, either from the outset or from the end of the third century,[62] but close attention to the hoard record suggests the process began later and was limited to Syria. In the late Seleucid period, there were reductions in the weight of the tetradrachm that required recoining of the entire silver stock of the shrunken realm of a particular ruler.

The first clear example of a politically motivated recoining is the disappearance of the precious metal coinage of the usurper Timarchus (c. 164–161). After his victory Demetrius I struck tetradrachms at Seleucia-Tigris celebrating his marriage to Queen Laodice, some of which were overstruck on the Seleucian tetradrachms of Timarchus.[63] The overstrikes can be recognized from traces of the undertypes of Timarchus and/or from spread flans which indicate that the coins were hammered to obliterate or at least mutilate the offensive designs. Demetrius's later Seleucian

[60] P.Cair.Zen. II 59176, l. 64 (255 BC). [61] Hoover (2011) 263–4.
[62] Aperghis (2001) 90–5; Aperghis (2004) 237–46; Houghton (2012) 240. [63] SC II /1, 183.

tetradrachms, depicting him alone, without his queen, no longer show evidence of overstriking. Evidently Timarchus's Seleucian coinage was not abundant, and this is consistent with other evidence suggesting that he occupied Seleucia only briefly.[64] Timarchus coined more extensively at his capital, Ecbatana, yet little of his precious metal currency has survived. Almost certainly it provided bullion for the voluminous silver issues of Demetrius I at Ecbatana. The drachms display a wide variety of styles, fabrics, and engraving techniques, including a heavy-handed use of the drill for some reverse dies.[65] It seems clear that the staff of the mint was enlarged and that production standards were relaxed or waived to enable a rapid conversion of Timarchus's drachms into drachms of the legitimate king.

Demetrius I apparently also changed long-standing Seleucid policy concerning the circulation of older coinage in Syria. Syrian hoards deposited before c. 160 often contain coins of the third-century Seleucid kings.[66] After that date kings earlier than Antiochus IV are represented in only two hoards, in one case certainly in small numbers.[67] The lifetime coinage of Alexander the Great and coins of the *Diadochi* also disappear from Syrian hoards after c. 160. Le Rider and de Callataÿ attributed their disappearance to the cessation of minting of posthumous Alexanders in western Asia Minor by c. 160, and they suggested that this change of fashion led to the recoining of the Alexanders by Seleucid mints.[68] But we have seen that older Seleucid coinage disappeared at the same time. Evidently Demetrius I ordered the reminting of all older coinage circulating in Syria. This change of policy, which is not reflected in eastern hoards, must be related to the emergence of Antiochia as the most productive mint of the empire.

It appears that subsequent rulers continued the program of recoining by recycling more recent coinage. Most Syrian hoards of the mid second century and later include coins of only one to three Seleucid reigns.[69]

---

[64] Babylonian cuneiform documents last mention Antiochus V on January 11, 161 and first mention Demetrius I on May 14, 161; see Le Rider (1965) 322, n. 3.
[65] *SC* II/1, 195.
[66] Latakia, 1979 (*IGCH* 1544), closure c. 169; Qal'at el-Moudiq, before 1966 (*SC* II/2, pp. 87–88), closure c. 165; Ma'aret en-Numan, 1960 (*CH* VI, 37 = *CH* VII, 98 = *CH* VIII, 433 = *CH* IX, 511), closure 162; Syria, 1990 (*CH* VIII, 434), closure c. 160.
[67] Syria, 1971 (*IGCH* 1555), closure c. 145; southeast Turkey, 1976 (*CH* III, 60 = *CH* IV, 64), closure 142.
[68] Le Rider and Callataÿ (2006) 96.
[69] Near East, 1977 (*CH* IV, 55); northern Syria, 1912 (*IGCH* 1548); Antakya, 1959 (*IGCH* 1553); Latakia, 1950 (*IGCH* 1561); Akkar, 1956 (*IGCH* 1559); Ghonsle, 1955 (*IGCH* 1560); Syria (?) before 1917 (*IGCH* 1554); Teffaha, 1954 (*IGCH* 1557); "Caiffa," c. 1905 (*IGCH* 1556); Syria, 1984 (*CH* VIII, 456); Ras Baalbek, 1957 (*IGCH* 1593), Demetrius I, Alexander I, Demetrius II first reign; Hama region, c. 2001 (*SC* II/2, p. 93), Demetrius I, Demetrius II first reign; unknown findspot (*CH* VII, 467),

The motive in these cases was not the eradication of rivals; the hoards in question typically include coins of kings who were overthrown by their successors. The recoining process probably helped to maintain the stable production level that has been documented for mid second-century Antiochia except in years of crisis.[70]

Our observations about the mid second-century Syrian hoards should be treated with a certain caution, because most of the relevant hoards were recorded from commerce and their integrity cannot be assured. Nevertheless, hoards of the last quarter of the second century, also recorded from commerce, typically have broader chronological samples and this may imply that Antiochus VIII and IX, despite their protracted civil war, reverted to a more passive monetary policy in Syria.

Foreign coinage of Attic weight, especially late posthumous tetradrachms of Alexander, Athenian "New Style" tetradrachms, and wreathed tetradrachms of western Asia Minor, continued to enter Syria after the reform of Demetrius I. They are represented in all but the smallest hoards deposited between c. 155 and c. 140. After this, the importation of foreign currency tapered off, so that Seleucid coins predominate in most hoards of the late second century.[71]

The fragmentation of the Seleucid kingdom under the sons of Antiochus VIII led to a revival of interventionist monetary policies. Seleucus VI based himself at Seleucia-Calycadnus as he prepared his invasion of Syria Seleukis. During his sojourn in Cilicia, he reduced the weight of his tetradrachm sharply, gaining an obol of silver for each recoined tetradrachm so that he could mint 25 tetradrachms from the silver reclaimed from 24 of the heavier coins.[72] His reform was motivated by his urgent need to finance his military adventure from a base with limited resources that could be used to raise money.

After gaining possession of Antiochia in 88/7, Philip I issued a massive coinage of tetradrachms. Their abundance is in sharp contrast to the rarity of tetradrachms of his older brothers and of his cousin Antiochus X. The explanation lies in another weight reduction, from an average weight of c. 16.00 grams under Antiochus X to 15.65 grams under

---

Demetrius I, Alexander I, Demetrius II first reign; Aleppo, c. 1930 (*IGCH* 1562), Tryphon; Khan el-Abde, 1938 (*IGCH* 1597), Tryphon, Antiochus VII; Syria or south Anatolia, 1999 (*SC* II/2, p. 94), Antiochus V, Demetrius I, Alexander I, Demetrius II first reign, Antiochus VI, Antiochus VII; Syria, 1997 (*SC* II/2, 94–95), Demetrius II first reign, Antiochus VII; Latakia, 1948 (*IGCH* 1563), Antiochus VII, Demetrius II second reign; Antakya? 1964 or earlier (*IGCH* 1564), Alexander II; Antakya, 1932–9 (*IGCH* 1565), Alexander II; coastal Syria or northern Lebanon, 2000 (*SC* I/2, p. 96), Alexander II; citadel of Amafya, May 1986 (*CH* VIII, 360), Demetrius II.

[70] Hoover (2011) 251–4.   [71] Le Rider and Callataÿ (2006) 82–4.   [72] *SC* II/1, 555.

Philip.⁷³ As was usual with such metrological reforms, it was necessary to recoin the entire existing stock of currency in order to enforce acceptance of the lightweight tetradrachms. This recoining effort no doubt accounts for the great rarity of the silver coinage of Philip's recent predecessors.⁷⁴ But he gained only half an obol of silver for each recoined tetradrachm. The modest gain suggests that his primary motive was not to expand his monetary supply but to eradicate the memory of other rulers and to create a monopoly for coinage bearing his name and portrait.

The process of regularly withdrawing older coinage to provide bullion for new issues is attested only by Syrian hoards, and episodes of recoining after weight reductions occurred only in the west. Numerous eastern hoards show that older coinage, even coinage of the first Seleucids, remained in circulation in the Upper Satrapies until the mid second century. This difference in monetary policies illustrates the degree of autonomy enjoyed by administrators in the eastern provinces.

6 Quantitative Comparisons

We have die studies for the Antiochia mint from Seleucus I through Antiochus V, and also for the reign of Antiochus VII.⁷⁵ A comprehensive die study of the coinage of Ptolemy V through Ptolemy IX⁷⁶ allows for comparisons of the output of silver tetradrachms at Antiochia and Alexandria at two different points in the second century. This method of comparison has been successfully tested recently.⁷⁷

Under Antiochus IV Epiphanes, the Antiochia mint employed 57 obverse dies over a period of twelve years, for an average of 4.75 dies per year (though the rate of die usage was lower at the start of the reign and increased over time). During this period Ptolemy VI revived the minting of silver in Egypt, which had lapsed by the end of the third century. He produced, or at least initiated, a large issue of unmarked, undated tetradrachms, that was surely intended at least in part to finance an attack on the Seleucid empire. The obverse die count for this coinage stands at 151 at a minimum,⁷⁸ but we do not know the duration of the minting and hence cannot calculate a yearly average. If the entire emission was produced intensively over a period of two or three years, for the sole purpose of financing a war against Antiochus IV, obverse die use could

---

⁷³ *SC* II/1, 596. ⁷⁴ Hoover (2011) 259–61. ⁷⁵ Le Rider (1999); Lorber (2016c).
⁷⁶ Olivier (2012). ⁷⁷ Iossif (2015). ⁷⁸ Faucher et al. (2017).

have averaged fifty to seventy-five dies per year, many multiples of the rate of die use at Antiochia, even though Epiphanes twice invaded Egypt, battled a revolt in Judea, celebrated a major international festival at Daphne, and organized an eastern campaign. If production of the unmarked Alexandrian emission lasted almost until the revival of regular tetradrachm production in 155,[79] obverse die use would have averaged around nine per year, still nearly double the rate at Antiochia under Antiochus IV.

During the reign of Antiochus VII, the Antiochia mint employed 116 tetradrachm obverse dies, for an annual average of 11.6 dies over the ten-year reign. This is more than double the rate of die consumption under Antiochus IV, but it falls within the average range for noncrisis years under Demetrius I through Demetrius II, second reign.[80] During the ten-year period when Antiochus ruled the Seleucid empire, the Alexandria mint under Ptolemy VIII was active intermittently, apparently failing to strike tetradrachms in 135/4 and 130/29 (the latter the beginning of the Alexandrian revolt against the king). The mint employed a total of 16 obverse dies, for an average of only 1.6 dies per year. This low rate of production may be attributable in part to the fact that the Ptolemaic empire was at peace and secure from any Seleucid threat, with Antiochus VII initially embroiled in civil war with Tryphon and later planning for the reconquest of the Upper Satrapies.

As these snapshots illustrate, levels of monetary production fluctuated over time in both empires, even at major mints which operated regularly, if not continuously. Other studies have demonstrated that production levels within each empire varied from mint to mint.[81]

7 Conclusions

Seleucid monetary policies changed in the course of the second century, but only in the western part of the empire. Demetrius I introduced new methods of managing and renewing the currency supply of Syria. Monetary policy in Coele Syria and Phoenicia was influenced by the Ptolemaic legacy in the region, as well as by Phoenician and Judean ethnic identities. The quasi-municipal bronze coinages of the Phoenician cities and the Seleucid eagles struck at some of the same cities may have

---

[79] Faucher et al. (2017) 221–2.   [80] Hoover (2011) 251–4.
[81] For the Seleucid empire, see Le Rider (1999) (Antiochia); and Boillet (2013) (Ecbatana). For the Ptolemaic empire, Olivier (2012).

integrated civic institutions into the royal administration, further blurring the distinction between royal and civic in this part of the Seleucid empire. The administration of the Upper Satrapies, however, maintained the original laissez-faire approach of Seleucus I. Coinage already in circulation was allowed to remain in circulation indefinitely, and all coinage of Attic weight was legal tender regardless of its issuing authority. In the east, in particular, this implied the circulation of coins bearing the names and portraits of non-Seleucid rulers, including the kings of Bactria, Parthia, Elymais, and Characene. It is difficult to define the Seleucid attitude toward the symbolic aspect of coins as expressions of royal authority. In the case of their own coinage, they seemed to exploit its potential (at least, to a certain extent), but they seemed to overlook it completely when the coinage emanated from other sovereigns, insofar as these coinages served their primary fiscal needs (i.e. the payment of the army and administrative transactions).

2B THE PTOLEMAIC EMPIRE
Catharine C. Lorber

1 Introduction

Ptolemaic rule, and in particular its first century, was distinguished by multiple monetary reforms which subjected the currency system and the economy to repeated episodes of transition and adaptation. Certain monetary policies were imposed throughout the Ptolemaic empire. In general, however, different policies obtained in each province, though on occasion some aspects were coordinated. The patterns suggest that monetary policies could be dictated from Alexandria, but in some cases or at some times, local governors or financial officials may have had discretion over the currency.

2 Late Fourth through Third Centuries

2.1 *Egypt*

The foundational currency reforms of the first two Ptolemies have been well studied, so we need mention only the most significant reforms here. The most consequential monetary reform of Ptolemy I was his abandonment of the Attic weight standard and his creation of a closed monetary zone in which his own coinage enjoyed a monopoly. Foreign coinages were subject to exchange at the points of entry to Egypt, no doubt yielding a profit to his administration. This policy was ultimately extended to most or all of his external possessions and was maintained by his successors.

The most consequential monetary reform of the second Ptolemy was his introduction in the mid to late 260s of a new bronze coinage, called Series 3 in current numismatic terminology, which for the first time provided a drachma in bronze. This reform took place in the context of broader economic reforms which affected the tax system, other royal revenues, and the financing of native temples, all of which seem designed to promote and indeed enforce the monetization of the Egyptian countryside. A preliminary survey of Egyptian excavation coins found that Series 2, which includes most bronze coinage of Ptolemy I and the pre-reform bronze coinage of Ptolemy II, is represented at eighteen sites throughout Egypt, from Alexandria to Elephantine.[82] The total number of sites is the same for Series 3, and the total number of coins retrieved is actually smaller. These patterns indicate that the monetization of the Egyptian *chora* was essentially a fait accompli before the celebrated reforms of Ptolemy II.[83] The archaeological finds are corroborated by Theban tax documents attesting the use of bronze coinage in tax payments in the last years of Ptolemy I. Such receipts are more numerous under Ptolemy II and from 264 they reflect the payment of the salt tax, a capitation tax levied on nearly every adult.[84]

Another common assumption is that Philadelphus's reformed bronze coinage was intended to replace the use of silver in the *chora*.[85] This had little or nothing to do with Egyptian traditions concerning the use of bronze – the use of silver coinage was well established in the fifth and fourth centuries BC – and should instead be related to the fiduciary character of the bronze coinage and to concerns over the stock of silver in Egypt. Indeed, by the reign of Ptolemy IV silver coinage largely disappears from documentary sources, and its disappearance has led papyrologists and economic historians to hypothesize a silver shortage. That hypothesis has been confirmed through the study of coin hoards (see below).

---

[82] Faucher (2011) 443.
[83] This conclusion differs from that of Faucher (2011) 438–9, who noted that Series 3–5 *combined* are represented at more Egyptian sites than Series 2.
[84] Muhs (2005) 6–8.
[85] Rostovtzeff (1941) I, 400; Gara (1984) 115; Mørkholm (1991) 105–6; von Reden (2007) 60–1.

The Zenon archive and other papyri from the Arsinoite nome inform us that salaries were often paid late or transmuted to payments in kind.[86] These phenomena and the widespread use of different forms of credit in the mid third century suggest that monetary supplies, whether of silver or of bronze, were inadequate to meet the needs of the Egyptian economy.[87]

For reasons which remain obscure, Ptolemy III revived the Attic weight standard for his precious metal coinage, probably upon his return from his Asian campaign. Subsequently production of precious metal coinage became episodic and was generally limited to times of military crisis. We can also observe a decline in the number of silver hoards closing in the reigns of Ptolemy III, IV, and V, a decrease in the size of the hoards, and the disappearance of older silver coinage from these hoards beginning in Philopator's reign.[88] This might be attributed to natural attrition were it not for the fact that silver hoards from Syria and Phoenicia show no comparable loss of older coinage; hoards deposited at the end of the Fifth Syrian War contain substantial quantities of old tetradrachms of Ptolemy I and II. The Egyptian hoards supplement the papyrological sources in that they show silver coinage disappeared from the Delta, a region scarcely represented in the papyrological record. Apparently, most older silver coinage was withdrawn from circulation in Egypt, and the state found mechanisms for attracting new silver issues back into the treasury not too long after they were placed into circulation.

A less noted reform of Ptolemy III was his restriction on the areas of circulation of the royal bronze coinage. Series 2 circulated very widely outside of Egypt, and issues struck under Ptolemy II are particularly well documented in Greece, where they financed Ptolemaic involvement in the Chremonidean War.[89] Series 3, the reformed bronze currency of Ptolemy II, circulated in Syria and Phoenicia, Cyprus, and Ptolemaic Asia Minor, as well as in Egypt. But beginning with Series 4, the first bronze coinage of Ptolemy III, the provenances are almost exclusively Egyptian. Corresponding bronze series were inaugurated in his foreign possessions, and these also tended to remain within their provinces.[90]

Ptolemy IV imposed a single administration over the production of bronze coins at Alexandria, in Cyprus, at Tyre, and in Cyrenaica, all of whose products were linked by shared controls.[91] This centralized

---

[86] Reekmans (1994). [87] Von Reden (2001) 70–3; (2007) 151–252.
[88] Lorber (2013) 136–8; 148–50. [89] Varoucha-Christodoulopoulou (1953–4).
[90] Provenances cited here and elsewhere in this chapter are recorded in Lorber (2018).
[91] Lorber (2016b) 107–8.

administration of the provincial bronze mints ended before the next currency reform in Egypt.

The final currency reform of third-century Egypt began with a demonetization of most existing bronze coinage in 207/6.[92] This demonetization is reflected in hoards found throughout Egypt, whose loss can be attributed to the outbreak of the Great Revolt of Upper Egypt as well as widespread disorders in the Delta.[93] The demonetization was followed by an episode of countermarking of two bronze denominations which were allowed to remain in circulation, then by the introduction of a new bronze coinage (Series 6).[94] Papyrological sources indicate that around this time the bronze drachm was drastically devalued, from a unit notionally equivalent to the silver drachm, to a unit worth only one sixtieth of a silver drachm.[95] The unfortunate residents of Egypt thus had to contend with three simultaneous crises: social unrest and civil war, demonetization of most of their savings (if they had any), and a drastic devaluation of the only currency available to most people.

The Alexandria mint produced substantial issues of silver and gold coinage in the early years of Ptolemy V, at least in part to finance the campaign to recover Syria and Phoenicia from Antiochus III. These coins left almost no trace in the papyrological sources, and none in the Egyptian hoard record. From literary sources we can infer that these precious metal emissions accrued to the accounts of elite soldiers like the mercenary general Scopas the Aetolian and his officers, who earned 10 gold *minae* and 1 gold *mina* per day, respectively (Polyb. 13.2.3), and probably also to high-ranking officials.

2.2 Syria and Phoenicia

For most of the third century, production of coinage in Syria and Phoenicia was managed through, or delegated to, established local polities. When Ptolemy I occupied the region for the final time before the battle of Ipsus, there was one active mint in his new territories. Since the late Persian period, Jerusalem had produced a coinage of small silver denominations inscribed with the name of the province of Judea in Hebrew (Yehud). This

---

[92] For the date, see Gorre and Lorber (2020).   [93] Lorber (2018) II, 146–153.
[94] Lorber (2000) 80–2; Huston and Lorber (2001).
[95] The 60 to 1 ratio was hypothesized by Heichelheim (1930) 12–21; 25–7; Reekmans (1951) 69–78; Maresch (1996) 6, 21; 55–6; 58–9; 72–3; von Reden (2007) 71. Strong support comes from a Cyrenean inscription attesting the adoption of this ratio at Cyrene at some point in the second century; see Rosamilia (2016); (2017).

was the only Palestinian coinage to survive Alexander's conquest, and under Ptolemy it adopted Lagid types modeled on those of Alexandria, though Judea was still named alone as the issuing authority, with no mention of the king's name or title. These coins had a very restricted circulation, consistent with their local issuing authority. We may envision a degree of local administrative autonomy in which the Judahite governor/high priest collected the taxes, converted them into coinage, and spent the coinage locally for public purposes, perhaps principally for the pay of soldiers in small guardposts.

The province of Syria and Phoenicia eventually became a closed monetary zone like Egypt, in which royal Ptolemaic coinage (supplemented by the Yehud coinage) enjoyed a monopoly. Apart from the Judahite coinage, production of precious metal currency was extremely episodic in the early Ptolemaic period, with one issue struck at Sidon and Tyre in 294, after their surrender to Ptolemy I, and no further coining at these coastal mints until the outbreak of the Second Syrian War c. 274.[96] Two extraordinarily large issues of Sidon and Tyre, perhaps datable to this period but in any case no later than 267/6, probably reflect the reminting of stocks of older coinage – local Phoenician issues and coinage of Alexander the Great and Philip Arrhidaeus.

The early issues of Sidon and Tyre are datable because of control links to the coinage of Alexandria, but they differ from Alexandrian coinage in that the mint cities are clearly identified by mint marks. This use of mint marks may follow the practice of Alexander, who inscribed his Phoenician coinage with the names of the mint cities, the names of local city-kings, and/or their regnal dates.

Beginning in 266/5 the pattern of coastal coin production transitioned from episodic to regular. Tyre struck modest issues of silver tetradrachms bearing the regnal dates of Ptolemy II, from year 20 through year 24. In 261/0, a major reconfiguration of the mint system introduced a twenty-year period of regular coin production at elevated levels. Sidon and Tyre were joined by three new coastal mints, Ptolemais, Jaffa, and Gaza, and the five mints produced annual issues of silver tetradrachms supplemented by less-regular issues of gold *mnaieia*, all dated by the regnal years of Ptolemy II. These coinages display additional controls in the form of letters or monograms. Many of the controls served to distinguish different emissions in the same year, and most were employed over several or even many years. Nine controls appear on the coinage of more than one mint, in some cases

---

[96] Lorber (2012a) 36–40.

contemporaneously. This sharing of controls proves that these markings were not part of an internal system by which each mint kept track of the workers responsible for the weight and purity of the coins; instead, the control system must have served administrative needs. Hypothetically, the Syro-Phoenician controls could connect the coinage with the fiscal cycle, that is, they could reflect each city's conversion of a year's taxes, or a portion of them, into a year's coinage/expenditures.[97] The output of Sidon and especially of Tyre is much larger than that of the other mints, consistent with their greater economic importance, and between them they account for nearly all the emissions of gold.

The Syro-Phoenician tetradrachms of this period feature an idealizing portrait of the dynastic founder and a new legend naming "Ptolemy Soter" instead of "Ptolemy the King."[98] These two traits allow for the identification of contemporary (but not explicitly dated) coinages at Alexandria and the Cypriote mints. The contemporary Alexandrian tetradrachms are small issues, soon discontinued in favor of decadrachms honoring Arsinoe Philadelphus. The termination of Alexandrian tetradrachms, considered alongside the very wide circulation of the Syro-Phoenician and Cypriote tetradrachms, points to a shift in imperial military finance away from Egypt to Syro-Phoenicia and Cyprus.

Regular production of precious metal coinage ended after 242/1. Its cessation coincides with the end of the Third Syrian War, but also, more generally, with the policy of Ptolemy III suspending the provision of new silver currency. The Jerusalem mint probably closed at this time. Production of Syro-Phoenician bronze coinage was now concentrated at Tyre, which imitated the denominations of Alexandrian Series 5 but identified its issues with a club symbol. From this time forward bronze coinage from Alexandria and Cyprus essentially ceased to enter the province of Syria and Phoenicia.

After 242/1 the Syro-Phoenician mints reverted to episodic production of precious metal coinage in connection with military crises. In 224/3 the five mints struck a coordinated issue linked by a shared control, probably in response to the death of Seleucus II and the threat of renewed hostilities with his successor.[99] After the battle of Raphia, Tyre, Sidon, and Ptolemais

---

[97] Lorber (2015a) 65; Iossif (2014a) 71.
[98] This is the first appearance of the *epiklesis* Soter in an official Ptolemaic document; it was not used in the dating protocols of papyri before 259; see Hazzard (2000) 3–24.
[99] Mørkholm (1980). The date of the issue is known because Jaffa and Gaza dated their share of the emission.

struck celebratory issues in silver and gold, undated as was usual with occasional emissions.

Shortly afterward, a modest attempt was made to restore a more regular rhythm of silver coin production. A new series of silver tetradrachms in the name of Ptolemy Soter bore numerals which are assumed to refer to an era beginning with year 48 and continuing to year 58.[100] Although various eras have been proposed, the current near-consensus places the start of the era in 262/1, in which case the Julian equivalents of the era dates are 215/4 to 205/4.[101] Unlike the dated coinages struck from 261/0 to 242/1, the era coinage does not advertise its mint, but provenances predominantly from Israel, Lebanon, and Syria point to an origin in Syria and Phoenicia. If we are correct in surmising a relation between annual dates and the fiscal cycle, the era coinage may have been struck from a revenue stream not connected with a city. The era coinage was later revived and from its beginning to its end was struck over more than half a century, with significant interruptions. Its mint was relocated from Syria and Phoenicia to Cyprus and back.[102] The event of 262/1 commemorated by the era must therefore have been an event of more than local significance. Past attempts to interpret the era have assumed commemoration of a political or cultic event,[103] but it is worth asking if the administrative reforms of Ptolemy Philadelphus could have created some new fiscal institution in these provinces with its own treasury and, perhaps, the authority to mint coinage.

The Syro-Phoenician mints were reactivated to finance the Fifth Syrian War. This complex coinage involved several series. The main series was neither dated nor identified as to mint.[104] A parallel undated series shared four obverse dies with the main series but was inscribed with the mint marks of several coastal cities including Sidon and Tyre as well as other cities (Tripolis, Byblus, Berytus, Dora, Strato's Tower) which had never before served as Ptolemaic mints. Jaffa and Ptolemais struck tetradrachms dated to regnal years 5, 6, and 7. The issues with mint marks evidently represent special contributions toward the war effort by the cities. The main series itself must reflect a non-civic revenue source, presumably the royal or provincial treasury. Two additional series were produced by uncertain mints in the final year of the war, one of which has been shown, through careful stylistic analysis, to have emanated from two different workshops or mints.[105] The diversity of these coinages points to

---

[100] Mørkholm (1975–76), concluding that the coinage was dated according to the Aradian era.
[101] Lorber (2007a) 106–10 for a summary of the proposals. [102] Olivier (2012) 571–8.
[103] See Mørkholm (1975–6) for a summary of earlier views; Lorber (2007a) 107–9.
[104] Mørkholm (1979). [105] Carlen (2019).

a major financial mobilization involving many different revenue sources and several administrative modalities. Alexandria's principal contribution to the war finances consisted of entirely unmarked tetradrachms.

2.3 Cyprus

Like Egypt and Syro-Phoenicia, Cyprus under the Ptolemies was a closed monetary zone. Its earliest explicitly Ptolemaic coinage was struck immediately after the island's recovery by Ptolemy I in 294 and shares controls with the coinage of Alexandria.[106] At this early stage, two series can be recognized on the basis of their controls, but they are not identified by mint marks. Later there are three principal series, no doubt corresponding to the output of Salamis, Citium, and Paphos, whose mint marks appear on gold *mnaieia* in the name of Arsinoe Philadelphus, but not on the silver coinage. Cypriote production of precious metal coinage was far more significant than that of Syria and Phoenicia before 261/0, but because the Cypriote coinage is undated, it is difficult to comment on rhythms of production. The presence of a Gallic shield on certain groups links them to Alexandrian issues struck during the First Syrian War, while a legend naming Ptolemy Soter implies that other groups were contemporary with the Syro-Phoenician coinage issued annually between 261/0 and 242/1. The Gallic shield groups, like their Alexandrian counterparts, are well represented in Greece, Syria and Phoenicia, and Cilicia, and also circulated in Egypt, whereas the Soter groups are found mainly in Syria and Phoenicia. These patterns suggest the role played by Cypriote silver in financing the Chremonidian War and the early Syrian Wars, illustrating once again how Alexandria shifted the burden of its imperial project to its provinces.

The groups with the Soter legend appear to represent the last Cypriote silver coinage of the third century. The production of precious metal coinage probably ceased after 242/1, as in Syria and Phoenicia, and in conformity with the policy of Ptolemy III concerning the provision of coined silver. Around this same time an increasing supply of bronze coinage was ensured when Paphos inaugurated a distinctive series depicting the cult statue of Aphrodite Paphia on the reverse, with denominations corresponding to Alexandrian Series 5. In an exception to the general rule that bronze coinages of this period did not circulate outside their home

[106] Lorber (2012a) 38.

provinces, these Aphrodite bronzes are well represented in Pamphylia and Cilicia.[107]

2.4 Asia Minor and Thrace

Ptolemaic Cilicia was probably a closed monetary zone. The enormous Meydancikkale hoard, found in a Ptolemaic fortress in the Taurus mountains of western Cilicia, included silver coins of Alexander and of various Hellenistic kings along with an especially large Ptolemaic component.[108] This was evidently a royal treasure, and its mixed character suggests that it was formed near the border of Ptolemaic territory, probably through money changing and customs duties collected at the fortress.

Matters were different in southwest Asia Minor. Roger Bagnall concluded that Ptolemaic coins played a very minor role in the monetary circulation of Asia Minor.[109] Recent research has confirmed the scarcity of Ptolemaic coins in most of southwest Asia Minor but has identified concentrations of Lagid bronze coins at three coastal cities firmly held by the Ptolemies – Halicarnassus, Telmessus, and Caunus.[110] These concentrations are the result of local coin production. In a departure from the usual pattern in which a single mint dominated bronze production for each province, there were two equally productive royal bronze mints in western Lycia under Ptolemy III, one of them certainly at Telmessus, the seat of his cousin Ptolemy, son of Lysimachus, the other probably at Caunus.[111]

Other coin series from Asia Minor and Thrace suggest an active role for certain *poleis* in the aftermath of the Third Syrian War. The clearest evidence comes from Lebedus in Ionia, which after its refoundation as Ptolemais produced a short-lived municipal bronze coinage in two series, one depicting Ptolemy III and the other depicting Berenice II, both signed with the names of local moneyers.[112] Various series of tetradrachms, usually portraying Ptolemy III, bear mint marks of Aenus, Ephesus, and other cities which cannot be identified.[113] Both their iconography and their titulature are extremely variable. The lack of consistency points to the argument that these coins were struck in civic mints under the control of local officials. The volume of

---

[107] Personal communication from A. Tolga Tek and H. Koker. A possible explanation for this phenomenon could be repatriation of Pamphylian and Cilician mercenaries who served on Cyprus.
[108] Davesne and Le Rider (1989).   [109] Bagnall (1976) 198–200.   [110] Cavagna (2015) 211–20.
[111] Ashton (2002) 8; 10; Konuk (2004).   [112] Dieudonné (1902).   [113] Lorber (2014a) 120–7.

production seems too small to have covered regular expenses such as the pay of garrisons, and the association of the cult title Soter with the third Ptolemy in some series suggests that the tetradrachms may have been minted to pay the costs of civic cults in his honor. Puzzlingly, however, the Asia Minor tetradrachms are not found in modern Turkey but almost exclusively in the Levant.

2.5 Cyrenaica

Ptolemaic Cyrenaica was definitely a closed monetary zone, but it had characteristics unlike any other province.[114] As *eparch* or king Magas minted silver with Ptolemaic types, on the Ptolemaic weight standard, as well as bronze coinage; but curiously, his silver is not found in Africa, only in Crete.[115] After Ptolemy III took possession of Cyrenaica, the province was deprived of precious metal coinage. The local mints produced bronze coinage only, usually featuring a head of Libya as patron goddess of the region. The bronze-only policy may have been punitive, for the *poleis* of Cyrenaica had revolted repeatedly against Ptolemaic rule; or it may have been a precaution against further revolts since silver was the currency for the engagement of mercenaries. But we must also note that in a few years Ptolemy III Euergetes would suppress the production of silver coinage throughout his empire and withdraw it from circulation in Egypt. His policy restricting the circulation of bronze coinage completed the monetary isolation of Cyrenaica: bronze coinage from Alexandria, Cyprus, or Tyre did not enter Cyrenaica, and similarly the bronze coinage of Cyrenaica did not circulate in the other provinces of the Ptolemaic empire.

Precious metal coinage should have been attracted to Cyrenaica by the famous trade in silphium, but no trace of it has been found archaeologically.[116] Most likely the silphium trade was conducted entirely on credit. The bronze-only policy did not affect the prosperity of the residents of the cities, if we can judge from the flourishing house and necropolis construction of the late third and early second centuries.[117]

The centralized administration of provincial bronze mints under Ptolemy IV (see 1.1 above) was extended to Cyrenaica later than to Cyprus and Tyre. It was associated with a revival of mint activity at Berenike-Euesperides, which displayed its civic *parasemon*, an apple

---

[114] Lorber (2016b).   [115] Fischer-Bossert (2016) 60; Stefanakis (2016).   [116] Crisafulli (2014).
[117] Laronde (1987) 423.

branch, on its coinage.[118] The occasion for granting this coining privilege was perhaps the enrollment of the city's namesake, Berenice II, in the Ptolemaic dynastic cult in 211/0.

2.6 Coin Production outside the Ptolemaic Empire

A few coin series can be associated with temporary Ptolemaic occupations of foreign territory or with alliances. During his Greek campaign of 308 the first Ptolemy occupied Corinth, Sicyon, and Megara, holding the two former for several years. The mints of these cities issued silver drachms of Ptolemaic type and weight, presumably as their contribution to the pay of the Lagid garrisons. The Corinthian drachms of Ptolemaic type were associated in the Chiliomodi hoard of 1932 (*IGCH* 85; *EH* I, 1) together with regular Corinthian coinage and with Ptolemaic tetradrachms from Alexandria, the latter perhaps implying that the occupied cities did not bear the full cost of their garrisons.

A Ptolemaic bronze mint operated briefly in eastern Sicily, probably about 264.[119] The coinage was most likely intended to pay a contingent of soldiers sent to support Hieron II in the early stages of his career. The alliance was ruptured when Hieron found himself at war with Rome, and thereafter Hieron struck imitative coins in the name of Ptolemy the King, but of Sicilian style.

In 254 a Ptolemaic fleet protected Byzantium from attack by Antiochus II.[120] A bronze coinage was issued in the name of King Ptolemy, depicting his deceased and deified sister-wife Arsinoe Philadelphus, with local Byzantine types on the smallest denominations.[121]

At the beginning of the Third Syrian War, Ptolemy III occupied Seleucia-Pieria and other territories on the northern Syrian coast. Associated with this occupation is a bronze coinage depicting and naming his queen, Berenice II, on the obverse, probably minted at Seleucia-Pieria itself or perhaps at Heraclea-by-the-Sea (Ras ibn Hani), site of a Ptolemaic garrison.[122]

A bronze coinage depicting the third Ptolemy is found abundantly in the Peloponnese, with the discoveries centering on Corinth.[123] It was probably struck locally to pay a Ptolemaic garrison at Corinth after 243, when Euergetes was elected *hegemon* of the Achaean League. An alternative

---

[118] Lorber (2016b) 108. [119] Wolf and Lorber (2011). [120] Psoma (2008).
[121] Arslan and Özen (2000), redated and reinterpreted by Psoma (2008). [122] Lorber (2007b).
[123] Chryssanthaki (2005) 168–9.

interpretation relates this coinage to the Ptolemaic alliance with Cleomenes of Sparta.[124]

3 The Second Century BC

3.1 Egypt

Papyrological sources provide no solid evidence for exchange between bronze and silver coinage in the first decades after introduction of the bronze standard in 207/6.[125] Apparently bronze and silver functioned as separate currencies, and silver was rarely spent as money, but instead was offered in pledges against loans. Under Ptolemy V the monopoly for currency exchange was farmed to goldsmiths,[126] a clue that it was not sufficiently profitable to attract bids on its own. It is only in the second sole reign of Ptolemy VI that exchange banks are again attested.[127] A clear definition of the relation of silver and bronze coinage, at a ratio of 1200 : 1,[128] may be one of the reforms that followed Philometor's return from exile on Cyprus.

The bronze coinage was subject to weight reductions before stabilizing in Philometor's second sole reign. Increases in the prices of basic commodities over the course of the second century, as expressed on the bronze standard, have been understood as evidence for devaluation of the bronze currency, but the sparseness of the data makes it impossible to coordinate these price increases with the declining weight of the coinage. The *timê* (price) of the silver stater with respect to bronze also increased moderately over time, with a gap in the evidence between 161/0 and the early 130s BC.[129] The stable metrology of the bronze coinage over this period compels us to conclude that exchange rates were established by fiat and were unrelated to the physical characteristics of the bronze coinage.[130]

Under Ptolemy VI the Alexandria mint produced a large mass of unmarked silver tetradrachms. The earliest datable examples occurred in a hoard in commerce in 2016, with a closing date of 174/3.[131] It seems plausible that an important portion of this coinage was struck to finance the campaign of Lenaeus and Eulaeus to recover Coele Syria from the Seleucids.

---

[124] Hackens (1968) 84–6.   [125] Lorber (2017) 24–39.
[126] P.Mich. XVIII, 771 (Arsinoites, 195) and 774 (Arsinoites, 194); *BGU* VI 1242 (Oxyrhynchus, 193).
[127] O.Bodl. I 50 (Thebes, 159/8).   [128] P.Mich. III 145.   [129] Lorber (2017).
[130] Faucher and Lorber (2010) 43–5; 48–9; 52–4.   [131] Carlen and Lorber (2018) 24–5.

In 155/4 the Alexandria mint initiated a new pattern of coin production which endured to the end of the dynasty. The mint struck regular annual issues of silver tetradrachms dated by the regnal year of the king, but with an enigmatic mint mark ΠΑ indistinguishable from the mint mark of Paphos. The identification of precious metal coin issues by means of regnal dates and mint marks was already well established on Cyprus (see Section 3.2). It might seem, then, that the practice of placing mint marks and dates on precious metal coins had become a convention, without particular administrative significance. Yet Alexandria continued to mint gold coins – *mnaieia* and occasional half-*mnaieia* in the name of Arsinoe Philadelphus – without corresponding mint marks and dates, whereas the *mnaieia* of the Cypriote mints bore both markings. Alexandrian bronze coinage, like Ptolemaic bronze coinage generally, was also undated.[132] The fact that in Egypt silver was the only one of the three monetary metals to be dated suggests a connection with the long-standing problem of Egypt's limited stock of silver.

The practice of dating the silver can be understood as an administrative tool for managing the orderly withdrawal of older silver coinage. Tacit recalls of various bronze series can be inferred from the record of bronze hoards.[133] Silver hoards are remarkably few in the second century but seem to attest a similar process. The Keneh hoard of 1923 (*IGCH* 1708; *EH* I, 209), closing in 145/4, still contained 17 examples of the undated tetradrachm issue of Ptolemy VI. The Tell Nebesheh hoard of 1886 (*IGCH* 1709; *EH* I, 210), closing in 131/0, contained only dated tetradrachms, perhaps only of Ptolemy VIII. A hoard in the Greco-Roman Museum of Alexandria, closing in 107/6, contained no coins earlier than year 50 of Ptolemy VIII.[134] Two hoards closing early in the joint reign of Cleopatra III and Ptolemy X – Avenue of the Sphinxes, Karnak, 1972–4 (*CH* III, 64; *EH* I, 215) and Dendera, 1918 (*EH* I, 216) – opened with tetradrachms of Cleopatra III and Ptolemy IX. The disappearance of older coinage evident in these hoards is too rapid and systematic to be attributable to natural attrition. In fact, it appears that the pace of the recalls quickened and that silver tetradrachms circulated for ever shorter periods before being recoined. A further inference is that there was some pressing need for

---

[132] The only exception was the short-lived Alexandrian Series 8, displaying the third and fourth regnal years of Ptolemy IX.

[133] Faucher and Lorber (2010) 35–6; 45–6.

[134] This hoard was included as part of the Kom Truga hoard of 1931 (*IGCH* 1719; *EH* I, 232) by Shahin (2005). Reconstruction of the GRM hoard is based on comparison with the original description of the Kom Truga find by Adriani, aided by the critique of J. Olivier.

fresh coinage driving this cycle. Possibly there was some requirement that state expenditures be made in coins dated to the current fiscal year and older coinage only circulated secondarily, in the private economy.

The regular provision of silver coinage did not imply an abandonment of the bronze standard, which continued in use until the fall of the Lagid dynasty and even beyond. The maintenance of a reliable supply of silver was probably intended to lubricate administrative processes, such as the payment of penalties, the conversion of taxes collected in bronze to silver, payment of gratuities to officials and their retainers, and likely the payment of (at least some) salaries of state officials.[135]

3.2 Cyprus

After the final settlement of the Fifth Syrian War, Cyprus became a center for minting precious metal coinage. The mints of Salamis, Citium, and Paphos produced regular annual issues of silver tetradrachms, supplemented by occasional issues of gold *mnaieia* in the name of Arsinoe Philadelphus. The silver and gold coinages both bear the mint marks of Salamis, Citium, or Paphos and the regnal date of the king, beginning in 193/2 at Salamis, 192/1 at Citium, and 180/79 at Paphos.[136] Amathus briefly functioned as a mint during the Sixth Syrian War, striking tetradrachms in 170/69 and 169/8.

If the mint marks and dates suggest a relation between these coinages and the fiscal cycle of the issuing cities, there are other markings whose administrative significance is far from obvious. The tetradrachms sometimes bear subsidiary symbols, usually of a religious, dynastic, or military character. The patterns of appearance are opaque – sometimes the same symbol appeared for several years in succession, some years lack symbols, Salamis and Citium occasionally coordinated their symbols, and Paphos rarely used symbols until the accession of Ptolemy IX.

A second series of era tetradrachms (see Section 2.2 above) was struck on Cyprus from 193/2 to 171/0. It has some characteristics not seen in the first series of era tetradrachms, notably contrasts of style implying that from year 86 (177/6) two workshops alternated in engraving the dies and perhaps in producing the coinage, while in year 90 (173/2) the two workshops collaborated.[137] Apparently the administrative entity which

---

[135] For examples of penalties and payments to officials, see Verhoogt (2005). For the conversion of taxes into silver, see P.Tebt. I 121 and the commentary of Hoogendijk (2010) 316–8.
[136] Mørkholm and Kromann (1984).   [137] Carlen (2015).

authorized this coinage contracted it out, and this is consistent with the absence of mint marks. As with the first series of era tetradrachms, the second series may represent disposition of revenues from sources not associated with the cities which operated the major mints.

Second-century Cyprus had a third silver coinage comprising denominations smaller than the tetradrachm: didrachms and drachms featuring a bust of Dionysus on the obverse, triobols and diobols portraying the reigning king. The values of these small denominations overlapped the values of bronze coins, and their exceptional types suggest some special function. The most intriguing hypothesis connects this coinage with the Artists of Dionysus on Cyprus.[138] The coins bear neither dates nor mint marks, yet it is clear from variations in their style and fabric that they were minted intermittently; in fact, their production ceased altogether at mid-century and resumed only in the final years of Ptolemy VIII.[139] In this latter period only the Dionysian types were revived, and the coins sometimes share the subsidiary symbols of tetradrachms. The exceptional obverse types of these Cypriote minor denominations mark them as an epichoric coinage that did not circulate outside the island. In contrast, Cypriote tetradrachms of the standard Ptolemaic design are found in Egyptian and especially Syro-Phoenician hoards.

There is no evidence that Cyprus adopted the bronze standard which dominated the monetary economy of Egypt. Cypriote bronze coinage under Ptolemy VI retained the denominational structure and fabric of third-century Egyptian bronze coinage, so that it was not easily compatible with the bronze coinage of contemporary Egypt. In an exception to the general practice of leaving bronze coinage undated, from 145/4 to 135/4 Ptolemy VIII issued a series of bronze coins dated by his regnal years, with a last isolated emission in 130/29. These bronzes differ in fabric and style from the bronzes of Ptolemy VI, reflecting a change in the methods of production. Although we have suggested that the display of regnal dates might relate silver coinage to the annual fiscal cycle or facilitate the systematic withdrawal of older coinage, it is difficult to offer hypotheses about the dating of bronze currency.

The voluminous bronze coinage of Ptolemy IX and X was undated, but the control system was more elaborate than usual for Cypriote bronze coinage, involving symbols, letters, or combinations of the two. Some

---

[138] Poole (1883) l–li. For a parallel from western Asia Minor, struck by the Artists of Dionysus based at Teos, see Lorber and Hoover (2003).

[139] This resumption may coincide with a refoundation or reorganization of the Artists of Dionysus in Cyprus; see Aneziri (1994).

specimens have been found in Israel, relics of the invasion of Soter II during the War of Scepters, while other specimens found in Egypt, in Alexandria and in the Fayum, provide evidence that his attempt to recover Egypt came closer to success than has been inferred from documentary papyri.[140]

3.3 Continued Circulation of Ptolemaic Silver in Seleucid Coele Syria and Phoenicia

The hoard record for the Seleucid province of Coele Syria and Phoenicia indicates that Antiochus III and his immediate successors maintained the closed monetary zone established by the Ptolemies, and they did not open it even to their own Attic-weight silver.[141] Furthermore, they were slow to mint a specifically Seleucid silver coinage on the lighter Ptolemaic weight standard which could circulate in the province. It was Alexander I Balas, a pretender supported by Ptolemy VI, who finally introduced a substantial coinage of this sort in 151/0. These policies allowed Ptolemaic silver coinage to maintain a monopoly in the province for nearly half a century after the Seleucid conquest of 198.

There may have been economic motives for Seleucid retention of the closed monetary zone, such as the unsupportable cost of reintroducing a heavier weight standard.[142] But these considerations do not explain why the Seleucid rulers did not immediately replace the Ptolemaic silver with a suitable lightweight currency of their own, or at least countermark the Ptolemaic coinage with a symbol of Seleucid authority. By permitting the continued monopoly of Ptolemaic coinage, they tended to undermine their own authority and legitimacy while promoting those of the rival dynasty. The ambiguity was increased by and probably related to the special status of Coele Syria and Phoenicia as the dowry of Cleopatra I (Joseph. *AJ* 12.154; App. *Syr.* 5; Por. *FGhist* 260 F47 *ap.* Hieron. *In Dan.* 11.17). As is clear from the account in Josephus, the dowry was not a return of territory but a gift of the revenues of the province. Initially, probably after the engagement of Cleopatra to Ptolemy V in 195, the revenues were divided equally between Antiochus III and the younger king, the division being made at the local level (Joseph. *AJ* 12.155). After their marriage in 194/3 Ptolemy V and Cleopatra I held an auction for the

---

[140] For the Israeli finds, Gitler and Stein-Kushnir (1999). For Egypt, see the hoards Alexandria, 1933 (*IGCH* 1717; *EH I* 224) and Karanis, 1924/5 (*IGCH* 1716; *EH* I, 226).
[141] Le Rider (1995). [142] Houghton and Lorber (2000–2) 55–7.

contract to farm the taxes on the cities of Coele Syria and Phoenicia, and the contract was won by Joseph, son of Tobias (Joseph. *AJ* 12.160–79).[143] Joseph farmed these taxes for twenty-two years (Joseph. *AJ* 12.186 and 224). Assuming he first won the contract for the fiscal year 193/2, the arrangement lasted until 172/1, shortly before the outbreak of the Sixth Syrian War. Maurice Sartre and Sylvie Honigman have argued that Seleucus IV and Antiochus IV sought to abrogate the tax-sharing arrangement and seize all the revenues for themselves.[144] The latter king formally repudiated the dowry in the diplomatic negotiations following his initial invasion of Egypt. It seems quite likely that he cancelled the tax-sharing agreement in 171 and that this provoked the disastrous attack by Eulaeus and Lenaeus which initiated the Sixth Syrian War.

Over the lifetime of the tax-sharing agreement, the remission of taxes to Alexandria should have reduced the amount of Ptolemaic silver circulating in Coele Syria and Phoenicia. Indeed, this could conceivably have been a goal of the Seleucid policy, to cleanse the province gradually of foreign coinage. No evidence confirms that the currency supply was continually replenished during this period by the arrival of more Ptolemaic silver through trade.[145]

Fresh Ptolemaic silver coins began to appear after 170, as attested by hoards closing between 164/3 and c. 154.[146] These hoards contain nothing earlier than issues of Ptolemy VI, including coins from Alexandria, Cyprus, and/or era coinage. As we observed with the late second-century Egyptian hoards, this time horizon is too short to reflect a natural process of attrition. The absence of older coinage could be consistent with an attempt by Antiochus IV, somewhere around 170, to ban Ptolemaic silver from Coele Syria and Phoenicia. Alternatively, it could be consistent with a recoining effort.

The era coinage was revived in this critical period. A third series of era coins, consisting of didrachms almost exclusively, was minted between 163/2 and 146/5. The era didrachms are found overwhelmingly in Israel and Lebanon. Metallurgical analyses conducted by Julien Olivier revealed that they share the lead-debased alloy of dated Syro-Phoenician tetradrachms of

---

[143] The passage in Josephus confusingly begins in the reign of Ptolemy III, but the account of the bidding process and surety reflects knowledge of actual Ptolemaic administrative practice, even if the details are fanciful.

[144] Sartre (2014); Honigman (2014a) 316–8; 342–3.   [145] Lorber (2021).

[146] Southern Palestine (*CH* IV, 58; *EH* I, 115); Bethlehem area, 1984 (*CH* VIII, 432; *EH* I, 113); Lebanon, 1968 (*CH* IV, 60; *EH* I, 116).

Ptolemy II and III.¹⁴⁷ Citing the findspots and his metallurgical analyses, Olivier suggested that the era didrachms were likely minted in Judea and that they represented a Ptolemaic subsidy for the Maccabean revolt.¹⁴⁸ Considering the absence of older coinage from the hoards, we might envision an operation in Judea reminting third-century Ptolemaic tetradrachms into didrachms, under the supervision of specialists sent from Egypt. This effort was supplemented by the continuing importation of new Ptolemaic coinage, as attested by the hoards cited above. Production of the era coinage ceased with the death of Ptolemy VI, but Ptolemaic silver continued to circulate alongside the metrologically compatible Seleucid eagles (see Chapter 7A), eventually disappearing in the reign of Antiochus VII.

3.4 Cyrenaica

The formal deification of Ptolemy V in 199/8 was commemorated by special emissions of bronze coinage at Tyre, in Cyprus, and in Cyrenaica.¹⁴⁹ These coinages were linked by shared iconographies, but in Cyrenaica, after decades in which the provincial coinage was dominated by the goddess Libya, the iconographies of apotheosis included elements alluding to the civic traditions of the three greatest *poleis* of the province, Cyrene, Berenike-Euesperides, and Ptolemais-Barce. This was the last occasion when the coinage of Ptolemaic Cyrenaica acknowledged the cities.

The records of the *damiergoi* of the temple of Apollo at Cyrene record changes in the values of commodities which indicate that the bronze standard was introduced to Cyrenaica at some point in the second century.¹⁵⁰ When Ptolemy VIII assumed the kingship of Cyrenaica, he introduced a new bronze coinage reviving the metrology and denominational system of third-century Egyptian coinage (Series 3 through 5), which had never before been employed in Cyrenaica but was used contemporaneously on Cyprus for the bronze coinage of Ptolemy VI. The new Cyrenaican coinage of the younger Ptolemy was further exceptional in that it bore his cult epithet along with his name and title, whereas all previous Ptolemaic bronze coinage, regardless of the province, had named 'Ptolemy the King' without stipulating an individual Ptolemy. Bronze coinage of traditional Cyrenaican type, with an abbreviated cult epithet, was also

---

[147] Olivier (2018) 38–9. [148] Olivier (2018) 40–4. [149] Lorber (2006); Lorber (2016b) 108–11.
[150] Rosamilia (2016); (2017).

issued under Euergetes II, probably during his reign in Egypt. His successor, Ptolemy IX, continued the practice of abbreviating his cult epithets on his Cyrenaican bronze coinage. A few of these coins have been found in Israel, evidence that Soter II had support from Cyrenaica for his Judean campaign.[151]

4 Conclusion

The monetary policies of the Ptolemies in Egypt can usually be related to the problem of managing a limited stock of silver. The policies affecting Cyprus, Syria, and Phoenicia were apparently driven by military needs, whereas policy in Cyrenaica seemingly alternated between controlling and courting the *poleis* of the province. The second century witnessed a trend toward dated annual issues of silver, beginning in Cyprus, taken up in Judea, and finally adopted in Egypt. François de Callataÿ has viewed this pattern as a trend toward simplification of control systems and has argued that simple controls involving a date imply the existence of secure written archives which preserved all essential information about the minting process, including the instructions given and the persons responsible for carrying them out.[152] This chapter suggests two additional administrative purposes for the dating of coinage. The first was to integrate coin production into the annual fiscal cycle, by having local taxes converted into coinage which could be spent either locally, to meet local needs, or diverted to broader purposes of imperial finance. The second was to manage the supply of silver, by systematically withdrawing and reminting older coins.

Common Conclusion

The Seleucid and Ptolemaic monetary systems began by looking vastly different according to several important measures. But in the second century the monetary policies of the two empires converged somewhat. Seleucid absorption of the Ptolemaic province of Syria and Phoenicia led to adoption of the local practice of dating coinages, though the Seleucid practice was inconsistent in its application and reckoned by the Seleucid Era rather than by regnal years. A second consequence of this annexation was that Antiochus III and his immediate successors apparently attempted to impose a monetary system relying more or less exclusively on coined bronze, following a trail blazed earlier in Ptolemaic Egypt. A final

---

[151] Syon (2016) 148, nos. 10–2.   [152] Callataÿ (2012).

consequence was surrender to Lagid symbolism on the Seleucid eagles which were minted for half a century.

In Syria, Demetrius I finally withdrew the older coinage which had provided the main stock of precious metal currency, some of it more than a century old, and converted it into fresh coinage in his own name. Subsequent rulers continued the policy of renewing the Syrian coinage by systematically withdrawing and recoining the oldest issues in circulation, a process that can also be documented in Egypt in the latter second and first centuries. Meanwhile the Seleucid east maintained the traditional open monetary system. The last Seleucids occasionally resorted to weight reductions which required recoining of the entire stock of currency, a type of reform famously used by the first Ptolemy to close the currency market of his kingdom.

When it comes to the integration and involvement of local polities and local elites in monetary production and reception, all our positive cases come from the west, and specifically from regions where the city had long been the fundamental unit of political organization: western and coastal Asia Minor, Cyrenaica, Cyprus, and the area of Coele Syria and Phoenicia. Coins struck in Asia Minor under both dynasties hint at a sharing of royal and civic authority, but the specific arrangements remain a matter of guesswork. In Ptolemaic Cyrenaica deprivation of precious metal coinage was a means of controlling the rebellious tendencies of the province; the bronze coinage normally expressed royal dominance, and allusions to individual cities may be related to benefactions granted on special occasions of importance to royal ideology. The use of civic mint marks in Ptolemaic Cyprus sheds little light on the relations between the crown and the cities, but the Dionysian silver coinage looks like a tool for reinforcing loyalty to the royal house through the celebration of festivals. The most intelligible examples come from Phoenicia and Coele Syria. The Ptolemies likely integrated coinage into the fiscal cycle of the Phoenician cities and at times of crisis certainly levied tribute payments on the cities in the form of freshly minted coinage. The Seleucids seemed to make use of local elites, at least at Tyre, for producing annual issues related to the fiscal cycle; in fact, one could even say that the Seleucid policy in the closed economy of Coele Syria and Phoenicia is in some respects a continuation of Ptolemaic practices in this area. However, Seleucid monetary production involved coastal cities only. Judea remained involved with Ptolemaic silver coinage as part of a Ptolemaic political intervention in the area, first through Tobiad tax farming, then through the receipt of Ptolemaic subsidies for the Maccabean revolt and production of the third series of era coins. Only in Egypt and in the Seleucid east do we find few or no allusions to cities on the coinage, even though Egypt, Mesopotamia, Babylonia, and Susiana were home to famous ancient cities. In the Seleucid case, it is especially mystifying that the second-century royal program of establishing *polis* institutions in eastern cities did not affect the coinage in any discernible way.

A recent article compared the overall monetary output of the two dynasties based on hoard evidence and extrapolation.[153] The conclusion was that the two economies were of comparable size, with almost identical levels of monetization, and identical percentages of precious metals transformed annually (on average) into fresh coinage. For methodological reasons, this study did not consider the important role of bronze coinage in the Ptolemaic empire. These bronze coins could be the Lagid counterpart of foreign Attic-weight coins entering the Seleucid economy. Both played an important role in supplementing the precious metal coins issued by the Seleucid and Ptolemaic authorities. It seems that the two dynasties adopted two different approaches to address similar problems.

[153] Iossif (2015).

PART III

Collaboration, Crisis, and Resistance

CHAPTER 8

Legitimizing the Foreign King in the Ptolemaic and Seleucid Empires
The Role of Local Elites and Priests

Stefan Pfeiffer and Hilmar Klinkott

Common Introduction

It is a well-established fact that foreign rulers in empires need to cooperate with local elites in order to execute power. These elites in the Ptolemaic and Seleucid empires were mainly the priests of local cults, and so we look above all at religious elites when we study the ideological integration of *basileis* into local milieus. When the Ptolemaic king appears in Egypt as 'pharaoh' or the Seleucid king in Mesopotamia as 'King of Babylon,' the use of these titles seems at first logical and natural. Yet on closer inspection, we find that this nomenclature in indigenous writing and visual culture was the result of a complex and highly sensitive process of communication, shaped by king and Greco-Macedonian court elites, on the one hand, and indigenous priests, on the other. After Alexander's invasions, no practice was regular or 'obvious' in the new Hellenistic monarchies – neither the continuation of traditions, nor the incorporation of foreign elements. The kings had to be crowned in the first instance,[1] to be accepted by the priests,[2] and to be accepted by the general public.[3] The early phase of Hellenistic monarchy was characterized by the establishment of sustained dynastic rule, which meant the 'indigenization' of pharaoh and king.[4]

Moreover, in both Hellenistic Egypt and Babylonia the priests had the power not only to legitimize but also to delegitimize the ruling king. If we look at Ptolemaic Egypt, inscriptions, papyri, and temple-reliefs offer rich material that points to the cultic relationship between king and priesthood. Inscriptions in particular shed light on many details of the complex process of royal-priestly communication. Not only can we

---

[1] Pfeiffer (2014b) 49; Klinkott (2014) 64–5. [2] Cf. Husson and Valbelle (1992) 170–4.
[3] For a different emphasis, compare Gorre and Clancier in this volume. [4] Huß (2001) 192–212.

observe the religious embedding of the king, but also the particular power priests had over the legitimization of kings in situations of crisis. Stefan Pfeiffer demonstrates in his part of the following chapter the extent to which the king was dependent on the priests. It has often been observed that the sacerdotal decrees known from the third and second century BC show an essentially precarious situation of Ptolemaic rule. Yet these texts also illuminate the various hazards for royal authority and hence the state. On the one hand, the priests legitimized the king only passively when there was active resistance against him in the homeland; on the other hand, they promoted the Ptolemaic rulers actively thanks to the form and intensity of formulations, in other words through active writing. The texts thus reveal the heterogeneity of the indigenous priesthood, their different political attitudes, the intensity of their influence, as well as the reaction of the king supporting specific loyal groups of priests. When looked at in detail, the synodal decrees highlight at a micro level a process that we usually treat only on a macro level in terms of its results for royal policy. Moreover, although the description and depiction of the Ptolemaic pharaoh was allegedly composed by all Egyptian priests during the synods, the priesthood of Memphis played an important and leading role. These priests and their peer group were the ones who indigenized the foreign pharaoh and mythologized his deeds in highly precarious situations for the legitimacy of the ruler, such as famines and indigenous revolts.

Hilmar Klinkott suggests in the second part of the joint chapter that the synodal decrees extant from Egypt can bring to the fore comparable processes of communication in Seleucid Babylonia where similar evidence is unfortunately lacking. Sacerdotal cuneiform texts seem to reflect the same process of royal establishment: The new Macedonian rulers were dependent on the support of Babylonian priests to create, formulate, and shape the perception of being legitimate and indigenized kings in the core region of their young empire. There was a king installed in the traditional manner, on the one side, and temples enjoying royal support and privileges, on the other, and they came together in great religious festivals. The Babylonian material offers another, though fragmentary, view of the same process of communication and negotiation between kings and priests with quite similar outcomes. It is therefore helpful, Klinkott suggests, to compare the Ptolemaic and Seleucid empires not just in order to demonstrate difference but also to tease out corresponding forms of politics and communication between local priests and the foreign king in the dynamic phase of establishing a new political regime.

A THE EGYPTIAN PRIESTS AND THE PTOLEMAIC KINGS

Stefan Pfeiffer

1 Introduction

In 306 BC Ptolemy, son of Lagos, declared himself *basileus* and was proclaimed pharaoh in 304, a ceremonial act that in my view should have included a formal coronation ceremony conducted by the high priest of Memphis.[5] Shortly afterward, king Ptolemy issued a decree which prohibited the sale of temples and the billeting of soldiers in sacred precincts and thereby put a stop to such practices which in the view of the Egyptian priests were extremely *contra mores* and *contra religionem* and thus posed a strong threat to the legitimacy of the newly crowned pharaoh.[6] From now on a boom of temple building and decoration started in Egypt.[7] The wealth which could now be achieved by those holding priesthoods can be detected in Thebes, for example, after suffering a rapid decline in the Persian period, by the growth of splendid funerary ensembles.[8] Therefore, in contrast to recent views, it was not Ptolemy II but already Ptolemy I who was intensely interested in good relations with the Egyptian priests.[9] This is underpinned by his bringing back of the statues of Egyptian gods that had allegedly been robbed by the Persians, a deed that became a topos of Ptolemaic religious policy for the first four kings.[10] It is also with Ptolemy I that the temples started receiving endowments of formerly 'secularized' possessions. This is shown not only in the case of the famous satrap stela for the temple of Buto but also on a small stela in hieroglyphic and demotic script from the Sigmund Freud Collection for a sanctuary in Tell el-Balamun.[11]

---

[5] *P. dem.* Louvre 2427; 2440, were dated to year 13 of Alexander IV; cf. Huß (2001) 191; Worthington (2016) 160–2; Caneva (2016) 69–71; on the ceremony, see Huß (1994) 51–2.
[6] *SB* 16.12519, with Hagedorn (1986) 65–70; Rigsby (1988) 273–4.
[7] Swinnen (1973); Chauveau and Thiers (2006) 375–404; Minas-Nerpel (2018); von Recklinghausen (2018), 316, n. 255, with further references.
[8] Schreiber (2007).
[9] Gorre (2009a) 99–114; Agut-Labordère and Gorre (2014) 39: 'The only known document on this matter is the Satrap Stele, often considered as the proof of Ptolemy I's interest for the temples. Its analysis shows, in reality, the purely economic character of the intervention of royal power reported on it.' 40: 'However, because of its insulation, this document cannot be considered as a supportive piece of evidence for a general policy towards the temples on the part of Ptolemy Satrap.'
[10] Cf. Satrap stela; Agut-Labordère (2017).
[11] Cf. Wells (1989) 54–5; Wells and Ueno (1996) no. 33; Meeks (1978) 684 no. 10; Vleeming (2001) no. 133.

As is well known, the indigenous priests on the other side presented the foreign king as an Egyptian pharaoh. In this position he was 'master of the ceremonies' (*nb jr.t iḥ.t*), and by performing the temple rituals he guaranteed the world order called Maat. If he failed to accomplish the prescribed rituals, this Maat would be deeply disturbed, and starvation and social unrest would explode in Egypt.

The ideal and automatic connection between ritual and Maat was explained, for example, by the priests of Mendes to Ptolemy II in a hieroglyphic stela:

> He recognized the order, given by Thot besides Ra for the kings of Upper and Lower Egypt, as follows: ... It is really useful for the king, if he lets flourish the bread offering for the Ram, the lord of Dejdet, in order that the offerings may be increased, his territory may be enlarged, something useful is done for his house. If (on the contrary) the offerings on the table are reduced, there will be disaster for mankind. If (instead) the offerings on the table are increased, he (the Ram) will give food for the whole land, because the Nile flood will overflow the arable land due to the bread offering. It (the Nile flood) is the father of the king.[12]

This is a textual transposition of what we can see in many temple reliefs, showing a pharaoh giving offerings to the gods.[13] However, what is rarely found is the clear explanation of the consequence of negative deeds given by the priests of Mendes: if a pharaoh reduces the amount of his offerings, there will be disaster. This attention to the consequences of negative deeds is also important for the late Egyptian prophecies, which have the following structure: illegitimate rule coincidences with the withdrawal of the benevolence of the gods towards Egypt, which leads directly to inadequate Nile floods from which starvation results.[14] This means that bad economic situations in Egypt were automatically interpreted from a religious perspective, but in contrast to other religions the fault lay not with the people who had neglected the gods but with the political leader, who was personally to blame because he was the only officiating priest of Egypt.

In the following remarks I aim to analyze how the Egyptian priests were able to maintain the concept of the foreign king as Egyptian pharaoh in situations which were highly dangerous for Ptolemaic rule, for instance when the king ran the risk of losing his legitimacy as pharaoh because of an impending famine or of social unrest. In this respect I want to look at the

---

[12] *CGC* 22181, l. 16–17; Schäfer (2011) 250.
[13] Cf. e.g. Edfou VIII 18,2–18,8 (Translation D. Kurth [1998]); Bonneau (1964).
[14] Quack (2002).

question of how priests reacted when the living reality clearly showed that the foreign king had failed to fulfill his duty as master of the ceremonies, which could easily be interpreted as a withdrawal of the gods' favor towards him. The first case focuses on inadequate Nile floods which could lead to starvation, the second turns to social unrest and insurrection in Egypt. Hence, it is obvious, both cases are closely intertwined.

As I will concentrate on the macro level of the relationship of *the* Egyptian priests to *the* Macedonian king, I must first make some preliminary methodological remarks, as there are three reasons that should lead us to avoid thinking in terms of a dichotomy of king *versus* priests:

1. From a cultic point of view such a dichotomy could not even exist, because there was no difference between them: the king was the first priest of Egypt, he was the *conditio sine qua non* of the existence of every priesthood, and he was the master of the ceremonies and all Egyptian priests only acted as his substitutes.[15]
2. There was not one single priesthood in Egypt, but many different priesthoods in the forty *nomes* of the land, including priests of large and important temples and priests of smaller and poorer temples, and priesthoods in competition or collaboration with the foreign regime or even with each other.[16] It is not even possible to determine the social structure of these priesthoods. It is certain that many of the priests belonged to the elite of Egypt, but there were also priests belonging to other strata of society.[17]
3. Taking an ethnic view of Macedonian *versus* Egyptian is problematic because from the second century at the latest members of the Greco-Macedonian elite became Egyptian priests as well.

Werner Huß was aware of these problems and, nevertheless, called his seminal book *Der makedonische König und die ägyptischen Priester*.[18] This view can be accepted up to a point in two ways, but we will also see that one cannot follow such a dichotomy.

1. The Ptolemies were foreign rulers and perceived themselves as non-Egyptians until the reign of Cleopatra VII. Their identity was Macedonian or Hellenic, eventually Alexandrian, which does not

---

[15] Cf. Chauveau (2000) 108–9.   [16] Ibid., 46–9; Gorre (2009a) xiv.
[17] Blasius (2002) 41–62, esp. 49; Chauveau (2000) 47: 'The very diversity of the Egyptian clergy, both in its geography and in its sociological makeup, affords a strong hint that unanimity, in one sense or another, could never have been achieved.'
[18] Cf. Huß (1994) 11, n. 5.

exclude that under certain circumstances they could assume other identities, for example, that of an Egyptian pharaoh. Every subject could easily experience the fact that the king was not an Egyptian *strictu sensu* when he came into contact with the Greek administration of Egypt.

2. Although there was not one single Egyptian priesthood, one 'clergy,' a term used somehow misleadingly, there is one group of sources which at least pretend that this was indeed the case:[19] the sacerdotal decrees from the times of Ptolemy III to Ptolemy VI, which were issued during regular synods that allegedly included all Egyptian priests in order to honor the pharaoh.

The analysis that follows focuses on the sacerdotal decrees of the Egyptian priests, which were formally adapted from the Hellenistic honorific decrees of Greek cities and corporations. These decrees are divided into two major parts: in the first part the priests extensively describe the good deeds of the king, while in the second part this description of deeds functions as a motivation for the bestowal of honors on him. The reasons invoked in the first part normally consist of topoi attached to the image of the good ruler (e.g. the privileges he gives to the priests or the people of Egypt and his funding of cults). However, besides these topoi, specific problems are also mentioned as well as the actions of the king to solve them. These problems are particularly interesting, as they allow us to explore in more detail two specific aspects of the religious legitimacy of a given pharaoh: his ability to maintain the natural as well as the social order.

2 The Pharaoh as 'Nile of Egypt'

One of the main problems faced by a foreign pharaoh was to maintain the natural order. By performing the prescribed rituals for the Egyptian gods, the pharaoh was responsible for the adequacy of the Nile flood. Reductions in the Nile flood and the resulting food shortages were a significant threat to the legitimacy of his rule. This happened for the first time in the early Ptolemaic period, when Ptolemy III was at the peak of his military career shortly after having ascended the throne. He was on his way to conquer the Seleucid empire when an insurrection broke out in Egypt that forced the king to return to Egypt. We do not know much about this insurrection, but there seems to

---

[19] Cf. Moyer (2011b).

have been a low Nile flood.[20] In combination with a firmer grasp over Egypt's economic resources, which Ptolemy needed for his Syrian campaign, a famine threatened the Egyptian subjects. The hardships of such economic oppression are reflected in Egyptian prophecies. In the *Oracle of the Potter*, for instance, the foreigners are equated to Typhonians, which means to followers of the god of evil, Seth-Typhon, who extracted everything from Egypt so that the peasants were going to starve.[21] The absence of the bulk of the army in 244 BC made it easy for the Egyptians to rise up against foreign rule, but order was quickly reestablished by the king on his return. Nevertheless, his rule was in danger of becoming delegitimized because of inadequate Nile floods and, above all, his inability to secure the well-being of his Egyptian subjects. Seven years later, therefore, the priests tried to reinterpret the whole affair, as reported in the sacerdotal decree of Canopus from 238 BC:

> and when the river once overflowed its banks insufficiently and all those in the country were terrified at this happening and were thinking upon the destruction that had taken place under some of the former kings, in whose reign those dwelling in the country met with droughts.[22]

By pointing to the fact that the Nile flood was inadequate, the priests indicate something might have been wrong with the temple cults. At the same time, they admit that such things also had happened under earlier Egyptian pharaohs. Such an event is, for instance, related on the well-known 'famine stela', cut into the rock on the island Sehel in the region of the first cataract in Ptolemaic times by the priests of Elephantine (Fig. 8.1). In its lunette the stela shows the famous pharaoh Djoser (2720–2700 BC) performing an unguent offering to Khnum, Satis and Anuket, the triad of Elephantine.

Khnum speaks out: 'I give to you the Nile every year at the right time.' The hieroglyphic text of the stela refers to a famine lasting seven years because of inadequate Nile floods. The Pharaoh gives a realistic description of the disaster:

> I was in mourning on my throne. Those of the palace were in grief. My heart was in great affliction, because Hapy had failed to come in time in a period of seven years. Grain was scant, kernels were dried up, scarce was every kind of food. Every man robbed his twin, those who entered did not go. Children cried, youngsters fell, the hearts of the old were grieving; legs drawn up, they

---

[20] *P. Haun* I 6; *FGrHist.* II 260, F 43; Justin XXVII 1, 9; McGing (1997) 275–7; Veïsse (2004) 3–5; Huß (1994) 373–5; Hauben (1990) 33–4; Manning and Ludlow (2016); Manning J. G. et al. (2017).
[21] Cf. Chauveau (2000) 50–1.
[22] OGIS I 56, 13–15 = Pfeiffer (2020) no. 14; translation: Bagnall and Derow (2004) no. 164.

Fig. 8.1 Famine stela, Sehel island, Ptolemaic period. © Stefan Pfeiffer

hugged the ground, their arms clasped about them. Courtiers were needy, temples were shut, shrines covered with dust, everyone was in distress.[23]

According to Egyptian traditions of the Ptolemaic period, similar famines had occurred in the times of pharaoh Neferkasokar (2744–2736 BC) from the second dynasty and Chufu (2620–2580 BC) from the fourth dynasty.[24] In a demotic text referring to a dream of Chufu, the pharaoh established a guideline as to how to react to such a famine:

> Make a trip to the south to [the cities] of Upper Egypt, make a trip down to the north, to the cities of Lower Egypt. May you find a temple for every god, may you provide the food in the manufacturing facilities of the gods, may you renew the lapsed, may you fill that which you have found empty, may you perform the rituals in the temples.[25]

The same was done by Djoser in Elephantine, and Ptolemy III followed this precedent as we learn from the decree of Canopus. He increased the incomes of the temples, he took care of the cults of Egypt and he rebuilt or founded temples. In Philae a similar attitude was also recorded on the

---

[23] Translation: Lichtheim (2006) 94–100; cf. Barguet (1953); Goedicke (1994) 562–7.
[24] Burkard (1990); Quack (1992–3).   [25] Quack (1999) 274.

Greek building inscription of the Naos of the temple of Isis.[26] And last but not least, Ptolemy and his wife were such capable rulers that they could prevent the threatening famine:

> exercising provident care over those in the temples and the others inhabiting the country, by exercising much forethought and forgoing not a little of their revenues for the sake of the safety of the people, and by sending for grain for the country from Syria and Phoenicia and Cyprus and many other places at rather high prices, they saved the inhabitants of Egypt, leaving behind an immortal benefaction and the greatest record of their virtue both for contemporaries and for future generations; in return for which the gods have granted them their kingdom peacefully established and will give them all the other good things for all time.[27]

As we can see, Ptolemy himself has taken over the function of Nile, and the gods gave him his rule in reward.[28] The priests therefore introduced a new feast in every Egyptian temple which was to be held on the heliacal rising of the Sirius-star which every year announces the coming of the Nile flood. A rebellion against such a good pharaoh from now on would be hybris against the Egyptian gods.

3 The Victorious Pharaoh

The honorific decrees of the Egyptian priests show that the priests were eager to present the Ptolemaic pharaoh in the same way as they presented him on temple reliefs: he is the one responsible for the rituals of the Egyptian cults by guaranteeing the provisioning of the gods and people of Egypt. This is also confirmed by the description of his military achievements, which were the main theme of nearly every sacerdotal decree we know. The Ptolemaic pharaohs are presented according to the important apotropaic ritual of smiting the enemy. According to temple reliefs, in exchange for 'smiting the enemy' the gods grant the pharaoh a firm and stable rule. This is, for instance, visible on the 'gate of Euergetes' in the temple of Karnak, in which Ptolemy III is depicted smiting the head of an Asian enemy with a mace in front of Osiris and Isis.[29] Osiris lauds the king for his deed: 'I praise your smiting of the enemy. You are my heir who follows me on the throne. I give you my position as ruler over the two lands, may your life be eternal.' And Isis

---

[26] OGIS I 61 = Pfeiffer (2020) no. 10.
[27] OGIS I 56, 15–20 = Pfeiffer (2020) no. 14; translation: Bagnall and Derow (2004) no. 164.
[28] Pfeiffer (2004) 219–20.   [29] Clère (1961) pl. 62; cf. fig. 2.

adds: 'I give you the position of my son Horus; may you rule legitimately on his throne.'

After Ptolemy IV gained his victory against the Seleucids in Raphia, the priests could present him in a similar way but adapted to Hellenistic iconography. The pharaoh is now spearing his enemy from horseback – a riding pharaoh was unknown to Egyptian conceptions of pharaonic representation but well known for Hellenistic kings, and one may also think of the Alexander mosaic from Pompeii.

The priests were furthermore able to put their Egyptian ritual principle of *do ut des* into the scheme of Greek honorific decrees just after the description of the deeds of the king. For example, in the Rosetta decree one reads: 'in return for which the gods have given him health, victory, power and [all] other good things, his kingdom remaining to him and his children for all time.'[30] The position of this formula – I call it the ἀνθ' ὧν or divine-reciprocity formula – just after the motivations is extremely important, as it was an innovation for Hellenistic decrees.[31] It was inserted in every sacerdotal decree we know and shows how the priests were not only copying Greek decrees but at the same time adapting them, also in terms of their structure, to their theological need. The general structure of a Hellenistic honorific decree augmented by the Egyptian priests looked as follows:[32]

1. Opening
2. motivations, beginning with ἐπειδή or similar
3. the ἀνθ' ὧν formula of the Egyptian priests
4. (hortatory intention)
5. resolution formula and decision beginning with ἀγαθῆι τύχηι and δεδόχθαι or similar
6. conclusion

However, showing the pharaoh, as master of ritual, smiting the enemies became problematic in the second century, because from the reign of Ptolemy V onward it was impossible for the priests to praise the pharaoh for smiting non-Egyptian adversaries. The four decrees we know from the reign of Ptolemy V, beginning with the Rosetta decree of 196 BC, followed by the so-called Philensis II (186 BC) and Philensis I (185 BC) decrees and

---

[30] OGIS I 90, 35–6 = Pfeiffer (2020) no. 22; translation: Bagnall and Derow (2004) no. 165.
[31] The Hellenistic decrees knew this formulation in different contexts. It is used sometimes in the motivation as well as in the resolution; cf. *IG* II² 1009 or 1326; cf. on the Egyptian perspective of the divine reciprocity formula von Recklinghausen (2018), 213–15.
[32] Cf. McLean (2002) 229–31; Clarysse (2000), 48–50.

ending with the decree of 182 BC,[33] are all related to the rebellions of Egyptian subjects in Egypt itself. These local rebellions were of utmost danger for the legitimacy of the foreign pharaoh as they were not only a political but also a religious proof of his inability to rule justly and according to the will of the Egyptian gods. They clearly showed that the king did not perform his office as master of ritual in a righteous way. This can easily be seen in a description of the famous Papyrus Jumilhac, which gives an account of aetiologies and myths of the 17th upper Egyptian *nome* (late Ptolemaic/early Roman). Here one reads:

> If one does not perform all rites of Osiris at the right time in every nome, and all his feasts that are prescribed in the calendar, then this land will be anarchic, the mob will let down its lord and no order will (hold its ground) in the crowd. Anubis, Horhekenu, the butcher demon and the Wanderers, who are armed with their knives, will come out according to his order and descend. If not all the rites are performed for Osiris at the right time, then the pestilence will come upon the whole of Egypt, the butcher demons will emerge looting, and the trappers of Osiris will set their traps all over Egypt.[34]

The Theban pharaohs presented the Ptolemies as foreign and Sethian adversaries who devastated and plundered Egypt. In contrast, they presented themselves as god-elected pharaohs, as a just and legitimate alternative for the local peasants. The Ptolemies were now forced to fight against their own Egyptian subjects, which was obviously at odds with the Egyptian world view whereby a pharaoh must look after his subjects. After the rebellious territories had been won back, the priests had to find a way to present the Ptolemaic winner as legitimate pharaoh again despite having killed thousands of Egyptians, and they found the perfect way to achieve this. In the decree of 186 BC they described the rule of the usurping pharaohs in Thebes as a time of impious rebels, who did wrong against the *nomes*, the sanctuaries, and the people of Egypt, who hindered the cults and destroyed the altars and statues of the gods, who even devastated the canals.[35] In this way, the Egyptian rebels were compared to the Typhonians of prophetic literature, and the Ptolemaic pharaoh who subdued them was the savior of Egypt. In the decree of 196 BC this salvation is described:

> And going to Lykonpolis in the Busurite (*nome*), which had been occupied and fortified against a siege with an abundant collection of arms and with all other provisions – for longstanding was the disloyalty of the *impious men*

---

[33] Cf. von Recklinghausen (2018), 8.   [34] P. Jumilhac 18, 5–9, in the translation of Pries (2012).
[35] Text and commentary: von Recklinghausen (2018), 61–81.

> gathered there, who had wrought much evil against the temples and those dwelling in Egypt – ... (and) in a short time he took the city by storm and destroyed all the *impious men* in it, just as [Herm]es and Horus (son) of Isis and Osiris subdued the former rebels in the same regions; and all those who led the rebels in his father's reign and troubled the country and did wrong to the temples, arriving in Memphis and avenging his father and his own throne he punished all fittingly at the time when he came for the performance of the proper rites for the assumption of the throne.[36]

As we can see, the rebels are called impious men, and Ptolemy is directly compared to Horus, the avenger of his father. However, the priests went a step further by claiming that Ptolemy did the same as Horus did with 'former rebels in the same region.' By doing this they mythologized the deed of Ptolemy, because every Egyptian knew what the priests alluded to: it was the myth of Horus. This myth was celebrated and reenacted every year, for example, in Edfu in a great festival, where it is also depicted and described on the inner side of the enclosure wall of the temple of Horus.[37] According to this myth the sun god Re, equated to Osiris, had grown old and weak, and rebels in Egypt had raised war against him. It was Horus who extinguished these rebels by harpooning them in every part of Egypt, travelling the Nile from lower Nubia down to the Delta. In the reenactment festival the rebels were depicted as hippopotami, crocodiles, antilopes, Nubians, or Asiatics and the god Seth was the evil adversary and murderer of Osiris. Because Horus had defeated the rebels and Seth with great perfection, he could claim to be pharaoh:

> O Horus the Behdetite, great god, lord of the sky ... When thou hast received thine office with crook and flail, and art crowned with the Double Diadem of Horus, ... Thine inheritance is thine, great god, son of Osiris. Now that thou hast smitten the Lower Egyptian Bull. Be glad of heart, ye inhabitants of the Great Seat, Horus has taken possession of the throne of his father.[38]

In 197/196 BC it was possible for the fourteen-year-old Ptolemy V to reenact the myth not only in a temple ritual and festival but also in reality. He had taken revenge for his father under whose reign the rebellion had started. This was a perfect prelude to his coronation as Egyptian pharaoh in Memphis. During this coronation the chiefs of the rebels were put to death by impalement in a ritual that belonged to 'the proper rites for the

---

[36] OGIS I 90, 22–8 = Pfeiffer (2020) no. 22; translation: Bagnall and Derow (2004) no. 165; cf. Polyb. XXII 17; for the mythological context: Plut. *de Is.* 19.
[37] Kurth (1998) 198–203; Leitz (2009) § 17.   [38] Fairman (1974) 105–6.

assumption of the throne.' The king was wearing the 'Pschent' crown that he had on his head when 'he entered the [temple] in Memphis in order to perform [in it] the rites for the assumption of the throne.'[39]

As Ptolemy did not extinguish Egyptians but impious rebels, his victory could also be depicted like the victory of Horus. The priests ordered that statues of the king should be set up in every Egyptian temple called 'Ptolemy the Avenger of Egypt' beside a statue of the god of the temple who gives him a sword of victory. The decree of 186 BC also prescribed that the stela should have a similar depiction which shows the god giving Ptolemy the sword and Ptolemy himself holding a disarmed captive and performing the act of smashing the head of the captive with a mace.[40]

4 Conclusion

The description and depiction of the Ptolemaic pharaoh was, as we could see, quite complex and demonstrated a deep understanding of Egyptian religion and ritual practice. In my view only Egyptian priests were able to construct this. However, we now must zoom in from the macro-perspective to the micro-perspective, because it is a fact that there was not one Egyptian 'clergy.' Therefore, it is likely that the decrees were composed not by all Egyptian priests during the synods, but rather by a special group of priests who had deep-rooted relations to the throne, who were furthermore of such prestige inside Egypt that they were accepted as the voice of all priests. And these were, as is often stated in literature, the high priests of Memphis. That they indeed were the authors of the decrees can be corroborated by further facts. When, for example, the king's care for animal cults is mentioned, it is the Memphite Apis and the Heliopolite Mnevis which are explicitly mentioned.[41] That Memphis in Ptolemaic times was of great importance can furthermore be seen by the fact that in 182 BC the Mnevis bull was not installed on his throne in Heliopolis but – at least according to Nespoulous-Phalippou – in Memphis.[42] Even when the priests refer to specific construction activities of the Ptolemies in the Egyptian temples, only Memphis is mentioned.[43] And the synods themselves were held either in or near Alexandria (in 243, 238, and 186 BC) or in Memphis (in 217, 196, 185, and 182 BC).

---

[39] OGIS I 90, 44–5; translation: Bagnall and Derow (2004) no. 165.
[40] Text and commentary: von Recklinghausen (2018), 91; depiction of such a scene: Nespoulous-Phalippou (2015), pl. 2 (decree of 182 BC).
[41] OGIS I 56, 9; Gozzoli (2006) 151; Blasius (2011) 148–9.
[42] Nespoulous-Phalippou (2015) 178–83.   [43] Ibid.; OGIS I 90, 33.

The high priests of Memphis called themselves 'leaders of the prophets of all gods and goddesses of Upper and Lower Egypt.'[44] The high priest Teos from the reign of Ptolemy III even referred to a synod, because he was the one 'who enters into the King's House on all its festive occasions *ahead* of priest(s) (and) all the prophets from the temples of Upper and Lower Egypt into the presence of him who summons them, great in his dignity of the great nobleman of Egypt.'[45]

These priests, who, interestingly, rarely held administrative positions, were the ones who were perfectly able not only to indigenize the foreign pharaoh but also to mythologize his deeds in the face of highly precarious situations for his legitimation as ruler, like threatening famines and indigenous revolts.[46] So to sum up: if we talk about *the* Egyptian priests and their presentation of the foreign pharaoh and by doing this look only at the sacerdotal decrees, we should bear in mind that, at least in my view, we actually mean, above all, the Egyptian priests of Memphis.

B THE BABYLONIAN PRIESTS AND THE SELEUCID KINGS

Hilmar Klinkott

1 Introduction

The synodal decrees of Ptolemaic Egypt offer a rich source for analyzing the processes of royal legitimation as well as for the political role the indigenous priesthoods played in this process, as Stefan Pfeiffer illustrates in this chapter.[47] They reflect an intensive exchange between priests and the Ptolemaic kings. Texts such as the Pithom stela or the Canopus and the Raphia decrees inform us that the kings summoned the priests of the whole country to common conventions (*sunhodoi*), and subsequently laid down the bilateral agreements between both parties, discussing the main and specific interests of the temples as well as those of the king.[48] The reign of the ruling king was accepted, legitimized and dynastically guaranteed by the Egyptian priests, while the priesthoods were granted royal support and

---

[44] Quaegebeur (1980) 295–6; Statue Alexandria 27806, 2.
[45] Stele Wien 154, 7–8; Quaegebeur (1980).
[46] On administrative positions rarely held by priests, see Klotz and LeBlanc (2012) 685.
[47] Pfeiffer, above; see also Blasius (2011), 140; 145–52; 163–79.
[48] Pfeiffer (2004) 57; 61: § 4–6, compare also: Spiegelberg (1925) 6: § 5f. Concerning the satrap's stela, the Pithom stela and their texts with translation, see Schäfer (2011). See also the overview by Huß (1991). Huß (1994) 46–7 assumes such conferences to have been a yearly occurrence.

privileges.⁴⁹ The stabilization of the royal position and the formulation of indigenous legitimization come across as intensive processes of communication, in which both parties negotiated their interests and which ultimately depended on priestly acceptance, as Gregor Weber has well demonstrated.⁵⁰

Texts revealing this communication process in similar detail are missing from the Seleucid empire. Nevertheless, the relationship between its kings and the priests of the Babylonian temples seems to be comparable. The political, economic, and social influence of Babylonian temples, their administrative correlation to the imperial structures, and not least their importance for religious legitimation through conveying an indigenous acceptance of royal rule perform similar functions. Thus, establishing the foreign supremacy of the Macedonians as regular and rightful kingship, with Babylonia at its core, was a complicated process. As the so-called *Dynastic Prophecy* shows, this process is also characterized by Babylonian hostilities against Macedonian rule.⁵¹ However, Susan Sherwin-White emphasizes 'the central importance of Babylonia' as 'the key to control of Alexander's empire' as well as the 'key for tapping the resources of the "outer satrapies".'⁵² By this account, Alexander had already planned to make Babylon the capital of his empire.⁵³ In any case, Babylon, as well as Uruk, remained traditional Mesopotamian cities, even if a community of Greek inhabitants was settled in Babylon under Antiochus III or Antiochus IV at the latest, as analyzed in detail by van der Spek.⁵⁴

This fact, too, is equivalent in principle to the conditions in Egypt during the installation of Ptolemaic kingship. The Egyptian cities, notably Memphis as an old religious center of Pharaonic rule, promoted the traditional character and indigenous prestige of kingship.⁵⁵ Yet, it was a long journey – in Hellenistic Egypt as well as in Babylonia – from the perception of the Macedonians as foreign rulers to their acceptance as legal indigenous kings (Pharaoh or King of Babylon).⁵⁶ This process was a core

---

⁴⁹ On the different kinds of priests participating in the synod of Raphia, see Pfeiffer (2004) 76–9; Huß (1994) 14–46; 69–71.
⁵⁰ Weber (2012).   ⁵¹ Grayson (1975) ch. 3; Sherwin-White (1987) 10; translation 12–14.
⁵² Sherwin-White (1987) 16.
⁵³ Strabo 15.2.10; Curt. 5.1.42; Arr. *An.* 3.16.4; 7.17.2; see also van der Spek (1987) 65.
⁵⁴ See van der Spek (1987) 65–74. Compare also the discussion of Gorre and Clancier in this volume.
⁵⁵ Pfeiffer, above, who emphasizes for the Ptolemies that they were 'proclaimed pharaoh, a ceremonial act that in my view should have included a formal coronation ceremony conducted by the high priest of Memphis.'
⁵⁶ For a different approach, which considers the local priests as deputies of the king, see Gorre and Honigman (2013) 107–10; and (2014) 308–10; and Gorre and Clancier in this volume.

element of the durable establishment of legitimized rule, essentially connected with the theological escrow of the local priests. Negotiating this relationship was a fundamental necessity for the new foreign rulers, while representing an opportunity for political influence for the priesthood as far as the (administrative, financial, personal, or cultic) equipment of the temples was concerned. Starting from the hypothesis that the Ptolemaic synodal inscriptions offer a parallel for understanding the relationship between the kings and Babylonian priests, I will argue that founding Seleucid rule was based on similar intense negotiation. The Babylonian sources do not document the negotiation in such detail but reflect them in their outcome. Thus, the interpretation of the Ptolemaic synodal decrees offers a quantity of information for analyzing the establishment of royal rule as a process of communication between king and priests. Transferring these methods and processes to a similar context in Seleucid Babylonia may help to understand the fragmentary puzzle of its priestly texts.

Susan Sherwin-White has stated:[57] 'This[58] and other Babylonian Hellenistic texts present a coherent picture of the Seleucids in which the king is no foreign enemy but a legitimate and just ruler in harmony with Babylonian gods, participating actively in Babylonian cult.' In consequence, we may ask whether the Seleucids achieved this role *because* of being in harmony with Babylonian gods and participating actively in Babylonian cults.

2 Antiochus I and the Borsippa Cylinder

The famous Antiochus cylinder, an official royal document dealing with the Babylonian temples, in this case the Esagila and Ezida of Borsippa, is perfect evidence for the interactive relationship between the king, Antiochus I Soter, and the Babylonian priesthood.[59] K. Stevens states: 'This in turn suggests a decree of active interchange and negotiations between the Seleucid court and the priestly and scholarly elite of Borsippa.' Because of the cylinder's singularity, Stevens could not study the operating principles of this communication process in detail.

They may become visible by comparing the cylinder with the Egyptian Synodic decrees, which provide much more information on, and details of,

---

[57] Sherwin-White (1987) 28. Cf. also Schäfer (2015) 631–3.
[58] This is the foundation inscription of Ezida at Borsippa (Pritchard [1955] 317; Austin [1981] no. 189).
[59] Stevens (2014) 67: 'The Antiochus cylinder itself tells us more about the relation between Antiochus I and the priestly elite of Borsippa than about Seleucid patronage of Babylonian cult or culture more generally, or Seleucid imperialism in a "global" sense.'

this 'interchange.'⁶⁰ At the very beginning the king gives a presentation of his status in a very typical way.⁶¹

> Antiochus, the great king, the mighty/legitimate king, king of the world, king of Babylon, king of lands, the caretaker of Esagila and Ezida, first son of Seleucus, the king, the Macedonian, king of Babylon, am I.

His titles show many similarities to those of the Achaemenid rulers, certainly alluding to a kind of manorial continuity: he is named 'great king, king of the world, . . . king of all countries' – a form we know, for example, from the Darius inscription of Naqsh-i Rustam (DNa).⁶²

But there are some other elements which are unusual for Achaemenid royal inscriptions and which seem to be a specific part of the local, Babylonian titulature.⁶³ In particular, Antiochus and his father Seleucus Nicator are each called 'king of Babylon.' From Xerxes I on, only a few of the Achaemenid rulers used this specific title in their official inscriptions, but always in a very local, Babylonian context.⁶⁴ In addition, the Achaemenid Great Kings – even in their specific function as kings of Babylon – refrained from restoration work on the Babylonian temples.⁶⁵

In contrast, Antiochus prominently demonstrated his role as the 'caretaker of the temples Esagila and Ezida.' On the one hand he is thus described as a king protecting the Babylonian temples in general; on the other hand, he is the one who favored these two specific temples, also in practice by means of new restoration work.

---

⁶⁰ See also Kosmin (2014a) 174–5; 188, who extends the comparability or similarity to Ptolemaic texts in general. But Kosmin does not study the parallels between the Antiochus cylinder and Ptolemaic synodal inscriptions in detail, nor ask about processes and actors behind the textual results.
⁶¹ Translation from Kuhrt and Sherwin-White (1991) 76; see also Pritchard (1955) 317; Stevens (2014) 68.
⁶² Concerning this specific form, also in other Achaemenid royal inscriptions, see Ahn (1992) 258–72.
⁶³ On the Assyrian and Babylonian elements in the titles, see Stevens (2014) 73f. with table 1. See also Kosmin (2014a) 189: 'a bricolage of Neo-Assyrian, Neo-Babylonian, and Achaemenid royal titles.'
⁶⁴ See also in the new-Babylonian legal and administrative documents: San Nicolò and Ungnad (1935) with the title 'king of Babylon' for Cyrus II: no. 6; 16–19; 30; 57; 67–9; 110; 177–9; 306–10; 348; 349; 416–19; 478; 479; 544; 586; 669; 670; 774–6; for Cambyses: no. 5; 20–3; 28; 29; 70–2; 99; 157; 180–5; 251–8; 305; 313–15; 350; 351; 379; 380; 420–2; 482–4; 545–8; 587; 628; 629; 671; 686; 712; 777; for Brdiya/Barzija: no. 24–6; 352; for Darius I: no. 7; 35; 37–42; 51–5; 58–62; 74–88; 100–2; 111; 112; 115–35; 137; 146; 147; 158; 186–218; 259–81; 316–39; 353–60; 362–4; 367; 368; 381–5; 424–60; 486–99; 501–7; 515–20; 522; 549–62; 564–72; 588–90; 592–604; 606–11; 630; 631; 653–55; 672–82; 687–94; 701; 702; 713; 717; 780; 781; for Xerxes I: no. (91); 138; 574; 575; 577; 616; 617; 635; 636; without the Babylonian royal title: San Nicolò and Ungnad (1935) for Cyrus II: no. 585; 782; 783; for Cambyses: no. 481; for Darius I: no. 361; 521; 563; 571; 632; for Xerxes I: no. 465–9; 472; 576; 784; 787; for Artaxerxes I: no. 10; 27; 284; 285; 340; 341; 387–9; 473; 637; 638; 643; for Darius II: no. 286; 287; 342; 390; 474.
⁶⁵ Schaudig (2010). See also Klinkott (2019) 128. On the Babylonian kingship in Achaemenid times, see also Scharrer (1999) 106–18. On the lack of restoration under Achaemenid rule: Scharrer (1999) 123.

With the Egyptian synodal decrees in mind, in particular the Canopus decree of Ptolemy III,[66] the following passage of the Borsippa cylinder reflects some elements of communication between the priests and the king. The cylinder reports of special privileges the king granted to the Borsippa temples:[67]

> When I decided to build Esagila and Ezida, the bricks for Esagila and Ezida I moulded with my pure hands (using) fine quality oil in the land of Hatti and for the laying of the foundation of Esagila and Ezida I brought (them). In the month of Addaru, on the twentieth day, year 43, the foundation of Ezida, the true temple, the house of Nabû which is in Borsippa I did lay.

The restoration of the temple and the statement that it is 'the only true ... in Borsippa' involves a financial and theological support of its priesthood. The cylinder itself records the results of such an exchange process, as Paul Kosmin demonstrated with the 'Akkadianization that deliberately identifies the Seleucid queen (that is: Stratonice's name) with the Syrian goddess Astarte.'[68] Furthermore, the syncretism of Apollo and Nabû visualizes the interweaving of Hellenistic ideology and Babylonian/Borsippan traditions – itself a proof of successful negotiations between king and priests.[69]

The content of the cylinder led Susan Sherwin-White to conclude that 'Antiochus (I) was responsive to Babylonian traditions, which required a king to be involved personally ... in the rituals concerning temple-building.'[70] Parallels to Nebuchadnezzar's cylinder are not the only ones in existence, as Kathryn Stevens has demonstrated; the parallels to the Ptolemaic Memphis decree, the so-called Rosetta Stone, are also striking.[71] There, the king expected the formulation of official acceptance and his royal legitimization by the priests in return.[72] Accordingly, the next section of the Babylonian cylinder declares:[73]

> (O) Nabû, lofty son, wise one of the gods, the proud one, worthy of praise, most noble son of Marduk, offspring of Erua, the queen, who formed mankind, regard (me) joyfully and, at your lofty command which is ever

---

[66] For the Greek text, see Pfeiffer (2015) 75–88 no. 14; Pfeiffer (2004).
[67] Kuhrt and Sherwin-White (1991) 76; cf. Pritchard (1955) 317. [68] Kosmin (2014a) 187.
[69] Kosmin (2014a) 176–80. Compare in addition Kosmin (2014a) 175 concerning the 'overlapping of indigenous and colonial symbolic systems,' especially in practicing the sacrifices. Critical of this Stevens (2014) 80. But she cannot deny the act of conscious construction, even in using 'standard phrasings' (ibid. 81) in the text.
[70] Sherwin-White (1987) 28. [71] Pfeiffer (2015) 111–26.
[72] See the recent German translation of Pfeiffer (2015) 117 § 19, here translated into English: 'Therefore the Gods gave him health, victory and power and all the other good things during the royal rule for him as well as for his children, everlasting.'
[73] Kuhrt and Sherwin-White (1991) 76–7; Pritchard (1955) 317.

unchanging, <u>may the overthrow of the countries of my enemies</u>, the achievement of my battle-wishes against my enemies, <u>permanent victories, just kingship, a happy reign, years of joy, children in satiety</u> be (your) <u>gift for the kingship of Antiochus and Seleucus, the king, his son, for ever</u>!

The king expected constant firm support of his royal legitimation ('my years many, my throne firm, my rule lasting') and promised in exchange permanent privileged treatment of the temple through financial support when he says: 'and may I personally conquer (all) the countries from sunrise to sunset, gather their tribute and bring it (home) for the perfection of Esagila and Ezida.'[74]

The result of the kings' respect for the temples and gods is the guarantee of the preservation of their dynastic kingship, granted by the Babylonian gods, as Cyrus once programmatically asked on an Akkadian clay cylinder from Ur: 'I returned the gods to their shrines ... let them dwell ... life of long days. Affirm the throne, an everlasting reign and kingship without equal, grant me as a gift.'[75] Similar to this are also the final statements of the Cyrus Cylinder and of the Borsippa inscription of Antiochus I.

At the end, Antiochus emphasizes once more the main topics: first, he confirms Ezida as the only true temple, then he is acknowledged as legal king by the favor of the god, that is by support of the priests, and in the same way Seleucus and Stratonike are recognized as king and queen from a dynastic perspective:[76]

> O Nabû, foremost son, when you enter Ezida, the true temple, may favor for Antiochus, the king of lands,[77] (and) favor for Seleucus, the king, his son, (and) for Stratonike, his consort, the queen, be in your mouth.

By using the style and form of a clay cylinder in cuneiform writing, Antiochus is presented as a Babylonian king according to the old, local traditions.[78] This document is somewhat reminiscent of the so-called Cyrus cylinder of Cyrus the Great.[79] Furthermore, the cuneiform writing emphasizes the participation of local priests in formulating and elaborating the decree of the Macedonian ruler. In other words, the priestly elite (of Borsippa) stood clearly behind the results of the exchange negotiating royal and priestly interests. This is demonstrated by formulating an elaborate

---

[74] Pritchard (1955) 317. [75] Translation by Kuhrt (2010) 75, no. 22 (III).
[76] Kuhrt and Sherwin-White (1991) 77; Pritchard (1955) 317.
[77] This title is important to use because – in contrast to the title of King of Babylon – its specific dimension refers to the financial support for the temple through foreign tributes.
[78] Kosmin (2014a) 173–6; 188–92; Haubold (2013a) 141 as an act of the king Antiochus himself.
[79] Kuhrt (2010) 70–4 with translation. For the Babylonian titles of Cyrus, see Ahn (1992) 131–9.

composition of Seleucid ideology and Borsippan theology in the Babylonian language.[80]

It is worth noticing the specific Babylonian elements present at the beginning of the inscription. They fill in a gap of late Achaemenid times, since the kings had not used the title of King of Babylon from the rule of Artaxerxes I onward.[81] Antiochus refers back to an older – Neo-Babylonian and Teispide –[82] tradition, in which the acting ruler is legitimized and first of all named as King of Babylon.[83] This title entails the king celebrating the so-called *akītu*-festival (every year) with the Babylonian priests.[84] These details, as well as the linguistic design of the cylinder, indicate a strategic involvement of the new royal family in the traditional framework of indigenous Babylonian theology. This means an active act of writing, consciously realized by the priests with their theological and literary knowledge.[85] Kathryn Stevens thus rightly states: 'Yet the royal titulary was typically selected with great care.'[86]

3 Kings and Babylonian Temple Rituals

As Babette Edelmann has pointed out, the *akītu*-festival can be seen as an annual interaction between the king, giving an account to the god Marduk of the fulfillment of his promises, and the god, that is, in fact, the priests, through the king's renewed election as king of Babylon.[87]

This crowning festival in the Esagil of Babylon from 1 to 12 Nisan of the year was celebrated by the Seleucids, some of them being known to have participated actively, such as Seleucus III, Antiochus II, and probably Antiochus III.[88] The ritual is best documented by a text of the Hellenistic period, dated to the reign of Seleucus III.[89] When the king received his royal regalia at Marduk's temple, he gave an account to the god in front of the high priest, a kind of negative confession, emphasizing that 'I did not destroy Babylon; I did not command its overthrow; I did not (...) the temple Esagil; I did not forget its rites.'[90]

---

[80] Stevens (2014) 85–6.   [81] Stevens (2014) 72.
[82] For the Teispide dynasty of Persian Great Kings: Rollinger (1998–9) 155–209.
[83] On the explicit link to Nebuchadnezzar II: Kosmin (2014a) 188–92; on the Assyrian link in the text in general: Stevens (2014) 73–5. See also on Persian inheritance of the Seleucids. Tuplin (2009) 119–21.
[84] Scharrer (1999) 105; on Antiochus, see Kosmin (2014a) 192.
[85] See e.g. Stevens (2014) 75: 'Assyrianizing titles (...) within a Babylonian structure.'
[86] Stevens (2014) 75.   [87] Edelmann (2007) 303.
[88] See Szelényi-Graziotto (1996) 176; 182f.; Edelmann (2007) 305. Cf. also Mitsuma (2013).
[89] See Erickson (2011) 56; 59.   [90] Translation by Pritchard (1955) 334.

Legitimizing the Foreign King: Local Elites and Priests

At the dawn of Macedonian rule, the Babylonian Astronomical Diaries refer to Alexander entering Babylon with offerings at the Esangila:[91]

> For 1 shekel of s(ilver . . .)
> That month, from the 1st to (. . .)
> **Came to Babylon saying: 'Esangila (. . .)'**
> **And the Babylonians for the property of Esangila** (. . .)
> On the 11th, in Sippar an order of A (lexander . . .)
> **(' . . .) I shall not enter your houses'. On the 13th,** (. . .)
> (. . .) to the outer gate of Esangila and (. . .)
> (. . .) on the 14th, these Ionians a bull (. . .)
> Short, fatty tissue (. . .)
> (. . .) **Alexander, king of the world, (came in) to Babylon** (. . .)
> (. . .) horses and equipment (. . .)
> (. . ..) and the Babylonians and the people of (. . ..)
> (. . ..) a message to (. . .)

Alexander's interest in the temple of Bêl can be seen, programmatically, as a religious act of the new king in accordance with traditional local habits in order to be accepted as Babylonian king.[92] More specifically, the fragmentary citation of line 7 seems to comply with the so-called negative confessions. Both parts, the offerings and the negative confessions, were typical and important elements of the *akītu* festival, as stressed by Amélie Kuhrt with regard to a similar cultic act by Cambyses as king of Babylon (before Nabû).[93] In fact, there is no other proof for Persian kings performing the *akītu* ritual. It is thus remarkable that Alexander fulfilled the ritual at the very beginning of his Babylonian occupation, consciously drawing on late Babylonian traditions of royal legitimation and dissociating himself from the Achaemenid policy.

Alexander's behavior in Babylon is used by the Seleucids to connect themselves to specific privileges attached to Babylonian kingship, which was itself one aspect of the Achaemenid legitimation of the status of Great Kings. This becomes evident in a fragmentary tablet of the Astronomical Diaries (BM 36613), lines 6'–10':[94]

---

[91] Sachs and Hunger (1988) 179 no. -330, 'Rev.'
[92] Boiy (2004) 111 according to Kuhrt (1990) 127. See also Scharrer (1999) 120–1.
[93] Kuhrt and Sherwin-White (1987a) 75. On the text: Grayson (1975) 111: Chronicle 7, ll. 24f.: 'On the fourth day, when Cambyses, son of C[yrus], went to Egidrikalammasummu, the . . . official of Nabu who . . . '. See also Heller (2010) 252–60; Kuhrt (1988) 122.
[94] For the text and translation, see Sachs (1977) 129–46.

> the ...]th [year] of Arsu the son of Umasu [called] Artaksats[u ......] (they) entered. And the temple of the goddess Anunîtu inside the cit[y ...... **Aleksan]darris, the great king, made** (or: did, or: built), **you Bab-[ylonians** ...... the ...]s and the houses returned to the possession of the temple Esaggil (sic!) **and the Babylonians (...) the temple Esaggil** they built (or: performed). The army (...).

Arrian reports that Alexander enacted his status as Great King according to the Persian tradition when he resided in Babylon in 323 BC. Having conquered Babylonia and the Persian residences, Alexander promised to restore and rebuild the temple of Bêl in Babylon itself (Arr. *Anab.* 3, 16, 4 f.; 7, 17, 1–5). Additionally, the Astronomical Diaries from Babylon inform us about the continuation of this restoration work at the Esagil even after Alexander's death.[95] All these royal commitments are a part, and result, of the negotiations between the Babylonian priests and the Macedonian conqueror. From the very beginning the Babylonian priests, called Chaldaeans by Arrian, wished communication with the new ruler.[96] Therefore, they offered Alexander helpful services, and he immediately reacted by promising the restoration of their temples. In consequence, Arrian tells us about a very first synod.[97]

> On entering Babylon, Alexander directed the Babylonians to rebuild the temple of Baal, whom the Babylonians honour more than any other god. (...) At Babylon too he met the Chaldaeans and carried out all their recommendations for the Babylonian temples, and in particular sacrificed to Baal, according to their instructions.

Arrian is absolutely clear: Alexander granted every cultic privilege the priesthood was interested in and actively took part in the offerings to the local deity. In particular, he followed the regulations and instructions of the priests, as Arrian knew from Aristobulus (Arr. *Anab.* 7, 17,5). The same respect towards the Babylonian temples, their cults and their properties is also documented by the *Astronomical Diaries*. Alexander respected the property of the temples.[98] But above all, the meeting of the new ruler with the most important priests of the city seems to follow a much older

---

[95] See Everling (2014) 17–24.
[96] On the role of the Babylonian (priestly) elite conferring royal legitimacy and maintaining the stability of rule, see Haubold (2016) 93–100. Concerning the Babylonian priests or 'Chaldeans' in Greek sources as a group which was responsible for the communication of Babylonian traditions, theology and philosophical questions – the so-called 'barbarian wisdom' – see Haubold (2013b) 35; 40–2.
[97] Arr. *Anab.* 3, 16, 4–5.
[98] Sachs and Hunger (1988) 179 no. -330, 'Rev.' See also Scharrer (1999) 119.

traditional procedure in this specific situation. In fact, an Akkadian *paean* in praise of Cyrus after he had entered the city explains in detail the meeting of the new (Persian) ruler with the priests and his care for the Babylonian temples. The poem informs us, in col. V, lines 23 and 24: 'Zeriya, the *šatammu*, crouched before him (and) Rimut, the *zazakku* (= the royal secretary), standing before him, confirmed the king's words, agreed with his declarations.'[99]

Alexander's presentation and his entry into the city of Babylon must be understood within a far older tradition that goes back to Sargon II in 710 BC and Cyrus II in 539 BC.[100] In particular, the famous Cyrus Cylinder explains the common features. Alexander and Cyrus both marched with their armies to liberate Babylon (Cyrus cyl. § 23 f.), defeating their enemies (Cyrus cyl. § 13), both kings entered the city peacefully (Cyrus cyl. § 17.22), they were both welcomed by the population and took up their residences in the royal palace (Cyrus cyl. § 23). Both Cyrus and Alexander immediately visited the temples (Cyrus cyl. § 26), they ordered the robbed deities brought back to the temples (Cyrus cyl. § 32)[101] and began with restoration work on the temples and the city (Cyrus cyl. § 38–43).[102] It may be a programmatic statement for a successful policy – even for Alexander – as well as a reflection of the priestly negotiations with the conqueror when the Cyrus cylinder quotes in direct speech: (§35) ... *say words in my favour and speak to Marduk, my lord: 'For Cyrus the king, who honours you, and Cambyses, his son,'* (36) [. . .] *the kingship.'*

4 Kings and the Babylonian Temple Rebuilding Program

One fact perfectly illustrates the conscious assumption of older Babylonian traditions by Macedonian rulers. As Alexander had done, Antiochus proclaimed the ceremonial restoration of the temples and gods and the political program of rebuilding Babylonian temples in general.[103] This support for the Babylonian temples is a clear recourse to late Babylonian forms of royal legitimation as Babylonian king. The last late Babylonian king, Nabonidus, extensively developed restoration

---

[99] Translation by Kuhrt (2010) 78. [100] See Boiy (2004) 106.
[101] See also in the Akkadian tablet of Ur: Kuhrt (2010) 75 no. 22 (III), and at the poetic condemnation of Nabonidus: Kuhrt (2010) 78: col. IV, l. 12.
[102] For a translation, see Kuhrt (2010) 72.
[103] See in detail Kuhrt and Sherwin-White (1991) 79–81 (ceremonial restoration); 81–2 (rebuilding program).

work and rebuilding, as reported in many texts and cylinder inscriptions.[104] Cyrus II assumed this specific kind of legitimation in his function as the new King of Babylon, but his royal building work at the Eanna temple of Uruk is the latest documented.[105] So the restoration and rebuilding of Babylonian temples by Alexander and the Seleucid kings[106] was not only an architectural necessity, it was first and foremost a political statement of dissociation from Achaemenid rule and a reference to the late Babylonian kings (perhaps to Cyrus in his very Babylonian tradition as well).[107] Last, but not least, all these acts of reference are unimaginable without a vigorous exchange with priestly interests. Its implementation in the texts, as well as in the building program, was preceded by a detailed consultation between the king (or his court) and the priests. The duration of these negotiations may be the reason for the gap in the rule of Seleucus I, who lacked the title of a Babylonian king.[108] Only the Borsippa cylinder of Antiochus I names him posthumously with this title.[109] In Babylonia – as well as in early Ptolemaic Egypt – it was a complicated process to win over the indigenous priesthood to confirm the legitimation of the new Macedonian ruler as the local king in a traditional form. The – possibly synodal – exchange and agreement of royal and priestly interests took place in the background.

This policy is certainly an important part of the specific legitimation as king of Babylon but does not mean automatic recognition as such. This becomes clear in the case of Alexander in the *Astronomical Diaries*. While one of the early Diaries (AD 1–330) gives Alexander the title 'king of the world,' a later one (AD 1–329) clearly depicts him as a foreign ruler: 'the eighth year of Alexander, the king from the land of Hanû.'[110] It is only the specific context of the Esagil temple in which some neo-Babylonian texts describe Alexander in the role of a Babylonian king.[111]

---

[104] Schaudig (2010).
[105] Kleber (2008) 259: Cyrus restored the pavement of the court and rebuilt the brickwork of the Eanna; Scharrer (1999) 107–10. For restoration work at the temples as an act of royal representation demonstrating the legitimization of rule in Neo-Babylonian times, see Schaudig (2010).
[106] See also Boiy (2010a) 211–19.
[107] The absence of this policy, in particular of restoration work and privileges for the temples under Achaemenid rule, is symptomatic. See (wrong and without proof) Boiy and Mittag (2011) 111.
[108] Scharrer (1999) 97–100.   [109] Scharrer (1999) 99; 127.
[110] Boiy (2004) 107. Concerning Hanû, see in detail Boiy (2004) 120–1. The title King of the World is also a traditional one, used, for example, by Cyrus on an Akkadian clay cylinder at Ur: Kuhrt (2010) 75 no. 22 (III).
[111] See Sachs (1977) 146–7; Edelmann (2007) 304.

Because Antigonus Monophthalmus treated Babylonia as enemy territory, sacking towns, temples, and the countryside in the struggle for that satrapy against Seleucus in 311 BC,[112] the resumption of old Babylonian traditions and the restoration of temples must be seen as a political program and a basic element for the Seleucids. They used it to distinguish themselves from Antigonus Monophthalmus, in order to establish themselves successfully as rulers. But Seleucus, too, had to strive to gain appreciation as king of Babylon. When he arrived in the city after the conference of Triparadisus in 320 BC, the *Chronicle of the Successors* describes him as 'satrap of Babylonia' (ABC 10: obv. 6).[113] When Antigonus controlled the city between 315 and 311 BC, the tablets (in particular the so-called brewer's archive from Borsippa) titled him 'Antigonus strategos.'[114] The so-called *Babylonian King List* explicitly remarks in this context: 'years there was no king in the land,' while all other rulers up to Antiochus IV are mentioned with the addendum 'ruled as king.'[115] When Seleucus (I) came back again to Babylon after the battle of Gaza, the *Chronicle of the Successors* (ABC 10: rev. 3–6) mentioned him as 'Seleucus, the army commander.'[116] From 305/4 BC Seleucus was given the full title of King of Babylon, while his son Antiochus I bore the official title of Crown Prince (*mâr šarri*), acting in the Babylonian temples of Esagil and Sîn-Egišnugal.[117] Finally, from November 294 BC onwards, Seleucus and Antiochus were both titled kings in co-regency.[118]

Amélie Kuhrt remarks with regard to the restoration works of the vast temple complexes at Uruk: 'It is in his (that is Antiochus's) co-regency and reign that one sees the beginnings of a definite interaction of Macedonian rulers and indigenous Babylonian subjects on both the administrative and cultural plane.'[119] We know from the *Astronomical Diaries* that Apammu, the eldest son of Antiochus II (AD 2 -245A), acted with the *šatammu* of Esagil, a *dâtabara* (?) and the *kiništu*, that means the assembly of Esagil temple, in the context of a Babylonian festival (AD 2– 245B).[120] That means, as Tom Boiy has pointed out, that the king's eldest son was present in Babylon and obviously in regular and close contact with the priestly

---

[112] See Sherwin-White (1987) 15. The Chronicle of the Successors reports of 'weeping and mourning in the land' and of 'plundering the city and the land.' See Boiy (2010b) 10.
[113] Boiy (2004) 119.   [114] Boiy (2004) 124.
[115] Sachs and Wiseman (1954) 202–11; concerning Antigonus see 203 ll. 3 and 204.
[116] Boiy (2004) 127.
[117] Boiy (2004) 139; Scharrer (1999) 99; Kuhrt and Sherwin-White (1991) 81.
[118] Boiy (2004) 139.   [119] Kuhrt (1987) 52.
[120] See on this assembly: Jursa (2005) 51; Sarkisjan (1997) 244–5.

administration.¹²¹ It is therefore unsurprising that the most extensive text describing the crowning ritual of the *akītu* festival dates to the time of Seleucus II.¹²² This text illustrates in detail the ritualized subordination of the king being enthroned by the high priest:¹²³

> (420) He (the high priest) will place [the king (?)] behind him. He will make him enter before Bêl.
>
> (421) [After this (?)] he will pull his ears, make him kneel on the ground.

The following lines cite the ritual concessions of the new king to the temple:

> (422) [Together w]ith (?) <u>the king he will say this once</u>:
>
> (423) [I have not] sinned, lord of the lands, I have not neglected your divinity,
>
> ... (425)[I have not] made Esagil tremble, I have not forgotten its rites, ...

This interaction is documented by the cultic calendar of Hellenistic Babylonia and the texts concerning the Babylonian cults,¹²⁴ which were continually practiced in the Hellenistic period with (almost) no differences to pre-Hellenistic times.¹²⁵ Marc Linssen has noted that 'even the Macedonian rulership took part in the Babylonian cults; they did not attempt to change the cults but themselves adapted to Babylonian customs.'¹²⁶ The interpretation of all these elements as part of the outlined communication process could be taken further.

5 Negotiating between Kings and Babylonian Priests

All these texts document in general an intensive relationship between the king and the Babylonian priests that shaped Seleucid kingship in Babylonia.¹²⁷ The privileges granted by the king, as well as the cuneiform cylinder inscriptions in an old Babylonian tradition, are witness to different parts of the same shaping of the communication process underpinning the acceptance, legitimation, and official representation of the ruling king. The negotiations between kings and Babylonian priests could not be documented in the Seleucid sources in as much detail as in the Ptolemaic

---

¹²¹ Boiy (2004) 147.
¹²² See Sherwin-White (1983c) 156–8; (1987) 11–14; Kuhrt and Sherwin-White (1991) 81–2.
¹²³ For the text, see Linssen (2004) 231–2.
¹²⁴ On the cultic calendar: Boiy (2004) 277–87. Concerning the festivals: Linssen (2004) 168.
¹²⁵ Linssen (2004) 168; Szelényi-Graziotto (1996) 178–82.   ¹²⁶ Linssen (2004) 168.
¹²⁷ See also Bioy and Mittag (2011) 111 with n. 25.

inscriptions.¹²⁸ But in my opinion there is a representative text of the *Babylonian Chronicles* that shows a striking correspondence.¹²⁹ Apart from the many difficulties, all discussed in detail by Susan Sherwin-White,¹³⁰ the text refers to the main aspects of the exchange process:¹³¹

> (3) The eighty-eighth year of Seleucus, the **king**: in the month Nisan, that same month, the eighth day, a Babylonian, the shatammu of Esagil, (4) established, according to **the command of the king**, precisely in accordance with the **parchment letter which the king had sent before**, as the [offer]ing of Esagil (5) [N] shekels of silver from the house of the king, from his own house, eleven fat oxen, one hundred fat ewes, (6) eleven fat ducks for the offering, within Esagil, (7) to Bel (Lord), Beltiia (Mistress), and the great gods and for the ritual of Seleucus, the king, (8) and his sons.

In one respect the text is absolutely clear: the king wrote to the priests of the Esagil at Babylon by parchment letter, obviously as part of a longer communication. We may suppose that the priests made clear that they would acknowledge Seleucus as king, as in the Ptolemaic texts. The Chronicle notice is the result of these negotiations, legalized by a royal edict called the command of the king. On the other hand, the king perhaps granted several donations from his own treasury to the Babylonian *šatammu* of the Esagil for regular offerings and cultic rituals – as we know from the Ptolemaic synodal inscriptions, for example, the Pithom stela.¹³² The practical implementation of the royal commitments is perfectly documented by an Astronomical Diary text (- 187), in which Antiochus III stayed for 10 days in Babylon and Borsippa, travelled repeatedly between the cities, and made offerings to the gods before he returned to Seleucia-Tigris.¹³³ The similarities with the Ptolemaic synodal inscriptions, in particular the Pithom stela, are evident. At the beginning, the text refers to Ptolemy II travelling – obviously from Alexandria – to the *nome* of harpoons, there to the temple of Per-Kecheret (§ 7) and equipping the sanctuary there (§ 8). Then Ptolemy turned to Marmi in Lower Egypt – in this part Ptolemy also bears only the title of King of Lower Egypt – where he visited his palace and donated support to the temple (§ 9).¹³⁴ In

---

¹²⁸ See in particular the Canopus decree: Pfeiffer (2004). ¹²⁹ Grayson (1975) 13b.
¹³⁰ Sherwin-White (1983c) 156–7. ¹³¹ Translation by Sherwin-White (1983c) 156.
¹³² For the Pithom stela, see Schäfer (2011) 216 § 8.9; 219 § 17; 221–2 §26–7. For the decree of Canopus of Ptolemy III (238 BC), see Pfeiffer (2004) 58–65 § 20–73, to be compared with the so-called Raphia decree of Ptolemy IV from 217 BC, see Thissen (1966) 17 § 19; 21 § 28–9.
¹³³ See Szelényi-Graziotto (1996) 182–4.
¹³⁴ See for the text in translation Schäfer (2011) 215–6.

the same way, the Raphia decree of 217 BC gives the following details about Ptolemy IV: 'He travelled by ship through Egypt. The occupants of the temples came out approaching him.'[135]

6 Conclusion

As van der Spek illustrated in 1987, the cuneiform archives document the workings of an intact temple administration with the *šatammu* (chief administrator at the temple)[136] and the *kiništu* (a temple board/council) at Babylon,[137] 'the leader of the temples of Uruk' (rab ša rêš ali (ša bît ilâni) ša Uruk) and a '*kinishtu* of the temples/of the Reš-sanctuary' at Uruk.[138] Van der Spek concluded from the cuneiform tablets 'that the temple in Babylon was governed by a *šatammu* and a council, and that this board formed, in fact, the highest local authority in the city as it also had power in civil matters.'[139] In other words, the Seleucid kings did not reduce the political and administrative influences of the local temples as the Achaemenid kings had tried to do. Quite the contrary: they established, in a traditional way, special officials as royal representatives in the temple and in close contact with its priestly administration. So we know in Babylon of the *pahatu* (the governor) and 'the deputy of Nicanor' who acted with the *šatammu* and the temple council,[140] or the 'overseer of the temples,' *uppudêtu*, maybe comparable to the *prostatai* in Egypt;[141] in Uruk we find the *šaknu* and the *paqdu*, who seems to have exercised royal control over the exploitation of the temple property.[142] The *Astronomical Diary* (- 187) quoted above illustrates king Antiochus III (line 9'; 10') acting in common with the *šatammu* of Esagil (line 8') and the *pahatu* of Babylon (line 9').[143]

The dissolution of the Seleucid empire seems to have coincided with the break-up of this bilateral relationship. When Antiochus IV started to neglect close relations with the Babylonian priests, he jeopardized the stability of Seleucid rule in Mesopotamia.

When Seleucus I moved some of the Babylonians to the newly founded Seleucia-on-the-Tigris but left the 'Chaldaeans' in the old city, as reported by Pausanias (1.16.3), this was not only a demonstration of piety and respect for the Babylonian religion. In my opinion and in comparison with the

---

[135] According to the German translation of Thissen (1966) 21 § 27.
[136] On the office of *šatammu*: Boiy (2004) 196–202.
[137] van der Spek (1987) 60–5. On *kiništu* in particular: Boiy (2004) 202–4.
[138] van der Spek (1987) 70–1. [139] van der Spek (1987) 64. [140] van der Spek (1987) 63.
[141] van der Spek (1987) 64. [142] van der Spek (1987) 71–2. [143] Szelényi-Graziotto (1996) 183.

Ptolemaic texts, it showed much more than an appreciation of the priests. It was more than a 'policy of tolerance and flexibility in accepting regional autonomy,' as David Engels passively characterized it.[144] Royal protection and support of the temples, the continuation of traditional structures in administration and cult, and performance of his religious role as Babylonian king are expressions of an active Seleucid policy for the formation of their empire in Mesopotamia. So, it is not by chance that, under the rule of Seleucus I, his son Antiochus is attested by a Babylonian tablet as offering sacrifices as crown prince to Sin in Babylon (BCHP 5) and on the ruins of Esagil (BCHP 6).[145]

Support for the temples, the continuity in administration and cult, and the Seleucids' fulfilment of their religious role as Babylonian kings are not simply aspects of a general record of religious structures and traditions in Hellenistic Babylonia. They are, in my opinion, at the same time elements of and evidence for a process of negotiation of royal and priestly interests. The final and essential act of these negotiations was celebrated at the end of the *akītu* festival by the ritual (re)installation of the Babylonian king. The priest revealed an oracle concerning the future of the ruling king and gave him back the royal insignia.[146] This resembles the biographical inscription of Psentptais III, high priest of Ptah in Memphis, which describes his leading the main Egyptian festivals in Memphis and crowning the king in the reign of Ptolemy XII.[147] The important occasion ostentatiously demonstrated royal legitimation substantially supported by the indigenous Babylonian priests, while conversely illustrating the reliance of the king on the priesthood, as shown in particular by his participation in the festival. Thus, it is unsurprising that there is clear evidence, in particular for the early Seleucid kings who were establishing their rule in Babylonia, for celebrating the festival in a way that resembles a synod.[148]

---

[144] Engels (2011) 21.   [145] Boiy (2013) 120; see also Kuhrt and Sherwin-White (1991) 81.
[146] See Boiy and Mittag (2011) 110, with the relevant sources in n. 21.
[147] See Blasius (2011) 140; 149 (text).
[148] There are obviously many more examples for royal participation in the festival than only for Antiochus III, as Boiy and Mittag (2011) 110, n. 22 suggest. As discussed above, there is also some evidence for (Seleucus I?), Antiochus I and Seleucus II.

CHAPTER 9

Antiochus III, Ptolemy IV, and Local Elites
Deal-Making Politics at Its Peak

Boris Dreyer and François Gerardin

Common Introduction

This chapter shows that communication between rulers and local elites, whose legitimation strategies responded to local conditions, reached its qualitative and quantitative peak under the reign of Antiochus III. The areas of conflict in which this king was involved provide the evidence for this claim. Two reasons have led us to privilege contested peripheries over the core territories of his kingdom. First, areas and periods of fierce diplomatic and military confrontation are exceptionally well documented in literary accounts as well as the epigraphical and papyrological sources. Second, the intensity of conflict in these territories throws into sharper relief the principles of interaction between the local elites and the agents of imperial power. Given the cost of coercion and direct control, competition assumed the form of increasing communication between imperial centers and local communities. In the conflict between the Seleucids and Ptolemies in Syria and Phoenicia in the reigns of Antiochus III, Ptolemy IV, and Ptolemy V, the competing empires followed the same system of rules. In the war between the Romans and the Seleucids in the 190s in the eastern Mediterranean, by contrast, Antiochus III, so far successful, faced the challenge of a rival – Rome – that had fundamentally changed the rules of the game. When both the Ptolemaic and the Seleucid empires began to decline, in 207 and 188 BC respectively, this evolution brought local, and to some degree national, uprisings, followed by royal repression.

As a starting point, we draw on the definition of local elites proposed by Peter Mittag and Boris Dreyer a few years ago:[1]

---

[1] Dreyer and Mittag (2011) 10. Boris Dreyer provided the inspiration for the project to examine local elites in contested areas in the time of Antiochus III. He and François Gerardin closely worked together in the writing and revision of their papers. They both would like to thank the editors of the volume for their kind invitation to speak at the conference and their unfailing assistance in the editorial process.

> The 'local elite' is a minority that is not necessarily homogeneous and emerges from a politically, socially, or ethnically defined social entity. Its composition greatly varies, depending on the criteria that apply in a given time and place. It plays a substantial role in making the decisions that will be relevant for its communities. The members of the local elite aim to regularly monopolize communication with the center of power, in the long term legitimize their actions vis-à-vis the majority of the local population, and thus perpetuate their privileged position.

The choice of areas of conflict requires two qualifications to be made to that initial definition. First, local elites are not necessarily a product of their society. In Syria and Phoenicia, for instance, they were normally Greek or hellenized leaders who were granted land by kings or other potentates or who inherited it. Second, the focus of this chapter is on communication between the king who laid claims to territories and the local elites that inhabited them. If officials of all ranks were supposed to represent royal authority on the ground, conversely the most successful members of the local elites could enter the narrow, Greek-speaking circle of the king and his court. In this process, both parties maneuvered to best preserve or promote their personal interests. On the one hand, the king sought to sustain communication between his administration and the local elites that had proved loyal in order to extend his sway over the region and secure imperial revenue in the form of tribute. Aiming to strengthen his influence on the ground, he could pursue various strategies: redistribute or reorganize the positions of authority held by elites at the local level; establish a local ruler cult financed by local resources; and create new social groups or rebrand old ones. Thus, he could rename the civic subdivisions, known as tribes (*phylai*), after a member of the dynasty who then held the position of founder hero of the tribe and received divine honors. Alternatively, he could take the radical step of modifying the constitution, especially if he was interacting with Greek cities. On the other hand, local elites sought to stabilize their influence by mediating the benefits provided by the new ruler. In so doing, these local power brokers could move up the ladder of the regional administration or the court hierarchy, offering exclusive contact with their local communities in matters of politics, diplomacy, and war in exchange for individual promotion.

To support this claim, François Gerardin first emphasizes the role of failed interactions between central power and political elites in the loss of Syria-Phoenicia and other external possessions to Antiochus III by Ptolemy IV and Ptolemy V. Boris Dreyer then examines the so-called Cold War between the Seleucids and Rome in the 190s, arguing that this context proved exceptionally favorable to the political action of local elites.

1A THE GREEK ELITES AND THE CRISIS OF THE PTOLEMAIC EMPIRE

François Gerardin

1 Introduction

In this contribution, I explore the role of local elites in the loss of Ptolemaic overseas possessions under Ptolemy IV and Ptolemy V. Local elites were a necessary component of Hellenistic rule. In Egypt, Pharaonic imagery and ideology presented the king as omnipotent. Yet the chain of command from king to subject was not unproblematic: a general on campaign could be lured into switching sides, an official could disobey royal orders, and peasants could – and did – refuse to pay taxes. Sole ruler he might be, but the monarch had to share power with local entities.[2] Accordingly, the Ptolemies from the very beginning had to reckon with the power of Egyptian temples. That was, however, only one of the 'ruling coalitions' on which they relied to take over Egypt.[3] Ptolemaic power, in its Greek incarnation, relied heavily on Greek elites, who had migrated from the cities of the Aegean and Greece. In the Ptolemaic kingdom, local power was to a large extent delegated to at least three categories of local elites: the entourage of the king, the Greek civic elites, and the native hellenized notables.[4] Ptolemaic pageantry, patronage of the arts, and propaganda toward the Greek world was directed primarily toward these local elites, who were the mainstay of the Ptolemaic imperial system.

Yet this network of Greek or hellenized elites, as I will argue, turned out to be a double-edged sword.[5] This is particularly clear at the moment of the so-called crisis of Ptolemaic power in the years of transition from Ptolemy IV to Ptolemy V, when most of the overseas possessions were lost. In a short period of time, the Ptolemaic kingdom was reduced from one of the superpowers in the Hellenistic world to a kingdom of regional significance. For a long time, following Polybius's account of the battle of Raphia, scholars have focused on the consequences of Egyptians' enrollment into the phalanx and the uprising against the Ptolemaic dynasty starting in 207

---

[2] This understanding of Ptolemaic power, which departs from the paradigm of the 'royal economy,' takes its inspiration from Manning (2010) esp. chapter 4.
[3] See Manning (2010) 84–9, who stresses "ruling coalitions" in the construction of the Ptolemaic state and cites previous literature.
[4] Dreyer and Mittag (2011) 10 for a definition of local elites; Savalli-Lestrade (2003) 61 rightly stresses the need to distinguish those three groups.
[5] Will (2003) 105–8 and, more recently, Eckstein (2008) 124–9 on the "crisis of Ptolemaic power."

Antiochus III, Ptolemy IV, and Local Elites: Deal-Making 265

BC.[6] In this part of the chapter I draw on evidence ranging from Polybius's *Histories* and Greek inscriptions to the hieroglyphic version of the Raphia decree to shift the perspective. I emphasize the role of Greek elites under Ptolemy IV and Ptolemy V and how they allowed the Ptolemaic imperial machinery to collapse so quickly. The defection of Greek elites at the local level and court rivalries at the center decisively contributed to the defeat of the Ptolemies by Antiochus III.[7] Recent interpretations of this important moment of Egyptian history have revolved around fiscal pressure and climatic shocks in the Nile Valley.[8] The perspective suggested here supplements this literature and offers a complementary explanation.

This section is primarily concerned with the reign of Ptolemy IV and the early reign of Ptolemy V in the years 220 to 200 BC. It covers the areas that became directly subject to the Ptolemies, or at least were in the Ptolemaic sphere of influence, but were contested by Antiochus III. Those are Syria and Phoenicia – recast as Coele Syria and Phoenicia by the Seleucids – and, in southern Asia Minor, Cilicia, Pamphylia, Lycia, and Caria. I pay particular attention to Syria and Phoenicia which had been a bone of contention between the two kingdoms since the age of the successors. I substantiate my argument with the stories of individuals and families who at turns supported and deserted Ptolemy IV and his contender Antiochus III. I first follow the trajectory of prominent families who, passing on power from one generation to the other, brought the Ptolemaic empire to its height under Ptolemy III and endeavored to sustain it under Ptolemy IV. In the confrontation with Antiochus III, this reliance on Greek elites, especially the Ptolemaic officers serving in Syria and Phoenicia, had the opposite effect of bringing about the collapse of the Ptolemaic imperial system. Conversely, the Seleucid king conquered Ptolemaic territories by winning over, and even stimulating the emergence of, local elites.

2 The Power of Greek Elites in Ptolemaic Overseas Possessions

Communication between elites at the center and elites at the periphery proved critical for the establishment and perpetuation of Ptolemaic

---

[6] Polyb. 5.107, translation in Austin (2006) no. 277; Will (2003) 40–4; and, more recently, McGing (2016).
[7] On priestly decrees, the literature has been growing; see Manning (2010) 97–102.
[8] Ludlow and Manning (2016) on volcanic eruptions, Nile failures, and bad harvests in ancient Egypt; one may add the secret pact between Antiochus III and Philip V to share the spoils of the Ptolemaic empire, on which see Dreyer (2002).

domination outside Egypt.⁹ This communication consisted of words, gestures, and goods that created a reciprocal relation between rulers and ruled. The king and his entourage disseminated royal portraiture, narratives of victory, and poetic recreations of imperial space in Egypt and overseas. The Greek local communities, toward whom these messages were directed, also took an active part in soliciting the king through embassies.

2.1 The Collaboration of Greek Civic Elites under Ptolemy III

Both forms of communication were at play during the so-called Third Syrian War that inaugurated the apogée of the Ptolemaic empire. In the year 246 BC, Ptolemy III dealt a severe blow to the Seleucid monarchy.¹⁰ Taking advantage of the dynastic crisis that followed the death of Antiochus II, he launched a campaign that carried him to the Seleucid capital cities of northern Syria and well into the Seleucid East, notably Babylon.¹¹ Whether the pro-Seleucid population of the city successfully resisted the siege, or unrest caused by a bad harvest and climatic stress called him back, he stopped his advance and returned to Egypt.¹² The king, however, was careful to capitalize symbolically on his success.

The fragment of a war bulletin, probably composed by Ptolemy III himself, describes the enthusiastic welcome he received upon entering the cities of Seleucia-Pieria and Antioch.¹³ Sacrifices, both public and private, are made in his honor: sacrificial victims (*hiera*) are brought to the city gate and altars are set up in front of houses. All constituencies within the city display great zeal (*ekteneia*) in showing their approval of Ptolemy's takeover. The narrative certainly embellishes reality. No external source indeed confirms that the city's population unanimously welcomed the new ruler. Yet, however fabricated, the bulletin disguises conquest as acceptance in a revealing way: in this text, Ptolemaic power conceives of itself as

---

⁹ For the shift from administration to communication, or "hard power" to "soft power," see Buraselis and Thompson (2013) 8 who define the latter as "the less tangible resources of power, such as are to be found, for instance, in the promulgation of cult and culture;" Bagnall (1976) on the administration of the Ptolemaic empire, with an up-to-date, but not definitive treatment in Huß (2011).

¹⁰ Grainger (2010) 153–70 on the Third Syrian War; see also Lehmann (1998).

¹¹ The cuneiform text (*BCHP* 11) that records this aspect of the campaign confirms the lofty claims contained in the so-called Adoulis inscription (OGIS I 54, l. 17–20, translation in Bagnall and Derow [2004] no. 26) that "he crossed the Euphrates river and after subjecting to himself Mesopotamia and Babylonia and Sousiane and Persis and Media and all the rest of the land up to Bactriane." Ptolemy III reached the city but may not have taken it: see new commentary, edition, and translation of *BCHP* 11 in Clancier (2012); see also Burstein (2016) on Ptolemy III's campaign.

¹² Manning et al. (2017) 6.   ¹³ BNJ 160, with translation in Bagnall and Derow (2004) no. 27.

communication both between city and king via the ruler cult, and between Egypt and the outside possessions via the bulletin itself, found in Gurob in the Fayyum, but celebrating military conquests in Syria.

Besides the ostensibly enthusiastic, and carefully staged, surrender of Antioch, most cities resorted to diplomatic channels in order to negotiate their subjection to Ptolemaic power. In the absence of the king, and in less exceptional places than the Seleucid capital, intermediaries were needed and concessions made. Tlepolemos, son of Artapates, conducted such business on behalf of Ptolemy III in the small city of Kildara, modern-day Kuzyaka southwest of Mylasa.[14] Tlepolemos was one of the governors (*strategos*) sent by the Ptolemies to rule their provinces. The four ambassadors sent by the city approached him with gifts (*xenia*). From the letter sent by Tlepolemos in response to this embassy, which is preserved in four fragments, it is hard to say what precisely they requested. According to Gauthier's restoration of fragment B, the community was subject to the payment of a contribution (*syntaxis*).[15] In the context of the new confrontation between Ptolemies and Seleucids, the city seems to have negotiated the reallocation of funds from this 'contribution' to a ruler cult: in effect, an abatement of taxes.[16] The last fragment mentions harbor dues or the affairs of the harbor, which was located 10 km away from the city.[17]

The letter's rhetoric tallies with that of other royal letters addressed to Greek cities. Clichés pervade the text: Kildara's ambassadors show dedication in their behavior and are received by Tleopolemos with generosity (*philanthrōpōs*). Whether the city was a former subject city or is a new ally, a ruler cult has been established in the form of "sacrifices for King Ptolemy, Queen Berenice, and other gods (or kings?)."[18] Tlepolemos entreats Kildara to continue this show of loyalty in exchange for the requested abatement of taxes.[19] The Ptolemaic official, who acts as proxy for the king, secures the loyalty of the city through the devolution of revenue to the city. But he does so in response to Kildara's diplomatic overtures. The

---

[14] SEG XLII 994 with the remarks by Gauthier, *BÉ* 1994.528; translation in Austin (2006) no. 267.
[15] SEG XLII 994 B l. 5 ἀφ' ἧς ἂν φέρητε συ[ντάξεως . . .], following Gauthier, *BÉ* 1994.528, who cites the Teian decrees for Antiochus III as a parallel; this would imply that Kildara was under the control of the Ptolemies before the outbreak of the war.
[16] SEG XLII 994 D l. 2: ἀτελεῖς εἶναι ἡμέρας ἑπτά "exempt for seven days" – the exemption must have been granted for a festival to honor Ptolemy III.
[17] SEG XLII 994 D l. 4: καὶ περὶ τῶν κατὰ τὸν λιμέ[να].
[18] SEG XLII 994 B l. 2–4: εἰς τὰς θυσίας τὰ[ς γιγνομένας ὑπὲρ τοῦ βασιλέως]| Πτολεμαίου καὶ τῆ[ς ἀδελφῆς αὐτοῦ βασιλίσσης Βερε]|νίκης καὶ τῶν ἄλλω[ν θεῶν ? or βασιλέων Chaniotis].
[19] SEG XLII 994 D l. 2 [- – - θ]υσίαν συντελεῖτε καθάπερ κα[ὶ πρότερον - - - - - - - - -].

concluding statements of his letter promise more "concessions" from the royal house and Tlepolemos's "care" for the fate of the city.[20]

Tlepolemos himself was also typical of the elites connecting the periphery to the center. His patronym, Artapates, betrays his Iranian origin and connects his own position of power under the Ptolemies with the preeminence of his family at the time of the Achaemenid kings.[21] As the descendant of a family that was well established in the city of Xanthos, Lykia, he made it to the top of the Ptolemaic hierarchy of honors, holding the prestigious priesthood of Alexander and the deified Ptolemies in Alexandria around the same time as the Third Syrian War, in the years 247/6 and 246/5.[22] His letter to Kildara testifies to his ability to communicate with the elites of a given city – here, ambassadors – in order to strengthen, or expand, Ptolemaic rule. This aptitude was intimately connected with a supra-civic system of communication among the Greek elites, for Tlepolemos is said by Pausanias to have won the foal race at the Olympic games.[23] The Ptolemaic state apparatus built on this network of communication between Greek elites to create its own connections between a small civic community and the royal house. In Egypt itself, Tlepolemos, if indeed he is identical with the official twice mentioned in the Zenon archive, held a top position in the Ptolemaic bureaucracy: a papyrus characteristically places him as the first mover in a chain of letters ordering the assignment of land plots.[24]

Not all Greek cities would have been made part of the Ptolemaic kingdom in the same way.[25] Under the reign of Ptolemy IV, Thraseas, the governor of Cilicia, communicated with the city of Nagidos on account of a territorial dispute with the new city of Arsinoe.[26] Aetos, the father of Thraseas and founder of Arsinoe, had implemented the settlement program of the Ptolemies in Asia Minor and the

---

[20] SEG XLII 994 D l. 15–6: [- - - τά τ]ε παρ' ἐκείνων ὑμῖν ὑπάρξι φιλάνθρω[πα· ἡμεῖς δὲ] | [- - - - - -] ροι ἐσόμεθα πρὸς τὸ τὴν ἐπιμέλειαν ὑ[μῶν γενέσθαι]; on such 'contract clauses' in royal letters see Ma (2002) 179–80.

[21] Robert and Robert (1983) 168–71.

[22] See nos. 44a and 45 in the chronological list of eponymous priests in Clarysse and Van der Veken (1983) 8–11.

[23] Paus. 5.8.11 with Habicht (1985) 87–8.

[24] *PSI* 5 513: chain of letters ordering the assignment of new κλῆροι; P. Cair. Zen. 2 59283, reedited by Ferretti, Schubert and Tomcik (2017) 217–18, provides another attestation for Tlepolemos in Egypt; P. Petrie Kleon 10, a private letter from the archive of the engineer Kleon, also makes reference to a Tlepolemos, but falls slightly earlier within the same chronological range (260–249 BC).

[25] On the relations between the Ptolemies and Greek cities, Buraselis (1993) is a starting point; analysis of prosopographical data in Paschidis (2008); Kossmann (2011) on the Ptolemies and Asia Minor.

[26] SEG XXXIX 1426: letter of Thraseas to Arsinoe followed by a decree of Nagidos recognizing the new city.

Aegean.²⁷ After the Ptolemies had lost control over the area and the foundation failed, Thraseas mediated between both communities in order to revive Arsinoe. Communication, in the form of a mediation between two cities in conflict with one another, occurred only as a second recourse. Direct control, although scarcely used, was also an option outside Egypt. In most cases, however, powerful "friends" of the king – a status not yet attested in the time of Tlepolemos – always served as intermediaries between Greek civic elites and the king.

2.2 Syria and Phoenicia an Exception?

One partial exception was the province of Syria and Phoenicia which did not fully conform to this pattern of rule. In this buffer zone with the Seleucid kingdom, the Phoenician cities were controlled by traditional notables, who were hellenized – if not Greek – elites. Functioning as entrepôts for trade with the East and a network of military bases against the Seleucids, the importance of those cities cannot be overstated. Accordingly, analyzing the variety of mint marks on Phoenician coinage, Iossif has argued that the cities were subject to the payment of a tribute and, in this manner, kept in check by Ptolemaic authorities.²⁸ Yet beyond the numismatic evidence, there is no evidence for direct communication between Phoenician cities and the Ptolemies. It is sometimes written that those cities became hellenized and therefore adopted the Greek model of government. But this assumption remains altogether unproven. Apicella and Briquel-Chatonnet, after a thorough examination of all the extant sources, concluded that in the Hellenistic period those cities were urban monarchies rather than cities on the Greek pattern.²⁹

Just as they did with Greek cities, however, the Ptolemies were content to leave Phoenician elites in power. The example of Diotimos, son of Dionysios, a winner at the chariot races in Argos, points to the uninterrupted social and political preponderance of Phoenician elites throughout the third century BC. The city of Sidon honored Diotimos for his victory with an inscribed statue.³⁰ He bears the title of judge (*dikastes*), which has

---

[27] See Fischer-Bovet in this volume on the settlement policy of the Ptolemies; and Fischer-Bovet (forthcoming).
[28] Iossif (2014a) 65–7.
[29] Apicella and Briquel Chatonnet (2015). For Greek text, see this book's web page (www.cambridge.org/9781108479257).
[30] *Nouveau Choix* 35; Bickerman (1939) 92 on the dating either at the end of Ptolemaic occupation or during the first years of Seleucid control over Sidon.

been taken to refer to the post of *suffete*, the highest magistracy in Tyre.³¹ In verse he is "very first among the citizens" and must have been so in reality.³²

These Phoenician elites adopted Greek modes of elite communication. In Kos, for instance, Abdalonymos, the Sidonian king and, according to Habicht, one of Diotimos' forbears, made a dedication to Aphrodite.³³ Yet the civic level of interaction between the king and the city did not follow the Greek pattern. Was that due to the limits of hellenization in Phoenicia? The structure of the poem itself, which moves from the glory earned by the winner to the rejoicing of Thebes for its *metropolis* and, finally, to the declaration by Greece of the excellence of Sidon, points to the Phoenician sense of cultural antecedence vis-à-vis the Greeks.³⁴ In all of this, the resilience of Phoenician self-consciousness and local power is revealed. There is scarce evidence for the royal cult in Phoenician cities. In Tyre, an altar was dedicated to the divine siblings.³⁵ In the aftermath of the battle of Raphia, the royal priest Anaxikles dedicated a statue to the Great King Ptolemy.³⁶ But we do not know how those cults fitted with the patterns of control over cities. Nor do we know how the representatives of Ptolemaic power, the governor (*strategos*) and managers (*oikonomoi*) appointed in Syria and Phoenicia, communicated with cities.³⁷

2.3 The Rise of Elites at the Ptolemaic Court under Ptolemy IV

The Ptolemies strove to preserve local power, not to replace it. This policy culminated during the reign of Ptolemy IV. Polybius paints the portrait of an incompetent king.³⁸ He had many reasons to give a negative appraisal of Ptolemy IV. Yet his judgment was predicated on the notion that a man's general 'conduct' (*proairesis*) makes good kings and, therefore, good government. The model of diffuse, localized, and informal power relations outlined above suggests that the king's attitude compounded the tendency to devolution. His promotion of the cult of Dionysus had more to do with political

---

³¹ Bickerman (1939) on the interpretation of δικαστής as suffete; see Apicella and Briquel-Chatonnet (2015) 20–5 for a new interpretation of the title as international judge.
³² *Nouveau Choix* 35, l.5: τῶγ [l. τῶν] γὰρ ἀστῶν πράτιστος.
³³ SEG XXXIX 758 (Kos): [Ἀφρ]οδίτηι ἱδρύσατο | [. . .]τιμος Ἀβδαλωνύμου | [Σιδ]ῶνος βασιλέως | [ὑπ]ὲρ τῶν πλεόντων; Habicht (2007) 126–7 suggests [Διό]τιμος.
³⁴ Insightful remarks in Bonnet (2014) 294–6 on the limits of hellenization in Phoenicia.
³⁵ Rey-Coquais (2006) 99–101.   ³⁶ *CIIP* 2172.
³⁷ Our chief evidence for those officials comes from the two ordinances for the registration of slaves and livestock, *C. Ord. Ptol.* 21–2, with analysis in Bagnall (1976) 18–21.
³⁸ Polyb. 5.34 on the lack of interest in the overseas possessions and 5.62 on the indifference of the king to the defense of Egypt; on this passage, see Erskine (2013) 83–92 and, more broadly on Polybius and the Ptolemies, Fischer-Bovet (2016) 210–16 and, on Polybius' opinion about the right behavior of kings, Dreyer (2013).

concerns than an inclination to debauchery.³⁹ His predecessors, as Polybius duly noted, had been greatly concerned with overseas possessions and devised indirect means to hold the empire together. Under Ptolemy IV, the logic of imperial expansion and the tricks of power delegation reached their apex. The power in the hands of local elites became unprecedented – a fact mirrored by the institution of aulic titles.⁴⁰ Now Ptolemy IV was not completely incompetent but, at the very least, passive, slow to respond, and of a contemplative character. And so, under such a king, the system would soon fall apart.

The reign of Ptolemy IV has been described as the era of Sosibios and Theogenes – and rightly so.⁴¹ The latter was the minister of finances (*dioiketes*) at least from 217 to 207.⁴² The former was the chief minister of the king, a position he had already held under Ptolemy III.⁴³ His four victories at the Nemean and Isthmian games were celebrated by Callimachus himself in a poem preserved in fragments.⁴⁴ Sosibios at some point received a gift-estate (*dorea*) as a reward for his services.⁴⁵ To Polybius's indignation, he displayed the perfect qualities of a courtier – "acuteness" and "exceeding mischievousness" – which enabled him to "manipulate king after king."⁴⁶ Yet Polybius also reports his successful reorganization of the Ptolemaic army before the battle of Raphia.⁴⁷ In that moment, he deftly put his diplomatic network among the Greek elites to work, soliciting embassies from the friendly cities of Rhodes, Byzantium and Cyzicus and so putting off the confrontation with Antiochus III.⁴⁸ With the aid of Agathocles, another prominent courtier, he harnessed peer-polity interaction among Greek poleis to give the Ptolemies more time to train the Egyptian contingent and muster new troops.

Long after the victory at Raphia, when Ptolemy IV passed away and was succeeded by his young son, external help from the Greek world was once again much needed. Sosibios, who had become the guardian of Ptolemy V and was de facto ruling as regent, planned to hire new mercenaries for the war against Antiochus and the settlement of new troops in the *chora*.⁴⁹ Agathocles,

---

³⁹ Huß (2001) 454–6 on Ptolemy IV and the cult of Dionysus.
⁴⁰ Mooren (1975), but inscriptions from the Boubasteion in Alexandria prove that aulic titles were already in use under Ptolemy IV, see Abd el-Fattah, Abd el-Maksoud, and Carrez-Maratray (2014) 153–4 on the earliest attestation for the title 'of the first friends'; on aulic titulature under the Seleucids see n. 117.
⁴¹ Huß (2001) 458–64 for a fuller analysis of their careers.   ⁴² Huß (2001) 463–4.
⁴³ This point is forcefully made in Holleaux (1942) 49–51 on the basis of a Delian decree.
⁴⁴ Callim. *Pf. fr.* 384, with Lelli and Parlato (2008) on the structure of the poem and the number of Panhellenic victories.
⁴⁵ P. Tebt. 3.2.860 l. 110 (account of receipts): Σω(σιβίου) δω(ρεᾶς).
⁴⁶ Polyb. 15.34.4: βασιλεῖς ἐκ βασιλέων μεταχειριζόμενος.   ⁴⁷ Polyb. 5.63.   ⁴⁸ Polyb. 5.65.
⁴⁹ Polyb. 15.25.27; note that the κατοικίαι are not foreign settlements but very probably new cleruchies in Egypt.

the successor of Sosibios, sent off Skopas, an Aetolian from Trichoneion, to hire new mercenaries. Before fleeing to Egypt, Skopas had been a general of the Aetolian League, had played a major role in the First Macedonian War, and had been appointed a lawgiver (*nomographos*).[50] Surely material reward would have motivated him to come to the court in Alexandria given that the Aetolian League sent off its citizens to make money as mercenaries.[51] Yet his share in Ptolemaic power must be placed in the context of the diplomatic contacts between Sosibios and Greek elites.[52] Skopas followed the logic of imperial power: that was nothing new in the land of the Nile. Egyptian history offers ample precedent for the rise of foreigners to the highest echelons of the state. The accession to power of Libyan families during the Third Intermediate Period is just one of many examples.[53]

3 The Treachery of Greek Elites?

Communication between elites at the center and elites at the periphery, albeit fundamental, is rarely adduced to explain the collapse of the Ptolemaic imperial system. The Egyptian national movement that followed the battle of Raphia is often said to have undermined Ptolemaic state power and thus precipitated the decline of the Ptolemaic empire.[54] Building on the results of the previous sections, I now make a case for the agency of Greek elites in this process. On the periphery, Ptolemaic officers defected to Antiochus III, who quickly conquered Syria and Phoenicia, whilst at the center, the leading men of the Alexandrian court depleted the royal treasury through lavish gifts on cities and the army. The generals on campaign and the courtiers at home, two groups that largely overlapped, operated in a world governed by the rules of the game played by Hellenistic kings and Greek elites, but this time to the Ptolemies' detriment.

3.1 The Defection of Ptolemaic Officers

The main source for the confrontation between Ptolemy IV and Ptolemy V on one side and Antiochus III on the other is Polybius.[55] During the first

---

[50] Flacelière (1937), see Index s.v. Scopas.
[51] The notice in the Suda, Adler IV p. 384, l. 6–16, which surely draws on a tradition hostile to him, claims that Skopas was "insatiable" and would request a salary of ten minas rather than one.
[52] Polyb. 16.22.2 on the court's appreciation of Sosibios's successful diplomatic policy.
[53] Kemp (2006) 42–6. [54] E.g. Will (2003) 40–4.
[55] Book 5 is fully extant; books 15 and 16 only in excerpts; Fischer-Bovet (2014b) 86–92 on the "war against the Egyptians" in 217; on the distinction between the "treatment of facts" and "treatment of characters" in Polybius, see the illuminating remarks in Préaux (1965).

phase of the conflict, conventionally called the Fourth Syrian War, Antiochus III recaptured Seleucia-Pieria, led his army down the Jordan Valley, and was stopped at Raphia in June 217. Fragments of Polybius, in which he criticizes Rhodian historians, give a sketch of the conflict which followed fifteen years later, the Fifth Syrian War.[56] After various campaigns in Asia Minor and the East, Antiochus III resumed the offensive, laid siege to Gaza, was pushed back by a Ptolemaic counteroffensive, and finally defeated the Ptolemaic army at Panion in 200. The war lingered on through 198, presumably owing to the resistance of several cities. Antiochus III, as he had already done in the East, concluded a peace treaty with Ptolemy V by giving him his daughter Cleopatra in marriage.[57]

As all parties had been aware, and above all the Ptolemaic court at Alexandria, the defection of Ptolemaic officers transformed the course of the conflict from the very beginning. During the Second Syrian War, the revolt of Ptolemy "the Son" at Miletus facilitated the capture of the city by Antiochus II. In the same way, Theodotos the Aetolian, the governor of Syria and Phoenicia, switched sides to Antiochus III. In fact, several defections broke down the Ptolemies' defense: along with Theodotos, Ptolemaic officers joined Antiochus III *en masse*. Polybius's narrative of the Fourth Syrian War is again the chief source of information for these defections. He records that Panaitolos and his "friends," and not only Theodotos, surrendered the cities of Tyre and Ptolemais to the Seleucid king.[58] From there, Antiochus reached Sidon, bypassed the city, and moved east to reach the north-south corridor of the Jordan Valley. In the region of Abila, he won over the Ptolemaic officer Ceraeas and, after him, Hippolochos and his four hundred horse. All those defectors were foreign to the lands of Syria and Phoenicia: Theodotos was an Aetolian, Ceraeas very probably a Pisidian; Lagoras, whose defection is deduced from his participation in the siege of Sardeis, came from Crete; Hippolochos from Thessaly.[59] These generals served in the subsequent Seleucid campaigns

---

[56] Holleaux (1942) 317–36 for the reordering of the chronological sequence; see also Will (2003) 118–19 and Dreyer (2008).
[57] Kaye and Amitay (2015) on this marriage and the status of Syria and Phoenicia as "Cleopatra's dowry."
[58] Polyb. 5.62; the *proditio Theodoti* resurfaces Porphyry's account of the Fourth Syrian War, as excerpted by Jerome, in BNJ 260 F 44; Balandier (2014) 216–18 conjectures that Theodotos was the founder of Hippos and Tel Anafa.
[59] Ceraeas is a Pisidian, Robert (1937) 367; none of the Ptolemaic mercenaries listed in SEG XXVII 973 bis is from Syria or Phoenicia (although many are Salaminians), except for the one bearing the ethnic Φιλωτέρειος l. 5, which refers to Philoteria – a demotic from Alexandria or Ptolemais is unlikely.

and were redeployed along with their troops: examples include Lagoras the Cretan in Lydia and Panaitolos in Baktria during Antiochus' *anabasis*.[60]

More defections followed Antiochus III's renewed military aggression during the Fifth Syrian War. Ptolemaios son of Thraseas, who had been one of the commanders of the Macedonian phalanx at Raphia, soon joined Antiochus at an undetermined moment in the war.[61] His father Thraseas, who had been the Ptolemaic governor of Cilicia, had been appointed to the same position in Syria and Phoenicia.[62] Because Ptolemaios is attested with the same title as his father, it is assumed that he joined Antiochus III in that capacity.[63] Tlepolemos, son of Artapates, and grandson of Tlepolemos the governor of Caria and priest of Alexander under Ptolemy III, had occupied an important position during the Fifth Syrian War. He had been appointed governor of Pelousion and became the chief rival of Agathocles when Ptolemy V was still a boy.[64] At the same time, he was priest *pro poleos* in his home city of Xanthos in the last years of Ptolemaic rule, and again in the city of Amyzon after its conquest by Antiochus III.[65] Although a former Ptolemaic minister, he accepted the Seleucid yoke in his home city, but may not have anticipated Antiochus' victory as Ptolemaios did.

3.2 *The Disruption of Political Communication at the Court*

Polybius explains these defections by the predicament of the court at Alexandria. Concerning Theodotos, he explicitly reports that despite his good services for Ptolemy during Antiochus' first campaign in the spring of 221, he was called back to Alexandria and encountered a real nest of vipers. This is why, Polybius writes, he "now formed the project of entering into communication with Antiochus and handing over to him the cities of Coele Syria."[66] Rivalries at the court worsened over time, reaching their climax during the Fifth Syrian War. Under the boy king Ptolemy V, the

---

[60] Polyb. 7.15–8: Lagoras; Polyb. 10.49.11: Panaitolos.   [61] Polyb. 5.65.3–4.
[62] *IGLTyr* 18 (dedication of an equestrian of Philopator): Thraseas son of Aetos is στρατηγὸς Συρίας καὶ Φοινίκης and bears the demotic Εὐσεβεῖος, which makes him a citizen of Alexandria; Habicht (2006) 243–74 on the entire family tree.
[63] Ma (2002) no. 21 for the dedication at Soloi, made probably in 197 BC, in which Ptolemaios bears the same title as his father.
[64] Polyb. 15.25.26.
[65] Bousquet (1988) 24–5 on the priesthood of Tlepolemos in Xanthos; Robert, Amyzon 15 B for the same priesthood in Amyzon.
[66] Polyb. 5.40.1–3; note the use of the verb "to speak" (λαλεῖν), which implies direct, oral communication between Theodotos and the king.

enmity (*echthra*) between Agathocles and Tlepolemos weakened the kingdom.[67] Agathocles, according to Polybius, was ruling de facto as king of Egypt.[68] Of unknown, but not obscure, origins, as his adversary would have it, he belonged to the circle of courtiers who controlled the state.[69] His career must have been no different from that of Sosibios or Tlepolemos.[70] He wrote a commentary on *Adonis*, a tragedy written by one of his friends, and was a favorite of Ptolemy IV.[71] This resulted in great hostility and invective against him. According to Porphyry, he was held responsible for the loss of Ptolemaic overseas dominions.[72]

The particularly sinister portrayal of Agathocles in Polybius certainly derives from a source hostile to the ruling faction.[73] Although emphasizing character as a rationale for the collapse of royal authority, Polybius also lays bare the disruption of communication between the king, or in fact his ministers, and the Greek elites. In his account, Agathocles replaced the king's 'friends' (*philoi*) with, among servants of lower rank, "those most remarkable for their effrontery and recklessness."[74] The entry of new men into the court no doubt elicited hostile reactions echoed by Polybius' source. Selection was no longer predicated on service but on allegiance to either Agathocles or his rival, and eventually successor, Tlepolemos, son of Artapates and grandson of Tlepolemos, the winner of the foal race at Olympia (see Fig. 9.1). Polybius depicts the streets and banquets as venues for political competition: against his enemy Agathocles, slander (*loidoria*) became for Tlepolemos the most effective weapon.[75] Agathocles retaliated by insinuating that Tlepolemos would betray the king and "call (*kalein*) Antiochus to the direction of the kingdom."[76] The contrast with the reign of Ptolemy III, and especially between Tleopolemos the Elder and Tlepolemos the Younger, is striking.

Under Ptolemy IV, and even more so in the troubled context of the regency, the proliferation of reward-seeking courtiers disturbed the system of political communication between ruler and elites. Monson ascribes the "fiscal crisis" under Philopator to what he calls "elite overproduction," or a

---

[67] Polyb. 15.25.34. [68] Polyb. 15.34.5.
[69] Just. *Epit.* 30.2.5: *Agathocles regis lateri iunctus civitatem regebat.*
[70] P. Oxy. 42 3052 l.7 records a military camp (παρεμβολή) of Agathocles.
[71] Huß (2001) 460–2; Porphyry, BNJ 260 F 45 claims that Agathocles was the *eromenos*/*concubinus* of the king.
[72] Porphyry, BNJ 260 F 45: *tantae enim dissolutionis et superbiae Agathocles fuit, ut subditae prius Aegypto provinciae rebellarent ipsaque Aegyptus seditionibus vexaretur.*
[73] Préaux (1965) 371–3 on the sources of Polybius. [74] Polyb. 15.25.20–1. [75] Polyb. 15.25.32.
[76] Polyb. 15.26.35.

Ἀρταπάτης - *Strategos* in Egypt -Dedicant in Delos ↓ **Τληπόλεμος Ἀρταπάτου** -Priest of Alexander the Great -Winner at the foal race at Olympia -Governor of Karia ↓ **Ἀρταπάτης Τληπολέμου** -Unknown ↓ **Τληπόλεμος Ἀρταπάτου** -Regent of the kingdom -Dedicant in Delphi -Priest *pro poleos* in Xanthos ⋮ **Τληπόλεμος** - Ambassador to Antiochus IV	According to Jeanne and Louis Robert, Tlepolemos son of Artapates the priest of Alexander and winner at the Olympic games ("Tlepolemos the Elder") was the grandfather of Tlepolemos son of Artapates the governor of Pelousion and regent of the Ptolemaic kingdom ("Tlepolemos the Younger"). The Artapates who made dedications in Delos in 278 must have been the father of Tlepolemos the Elder. Following Wilhelm (1974), the *strategos* Artapates who left graffiti at Silsilis, Egypt, must have been a member of the same family, perhaps the same as the Artapates who made dedications in Delos. The Tlepolemos attested twice in the Zenon archive should be the same as Tlepolemos the Elder, at least "possibly" according to Pap. Lugd. Bat. XXI A p. 430, but it is unlikely that two people named Tleopolemos were both very high up in the state hierarchy at the same time. Artapates, who was sent as ambassador to Rome by Xanthos may have been a member of the same family, perhaps the son of Tlepolemos the Younger. Tlepolemos the ambassador sent by Philometor to Antiochus IV probably belonged to the same family (Polyb. 28.19.6). For a summary of the history's family, see Dreyer (2007) 254 n. 77.

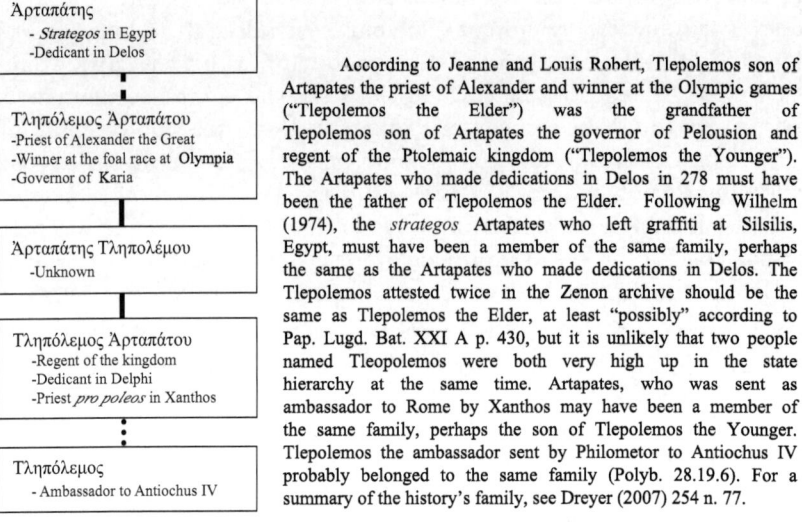

Figure 9.1 Empire-Builders from Lycia: The Family of Tlepolemos son of Artapates.

context in which too many local elites were competing for a share in the surplus collected by the state.[77] A close reading of Polybius on Tlepolemos, who ruled "more like an heir than like a trustee," confirms this intuition. When the Megalopolitan historian describes how the regent depleted royal funds through lavish donations to ambassadors from Greek cities and Dionysiac artists, he employs the same language as civic decrees acknowledging the benefactions of the king and his agents. In exchange for his lavish gifts, Tlepolemos received "expressions of thanks."[78] Those *logoi* are the institutionalized language of reciprocity between king and city, suffused with references to benefactions past and future and the generalization of the reference to all Greeks.[79] Polybius explicitly mentions inscriptions set up, and songs performed, in honor of Tlepolemos.[80] His story is very much that of an exchange of *charis* used and abused.

---

[77] Monson (2015) 179–80. [78] Polyb. 16.21.11–12.
[79] Ma (2002) 182–94 on the "vertical" dimension in the language of reciprocity, which refers to an invented past and points to a promising future, and the "horizontal" dimension, which refers to "all the Greeks" as beneficiaries of the king's largesse.
[80] Polyb. 16.21.12.

The communication among elites that had allowed the expansion of the Ptolemaic kingdom was now working against the interests of the Ptolemies. Defections arose from the inability of the boy king Ptolemy V and, to a lesser extent before him, Ptolemy IV, to project a legitimate image of themselves, attract new elites, and reward them as expected. Yet the system itself, which had thrived on the promotion of Greek elites to the highest positions, must be seen as the fundamental reason. The Ptolemaic machinery of political communication was exhausted. The vocabulary used to characterize these defections suggests that they were in the nature of things. Theodotos and subsequent defectors are not defined as traitors, but as apostates or, in the Demotic version of the Raphia decree, as men of "deceit."[81] In the world of Greek cities, the traitor was considered one of the worst criminals, but in the world of kings, only the relation between monarch and subject had been broken. The act was considered apostasy (*apostasia*) rather than treason (*prodosia*).[82] Accordingly, Ptolemaic envoys, in the peace talks that followed the loss of Seleucia-Pieria, pointed out that the betrayal of the Ptolemaic governor had been "trickery" (*paraspondema*) – in fact, Antiochus had only been able to play the game better.[83]

4 Antiochus III, Winner and Promoter of Local Elites?

Antiochus III, I argue in this final section, owed the recovery of Coele Syria to his ability to gain the support of local elites, from local communities as well as former Ptolemaic officers. He won the war on the diplomatic as well as the military front. He also promoted new elites by granting settlements city status and inviting local notables to participate in the peer-polity interaction of Greek cities.

4.1 Local Elites and the Conquest of Syria and Phoenicia by Antiochus III

During his campaign, Antiochus III received support from various communities. At the beginning of the Fourth Syrian War, before

---

[81] CGC 31088, l. 25: "the acts of treachery which the officers had committed" (*nꜣ qrf(.w) r ir nꜣ ts-mšꜣ.w r.ir=f*); the work for treachery, *qrf*, is best translated as "guile, treachery, ambush" (CDD q 60); it is the opposite of the just and obedient behavior implied in the notion of Maat; for further reference on this passage, see below n. 96.
[82] Mélèze-Modrzejewski (2011) 296–7.   [83] Polyb. 5.67.

confronting the Ptolemaic general Lagoras who had been sent to block his advance, he encountered a delegation from Arados. This Phoenician city had enjoyed a special status within the Seleucid kingdom.[84] As allies of the king, they offered military support (*symmachia*).[85] At the same time, they petitioned the king that he might arbitrate a dispute (*diaphora*) between the Aradians living on the island and the Aradians living on the mainland. Polybius' report of the affair provides few details, but parallels suggest that Aradians who had settled on the mainland paid tribute, or were subject to increasingly ill-accepted control by civic authorities on the island.[86] This settlement, which was not yet called Antarados, must have been the nucleus of the community that would receive city status under Constantine and be renamed Constantina.[87] After Antiochus III managed to settle this conflict, he received naval reinforcements from a Phoenician settlement. In a memorandum to Antiochus V, the short-lived son of Antiochus IV and grandson of Antiochus III, the Sidonians from the harbor of Iamnia, modern-day Yavne Yam in Israel, claimed fiscal exemption on the grounds that they served his grandfather well during the war.[88] Two generations later, the petition still recalls the interaction between local communities and the Seleucid king.

During the campaign of the Fourth Syrian War, and despite the wave of defections, some places remained loyal to the Ptolemies.[89] Cities on the coast even participated in the celebration of the Ptolemaic victory at Raphia, at least according to one piece of evidence from Ioppe, modern-day Jaffa.[90] Yet, on the whole, Antiochus III seems to have been a better player in the game of local politics. After the Fifth Syrian War, he is often

---

[84] Capdetrey (2007) 212–13 for summary and previous literature.
[85] Polyb. 5.68.7; on the meaning of συμμαχία, see Holleaux (1942) 81 commenting on κατὰ συμμαχίαν in Choix Délos I 92 l. 31 (decree of the Cretan auxiliaries for Aglaos son of Theokles).
[86] In addition to the stone from Arsinoe in Cilicia (SEG XXXIX 1426), the copy of a Seleucid grant to the temple of Zeus Baitokaike (RC 70), whether from the time of Antiochus I or a late Seleucid (Antiochus VIII?), offers an interesting parallel: formerly given as a gift-estate (δωρεά) to one Demetrios son of Demetrios, the revenues of the sanctuary are now the property of the god and his priesthood.
[87] Lenski (2016) 155–8.
[88] SEG XLI 1556 l. 9: [- - τῶ]ι πάππωι ἐν τοῖς κατὰ τὴν ναυτικὴν χρε[ίαν - -].
[89] That was also the case of Gaza at the beginning of the Fifth Syrian War; see Polyb. 16.22a.
[90] That is the assumed context for the dedication by Anaxikles in honor of Ptolemy IV "the Great King"; see CIIP 2172 for text and commentary.

said to have inherited the Ptolemaic administration wholesale, in particular the Ptolemaic monetary system with a reduced standard. But he also innovated. In financial matters, for instance, he allowed the cities of Tyre and Ptolemais to issue royal bronze coinage in four denominations.[91] Hoover has argued, on the basis of the types on the reverse – a palm tree, the stern of a galley – of coins from Tyre that Antiochus III had granted the city a preferential status.[92] Iossif, on the other hand, has pointed out the military destination of those issues, namely the payment of troops.[93] Whatever the true objective followed by Antiochus III, this bronze coinage, broadly circulated in Phoenicia, put the mint officials in Tyre to work for him rather than against him. Local power was Antiochus III's strongest weapon.

Antiochus III responded to the needs of powerful people on the ground. During the Fifth Syrian War, former Ptolemaic officers sought opportunities to reinforce their local authority by petitioning him. An important inscription discloses these interests. The stela, found near ancient Scythopolis, Hefzibah in modern-day Israel, contains a series of letters and memoranda addressed by Ptolemaios son of Thraseas, discussed above, to Antiochus, along with the king's replies.[94] In the first memorandum, Ptolemaios adjudicates disputes between the inhabitants of the villages who belong to him. In the second memorandum, which is addressed to Antiochus as Great King, he requests no billeting and a ban on the enslavement of the local population. Those local people live in "villages" that he either purchased, inherited, or was granted by royal ordinance (*prostagma*).[95] The inheritance of those villages is consistent with the passing on of the title of governor from Thraseas to Ptolemaios. Further acquisition, along with royal grants, made him an important landowner. The Ptolemaic officers who defected with Theodotos during the Fourth Syrian War must have found themselves in the same situation. The so-called Raphia decree, which narrates the campaign of Philopator after Raphia, and his return to Egypt for the festival of the birthday of

---

[91] *SC* 1078–83.   [92] Hoover (2004) 487.   [93] Iossif (2014a) 78–9.
[94] SEG XXIX 1613, with comprehensive analysis in Feyel (2017) and earlier dating in Savalli-Lestrade (2018).
[95] SEG XXIX 1613 l. 23–4 εἰς τὰς ὑπ[αρχ]ούσας μοι κώ[μ]ας | [ἐγ] κτήσει καὶ εἰς [τ]ὸ πα[τ]ρικὸν καὶ εἰς [ἃ]ς σὺ προ[σ]έταξας.

Horus, refers to those defections, which may have taken place after, and despite, the victory at Raphia.[96] The desire to preserve property and privilege in Syria and Phoenicia undoubtedly motivated the defection.

Antiochus III lured networks of local elites into Seleucid domination through his ability to reward and, more importantly, communicate. The adverbs used by Polybius to describe the encounter between Antiochus III and the Ptolemaic defectors – "courteously," or even "with magnificence" – suggest munificent treatment on the part of the Seleucid king. His campaign in the East, commonly referred to as his *anabasis*, had earned him a great deal of prestige. After his victory at Panion, he assumed the title of Great King.[97] Antiochus made it one of the themes of his propaganda toward Greek cities in western Asia Minor. In one of his memoranda, Ptolemaios son of Thraseas addressed him as Antiochus the Great King and so relayed royal discourse locally. Through exemption from billeting and the prohibition of enslavement, Ptolemaios aimed to restore security and, therefore, peace.[98]

In accordance with this theme of royal propaganda, Antiochus III reorganized local communities. On many occasions, he resettled a city which had been destroyed or depopulated by war.[99] In his dealings with Jerusalem, he was content to recognize the local authorities as long as they displayed loyalty toward him. In the letter to Ptolemaios copied by Flavius Josephus, he orders that the scattered inhabitants be brought back. He grants a three-year tax exemption, pays an allowance for sacrifices and the repair of the Temple, sets free enslaved inhabitants, and restores their property.[100] For all the emphasis Josephus lays on the king's piety, Antiochus III's behavior was not peculiar to Jerusalem. He acted in keeping with a strategy of remote control. This strategy seems to stand in contrast to the active policy of city foundation implemented by Antiochus IV, whereby the king selected new local elites and promoted the institutions of the Greek city.[101]

---

[96] For text, see n. 81 above; the defection of Ptolemaic officers *after* Raphia is Winnicki's hypothesis, discussed by Fischer-Bovet (2014b) 88 n. 131; a definitive, and clearer, edition of this part of the text remains a desideratum.

[97] Ma (2002) 272–6; and Dreyer (2007) 291 n. 257; Antiochus III also bears the title of Great King in the Cuneiform documentation, although in one attestation: *CT* 49.34 to be read with Graslin-Thomé (2017).

[98] Feyel (2017) 128–9 emphasizes this dimension in the royal correspondence of Antiochus III.

[99] Robert and Robert (1983) 188–91 on the resettlement (*synoikismos*) of cities by Antiochus III.

[100] Joseph. *AJ* 12.138–44, translation and commentary in Austin (2006) no. 215; fundamental is Bickerman (2007) 315–56; the gift of timber is paralleled by the letters of Antiochus III to Sardeis, see Ma (2002) no. 1.

[101] For a summary of the literature on Antiochus IV and cities, see Mittag (2006) 182–208.

And yet Antiochus III anticipated, or at least foreshadowed, this policy. More evidence has come along to suggest that, in addition to repopulating existing cities, he also founded, or at least refounded, new cities. The cuneiform scholarly literature from Hellenistic Babylon attests to the presence of "citizens" starting under the reign of Antiochus IV.[102] An entry in the *Astronomical Diaries* suggests the possibility that the city was in fact founded before 187 BC, under Antiochus III.[103] Although the nature of these "citizens" is debated, Clancier, in his contribution to this volume, argues that Babylon was refounded as a Greek city (*polis*) and that former members of the council of the Esagil entered the civic body. Similarly, Antiochus III may have refounded Gadara as Antiochia, thus anticipating the policy of his sons Seleucus IV and Antiochus IV in the Dekapolis.[104]

4.2 New Civic Elites at Antiochia-Pyramos

Asia Minor, especially Cilicia, provides better evidence for the redefinition of local power networks by Antiochus III. With the foundation of Arsinoe in Cilicia near the city of Nagidos, the Ptolemies had already used new settlement to assert their rule in the region.[105] Antiochus III applied the same method to attain opposite goals – a reversal of local power dynamics in his favor. The city of Mallos, which is included in the list of cities in Cilicia conquered by Antiochus III on his way to Ephesos in 197 BC, had been a pro-Ptolemaic bastion.[106] Savalli-Lestrade made a masterful edition of a civic decree of Antiochia-Pyramos, dated to the first half or the second third of the second century BC.[107] This city was created out of the modest, and formerly dependent, harbor settlement of Magarsos, as an attempt to put down Mallos. Evidently, Antiochia-Pyramos owed its very existence to a Seleucid king, but which one? Examining the attestation of ethnic titles in the Delphic list of those who receive the sacred envoys, the *theorodokoi*, and a Boeotian list of victors at a musical contest, Savalli-Lestrade has

---

[102] See Clancier and Gorre in this volume.
[103] Boiy (2004) 207 on AD 2:331 no. 187 A Rev. 9–10.
[104] Wörrle (2000) for this argument based on SEG L 1479 and Steph. Byz. s.v., who indicates that Gadara was renamed Antiochia and then Seleucia, possibly by Antiochus III and then by Seleucus IV.
[105] See Fischer-Bovet in this volume.
[106] BNJ 260 F 46: *Eo enim tempore captae sunt Aphrodisias et Soloe et Zephyrion et Mallos et Anemurium et Selenum et Coracesium et Coricus et Andriace et Limyra et Patara et Xanthus et ad extremum Ephesus*; but see Chrubasik (2016) 247–50 on the conquest of Cilicia by Seleucus II and the problematic conciliation of this text with coin evidence.
[107] First published in SEG XII 551, now fully republished and analyzed in Savalli-Lestrade (2006).

postulated a *terminus ante quem* of 209/8 BC and raises the possibility that Antiochia-Pyramos was refounded under Antiochus III between 216 and 213 BC rather than under one of his predecessors.[108] If so, after the conquest of the entirety of Cilicia, Antiochus III must have transferred a large chunk of civic territory to Antiochia-Pyramos and thus caused the temporary decline of Mallos.

This transformation went hand in hand with the redistribution of power among local elites. Interactions between Seleucid royal foundations gave prominent citizens the opportunity to assert their privileged positions through embassies. This is precisely what happens at Antiochia-Pyramos in the preserved decree, albeit at a moment when the city was probably declining. On the occasion of a civic procession to the sanctuary of Athena Magarsios, the citizens of Antiochia-Kydnos – the new name given to the city of Tarsos by the Seleucids – are proclaimed "parents and friends." Ambassadors are chosen to go to Antiochia-Kydnos. It became important for royal and civic officials alike to show citizenship from one of the Syrian royal cities. A statue base recalls the presence of two brothers from Antiochia-Daphne and, more importantly, Diomedes son of Asklepiades, from Seleucia-Pieria, who was honored by Antiochia-Pyramos for his good services in the capacity of an "official in charge of revenues."[109] Parallels for this position suggest that he was competent on a supra-regional scale, presumably over Syria and Phoenicia as well as Cilicia.[110] In this refashioned political landscape, Antiochia-Pyramos and the cities of Cilicia lacked any substantial autonomy: the episode related by Jason of Cyrene of the grant of Tarsos and Mallos to the mistress of the king, if true, was conceivable only because these cities were entirely subjected to Seleucid royal power.[111] A city like Antiochia-Pyramos was a tool in the hands of Antiochus III.

One family became prominent in the new city. In the decree for the celebration of the kinship and friendship between Antiochia-Pyramos and Antiochia-Kydnos (Tarsos), the highest official of the city, the *demiourgos*, very probably the eponymous magistrate, leads the embassy to the parent

---

[108] Cohen (1995) 360–1 favors Seleucus I, but Heberdey-Wilhelm, *Kilikien* 14, which he adduces, is redated from the mid third century to the early second century by Savalli-Lestrade (2006) 165–6.

[109] Heberdey-Wilhelm, *Kilikien* 26 for the two brothers; Heberdey-Wilhelm, *Kilikien* 16 for the statue base of Diomedes son of Asclepiades.

[110] Chrubasik (2016) 127–9 on Timarchos and the title ὁ ἐπὶ τῶν προσόδων in App. *Syr.* 45; see also Capdetrey (2007) 314–16.

[111] 2 *Macc.* 4.30–1.

city.¹¹² The text gives the names of his father and grandfather which, with the help of another dedication from Antiochia-Pyramos and a list of *proxenoi* from Delphi, allows the reconstruction of the family tree.¹¹³ The father of the *demiourgos* Demetrios had the same name as his son and was sent on an embassy to Delphi in the year 172/1 BC. Like his son, he was a prominent citizen of Antiochia-Pyramos. He had two brothers, Diodoros and Artemidoros, and together they set up a statue for their father Anaxippos, who was priest of Athena and Zeus Polias. The relation between those cults and the sanctuary of Athena Magarsios is unclear. But this position undoubtedly made Anaxippos one of the chief members of the civic elite at Antiochia-Pyramos. If his son was active in 172/1 BC, he might have been in office if not in 216/5, at least in 197 BC when Antiochus III conquered the rest of Cilicia. His family exemplifies the creation of specifically civic elites, who took advantage of the policy of the Seleucid king and his successors toward cities and thus took part in the regional and supra-regional peer-polity interactions of Greek cities.

5 Conclusion

Greek elites, whether at the center – the 'friends' – or on the periphery, reversed the power dynamics between the Ptolemies and Seleucids under Ptolemy IV and Antiochus III.¹¹⁴ Political communication as it was defined in the introduction and has been analyzed throughout this chapter fed on and promoted individuals who adopted the norms of elite Greek behavior: at the civic level, tenure as a priest of the royal cult and, at the supra-civic level, participation in festivals and competitions. This two-level dialog between the king and local communities underlay the expansion of the Ptolemaic kingdom. Roger Bagnall, in his classic study, wrote that "the Ptolemaic empire was in the main an empire grouping Greek cities."¹¹⁵ One may as well say that those overseas possessions were held together by the Greek elites in communication with the Ptolemies.¹¹⁶ This system was

---

[112] SEG XII 511 l. 34–6.
[113] *Syll.*³ 585 280–6 for the list of *proxenoi* from Delphi; Robert's edition of the dedication is published in Savalli-Lestrade (2006) 229.
[114] Grainger (2010) 219–20 overlooks this dimension when he writes of the "complacency" of Philopator after the victory at Raphia.
[115] Bagnall (1976) 235.
[116] That those elites communicated through waterways, and the Ptolemaic empire was primarily a maritime one, is a central theme in the collection of essays published in Buraselis, Stefanou, and Thompson (2013); this approach is shared by Fischer-Bovet (forthcoming) in her discussion of Ptolemaic expansion in southern Anatolia.

used and abused. On the periphery, its extension was limited by the existence of non-Greek communities, for instance in Syria and Phoenicia. At the center, it led to the concentration of power in the hands of courtiers and ministers who, under Ptolemy IV and the boy king Ptolemy V, held the de facto positions of kings.

Antiochus III, in his confrontation with the Ptolemies, won on account of his ability to rob the Ptolemaic empire of its connections with local power networks. There was a marked difference between the civic elites of Greek *poleis* in western and southern Asia Minor and the free-floating, supra-civic elites that controlled Syria and Phoenicia – a difference that deserves strong emphasis here. Just as local power had reached its apex in the Ptolemaic kingdom under Ptolemy III and Ptolemy IV, so the Seleucids were then reversing the power dynamics by showing themselves better players at this game. It is no coincidence that Seleucid power networks were formalized into the court hierarchy during the reign of Antiochus III.[117] He prevailed over the Ptolemies in appropriating the themes of Achaemenid ideology for himself, such as the title of Great King, and presented himself as an agent of peace in the conquered territories.[118] In some cases, he promoted loyal civic elites in cities of which he was the founder; but Antiochia-Pyramos is the only attested, and not entirely certain, instance of this. Antiochus III continued this policy on an even grander scale in western Asia Minor, where civic communities were far more numerous. But there, as Dreyer argues in the next part of this chapter, he had to reckon with a newcomer in the competition: Rome.

2B THE GREEK ELITES BEFORE AND DURING THE SELEUCID-ROMAN WAR*

Dreyer Boris

1 Introduction

The ability of (local) elites to act at every level changed according to political conditions, as the previous section by Gerardin has already shown. Ancient

---

[117] Dreyer (2011b) on court hierarchy under Antiochus III; see n. 40 above on the Ptolemies.
[118] Gerardin (2017) on the ideological debate between Ptolemies and Seleucids for the title of Great King.
* Thanks to Arthur Eckstein for having improved the English of my translations of Greek documents.

historians, unfortunately, suffer from a notorious scarcity of relevant sources that could provide information on the motivations of the groups determining these processes and developments. Modern historians seem to have a much easier task. In his article "The Middle States in the System of the Great Powers," historian Theodor Schieder empirically examined different international scenarios in order to assess the freedom of the "middle states" (*Mittelstaaten*) and their diplomats within the political framework set by the great powers.[119] One scenario was embedded in the conflicts at the European level during the years following 1866 up to the Franco-Prussian War of 1871, and the other at a global level during the years following the German capitulation in 1945. His analysis ends in stating how fatal the policy of the "middle states" and the ambitions of their politicians could be whenever the big powers were in a stalemate – with global consequences. But the famous historian does not answer the following question: which factors within the "middle states" led to this fatal outcome?

This role of the "middle states" and their elites which form our focus, can, however, be demonstrated for the 190s BC. For this period we possess exceptionally good evidence: the Polybian material (Livy and the Byzantine excerptors of the original Polybian books) and the documents of that period. Above all, the latter enable us to demonstrate the vast influence, both positive and negative, that local elites in Greek states could exert. While this question will be examined in the second part of this section, I will first outline the specific ways in which Seleucid rule was organized in order to clarify the conditions faced by local elites within the area of conflict between the Seleucids and the Romans. I will there point out the exceptional influence exerted by these elites in contrast to those in the area of conflict between the Seleucids and the Ptolemies analyzed by François Gerardin in his parallel contribution.

2 The Organization of Seleucid Rule

The stability of Seleucid domination has long been an object of research.[120] Despite the general impression of instability within the Seleucid empire, it is striking how solid Seleucid rule remained in Asia Minor even after the defeat of Antiochus III on the Greek mainland in 191 BC, although the Roman naval and infantry forces, together with their Pergamene and

---

[119] Schieder (1981).
[120] E.g.: Heuss (1937); Bickerman (1938); Orth (1977); Habicht (1989); Kuhrt (1996); Mehl (1999); Ma (2002); and Dreyer (2007).

Rhodian allies, were heading toward the straits before finally crossing them. One reason for their loyalty was the countermeasures taken by the Seleucids, especially Antiochus III's successor Seleucus IV. The cities near the straits were heavily disputed. Livy (37.9.1–4) as well as Polybius (21.6.1–6) both record that Phokaia switched sides to Seleucus before the battle of Myonnesos. According to these accounts, riots arose there because of the tribute that the occupying Roman forces imposed. Adherents of both the competing groups within the city appeared before Seleucus, whose army was nearby and ready to take it over:

> In Phokaia, riots arose partly because they were affected by the billeting of those Romans that were left behind on the ships, partly because they were irritated by the imposed contributions. About this time, the leading magistrates of Phokaia – moved by the riots of the masses due to the scarcity of bread and by the activity of the partisans of Antiochus – sent envoys to Seleucus, who stood at the edge of their territory. And they asked him to keep away from the city because they would hold back and wait for the decision of the war. Then they would obey the orders of the winner. Among the envoys, Aristarchos, Kassandros, and Rhodon were partisans and friends of Seleucus. Hegias and Gelias stood on the opposite side and favored the Romans. When they arrived, Seleucus immediately approached Aristarchos and his companions to speak with them, secretly neglecting those who attended Hegias. When he heard about the mood of the masses and about the scarcity of bread, he refused to welcome the envoys officially and to negotiate with them, but advanced against the city. (Polyb. 21.6.1–6)

Therefore, Seleucus suspended negotiations with the ambassadors of the city, and the adherents of the party of Antiochus indeed opened the gates for him. It seems that this was not an isolated case, if we can believe the account of Livy, whose source was Polybius:

> At the same time, Seleucus seized Phokaia by treason because one of the guards opened a gate. Kyme, as well as other cities on that coastline, surrendered because they feared him. (Livy 37.11.15)

The Romans were able to regain the city of Phokaia, but only after the victorious sea battle of Myonnesos. In the course of doing so, they imposed laws while pretending to reinforce the original laws:

> The Roman fleet sailed from Chios to Phokaia. ... As soon as the Roman fleet occupied these very safe harbors, the *praetor* decided that, before he attacked the wall with scaling ladders and equipment, he should send envoys to try to win over the leading men and politicians. When he saw them resisting, he began to attack at two places simultaneously. ... When they (sc. the citizens) heard this, they asked for five days to think about it.

> Meanwhile they tried to find out whether Antiochus could come to their support. When the envoys sent to the king reported that no help could be expected from him, they opened the gates under the condition that they would not endure hostile acts. ... He (sc. the *praetor*) restored to them their city, its territory and their own laws. (Livy 37.31.8–32.14)

This means that the former Seleucid rule was connected with constitutional changes, which required a constitutional revision when the Romans took over the rule. The conclusion is thus twofold. The transition of cities like Phokaia to the Roman side had consequences that went far beyond a simple replacement of one elite group by the other. The transition could also affect the constitution, which was changed to the "original" or "traditional" arrangement on that occasion. Additionally, it is remarkable that only a few cities defected to the Roman side, even though Antiochus III turned out to be hesitant after his defeat in 192/1. While until then he had proved to be irresistible, this caused his contemporaries disappointment:

> The king Antiochus initially seemed to be a personality who was able not only to plan, to dare, and to try, but also to fulfill great plans. When he got older, though, he fell far short of the expectations he himself elicited and became a disappointment to all. (Polyb. 15.34)

It was not until the experience of the Seleucid disaster at the battle of Magnesia near Sipylos that a higher number of Greek cities changed sides, especially those near to the western coast. This movement was so remarkable that it became a criterion for the reorganization of the territory of Asia Minor by the Romans at the peace treaty of Apamea in 188 BC. Henceforth, only those communities that dared to join the Roman side before the battle of Magnesia could enjoy freedom without restrictions. This was a privilege reserved for the minority of cities. Nevertheless, the Greek cities of the Anatolian hinterland – and even Ephesos on the coast – remained loyal to Antiochus III after the Seleucid defeat. It was not until the campaign of Vulso against the Galatians in 188 BC that the backbone of Seleucid rule in Asia Minor was broken.

There are various explanations for this. First, the Galatians were allies of Antiochus in the Roman-Seleucid War, so any threat from the barbarians was greatly reduced, especially inland. Second, the Seleucid military colonies – which are well attested inland – still existed and ensured imperial control.[121] In particular, the case of Toriaion shows that after the peace of

---

[121] If Joseph. *AJ* 12.147–53 about the settlement of 2,000 Jewish mercenaries after an uprising – perhaps that of Achaios – is historically correct, see Gauthier (1989), 41 with literature in n. 89; Bringmann (1983) 63 and 128.

Apamea the successors to Seleucid power in the area, such as the Attalids, also encountered difficulties maintaining the loyalty of certain communities.[122]

> With Good Fortune. King Eumenes sends greetings to the settlers at Toriaion. Your citizens Antigenes, Brennus, and Heliades, whom you have sent in order to congratulate us (l. 5), that we have accomplished everything and that things are now in good shape, and to inform us that you have therefore added the proper sacrifices of thanksgiving, celebrating a festival as gratitude to the gods ... because of your loyalty toward our rule ... they (sc. the ambassadors) asked us to grant you a constitution (l. 10), your own laws, a gymnasium, and what eventuates from all this. ...
>
> I recognized that granting your requests would not only mean a minor loss for me, but result in a great and abundant advantage for you. (l. 20) The present conditions, granted by me, will be long-lasting for you, because I received possession in a legitimate way, because I got it from the Romans, who gained their hegemony by war and treaty from those who are not in power any more. ... You should try now, since you have received these great honors from me, to demonstrate honestly your loyalty by acts on every occasion.

The third and most important reason for the lasting support of the Seleucids was their long tradition of rule in Asia Minor. Seleucid power was deeply rooted inland and well organized. This explains the defeat of Achaios, the viceroy in Sardeis. He failed at the very moment when young Antiochus decided to cross the Tauros into Asia Minor. Some reorganization is attested after the violent death of Achaios. These rearrangements comprised especially the installation of cults emphasizing loyalty toward the members of the royal family.[123]

> Queen Laodice sends greetings to the Council and People of Sardeis: Metrodoros, Metrophanes, Sokrates, and Herakleides, your ambassadors (line 10), have handed over the decree, according to which you have decided to consecrate a sacred enclosure called Laodikeion and to establish an altar and to organize as a yearly festival the Laodicia on every 15th of the month Hyperberetaios, and to carry out a procession and a sacrifice to Zeus Genethlios for the safety of our brother, King Antiochus, the safety of myself, and the safety of our children (line 15). Your ambassadors also urged us strongly in accordance with the content of the decree (to accept

---

[122] L. Jonnes – M. Ricl, EA 29 (1997) 1–30. King Eumenes II granted Toriaion, in Phrygia Paroreios, the status of a city. The date is shortly after 188 BC, see editorial comments; see also Schuler (1999). For Greek text, see this book's web page (www.cambridge.org/9781108479257).

[123] Antiochus III, Laodice and Sardeis between spring and midsummer 213 BC. Ed. Gauthier (1989); for Greek text, see the book's web page (www.cambridge.org/9781108479257).

the honors), (and) we have accepted these honors with pleasure. And we praise the eager attitude of the People and we will always [try] to produce good things for the city. Your ambassadors will report to you on these matters (line 20). On the 10th of Panemos, year 99.

Later on, this cult was reorganized according to a hierarchy for those regions of the empire which were subjected (and not formally associated).[124] It aimed at binding the local elites to the Seleucid dynasty at all levels by celebrating the birthdays of their members, by worshipping the joint rule of the royal couple, and by honoring Laodice, the predecessors of Antiochus (*progonoi*) and Antiochus himself. This was a response to the crisis of the previous years. Likewise, when Antiochus established these bonds of loyalty, he could build on structures that existed before the crisis.[125]

This had far-reaching consequences with respect to the elites. Our evidence for the personnel who served in these cults of loyalty records the privileged position gained by the holders of these cult-offices. In addition, they gave their relatives the most important functions. These personnel (and their families), who had developed close connections with their Seleucid "patrons," were interested in perpetuating these political circumstances. The regulations of 209 BC mentioned above demonstrate the consequences of these changes at all levels, starting from the capital of Asia Minor, Sardeis, down to the local entities at the bottom.[126] Since these privileged offices were new, or at least renewed, they had effects on the structure of the regional and local (urban) administration and constitution: a new hierarchy, new eponymous offices. The aforementioned dossier of Sardeis shows the advantages gained by the whole community when the royal cult and its priesthoods were established (see above.)[127] A precondition of this (new) arrangement in the case of Sardeis and certainly elsewhere was the unconditional surrender of the community. Troops were

---

[124] Convincingly described by Gauthier (1989).
[125] Dreyer (2011b) and (2010c). Ma (2002) no. 4, 288–92:

ὠιόμεθα δὲ δεῖν εἶναι αὐ
τὸν καὶ ἐπὶ τῶν ἱερῶν καὶ τὰς προσό
δους τούτων, καὶ τἄλλα διεξάγεσ
θαι ὑπ' αὐτοῦ καθὰ καὶ ἐπὶ τοῦ πάπ
που ἡμῶν ὑπὸ Δίωνος·

"We think it necessary that he should also be in charge of the sanctuaries, and that their revenues and the other matters should be administered by him (line 40), just as was done by Dion during the reign of our grandfather."

[126] Ma (2002) no. 4, 288–92.   [127] IK 28,1, no. 4, p. 20; Ma (2002) nos. 26–28, 329–337.

quartered in the city to ensure loyalty. These factors help to explain the adhesion of the region to Seleucid rule even after the defeat and the resignation of the monarch.

The Seleucid practice of intervening at the local level was therefore not negligible on the whole. Yet this hypothesis seems to contradict the bon mot attributed to Antiochus III in which the king stated that all his orders that could not be harmonized with the constitution of a community should be ignored.[128] Even if we suppose that these words concerned only those cities that were formally free and only associated with the Seleucid sphere of hegemony – they were nevertheless part of the *pragmata* ("affairs") of the king himself – the documentary evidence on constitutional intervention by the Seleucids cannot be rejected.[129] The following document from Euromos, a city that was under Philip V's control and bore the name Philippi, is a good example:[130]

> Under the rule of King Antiochus and Antiochus the son, in the 115th year [of the Seleucid era], in the month Gorpiaios [August]: On the following items, Zeuxis, appointed by King Antiochus to rule all territory on this side of the Tauros Mountains, and the citizens of Philippi [Euromos], through their ambassadors sent by the city – Andronomos, son of Sotades, and Antiochus, son of Chenon – have agreed:
>
> The citizens of Philippi will be friends and allies of King Antiochus and his descendants, and they will preserve the friendship and military alliance for all time, without hidden motives, and voluntarily.

Antiochus III took advantage of the temporary weakness of the Macedonian king in the context of the defeat of Kynoskephalai in May 197 BC, cancelled the *koinopragia* of 203 BC, the so-called "secret pact" (*Raubvertrag*), and conquered the Macedonian possessions in southwest Asia Minor (197/6). In the case of Euromos, this meant a constitutional revision in addition to the "usual" replacement of one local dominant elite group by the other, as negotiated in the contract guaranteeing Seleucid control. This constitutional change is only partially preserved, and its target is not easily determined.[131] But it is certain that the Seleucids

---

[128] Plut. *reg. et imp. apophth.* 183e.
[129] On the *pragmata*, see the document of Antiocheia in Persis: OGIS 231 = *IM* 18 = *IK* 65, no. 250, ll. 25–8: γεγράφαμεν δὲ καὶ τοῖς ἐπὶ τῶν πραγμάτων τεταγμένοις, ὅπως καὶ αἱ πόλεις ἀκολούθως ἀποδέξωνται.
[130] Euromos and Antiochus, August 197 BC, ed. Errington *EA* 8, 1986, 1; for Greek text see the book's web page (www.cambridge.org/9781108479257).
[131] De Ste Croix (1981) 304; Dreyer (2007) 309.

aimed to secure their influence among the local elites and their community with these constitutional modifications:[132]

> [It was decided that the following changes in the government should be instituted] ... first, the election to office of the three *kosmoi*; after them, the three *prostatai* of the People; the elections for the offices should be held on a rotating basis by the tribes [*phylai*]. To the *kosmoi* should be transferred all affairs concerning the protection of the city and its territory, and the keys to the city gates should be handed over to them. Additionally, the care of the fortresses should be turned over to them, as well as command in campaigning, as well as whatever concerns the treaty of alliance that was concluded with Antiochus the Great King through the negotiations with Zeuxis.
>
> Under no circumstances should any office be more powerful than this – with the exception of the powers of the City Council – and this office should not be subordinated to any other office.
>
> To the *prostatai* should be given competence over daily political business, and everything else as far as determined by the laws.
>
> If messages need to be sent elsewhere concerning the affairs of the city or any other matters, they should be sent after they have been written by the *kosmoi* and the *prostatai*; no other public officials are allowed to send letters concerning the city on their own authority.
>
> [No one may] be elected [two times to the same] office out of the three tribes on their rotating basis. The chief priests and the priests of Cretan Zeus [and Dictynna] [should be elected] each year in elections on a rotating basis [out of the three tribes].

It can be demonstrated that these and other similar activities were successful and took place in cooperation with the pro-Seleucid section of the local elites. The rapid Seleucid success was immediately recognized by the Roman ambassadors, as they tried to free the Antigonid communities in Asia Minor in the aftermath of the battle of Kynoskephalai according to the law of the victor. They tried but, when they arrived, the communities were already 'liberated' by the Seleucids.

3 The "Cold War" Situation of the 190s BC and the Local Elites

Though the fast Seleucid advance was successful in gaining influence among the Greek coastal cities and their elites, the uncertain situation in which Antiochus found himself when he met the Roman ambassadors for

---

[132] Change of constitution in Euromos under the 'rule' of Antiochus, after 197 BC, ed. Errington EA 21, 1993, 24 (with amendments of Brixhe, *BÉ* 1995, 526); for Greek text, see the book's web page (www.cambridge.org/9781108479257).

the first time was quite obvious. Both the Roman and Seleucid powers indisputably had opposing interests but also felt mutual respect, as their power balanced each other. This tense situation became clear in the words of Antiochus to the Roman ambassadors, as reported by Polybius (18.51.9): "The autonomous cities in Asia could not obtain freedom by Roman order, but by an act of grace of himself." In my opinion, this act of grace could only be explained by initiating an arrangement negotiated with the elites. It was known and well established as a model of treatment of Greek cities at the edge of Antiochus's *pragmata*. This arrangement avoided the formal subjugation of the city and introduced the moderate hegemony of the Seleucids.

Some of these cities did not behave according to this established "rule" anymore, which explains the behavior of the king. These rule-breakers had an advocate in the republic of Rhodes, which already opposed Antiochus' advance in the south. Since Antiochus had to act in his role as liberator in order to continue his overwhelmingly fast recovery, he had to accept it. Even more problematic was the opposing attitude of communities like Smyrna, Lampsakos, and Alexandria in the Troas that closed their gates to the advancing Antiochus. Considering the far superior power of the king, the behavior of these cities was possible only because their political elites had another point of reference.

In the year 196 BC, Rome declared unconditional freedom for the states on the Greek mainland, and indeed only withdrew her troops in 194 BC. The impact on Asia Minor was immediately visible; Smyrna established a loyalty cult for the personified goddess "Roma." This happened according to the usual "rules" that cities in the east followed. Accordingly, Smyrna wanted above all to take the initiative in expressing loyalty toward Rome (i.e. with the appearance of doing so voluntarily), especially as Antiochus was approaching. Additionally, with this new deity and its cult personnel the community authorized the group of politicians responsible for this policy to determine a further course of action. On the contrary, the Romans played no active role in this context and in this region yet.

This obviously anti-Seleucid behavior at this early stage (i.e. in the year 195 BC) was very risky for those who stood for this policy, and the commitment of the elites was high. This can also be demonstrated in the case of Lampsakos:[133]

---

[133] Honorary decree for Hegesias in Lampsakos, *IK* 6 no. 4; cf. Ma (2002) 87; for Greek text see the book's web page (www.cambridge.org/9781108479257).

[When the people looked for volunteers] and appealed urgently (...) made the decision (line 5) according to which those who would undertake for the sake of the city an embassy to the Massaliots and the Romans would be honored by the people, (...). When some were suggested but would not undertake [the task], (...) then Hegesias [took it up], (...), he disregarded his personal interests for the benefit of the city (line 15).

When he took up the journey and arrived in Hellas, he and his colleagues on the embassy met there with Lucius, the general of the Roman fleet [the *praetor* L. Quinctius Flamininus]; (...) and requested of Lucius, since we are relatives of the Romans, [to take care] of our city, so that what seems useful for our people could indeed be achieved (...)

(...) He took up also the long and dangerous journey to Massilia (line 45), and appeared before the Council of Six Hundred, and persuaded them to agree to a joint embassy to the city of Rome. (...)

When he arrived (line 50) [at Rome, together with] the colleagues of the embassy and with those sent with him [from] Massilia, he started talks with the Senate together with his colleagues, (...)

And when the embassy [was pleading] that we (line 65) be included in the [treaty] made between the Romans and [King Philip], [the senate] did include us in the treaty [with the king], as they themselves wrote to us. Concerning (all) the remaining issues, the Senate referred us to the [Roman] consul Titus [Quinctius Flamininus] and the Commission of Ten, which were concerned with (line 70) affairs in Hellas. And having come to Corinth together with (...), he met the Roman commander [and the Commission of Ten] and talked to them about the situation of our city. (...) he received on these issues a favorable answer, as well as letters to the kings, and perceiving they were useful, he sent (...) as it had been decreed before (...).[134]

Clearly, Hegesias assumed the leadership over a majority in council and assembly, even in the face of the threat of Seleucid power. His declared aim was to convince the Romans to include the city in the peace treaty between Rome and the Antigonids (line 65ff.) in order to be protected by the Romans – as those *adscripti* of the attested peace of Phoenice had been. The abovementioned answer of Antiochus to the Roman ambassadors demonstrates his view that Roman claims on those communities in accordance with the law of the victor, insofar as they previously belonged to Philip, were unacceptable. And although both sides were only pretending to liberate the Greek cities, this challenged his hegemony in this part of his realm.

---

[134] Transl. Bagnall and Derow (2004) 70 no. 35.

In contrast, the official "act of liberation" was crucial for installing a moderate form of rule in this area that was mostly under his hegemony and at the edge of his *pragmata*. This form of rule is reflected in the peace of Apamea and carried a financial aspect in addition to having consequences at both the institutional and the personal level. Since a "freed" city could not officially pay tribute, this category of subject city paid its tribute by contributing levies to the new protecting deity. This is implied by paragraphs in the peace of Apamea requiring the reorientation of the levies of those cities which were formally liberated by Antiochus from the Seleucids to Pergamum – insofar as those cities remained on the Seleucid side until the battle of Magnesia.[135] If this is correct, then the Seleucid version of freeing the cities looked different from what the Romans offered in 196 BC and fulfilled in 194 BC when they withdrew their troops from the Greek mainland.

While the largest powers were in a stalemate (also, to a certain extent, in Palestine and Coele Syria), the situation of the 190s BC offered alternatives, especially at the edges of their sphere of influence. It provided freedom for politicians in cities and intermediate powers – at their personal risk – to act or to choose between two versions of liberation (unlike in Palestine and Coele Syria). The petulant answer of the king cited above touched on a sensitive point. The elites and the representatives of the regional powers could exercise significant influence, resulting in a good or a bad outcome, in peace or war.

An important possible reason for the bad outcome of the 190s BC was the fact that Antiochus offered refuge to Hannibal at his court when he escaped from Carthage. After the Second Punic War, Hannibal had also pursued a policy for his home city. This aimed at weakening the constitutional bodies that were dominated by the traditional merchant families. His internal enemies, who feared for their privileged position in Carthage, denounced him in Rome. Hannibal escaped to Ephesus and into the Seleucid sphere, where he gained great influence over the king, especially on his military strategies, in the following years (196 to 193 BC).

---

[135] Polyb. 21.46.2–3; cf. Dreyer (2007) 355. To the last group Polybius mentions here belonged Tralles and Nysa (?) (Schmitt [1964] 281), Ephesos and Telmessos (Polyb. 21.46.10), Magnesia near Sipylos (Livy 37.56.3), Thyateira (Livy 37.44.4), Skepsis (Strabo 13.1.54 C 609), Abydos (Strabo 13.1.128 C 595); Niese (1903) 62, n. 10; Bengtson (1944) 242, n. 5), Priapos (Strabo 13.1.14 C 588). The case of Phokaia is disputed (see above: first it moved to the Roman side, then to the Seleucid side, afterwards – before the battle of Magnesia, Livy 37.37 etc. – again to the Roman side, Livy 37.32.14): Ma (2002) 282 according to Mastrocinque (1994) 452, is tending to count the city to this group. But Phokaia seems to be counted among those special cases (not explicitly though), which were granted freedom; Polyb. 21.46.7; Livy 38.39.12.

As with Hannibal's reform plans, the military plans of Antiochus III quickly found their way to Rome, where the Senate was still in 192 BC preparing its response of 191 BC. It distributed the *provinciae* among the consuls with the aim of renewing the war in southern Italy and Sicily, Carthage being a target.

Surprisingly, just before the war started, Hannibal's influence on Antiochus was undermined. As soon as the Romans had completely left the Greek mainland in 194 BC, according to their promise, Antiochus rejoiced, hoping that the occupation of Greece was now at hand. But he had to wait, because according to his own propaganda he could take the offensive only in response to an invitation to liberate the cities by the local elites. Moreover, he had to take into account the facts that his troops were tied up in Thrace and that preparation of the fleet had only just started.

In spring 193 BC, negotiations were held in Rome with ambassadors from the king, with representatives of the cities and of federal states also present. Mutual respect was obvious. This can be demonstrated by the servile behavior of the Romans toward the leader of the Seleucid embassy, Menippos.[136]

> (From the) Romans. Marcus Valerius, (son) of Marcus, *praetor*, and the tribunes of the *plebs* and the Senate, to the *boule* and the *demos* of the Teans, greeting. Menippos, the ambassador sent to us by King Antiochus, chosen also by you as ambassador concerning your city, presented the decree and himself spoke with all zeal in accordance with it. We received the man both on account of his previous reputation and on account of his innate good character, and we listened favorably to his requests. . . . Wherefore, for these reasons and on account of our goodwill toward you and on account of the esteemed ambassador, it is our decision that your city and land are to be sacred, as is even now the case, and inviolable and free from the tribute at the hands of the *demos* of the Romans, and we shall try to increase both the honors to the god and our kindnesses to you, so long as you maintain your goodwill toward us even after this. Farewell.[137]

This document was a response to a request for asylum by the city of Teos. This initiative resurrected an action that had started ten years earlier and was used by Seleucid and Macedonian diplomats – Hagesandros (Seleucid) and Perdikkas (Antigonid who was honored with Tean citizenship) – as a well-established instrument to calm down the tension between both kingdoms in the context of the "secret pact." In this situation, representatives of

---

[136] Letter of Messala to Teos, ed. Sherk *RDGE* 34, 193 BC; for Greek text see the book's web page (www.cambridge.org/9781108479257).
[137] Translation Bagnall and Derow (2004) 75–6 no. 39.

the two big powers and ambassadors of the local elites of Teos, Apollodotos and Kollatas, cooperated.[138] The target was twofold. First, the region of Teos and its territory were appeased. Additionally, the two kingdoms acknowledged their wish not to go to war with each other, at least within this region. In this respect, the local elites cooperated with the representatives of the king to the benefit of their city and they used their connections.

The request for asylum of 193 BC, without any representative of Teos present, stood out because of its programmatic character. The wording of the preserved document itself marks out the exceptional nature of the event. It was officially stated that both sides were not interested in war. Moreover, each party declared it would work on de-escalating the tensions in western Asia Minor, at least for the territory of Teos, for which Menippos had negotiated.

But the influence of the urban and royal representatives had its limits. In view of the (officially) frozen negotiations, the Roman senators and Antiochus's ambassadors alike were looking for alternatives in secret. The Romans created a surprise with their suggestion of negotiating about a sphere of influence and they put forward the straits as a limit. An agreement on this basis would have necessitated the abandonment of important allies on both sides. None of the regimes in the cities on the other side of the straits, which had so far counted on Roman support, could now be sure about Roman loyalty. If the Seleucids agreed to this suggestion, they would have fallen under their dominion sooner or later. The pro-Roman elites there would have been the first victims of a settlement of that kind.

Yet they could soon breathe freely. The suggestion to declare the straits as a limit for the spheres of influence between the Romans and Seleucids failed. Instead, the two big powers again tried to win over the local elites of the cities to their cause, not only in Rome but also later in the Greek mainland. The Seleucid envoys secured Aetolian support for themselves. A competing mission from Titus Quinctius Flamininus, who worried about the balance of power that was established in Greece between 197 and 194 BC, tried in vain to convince the Aetolians to remain loyal to their obligations. The representatives of those cities and federal states that would have lost their independence, had the Roman suggestion been successful, were also working against an agreement of the big powers. Until 193 BC, the Rhodians and the king of Pergamum tried to convince the Roman representatives not to accede to the Seleucid claims.

---

[138] Dreyer (2010b); Dreyer (2011a).

Even worse was the role of the Aetolians: a group of the *apokletoi* under the leadership of Thoas got access to Antiochus without authorization of their own assembly. Contrary to all the plans and strategies favored by the king in the past, they convinced him to risk a conflict with the Romans on the Greek mainland. This Aetolian group was supported by a camarilla at court under the auspices of Minnion. A majority at court favored the war on the Greek mainland in the hope of undermining Hannibal's influence on the king. In addition, their adherents believed that a war in Greece could be easily and safely carried out according to the promises of the Aetolian war party at the court.

In any case, the final decision was to be made by the king. His behavior is not easy to understand, though. During the second meeting with the Roman ambassadors in Ephesus in 193 BC, Antiochus handed the decision over to his chancellor Minnion as head of the hawks aiming at war. Though the death of Antiochus's son and successor does not explain the failure of the king, this event had consequences for queen Laodice, who seemingly fell into disgrace on that occasion. Antiochus should have known that at this very moment his fleet and his army, currently occupying Thrace, were not able to face the Romans. On the contrary, the king, bound to his propaganda as an invincible liberator, promised – probably in good faith – the support of the Seleucid army as soon as the Greek cities would rise against the Romans.

The first minister Minnion could be sure of the king's attitude when negotiating with the Romans, but otherwise there would be time enough afterwards to revise the results. One must assume that the Seleucid headquarters – the king included – shared the opinion of the Aetolian war party under the leadership of Thoas without any attempt to verify it. They believed that the Greek cities would support their case as soon as Antiochus landed in Greece with his army as liberator. Therefore, it was his propaganda as the agent of Greek freedom that made Antiochus a servant of the Greek elites in this period of stalemate. This situation enabled elites, in this case the Aetolians, to decide upon war and peace.

But on the other side, the self-declared representatives of the Aetolian federal state believed the king's promise to send a great army as soon he was called on to do so. Mutual disappointment was therefore inevitably great in 192 BC. After the Seleucid army had landed on the invitation of the Aetolians, it was not initially possible to achieve a declaration of war by the Aetolian assembly, even though this was *the* precondition of the military alliance with the Seleucids.

Meanwhile, the lack of support for Antiochus in Greece cannot only be explained by the unpopularity of his allies the Aetolians, but also by the disappointing inactivity of the king. The political elites were aware of the difference between the Roman and Seleucid claims to free the Greek cities. Whereas the Seleucid king liberated a Greek city in order to perpetuate the actual hierarchy by installing a royal cult to trigger loyalty and imposing regular tribute, the Romans declared the liberation of the Greeks in 196 BC and left the Greek mainland in 194 BC after reorganizing the relationship between the powers in Greece as well as the political system of some cities, federal states and monarchies. This meant that the cities could rule themselves without hegemonial predominance (within Greece). This policy, strongly influenced by Titus Quinctius Flamininus, was no act of altruism. The Romans withdrew their troops to avoid their presence under the command of a senator and established a sphere of stability among loyal and grateful states – *grateful* as clients should be when granted benefits by their patrons. But they failed: the Aetolian call to Antiochus for help against Roman "rule" in Greece ended this Roman policy.

The end of this policy can be studied in the Polybian account of the negotiations in the Senate in 189 BC, which is based on good documentary material. The Rhodian ambassadors clearly argued that the principle of (city) freedom and monarchical rule (here of Pergamum) were incompatible. This freedom could only be guaranteed by republican states (like Rhodes and Rome).[139] This speech is based on actual experience for those areas under Seleucid dominance, which were never legally subjugated but officially "liberated." The regimes in those cities remained loyal to the Seleucid king, who ensured their development by installing a loyal elite (notably serving as personnel in royal cults) who had an interest in the continuity of royal rule, a course that could not be harmonized with republican ideals.

4 Conclusion

The fact that the Roman-Seleucid confrontation evolved into a bipolar stalemate, well known in modern times, offered hitherto unknown possibilities to the political elites at all levels: at the court, in the regional administration, and in the cities. This was demonstrated in several cases, though not all. The elites of Coele Syria could not gain the freedom to act because the Ptolemies and Seleucids adhered to the same principles and

---

[139] Polyb. 21.18–24; Livy 37.52–6; Dreyer (2007) 328–33.

Antiochus III, Ptolemy IV, and Local Elites: Deal-Making

played the same "game." There was a crucial difference in the situation with the Romans in the Aegean and in western Asia Minor: the Romans and Seleucids blocked each other with their propaganda, yet with mutual respect, between 197 and 192 BC.

The different policies caused the influence of the local Greek elites to grow, constructively ensuring peace in one case and stimulating conflict in another. The local politicians, especially a group of plotters among the Aetolian *apokletoi*, a camarilla at the Seleucid court, gained influence over Antiochus at a key moment. Contrary to the impression given by his propaganda, the king was bound to his policy of liberation toward the Greek cities and felt himself under pressure in the face of the Roman challenge. This resulted not only in the destabilization of the Seleucid empire but also in the end of the policy toward the Greek cities so far applied by the majority in the senate. This challenged the Seleucids, and it put an end to the king's prewar policy toward the Greek states.

Common Conclusion

This chapter has compared two conflict areas in which Antiochus III was involved as the main protagonist. Four salient points emerge from our investigation.

1. Where Greek cities were the predominant form of social organization, well-established rules governed the communication between kings and local elites, whether at the royal court itself or at any level of interaction between the local communities and the center of imperial power. These rules had not been created by the Hellenistic monarchs, but became the general medium of interaction among Greek, Macedonian, and hellenized elites after the conquests of Alexander the Great. The Greek documentation amply attests to these rules, at least until the beginning of the second century BC.
2. Regions of conflict provide the best case studies for this phenomenon because evidence there is comparatively good, although scarcer in Coele Syria and Phoenicia, the conflict area between the Ptolemies and Antiochus III, than in western Asia Minor and Greece, the region disputed by Antiochus III and Rome in the eastern Mediterranean during the so-called Cold War period of the 190s BC. The communication of local elites on the Phoenician seaboard and in Coele Syria often assumed distinctive forms, for instance by acknowledging and celebrating a ruler as Great King.

3. Antiochus III defeated the Ptolemies because, with more generous promises, he managed to entice the elites in the region of Coele Syria and Phoenicia to defect. Ptolemy IV, a lethargic ruler according to Polybius (Polyb. 5.34), proved unable to sustain effective communication. Furthermore, the core area of the kingdom, Egypt, entered a phase of crisis and transition in its relations with the Ptolemaic dynasty between 207 and the 180s BC.

   Both dynasties, however, followed the same rules in their interactions with local elites. Antiochus III lost his war against Rome in the 190s BC because the Romans, in their dealings with the states of the Greek mainland, employed a vocabulary that was familiar to them but endowed with a different meaning on the Greek side. Initially at least, the promises made by the Romans proved more attractive and so they got the upper hand.

4. The second century BC brought new developments that had major effects on the communication between kings and local elites. Rome's rise to the status of dominant power in the *oecumene* constituted a major factor of change. At the same time, a native insurrectional movement within the Ptolemaic and Seleucid empires began to challenge the monopoly of Greek and Macedonian elites over communication with the king. The era of deal-making politics, as it had been practiced in the third century BC and reached its peak under Antiochus III, had come to an end.

CHAPTER 10

Regional Revolts in the Seleucid and Ptolemaic Empires

Sylvie Honigman and Anne-Emmanuelle Veïsse

1 Introduction

The most prominent feature shared by the Great Revolt of the Thebaid against the Ptolemies of Alexandria (206–186 BCE) and that of Judea against the Seleucids (which began in the 160s) is that scholars studying these respective uprisings tend to describe them as unique events.[1] For this reason, despite their close chronological connection, they have seldom been studied in a comparative perspective.[2] Our purpose is to show that such a comparison is not only appropriate, but enlightening. This is not to deny, of course, that these two events had their respective specificities, but we firmly reject claims that the revolts in question were as exceptional as they are made out to be. Indeed, the common view that the Maccabean revolt in Judea was caused by religious persecution – the factor that makes the episode allegedly unique – is to our mind an uncritical endorsement of a stock narrative through which the rebellion has been memorialized in the subsequent Jewish tradition; and while the troubles in Judea did indeed have a strong religious component, other more 'standard' factors (so to speak) were also in play, and in no small measure.[3] Likewise, the belief that the Great Theban Revolt was the consequence of Egyptian nationalism combined with the alleged Theban tradition of feudal independence – an assumption which used to prevail – should be definitively discarded in view of recent studies highlighting the impact of far-reaching changes in the Ptolemaic way of ruling the region in the decades running up to the revolt – a process that Joseph Manning has dubbed

---

[1] The reason for leaving an open date for the end of the Judean revolt will be addressed in Section 2.2 below.
[2] The most prominent exception is Eddy (1961).
[3] For an historiographical overview of studies on the Maccabean revolt, see Honigman (2014a) 17–32. On claims of uniqueness, see ibid. 239 and Honigman (2014b) 60.

as the 'Ptolemaicizing' of Upper Egypt.[4] Taking these revised premises as our cue, we will treat the Great Revolt of the Thebaid and the Maccabean revolt of Judea as two case studies that realistically bear comparison, whatever their individual specificities.

Admittedly, at first glance the comparison looks unpromising, or even far-fetched. For a start, in geopolitical terms the status of the Thebaid and Judea within their respective settings of the Ptolemaic kingdom and Seleucid empire differed considerably. Moreover, as just noted, the respective sources documenting the revolts are also of a different nature. The Judean events are narrated in literary sources – the first two Maccabees books, Josephus, *Antiquities*, 12, and the Book of Daniel, 11 – offering both a coherent storyline and an explicit causal interpretation. While we are only beginning to realize how biased their narrative is, the documentary evidence that could offer a counterpoint is scarce, and the debate continues over the relevance to the revolt of specific documents.[5] In contrast, for the Great Theban Revolt the main sources of evidence are numerous papyri and inscriptions, each one documenting some tiny aspect of the events, leaving it therefore to modern scholars to piece together a coherent picture of the events from these scraps of evidence.[6] Moreover, the only text providing a narrative, the so-called Second Philae decree, is basically propaganda. It was promulgated in 186 BCE by a gathering of Egyptian priests held in Alexandria to celebrate the defeat of the rebel Chaonnophris a few days earlier, and its claim that the troubles were caused by impious plunderers is a traditional *topos* and can by no means be accepted at face value.[7]

As noted above, the purpose of drawing comparisons between the two revolts is not to artificially endorse the similarities. Although they shared some key affinities – in particular their respective timing coincided with thorough social, economic and political changes – the principal factors that triggered the respective uprisings were, as we shall see, quite different.[8] While they began on distinct footings, once the revolts were under way, their development basically followed variations of pre-scripted scenarios. Although ideological discourses may attempt to take a new slant, they

---

[4] Manning (2003a) 69; 73. [5] See below, Section 2.2.
[6] Pestman (1995); Veïsse (2004); and Veïsse (forthcoming a).
[7] Two versions of the decree are preserved, see von Recklinghausen (2018). Beside the Philae decree, the only narrative alluding to the revolt are fragments from a story situated in Moses's time by the Judean Alexandrian author Artapanus, in which he refers to the wicked pharaoh 'Chenephres' (probably Chaonnophris). See Veïsse (2013).
[8] The state of the evidence does not allow full comparison of the causes, in particular because we lack a comprehensive narrative about the causes of the rebellion in the Thebaid.

cannot afford to altogether break with established traditions lest they lose the power of persuasion. By the same chalk, because innovation itself is a costly business, the material response of any given central power toward a revolt will be essentially a replay, at least in its early phases, though they may of course differ in scale as needs require. Therefore, based on our premise that the Theban and Maccabean revolts share certain typical features alongside their peculiarities, we will take them as case studies for comparing the Ptolemaic and Seleucid responses to native revolts, respectively. This choice stems from the fact they are by far the best-documented case studies of native revolts in these two kingdoms. By breaking down the events into basic conceptual units – the run-up to the revolts, the ideological discourses of the rebel leaders, those of the kings, the immediate royal responses, and the aftermath of each revolt – our comparison of the two will cast light on what we see as the structural features of these historical episodes.

With this assumed comparability as our starting point, there are three aspects which, in our view, carried weight in the strategic decisions of both sides and in their respective representations of the conflict, both in Egypt and Judea: the distinct territorial configuration of the areas in question; the different historical contexts (in particular, the interference – or not – of dynastic struggles with the revolt management); and the different mobilization of cultural memories to reshape the ideologies of power. Our interpretation of the revolts involves exploring how these three major aspects interacted to influence both the symbolic representations and the concrete actions of the two sides engaged in both conflicts, respectively. In the aftermath, while in Judea the Seleucids eventually acknowledged the emergence of local dynasts (who ultimately assumed the title of kings), the Ptolemies never once relented until they had completely crushed the Theban pharaoh.

2   The Storylines

To complement the discussions that follow, we can start by summarizing the two revolts, in chronological order: note that the difference in length of the two summaries reflects the different nature of the sources of evidence.

2.1   *The Thebaid*

In the Thebaid the revolt started in 207/6 BCE, at the very end of Ptolemy IV Philopator's reign. In the autumn of 205 BCE a certain Haronnophris seized power in Thebes, assumed the title of 'pharaoh,' and was acknowledged by the priests of Amon. Based on documents dating between 204 and 201/0 BCE, his authority was also acknowledged southwards in Pathyris, and northwards in the Coptite *nome* and Abydos, although the precise chronology of how his area of influence extended remains elusive. In the context of a large-scale Ptolemaic counterattack, in the summer or autumn of 199 he was either succeeded by Chaonnophris or (more likely) assumed this new name for his reign.[9] In Thebes, the authority of Ptolemy V was temporarily reinstated between the end of 199 and late 198 BCE. But the city was lost again to Chaonnophris and was finally reconquered only around the autumn of 191 BCE. Chaonnophris was ultimately defeated by the Ptolemaic forces on 27 August 186 BCE in a battle that took place at an unknown site in Upper Egypt. The Ptolemaic victory was celebrated by a gathering of Egyptian priests in Alexandria and commemorated in the so-called Second Philae decree. Altogether, the unrest lasted twenty years.

2.2 *Judea*

Whereas the beginning and end of the Theban revolt are (relatively) easy to delineate, the end of the Judean uprising is harder to pin down. Admittedly, the texts themselves emphasize such an end, namely Judas Maccabee's refounding of the temple; and, to go by historical parallels, we might end the chronological survey with the settlement granted by Antiochus V at the beginning of his reign (early 163 BCE).[10] But the troubles resumed soon afterwards, and in accordance with our understanding of the nature of the Seleucids' management of the revolt, we take this survey down to John Hyrcanus (135/4–104 BCE), Simon Maccabee's son, and seemingly the first Hasmonean to assume the title of king.

Leaving aside their assorted contradicting details, 1 and 2 Maccabees offer a coherent storyline.[11] According to 2 Maccabees (4:7–10), the sequence of events begins immediately after Antiochus IV became king in 175 BCE, when Jason, the brother of the Jerusalem high priest Onias III, usurped the high priesthood by offering money to the king. Jason further obtained from the king the right to found a *polis* and a *gymnasion* in Jerusalem. Two years later, Jason was forced into exile by one Menelaus,

---

[9] Veïsse (2013); and Veïsse (forthcoming a). The Ptolemaic military response was first delayed by troops being mobilized to deal with the Fifth Syrian War and revolts in the delta.

[10] See below, n. 14.

[11] Here and below, Josephus's account in *Antiquities* 12 is omitted when it simply paraphrases 1 Maccabees. See Honigman (2014a) 5.

who became high priest by offering an even higher sum of money to the king (2 Macc. 4:23–5). When (either during his first or second campaigns of 169 and 168 BCE, respectively) a false rumor reached Judea that Antiochus IV had been slain in Egypt, Jason attempted to retrieve power and laid siege to Menelaus and his partisans in Jerusalem's citadel, but to no avail (2 Macc. 5:1–7). As he returned from his campaign in Egypt, Antiochus IV 'believed' (διέλαβεν) that Judea was in revolt because of the civil war between Jason and Menelaus, and he stormed the city, massacring its population and plundering the temple (2 Macc. 5:11–26). Shortly afterwards, he sent an envoy to compel the Judeans to forsake the laws of their ancestors and to relinquish God's laws (6:1–11). Judas Maccabee led the revolt that followed and within two years reconquered Jerusalem. Shortly after Antiochus V succeeded his father, he rescinded the decree of persecution (early 163).

According to 1 and 2 Maccabees, the Maccabean wars against the Seleucid armies and the neighboring populations resumed in 162. When Judas was killed in the battlefield in 161 or 160, he was succeeded by his brother, Jonathan (161/0–143), who waged war intermittently against the Seleucids.[12] In the years 152–150, Jonathan shrewdly exploited Demetrius I's and Alexander Balas's rivalry over the Seleucid succession. Balas acknowledged him as high priest and 'kin of the king' (*sungenes*; 1 Macc. 10:15–20) and subsequently promoted him as 'one of the First Friends' (*tôn prôtôn philôn*) and appointed him 'district governor' (*strategos* and *meridarches*) in Judea (1 Macc. 10:59–66, esp. 66). Jonathan was succeeded by the youngest Maccabee brother, Simon (143–ca. 135/4), and in 141, Demetrius II granted him autonomy; thereupon Simon initiated his own era (1 Macc. 13: 36–42). Simon was in turn succeeded by his son, John Hyrcanus (135/4–104 BCE), as high priest and 'head of the nation' (*ethnarches*), thereby establishing the principle of dynastic transmission of power within the Hasmonean family. Hyrcanus started to mint coinage in 110, and he may have taken the title of king, although the latter is formally attested only with Aristobulus (104–103 BCE).

1 and 2 Maccabees were most likely composed by court historians under Hyrcanus's reign.[13] Consequently, it is likely that the storyline based on the ancient sources that we just offered above was advanced

---

[12] 2 Maccabees' account of the wars terminates before Judas's death. The subsequent events are covered by 1 Maccabees.
[13] Honigman (2014a) 65–94.

and possibly contrived to legitimize the Hasmoneans' usurpation of power. Whereas this storyline gains some credibility starting with Jonathan, every single episode from the deposition of Onias III in 175 up to the initial restoration of the peace at the beginning of Antiochus V's reign is debated, owing either to contradictions between the literary sources or to modern controversies about their reliability. In particular, in contrast with Jonathan and Simon, in historical terms the figure of Judas Maccabee remains elusive, and given that the founding (or refounding) of the Jerusalem temple was the primary source of a ruler's legitimacy in the Judean tradition, it is hard to know which elements in the extant descriptions of this episode are based on genuine events, if any.[14]

The literary deconstruction of 2 Maccabees' narrative suggests that when Antiochus IV returned from his Egyptian campaign, he was not mistaken about Judea being in revolt, and his assault on Jerusalem must be seen as the first step in the revolt's suppression.[15] The building of a citadel watching over the temple, installation of a garrison, and confiscations of lands from the rebels – both as a punitive step and to provide land plots for the soldiers – followed suit. This suppression of the revolt was subsequently emplotted as an act of religious persecution according to a well-documented narrative pattern and was transformed into the cause – and not the consequence – of the revolt, turning Antiochus IV into an archvillain who assaulted Jerusalem for no reason.[16]

---

[14] On the Judean ideology of power, see Honigman (2014a) 95–118, and further below, Sections 4.1 and 4.3. For chronological reasons, John Ma (2013a; and 2020) questioned the ancient sources' twofold claim that Jerusalem was militarily reconquered by Judas and his brothers and that they purified the temple, and in this way allowed for the sacrifices to be resumed. Instead, based on his revision of the order of the four royal letters gathered in 2 Maccabees 11, Ma suggested that peace was restored in Judea in the same way as in Greek cities that had revolted and been taken back. That is, the temple was returned to the Judeans by Antiochus V, at the outcome of negotiations between the high priest Menelaus and the king. Likewise, there is no archaeological evidence of troubles in the region at the supposed date of Judas's military campaigns (Berlin [1997]), while Katell Berthelot (2018) has shown that the literary accounts in 1 and 2 Maccabees are heavily informed by literary (biblical) models. In contrast, although the details and chronology of Jonathan's and Simon's regional conquests are also suspect on both literary and archaeological grounds (Berthelot [2018]; Berlin and Herbert [2015]), archaeological finds certainly attest that there were troubles in the 140s. See the collected papers in Berlin and Kosmin (2021).

[15] For the problems surrounding the historicity of Judas's deeds, see previous note.

[16] For a detailed study, see Honigman (2014a) 378–404. For a critical reading of the persecution accounts, see ibid. 22–58, and Honigman (2014b). On land confiscations, see further Honigman (2014a) 281–4.

3 The Run-up to the Revolts

Despite obvious differences that will be detailed below, the events that catalyzed the two revolts offer some interesting points of comparison.

3.1 Catalysts for the Great Revolt in the Thebaid (206–186 BCE)

The Great Revolt of the Thebaid resulted from a particular contingency of local and more general factors. Notably, troubles also broke out in the Delta and the Fayum at about the same time (the end of Ptolemy IV's reign), suggesting that various general factors were at play. In particular, it appears that the Fourth Syrian War, which ended with the battle of Raphia in 217 BCE, had lasting consequences. Whereas we may assume that the abrupt demobilization of a great number of soldiers at the end of the war had a destabilizing social effect, we are on firmer ground in stating that the military campaigns had strained royal finances to the breaking point.[17] There are also clues that prices likewise rose in the late third century and that the demonetization of some of the Ptolemaic bronze coinage that resulted from the accounting and monetary reforms known as the 'Grand Mutation' had negative repercussions.[18]

That said, alongside this general context, the scope and length of the revolt in Upper Egypt can be explained only by specific local factors, corresponding to the 'Ptolemaicizing' of Upper Egypt, that is, a package of changes implemented in the second half of the third century BCE, by means of which the Ptolemies tightened their grip on the area in question.[19] One move in particular involved imposing a tighter control on land. In the southern Thebaid, from the 220s on, confiscated lands were reassigned through 'auctions of Pharaoh,' that is, public sales, a practice which had no precedent in Egyptian history.[20] At about the same time, in the Theban area the levy of the 'harvest-tax' (*shemou*) that bore upon temple land was transferred from the 'scribes of the temple of Amon' to the 'scribes of Pharaoh,' that is, governmental officials, and the grains

---

[17] We have no means to assess what part exactly the demobilization of soldiers played in the troubles. On the royal finances, see Fischer-Bovet (2014b) 88–9; Hazzard and Huston (2015) 113–14; Agut-Labordère and Moreno-García (2016) 711–12; 715. A dire need for liquidity may explain why the *telestikon*, the tax that priests paid on assuming office, was raised under Ptolemy IV (see OGIS I 90, l. 16).

[18] On prices rising, see Hazzard and Huston (2015). On the demonetisation, see Picard and Faucher (2012) 50–1; 60–108; and Gorre and Lorber (2020). According to Gorre and Lorber's revised dating the reform occurred ca. 207/6.

[19] See above, n. 4.   [20] Manning (2003b) 160–1.

delivered as tax payments were stored in the royal granary, and no longer that of Amon.[21] As a consequence, the temple of Amon was deprived of an important source of income, all the more since this transfer also applied to the taxes that were levied on the temple lands rented out on hereditary lease and whose revenues served to finance the cults and priestly prebends. It seems that the *syntaxis* (the royal subsidies to the temples) was intended to make up for the resulting loss of revenues.[22] However, because of the financial strictures that befell the royal treasury following the Fourth Syrian War, we may surmise that the sums actually allocated were far below the temples' needs (and expectations).[23] In particular, given that the *syntaxis* financed not only the cult but also the payment of the priestly personnel, the priests' incomes may have been substantially reduced as a consequence.

Moreover, there is evidence that the Ptolemaic administration in Upper Egypt increasingly interfered in the temples' internal management, according to a pattern that had occurred earlier in the temples of Lower and Middle Egypt.[24] Two royal 'commissioners of the temples' (*praktores tôn hierôn*) were sent to Edfu in the 220s to put the temple's finances right following their mismanagement by the temple administrators (*lesoneis*).[25] Ralph Birk has recently shown that the hierarchic structure of the priesthood in the temple of Amon in Thebes was reorganized already by the mid third century: the roles of 'great governor of Thebes' and 'second governor of Thebes' were created, and their incumbents became the highest priestly authorities of the temple. Given that similar roles appeared in Edfu and Denderah in Upper Egypt and in temples located in the Delta, we may safely assume that the reform was implemented, or at least supported, by the Ptolemies.[26]

There can be little doubt that the revolt that started in 207/6 BCE responded to these moves geared to tightening the Ptolemies' control on the southern part of Egypt in the latter half of the third century BCE, and the unfortunate coincidence of these moves with the turmoil and financial

---

[21] Vandorpe (2000b) 176–7; 195–6; and Vandorpe (2005). See also Manning (2003a) 71; and Monson (2012) 165–7.
[22] Vandorpe (2000b) 177, n. 20; 196; Vandorpe (2005) 168–9. The *syntaxis* is first recorded in the Memphis decree of 196 BCE but is not presented as an innovation and therefore must have been created earlier.
[23] Agut-Labordère and Moreno-García (2016) 710–12.
[24] Gorre (2009a); Gorre and Honigman (2014); and Clancier and Gorre in this volume.
[25] Clarysse (2003); Manning (2003b) 83–5. Manning also suggests that the building of the Edfu temple may have been a way of asserting financial control on the temple ([2003b] 85; 162).
[26] See Birk (2016; and 2020).

strictures that followed the Fourth Syrian War only worsened the situation. The authority of the Ptolemies had long been established in Upper Egypt, but until then had prompted no turmoil. Therefore, what sparked the unrest was the change in the way of domination, and not the domination per se, as the established view has it. As in Judea, the temples were particularly affected by the increasing control of the king. However, given that Haronnophris's social background is unknown, we have no positive evidence that the revolt originated in the temples themselves.[27]

3.2 The Catalysts of the Revolt in Judea (ca. 168–ca. 163 BCE)

The question of how to explain the Judean revolt against Antiochus IV is a particularly vexed one, given that the literary sources offer a version designed to legitimize the Hasmonean rise to power, whereas documentary sources are scarce.

It is ultimately uncertain whether or not and to what extent the geopolitical context played any role in the Judean crisis. Because the author of 2 Maccabees claims that in attacking Judea, the Seleucid general Nikanor intended to pay off the war indemnity that the Seleucid dynasty owed to the Romans with the proceeds from the sale of Judean prisoners of war (2 Macc. 8:10), it is widely assumed that the financial clause of the Apamea treaty of 188 BCE impacted the Judean crisis, although how it did so precisely remains uncertain. Moreover, we cannot rule out that the author's allusion to Apamea was a decoy. Both 1 and 2 Maccabees insist time and again that the Seleucids attacked Judea for no reason, and therefore they needed either to erase causal factors altogether (as in 1 Maccabees) or to point to evil purposes – such as the civil war between Jason and Menelaus (not coincidentally, the Maccabees' rivals to power), and lust for booty.[28] Likewise, an inscription advertising Seleucus IV's appointment in 178 BCE of a certain Olympiodoros to 'take care' (*epimeleia*) of the sanctuaries in the satrapy of Coele Syria and Phoenicia drew much attention (*SEG* 57 1838, l. 25), as this appointment was interpreted as an administrative reform aimed at tightening the royal control over the temples' revenues. It was suggested that this reform cast new light on the episode of Heliodorus, Seleucus's vizier, visiting Jerusalem and claiming monies kept in the city's temple, which is told in 2 Maccabees (3:4–4:6).

---

[27] The old view that Haronnophris was of Nubian extraction should be discarded. See Veïsse (forthcoming a).
[28] For a detailed discussion, see Honigman (2014a) 234–6; 284–6. On alleged royal greed, compare 1 Maccabees 1:20–4.

Although the details of the story remain obscure, if we are to believe 2 Maccabees the incident ended with the high priest successfully withstanding the attempts of a high-ranking royal official to seize monies deposited in the temple. But scholars disagree over whether or not this episode had any part in the events that followed, namely Jason's deposing of the Jerusalem high priest and the institution of a *polis* at the beginning of Antiochus IV's reign.[29]

As archaeological data have revealed, at this time Jerusalem was a small town, first and foremost accommodating the temple personnel and various members of the elite, while the material culture in Judea was far less open to foreign importations than neighbouring regions.[30] Due to an uncertainty in translation (2 Macc. 4:9), it is unclear whether the *polis* comprised all the urban population or only a fraction of it.[31] Whatever the case, the description of Jason's deeds in 2 Maccabees 4:7–15 dovetails overstated accusations of impiety – such as the priests allegedly neglecting the temple service to run to the *palaestra*, while Jason is castigated as a fake high priest – with allegations of a more plausible nature.[32] First, we may accept the author's claim that the cultural novelties entailed by the establishment of the gymnasium and ephebic class had a destabilizing social effect, as the sons of (part of) the social elites engaged in what seems to have been regular military instruction.[33] Second, he also insists on the financial repercussions of the city's poliadization. In particular, it seems that the founding of the *polis* entailed overhauling the tax system, presumably at the expense of the non-citizen population, and according to 2 Maccabees 4:11, this included raising the provincial tribute (presumably) by one third relative to the financial settlement that had been negotiated when Antiochus III conquered the region in 200 BCE.[34] In the references to the causes of the crisis in the ensuing chapters of 2 Maccabees, financial issues feature prominently alongside accusations that the high priests appointed by the Seleucid kings were unworthy; whereas the parallel sections of 1 Maccabees dwell on the issue of land confiscations.[35] While the latter are presented as a consequence of a military colony (*katoikia*) being settled in Judea after the revolt, we cannot rule out that the poliadizing had already sparked tensions on the land, since

---

[29] See the contrasting views in Honigman (2014a) 316–44; Eckhardt (2016b); and Muccioli (2019).
[30] Lipschits and Tal (2007) 34.
[31] See the opposed translations and discussions in Kennell (2005); and Doran (2012) ad loc.
[32] On the ideological usefulness of these accusations of impiety, see below, Section 4.1.
[33] See Kennell (2005).
[34] On the meaning of *philanthropa basilika* in 2 Maccabees 4:11, see Honigman (2014a) 264–6.
[35] On the causal analysis of the ancient authors, see Honigman (2014a) 259–95.

swaths of the agricultural territory encircling the city were incorporated into the *polis*.

Altogether, several short-term factors that appear to have played a part in destabilizing the region may be identified, the two most obvious being the creation of the *polis* itself, entailing not only cultural but also (and more decisively) social and economic upheavals; and the ensuing struggle for power among local priestly families when Jason ousted his brother Onias III. Between 175 and 152 BCE, five individuals from four different families (Onias III, his brother Jason, Menelaus, Alcimus, and Jonathan Maccabee) served as high priests. If 2 Maccabees is to be trusted, Jason and Menelaus waged a civil war in Jerusalem in the summer of either 169 or 168 BCE, and the office lay vacant for seven years (159–152 BCE). In addition, 2 Maccabees (4:11; cf. 4:27–8) mentions a sharp rise in the tributes paid to the king. Finally, it seems that the final trigger to the revolt was the rumour that Antiochus IV had died in Egypt (2 Macc. 5:5). The structural and midterm factors behind the uprising are more tricky to determine – a possible administrative reform by Seleucus IV in 178 BCE, perhaps linked to renewed tensions between the Seleucids and the Ptolemies;[36] the consequences of Antiochus III's settlement of 200 BCE (Josephus, *Ant.* 12.138–45), whereby the conqueror granted innovative political and economic powers to the high priest;[37] the consequences of the Apamea treaty; and conceivably various social and cultural undercurrents internal to Judean society that so far elude us.

3.3 Some Common Points

Although the causes in Judea were different from those in the Thebaid,[38] in both cases the revolt occurred at a time of social and economic upheaval. Moreover, it seems that in these two regions some political miscalculation also played its part. In the Thebaid, the revolt responded to administrative steps taken in the last decades of the third century BCE aimed at tightening the royal control over the region. On the face of it, these steps were not dissimilar to the reforms that Ptolemy II Philadelphus had carried out in Lower and Middle Egypt in the 270s and 260s BCE. But whereas Ptolemy II's reforms were implemented without incurring any particular opposition in these regions, in the Thebaid their unfortunate chronological coincidence with the Fourth Syrian War ultimately prompted outright rebellion.

---

[36] See Sartre (2014). [37] See Honigman et al. (2017); and Honigman (2021).
[38] With the provision stated above, n. 8.

In founding a *polis* in Jerusalem, Jason may have sought to make up for his lack of dynastic legitimacy by strengthening his symbolic and practical association with the king, but his calculation proved double-edged.

4 Ideological Discourses: Between Inherited and Reinvented Traditions

Although the events preceding the revolts differ widely, responses from the central power tended to begin with a similar (military) response, and therefore at this stage some structurally significant comparisons may be made. In our view, this is also true for the ideological constructs through which the respective ruling kings and rebel leaders legitimized their actions. In short, alongside their evident distinctions, the pre-Achaemenid royal ideologies in Egypt and the Near East (including Judea) shared certain affinities, such as the definition of royal legitimacy in terms of the king's guaranteeing cosmic order ('justice,' Egyptian Maat, and Hebrew *ṣedeq*) on earth. Moreover, both Egypt and Judea shared a history as former parts of the Achaemenid empire, giving them a potential ground for a common heritage informing both memories of the past and present ideologies of kingship in Egypt and Judea. Hence the interest in the different ways in which each side constructed its legitimizing discourse in the course of the revolts, respectively. In particular, while it comes as no surprise that the respective leaders of the revolts reinvented rather than revived their respective native traditions about kingship, the resulting ideologies took very different paths. Likewise, the corresponding responses of the kings are notably contrasting. We will dwell on these ideological aspects first, starting with Judea, given that the ideological discourses of the rebels[39] (or at least their descendants, the Hasmoneans) are amply documented by the literary sources.

4.1 Judea

4.1.1 How the Hasmoneans Memorialized the Revolt

Because the Judean revolt that began under Antiochus IV eventually led to the emergence and rise of a local dynasty, and because the literary works advocating the official version of these events were later canonized by the Christian Fathers, we have first-hand evidence regarding the ideological

---

[39] The label of 'rebels' is, of course, ideologically loaded. We employ it here because it is convenient, but we bear in mind that the said rebels never described themselves in this way.

discourse behind the actions of the Judean rebels – or more accurately, that which crystallized under (presumably) John Hyrcanus. The two books of the Maccabees illustrate how the Hasmoneans transformed a specific episode of the revolt – namely the interruption of the sacrifices in the Jerusalem temple for two years and their eventual resumption – into the dynasty's founding myth. To this end, the story of this event was cast into the stock narrative pattern of a king founding a temple, a trope which in the Judean tradition served to proclaim both the legitimacy of a specific ruler and that of his specific form of rule.

This narrative pattern was originally devised as a vehicle of the royal ideology to validate the claim that the king was elected by a divine patron, and it spread across Mesopotamia, northern Syria (Ugarit), and Judah/Judea.[40] In substance, according to it the deity chose the man who would build His or Her 'house' (that is, temple), and in return the deity built the chosen one's house (that is, royal dynasty). In the Judean literary tradition, the pattern informs all the texts describing the construction of the Tabernacle in the desert; Solomon's building of the temple; its reconstruction in Persian times; the story of Hanukkah in 1 and 2 Maccabees (1 Macc. 3:1–9:22; 2 Macc. 4:7–13:26; cf. also; and 2 Macc. 14:1–15:36); and Josephus's description of Herod's rebuilding of the temple in the *Antiquities* (Joseph. *AJ* 15.380–425). It also shapes accounts of the construction of other royal monuments, such as the story of the rebuilding of Jerusalem's walls in the Book of Nehemiah, and that of Simon building his palace in 1 Maccabees (13:1–16:22).

Traditionally, stories of temple building came in handy for usurpers unable to rely on the argument of lineage as a source of legitimacy. In these cases, the accounts described at length how the deposed predecessor had neglected his duties toward the deity and allowed His or Her temple to fall into ruin – this was evidence of his wickedness, and hence justification for being ousted. This *topos* can easily be traced in both 1 and 2 Maccabees, respectively targeting Jason and Menelaus (2 Macc. 4:6–5:26), and Alcimus (1 Macc. 7:5–25; 9:1, 54–7), that is, the three high priests who ruled between Onias III and Jonathan – the first member of the Hasmonean family to hold this position.[41]

Finally, with the demise of native kingship in Judea, the use of the narrative pattern continued as a means to support the legitimacy of a ruler, regardless of the nature of his power, and the legitimacy of whatever social

---

[40] This overview summarizes Honigman (2014a) 95–182. For further bibliography, see there.
[41] For a detailed analysis, see Honigman (2014a) 197–228.

order he embodied until that moment. To this effect, narrative details were adjusted to suit each new circumstance. In both 1 and 2 Maccabees, the pattern is duplicated as a means to dramatize the Hasmonean dynasty simultaneously holding the two titles of high priest and king. To achieve this 1 Maccabees juxtaposes the story of Judas's refounding of the temple (3:1–9:22) with that of Simon building his palace (13:1–16:22), whereas 2 Maccabees complemented the foundational story of Judas refounding the temple (4:7–13:26a, being the etiological myth of the Jewish Hanukkah festival) with a second episode of a similar nature (14:1–15:36). In this way, the traditional narrative pattern was revisited to legitimize an unprecedented form of power – the same person being both king and high priest.

4.1.2 *The Image of the Seleucid Kings in 1 and 2 Maccabees*

Although in both 1 and 2 Maccabees Antiochus IV is depicted as a wicked king, neither work expresses a sweeping condemnation of foreign domination per se. Actually, the way the king is portrayed belongs to a well-established literary tradition that defines the nature of proper kingship and governance by means of portrayals of historical kings, in which the biographical details were adjusted in order to 'retrofit' a given figure to match archetypes of either righteous or wicked kings. Both in 2 Maccabees and 1 Maccabees the life of Judas Maccabee, as the temple refounder, is heavily embroidered, not to say mythologized, while the brass-tacks depiction of Antiochus Epiphanes is part of this method of memorializing a chosen figure.[42]

At the same time, the negative impact of Antiochus's portrayal is counterbalanced in different ways in the two works. In 2 Maccabees, the narrative pattern of founding the temple was primarily exploited to delegitimize the rival high priests, that is, the local competitors, and only secondarily Antiochus IV himself. Moreover, Antiochus V put an end to the first phase of the Judean crisis by restoring the Judeans' institutions and control over their temple, and the dossier of letters announcing the new settlement are duly copied in 2 Maccabees (11:16–38).

In 1 Maccabees, the negative portrayal of the king in the section narrating Judas's life is limited to the characterizing of Antiochus, specifically. In contrast, as Boris Chrubasik has argued, the sections covering Jonathan's and Simon's biographies in 1 Maccabees offer a complex picture of the relations between the Judean strongmen and the Seleucids.[43] The author carefully recorded the occasions in which Seleucid kings and pretenders

---

[42] On Judas, see n. 14 above.   [43] Chrubasik (2021).

acknowledged Jonathan and Simon as high priests and moreover eagerly advertized all the administrative titles and honors granted to them.[44] As Chrubasik noted, had the author of 1 Maccabees so wanted, he could have omitted any mention of Jonathan's and Simon's personal relations with the Seleucids. The fact that he chose to emphasize them is evidence that the Maccabees recognized the Seleucid dynasty as the very source of their legitimacy.

4.2 The Thebaid

In contrast with Judea, we have no narrative from the Theban rebels.[45]

4.2.1 The Side of the Thebans

In the absence of a proper narrative, we may nevertheless gain some sense of how the rebel leaders perceived their status from their assumption of the title of 'pharaoh' and also from the names by which they were known, which (as their parallel linguistic forms suggest) were self-styled regal names and not their birthnames. So, both 'Haronnophris' ($Ḥr$-wn-nfr, 'Horus-Onnophris') and 'Chaonnophris' ($'nḫ$-wn-nfr, 'Onnophris lives' or 'May Onnophris live') include the component Onnophris (Wn-nfr) – an epithet of the god Osiris – which since the Late Period had become the model of kingship.[46] By adopting these names, Haronnophris and Chaonnophris (assuming that they were two distinct persons) chose to reference an ideal past and in this way to counter-challenge the Ptolemies' legitimacy as pharaohs.[47] If we are right in believing that actually these two names were used in succession by a single person, the shift from 'Horus-Onnophris' to 'Chaonnophris' in 199 BCE incorporates the oblique comment that despite the early successes of the Ptolemaic counterattack in the summer of 199 BCE, the pharaoh was still alive and ready to defend his position.[48] (Even if the two names indicate a succession, the

---

[44] For the main details, see the overview, Section 2.2 above.
[45] The so-called apocalyptic texts, which are often cited as a case of 'resistance literature,' are not relevant to our concern. The *Oracle of the Lamb* and the *Demotic Chronicle* relate to the period prior to the Ptolemaic era. While the *Oracle of the Potter* seems to display an anti-Alexandrian slant, nothing in it suggests a connection with the Theban revolt. On these texts, see Felber (2002); Koenen (2002); and Chauveau (2017).
[46] Clarysse (1978) 252–3; and Coulon (2010).
[47] Consequently, they also challenged the link established in priestly circles between the Ptolemaic kings and the god Osiris during the third century. See Coulon (2005); and Preys (2015).
[48] See Veïsse (forthcoming b). Abydos was besieged during the summer of 199 BCE, and the Ptolemaic forces temporarily reconquered Thebes at the end of this year.

implications are much the same: the first 'rebel pharaoh' Haronnophris may have died during the counterattack, but the sovereignty remained.)[49]

The assumption of the title of pharaoh by the leader of the Theban revolt is reasonable evidence that he contested the legitimacy of the Ptolemies altogether: there could only be a single pharaoh, sacred mediator between mankind and the gods. Hence, the name chosen by Haronnophris in 205 BCE – which programmatically referred to Onnophris/Osiris – indicates his claim to restore rightful kingship over Egypt. Further evidence of this 'return to the past' may be found in the new administration set up as early as 205 BCE, which not only used the Egyptian language but adopted such archaizing phrases as 'scribe of the king' (*sḫ nsw*) instead of the more modern term 'scribe of [the] Pharaoh' (*sḫ pr-'3*).[50] At the same time, even though his innovations were not as far-reaching as those of the Hasmoneans, this Haronnophris introduced some selective alterations to the pharaonic tradition. In the Demotic notarial contracts dating from his reign, his name is associated with the epithets of 'beloved by Isis, beloved by Amonrasonther.' In Demotic contracts, no epithets referring to Egyptian gods were ever used, neither in the days of Ptolemaic or Persian rule, nor in the Saitic Period, when the pharaohs were still Egyptian. Therefore, it seems that Haronnophris took over the Ptolemaic practice of adding royal epithets (such as 'Philopator' and 'Epiphanes') in the dating formulas of documents, adapting this custom to his own needs. But although the invented tradition of the Hasmoneans accepted that Judean rulers were perforce subordinate to an imperial overlord, Haronnophris staunchly upheld the pharaonic ideology of exclusive and independent rule. This firm ideological stance also explains why the response of the Ptolemaic kings to the uprising markedly differed from that of the Seleucids.

4.3 A Common Trope: The Guardian of Divine Order and His Havoc-Wreaking Opponent

Before venturing an interpretation of why the separate ideological constructions of the Theban and Judean rebel leaders differed so greatly, let us

---

[49] On the simultaneous adoptions of the name Chaonnophris on the one hand and of Ptolemy V's epithets *Epiphanes* and *Eucharistos* on the other as a clue to an ideological war between the two sides, see Uggetti ('Les archives bilingues de Totoès et de Tatéhathyris,' PhD dissertation, École Pratique des Hautes Études, Paris).

[50] Depauw (2006).

examine a common trope of the period to establish how these differences emerged from a representation of power which, albeit with local variants, was basically common to the entire ancient Near East, including Egypt. The trope in question is that the legitimate ruler guarantees divine order on earth, and hence his adversary (or predecessor, when the speaker is a usurper) promotes chaos. From our sources we can see that the comparison switches sides – in Egypt the wicked are the rebels, while in Judea the wrongdoers are the king and the rival high priests (Jason, Menelaus, and Alcimus) – but this switch merely strengthens rather than weakens the notion that this was a common trope in the definition of power.

The source for Egypt is the Second Philae decree, promulgated on 6 September 186 BCE to celebrate the defeat of Chaonnophris a few days earlier.[51] As one might expect, the picture here is the opposite of the one suggested by the names Haronnophris and Chaonnophris. Here the ruling king Ptolemy V is depicted as the legitimate pharaoh who by crushing the revolt and restoring order in Egypt in accordance with the will of the Egyptian gods re-enacts the mythical battle between Horus and the supporters of Seth. Logically, the rebels and their leader are painted as impious individuals who slew, plundered, and indiscriminately desecrated all that is revered – in other words, they turned the world into chaos. In the Hieroglyphic version, the name *'nḫ-wn-nfr* (Chaonnophris) is transmogrified into *ḫr-wn-nfr*, whereby the symbol of life *'nḫ* is replaced with the phoneme *ḫr* as a way of branding the rebel as an impostor.[52]

In 2 Maccabees, the roles are distributed according to two intertwined scripts, both elaborating on the notion that the legitimate king builds (or rebuilds) the temple. As noted earlier, in the persecution accounts, Antiochus IV is depicted as an archetypical wicked king doing the opposite of what a good king is supposed to do – plundering the temple, disrupting the sacrifices, and compelling the Judean to infringe divine law.[53] In 2 Maccabees, a complementary narrative thread targets the rival high priests. While Onias III is depicted as an ideal high priest, Jason deposes him, Menelaus assassinates him, and eventually the late Onias III appears to Judas Maccabee in a dream and acknowledges him as his successor. Likewise, the gymnasium that Jason established in Jerusalem is depicted as a kind of 'anti-temple' – allegedly, the priests neglect the cult's service to run to the *palaestra*. Menelaus steals the holy vessels (which in the Jerusalem temple held the same symbolic importance as divine statues elsewhere) and later on even assists Antiochus IV as the king plundered the

---

[51] See n. 7 above. [52] Vittmann (2005) 210–11. [53] Weitzman (2004); and Honigman (2014b).

temple, whereas Judas Maccabee notably devotes himself to restoring the temple.[54]

5 The Impact of Territory, History, and Assumed Heritages

These parallel (albeit, admittedly, not identical) ways of conceptualizing the legitimate and illegitimate ruler by referring to the notions of divine order and cosmic chaos highlights a major difference in the respective representations of power associated with the Theban and Judean revolts: the discourses of exclusive power shared by the king and the rebel leaders in Egypt offer a cogent contrast with the notion of indirect rule within the imperial setting of Judea. Although the approach tabled here is admittedly speculative, in this section we aim to fathom which factors contributed to producing these opposing discourses and will focus on three major ingredients involved: territory and space; history (in particular, to what degree dynastic struggles influenced the unfolding of the revolts); and the selective promotion of cultural memories.

5.1 Judea: Persian Heritage and the Practice of Indirect Rule

5.1.1 The Seleucid Side

The successive settlements concluded by Antiochus V in early 163 BCE and Demetrius II in 141 BCE show the governing Seleucid culture adapting with a certain ease to the changing circumstances. In the year 163 the king basically granted a return to the previous status quo, and this settlement was similar to those negotiated with cities that had first rebelled and then been recaptured.[55] In 141 Demetrius II ordered the withdrawal of the Seleucid troops from the Jerusalem citadel, granting Simon not only exemptions from tributes and all taxes but also the right to uphold the strongholds that the Judeans had built, in exchange for his allegiance (1 Macc. 13:36–42). Simon started his own era (ibid.) and had a local assembly acknowledge his powers as high priest, *strategos* and *ethnarchês* (1 Macc. 14:25–49).

In sum, although the Seleucids made protracted attempts to reconquer the region through military means whenever circumstances allowed, a regime of indirect rule was progressively established. This method of governing ideally suited to the sheer extension of the imperial territory

---

[54] Honigman (2014a) 197–228.   [55] Ma (2013a; and 2020). See above, n. 14.

proved a precious resort whenever the political or geopolitical situation became adverse.[56]

But while this picture of local aspirations to autonomy offset by the power struggle among claimants to the Seleucid throne is familiar, the case study of Judea is particularly interesting because it is difficult – even fruitless – to try to pinpoint precisely when the state of open revolt ended, and when more fluid relations between local leaders and kings were restored in Judea, whereby local leaders aspired to as much autonomy as possible, and kings tightened and slackened their domination as circumstances required.

The author of 1 Maccabees chronicles in detail how in 151–150 BCE, Demetrius I and Alexander Balas outbid each other in their attempts to win over Jonathan's support. For his part, Demetrius granted Jonathan the right to recruit troops and – of course – to become his ally (1 Macc. 10:6), while letting him take up residence in Jerusalem and fortify the city (1 Macc. 10:10), whereas Balas appointed Jonathan high priest and *philos*, and – of course – urged him 'to take [his] side and keep friendship with [him]' (1 Macc. 10:18–20).[57]

5.1.2 The Side of the Hasmoneans

At the same time, as noted above, the fact that the author of 1 Maccabees chronicled with such details the occasions in which the various Seleucid contenders honoured the Maccabean brothers shows how the former were able to play off local rivals against each other, just as local leaders played off the Seleucid contenders, eliciting the need for each successful local contender (successively, in Judea, Jonathan and Simon) to advertize his personal ties with the king.[58] Moreover, there are grounds to believe that Jonathan and Simon, respectively, waged war basically as Seleucid mercenaries (albeit of dubious faithfulness) and not (or not only) on their own accounts.[59]

The bearings of the regime of indirect rule (or autonomy) are particularly interesting to examine when it comes to the period of the Hasmonean dynasty. Not only did the Hasmoneans introduce singular innovations by

---

[56] Chrubasik (2016).
[57] Cf. the motives attributed to Demetrius in 1 Macc. 10:3–5. A similar scenario was repeated in the days of the struggle between Demetrius II and Trypho (1 Macc. 11:28–36). Alliances could work the other way around, as the episode narrated in 1 Macc. 16:11–18 shows.
[58] See Chrubasik (2016; and 2021). Eckhardt (2016a) cogently argued that the account of 1 Maccabees obscured the role of rivals to the Maccabees, who had similar access to Seleucid pretenders. On contenders, see, in particular, 1 Maccabees 16:11–24.
[59] On Jonathan, see Josephus, *Ant.* 13.148–53. See Berlin and Herbert (2015).

assuming the dual title of high priest and king jointly, but the situation whereby a king was subject to another king in Judea was equally innovative.[60]

The juxtaposition of clashing ideological discourses in 1 Maccabees reflects the tensions, as John Hyrcanus struggled to reconcile two patently incompatible sources of legitimacy. On the one hand, the narrative template of the ruler building the temple stemmed from the days of native kingship and was devised to promote the ideology whereby the king's legitimacy derived from divine will itself. In 1 Maccabees (and 2 Maccabees) this ideological undertow comes to the fore in the story of Judas Maccabee and his brothers refounding the Jerusalem temple. On the other hand, the biography of Jonathan trumpets the honours received from Seleucid pretenders as his main fount of legitimacy. Simon's life neatly combines these two discourses.[61]

Ever since Persian times, Judea had been part of an empire, and the Judean literary works written in this period (such as the prophetic books of Haggai and Zechariah 1–8) clearly show that the Judean scribes were quite comfortable acknowledging the Persian king as their own.[62] Moreover, works referring to the Persian era but composed in Hellenistic times (such as the Septuagint book of 1 Esdras) prove that the memory of the Achaemenid dynasty (and hence of the imperial structure itself) remained positive.[63] Ultimately, 1 Maccabees does not break with this tradition – it actually elaborates things further so as to accommodate the Hasmoneans' royal ambitions.

5.2 *The Pharaonic Ideology of the Exclusive Ruler*

By contrast, in the case of the Theban revolt nothing close to this model of indirect rule was even considered – either by the rebels or by the Ptolemies.

---

[60] Although, of course, this pattern must have been familiar from the title of 'King of Kings' used by the Achaemenids, and from the existence of vassal kings elsewhere in the Seleucid empire. See Chrubasik (2016).
  According to Josephus (*Ant.* 13.299–300), Hyrcanus further claimed that he was a prophet. The association between high priesthood and prophecy was all but traditional in Judea (in traditional terms, these functions were opposed), let alone in combination with the military powers of the *ethnarchês* or king.
[61] Simon's building of the ruler's palace is associated with his purifying of the Akra, the Seleucid citadel that watched over the temple, and this deed is explicitly depicted as completing Judas's purifying of the temple. See Honigman (2014a) 160–9.
[62] In particular, the dating system refers to the reigning years of the Persian kings.
[63] The precise date of LXX 1 Esdras is debated, but there is a wide consensus that the book is Hellenistic. Theories about the date of the Masoretic book of Ezra-Nehemiah range from Persian times to the Hasmoneans.

In contrast with the Seleucids, there was no way the Ptolemies would ever tolerate the emergence of local dynasts in Upper Egypt, owing to the territorial organization of Egypt and because of the entrenched native ideology of how power should work. The control of southern Egypt was crucial to the Ptolemies for maintaining the economic interdependence between Upper and Lower Egypt, and allowed access to the eastern coastline and the western oases, along with control of the border with the Meroitic kingdom.[64] Likewise, the pharaonic ideology of command was exclusive, ruling out the notion that a pharaoh could ever countenance another pharaoh.[65] Had they accepted the presence of Haronnophris in Upper Egypt – as the Seleucids did with the Hasmoneans in Judea – the Ptolemies would have irremediably undermined their legitimacy as pharaohs in the minds of their Egyptian subjects. Ultimately, in Egypt the legacy of Persian times was different from how it was perceived in Judea: while the Judean elites managed the ideological complexities of living without a king in an imperial setting, in Egypt the Achaemenids (like the Ptolemies) strove to be acknowledged as pharaohs.[66] In sum, location and the ruling ideology were major factors determining the campaigns of re-conquest promoted by the Ptolemies, who would not settle for less than the complete suppression of the rebellion. From the Ptolemaic perspective, there could be no alternative. The same holds true with Haronnophris: even though his revolt led to a *de facto* secession of the Thebaid, his declared aim cannot have been only that. Incidentally, had the Theban revolt occurred in the midst of dynastic struggles, as in Judea, we may reasonably assume that the Ptolemies would have handled it in a substantially similar way. Because of this ideology of the exclusive ruler, no Ptolemaic contender to power in Alexandria would have been able – or willing – to acknowledge a second pharaoh at his side to advance his struggle.

5.3 The Distinct Status of the External Possessions of the Ptolemies

The impact of territorial organization, history, and inherited representations of power comes to the fore not only in the different ways the

---

[64] During the revolt, the Meroitic kings extended their domination northwards, and Nubian troops joined Chaonnophris's side in the final battle of 186 BCE.

[65] In the course of Egyptian history, there were periods during which different dynasts assumed the title of 'pharaoh' simultaneously, but this does not mean that they acknowledged each other.

[66] In contrast with the short-lived Assyrian domination (first decades of the seventh century BCE), the Persian domination was not perceived by the Egyptians in an entirely negative way, even though the two invasions tended to be conflated to shape an 'anti-Persian' memory at the time of the Ptolemies. See Agut-Labordère (2017); and Gorre (2017).

Seleucids and Ptolemies responded to the revolts respectively, but also in how the Ptolemies handled Egypt, on the one hand, and their so-called external possessions, on the other. While the unity of Egypt was non-negotiable, the Ptolemies in the third century tolerated the emergence of local dynasts such as Ptolemy of Telmessos in Asia Minor[67] and grudgingly adapted to the secession of Cyrenaica under Magas.[68] Moreover, in the second century the Ptolemies used Cyrenaica and Cyprus as assets to placate contenders in the context of the ongoing dynastic quarrels.[69] Following the struggle for power between Ptolemy VI and Ptolemy VIII in Egypt (164–163 BCE), Ptolemy VIII was granted Cyrenaica in 163 BCE as a means toward reconciliation; likewise, in 114/3 BCE Ptolemy X was made king of Cyprus, probably to ward off possible conflicts with his brother Ptolemy IX. The situation was different when Ptolemy IX took Cyprus by force around 105 BCE, in retaliation for having been replaced on the Egyptian throne in 107 BCE by Ptolemy X. Nevertheless, his domination on the island eventually helped reach a status quo between the two from 101 to 88 BCE. In conclusion, it appears that all these territorial concessions were made exclusively for the benefit of the closed group of members of the Ptolemaic dynasty – in neat contrast with how things evolved in the Seleucid realm.[70]

6 The Aftermath of the Settlements

The respective responses of the Seleucids and the Ptolemies to the rebellions had lasting consequences over the relations between these regions and the ruling dynasties that followed the respective quelling of the revolts – the Ptolemaic reconquest of the Thebaid in 186, and Demetrius II's acknowledgement of the Judeans' autonomy under Simon's leadership in 141 BCE. In Egypt, it is particularly worth following the behaviour of the population in the Thebaid in the era

---

[67] See Capdetrey (2007) 122–3, and Bennett (online, 2001–13), with further bibliography.
[68] See Bennett (online, 2001–13), with further bibliography; and Laronde (1987), 361–2, 379–80. Magas was the firstborn son of Queen Berenice I. He was appointed governor of Cyrenaica by Ptolemy I around 300 BCE and proclaimed himself independent at the beginning of Ptolemy II's reign. After his plan to wage war against Magas in the 270s fell through because of his Gallic mercenaries' mutiny (Pausanias 1.7), there is no evidence that Ptolemy II ever intended to reconquer Cyrenaica by force. Egypt and Cyrenaica were eventually united again through the wedding of Ptolemy III and Berenice II, Magas's daughter.
[69] See Vandorpe (2010) 170.
[70] As the son of King Lysimachus and Arsinoe II, Ptolemy of Telmessos was the nephew and then stepson of Ptolemy II, whereas Magas of Cyrene was Ptolemy II's half-brother.

of the dynastic struggles that started in the context of Antiochus IV's invasion of the country in 170/169 BCE and reached its climax with the civil war between Ptolemy VIII Euergetes II and Cleopatra II in the 130s. Whereas, as we saw, the dynastic struggles in the Seleucid empire that started shortly after Antiochus V's death in 162 BCE overlapped with the rise of the Hasmoneans to power, and the autonomy granted to the Judean dynasts did not end their subordination to the imperial state.

6.1 The Thebaid

Whereas Judea was eventually granted autonomy, the Ptolemaic authority was reinstated in Upper Egypt and even enhanced after the end of the revolt.[71] In the decades that followed its suppression, new military camps – mainly of native soldiers – were established south of Thebes in Hermonthis, Crocodilopolis, Pathyris, and Latopolis, and the number of royal banks, granaries, and Greek notarial offices gradually increased. The impact of this process of integration was keenly felt. It is striking that no major uprising occurred in the Thebaid in the second century BCE, even though the dynastic struggles generated a potentially favourable context for troubles to resume.[72]

The city of Thebes itself, which was the primary seat of Haronnophris's power, patently refrained from taking sides during the civil war that pitted Cleopatra II and Ptolemy VIII Euergetes II against each other in the late 130s BCE.[73] A striking evidence to its neutrality is provided by the quick and seemingly erratic pace at which dates referring to Cleopatra II and Euergetes II, respectively, alternated in Theban documents in the second half of the year 131 BCE: Euergetes on 26 July, Cleopatra on 4 and 15 October, Euergetes on 10 November, Cleopatra on 13, 18, and 22 November, and then Euergetes permanently from 4 December.[74] Papyrus *UPZ* II 217 in particular, dated 22 November 131 BCE, attests that troops acknowledging Cleopatra's authority were stationed in Thebes

---

[71] Vandorpe (2011; 2014); Vandorpe and Waebens (2009) 38–50.
[72] Although troubles are documented in the Panopolite in the 160s and again in the 130s, the events can by no means be compared with the Great Theban Revolt, either in scale or in scope. Furthermore, they affected the northernmost part of the Thebaid and not the Theban area itself, which had been the core of the revolt in Haronnophris's days. The so-called 'pharaoh Harsiesis' who allegedly took control of Thebes in 131 is a historiographical myth; see Veïsse (2011).
[73] See Lanciers (2020).   [74] See Veïsse (2004) 50–1 (add *O. Louvre* n°73 for 4 December 131).

at that time.⁷⁵ Despite this military presence in the city, though, the content of the documents dating from July to December 131 BCE shows that the business of daily life continued as usual, suggesting that the struggle for the control of Thebes was actually taking place elsewhere, and not in the city.

The attitude of Pathyris and Hermonthis, located respectively around twelve and twenty-five miles south of Thebes, confirms rather than invalidates our suggestion that the crushing of the Theban revolt in 186 BCE was final. At the early stage of the Great Theban Revolt, Pathyris had acknowledged Haronnophris's authority.⁷⁶ Between 165 and 161 BCE, a military camp subsidiary to that of Crocodilopolis was created and many Egyptian soldiers were recruited as *misthophoroi* (soldiers receiving a pay, not land slots), most of them receiving the pseudo-ethnic of *Persian of the descent (tes epigones)*.⁷⁷ During the civil war of the 130s BCE the city remained loyal to Euergetes II, whereas the Hermonthites stood for Cleopatra. In a well-known private letter dated to 15 January 130 BCE, Esthladas, the son of the cavalry-officer Dryton, informed his parents, who lived in Pathyris, of the wide-scale offensive that was being planned by Euergetes II's forces, under the command of the general (*strategos*) of the Thebaid Paos, against the people of Hermonthis for the month of Tybi (23 January to 21 February):

> As I often write you to be of good heart and to look after yourself until things get back to normal, it would be good if you put heart into yourself and our family. For it has come to our ears that in the month of Tybi Paos [the *strategos* of the Thebaid] is sailing up the Nile with sufficient forces to suppress the rabble in Hermonthis [*tous en Hermonthei ochlous*] [and] that he will treat them as rebels [*ôs apostatais*].⁷⁸

Were we to base our conclusion on this testimony alone, we might deduce that a new 'Egyptian uprising' had recurred in the Thebaid in the wake of the civil war between Cleopatra II and Euergetes II. In truth, however, the people in Hermonthis supported Cleopatra II, as is clearly shown by a legal document (a loan agreement) drawn up in the city ('in Hermonthis of the Thebaid') and dated to her third year as 'Queen Cleopatra Philometor

---

⁷⁵ The document is a royal oath by which one Demetrius provides a guarantee to a certain Ptolemaios, recently incorporated into the military administration as secretary (*grammateus*) of the 'infantrymen of Diospolis.' The oath is taken in the name of 'queen Cleopatra *thea Philometor Soteira*.'
⁷⁶ See Chaufray and Wegner (2016). The demotic papyri P.BM EA 10486 and P.Ryl.Dem. 32 were written in Haronnophris's name on 27 September and between 12 November and 11 December 204 BCE, respectively.
⁷⁷ Vandorpe (2008; 2014).   ⁷⁸ P.Dryton 36, ll. 2–12, trans. K. Vandorpe.

Soteira' on 29 October 130 BCE.[79] Apart from the protocol in the name of Cleopatra II, the main point of interest lies in rare and meaningful titles borne by some of the protagonists. Both Dionysios, the brother and guardian (*kurios*) of Isidora, the lender, and one of the witnesses belong to the 'brothers cavalry settlers' (*adelphoi katoikoi hippeis*),[80] a military title otherwise attested in one or two other documents only.[81] The five other witnesses are labelled as *tetartomeritai*, once again a rare term that apparently designates soldiers receiving extra salary.[82]

The title of 'brother cavalry settler' was likely a distinction awarded for loyalty. Not only does it appear precisely in one of the few documents dated according to Cleopatra II's reign, but it continues a policy implemented by Ptolemy VI, who in the 160s BCE granted the title of 'relative cavalry settler' (*sungenes katoikos hippeus*) to particularly deserving soldiers.[83] The salary bonus which the five *tetartomeritai* were granted may be explained as a reward in a context of war.[84] These various recipients of Cleopatra II's gratitude must have been members of the local garrison, since one of them is the brother of the woman acting as lender: we may infer that he belonged to a family already settled in Hermonthis.[85] The eminent services that had been recompensed by the queen are probably linked to the wide-scale offensive launched by Euergetes II against Hermonthis at the beginning of 130 BCE, under the command of the *strategos* Paos. Obviously, the offensive was a failure because Cleopatra was still recognized in the town by late October 130 BCE. However, Ptolemy's authority was ultimately reinstated, before January 127 BCE by the latest, and probably well before.[86]

We may ask why Hermonthis stood by Cleopatra, whereas Pathyris – and presumably also Crocodilopolis, since the military camp of Pathyris was a branch of that of Crocodilopolis – remained loyal to Ptolemy VIII.[87]

---

[79] P.Bad. 2.2. It was in Hermonthis that the queen's authority was acknowledged for the longest period: at that time (October 130 BCE) the few other cities in Upper and Middle Egypt which had rallied the queen (Edfu, Elephantine, and Heracleopolite nome) had already acknowledged Euergetes II's authority.
[80] Mooren (1975), nos. 252 and 253.
[81] SB XX 14083 and *BGU* VI 1285; the first text is dubious. See Scheuble-Reiter (2012) 78.
[82] See Van't Dack (1988) 61–3; and Vandorpe (2014) 118 and n. 36.
[83] See Scheuble-Reiter (2012) 78–9.
[84] The five *tetartomeritai* may have also belonged to the group of the *adelphoi*, see Mooren (1975) nos. 254–8; Vandorpe (2014) 118 and n. 36.
[85] We may surmise that the borrower, Ptolemaios son of Apollonios, also belonged to the garrison and, based on his ethnic ('Persian of the descent'), that he was of Egyptian descent, despite his name.
[86] BGU III 993.
[87] On the link between the camps of Pathyris and Crocodilopolis, see Vandorpe and Waebens (2009) 36.

Various clues suggest that the answer lies in the protracted local feuds between the three cities:[88] various papyri document an ongoing legal dispute between the priests of Hermonthis and those of Pathyris about the ownership of a plot of land, a quarrel that lasted at least from 181/0 and still remained unsettled in 148 BCE. Despite various legal recourses on both sides, throughout this period people from the two cities engaged in mutual skirmishes a number of times.[89] In September 123 BCE – that is, after Cleopatra II and Ptolemy VIII had reconciled – a full-fledged local war broke out between Hermonthis and Crocodilopolis, pitting the two garrisons against each other – namely, no less than 500 infantry and 20 cavalry on the Crocodilopolite side, and 40 cavalry and an unknown number of infantry on the Hermonthite one.[90] Hints of hostility between the Pathyrites and the Hermonthites can still be detected in a letter of 103 BCE addressed by an officer of the troops of Pathyris to his fellow soldiers, which mentions the 'impious inhabitants of Hermonthis.'[91]

In light of these details, it seems that the main reason for the Hermonthites' decision to rally behind Cleopatra II during the civil war was continuing poor relations with their neighbours in Pathyris and Crocodilopolis, who remained faithful to Ptolemy VIII. While in sociostructural terms this scenario of political rallying driven by local rivalry has parallels in specific regions of the Seleucid empire – such as Judea and Phoenicia – in the context of the Syrian wars, in the present case of Upper Egypt, the engagement of local cities in a dynastic war seems to evince that in the aftermath of the Great Theban Revolt the region had been lured deep into the political stand-offs of the Ptolemaic kingdom. It seems that the same holds true for the 'Theban uprising' of 88 BCE, which broke out at the time of the war between Ptolemy IX and Ptolemy X.[92] By this token, we may understand the expedition of Ptolemy IX against Thebes in this year as aimed against local supporters of Ptolemy X, paralleling Paos's expedition against Cleopatra II's supporters in Hermonthis.[93]

---

[88] For an overview of the bad relationship of the Pathyrites and Crocodilopolites with the Hermonthites during the second century, see Van't Dack et al. (1989) 42–3; and further Veïsse (2004) 60–1.
[89] P.Lond. VII 2188 + P.Lond. VII, p. 275. See Monson (2012) 133–4.
[90] Chrest.Wilck. II. Several people were killed during the fight. A demotic papyrus from the Louvre refers either to the same events or to another clash between Hermonthites and Pathyrites. See Devauchelle, de Cenival and Pezin (2018); and Chauveau (2019).
[91] C.Jud.Syr.Eg. 1 (29 June 103).   [92] Agut-Labordère and Moreno García (2016) 725.
[93] For an overview of the events of 88 BCE, see Van't Dack et al. (1989) 146–9; and Veïsse (forthcoming b).

6.2 Judea

Relations between the Hasmoneans and the Seleucids after Demetrius II withdrew his troops from Judea in 141 were typical of the rapport between the Seleucid kings and local dynasts, which fluctuated according to the shifting circumstances. For instance, shortly after John Hyrcanus succeeded Simon in 135/4, Antiochus VII Sidetes besieged Jerusalem for up to a year, seemingly to curb the Hasmoneans' growing ascendency. When Hyrcanus eventually surrendered, he was compelled to pay an indemnity for several Greek cities that his father had conquered, to offer up hostages, to demolish the city walls, and to accompany Antiochus VII in his campaign against the Parthians.[94] The alliance between Antiochus VII and Hyrcanus is reminiscent of the coalitions sealed between Seleucid kings and Greek cities or other dynasts. A royal mint was opened in Jerusalem, but between 134 and 131 it issued only coins in Antiochus VII's name, and not until either 129 (Antiochus VII's death) or 125 (Demetrius II's death) did it start issuing coinage bearing Hyrcanus's title. These successive minting policies indicate that Judea's status of autonomy was temporarily suspended but was reinstated at the earliest opportunity. Considering its strategic patterns of diffusion, the Hasmonean coinage has been plausibly defined as 'a political statement of a new ethnic power.'[95]

7 Conclusions

Although the details differ, the Theban and Judean revolts offer valid points of comparison because of certain basic similarities. First, both rebellions erupted at a time of deep social and political upheavals, which likely catalyzed them in the first place; second, the ideology of power in both regions was that the king himself was the supreme guardian of the cosmic order; and lastly, contingent factors such as miscalculations (the unfortunate timing of the reforms in Upper Egypt that coincided with the turmoil that followed the Fourth Syrian War; and Jason's founding of a *polis* in Jerusalem) undoubtedly interfered. Despite these common factors, the consequences of the revolts were respectively very different. Whereas in the Seleucid empire the practice of indirect rule resulted in an exponential rise in the number of regions and urban communities being

---

[94] Josephus, *Ant.* 13.236–50, based on Nicolaus of Damascus; Diod. Sic. 34.1; and Just. 36.1.10. On this episode, see, for instance, Rajak (1981).
[95] Syon (2015) 59.

granted local autonomy at each new wave of dynastic struggle, in Egypt the centralized culture of government explains why the dynastic struggles never had similar consequences there.

This exercise in comparison between the two revolts also has a healthy, defamiliarizing effect. Certain aspects that their respective experts tend to hold as simple givens appear instead to be specific and therefore deserve renewed attention. Key instances are as follows: the fact that the Ptolemies never considered tolerating Haronnophris as a local dynast; the different relations the Ptolemies had regarding Egypt and their foreign possessions, respectively; and the fact that political manipulations of the notions of piety and impiety were not specific to Judean monotheism.

Bibliography

Abd El-Fattah, A. T., Abd El-Maksoud, M. D., and Carrez-Maratray, J.-Y. 'Deux inscriptions grecques du "Boubasteion" d'Alexandrie', *Ancient Society*, 44 (2014), 149–77.

Abdullaev, K., Franceschini, F., and Raimkulov, A. 'The tetradrachm of Seleucos I from Sazagan Region of Uzbekistan', *Circle of Inner Asian Art and Archaeology*, 19 (2004), 10–13.

Acosta-Hughes, B. and Stephens, S. A. *Callimachus in Context. From Plato to the Augustan Poets* (Cambridge University Press, 2012).

Agut-Labordère, D. 'Les "petites citadelles". La sociabilité du *tmy* "ville", "village", à travers les sagesses démotiques' in G. Gorre and P. Kossman (eds.), *Espaces et territoires de l'Égypte gréco-romaine. Actes des journées d'étude, 23 juin 2007 et 21 juin 2008* (Genève: Droz, 2013), 107–22.

Agut-Labordère, D. 'Persianism through Persianization. The case of Ptolemaic Egypt' in R. Strootman and M. J. Versluys (eds.), *Persianism in Antiquity* (Stuttgart: Steiner, 2017), 147–62.

Agut-Labordère, D. 'Gods in the gray area. A political history of the Egyptian temples from Artaxerxes III to the end of the Argeadai (342– *ca.* 305 BC)' in S. Honigman, O. Lipschits, and C. Nihan (eds.), *Times of Transition: Judea in the Early Hellenistic Period* (Philadelphia, Pa: Penn State University Press, 2021) 177–86.

Agut-Labordère, D. and Gorre, G. 'De l'autonomie à l'intégration. Les temples égyptiens face à la couronne des Saïtes aux Ptolémées (VIe–IIIe siècle av. J.-C.)', *Topoi*, 19.1 (2014), 17–55.

Agut-Labordère, D. and Moreno-García, J. C. *L'Égypte des pharaons. De Narmer à Dioclétien, 3150 av. J.-C.–284 apr. J.-C.* (Paris: Belin, 2016).

Ahn, G. *Religiöse Herrscherlegitimation im achämenidischen Iran. Die Voraussetzungen und die Struktur ihrer Argumentation* (Leiden: Brill, 1992).

Alcock, S. E., D'Altroy, T. N., Morrison, K. D., and Sinopoli, C. M. (eds.), *Empires. Perspectives from Archaeology and History* (Cambridge University Press, 2001).

Alföldi, A. 'From the *Aion Plutonios* of the Ptolemies to the *Saeculum Frugiferum* of the Roman Emperors' in K. H. Kinzl (ed.), *Greece and the Eastern Mediterranean in Ancient History and Prehistory. Studies Presented to Fritz Schachermeyr on the Occasion of His 80th Birthday* (Berlin: de Gruyter, 1977), 1–30.

Allsen, T. T. 'Pre-modern empires' in J. H. Bentley (ed.), *The Oxford Handbook of World History* (Oxford University Press, 2011), 361–78.
Ameling, W. '"Market-place" und Gewalt. Die Juden in Alexandrien 38 n.Chr.', *WürzJbb N.F.*, 27 (2003), 71–123.
Ameling, W. 'Die jüdische Gemeinde von Leontopolis nach den Inschriften' in M. Karrer and W. Kraus (eds.), *Die Septuaginta – Texte, Kontexte, Lebenswelten. Internationale Fachtagung veranstaltet von Septuaginta Deutsch (LXX.D), Wuppertal 20.–23. Juli 2006* (Tübingen: Mohr Siebeck, 2008), 117–33.
Ando, C. 'Introduction. States and state power in antiquity', in C. Ando and S. Richardson (ed.), *Ancient States and Infrastructural Power. Europe, Asia and America* (Philadelphia, PA: University of Pennsylvania Press, 2017), 1–16.
Ando, C. and Richardson, S. (eds.), *Ancient States and Infrastructural Power. Europe, Asia, and America* (Philadelphia, PA: University of Pennsylvania Press, 2017).
Andrade, N. J. *Syrian Identity in the Greco-Roman World* (Cambridge University Press, 2013).
Aneziri, S. 'Zwischen Musen und Hof. Die dionysischen Techniten auf Zypern', *ZPE* 104 (1994), 179–98.
Aperghis, G. G. 'Population – production – taxation – coinage. A model for the Seleukid economy' in Z. H. Archibald, J. Davies, G. J. Oliver, and V. Gabrielsen (eds.), *Hellenistic Economies* (London: Routledge, 2001), 69–102.
Aperghis, G. G. *The Seleukid Royal Economy. The Finances and Financial Administration of the Seleukid Empire* (Cambridge University Press, 2004).
Aperghis, G. G. 'Recipients and end-users on Seleucid coins', *BICS*, 53.2 (2010), 55–84.
Apicella, C. and Briquel Chatonnet, F. 'La transition institutionnelle dans les cités phéniciennes, des Achéménides à Rome' in J. Aliquot and C. Bonnet (eds.), *La Phénicie hellénistique. Actes du colloque international de Toulouse (18–20 féviert 2013)* (Paris: de Boccard, 2015), 9–29.
Arnold, F., et al. 'Report on the excavations at Elephantine by the German Archaeological Institute and the Swiss Institute from autumn 2013 to spring 2014', published online at www.dainst.org/documents/10180/384618/Elephantine+-+Report+on+the+43rd+Season+(ENGLISH)/db559a8 f-a0ce-40e0-a3a4-b6bbe7530af6;jsessionid=E09107174292E5AC6782CCC27584093 F?version=1.0 (2014).
Arslan, M. and Özen, A. 'A hoard of unpublished bronze coins of Ptolemy Ceraunus', *AJN*, 12 (2000), 59–66.
Arzt-Grabner, P. 'Die Stellung des Judentums in neutestamentlicher Zeit anhand der Politeuma-Papyri und anderer Texte' in J. Herzer (ed.), *Papyrologie und Exegese. Die Auslegung des Neuen Testament im Licht der Papyri* (Tübingen: Mohr Siebeck, 2012), 127–58.
Ashton, R. H. J. 'Ptolemaic coins from Fethiye Museum', *NCirc*, 110.1 (2002), 7–12.
Ashton, S.-A. *Ptolemaic Royal Sculpture from Egypt. The Interaction between Greek and Egyptian Traditions* (Oxford: Archaeopress, 2001).

Austin, M. M. *The Hellenistic World from Alexander to the Roman Conquest. A Selection of Ancient Sources in Translation*, 2nd ed. (Cambridge University Press, 2006 [1981]).
Bach, J. 'Berossos, Antiochos und die Babyloniaka', *Ancient West and East*, 12 (2013), 157–80.
Bader, A., Callieri, P., and Khodzhaniyazov, T. 'Survey of "Antiochus' Wall". Preliminary report on the 1993–1994 campaigns' in A. Gubaev, G. Koshelenko, and M. Tosi (eds.), *The Archaeological Map of the Murghab Delta. Preliminary Reports 1990–95* (Rom: IsIAO, 1998), 159–86.
Bagnall, R. S. *The Administration of the Ptolemaic Possessions outside Egypt* (Leiden: Brill, 1976).
Bagnall, R. S. 'The origins of Ptolemaic cleruchs', *BASP*, 21 (1984), 7–20.
Bagnall, R. S. 'The people of the Roman Fayum' in R. S. Bagnall (ed.), *Hellenistic and Roman Egypt. Sources and Approaches* (Aldershot: Ashgate, 2006), 1–19.
Bagnall, R. S. and Derow, P. *The Hellenistic Period. Historical Sources in Translation*, 2nd ed. (Malden, MA: Blackwell, 2004).
Bagnall, R. S. and Rathbone, D. W. *Egypt. From Alexander to the Early Christians. An Archaeological and Historical Guide* (Los Angeles, CA: Getty Publications, 2004).
Baker, H. D. 'The image of the city in Hellenistic Babylonia' in E. Stavrianopoulou (ed.), *Shifting Social Imaginaries in the Hellenistic Period. Narrations, Practices, and Images* (Leiden: Brill, 2013), 51–65.
Baker, H. 'Temple and city in Hellenistic Uruk. Sacred space and the transformation of late Babylonian society' in E. Frood and R. Raja (eds.), *Redefining the Sacred. Religious Architecture and Text in the Near East and Egypt, 1000 BC–AD 300* (Turnhout: Brepols, 2014), 183–208.
Balandier, C. *La défense de la Syrie-Palestine des Achéménides aux Lagides. Histoire et archéologie des fortifications à l'ouest du Jourdain de 532 à 199 avant J.-C. Avec appendices sur Jérusalem et sur les ouvrages fortifiés de Transjordanie et du nord du Sinaï*, 2 vols. (Pendé: Gabalda, 2014).
Bang, P. F. 'Between Aśoka and Antiochos. An essay in world history on universal kingship and cosmopolitan culture in the Hellenistic ecumene' in P. F. Bang and D. Kołodziejczyk (eds.), *Universal Empire. A Comparative Approach to Imperial Culture and Representation in Eurasian History* (Cambridge University Press, 2012), 60–75.
Bang, P. F. and Bayly, C. A. *Tributary Empires in Global History* (Basingstoke and New York, 2011).
Baratin, C. 'Le grenier grec de Samarkand', *Hyper Article en Ligne – Sciences de l'Homme et de la Société*. Accessed 4 October 2010 at http://hal.archives-ouvertes.fr/hal-00483708/fr/,
Barguet, P. *La stèle de la famine, à Séhel* (Cairo: IFAO, 1953).
Barkey, K. *Empire of Difference. The Ottomans in Comparative Perspective* (Cambridge University Press, 2008).
Barkey, K. and Batzell, R. 'Comparisons across empires. The critical social structures of the Ottomans, Russians and Habsburgs during the seventeenth

century' in P. F. Bang and C. A. Bayly (eds.), *Tributary Empires in Global History* (Basingstoke: Palgrave Macmillan, 2011), 227–61.

Bar-Kochva, B. *The Image of the Jews in Greek Literature. The Hellenistic Period* (Berkeley, CA: University of California Press, 2010).

Bartman, E. 'Review of: C. Hallett, The Roman nude. Heroic portrait statuary 200 B.C.–A.D. 300 (Oxford University Press, 2005)', *CW*, 100.3 (2007), 310–12.

Beaulieu, P.-A. 'The descendants of Sîn-lēqi-unninni' in J. Marzahn and H. Neumann (eds.), *Assyriologica et Semitica. Festschrift für Joachim Oelsner anläßlich seines 65. Geburtstages am 18. Februar 1997* (Münster: Ugarit 2000), 1–16.

Bengtson, H. *Die Strategie in der hellenistischen Zeit. Ein Beitrag zum antiken Staatsrecht*, vol. 2 (Munich: Beck, 1944).

Bengtson, H. *Die Strategie in der hellenistischen Zeit. Ein Beitrag zum antiken Staatsrecht*, vol. 3 (Munich: Beck, 1952).

Bennett, C. "Ptolemy 'the Son'" in *The Ptolemaic Dynasty* at www.instonebrewer.com/TyndaleSites/Egypt/ptolemies/nios_i_fr.htm

Bennett, C. "Magas of Cyrene" in *The Ptolemaic Dynasty* at www.instonebrewer.com/TyndaleSites/Egypt/ptolemies/magas_i_fr.htm (online, 2001–13).

Bennett, C. *Alexandria and the Moon. An Investigation into the Lunar Macedonian Calendar of Ptolemaic Egypt* (Leuven: Peeters, 2011).

Bennett, C. 'Soter and the calendars' in P. McKechnie and J. A. Cromwell (eds.) *Ptolemy I and the Transformation of Egypt, 404–282 BCE* (Leiden: Brill, 2018), 46–69.

Bergmann, M. *Die Strahlen der Herrscher. Theomorphes Herrscherbild und politische Symbolik im Hellenismus und in der römischen Kaiserzeit* (Mainz: von Zabern, 1998).

Bergmann, M. 'Sarapis im 3. Jh. v. Chr.' in G. Weber (ed.), *Alexandreia und das ptolemäische Ägypten. Kulturbegegnungen in hellenistischer Zeit* (Berlin: Verlag Antike, 2010), 109–35.

Berlin, A. M. 'Between large forces. Palestine in the Hellenistic period', *Biblical Archaeologist*, 60 (1997), 2–51.

Berlin, A. M. 'Egypt. Something old, something new. Native cultures under Ptolemaic rule' in N. Fenn and C. Römer-Strehl (eds.), *Networks in the Hellenistic World. According to the Pottery in the Eastern Mediterranean and Beyond* (Oxford: Archeopress, 2013), 229–37.

Berlin, A. M. , 'Old stories and new actors. The case of Qedesh' in A. M. Berlin and P. J. Kosmin (eds.), *The Middle Maccabees. Archaeology, History, and the Rise of the Hasmonean Kingdom* (SBL Press: Archaeology and Biblical Studies Series, 2021).

Berlin, A. M. and Herbert, S. C. 'Kedesh of the Upper Galilee' in D. A. Fiensy and J. R. Strange (eds.), *Galilee in the Late Second Temple and Mishnaic Periods, vol.*

2: *The Archaeological Record of Galilean Cities, Towns, and Villages* (Minneapolis, MN: Fortress Press, 2015), 424–41.

Berlin, A. M. and Kosmin, P. J. (eds.), *The Middle Maccabees. Archaeology, History, and the Rise of the Hasmonean Kingdom* (SBL Press: Archaeology and Biblical Studies Series, 2021).

Bernand, A. *De Thèbes à Syène* (Paris: CNRS, 1989).

Bernand, A. *La prose sur pierre dans l'Égypte hellénistique et romaine*, 2 vols. (Paris: CNRS, 1992).

Bernand, É. *Recueil des inscriptions grecques du Fayoum, vol. 1: La "méris" d'Hérakleidès* (Leiden: Brill, 1975).

Bernand, É. *Inscriptions grecques d'Égypte et de Nubie au Musée du Louvre* (Paris: CNRS, 1992).

Bernand, É. *Inscriptions grecques d'Hermoupolis Magna et de sa nécropole* (Cairo: IFAO, 1999).

Bernard, P. 'Diodore XVII, 83, I. Alexandrie du Caucase ou Alexandrie de l'Oxus?', *JSav*, no. 3–4 (1982), 217–42.

Bernard, P. 'Maracanda-Afrasiab colonie grecque' in Accademia Nazionale dei Lincei (eds.), *La Persia e l'Asia Centrale da Alessandro al X secolo* (Rome: Accademia Nazionale dei Lincei, 1996), 331–65.

Bernard, P. *Fouilles d'Aï Khanoum, vol. 4: Les monnaies hors trésors. Questions d'histoire gréco-bactrienne* (Paris: de Boccard, 1985).

Bernard, P. 'Hellenistic Arachosia. A Greek melting pot in action', *EW*, 55 (2005), 13–34.

Bernard, P., Grenet, F. and Isamiddinov, M. 'Fouilles de la mission franco-ouzbèque à l'ancienne Samarkand (Afrasiab) en 1990 et 1991, '*Comptes-rendus de l'Académie des inscriptions et belles-lettres* 136 (1992), 275–311.

Bernard, P., Grenet, F. and Isamiddinov, M. Kh. "Основные результаты узбекской-французской экспедиции на Афрасиабе в 1990–1991 гг.," Общественные науки в Узбекистане 3–4 (1996), 34–42. ['New Results of the Uzbek-French Expedition at Afrasiab, 1990–1991,' Obshchestbennye nauki v Uzbekistane.]

Bernard, P., Pinault, G.-J., and Rougemont, G. 'Deux nouvelles inscriptions grecques de l'Asie centrale', *JSav*, no. 2 (2004), 227–356.

Berthelot, K. *In Search of the Promised Land? The Hasmonean Dynasty between Biblical Models and Hellenistic Diplomacy* (Göttingen: Vandenhoeck & Ruprecht, 2018).

Bickerman, E. J. *Intitutions des Séleucides* (Paris: P. Geuthner, 1938).

Bickerman, E. J. 'Sur une inscription grecque de Sidon' in Académie des Inscriptions & Belles-Lettres (ed.) *Mélanges syriens offerts à Monsieur René Dussaud* (Paris: Geuthner, 1939), 91–99.

Bickerman, E. J. *Studies in Jewish and Christian History*, new ed. (Leiden: Brill, 2007).

Birk, R. 'Genormt? Zur überregionalen Normierung von priesterlichen Epitheta in der Ptolemäerzeit' in M. Ullmann (ed.), *10. Ägyptologische Tempeltagung. Ägyptische Tempel zwischen Normierung und Individualität. München, 29.-31. August 2014* (Wiesbaden: Harrassowitz, 2016), 17–35.

Birk, R. *Türöffner des Himmels. Prosopographische Studien zur thebanischen Hohepriesterschaft der Ptolemäerzeit* (Wiesbaden: Harrassowitz Verlag, 2020).

Biscardi, A. 'Polis, politeia, politeuma' in International Congress of Papyrologists (ed.) *Atti del XVII Congresso Internazionale di Papirologia III (Napoli, 19–26 maggio 1983)* (Napoli: Centro Internazionale per lo Studio dei Papiri Ercolanesi, 1984), 1201–15.

Blanshard, A. J. L., 'Alexander's mythic journey into India' in H. Prabha Ray and D. T. Potts (eds.), *Memory as History. The Legacy of Alexander in Asia* (New Delhi: Ayran Books International, 2007), 28–40.

Blasius, A. 'Army and society in Ptolemaic Egypt – a question of loyalty', *ArchPF*, 47.1 (2001), 81–98.

Blasius, A. 'Zur Frage des geistigen Widerstandes im griechisch-römischen Ägypten. Die historische Situation' in A. Blasius and B. U. Schipper (eds.), *Apokalyptik und Ägypten. Eine kritische Analyse der relevanten Texte aus dem griechisch-römischen Ägypten* (Leuven: Peeters, 2002), 41–62.

Blasius A. '"It was Greek to me ... "– Die lokalen Eliten im ptolemäischen Ägypten' in B. Dreyer and P .F. Mittag (eds.), *Lokale Eliten und hellenistische Könige. Zwischen Kooperation und Konfrontation* (Berlin: Verlag Antike, 2011), 132–90.

Bloch, E. 'Nonsynchronism and the obligation to its dialectics', *New German Critique*, 11 (1977), 22–38.

Bohm, C. *Imitatio Alexandri im Hellenismus. Untersuchungen zum politischen Nachwirken Alexanders des Großen in hoch- und späthellenistischen Monarchien* (Munich: Tuduv, 1989).

Boillet, P.-Y. 'La production de l'atelier monétaire d'Ecbatane. Mise en perspective historique et financière', *RN*, 170 (2013), 191–211.

Boiy, T. *Late Achaemenid and Hellenistic Babylon* (Leuven: Peeters, 2004).

Boiy, T. 'Temple building in Hellenistic Babylonia' in M. J. Boda and J. Novotny (eds.), *From the Foundations to the Crenellations. Essays on Temple Building in the Ancient Near East and Hebrew Bible* (Münster: Ugarit, 2010a), 211–20.

Boiy, T. 'Royal and satrapal armies in Babylonia during the Second Diadoch War. The "Chronical of Successors" on the events during the seventh year of Philip Arrhidaeus (= 317/316 BC)', *JHS*, 130 (2010b), 1–13.

Boiy, T. 'Babylon during Berossos's lifetime' in J. Haubold, G. B. Lanfranchi, R. Rollinger, and J. M. Steele (eds.), *The World of Berossos. Proceedings of the 4th International Colloquium on "The Ancient Near East between Classical and Ancient Oriental Traditions", Hatfield College, Durham 7th–9th July 2010* (Wiesbaden: Harrassowitz, 2013), 99–106.

Boiy, T. and Mittag, F. P. 'Lokale Eliten in Babylonien' in B. Dreyer and P. F. Mittag (eds.), *Lokale Eliten und hellenistische Könige. Zwischen Kooperation und Konfrontation* (Berlin: Verlag Antike, 2011), 105–31.

Boncquet, B. *Diodorus Siculus (II, 1–34) over Mesopotamië. Een historische commentaar* (Brussels: Verhandelingen van de Koninklijke Academie van Wetenschappen, Letteren en Schone Kunsten van België, 1987).
Bongenaar, A. *The Neo-Babylonian Ebabbar Temple at Sippar. Its Administration and Its Prosopography* (Leiden: Nederlands Historisch-Archaeologisch Instituut te Istanbul, 1997).
Bonneau, D. *La crue du Nil. Divinité égyptienne à travers mille ans d'histoire, 332 av.-641 ap. J.-C. d'après les auteurs grecs, latins, et les documents des époques ptolémaique, romaine, et byzantine* (Paris: Klincksieck, 1964).
Bonnet, C. 'Phoenician identities in Hellenistic times. Strategies and negotiations' in J. C. Quinn and N. C. Vella (eds.), *The Punic Mediterranean. Identities and Identification from Phoenician Settlement to Roman Rule* (Cambridge University Press, 2014), 282–98.
Bopearachchi, O. 'Les monnaies séleucides de l'Asie centrale et l'atelier de Bactres', in M. Amandry and S. Hurter (eds.), *Travaux de numismatique grecque offerts à Georges Le Rider* (London: Spink, 1999), 77–93.
Bopearachchi, O. 'La politique monétaire de la Bactriane sous les Séleucides' in V. Chankowski and F. Duyrat (eds.) *Le roi et l'économie. Autonomies locales et structures royales dans l'économie de l'empire séleucide* (Lyon: Maison de l'Orient Méditerranéen), 349–69.
Boraik, M., el-Masekh, S. , Guimier-Sorbets, A.-M. , and Redon, B. 'Ptolemaic baths in front of Karnak temples. Recent discoveries (season 2009–2010)', *Cahiers de Karnak*, 14 (2013), 47–77.
Bousquet, J. 'La stèle des Kyténiens à Xanthos de Lycie', *RÉG*, 101 (1988), 12–53.
Boussac, M.-T., Fournet, T., and Redon, B. *Le bain collectif en Egypte. Origine, évolution et actualités des pratiques. Actes du colloque Blanéorient, Alexandrie, 1–4 décembre 2006* (Cairo: IFAO, 2009).
Bowman, A. K. and Rathbone, D. 'Cities and administration in Roman Egypt', *JRS*, 82 (1992), 107–27.
Boym, S. *The Future of Nostalgia* (New York, NY: Basic, 2001).
Briant, P. 'The Seleucid kingdom, the Achaemenid empire and the history of the Near East in the first millennium BC' in P. Bilde, T. Engberg-Pedersen, L. Hannestad, and J. Zahle (eds.), *Religion and Religious Practice in the Seleucid Kingdom* (University of Aarhus Press, 1990), 40–65.
Briant, P. *From Cyrus to Alexander. A History of the Persian Empire* (Winona Lake, IN: Eisenbrauns, 2002).
Briant, P. *Kings, Countries, Peoples. Selected Studies on the Achaemenid Empire* (Stuttgart: Steiner, 2017).
Bringmann, K. *Hellenistische Reform und Religionsverfolgung in Judäa. Eine Untersuchung zur jüdisch-hellenistischen Geschichte (175–163 v. Chr.)* (Göttingen: Vandenhoeck & Ruprecht, 1983).
Brown, B. R. *Royal Portraits in Sculpture and Coins. Pyrrhos and the Successors of Alexander the Great* (Frankfurt a. M.: Lang, 1995).
Buraselis, K. 'Ambivalent roles of centre and periphery. Remarks on the relations of the cities of Greece with the Ptolemies until the end of the

Philometor's age' in P. Bilde, T. Engberg-Pedersen, L. Hannestad, and J. Zahle (eds.), *Centre and Periphery in the Hellenistic World* (Aarhus University Press, 1993), 251–70.

Buraselis, K. 'A lively "Indian Summer". Remarks on the Ptolemaic role in the Aegean under Philometor' in A. Jördens and J. F. Quack (eds.), *Ägypten zwischen innerem Zwist und äußerem Druck. Die Zeit Ptolemaios' VI. bis VIII. Internationales Symposion Heidelberg 16.–19.9. 2007* (Wiesbaden: Harrassowitz, 2011), 151–60.

Buraselis, K., Stefanou, M. and Thompson, D. J. (eds.), *The Ptolemies, the Sea and the Nile. Studies in Waterborne Power* (Cambridge University Press, 2013).

Burbank, J. and Cooper, F. *Empires in World History. Power and the Politics of Difference* (Princeton University Press, 2010).

Burkard, G. 'Frühgeschichte und Römerzeit. P. Berlin 23071 VSO', *Studien zur Altägyptischen Kultur*, 17 (1990), 107–34.

Burkert, W. 'Lydia between East and West or how to date the Trojan War. A study in Herodotus' in J. Carter and S. Morris (eds.), *The Ages of Homer. A Tribute to Emily Townsend Vermeule* (Austin, TX: University of Texas Press, 1995), 139–48.

Burstein, S. M. *The Babyloniaca of Berossus* (Malibu, CA: Undena 1978).

Burstein, S. M. *The Hellenistic Age from the Battle of Ipsos to the Death of Kleopatra* (Cambridge University Press, 1985).

Burstein, S. M. 'Elephants for Ptolemy II. Ptolemaic policy in Nubia in the third century BC' in P. McKechnie and P. Guillaume (eds.), *Ptolemy II Philadelphus and His World* (Leiden: Brill, 2008), 135–47.

Burstein, S. M. 'Ptolemy III and the dream of reuniting Alexander's empire', *The Ancient History Bulletin*, 30.3–4 (2016), 77–86.

Cadell, H. 'Pour une recherche sur *astu* et *polis* dans les papyrus grecs d'Égypte', *Ktèma*, 9 (1984), 235–46.

Callataÿ, F. de 'Quantifying monetary production in Greco-Roman times. A general frame', in F. de Callataÿ (ed.), *Quantifying Monetary Supplies in Greco-Roman Times* (Bari: Edipuglia, 2011), 7–29.

Callataÿ, F. de 'Control marks on Hellenistic royal coinages. Use, and evolution toward simplification?', *RBN*, 158 (2012), 39–62.

Callieri, P. 'Margiana in the Hellenistic period. Problems of archaeological interpretation' in E. Acquaro (ed.), *Alle soglie della classicità. Il Mediterraneo tra tradizione e innovazione. Studi in onore di Sabatino Moscati, vol. 2: Archeologia e arte* (Pisa: Istituti Editoriali e Poligrafici Internazionali, 1996), 569–78.

Canepa, M. P. *The Two Eyes of the Earth. Art and Ritual of Kingship between Rome and Sasanian Iran* (Berkeley, CA: University of California Press, 2009).

Caneva, S. G. *From Alexander to the Theoi Adelphoi. Foundation and Legitimation of a Dynasty* (Leuven: Peeters, 2016).

Capdetrey, L. *Le pouvoir séleucide. Territoire, administration, finances d'un royaume hellénistique (312–129 av. J.-C.)* (Presses Universitaires de Rennes, 2007).

Capdetrey, L. 'Le royaume séleucide. Un empire impossible?' in F. Hurlet (ed.), *Les empires. Antiquité et Moyen Âge. Analyse comparée* (Presses Universitaires de Rennes, 2008), 57–80.

Capponi, L. *Il tempio di Leontopoli in Egitto. Identità politica e religiosa dei Giudei di Onia (c. 150 a.C.–73 d.C.)* (Pisa: Edizioni ETS, 2007).

Carlen, E. 'The final phase coinage of ΠΤΟΛΕΜΑΙΟΥ ΣΩΤΗΡΟΣ tetradrachms dated according to an uncertain era', *AJN*, 27 (2015), 99–140.

Carlen, E.A. (2019) "The spearhead and monogram coinage of Ptolemy V," *AJN* 31: 95–116.

Carlen, E. A. and Lorber, C. C., 'Silver coinage from the co-regency of Ptolemy VI and VIII', *Israel Numismatic Research*, 13 (2018), 3–33.

Cartledge, P. *The Greeks. A Portrait of Self and Others*, 2nd ed. (Cambridge University Press, 2002).

Casagrande-Kim, R. 'The way they looked. Dynastic portraiture on Ptolemaic coins' in R. Casagrande-Kim (ed.), *When the Greeks Ruled Egypt. From Alexander the Great to Cleopatra* (Princeton University Press, 2014) 58–71.

Cavagna, A. 'L'oro dei *theoi adelphoi*' in G. Zanetto, S. Martinelli Tempesta, and M. Ornaghi (eds.), *Nova vestigia antiquitatis. Seminari 2006–2007* (Milan: Cisalpino, 2008), 161–82.

Cavagna, A. *Monete tolemaiche oltre l'Egitto* (Milan: Cisalpino, 2015).

Chaniotis, A. 'Ein diplomatischer Statthalter nimmt Rücksicht auf den Verletzten Stolz zweier hellenistischer Kleinpoleis (Nagidos und Arsinoe)', *Epigraphica Anatolica* 31 (1993), 33–42.

Chaufray, M.-P. and Wackenier, S. *Papyrus de la Sorbonne, IV (n° 145–160)* (Paris: PUPS, 2016).

Chaufray, M.-P. and Wegner, W. 'Two early Ptolemaic documents from Pathyris' in S. L. Lippert, M. Schentuleit and M. A. Stadler (eds.), *Sapientia Felicitas. Festschrift für Günter Vittmann zum 29. Februar 2016* (Montpellier: Université Paul Valéry, 2016), 23–49.

Chauveau, M. *Egypt in the Age of Cleopatra. History and Society under the Ptolemies* (Ithaca, NY: Cornell University Press, 2000).

Chauveau, M. 'L'*Agneau* revisité ou la révélation d'un crime de guerre ignoré' in R. Jasnow and G. Widmer (eds.), *Illuminating Osiris. Egyptological Studies in Honor of Mark Smith* (Atlanta, GA: Lockwood Press, 2017), 37–70.

Chauveau, M. 'Démotique', *Annuaire de l'École pratique des hautes études (EPHE), Section des sciences historiques et philologiques* [on line], 150, 2019, http://journals.openedition.org/ashp/2851.

Chauveau, M. and Thiers, C. 'L'Égypte en transition. Des Perses aux Macédoniens' in P. Briant and F. Joannès (eds.), *La transition entre l'empire achéménide et les royaumes hellénistiques (vers 350–300 av. J.-C.)* (Paris: de Boccard, 2006), 375–404.

Cheshire, W. A. *The Bronzes of Ptolemy II Philadelphus* (Wiesbaden: Harrassowitz, 2009).

Chichkina, G. V. 'Les remparts de Samarcande à l'époque hellénistique' in P. Leriche and H. Tréziny (eds.), *La fortification dans l'histoire du monde grec*.

Actes du Colloque international La Fortification et sa Place dans l'Histoire Politique, Culturelle et Sociale du Monde Grec, Valbonne, décembre 1982 (Paris: CNRS, 1986), 71–8.

Chrubasik, B. *Kings and Usurpers in the Seleukid Empire. The Men Who Would Be King* (Oxford University Press, 2016).

Chrubasik, B. 'Sanctuaries, priest-dynasts and the Seleukid empire' in S. Honigman, O. Lipschitz, and C. Nihan (eds.), *Times of Transition: Judea in the Early Hellenistic Period* (Philadelphia, Pa: Penn State University Press, 2021) 161–76.

Chrysostoumou, P. 'Οι θεσσαλομακεδονικοί θεοί των καθαρμών και η μακεδονική γιορτή Χανδικά', *Makedonika*, 29 (1993–4), 175–201.

Chryssanthaki, K. 'Les monnaies lagides en Égée' in F. Duyrat and O. Picard (eds.), *L'exception égyptienne? Production et échanges monétaires en Égypte hellénistique et romaine. Actes du colloque d'Alexandrie, 13–15 avril 2002* (Cairo: IFAO, 2005), 159–75.

Clancier, P. '"Le *rab sikkati*" de Babylone contre "l'homme de renom venu d'Égypte". La troisième Guerre Syrienne dans les rues de Babylone' in P. Goukowski and C. Feyel (eds.), *Folia Graeca in honorem Edouard Will: Historica* (Nancy: ADRA, 2012), 9–31.

Clancier, P. 'The *polis* of Babylon. An historiographical approach' in B. Chrubasik and D. King (eds.), *Hellenism and the Local Communities of the Eastern Mediterranean, 400 BCE—250 CE* (Oxford University Press, 2017), 53–81.

Clancier, P. and Monerie, J. 'Les sanctuaires babyloniens à l'époque hellénistique. Évolution d'un relais de pouvoir', *Topoi* 19.1 (2014), 181–237.

Clarysse, W. 'Notes de prosopographie thébaine 7. Hurgonaphor et Chaonnophris, les derniers pharaons indigènes', *ChrÉg*, 53 (1978), 243–53.

Clarysse, W. 'Ptolemaeïsch Egypte. Een maatschappij met twee gezichten' *Handelingen van de Koninklijke Zuidnederlandse Maatschappij voor Taal- en Letterkunde en Geschiedenis*, 45 (1991a), 21–38.

Clarysse, W. *The Petrie Papyri*, vol. 1: *The Wills (P. Petrie 2)*, 2nd ed. (Brussels: Peeters, 1991b).

Clarysse, W. 'Greeks in Ptolemaic Thebes' in S. P. Vleeming (ed.), *Hundred-Gated Thebes. Acts of a Colloquium on Thebes and the Theban Area in the Graeco-Roman Period* (Leiden: Brill, 1995), 1–19.

Clarysse, W. 'Ethnic diversity and dialect among the Greeks in Ptolemaic Egypt' in A. M. F. W. Verhooght and S. P. Vleeming (eds.), *The Two Faces of Graeco-Roman Egypt. Greek and Demotic and Greek-Demotic Texts and Studies Presented to P. W. Pestman* (Leiden: Brill, 1998), 1–13.

Clarysse, W. 'Ptolémées et temples' in D. Valbelle and J. Leclant (eds.), *Le Décret de Memphis. Colloque de la Fondation Singer-Polignac à l'occasion de la célébration du bicentenaire de la découverte de la Pierre de Rosette* (Paris: Fondation Singer-Polignac, 2000a), 41–65.

Clarysse, W. 'The Ptolemies visiting the Egyptian chora' in L. Mooren (ed.), *Politics, Administration and Society in the Hellenistic and Roman World. Proceedings of the International Colloquium, Bertinoro 19–24 July 1997* (Leuven: Peeters, 2000b), 29–53.

Clarysse, W. 'The archive of the praktor Milon' in W. Clarysse and K. Vandorpe (eds.), *Edfu, an Egyptian Provincial Capital in the Ptolemaic Period. Brussels, 3 September 2001* (Brussels: Koninklijke Vlaamse Academie van België voor Wetenschappen en Kunsten, 2003), 17–27.

Clarysse, W. 'Toponymy of Fayum villages in the Ptolemaic period' in M. Capasso and P. Davoli (eds.), *New Archaeological and Papyrological Researches on the Fayyum. Proceedings of the International Meeting of Egyptology and Papyrology, Lecce, June 8th–10th 2005* (Lecce: Congedo Editore, 2007), 67–81.

Clarysse, W. and Thompson, D. J. *Counting the People in Hellenistic Egypt*, 2 vols. (Cambridge University Press, 2006).

Clarysse, W. and Vandorpe, K. *Zénon, un homme d'affaires grec à l'ombre des Pyramides* (Leuven University Press, 1995).

Clarysse, W. and Vandorpe, K. 'The Ptolemaic apomoira' in H. Melaerts (ed.), *Le culte du souverain dans l'Égypte ptolémaïque au IIIe siècle avant notre ère. Actes du colloque international, Bruxelles 10 mai 1995* (Leuven: Peeters, 1998), 5–42.

Clarysse, W., and van der Veken, G. *The Eponymous Priests of Ptolemaic Egypt. Chronological Lists of the Priests of Alexandria and Ptolemais with a Study of the Demotic Transcriptions of Their Names* (Leiden: Brill, 1983).

Claußen, C. *Versammlung, Gemeinde, Synagoge. Das hellenistisch-jüdische Umfeld der frühchristlichen Gemeinden* (Göttingen: Vandenhoeck & Ruprecht, 2002).

Clère, P. *La porte d'Evergète à Karnak* (Cairo: IFAO, 1961).

Cline, E. H. and Graham, M. W. (eds.) *Ancient Empires. From Mesopotamia to the Rise of Islam* (Cambridge University Press, 2011).

Coe, J. J. 'Disease as portrayed on ancient coins', *Journal of the Society for Ancient Numismatics*, 17.2 (1987), 36–8.

Cohen, G. M. 'Colonization and population transfer in the Hellenistic world' in E. Van 't Dack, P. van Dessel, and W. van Gucht (eds.), *Egypt and the Hellenistic World. Proceedings of the International Colloquium, Leuven, 24–26 May 1982* (Leuven: Orientaliste, 1983), 63–74.

Cohen, G. M. '"Katoikiai, katoikoi" and Macedonians in Asia Minor', *Ancient Society*, 22 (1991), 41–50.

Cohen, G. M. *The Hellenistic Settlements in Europe, the Islands, and Asia Minor* (Berkeley, CA: University of California Press, 1995).

Cohen, G. M. *The Hellenistic Settlements in Syria, the Red Sea Basin, and North Africa* (Berkeley, CA: University of California Press, 2006).

Cohen, G. M. *The Hellenistic Settlements in the East from Armenia and Mesopotamia to Bactria and India* (Berkeley, CA: University of California Press, 2013).

Collingwood, R. *The Idea of History* (Oxford University Press, 1946).

Coloru, O. 'Seleukid settlements. Between ethnic identity and mobility', *Electrum*, 20 (2013a), 37–56.

Coloru, O. 'Margiana' in R. S. Bagnall, et al. (eds.), *The Encyclopedia of Ancient History* (Malden, MA: Wiley, 2013b), 4300–01.

Connelly, J. B. *Votive sculpture of Hellenistic Cyprus* (New York University Press, 1988).

Coqueugniot, G. 'The Hellenistic public square in Europos in Parapotamia (Dura-Europos, Syria) and Seleucia on the Tigris (Iraq) during Parthian and Roman times' in S. Chandrasekaran and A. Kouremenos (eds.), *Continuity and Destruction in the Greek East. The Transformation of Monumental Space from the Hellenistic Period to Late Antiquity* (Oxford: British Archaeological Reports, 2015), 71–82.

Coulon, L. 'Quand Amon parle à Platon (la statue Caire JE 38033)', *RÉg*, 52 (2001), 85–112.

Coulon, L. 'Les reliques d'Osiris en Égypte ancienne. Données générales et particularismes thébains' in P. Borgeaud and Y. Volokhine (éd.), *Les objets de la mémoire. Pour une approche comparatiste des reliques et de leur culte* (Frankfurt a. M.: Peter Lang, 2005), 15–46.

Coulon, L. 'Le culte osirien au Ier millénaire av. J.-C. Une mise en perspective(s)' in L. Coulon (ed.), *Le culte d'Osiris au Ier millénaire av. J.-C. Découvertes et travaux récents. Actes de la table ronde internationale tenue à Lyon, Maison de l'Orient et de la Méditerranée (unversité Lumière-Lyon 2) les 8 et 9 juillet 2005* (Cairo: IFAO, 2010) 1–17.

Couvenhes, J.-C. and Heller, A. 'Les transferts culturels dans le monde institutionnel des cités et des royaumes à l'époque hellénistique' in J.-C. Couvenhes and B. Legras (eds.), *Transferts culturels et politique dans le monde hellénistique. Actes de la table ronde sur les identités collectives, Sorbonne, 7 février 2004* (Paris: Publications de la Sorbonne, 2006), 15–52.

Cowey, J. M. S. 'Das ägyptische Judentum in hellenistischer Zeit – neue Erkenntnisse aus jüngst veröffentlichten Papyri' in S. Kreuzer and J. P. Lesch (eds.), *Im Brennpunkt. Die Septuaginta. Studien zur Entstehung und Bedeutung der Griechischen Bibel*, vol. 2 (Stuttgart: Kohlhammer, 2004), 24–43.

Cowey, J. M. S. and Maresch, K. *Urkunden des Politeuma der Juden von Herakleopolis (144/3–133/2 v. Chr.)* (Wiesbaden: Westdeutscher Verlag, 2001).

Crawford, D. J. *Kerkeosiris. An Egyptian Village in the Ptolemaic Period* (Cambridge University Press, 1971).

Crisafulli, C. 'Presenza di moneta "straniera" di età greca e romana in Cirenaica dagli scavi urbinati e dal medagliere del Museo Archeologico di Cirene' in M. Luni (ed.), *Cirene greca e romana* (Rome: Bretschneider, 2014), 333–55.

Dahmen, K. *The Legend of Alexander the Great on Greek and Roman Coins* (London: Routledge, 2007).

Dale, S. F. *The Muslim Empires of the Ottomans, Safavids, and Mughals* (Cambridge University Press, 2010).

Dandamayev, M. A. 'The Neo-Babylonian *zazakku*', *Altorientalische Forschung*, 21 (1994), 34–40.

Darwin, J. *After Tamerlane: The Rise and Fall of Global Empires, 1400–2000* (London: Allen Lane, 2007).

Daubner, F. 'Seleukidische und attalidische Gründungen in Westkleinasien – Datierung, Funktion und Status' in F. Daubner (ed.), *Militärsiedlungen und Territorialherrschaft in der Antike* (Berlin: de Gruyter, 2011), 41–63.

Davesne, A. 'La deuxième guerre de Syrie (ca. 261–255 avant J.C.) et les témoignages numismatiques' in M. Amandry and S. Hurter (eds.), *Travaux de numismatique grecque offerts à Georges Le Rider* (London: Spink, 1999), 123–34.
Davesne, A. 'Les monnaies des premiers Ptolémées en Asie Mineure et à Chypre' in F. Duyrat and O. Picard (eds.), *L'exception égyptienne? Production et échanges monétaires en Égypte hellénistique et romaine. Actes du colloque d'Alexandrie, 13–15 avril 2002* (Cairo : IFAO, 2005), 177–87.
Davesne, A., and Le Rider, G. *Le trésor de Meydancıkkale (Cilicie Trachée, 1980)* (Paris: Éditions Recherche sur les Civilisations, 1989).
Davis, K. *Periodization and Sovereignty. How Ideas of Feudalism and Secularization Govern the Politics of Time* (Philadelphia, PA: University of Pennsylvania Press, 2008).
Davoli, P. *Archaeologia e papyri* (Naples: Eurocomp, 2001).
Davoli, P. 'Reflections on urbanism in Graeco-Roman Egypt. A historical and regional perspective' in E. Subías, P. Azara, J. Carruesco, I. Fiz, and R. Cuesta (eds.), *The Space of the City in Graeco-Roman Egypt. Image and Reality* (Tarragona: Institut Català d'Arqueologia Clàssica, 2011), 69–92.
de Cenival, F. *Papyrus démotiques de Lille*, vol. 3 (Cairo: IFAO, 1984).
de Certeau, M. *The Writing of History* (New York, NY: Columbia University Press, 1988).
de Meulenaere, H. 'Les stratèges indigènes du nome de Tentyrite à la fin de l'époque ptolémaïque et au début de l'occupation romaine', *RSO* 34.1–2 (1959), 1–25.
de Meulenaere, H. 'Ptolémée IX Sôter II à Kalabcha', *ChrÉg*, 36 (1961), 98–105.
de Polignac, F. 'Rome et Alexandrie métropoles universelles. Une rhétorique en miroir', *Métis*, n.s. 3 (2005), 307–18.
de Ste. Croix, G. E. M. *The Class Struggle in the Ancient Greek World. From the Archaic Age to the Arab Conquest* (London: Duckworth, 1981).
del Monte, G. F. *Testi dalla Babilonia ellenistica, vol. 1: Testi cronografic* (Pisa: Istituti Editoriali e Poligrafici Internazionali, 1997).
Delanty, G. and Kumar, K. *The SAGE Handbook of Nations and Nationalism* (London: SAGE, 2006).
Depauw, M. *A Companion to Demotic Studies* (Brussels: Fondation Égyptologique Reine Élisabeth, 1997).
Depauw, M. 'Egyptianizing the chancellery during the Great Theban Revolt (205–186 BC). A new study of limestone tablet Cairo 38258', *Studien zur Altägyptischen Kultur*, 34 (2006), 97–105.
Devauchelle, D., de Cenival, F. and Pezin, M. 'Les "révoltés" d'Hermonthis (Pap. Louvre AF 13584 R°)' in K. Donker van Heel, F. A. J. Hoogendijk and C. J. Martin (eds.), *Hieratic, Demotic and Greek Studies and Text Editions. Of Making Many Books There Is No End. Festschrift in Honour of Sven P. Vleeming* (Leiden: Brill, 2018), 233–48.
Dietze, G. 'Philae und die Dodekaschoinos in ptolemäischer Zeit. Ein Beitrag zur Frage ptolemäischer Präsenz im Grenzland zwischen Ägypten und Afrika an Hand der architektonischen und epigraphischen Quellen', *Ancient Society*, 25 (1994), 63–110.

Dietze, G. 'Der Streit um die Insel Pso. Bemerkungen zu einem epigraphischen Dossier des Khnumtempels von Elephantine (Th. Sy. 244)', *Ancient Society*, 26 (1995), 157–84.

Dietze, G. 'Temple and soldiers in southern Ptolemaic Egypt. Some epigraphic evidence' in L. Mooren (ed.), *Politics, Administration and Society in the Hellenistic and Roman World. Proceedings of the International Colloquium, Bertinoro 19–24 July 1997* (Leuven: Peeters, 2000), 77–89.

Dieudonné, A. 'Ptolemais-Lebedus', *JIAN*, 5 (1902), 45–60.

Dillery, J. *Clio's Other Sons. Berossus and Manetho* (Ann Arbor, MI: University of Michigan Press, 2015).

Dillon, S. *Ancient Greek Portrait Sculpture. Contexts, Subjects, and Styles* (Cambridge University Press, 2006).

Doran, R. *2 Maccabees. A Critical Commentary* (Minneapolis, MN: Fortress Press, 2012).

Doty, L. *Cuneiform Archives from Hellenistic Uruk* (Ann Arbor, MI: ProQuest 1977).

Downey, G. A. *A History of Antioch in Syria. From Seleucus to the Arab Conquest* (Princeton University Press, 1961).

Doyle, M. *Empires* (Ithaca, NY: Cornell University Press, 1986).

Doyle, L. 'Inter-imperiality', *Interventions*, 16.2 (2014a), 159–96.

Doyle, L. 'Dialectics in the longue durée. The IIPEC model of inter-imperial economy and culture', *Globalizations*, 11.5 (2014b), 689–709.

Draganov, D. *The Coinage of Cabyle* (Sofia: DIOS, 1993).

Dreyer, B. 'Der "Raubvertrag" des Jahres 203/2 v.Chr. Das Inschriftenfragment von Bargylia und der Brief von Amyzon', *EpigAnat*, 34 (2002), 119–38.

Dreyer, B. *Die römische Nobilitätsherrschaft und Antiochos III. (205 bis 188 v.Chr.)* (Hennef: Clauss, 2007).

Dreyer, B. 'Phönizien als Spielball zwischen den Großmächten– Der sogenannte Raubvertrag von 203/2 v. Chr. Dimensionen und Konsequenzen' in M. Witte and J. F. Diehl (eds.), *Israeliten und Phönizier. Ihre Beziehung im Spiegel der Archäologie und der Literatur des Alten Testaments und seiner Umwelt* (Göttingen: Vandenhoeck & Ruprecht, 2008), 215–31.

Dreyer, B. 'Die Rolle der lokalen Eliten abhängiger griechischer Städte vor dem Hintergrund der Entwicklung königlicher Administration und städtischer Politik im 2. Jahrhundert v. Chr.', *Klio*, 92.2 (2010a), 344–68.

Dreyer, B. '"L'asilo territoriale" dal periodo tardo-classico fino al dominio degli imperatori romani', *Geographia Antiqua*, 19 (2010b), 91–8.

Dreyer, B. 'Wie man "Verwandter" des Königs wird – Karrieren und Hierarchie am Hofe von Antiochos III.' in E. Dabrowa (ed.), *New Studies on the Seleucids* (Cracow: Wydawnictwo UJ, 2010c), 97–114.

Dreyer, B. 'Das Asylrecht als Mittel der Deeskalation in der Epoche des Hellenismus' in M. Linder and S. Tausend (eds.), *'Böser Krieg'. Exzessive Gewalt in der antiken Kriegsführung und Strategien zu deren Vermeidung* (Grazer Universitätsverlag Nummi et Scriptae, 2011a), 133–51.

Dreyer, B. 'How to become a "relative" of the king. Careers and hierarchy at the court of Antiochus III', *AJP*, 132.1 (2011b), 45–57.
Dreyer, B. 'Polybios und die hellenistischen Monarchien' in V. Grieb and C. Koehn (eds.), *Polybios und seine Historien*, Wiesbaden: Franz Steiner, 2013), 233–249.
Dreyer, B. and Mittag, P. F. (eds.), *Lokale Eliten und hellenistische Könige. Zwischen Kooperation und Konfrontation* (Berlin: Antike Verlag, 2011).
Droysen, J. G. *Geschichte des Hellenismus*, 3 vols. (Gotha: Perthes, 1877–8).
Dubs, H. H. 'A Roman city in ancient China', *GaR*, 4.2 (1957), 139–48.
Dumke, G. 'Diadem = Königsherrschaft? Der Fall des Diodotos I. von Baktrien' in A. Lichtenberger, K. Martin, H.-H. Nieswandt and D. Salzmann (eds.), *Das Diadem der hellenistischen Herrscher. Übernahme, Transformation oder Neuschöpfung eines Herrschaftszeichens. Kolloquium vom 30.–31. Januar 2009 in Münster* (Bonn: Habelt, 2012), 385–93.
Duncan-Jones, R. *Money and Government in the Roman Empire* (Cambridge University Press, 1994).
Düring, B. S. and Stek, T. D. (eds.) *The Archaeology of Imperial Landscapes. A Comparative Study of Empires in the Ancient Near East and Mediterranean World* (Cambridge University Press, 2018).
Eck, B. *Diodore de Sicile, bibliothèque historique Tome II Livre II* (Paris: Belles Lettres, 2003).
Eckhardt, B. 'The Hasmoneans and their rivals in Seleucid and post-Seleucid Judea', *Journal for the Study of Judaism* 47.1 (2016a), 55–70.
Eckhardt, B. 'The Seleucid administration of Judea, the high priesthood and the rise of the Hasmoneans', *Journal of Ancient History*, 4.1 (2016b), 57–87.
Eckstein, A. M. *Rome Enters the Greek East. From Anarchy to Hierarchy in the Hellenistic Mediterranean, 230–170 BC* (Malden, MA: Blackwell, 2008).
Eco, U. *The Infinity of Lists. From Homer to James Joyce* (London: MacLehose, 2009).
Eddy, S. K. *The King Is Dead. Studies in the Near Eastern Resistance to Hellenism, 334–31 B.C.* (Lincoln, NE: University of Nebraska Press, 1961).
Edelmann, B. *Religiöse Herrschaftslegitimation in der Antike. Die religiöse Legitimation orientalisch-ägyptischer und griechisch-hellenistischer Herrscher im Vergleich* (St. Katharinen: Scripta Mercaturae, 2007).
Edensor, T. 'Reconsidering national temporalities. Institutional times, everyday routines, serial spaces and synchronicities', *European Journal of Social Theory*, 9.4 (2006), 525–45.
Edwards, C. *Writing Rome. Textual Approaches to the City* (Cambridge University Press, 1996).
Eide, T., Hägg, T., and Pierce, R. H. *Fontes Historiae Nubiorum*, 4 vols. (University of Bergen Press, 1994–2000).
Eliade, M. *Le mythe de l'éternel retour. Archétypes et répétition* (Paris: Gallimard, 1969).
Engels, D. 'Middle Eastern "feudalism" and Seleucid dissolution' in K. Erickson and G. Ramsey (eds.), *Seleucid Dissolution. The Sinking of the Anchor* (Wiesbaden: Harrassowitz, 2011), 19–36.

Erickson, K. 'Apollo-Nabû. The Babylonian policy of Antiochus' in K. Erickson and G. Ramsey (eds.), *Seleucid Dissolution. The Sinking of the Anchor* (Wiesbaden: Harrassowitz, 2011), 51–66.

Eriksen, T. H. *Ethnicity and Nationalism. Anthropological Perspectives*, 3rd ed. (London: Pluto Press, 2010).

Erskine, A. 'Polybius and Ptolemaic sea power' in K. Buraselis, M. Stefanou and D. J. Thompson (eds.), *The Ptolemies, the Sea and the Nile. Studies in Waterborne Power* (Cambridge University Press, 2013), 82–96.

Everling, J. 'A Babylonian tablet from the time of Alexander IV' in M. Krebernik and H. Neumann (eds.), *Babylonien und seine Nachbarn in neu- und spätbabylonischer Zeit. Wissenschaftliches Kolloquium aus Anlass des 75. Geburtstages von Joachim Oelsner, Jena, 2. Und 3. März 2007* (Münster: Ugarit, 2014), 17–24.

Fairman, H. W. 'A statue from the Karnak cache', *JEA*, 20.1–2 (1934), 1–4.

Fairman, H. W. *The Triumph of Horus. An Ancient Egyptian Sacred Drama* (Berkeley, CA: University of California Press, 1974).

Falivene, M. R. 'Review of P.Polit.Iud.', *BibO*, 59 (2002), 541–50.

Farid, A. *Die demotischen Inschriften der Strategen* (San Antonio, TX: van Siclen Books, 1993).

Faroqhi, S. *The Ottoman Empire and the World around It* (London: I. B. Tauris, 2004).

Fasolt, C. *The Limits of History* (University of Chicago Press, 2004).

Faucher, T. 'La circulation monétaire en Égypte hellénistique' in T. Faucher, M.-C. Marcellesi, and O. Picard (eds.), *Nomisma. La circulation monétaire dans le monde grec antique. Actes du colloque international, Athènes, 14–17 avril 2010* (Paris: École Française d'Athènes, 2011), 433–54.

Faucher, T., and Lorber, C. C. 'Bronze coinage of Ptolemaic Egypt in the second century BC' *AJN*, 22 (2010), 35–80.

Faucher, T., Olivier, J., Brissaud, P., and Desbordes, C. '*EH* 208. Trésor de Tanis, 1986' in T. Faucher, A. Meadows, and C. C. Lorber (eds.), *Egyptian Hoards I. The Ptolemies* (Cairo: IFAO, 2017), 203–22.

Felber, H. 'Die demotische Chronik' in A. Blasius and B. U. Schipper (eds.), *Apokalyptik und Ägypten. Eine kritische Analyse der relevanten Texte aus dem griechisch-römischen Ägypten* (Leuven: Peeters, 2002), 65–111.

Ferretti, L., Schubert, P. and Tomcik, M. 'Three notes on some papyri from the Zenon Archive', *ZPE*, 201 (2017), 215–18.

Feyel, C. 'Le dossier épigraphique de Skythopolis (Hefzibah)' *Antiochos III et l'Orient. Journées d'études franco-allemandes, Nancy, 6–8 juin 2016* (Nancy: ADRA, 2017), 105–40.

Feyel, C. and Graslin, L. (eds.), *Le projet politique d'Antiochos IV. Journées d'études franco-allemandes, Nancy 17–19 juin 2013* (Nancy: ADRA, 2014).

Fischer-Bossert, W. 'The didrachm coinage of Magas' in M. Asolati (ed.), *Le monete di Cirene e della Cirenaica nel Mediterraneo. Problemi e prospettive. Atti del V Congresso Internazionale di Numismatica e di Storia Monetaria, Padova, 17–19 marzo 2016* (Padua: Esedra Editrice, 2016), 57–64.

Fischer-Bovet, C. 'Counting the Greeks in Egypt. Immigration in the first century of Ptolemaic rule' in C. Holeran and A. Pudsey (eds.), *Demography in the*

Graeco-Roman World. New Insights and Approaches (Cambridge University Press, 2011), 135–54.
Fischer-Bovet, C. 'Katoikoi' in R. S. Bagnall et al. (eds.), *The Encyclopedia of Ancient History* (Malden, MA: Wiley, 2013), 3712–13.
Fischer-Bovet, C. 'Est-il facile de conquérir l'Egypte? L'invasion d'Antiochus IV et ses conséquences' in C. Feyel and L. Graslin (eds.), *Le projet politique d'Antiochos IV. Journées d'études franco-allemandes, Nancy 17–19 juin 2013* (Nancy: ADRA, 2014a), 209–59.
Fischer-Bovet, C. *Army and Society in Ptolemaic Egypt* (Cambridge University Press, 2014b).
Fischer-Bovet, C. 'Hellenistic Empires. The dynasties of the Ptolemies and the Seleucids', in P. F. Bang, C. A. Bayly, and W. Scheidel (eds.), *The Oxford World History of Empire, Volume 2: The History of Empires* (Oxford, 2020) 167–97.
Fischer-Bovet, C. 'Ptolemaic imperialism in southern Anatolia (Lycia, Pamphylia and Cilicia)' in M. Munn (ed.), *Building a New World Order. Hellenistic Monarchies in the Ancient Mediterranean World* (forthcoming).
Fittschen, K. *Griechische Porträts* (Darmstadt: Wissenschaftliche Buchgesellschaft, 1988).
Fittschen, K. 'Zur Rekonstruktion griechischer Dichterstatuen 1. Die Statue des Menander', *AM*, 106 (1991), 243–79.
Fittschen, K. 'Zur Rekonstruktion griechischer Dichterstatuen 2. Die Statuen des Poseidippos und des Pseudo-Menander', *AM*, 107 (1992), 229–71.
Fittschen, K. 'The portraits of Roman emperors and their families. Controversial positions and unsolved problems' in B. C. Ewald and C. F. Noreña (eds.), *The Emperor and Rome. Space, Representation and Ritual* (Cambridge University Press, 2010), 221–46.
Flacelière, R. *Les Aitoliens à Delphes. Contribution à l'histoire de la Grèce centrale au IIIe siècle av. J.-C.* (Paris: de Boccard, 1937).
Fleischer, R. 'Physiognomie, idéologie, politique dynastique. Les portraits sur les monnaies des rois séleucids' in *Ο ελληνισμός στην Ανατολή* (Athens: European Cultural Centre of Delphi, 1991a), 303–9.
Fleischer, R. *Studien zur seleukidischen Kunst, vol. 1: Herrscherbildnisse* (Mainz: von Zabern, 1991b).
Fleischer, R. 'Hellenistic royal iconography on coins' in P. Bilde, T. Engberg-Pedersen, L. Hannestad, and J. Zahle (eds.), *Aspects of Hellenistic Kingship* (Aarhus University Press, 1996), 28–40.
Fleischer, R. 'True ancestors and false ancestors in Hellenistic rulers' portraiture' in J. M. Højte (ed.), *Images of Ancestors* (Aarhus University Press, 2002), 59–74.
Flood, F. B. *Objects of Translation. Material Culture and Medieval "Hindu-Muslim" Encounters* (Princeton University Press, 2009).
Förster, H. and Sänger, P. 'Ist unsere Heimat im Himmel? Überlegungen zur Semantik von πολίτευμα in Phil 3,20', *Early Christianity*, 5.2 (2014), 149–77.
Fournet, T., Lucore, S. K., Redon, B., and Trümper, M. 'Catalog of Greek baths' in S. K. Lucore and M. Trümper (eds.), *Greek Baths and Bathing Culture. New Discoveries and Approaches* (Leuven: Peeters, 2013), 269–334.

Fournet, T. and Redon, B. R. R. 'Un édifice exceptionnel de la chôra alexandrine. Les bains souterrains de Taposiris Magna', *Archéologia*, 439 (2006), 52–9.

Fournet, T. and Redon, B. R. R. 'Le bain grec à l'ombre des thermes romains', *Les Dossiers d'Archéologie*, 342 (2010), 56–63.

Fraser, P. M. 'Two studies on the cult of Sarapis in the Hellenistic world', *OpAth*, 3 (1960), 1–54.

Fraser, P. M. 'Current problems concerning the early history of the cult of Sarapis', *OpAth*, 7 (1967), 23–45.

Fraser, P. M. *Ptolemaic Alexandria*, 3 vols. (Oxford: Clarendon Press, 1972).

Fraser, P. M. *The Cities of Alexander the Great* (Oxford: Clarendon Press, 1996).

Fulińska, A. 'Iconography of the Ptolemaic queens on coins. Greek style, Egyptian ideas?', *Studies in Ancient Art and Civilization*, 14 (2010), 73–92.

Gara, A. 'Limiti strutturali dell'economia monetaria nell'Egitto tardo-tolemaico', *Studi ellenistici*, 1 (1984), 107–34.

Gardin, J.-C. 'Les relations entre la Méditerranée et la Bactriane dans l'antiquité, d'après des données céramologiques inédites' in J.-L. Huot, M. Yon, and Y. Calvet (eds.), *De l'Indus aux Balkans. Recueil à la mémoire de Jean Deshayes* (Paris: Éd. Recherche sur les Civilisations, 1985), 447–60.

Garstad, B. 'Pausanias of Antioch. Introduction, translation, and commentary', *ARAM*, 23 (2011), 669–91

Gauthier, P. *Nouvelles inscriptions de Sardes II* (Geneva: Droz, 1989).

Gehler, M. and Rollinger, R. (eds.), *Imperien und Reiche in der Weltgeschichte. Epochenübergreifende und globalhistorische Vergleiche*, 2 vols. (Wiesbaden: Harrassowitz, 2014).

Gehler, M. and Rollinger, R. 'Imperien und Reiche in der Weltgeschichte. Epochenübergreifende und globalhistorische Vergleiche' in M. Gehler and R. Rollinger (eds.) *Imperien und Reiche in der Weltgeschichte. Epochenübergreifende und globalhistorische Vergleiche, vol. 1: Imperien des Altertums, mittelalterliche und frühneuzeitliche Imperien* (Wiesbaden: Harrassowitz, 2014b), 1–32.

George, A. 'Xerxes and the Tower of Babel', in J. Curtis and St J. Simpson (ed.), *The World of Achaemenid Persia. History, Art and Society in Iran and the Ancient Near East. Proceedings of a Conference at the British Museum, 29th September – 1st October 2005* (London: I. B. Tauris, 2010), 471–80.

Gerardin, F . 'D'un grand roi à l'autre. La Syrie-Coelé entre rivalités idéologiques et transition impériale de Ptolémée IV à Antiochos III' in C. Feyel and L. Graslin-Thomé (eds.) *Antiochos III et l'Orient. Journées d'études franco-allemandes, Nancy, 6–8 juin 2016* (Nancy: ADRA, 2017), 81–106.

Gerardin, F. 'City foundations in Egypt and Western Asia in the second century B.C.', unpublished dissertation, Yale University (2018).

Ghirshman, R. *Bégram: Recherches archéologiques et historiques sur les Kouchans. Mémoires de la Délégation Archéologique Française en Afghanistan 12. Mémoires de l'Institut Français d'Archéologie Orientale du Caire 79* (Cairo: IFAO 1946).

Gitler, H. and Stein-Kushnir, A. 'The chronology of a late Ptolemaic bronze coin-type from Cyprus', *INJ*, 13 (1994–9), 46–53.

Goedicke, H. *Comments on the 'Famine Stela'* (San Antonio, TX: Van Siclen Books, 1994).

Goodrich, L. C. 'Homer Dubs (1892–1969)', *The Journal of Asian Studies*, 29.4 (1970), 889–91.

Gorin, A. N. 'Новый селевкидский монетный двор: Сарамканд-Мараканда' in A. A. Khakimov and S. R. Baratov (eds.), *Материалы по художественной и духовной культуре Узбекистана* (Tashkent, 2014), 29–48.

Gorre, G. 'Identités et représentations dans l'Égypte ptolemaïque', *Ktèma*, 32 (2007), 239–50.

Gorre, G. *Les relations du clergé égyptien et des Lagides d'après les sources privées* (Leuven: Peeters, 2009a).

Gorre, G. '"Nectanébo-le-faucon" et la dynastie lagide', *Ancient Society*, 39 (2009b), 55–69.

Gorre, G. 'The Satrap Stela. A middle ground approach', *Journal of Egyptian History*, 10.1 (2017), 51–68.

Gorre, G. 'The Egyptian *temenē* in the third century B.C.E. Profane and holy uses' in S. Honigman, O. Lipschitz, and C. Nihan (eds.), *Times of Transition: Judea in the Early Hellenistic Period* (Philadelphia, Pa: Penn State University Press, 2021) 187–98.

Gorre, G. and Honigman, S. 'Kings, taxes and high priests. Comparing the Ptolemaic and Seleukid policies' in S. Bussi (ed.), *Egitto. Dai Faraoni agli Arabi. Atti del convegno Egitto. Amministrazione, economia, società, cultura dai Faraoni agli Arabi. Égypte. Administration, économie, société, culture des pharaons aux arabes, Milano, Università degli Studi, 7–9 gennaio 2013* (Fabrizio Serra, 2013), 105–20.

Gorre, G. and Honigman, S. 'La politique d'Antiochos IV à Jérusalem à la lumière des relations entre rois et temples aux époques perse et hellénistique' in C. Feyel and L. Graslin (eds.), *Le projet politique d'Antiochos IV. Journées d'études franco-allemandes, Nancy 17–19 juin 2013* (Nancy: ADRA, 2014), 301–38.

Gorre, G. and Lorber, C. 'The survival of the silver standard after the Grand Mutation', in T. Faucher (ed.), *Money Rules! The Monetary Economy of Egypt, from Persians until the Beginning of Islam* (Cairo, 2020), p. 147–68.

Gorre, G. and Veïsse, A.-E. 'Birth and disappearance of the priestly synods in the time of the Ptolemies', in G. Gorre and S. Wackenier (eds.), *Quand la fortune du royaume ne dépend pas de la vertu du prince: un renforcement de la monarchie lagide de Ptolémée VI à Ptolémée X (169–88 av. J.-C.)?* (Leuven, Paris, Bristol: Peeters 2020) 113–40.

Goukowsky, P. *Essai sur les origines du mythe d'Alexandre (336–270 av.J.-C.), vol. 2: Alexandre et Dionysos* (Presses universitaires de Nancy, 1981).

Gozzoli, R. B. *The Writing of History in Ancient Egypt during the First Millennium BC (ca. 1070–180). Trends and Perspectives* (London: Golden House, 2006).

Grainger, J. D. *The Syrian Wars* (Leiden: Brill, 2010).

Graslin-Thomé, L. 'Le règne d'Antiochos III vu depuis Babylone. Antiochos III dans les sources cunéiformes' in C. Feyel and L. Graslin-Thomé (eds.) *Antiochos III et l'Orient. Journées d'études franco-allemandes, Nancy, 6–8 juin 2016* (Nancy: ADRA, 2017), 211–42.

Grayson, A. K. *Assyrian and Babylonian Chronicles* (Locust Valley, NY: Augustin, 1975).

Grenet, F. and Isamiddinov, M. (2001) 'Brève chronique des fouilles de la MAFOUZ (Mission Archéologique Franco-Ouzbèke) en 2000,' *Cahiers d'Asie Centrale* 9 (2001), 237–42.

Griesbach, J. 'Porträts als Kommunikationsmittel in der hellenistischen Polis' in J. Griesbach (ed.), *Polis und Porträt. Standbilder als Medien öffentlicher Repräsentation im hellenistischen Osten* (Wiesbaden: Reichert, 2014), 11–19.

Griffith, G. T. *The Mercenaries of the Hellenistic World* (Cambridge University Press, 1935).

Grimal, N. *A History of Ancient Egypt* (Oxford: Blackwell, 1992).

Gruen, E. S. 'The origins and objectives of Onias' temple', *Scripta Classica Israelica*, 16 (1997), 47–70.

Günther, L.-M. 'Herrscher als Götter– Götter als Herrscher? Zur Ambivalenz hellenistischer Münzbilder' in L.-M. Günther and S. Plischke (eds.), *Studien zum vorhellenistischen und hellenistischen Herrscherkult* (Mainz: Verlag Antike, 2011), 98–113.

Haake, M. 'Das Diadem– königliches Symbol in hellenistischer Zeit' in K. Ehling and G. Weber (eds.), *Hellenistische Königreiche* (Darmstadt: von Zabern, 2014), 24–8.

Habicht, C. *Pausanias' Guide to Ancient Greece* (Berkeley, CA: University of California Press, 1985).

Habicht, C. 'The Seleucids and their Rivals', CAH^2, VIII (1989), 324–82.

Habicht, C. *The Hellenistic Monarchies. Selected papers* (Ann Arbor, MI: University of Michigan Press, 2006).

Habicht, C. 'Neues zur hellenistischen Geschichte von Kos', *Chiron*, 37 (2007), 123–52.

Habicht, C. and Jones, C. P. 'A Hellenistic inscription from Arsinoe in Cilicia', *Phoenix*, 43.4 (1989), 317–46.

Hackens, T. 'A propos de la circulation monétaire dans le Péloponnèse au IIIe s. av. J.-C.' in *Antidorum W. Peremans sexagenario ab alumnis oblatum* (Publications Universitaires de Louvain, 1968), 69–95.

Hackin, J. *Recherches archéologiques à Begram.* (Mémoires de la Délégation Archéologique Française en Afghanistan 9) (Paris: Les Éditions d'Art et d'Histoire 1939).

Hackin, J. *Nouvelles recherches archéologiques à Begram. Mémoires de la Délégation Archéologique Française en Afghanistan 11* (Paris: Imprimerie Nationale-Presses Universitaires 1954).

Hackl, J. 'The Esangila temple during the late Achaemenid period and the impact of Xerxes' reprisals on the northern Babylonian temple households' in

C. Waerzeggers (ed.), *Xerxes and Babylon – The Cuneiform Evidence* (Leuven: Peeters, 2018).
Hagedorn, D. 'Ein Erlaß Ptolemaios' I. Soter', *ZPE*, 66 (1986), 65–70.
Hallo, W. W. 'On the antiquity of Sumerian literature', *JAOS*, 83.2 (1963), 167–76.
Handelman, D. 'The organization of ethnicity', *Ethnic Groups: An International Periodical of Ethnic Studies*, 1 (1977), 187–200.
Hansen, M. H. *Polis. An Introduction to the Ancient Greek City-State* (Oxford University Press, 2006).
Harder, M. A. *Callimachus. Aetia, vol. 2: Commentary* (Oxford University Press, 2012).
Hartog, F. *The Mirror of Herodotus. The Representation of the Other in the Writing of History* (Berkeley, CA: University of California Press, 1988).
Hatzopoulos, M. B. *Bull. Epig.* (1997) no. 356.
Hauben, H. 'L'expedition de Ptolémée III en Orient et la sédition domestique de 245 av. J.-C.', *ArchPF*, 36 (1990), 29–38.
Hauben, H. and Meeus, A. *The Age of the Successors and the Creation of the Hellenistic Kingdoms (323–276 B.C.)* (Leuven: Peeters, 2014).
Haubold, J. *Greece and Mesopotamia. Dialogues in Literature* (Cambridge University Press, 2013a).
Haubold, J. 'The wisdom of the Chaldeans'. Reading Berossos, *Babyloniaca* Book 1' in J. Haubold, G. B. Lanfranchi, R. Rollinger, and J. M. Steele (eds.), *The World of Berossos. Proceedings of the 4th International Colloquium on 'The Ancient Near East between Classical and Ancient Oriental Traditions', Hatfield College, Durham 7th–9th July 2010* (Wiesbaden: Harrassowitz, 2013b), 31–45.
Haubold, J. 'Hellenism, cosmopolitanism, and the role of Babylonian elites in the Seleucid empire' in M. Lavan, R. E. Payne and J. Weisweiler (eds.), *Cosmopolitanism and Empire. Universal Rulers, Local Elites, and Cultural Integration in the Ancient Near East and Mediterranean* (Oxford University Press, 2016), 89–102.
Hazzard, R. A. *The Imagination of a Monarchy. Studies in Ptolemaic Propaganda* (University of Toronto Press, 2000).
Hazzard, R. A., and Huston, S. M. 'The surge in prices under Ptolemies IV and V', *ChrÉg* 90 (2015), 105–20.
Heichelheim, F. *Wirtschaftliche Schwankungen der Zeit von Alexander bis Augustus* (Jena: Fischer, 1930).
Heilporn, P. 'La provenance de la dédicace I.Th. Sy. 302.', *CE*, 65 (1990), 116–21.
Heilporn, P. *Thèbes et ses taxes. Recherches sur la fiscalité en Égypte romaine (Ostraca de Strasbourg II)* (Paris: de Boccard, 2009).
Heinen, H. 'Die Tryphè des Ptolemaios VIII. Euergetes II. Beobachtungen zum ptolemäischen Herrscherideal und zu einer römischen Gesandtschaft in Ägypten (140–139 v. Chr.)' in H. Heinen (eds.), *Althistorische Studien. Hermann Bengtson zum 70. Geburtstag dargebracht von Kollegen und Schülern* (Wiesbaden: Franz Steiner, 1983), 116–28.
Heinen, H. 'Ein griechischer Funktionär des Ptolemäerstaates als Priester ägyptischer Kulte' in B. Funck (ed.), *Hellenismus. Beiträge zur Erforschung von*

Akkulturation und politischer Ordnung in den Staaten des hellenistischen Zeitalters. Akten des Internationalen Hellenismus-Kolloquiums, 9.–14. März 1994 in Berlin (Tübingen: Mohr, 1996), 339–53.

Heinen, H. 'Der κτίστης Boethos und die Einrichtung einer neuen Stadt. Teil II', *ArchPF*, 43 (1997), 340–63.

Heinen, H. 'Boéthos, fondateur de *poleis* en Égypte ptolémaïque (OGIS I III et un nouveau papyrus de la collection de Trèves)' in L. Mooren (ed.), *Politics, Administration and Society in the Hellenistic and Roman World. Proceedings of the International Colloquium, Bertinoro 19–24 July 1997* (Leuven: Peeters, 2000), 123–53.

Heinen, H. 'Hunger, Not und Macht. Bemerkungen zur herrschenden Gesellschaft im ptolemäischen Ägypten', *Ancient Society*, 36 (2006), 13–44.

Held, W. 'Die Residenzstädte der Seleukiden. Babylon, Seleucia am Tigris, Aï Khanum, Seleucia in Pieria, Antiocheia am Orontes', *JdI*, 117 (2002), 217–49.

Heller, A. *Das Babylonien der Spätzeit (7.-4. Jh.) in den klassischen und keilschriftlichen Quellen* (Berlin: Verlag Antike, 2010).

Helms, S. W. 'Old Kandahar Excavations, 1976: Preliminary Report', *Afghan Studies* 2 (1979), 1–8.

Helms, S. W. 'Excavations at 'the City and the Famous Fortress of Kandahar, the Foremost Place in all of Asia', *Afghan Studies* 3–4 (1982), 1–24.

Helms, S. W. *Excavations at Old Kandahar in Afghanistan 1976–1978: Conducted on Behalf of the Society for South Asian Studies (Society for Afghan Studies). Stratigraphy, Pottery and Other Finds. BAR International Series 686; Society for South Asian Studies Monograph 2* (Oxford: Archaeopress 1997).

Heuss, A. *Stadt und Herrscher des Hellenismus in ihren staats- und völkerrechtlichen Beziehungen* (Leipzig: Dieterich, 1937/ND 1963).

Hoffmann, F. *Ägypten. Kultur und Lebenswelt in griechisch-römischer Zeit. Eine Darstellung nach den demotischen Quellen* (Berlin: Akademie Verlag, 2000).

Hölbl, G. *Geschichte des Ptolemäerreiches. Politik, Ideologie und religiöse Kultur von Alexander dem Großen bis zur römischen Eroberung* (Darmstadt: Wissenschaftliche Buchgesellschaft, 1994).

Hölbl, G. *A History of the Ptolemaic Empire* (London: Routledge, 2001).

Holleaux, M. *Études d'épigraphie et d'histoire grecques, vol. 3: Lagides et séleucides* (Paris: de Boccard, 1942).

Hölscher, T. *Ideal und Wirklichkeit in den Bildnissen Alexanders des Großen* (Heidelberg: Winter, 1971).

Holt, F. L. *Alexander the Great and Bactria: The Formation of a Greek Frontier in Central Asia* (Leiden: Brill, 1988).

Honigman, E. 'Historische Topographie von Nordsyrien im Altertum', *Zeitschrift des deutschen Palästina-Vereins*, 47 (1923), 149–93; 48 (1924), 1–64.

Honigman, S. 'Philon, Flavius Josèphe, et la citoyenneté alexandrine. Vers une utopie politique', *Journal of Jewish Studies*, 48.1 (1997), 62–90.

Honigman, S. 'The Jewish politeuma at Heracleopolis (Urkunden des Politeuma der Juden von Heracleopolis [144/3–133/2 v. Chr.] [P. Polit. Iud.]', *Scripta Classica Israelica*, 21 (2002), 251–66.

Honigman, S. '"Politeumata" and ethnicity in Ptolemaic and Roman Egypt', *Ancient Society*, 33 (2003), 61–102.

Honigman, S. 'Jewish communities in Hellenistic Egypt. Different responses to different environments' in L. I. Levine and D. R. Schwartz (eds.), *Jewish Identities in Antiquity. Studies in Memory of Menahem Stern* (Tübingen: Mohr Siebeck, 2009), 117–35.

Honigman, S. *Tales of High Priests and Taxes: The Books of the Maccabees and the Judean Rebellion Against Antiochus IV* (Berkeley, CA: University of California Press, 2014a).

Honigman, S. 'The religious persecution as a narrative elaboration of a military suppression' in M.-F. Baslez and O. Munnich (eds.), *La Mémoire des persecutions. Autour des livres des Maccabées* (Leuven: Peeters, 2014b), 59–76.

Honigman, S. 'The Ptolemaic and Roman definitions of social categories and the evolution of Judean communal identity in Egypt' in Y. Furstenberg (ed.) *Jewish and Christian Communal Identities in the Roman World* (Leiden: Brill, 2016), 25–74.

Honigman, S. 'Searching for the social location of literate Judean elites in Early Hellenistic Times: A non-linear history of the Temple and Royal administrations in Judea' in S. Honigman, O. Lipschits, and C. Nihan (eds.), *Times of Transition: Judea in the Early Hellenistic Period* (Philadelphia, Pa: Penn State University Press, 2021) 199–228.

Honigman, S., Ecker, A., Finkielsztejn, G., Gorre, G, and Syon, D. 2017. 'The southern Levant in Antiochos III's time. Between continuity and immediate or delayed changes' in C. Feyel and L. Graslin-Thomé (eds.), *Antiochos III et l'Orient. Journées d'études franco-allemandes, Nancy, 6–8 juin 2016* (Nancy: ADRA, 2017), 161–207.

Hoogendijk, F. A. J. 'The practice of taxation in three late Ptolemaic papyri' in T. Gagos (ed.), *Proceedings of the 25th International Congress of Papyrology, Ann Arbor, July 29–August 4, 2007* (Ann Arbor, MI: Scholarly Publishing Office, 2010), 313–22.

Hoover, O. 'Ceci n'est pas l'autonomie. The coinage of Seleucid Phoenicia as royal and civic power discourse' in V. Chakowski and F. Duyrat (eds.), *Le roi et l'économie. Autonomies locales et structures royales dans l'économie de l'empire séleucide* (Paris: de Boccard, 2004), 485–507.

Hoover, O. 'Time is money? A second look at production, quantification and chronology in the late Seleucid period', in F. de Callataÿ (ed.), *Quantifying Monetary Supplies in Greco-Roman Times* (Bari: Edipuglia, 2011), 251–65.

Hornung, E. *Geschichte als Fest. Zwei Vorträge zum Geschichtsbild der frühen Menschheit* (Darmstadt: Wissenschaftliche Buchgesellschaft, 1966).

Hornung, E. *Idea into Image. Essays on Ancient Egyptian Thought* (New York, NY: Timken, 1992).

Houghton, A. 'A double portrait coin of Alexander I Balas and Cleopatra Thea', *SNR*, 67 (1988), 85–93.

Houghton, A. 'The Seleucids' in W. E. Metcalf (ed.), *The Oxford Handbook of Greek and Roman Coinage* (Oxford University Press, 2012), 235–51.

Houghton, A. and Lorber, C. C. 'Antiochus III in Coele-Syria and Phoenicia', *INJ*, 14 (2000–2), 44–58.

Houghton, A., Lorber C. C. and Hoover, O. *Seleucid Coins. A Comprehensive Catalogue, part 2: Seleucus IV through Antiochus XIII*, 2 vols. (New York, NY: American Numismatic Society, 2008).

Houghton, A., Lorber C. C. and Kritt, B. *Seleucid Coins. A Comprehensive Catalogue, part 1: Seleucus I through Antiochus III*, 2 vols. (New York, NY: American Numismatic Society, 2002).

Houroth, W., Rubensohn, O., and Zücker, F. 'Bericht über die Ausgrabungen auf Elephantine in den Jahren 1906–1908', *ZÄS* 46 (1909), 14–61.

Howe, T. 'Founding Alexandria. Alexander the Great and the politics of memory' in P. R. Bosman (ed.), *Alexandria in Africa* (Pretoria: Classical Association of South Africa, 2014), 72–91.

Hurlet, F. *Les empires. Antiquité et Moyen Âge. Analyse comparée* (Presses Universitaires de Rennes, 2008).

Huß, W. 'Die in ptolemaiischer Zeit verfaßten Synodal-Dekrete der ägyptischen Priester', *ZPE*, 88 (1991), 189–204.

Huß, W. *Der makedonische König und die ägyptischen Priester. Studien zur Geschichte des ptolemaiischen Ägypten* (Stuttgart: Steiner, 1994).

Huß, W. 'Ptolemaios der Sohn', *ZPE*, 121 (1998), 229–50.

Huß, W. *Ägypten in hellenistischer Zeit, 332–30 v. Chr.* (Munich: Beck, 2001).

Huß, W. *Die Verwaltung des ptolemaiischen Reichs* (Munich: Beck, 2011).

Husson, G. and Valbelle, D. *L'état et les institutions en Égypte des premiers pharaons aux empereurs romains* (Paris: Colin, 1992).

Huston, S. M. and Lorber, C. C. 'A hoard of Ptolemaic bronze coins in commerce, October 1992 (*CH* 8, 413)', *NC*, 161 (2001), 11–40.

Hutmacher, R. *Das Ehrendekret für den Strategen Kallimachos* (Meisenheim a. Glan: Hein, 1965).

Iliakis, M. 'Greek mercenary revolts in Bactria. A re-appraisal', *Historia*, 62.2 (2013), 182–95.

Invernizzi, A. 'Seleucia on the Tigris. Centre and periphery in Seleucid Asia' in P. Bilde, T. Engberg-Pedersen, L. Hannestad, and J. Zahle (eds.), *Centre and Periphery in the Hellenistic World* (Aarhus University Press, 1993), 230–50.

Invernizzi, A. (ed.), *Seleucia al Tigri. Le impronte di sigillo dagli Archivi*, 3 vols. (Alessandria: Edizioni dell'Orso, 2004).

Iossif, P. P. 'Seleucid religion through coins. Is it possible to quantify "iconography" and "religion"?' in F. de Callataÿ (ed.), *Quantifying Monetary Supplies in Greco-Roman Times* (Bari: Edipuglia, 2011), 213–49.

Iossif, P. P. 'Apollo *Toxotes* and the Seleukids. *Comme un air de famille*' in P. P. Iossif, A. S. Chankowski and C. C. Lorber (eds.), *More than Men, Less than Gods. Studies on Royal Cult and Emperor Worship. Proceedings of the*

International Colloquium Organized by the Belgian School at Athens (1–2 November 2007) (Leuven: Peeters, 2011a), 229–91.

Iossif, P. P. 'Seleucid "eagles" from Tyre and Sidon. Preliminary results of a die-study' in N. Holmes (ed.), *Proceedings of the XIVth International Numismatic Congress, Glasgow 2009* (Glasgow: International Numismatic Council, 2011b), 213–29.

Iossif, P. P. 'Imago mundi. Expression et représentation de l'idéologie royale séleucide. La procession de Daphné', *Electrum*, 18 (2011c), 125–57.

Iossif, P. P. 'Les "cornes" des Séleucides. Vers une divinisation "discrète"', *CahÉtAnc*, 49 (2012), 45–150.

Iossif, P. P. 'The last Seleucids in Phoenicia. Juggling civic and royal identity', *AJN*, 26 (2014a), 61–87.

Iossif, P. P. 'Seleucia on the Tigris under the Seleucids. "Monetary" pantheon vs. "glyptic" pantheon', *Mythos. Rivista di storia delle religioni*, 8 (2014b), 35–54.

Iossif, P. P. 'Who's wealthier? An estimation of the annual coin production of the Seleucids and the Ptolemies', *RNB*, 161 (2015), 233–72.

Iossif, P. P. 'Using site finds as basis for statistical analyses of the Seleucid numismatic production and circulation. An introduction to the method' in F. Duyrat and C. Grandjean (eds.), *Les monnaies de fouille du monde grec (VIe–Ier s. a.C.). Apports, approches et méthodes* (Bordeaux: Ausonius, 2016), 263–96.

Iossif, P. P. 'Antiochos' III precious metal numismatic production seen through hoard data. A quantitative perspective' in C. Feyel and L. Graslin-Thomé (eds.), *Antiochos III et l'Orient. Journées d'études franco-allemandes, Nancy, 6–8 juin 2016* (Nancy: ADRA, 2017), 37–77.

Iossif, P. P. and Lorber, C. C. 'Celestial imagery on the eastern coinage of Antiochus IV', *Mesopotamia*, 44 (2009), 129–46.

Iossif, P. P. and Lorber, C. C. The rays of the Ptolemies', *RN*, 168 (2012), 197–224.

Jaeggi, O. *Die griechischen Porträts. Antike Repräsentation, moderne Projektion* (Berlin: Reimer, 2008).

Jasnow, R. 'The Greek Alexander romance and Demotic Egyptian literature', *JNES*, 56.2 (1997), 95–103.

Joannès, F. 'À propos du *zazakku* à l'époque néo-babylonienne', *Nouvelles Assyriologiques Brèves et Utilitaires*, no. 4 (1994), 93–4.

Johnson, C. G. 'The divinization of the Ptolemies and the gold octadrachms honoring Ptolemy III', *Phoenix*, 53.1–2 (1999), 50–6.

Johnson, J. H. 'Is the Demotic chronicle an anti-Greek tract?' in H.-J. Thissen and K.-T. Zauzich (eds.), *Grammata Demotika. Festschrift für Erich Lüddeckens zum 15. Juni 1983* (Würzburg: Gisela Zauzich 1984), 107–24.

Jouanno, C. *Naissance et metamorphoses du Roman d'Alexandre* (Paris: CNRS Editions, 2002).

Jursa, M. *Neo-Babylonian Legal and Administrative Documents. Typology, Contents and Archives* (Münster: Ugarit, 2005).

Jursa, M. 'Agricultural management, tax farming and banking. Aspects of entrepreneurial activity in Babylonia in the late Achaemenid and Hellenistic periods' in P. Briant and F. Joannès (eds.), *La transition entre l'empire achéménide et les royaumes hellénistiques (vers 350–300 av. J.-C.)* (Paris: de Boccard, 2006), 137–222.

Kampakoglou, A., 'Danaus βουγενής. Greco-Egyptian mythology and Ptolemaic kingship', *GRBS*, 56.1 (2016), 111–39.

Kansteiner, S., Hallof, K., Lehmann, L., Seidensticker, B. and Stemmer, K. (eds.) *Der Neue Overbeck. Die antiken Schriftquellen zu den bildenden Künstlern, vol. 3: Spätklassik. Bildhauer des 4. Jh. V. Chr.* (Berlin: de Gruyter, 2014).

Karageorgis, V. *Ancient Art from Cyprus. The Cesnola Collection in the Metropolitan Museum of Art* (New York, NY: Metropolitan Museum of Art, 2000).

Karttunen, K. 'King Eucratides in literary sources', *Silk Road Art and Archaeology*, 6 (1999–2000), 115–18.

Kasher, A. *The Jews in Hellenistic and Roman Egypt. The Struggle for Equal Rights* (Tübingen: Mohr, 1985).

Kasher, A. 'Review essay of: J. M. S. Cowey and K. Maresch, Urkunden des Politeuma der Juden von Herakleopolis (144/3–133/2 v. Chr.) (P. Polit. Iud.) (Wiesbaden: Westdeutscher Verlag, 2005)', *JQR*, 93 (2002), 257–68.

Kasher, A. 'The Jewish *politeuma* in Alexandria. A pattern of Jewish communal life in the Greco-Roman diaspora' in M. Rozen (ed.), *Homelands and Diasporas. Greek, Jews and Their Migrations* (London: I. B. Tauris, 2008), 109–25.

Kaye, N. and Amitay, O. 'Kleopatra's dowry. Taxation and sovereignty between Hellenistic kingdoms', *Historia*, 64.2 (2015), 131–55.

Kayser, F. *Recueil des inscriptions grecques et latines (non funéraires) d'Alexandrie impériale (Ier–IIIe s. apr. J.-C.)* (Cairo: IFAO, 1994)

Keesling, C. M. *Early Greek Portraiture. Monuments and Histories* (Cambridge University Press, 2017).

Kemp, B. J. *Ancient Egypt. Anatomy of a Civilization*, 2nd edn. (London: Routledge, 2006).

Kennell, N. M. 'New light on 2 Maccabees 4: 7–15', *Journal of Jewish Studies*, 56.1 (2005), 10–24.

Kienitz, F. K. *Die politische Geschichte Aegyptens vom 7. bis zum 4. Jahrhundert vor der Zeitwende* (Berlin: Akademie-Verlag, 1953).

Kirby, C. and Rathbone, D. 'Kom Talit. The rise and fall of a Greek town in the Faiyum', *Egyptian Archaeology*, 8 (1996), 29–31.

Kleber, K. *Tempel und Palast. Die Beziehungen zwischen dem König und dem Eanna-Tempel im spätbabylonischen Uruk* (Münster: Ugarit, 2008).

Klinkott, H. 'Die Satrapenstele von Ptolemaios (I.) Lagou' in K. Ehling and G. Weber (eds.), *Hellenistische Königreiche* (Darmstadt: von Zabern, 2014), 61–5.

Klinkott, H. 'Heiligtum und Herrschaft. Zum Verhältnis von Lokalheiligtümern und Reichsverwaltung am Beispiel der Satrapienteilung von Babylonien' in R. Achenbach and P. Funke (eds.), *Persische Reichspolitik und lokale*

Heiligtümer. *Internationale Tagung des Exzellenzclusters "Religion und Politik in Vormoderne und Moderne" vom 24.–26. Februar 2016 in Münster (Westfalen)* (Wiesbaden: Harrassowitz, 2019), 121–146.

Klotchkoff, I. 'The Late Babylonian list of scholars' in H. Klengel (ed.), *Gesellschaft und Kultur im alten Vorderasien* (Berlin: Akademie-Verlag, 1982), 149–54.

Klotz, D. and LeBlanc, M. 'An Egyptian priest in the Ptolemaic court. Yale Peabody Museum 264191' in C. Zivie-Coche and I. Guermeur (eds.), *"Parcourir l'éternité." Hommages à Jean Yoyotte* (Turnhout: Brepols, 2012), vol. 2, 645–98.

Knobloch, J. 'Eine etymologische Fabel im Sintflutbericht bei Berossos', *Glotta*, 63 (1985), 1.

Koenen, L. 'Die Prophezeiungen des "Töpfers"', *ZPE*, 2 (1968), 178–209.

Koenen, L. 'A supplementary note on the date of the Oracle of the Potter', *ZPE*, 54 (1984), 9–13.

Koenen, L. 'The Ptolemaic king as a religious figure' in A. Bulloch, E. S. Gruen, A. A. Long and A. Stewart (eds.) *Images and Ideologies. Self-Definition in the Hellenistic World. Papers presented at a Conference Held April 7–9,1988, at the University of California at Berkeley* (Berkeley, CA: University of California Press, 1993), 25–115.

Koenen, L. 'Die Apologie des Töpfers an König Amenophis oder das Töpferorakel' in A. Blasius and B. U. Schipper (eds.), *Apokalyptik und Ägypten. Eine kritische Analyse der relevanten Texte aus dem griechisch-römischen Ägypten* (Leuven: Peeters, 2002), 139–87.

Konuk, K. 'The Ptolemaic coins in the Bodrum Underwater Archaeology Museum' in S. Isager and P. Pederson (eds.), *The Salmakis Inscription and Hellenistic Halikarnassus* (Odense: University Press of Southern Denmark, 2004), 165–75.

Kopp, P., et al. 'Report of the 40th season of excavation and restoration on the island of Elephantine', *Online Reports of the Deutsches Archäologisches Institut* (2011), www.dainst.org/.

Koshelenko, G., Gaibov, V., and Bader, A. 'Evolution of the settlement patterns in the Merv Oasis (Turkmenistan) from Alexander the Great to Arab conquest' in Istituto Italiano per il Medio ed Estremo Oriente (ed.), *La Persia e l'Asia Centrale da Alessandro al X secolo* (Rome: Accademia Nazionale dei Lincei, 1996), 305–17.

Kosmin, P. 'Seleucid ethnography and indigenous kingship. The Babylonian education of Antiochus I' in J. Haubold, G. B. Lanfranchi, R. Rollinger, and J. M. Steele (eds.), *The World of Berossos. Proceedings of the 4th International Colloquium on 'The Ancient Near East between Classical and Ancient Oriental Traditions', Hatfield College, Durham 7th–9th July 2010* (Wiesbaden: Harrassowitz, 2013), 199–212.

Kosmin, P. *The Land of the Elephant Kings. Space, Territory, and Ideology in the Seleucid Empire* (Cambridge, MA: Harvard University Press, 2014a).

Kosmin, P. 'Seeing double in Seleucid Babylonia. Rereading the Borsippa Cylinder of Antiochus I' in A. Moreno and R. Thomas (eds.), *Patterns of the Past. Epitedeumata in the Greek Tradition* (Oxford University Press, 2014b), 173–98.

Kosmin, P. J. 'The politics of science. Eratosthenes' Geography and Ptolemaic imperialism', *Orbis Terrarum*, 15 (2017), 85–96.

Kosmin, P. *Time and Its Adversaries in the Seleucid Empire* (Cambridge, MA: Harvard University Press, 2018).

Kossmann, P. 'Les Lagides et l'Asie Mineure', unpublished PhD thesis, École Pratique des Hautes Études, Paris (2011).

Kovacs, M. '*Imitatio Alexandri* – zu Aneignungs- und Angleichungsphänomenen im römischen Porträt' in R. von den Hoff, F. Heinzer, H. W. Hubert and A. Schreurs-Morét (eds.), *Imitatio heroica. Heldenangleichung im Bildnis* (Würzburg: Ergon, 2015), 47–84.

Kovacs, M. 'Vom Herrscher zum Heros – Die Bildnisse Alexanders des Großen und die *Imitatio Alexandri*', unpublished thesis of habilitation, University of Freiburg i. Br. (2017).

Kramer, B. 'Der κτίστης Boethos und die Einrichtung einer neuen Stadt. Teil I', *ArchPF*, 43 (1997), 315–39.

Kritt, B. *Seleucid Coins of Bactria* (Lancaster, PA: Classical Numismatic Group, 1996).

Kritt, B. *The Early Seleucid Mint of Susa* (Lancaster, PA: Classical Numismatic Group, 1997).

Kroll, J. H. 'The emergence of ruler portraiture on early Hellenistic coins. The importance of being divine' in R. von den Hoff and P. Schultz (eds.), *Early Hellenistic portraiture. Image, Style, Context* (Cambridge University Press, 2007), 113–22.

Krug, A. *Binden in der griechischen Kunst. Untersuchungen zur Typologie (6.–1. Jahrh. v. Chr.)* (Mainz Univ. Diss.: Hösel, 1968).

Krul, J. '"The beautiful image has come out". The nocturnal fire ceremony and the revival of the Anu cult at late Babylonian Uruk', unpublished PhD thesis, Westfälische Wilhelms-Universität (2014).

Kruse, T. 'Das *politeuma* der Juden von Herakleopolis in Ägypten' in M. Karrer and W. Kraus (eds.), *Die Septuaginta – Texte, Kontexte, Lebenswelten. Internationale Fachtagung veranstaltet von Septuaginta Deutsch (LXX.D), Wuppertal 20.–23. Juli 2006* (Tübingen: Mohr Siebeck, 2008), 166–75.

Kruse, T. 'Das jüdische *politeuma* von Herakleopolis. Zur Methode der Integration ethnischer Gruppen in den Staat der Ptolemäer' in V. V. Dement'eva and T. Schmitt (eds.), *Volk und Demokratie im Altertum* (Göttingen: Ruprecht, 2010), 93–105.

Kruse, T. 'Die Festung in Herakleopolis und der Zwist im Ptolemäerhaus' in A. Jördens and J. F. Quack (eds.), *Ägypten zwischen innerem Zwist und äußerem Druck. Die Zeit Ptolemaios' VI. bis VIII. Internationales Symposion Heidelberg 16.–19.9. 2007* (Wiesbaden: Harrassowitz, 2011), 255–67.

Kruse, T. 'Zwischen Integration, Assimilation und Selbstbehauptung. Das Politeuma der Juden von Herakleopolis in Mittelägypten' in A. Pülz and E. Trinkl (eds.), *Das Eigene und das Fremde. Akten der 4. Tagung des Zentrums Archäologie und Altertumswissenschaften an der Österreichischen Akademie der Wissenschaften, 26.–27. März 2012* (Vienna: Verlag der Österreichischen Akademie der Wissenschaften, 2015a), 73–81.

Kruse, T. 'Ethnic *koina* and *politeumata* in Ptolemaic Egypt' in V. Gabrielsen and C. A. Thomsen (eds.), *Private Associations and the Public Sphere. Proceedings of a Symposium Held at the Royal Danish Academy of Sciences and Letters, 9–11 September 2010* (Copenhagen: Det Kongelige Danske Videnskabernes Selskab, 2015b), 270–300.

Kuhrt, A. 'Berossus' Babyloniaka and Seleucid rule in Babylonia' in A. Kuhrt and S. M. Sherwin-White (eds.), *Hellenism in the East. The Interaction of Greek and Non-Greek Civilisations from Syria to Central Asia after Alexander* (Berkeley, CA: University of California Press, 1987), 32–56.

Kuhrt, A. 'Babylonia from Cyrus to Xerxes', *CAH*, IV^2 (1988), 112–28.

Kuhrt, A. 'Alexander and Babylon' in H. Sancisi-Weerdenburg and J. W. Drijvers (eds.), *Achaemenid History, vol. 5: The Roots of the European Tradition. Proceedings of the 1987 Groningen Achaemenid History Workshop* (Leiden: Nederlands Instituut voor het Nabije Oosten, 1990), 121–30.

Kuhrt, A. 'The Seleucid kings and Babylonia. New perspectives on the Seleucid realm in the East' in P. Bilde, T. Engberg-Pedersen, L. Hannestad, and J. Zahle (eds.), *Aspects of Hellenistic kingship* (Aarhus University Press, 1996), 41–54.

Kuhrt, A. *The Persian Empire. A Corpus of Sources from the Achaemenid Period*, 2nd ed. (London: Routledge, 2010).

Kuhrt, A. and Sherwin-White, S., 'Xerxes' Destruction of Babylonian Temples' in H. Sancisi-Weerdenburg and A. Kuhrt (eds.), *Achaemenid History, vol. 2: The Greek Sources. Proceedings of the Groningen 1984 Achaemenid History Workshop* (Leiden: Nederlands Instituut voor het Nabije Oosten, 1987), 69–78.

Kuhrt, A. and Sherwin-White, S. 'Aspects of Seleucid royal ideology. The Cylinder of Antiochus I from Borsippa', *JHS*, 111 (1991), 71–86.

Kurth, D. *Treffpunkt der Götter. Inschriften aus dem Tempel des Horus von Edfu* (Düsseldorf: Artemis und Winkler, 1998).

Kyrieleis, H. *Bildnisse der Ptolemäer* (Berlin: Mann, 1975).

Kyrieleis, H. *Ein Bildnis des Königs Antiochos IV. von Syrien* (Berlin: de Gruyter, 1980).

Kyrieleis, H. 'θεοὶ ὁρατοί. Zur Sternsymbolik hellenistischer Herrscherbildnisse' in K. Braun and A. Furtwängler (eds.), *Studien zur klassischen Archäologe. Friedrich Hiller zu seinem 60. Geburtstag am 12. März 1986* (Saarbrücken: Saarbrücker Druck und Verlag, 1986) 55–67.

Kyrieleis, H. 'Griechische Ptolemäerbildnisse. Eigenart, Unterschiede zu anderen Herrscherbildnissen' in H. Beck, P. C. Bol and M. Bückling (eds.), *Ägypten, Griechenland, Rom. Abwehr und Berührung* (Tübingen: Wasmuth, 2005), 235–43.

Kyrieleis, H. *Hellenistische Herrscherporträts auf Siegelabdrücken aus Paphos (Paphos IV B)* (Wiesbaden: Reichert, 2015).
La Rocca, E. and Bucchino, L. (eds.) *Ritratti. Le tante facce del potere* (Rome: Zetemata, 2011).
Ladynin, I. 'The Argeadai building program in Egypt in the framework of Dynasties' XXIX–XXX temple building' in V. Grieb, K. Nawotka, and A. Wojciechowska (eds.), *Alexander the Great and Egypt* (Wiesbaden: Harrassowitz, 2014) 221–40.
Lambert, W. G. 'A catalogue of texts and authors', *JCS*, 16.3 (1962), 59–77.
Lambert, W. G. and Walcot, P. 'A new Babylonian theology and Hesiod', *Kadmos* 4.1 (1965), 64–72.
Lanciers, E. 'Die ägyptischen Priester des ptolemäischen Königskultes', *RÉg*, 42 (1991), 117–45.
Lanciers, E., 'The civil war between Ptolemy VIII and Cleopatra II (132–124). Possible causes and key events' in G. Gorre and S. Wackenier (eds.), *Quand les vertus du prince ne font pas l'État. Un renforcement de la monarchie lagide de Ptolémée VI à Ptolémée X?* (Leuven: Peeters, 2020), 21–54.
Lang, M. 'Book two. Mesopotamian early history and the flood story' in J. Haubold, G. B. Lanfranchi, R. Rollinger, and J. Steele (eds.) *The World of Berossos. Proceedings of the 4th International Colloquium on "The Ancient Neat East between Classical and Ancient Oriental Traditions", Hatfield College, Durham 7th–9th July 2010* (Wiesbaden: Harrassowitz, 2013), 47–60.
Laronde, A. *Cyrène et la Libye hellénistique. Libykai historiai de l'époque républicaine au principat d'Auguste* (Paris: CNRS, 1987).
Laubscher, H. P. 'Hellenistische Herrscher und Pan', *AM*, 100 (1985), 333–53.
Laubscher, H. P. 'Triptolemos und die Ptolemäer', *Jahrbuch des Museums für Kunst und Gewerbe Hamburg*, 6–7 (1988), 11–40.
Laubscher, H. P. 'Ptolemäische Reiterbilder', *AM*, 106 (1991), 223–38.
Laubscher, H. P. 'Ein Ptolemäer als Hermes' in H. Froning, T. Hölscher and H. Mielsch (eds.), *Kotinos. Festschrift für Erika Simon* (Mainz: von Zabern, 1992), 317–22.
Launey, M. *Recherches sur les armées hellénistiques* (Paris: de Boccard, 1949–50).
Lauter, H. 'Lysipp als Porträtist' in J. Chamay and J. L. Maier (eds.), *Lysippe et son influence. Études de divers savants* (Geneva: Hellas et Roma, 1987), 57–75.
Le Rider, G. *Suse sous les Séleucides et les Parthes. Les trouvailles monétaires et l'histoire de la ville* (Paris: Geuthner, 1965).
Le Rider, G. 'La politique monétaire des Séleucides en Coelé Syrie et en Phénicie après 200. Réflexions sur les monnaies d'argent lagides et sur les monnaies d'argent séleucides à l'aigle', *BCH*, 119.1 (1995), 391–404.
Le Rider, G. *Séleucie du Tigre. Les monnaies séleucides et parthes* (Florence: Le Lettere, 1998).
Le Rider, G. *Antioche de Syrie sous les Séleucides. Corpus des monnaies d'or et d'argent de Séleucos I à Antiochos V, c. 300–161* (Paris: Institut de France, 1999).

Le Rider, G. and Callatay, F. de *Les Séleucides et les Ptolémées. L'héritage monétaire et financier d'Alexandre le Grand* (Paris: Éditions du Rocher, 2006).
Legras, B. *Les Reclus grecs du Sarapieion de Memphis. Une enquête sur l'hellénisme égyptien* (Leuven: Peeters, 2011).
Legras, B. 'Sarapis, Isis et le pouvoir lagide' in L. Bricault and M. J. Versluys (eds.), *Power, Politics, and the Cult of Isis. Proceedings of the Vth International Conference of Isis Studies, Boulogne-sur-Mer, October 13–15, 2011* (Leiden-London: Brill, 2014), 95–115.
Lehmann, G. A. *"Römischer Tod" in Kolophon/Klaros. Neue Quellen zum Status der "freien" Polisstaaten an der Westküste Kleinasiens im späten zweiten Jahrhundert v. Chr.* (Göttingen: Vandenhoeck & Ruprecht, 1998), 146–51.
Leitz, C. *Quellentexte zur ägyptischen Religion, vol. 1: Die Tempelinschriften der griechisch-römischen Zeit*, 3rd ed. (Münster: LIT, 2009).
Lelli, E. and Parlato, G. 'Le vittorie di Sosibio', *ZPE*, 166 (2008), 59–65.
Lenski, N. E. *Constantine and the Cities. Imperial Authority and Civic Politics* (Philadelphia, PA: University of Pennsylvania Press, 2016).
Lenzi, A. 'The Uruk list of kings and sages and late Mesopotamian scholarship', *JANER*, 8.2 (2008), 137–69.
Lerner, J. D. 'The Aï Khanoum philosophical papyrus', *ZPE*, 142 (2003), 45–51.
Lichtenberger, A., Martin, K., Nieswandt, H.-H, and Salzmann, D. (eds.) *Das Diadem der hellenistischen Herrscher. Übernahme, Transformation oder Neuschöpfung eines Herrschaftszeichens. Kolloquium vom 30.–31. Januar 2009 in Münster* (Bonn: Habelt, 2012).
Lichtenberger, A., Nieswandt, H.-H. and Salzmann, D. (eds.) 'Ein Porträt des Lysimachos? Anmerkungen zu einem anonymen Herrscherbild auf den Münzen von Lysimacheia' in E. Winter (ed.), *Vom Euphrat bis zum Bosporus. Kleinasien in der Antike. Festschrift für Elmar Schwertheim zum 65. Geburtstag* (Bonn: Habelt, 2008), 391–407.
Lichtheim, M. *Ancient Egyptian Literature, vol. 2: The New Kingdom* (Berkeley, CA: University of California Press, 1976).
Lichtheim, M. *Ancient Egyptian Literature*, 3 vols. (Berkeley, CA: University of California Press, 2006).
Lieven, D. , *Empire: The Russian Empire and Its Rivals* (London: John Murray, 2000).
Linssen, M. *The Cults of Uruk and Babylon. The Temple Ritual Texts as Evidence for Hellenistic Cult Practice* (Leiden: Brill, 2004).
Lipiński, E. *The Aramaeans. Their Ancient History, Culture, Religion* (Leuven: Peeters, 2000).
Lippert, S. L. and Schentuleit, M. 'Die Tempelökonomie nach den demotischen Texten aus Soknopaiu Nesos' in S. L. Lippert and M. Schentuleit (eds.), *Tebtynis und Soknopaiu Nesos. Leben im römerzeitlichen Fajum. Akten des Internationalen Symposions vom 11. bis 13. Dezember 2003 in Sommerhausen bei Würzburg* (Wiesbaden: Harrassowitz, 2005), 71–8.
Lipschits, O. and Tal, O. 'The settlement archaeology of the province of Judah. A case study' in O. Lipschits, G. N. Knoppers, and R. Albertz, R. (eds.), *Judah*

and the Judeans in the Fourth Century B.C.E (Winona Lake, IN: Eisenbrauns, 2007), 33–52.

Liverani, M. 'The growth of the Assyrian empire in the Habur/Middle Euphrates area. A new paradigm', *State Archive of Assyria Bulletin*, 2.2 (1988), 81–98.

Locher, J. *Topographie und Geschichte der Region am ersten Nilkatarakt in griechisch- römischer Zeit* (Leipzig: Teubner, 1999).

Lorber, C. C. 'Large Ptolemaic bronzes in third-century Egyptian hoards', *AJN*, 12 (2000), 67–92.

Lorber, C. C. 'A revised chronology for the coinage of Ptolemy I', *NC*, 165 (2005), 45–64.

Lorber, C. C. 'The last Ptolemaic bronze issue of Tyre', *INR*, 1 (2006), 15–20.

Lorber, C. C. 'The Ptolemaic era coinage revisited', *NC*, 167 (2007a), 105–17.

Lorber, C. C. 'The Ptolemaic mint of Ras Ibn Hani', *INR*, 2 (2007b), 63–75.

Lorber C. C. 'Theos *Aigiochos*. The *aegis* in Ptolemaic portraits of divine rulers' in P. P. Iossif, A. S. Chankowski and C. C. Lorber (eds.), *More than Men, Less than Gods. Studies on Royal Cult and Emperor Worship. Proceedings of the International Colloquium Organized by the Belgian School at Athens (1–2 November 2007)* (Leuven: Peeters, 2011), 293–355.

Lorber, C. C. 'Dating the portrait coinage of Ptolemy I', *AJN*, 24 (2012a), 33–44.

Lorber, C. C. 'The coinage of the Ptolemies' in W. E. Metcalf (ed.), *The Oxford Handbook of Greek and Roman Coinage* (Oxford University Press, 2012b), 211–34.

Lorber, C. C. 'An Egyptian interpretation of Alexander's elephant headdress', *AJN*, 24 (2012c), 21–31.

Lorber, C. C. 'The grand mutation. Ptolemaic bronze coinage in the second century B.C.' in S. Bussi (ed.), *Egitto. Dai Faraoni agli Arabi. Atti del convegno Egitto. Amministrazione, economia, società, cultura dai Faraoni agli Arabi. Égypte. Administration, économie, société, culture des pharaons aux arabes, Milano, Università degli Studi, 7–9 gennaio 2013* (Fabrizio Serra, 2013), 135–57.

Lorber, C. C. 'The royal portrait on Ptolemaic coinage' in A. Lichtenberger, K. Martin, H.-H. Nieswandt and D. Salzmann (eds.), *BildWert: Nominalspezifische Kommunikationsstrategien in der Münzprägung hellenistischer Herrscher, Kolloquium vom 17.–18. Juni 2010 in Münster* (Bonn: Habelt, 2014a), 111–81.

Lorber, C. C. 'Ptolemy I and Hermes-Thot. A new Ptolemaic gold issue', *NumAntCl*, 43 (2014b), 205–20.

Lorber, C. C. 'Royal coinages in Hellenistic Phoenicia. Expressions of continuity, agents of change' Rome' in J. Aliquot and C. Bonnet (eds.), *La Phénicie hellénistique. Actes du colloque international de Toulouse (18–20 féviert 2013)* (Paris: de Boccard, 2015a), 55–88.

Lorber, C. C. 'The gold mnaieia of autonomous Tyre with the double cornucopiae', *NumAntCl*, 44 (2015b), 177–94.

Lorber, C. C. 'Cryptic portraits of Ptolemaic kings on silver coins of the second and first centuries B.C., *NumAntCl*, 45 (2016a), 79–98.

Lorber, C. C. 'Cyrenaican coinage and Ptolemaic monetary policy' in M. Asolati (ed.), *Le monete di Cirene e della Cirenaica nel Mediterraneo. Problemi e prospettive. Atti del V Congresso Internazionale di Numismatica e di Storia Monetaria, Padova, 17–19 marzo 2016* (Padua: Esedra Editrice, 2016b), 101–26.

Lorber, C. C. 'Die study of the Antioch tetradrachms of Antiochus VII Euergetes', *NC*, 176 (2016c), 21–82.

Lorber, C. C. 'The price (*timê*) of the silver stater in Ptolemaic Egypt', *Ancient Society*, 47 (2017), 19–61.

Lorber, C. C. *The Coins of the Ptolemaic Empire, part 1: Ptolemy I through Ptolemy IV*, 2 vols. (New York, NY: American Numismatic Society, 2018).

Lorber, C. C. 'Silver coinage in Seleucid Coele Syria and Phoenicia. Implications for the history of Judah' in A. Berlin and P. Kosmin (eds.), *The Middle Maccabees. Archaeology, History, and the Rise of the Hasmonean Kingdom* (2021).

Lorber, C. C. and Hoover, O. D. 'An unpublished tetradrachm issued by the Artists of Dionysus', *NC*, 163 (2003), 59–68.

Lorber, C., and Iossif, P. P. 'Seleucid campaign beards', *AntCl*, 78 (2009), 87–115.

Lüderitz, G. *Corpus jüdischer Zeugnisse aus der Cyrenaika* (Wiesbaden: Reichert, 1983).

Lüderitz, G. 'What is the politeuma?' in J. W. van Henten and P. W. van der Horst (eds.), *Studies in Early Jewish Epigraphy* (Leiden: Brill, 1994), 183–225.

Ludlow, Francis and Manning, Joseph G. "Revolts under the Ptolemies: A Paleoclimatical Perspective" in J. J. Collins /J. G. Manning (eds.) *Revolt and Resistance in the Ancient Classical World and the Near East: In the Crucible of Empire* (Leiden, 2016), 154–71.

Ma, J. *Antiochos III and the Cities of Western Asia Minor* (Oxford University Press, 1999 [2nd ed., 2002]).

Ma, J. 'Le roi en ses images. Essai sur les représentations du pouvoir monarchique dans le monde hellénistique' in I. Savalli-Lestrade and I. Cogitore (eds.), *Des rois au prince. Pratiques du pouvoir monarchique dans l'Orient hellénistique et romain (IVe siècle avant J.-C.– IIe siècle après J.-C.)* (Grenoble: ELLUG, 2010), 147–64.

Ma, J. 'Re-examining Hanukkah', http://marginalia.lareviewofbooks.org/re-examining-hanukkah/ [2013a, accessed 20 January 2016].

Ma, J. *Statues and cities. Honorific Portraits and Civic Identity in the Hellenistic World* (Oxford University Press, 2013b).

Ma, J. 'Lire le portrait hellénistique. Pistes' in D. Boschung and F. Queyrel (eds.), *Bilder der Macht. Das griechische Porträt und seine Verwendung in der antiken Welt* (Paderborn: Wilhelm Fink, 2017), 49–66.

Ma, J. 'The Restauration of the Temple in Jerusalem by the Seleukid State: 2 Macc 11:16–38' in R. Oetjen (ed.), *New Perspectives in Seleucid History, Archaeology and Numismatics. Studies in Honor of Getzel M. Cohen* (Berlin; Boston: de Gruyter, 2020), 80–93.

Macdonald, G. 'Early Seleucid portraits', *JHS*, 27 (1907), 145–59.

MacGinnis, J. 'A further note on the *zazakku*', *Nouvelles Assyriologiques Brèves et Utilitaires*, no. 1 (1996), 19–20.

Macridy-Bey, T. 'À travers les nécropoles sidoniennes', *Rbibl N.S.*, 1 (1904), 547–72.

Madreiter, I. 'Antiochos the Great and the robe of Nebuchadnezzar. Intercultural transfer between Orientalism and Hellenocentrism' in S. Svärd and R. Rollinger (eds.), *Cross-Cultural Studies in Near Eastern History and Literature* (Münster: Ugarit, 2016), 111–36.

Mairs, R. 'The places in between. Model and metaphor in the archaeology of Hellenistic Arachosia' in A. Kouremenos, S. Chandrasekaran, and R. Rossi (eds.), *From Pella to Gandhara. Hybridisation and Identity in the Art and Architecture of the Hellenistic East* (Oxford: Archaeopress, 2011), 177–89.

Mairs, R. 'Glassware from Roman Egypt at Begram (Afghanistan) and the Red Sea trade', *British Museum Studies in Ancient Egypt and Sudan*, 18 (2012), 61–74.

Mairs, R. 'The Hellenistic Far East. From the *oikoumene* to the community' in E. Stavrianopoulou (ed.), *Shifting Social Imaginaries in the Hellenistic Period. Narratives, Practices, and Images* (Leiden: Brill, 2013), 365–85.

Mairs, R. 'Models, moulds and mass production. The mechanics of stylistic influence from the Mediterranean to Bactria', *Ancient West and East*, 13 (2014a), 175–95.

Mairs, R. *The Hellenistic Far East. Archaeology, Language and Identity in Greek Central Asia* (Berkeley, CA: University of California Press, 2014b).

Mairs, R. 'Achaemenid Ai Khanoum', *AMIran*, 46 (2014c).

Mairs, R. 'The founder shrine and the "Foundation" of Ai Khanoum' in N. Mac Sweeney (ed.), *Foundation Myths in Dialogue. Discourses about Origins in Ancient Societies* (Philadelphia, PA: University of Pennsylvania Press, 2015), 103–28.

Mann, M. *The Sources of Social Power, vol 1: A History of Power from the Beginning to A.D. 1760* (Cambridge University Press, 1986).

Manning, J. G. 'Edfu as a central place in Ptolemaic history' in W. Clarysse and K. Vandorpe (eds.), *Edfu, an Egyptian Provincial Capital in the Ptolemaic Period. Brussels, 3 September 2001* (Brussels: Koninklijke Vlaamse Academie van België voor Wetenschappen en Kunsten, 2003a), 61–73.

Manning, J. G. *Land and Power in Ptolemaic Egypt. The Structure of Land Tenure* (Cambridge University Press, 2003b).

Manning, J. G. *The Last Pharaohs. Egypt under the Ptolemies, 305–30 BC* (Princeton University Press, 2010 [3rd printing, 2012]).

Manning, J. G. 'Elephantine, Ptolemaic and Roman' in R. S. Bagnall, et al. (eds.), *The Encyclopedia of Ancient History* (New York: Wiley, 2012), 2.366–2.367.

Manning, J. G. and Ludlow, F. 'Revolts under the Ptolemies. A paleoclimatological perspective' in J. J. Collins and J. G. Manning (eds.), *Revolt and Resistance in the Ancient Classical World and the Near East. In the Crucible of Empire* (Leiden: Brill, 2016), 154–71.

Manning J. G. et al. 'Volcanic suppression of Nile summer flooding triggers revolt and constrains interstate conflict in ancient Egypt', *Nature Communications*, 8.1 (2017), article no. 900.

Marcus, R. *Josephus IX (LCL 365): Josephus, Jewish Antiquities, Books XII–XIII* (Cambridge, MA: Harvard University Press, 1943).

Maresch, K. *Bronze und Silber. Papyrologische Beiträge zur Geschichte der Währung im ptolemäischen und römischen Ägypten bis zum 2. Jahrhundert n. Chr.* (Opladen: Westdeutscher Verlag, 1996).

Maresch, K. and Cowey, J. M. S. '"A recurrent inclination to isolate the case of the Jews from their Ptolemaic environment"? Eine Antwort auf Sylvie Honigman', *Scripta Classica Israelica*, 22 (2003), 307–10.

Marinoni, E. 'Le capitale del regno di Seleuco I', *RendItsLomb*, 106 (1972), 579–631.

Marouard, G. 'Rues et habitats dans les villages de la chora égyptienne à la période gréco-romaine (IIIe s. av.-IVe s. apr. J.-C.). Quelques exemples du Fayoum (nome arsinoïte)' in P. Ballet, N. Dieudonné-Glad, and C. Saliou (eds.), *La rue dans l'Antiquité. Définition, aménagement et devenir de l'Orient méditerranéen à la Gaule. Actes du colloque de Poitiers, 7–9 septembre 2006* (Presses Universitaires de Rennes, 2008), 117–28.

Marouard, G. 'Les données archéologiques et architecturales des quartiers domestiques et des habitats dans les fondations et les refondations lagides de la chôra égyptienne. Une révision archéologique ' in P. Ballet (ed.), *Grecs et Romains en Égypte. Territoires, espaces de la vie et de la mort, objets de prestige et du quotidien* (Cairo: IFAO, 2012), 121–40.

Marouard, G. 'Maisons-tours et organisation des quartiers domestiques dans les agglomérations du Delta. L'exemple de Bouto de la Basse Époque aux premiers lagides' in S. Marchi (ed.), *Les maisons-tours en Égypte durant la basse-époque, les périodes ptolémaique et romaine. Actes de la table-ronde de Paris Université Paris-Sorbonne (Paris IV) 29–30 Novembre 2012* (Paris: de Boccard, 2014), 105–33.

Marouard, G. '"Completamente distrutte". Réévaluation archéologique de Philadelphie du Fayoum, Égypte' in R. K. Ritner (ed.), *Essays for the Library of Seshat. Studies Presented to Janet H. Johnson on the Occasion of Her 70th Birthday* (Chicago, IL: Oriental Institute of the University of Chicago, 2017), 119–52.

Marshall, F. H. 'MLXVI. Syene (Aswan)' in C. T. Newton (ed.), *The Collection of Ancient Greek Inscriptions in the British Museum*, vol. 4 (Oxford: Clarendon Press, 1916), 198–202.

Martin, K. 'Königin und Göttin. Zur Präsenz des Diadems auf Königinnen-Münzen' in A. Lichtenberger, K. Martin, H.-H. Nieswandt and D. Salzmann (eds.), *Das Diadem der hellenistischen Herrscher. Übernahme, Transformation oder Neuschöpfung eines Herrschaftszeichens. Kolloquium vom 30.–31. Januar 2009 in Münster* (Bonn: Habelt, 2012a), 395–423.

Martin, K. 'Der König als Heros? Das Diadem und die Binden von (Gründer-) Heroen' in A. Lichtenberger, K. Martin, H.-H. Nieswandt and D. Salzmann (eds.), *Das Diadem der hellenistischen Herrscher. Übernahme, Transformation oder Neuschöpfung eines Herrschaftszeichens. Kolloquium vom 30.–31. Januar 2009 in Münster* (Bonn: Habelt, 2012b), 249–78.

Maschek, D. 'Zum Phänomen der Bildnisangleichung im traianischen Männerporträt', *ÖJh*, 73 (2004), 171–88.

Maßner, A.-K. *Bildnisangleichung. Untersuchungen zur Entstehungs- und Wirkungsgeschichte des Augustusporträts (43 v. Chr.– 68 n. Chr.)* (Berlin: Mann, 1982).

Mastrocinque, A. 'Review of: K. Brodersen, Appians Antiochike (Syriake 1,1–44,232). Text und Kommentar. Nebst einem Anhang: Plethons Syriake-Exzerpt (Munich: Editio Maris, 1991)', *Gnomon* 66.5 (1994), 451–3.

Mastrocinque, A. 'Zeus Kretagenès seleucidico. Da Seleucia a Praeneste (e in Giudea)', *Klio*, 84.2 (2002), 355–72.

Matthew, C. A. 'Greek hoplites in an ancient Chinese siege', *Journal of Asian History*, 45 (2011), 17–37.

McEwan, G. *Texts from Hellenistic Babylonia in the Ashmolean Museum Oxford* (Oxford: Clarendon Press, 1982).

McGing, B. 'Revolt Egyptian style. Internal opposition to Ptolemaic rule', *ArchPF*, 43 (1997), 273–314.

McGing, B. 'Revolting subjects. Empires and insurrection, ancient and modern' in J. J. Collins and J. G. Manning (eds.), *Revolt and Resistance in the Ancient Classical World and the Near East. In the Crucible of Empire* (Leiden: Brill, 2016), 139–53.

McLean, B. H. *An Introduction to Greek Epigraphy of the Hellenistic and Roman periods from Alexander the Great down to the Reign of Constantine (323 B.C.–A.D. 337)* (Ann Arbor, MI: University of Michigan Press, 2002).

McMichael, P. 'Incorporating comparison within a world-historical perspective. An alternative comparative method', *American Sociological Review*, 55.3 (1990), 385–97.

McNicoll, A. 'Excavations at Kandahar, 1975: Second Interim Report', *Afghan Studies* 1 (1978), 41–66.

McNicoll, A. and Ball, W. *Excavations at Kandahar 1974 and 1975: The First Two Seasons at Shahr-i Kohna (Old Kandahar) Conducted by the British Institute of Afghan Studies. (BAR International Series 641; Society for South Asian Studies Monograph 1)* Oxford: Tempus Reparatum 1996.

Meadows, A. R. 'Money, freedom, and empire in the Hellenistic world' in A. R. Meadows and K. Shipton (eds.), *Money and Its Uses in the Ancient Greek World* (Oxford University Press 2001), 53–63.

Meadows, A. R. 'Ptolemaic possessions outside Egypt', in R. S. Bagnall, et al. (eds.), *The Encyclopedia of Ancient History* (New York, 2012) 5625–9.

Meadows, A. R. 'Ptolemaic possessions outside Egypt', in R. S. Bagnall, et al. (eds.), *The Encyclopedia of Ancient History* (Malden, MA: Wiley, 2013), 5625–9.

Meadows, A. R. 'The Ptolemaic league of islanders', in K. Buraselis, M. Stefanou and D. J. Thompson (eds.), *The Ptolemies, the Sea and the Nile. Studies in Waterborne Power* (Cambridge University Press, 2013a), 24–42.

Meeks, D. 'Les donations aux temples dans l'Égypte du Ier millénaire avant J.-C.' in E. Lipiński (ed.), *State and Temple Economy in the Ancient Near East. Proceedings of the International Conference Organized by the Katholieke*

Universiteit Leuven from the 10th to the 14th of April 1978, vol. 2 (Leuven: Katholieke Universiteit, Dep. Oriëntalistiek, 1978), 605–87.

Mehl, A. 'Zwischen West und Ost / Jenseits von West und Ost. Das Reich der Seleukiden' in K. Brodersen (ed.), *Zwischen Ost und West. Studien zur Geschichte des Seleukidenreiches* (Hamburg: Kovač, 1999), 9–43.

Meißner, B. *Historiker zwischen Polis und Königshof. Studien zur Stellung der Geschichtsschreiber in der griechischen Gesellschaft in spätklassischer und frühhellenistischer Zeit* (Göttingen: Vandenhoeck & Ruprecht, 1992).

Mekis, T. 'Quelques données nouvelles sur les stèles Budapest MBA inv. n°51.1928 et Prague MN P 1636, et sur la famille de Iâhmès fils de Smendès, propriétaire de la statue Caire JE 37075' in L. Coulon (ed.), *La cachette de Karnak. Nouvelles perspectives sur les découvertes de Georges Legrain* (Cairo: IFAO, 2016), 383–98.

Mélèze Modrzejewski, J. 'Le statut des Hellènes dans l'Égypte lagide. Bilan et perspectives des recherches', *RÉG*, 96 (1983), 241–68.

Mélèze Modrzejewski, J. *The Jews of Egypt. From Ramses II to Emperor Hadrian* (Princeton University Press, 1997).

Mélèze-Modrzejewski, J. *Droit et justice dans le monde grec et hellénistique* (Warsaw: Faculty of Law and Administration, 2011).

Messina, V. 'Da Uruk a Seleucia. Pratiche amministrative e archivi della Babilonia seleucide', *Mesopotamia*, 40 (2005), 125–44.

Meyer, H. *Ein Seleukide in Ägypten* (Munich: Staatliches Museum Ägyptischer Kunst, 2000).

Mileta, C. 'Überlegungen zum Charakter und zur Entwicklung der neuen Poleis im hellenistischen Kleinasien' in A. Matthaei and M. Zimmermann (eds.), *Stadtbilder im Hellenismus* (Berlin: Verlag Antike, 2009), 70–89.

Milne, J. G. *Greek Inscriptions* (Oxford University Press, 1905).

Minas, M. *Die hieroglyphischen Ahnenreihen der ptolemäischen Könige. Ein Vergleich mit den Titeln der eponymen Priester in den demotischen und griechischen Papyri* (Mainz: von Zabern, 2000).

Minas-Nerpel, M. 'Pharaoh and temple building in the fourth century BCE' in J. Cromwell and P. McKechnie (eds.), *Ptolemy I Soter and the Transformation of Egypt, 404–282 BC* (Leiden: Brill, 2018), 120–65.

Mitsuma, Y. 'The offering for the ritual of King Seleucus III and his offspring' in J. Feliu, J. Llop, A. Millet Albà and J. Sanmartín (eds.), *Time and History in the Ancient Near East. Proceedings of the 56th Rencontre Assyriologique Internationale at Barcelona 26–30 July 2010* (Winona Lake, IN: Eisenbrauns, 2013), 739–44.

Mittag, P. F. *Antiochos IV. Epiphanes. Eine politische Biographie* (Berlin: Akademie-Verlag, 2006).

Möller, A. 'Epoch-making Eratosthenes', *GRBS*, 45 (2005), 245–60.

Momigliano, A. 'J. G. Droysen between Greeks and Jews', *History and Theory*, 9 (1970), 139–53.

Monerie, J. *D'Alexandre à Zoilos. Dictionnaire prosopographique des porteurs de nom grec dans les sources cunéiforms* (Stuttgart: Steiner, 2014).

Monson, A. *From the Ptolemies to the Romans. Political and Economic Change in Egypt* (Cambridge University Press, 2012).

Monson, A. 'Hellenistic empires' in A. Monson and W. Scheidel (eds.) *Fiscal Regimes and the Political Economy of Premodern States* (Cambridge University Press, 2015), 169–207.

Mooren, L. *The Aulic Titulature in Ptolemaic Egypt. Introduction and Prosopography* (Brussels: Verhandelingen van de Koninklijke Academie van Wetenschappen, Letteren en Schone Kunsten van België, 1975).

Mooren, L. *La hiérarchie de cour ptolémaïque. Contribution à l'étude des institutions et des classes dirigeantes à l'époque hellénistique* (Leuven: Publications Universitaires de Louvain, 1977).

Moreno, P. *Lisippo* (Bari: Dedalo Libri, 1974).

Moreno García, J. C. 'Village' in W. Wendrich, et al. (eds.), *UCLA Encyclopedia of Egyptology* (Los Angeles: UCLA Press, 2011).

Mørkholm, O. *Studies in the Coinage of Antiochus IV of Syria* (Copenhagen: Munksgaard, 1963).

Mørkholm, O. 'The municipal coinages with portrait of Antiochus IV' in *Congresso Internazionale di Numismatica, Roma 1961 II* (Rome: Istituto Italiano di Numismatica, 1965), 63–7.

Mørkholm, O. 'The Ptolemaic "coins of an uncertain era"', *NNÅ* (1975–76), 23–58.

Mørkholm, O. 'The portrait coinage of Ptolemy V. The main series' in O. Mørkholm and N. M. Waggoner (eds.), *Greek Numismatics and Archaeology. Essays in Honor of Margaret Thompson* (Wetteren: Cultura, 1979), 203–14.

Mørkholm, O. 'A group of Ptolemaic coins from Phoenicia and Palestine', *INJ*, 4 (1980), 4–7.

Mørkholm, O. 'The monetary system in the Seleucid empire after 187 B.C.' in W. Heckel and R. Sullivan (eds.), *Ancient Coins of the Graeco-Roman World. The Nickle Numismatic Papers* (Waterloo, ON: Wilfried Laurier University Press, 1984), 93–113.

Mørkholm, O. *Early Hellenistic Coinage from the Accession of Alexander to the Peace of Apameia (336–188 B.C.)* (Cambridge University Press, 1991).

Mørkholm, O. and Kromann, A. 'The Ptolemaic silver coinage on Cyprus, 192/1–164/3 B.C.' *Chiron*, 14 (1984), 149–74.

Moses, S. *Der Engel der Geschichte. Franz Rosenzweig, Walter Benjamin, Gershom Scholem* (Frankfurt a. M.: Jüdischer Verlag, 1994).

Motyl, A. J. 'Thinking about Empire' in K. Barkey and M. von Hagen (eds.) *After Empire. Multiethnic Societies and Nation Building. The Soviet Union and the Russian, Ottoman and Habsburg Empires* (Boulder, CO: Westview Press, 1997), 19–29.

Motyl, A. J. *Imperial Ends. The Decay, Collapse, and Revival of Empires* (New York, NY: Columbia University Press, 2001).

Moyer, I. S. *Egypt and the Limits of Hellenism* (Cambridge University Press, 2011a).

Moyer, I. S. 'Finding a Middle Ground: Culture and Politics in the Ptolemaic Thebaid' in P. F. Dorman and B. M. Bryan (eds.), *Perspectives on Ptolemaic Thebes. Papers from the Theban Workshop 2006* (Chicago, IL: The Oriental Institute of the University of Chicago, 2011b), 115–45.

Moyer, I. S. 'Berossos and Manetho' in J. Haubold, G. B. Lanfranchi, R. Rollinger, and J. M. Steele (eds.), *The World of Berossos. Proceedings of the*

4th International Colloquium on "The Ancient Near East between Classical and Ancient Oriental Traditions", Hatfield College, Durham 7th–9th July 2010 (Wiesbaden: Harrassowitz, 2013), 213–33.

Muccioli, F. 'L'ἐπιστάτης et le στρατηγός καί ἐπιστάτης τῆς πόλεως. Problèmes ouverts d'administration du pouvoir entre Séleucides et Parthes', *Ktèma*, 39 (2014), 171–84.

Muccioli, F. 'La "stele di Eliodoro", i Seleucidi e i Giudei. Alcune considerazioni' in L. Capponi (ed.), *Tra politica e religione: I Giudei nel mondo greco-romano. Studi in onore di Lucio Troiani.* (Bologne: Jouvence, 2019), 49–79.

Mueller, K. *Settlements of the Ptolemies. City Foundations and New Settlement in the Hellenistic World* (Leuven: Peeters, 2006a).

Mueller, K. 'Did Ptolemais Theron have a wall? Hellenistic settlement on the Red Sea coast in the Pithom Stela and Strabo's *Geography*', *ZÄS*, 133 (2006b), 164–74.

Muhs, B. P. *Tax Receipts, Taxpayers and Taxes in Early Ptolemaic Thebes* (Chicago, IL: The Oriental Institute of the University of Chicago, 2005).

Müller, S. *Das hellenistische Königspaar in der medialen Repräsentation. Ptolemaios II. und Arsinoe II* (Berlin: de Gruyter, 2009).

Müller, W. 'Urbanism in Graeco-Roman Egypt' in M. Bietak, E. Czerny, and I. Forstner-Müller (eds.), *Cities and Urbanism in Ancient Egypt* (Vienna: Verlag der Österreichischen Akademie der Wissenschaften, 2010), 217–56.

Nadig, P. *Zwischen König und Karikatur. Das Bild Ptolemaios' VIII. im Spannungsfeld der Überlieferung* (Munich: Beck, 2007).

Nadig, P. 'Zur Rolle der Juden unter Ptolemaios VI. und Ptolemaios VIII.' in A. Jördens and J. F. Quack (eds.), *Ägypten zwischen innerem Zwist und äußerem Druck. Die Zeit Ptolemaios' VI. bis VIII. Internationales Symposion Heidelberg 16.–19.9. 2007* (Wiesbaden: Harrassowitz, 2011), 186–200.

Nawotka, K. *The Alexander Romance by Ps-Callisthenes. A Historical Commentary* (Leiden: Brill, 2017).

Nespoulous-Phalippou, A. *Ptolémée Épiphane, Aristonikos et les prêtres d'Égypte. Le Décret de Memphis (182 a.C.). Édition commentée des stèles Caire RT 2/3/25/7 et JE 44901* (Montpellier: Université Paul Valéry, 2015).

Neusner, J. 'The Mishnah's generative mode of thought. *Listenwissenschaft* and analogical-contrastive reasoning', *JAOS*, 110.2 (1990), 317–21.

Newell, E. T. *The Coinages of Demetrius Poliorcetes* (Oxford University Press, 1927).

Newell, E. T. *The Coinage of the Eastern Seleucid Mints from Seleucus I to Antiochus III* (New York, NY: The American Numismatic Society, 1938).

Newell, E. T. *The Coinage of the Western Seleucid Mints from Seleucus I to Antiochus III* (New York, NY: The American Numismatic Society, 1941).

Newsom, C. A. *Daniel. A Commentary* (Louisville, KY: Westminster, 2014).

Nielsen, I. *Hellenistic Palaces. Tradition and Renewal* (Aarhus University Press, 1994).

Niese, B. *Geschichte der griechischen und makedonischen Staaten seit der Schlacht bei Chaeronea, vol. 3: Von 188 bis 120 v. Chr.* (Gotha: Perthes, 1903).

Oelsner, J. *Materialien zur Babylonischen Gesellschaft und Kultur in Hellenistischer Zeit* (Budapest: Eötvös University, 1986).

Oetjen, R. *Athen im dritten Jahrhundert v. Chr. Politik und Gesellschaft in den Garnisonsdemen auf der Grundlage der inschriftlichen Überlieferung* (Duisburg: Wellem, 2014).

Ogden, D. 'Alexander's snake sire' in P. V. Wheatley and R. Hannah (eds.), *Alexander and His Successors. Essays from the Antipodes* (Claremont CA: Regina Books, 2009), 136–78.

Ogden, D. 'Seleucid dynastic foundation myths. Antioch and Seleucia-in-Pieria' in K. Erickson and G. Ramsey (eds.), *Seleucid Dissolution. The Sinking of the Anchor* (Wiesbaden: Harrassowitz, 2011), 149–60.

Ogden, D. 'Alexander, Agathos Daimon, and Ptolemy. The Alexandrian foundation myth in dialogue' in N. MacSweeney (ed.), *Foundation Myths in Ancient Societies. Dialogues and Discourses* (Philadelphia: University of Pennsylvania Press, 2014), 129–50.

Ogden, D. *The Legend of Seleucus. Kingship, Narrative and Mythmaking in the Ancient World* (Cambridge University Press, 2017).

Olbrycht, M. J. 'Ethnicity of settlers in the colonies of Alexander the Great in Iran and Central Asia', *Bulletin of International Institute for Central Asia Studies*, 14 (2011), 22–35.

Olivier, J. '*Archè et chrèmata* en Égypte au IIe siècle avant J.-C. (204–81 av. J.-C.). Étude numismatique et d'histoire', unpublished PhD diss., Université d'Orleans (2012).

Olivier, J. 'Coinage as a tool of Ptolemy VI Philometor's policies. Ptolemaic coins in Coele Syria and Phoenicia in the middle of the second century BCE', *Israel Numismatic Research*, 13 (2018), 35–54.

Olivier, J. and Lorber, C. C. 'Three gold coinages of third-century Ptolemaic Egypt', *RBN*, 159 (2013), 49–150.

Olshausen, E. *Prosopographie der hellenistischen Königsgesandten*, vol. 1: *Von Triparadeisos bis Pydna* (Leuven: privately published, 1974).

Orth, W. *Königlicher Machtanspruch und städtische Freiheit. Untersuchungen zu den politischen Beziehungen zwischen den ersten Seleukidenherrschern (Seleukos I., Antiochos I., Antiochos II.) und den Städten des westlichen Kleinasien* (Munich: C. H. Beck, 1977).

Osterhammel, J. *Geschichtswissenschaft jenseits des Nationalstaats. Studien zu Beziehungsgeschichte und Zivilisationsvergleich* (Göttingen: Vandenhoek & Ruprecht, 2001).

Palagia, O. 'A new interpretation of Menander's image by Kephisodotos II and Timarchos', *ASAtene*, 83 (2005), 287–97.

Palagia, O. 'Aspects of the diffusion of Ptolemaic portraiture overseas' in K. Buraselis, M. Stefanou and D. J. Thompson (eds.), *The Ptolemies, the Sea and the Nile. Studies in Waterborne Power* (Cambridge University Press, 2013), 143–59.

Panagopoulou, K. 'Cross-reading images. Iconographic "debates" between Antigonids and Ptolemies during the third and second centuries B.C.', *Eulimene*, 6–7 (2005–6), 163–81.

Parente, F. 'Onias III's death and the founding of the temple of Leontopolis' in F. Parente and J. Sievers (eds.), *Josephus and the History of the Greco-Roman Period. Essays in Memory of Morton Smith* (Leiden: Brill, 1994), 69–98.

Paschidis, P. *Between City and King. Prosopographical Studies on the Intermediaries between the Cities of the Greek Mainland and the Aegean and the Royal Courts in the Hellenistic Period, 322–190 BC* (Paris: de Boccard, 2008).

Peremans, W. 'Les lagides, les élites indigènes et la monarchie bicéphale' in E. Lévy *Le système palatial en Orient, en Grèce et à Rome. Actes du Colloque de Strasbourg 19–22 juin 1985* (Leiden: Brill, 1987), 327–43.

Peremans, W. and Van 't Dack, E. *Prosopographia Ptolemaica* (Leuven: Peeters, 1950–81).

Pestman, P. W. 'Haronnophris and Chaonnophris, Two indigenous pharaohs in Ptolemaic Egypt (205–186 B.C.)' in S. P. Vleeming (ed.), *Hundred-Gated Thebes. Acts of a Colloquium on Thebes and the Theban Area in the Graeco-Roman Period* (Leiden: Brill, 1995), 101–37.

Petzl, G. 'Das Inschriftendossier zur Neugründung von Arsinoë in Kilikien. Textkorrekturen', *ZPE*, 139 (2002), 83–8.

Pfeiffer, S. *Das Dekret von Kanopos (238 v. Chr.). Kommentar und historische Auswertung eines dreisprachigen Synodaldekretes der ägyptischen Priester zu Ehren Ptolemaios' III. und seiner Familie* (Leipzig: Saur, 2004).

Pfeiffer, S. 'Die Entsprechung ägyptischer Götter im griechischen Pantheon. Bemerkungen zur Überwindung interkultureller Differenz' in H. Beck, P. C. Bol and M. Bückling (eds.), *Ägypten, Griechenland, Rom. Abwehr und Berührung* (Tübingen: Wasmuth, 2005), 285–91.

Pfeiffer, S. 'The god Serapis, his cult and the beginning of the ruler cult in Ptolemaic Egypt' in P. McKechnie and P. Guillaume (eds.), *Ptolemy II Philadelphus and His World* (Leiden: Brill, 2008), 387–408.

Pfeiffer, S. 'Alexander der Große in Ägypten. Überlegungen zur Frage seiner pharaonischen Legitimation' in: V. Grieb, K. Nawotka and A. Wojciechowska (eds.), *Alexander the Great and Egypt. History, Art, Tradition* (Wiesbaden: Harrassowitz, 2014a), 89–106.

Pfeiffer, S. 'Das Ptolemäerreich' in K. Ehling and G. Weber (eds.), *Hellenistische Königreiche* (Darmstadt: von Zabern, 2014b), 48–54.

Pfeiffer, S. *Griechische und lateinische Inschriften zum Ptolemäerreich und zur römischen Provinz Aegyptus* (Berlin: LIT, 2020).

Picard, O. 'Le portrait de Ptolémée I ou comment construire la monnaie d'un nouveau royaume', *CahÉtAnc*, 49 (2012), 19–41.

Picard, O. and Faucher, T. 'La grande mutation des bronzes lagides. L'adoption d'une comptabilité décimale' in O. Picard, C. Bresc, T. Faucher, G. Gorre, M.-C. Marcellesi, and C. Morrisson (eds.), *Les Monnaies des fouilles du Centre d'Études Alexandrines. Les monnayages de bronze à Alexandrie de la conquête d'Alexandre à l'Égypte moderne* (Alexandria: Centre d'Études Alexandrines, 2012), 60–108.

Piejko, F. 'The relations of Ptolemies VIII and IX with the temple of Chnum at Elephantine', *BASP*, 29.1–2 (1992), 5–24.

Platz-Horster, G. 'Der Capita-iugata-Kameo in Berlin' in M. Avisseau-Broustet (ed.), *La glyptique des mondes classiques. Mélanges en hommage à Marie-Louise Vollenweider* (Paris: Bibliothèque Nationale de France, 1997), 55–82.

Plischke, S. *Die Seleukiden und Iran. Die seleukidische Herrschaftspolitik in den östlichen Satrapien* (Wiesbaden: Harrassowitz Verlag, 2014).

Poland, F. *Geschichte des griechischen Vereinswesens* (Leipzig: Teubner, 1909).

Poole, R. S. *Catalogue of Greek Coins in the British Museum. The Ptolemies, Kings of Egypt* (London: Longmans & Co., 1883).

Préaux, C. 'Polybe et Philopator', *ChrÉg*, 40 (1965), 364–75.

Préaux, C. *Le monde hellénistique. La Grèce et l'Orient de la mort d'Alexandre à la conquête romaine de la Grèce (323–146 avant J.C.)*, 2 vols. (Paris: Presses Universitaires de France, 1978).

Preys, R. 'La royauté lagide et le culte d'Osiris d'après les portes monumentales de Karnak' in C. Thiers (ed.), *Documents de théologies thébaines tardives (D3 T 3)* (Montpellier: Université Paul Valéry, 2015), 159–215.

Pries, A. H. 'Le roi est mort, vive le dieu ou le dieu est mort, vive le roi? Königsideologische Konzepte aus dem Umfeld der Lebenshäuser in griechisch-römischer Zeit' in H. Beinlich (ed.), *'Die Männer hinter dem König'. 6. Symposium zur ägyptischen Königsideologie Iphofen, 16.–18. Juli 2010* (Wiesbaden: Harrassowitz, 2012), 103–22.

Primo, A. *La Storiografia sui Seleucidi da Megastene a Eusebio di Cesarea* (Pisa: Serra, 2009).

Pritchard, J. B. *Ancient Near Eastern Texts Relating to the Old Testament*, 2nd ed. (Princeton University Press, 1955).

Psoma, S. 'Numismatic evidence on the Ptolemaic involvement in Thrace during the Second Syrian War', *AJN*, 20 (2008), 257–63.

Quack, J. F. 'Eine demotische Übersetzung aus dem Mittelägyptischen', *Enchoria*, 19–20 (1992–3), 125–9.

Quack, J. F. 'Der historische Abschnitt des Buches vom Tempel' in J. Assmann and E. Blumenthal (eds.), *Literatur und Politik im pharaonischen und ptolemäischen Ägypten. Vorträge der Tagung zum Gedenken an Georges Posener, 5.–10. September 1996 in Leipzig* (Cairo: IFAO, 1999), 267–78.

Quack, J. F. 'Ein neuer prophetischer Text aus Tebtynis' in A. Blasius and B. U. Schipper (eds.), *Apokalyptik und Ägypten. Eine kritische Analyse der relevanten Texte aus dem griechisch-römischen Ägypten* (Leuven: Peeters, 2002), 253–74.

Quack, J. F. *Einführung in die altägyptische Literaturgeschichte, vol. 3: Die demotische und gräko-ägyptische Literatur* (Berlin: LIT Verlag, 2009).

Quaegebeur, J. 'Documents égyptiens et rôle économique du clergé en Egypte hellénistique' in E. Lipiński (ed.), *State and Temple Economy in the Ancient Near East. Proceedings of the International Conference Organized by the Katholieke Universiteit Leuven from the 10th to the 14th of April 1978, vol. 2* (Leuven: Katholieke Universiteit, Dep. Oriëntalistiek, 1979), 707–29.

Quaegebeur, J. 'The genealogy of the Memphite high priest family in the Hellenistic period' in D. J. Crawford, J. Quaegebeur, and W. Clarysse (eds.), *Studies on Ptolemaic Memphis* (Leuven: Peeters, 1980), 43–81.

Quaegebeur, J. 'The Egyptian clergy and the cult of the Ptolemaic dynasty', *Ancient Society*, 20 (1989), 93–116.
Queyrel, F. 'Kastalia (II). Personnification de la source Castalie du sanctuaire de Daphné près d'Antioche', *LIMC* 5.1 (Zurich: Artemis & Winkler, 1990), 971–2.
Queyrel, F. 'Les portraits de Ptolemée III Évergète et la problématique de l'iconographie lagide de style grec', *JSav*, no. 1 (2002), 3–73.
Queyrel, F. 'Iconographie de Ptolémée II' in J.-Y. Empereur (ed.), *Alexandrina*, vol. 3 (Cairo: IFAO, 2009), 7–61.
Rabe, B. 'Zur Herstellung und Bedeutung der ptolemäischen Ringergruppen', *AntK*, 53 (2010), 49–61.
Rajak, T. 'Roman intervention in a Seleucid siege of Jerusalem?', *GRBS*, 22.1 (1981) 65–81.
Rapaport, U. 'Les Iduméens en Égypte', *RPhil*, 43 (1969), 73–82.
Rapin, C. and Isamiddinov, M. 'Fortifications hellénistiques de Samarcande (Samarkand-Afrasiab)', *Topoi*, 4.2 (1994), 547–65.
Raue, D., et al. 'Report on the 36th season of excavation and restoration on the island of Elephantine', *Online Reports of the Deutsches Archäologisches Institute* (2007), www.dainst.org/.
Raue, D., et al. 'Report on the 37th season of excavation and restoration on the island of Elephantine', *Online Reports of the Deutsches Archäologisches Institute* (2008), www.dainst.org/.
Redon, B. 'New architectural practices and urbanism' in K. Vandorpe (ed.), *A Companion to Greco-Roman and Late Antique Egypt* (Oxford: Wiley-Blackwell, 2019), 519–32.
Redon, B. and Faucher, T. 'Les Grecs aux portes d'Amon. Les bains de Karnak et l'occupation ptolémaïque du parvis ouest du temple de Karnak' in G. Gorre and A. Marangou (eds.), *La présence grecque dans la vallée de Thèbes* (Presses Universitaires de Rennes, 2015), 121–34.
Reekmans, T. 'The Ptolemaic copper inflation' in E. Van 't Dack and T. Reekmans (eds.), *Ptolemaica* (Leuven: Bibliotheca Universitatis, 1951), 61–119.
Reekmans, T. 'The behaviour of consumer in the Zenon papyri', *Ancient Society*, 25 (1994), 119–40.
Reiner, E. 'The etiological myth of the "seven sages"', *Orientalia*, 30.1 (1961), 1–11.
Reinsberg, C. 'Alexanderbilder in Ägypten. Manifestationen eines neuen Herrscherideals' in P. C. Bol, G. Kaminski and C. Maderna (eds.), *Fremdheit– Eigenheit. Ägypten, Griechenland und Rom. Austausch und Verständnis* (Stuttgart: Scheufele, 2004), 319–39.
Rey-Coquais, J.-P. 'Inscriptions et toponymes hellénistiques de Phénicie', *Studi Ellenistici*, 19 (2006), 99–117.
Rice, E. *The Grand Procession of Ptolemy Philadelphus* (Oxford University Press, 1983).
Rigsby, K. J. 'An edict of Ptolemy I', *ZPE*, 72 (1988), 273–4.
Ristvet, L. *Ritual, Performance, and Politics in the Ancient Near East* (Cambridge University Press, 2015).
Ritter, B. 'On the "politeuma in Heracleopolis"', *Scripta Classica Israelica*, 30 (2011), 9–37.

Robert, J. and Robert, L. *Fouilles d'Amyzon en Carie, vol. 1: Exploration, histoire, monnaies et inscriptions* (Paris: de Boccard, 1983).
Robert, L. *Études anatoliennes. Recherches sur les inscriptions grecques de l'Asie Mineure* (Paris: de Boccard, 1937).
Röllig, W. 'Hellenistic Babylonia. The evidence from Uruk' in *Ο Ελληνισμος στην Ανατολη. Πρακτικά Α' διεθνούς αραχαιολογιηού συνεδρίου: Δελφοί 6–9 Νοεμβρίου 1986* (Athens: European Cultural Centre, 1991), 121–9.
Rollinger, R. 'Der Stammbaum des achaimenidischen Königshauses oder die Frage der Legitimität der Herrschaft des Dareios', *AMIran* 30 (1998–9), 155–209.
Rosamilia, E. 'Numismatica e documentazione epigrafica. I piedi monetali e l'introduzione del "bronze standard" a Cirene' in M. Asolati (ed.), *Le monete di Cirene e della Cirenaica nel Mediterraneo. Problemi e prospettive. Atti del V Congresso Internazionale di Numismatica e di Storia Monetaria, Padova, 17–19 marzo 2016* (Padua: Esedra Editrice, 2016), 83–100.
Rosamilia, E. 'The introduction of the bronze standard in Cyrenaica. Evidence from the *damiergoi* accounts', *ZPE*, 201 (2017), 139–54.
Rose, P. 'Dodekaschoinos' in R. S. Bagnall, et al. (eds.), *The Encyclopedia of Ancient History* (Malden, MA: Wiley, 2012), 2184.
Rostovtzeff, M. 'ΠΡΟΓΟΝΟΙ' *JHS*, 55.1 (1935), 56–66.
Rostovtzeff, M. *The Social and Economic History of the Hellenistic World*, 3 vols. (Oxford: Clarendon, 1941).
Rougemont, G. *Inscriptions grecques d'Iran et d'Asie centrale* (London: School of Oriental and African Studies, 2012).
Rtweladse, E. V. 'Kampyr-Tepe-Pandocheion – Alexandria Oxiana' in S. Hansen, A. Wieczorek, and M. Tellenbach (eds.), *Alexander der Grosse und die Öffnung der Welt. Asiens Kulturen im Wandel* (Regensburg: Schnell & Steiner, 2009), 169–75.
Ruppel, W. 'Politeuma. Bedeutungsgeschichte eines staatsrechtlichen Terminus', *Philologus*, 82 (1927), 269–312 and 433–54.
Rutherford, I. 'Mythology of the black land. Greek myths and Egyptian origins' in K. Dowden and N. Livingston (eds.), *A Companion to Greek Mythology* (Malden, MA: Wiley-Blackwell, 2011), 459–70.
Ryholt, K. 'The Turin king-list', *Ägypten und Levante*, 14 (2004), 135–55.
Rzepka, J. '*Ethnos, koinon, sympoliteia*, and Greek federal states' in T. Derda, J. Urbanik, and M. Wecowski (eds.), *Euergesias Charin. Studies Presented to Benedetto Bravo and Ewa Wipszycka by Their Disciples* (Warsaw: Rafala Taubenschlaga, 2002), 225–47.
Sabottka, M. *Das Serapeum in Alexandria. Untersuchungen zur Architektur und Baugeschichte des Heiligtums von der frühen Ptolemäischen Zeit bis zur Zerstörung 391 n. Chr.* (Cairo: IFAO, 2008).
Sachs, A. J. 'Achaemenid royal names in Babylonian astronomical texts', *AJAH*, 2 (1977), 129–46.
Sachs, A. J. and Hunger, H. *Astronomical Diaries and Related Texts from Babylon, vol. 1: Diaries from 652 B.C. to 262 B.C.* (Vienna: Verlag der österreichischen Akademie der Wissenschaften, 1988).

Sachs, A. J. and Wiseman, D. J. 'A Babylonian King list of the Hellenistic period', *Iraq*, 16 (1954), 202–12.
Sahlins, M. D. *Islands of History* (University of Chicago Press, 1985).
Salvatori, S. 'The Margiana settlement pattern from the Middle Bronze Age to the Parthian-Sasanian period. A contribution to the study of complexity' in S. Salvatori and M. Tosi (eds.), *The Archaeological Map of the Murghab Delta II. The Bronze Age and Early Iron Age in the Margiana Lowlands. Facts and Methodological Proposal for a Redefinition of the Research Strategies* (Oxford: Archaeopress, 2008), 57–74.
Samuel, A. E. *Ptolemaic Chronology* (Munich: Beck, 1962).
San Nicolò, M. *Ägyptisches Vereinswesen zur Zeit der Ptolemäer und Römer, vol. 1: Die Vereinsarten* (Munich: Beck, 1913).
San Nicolò, M. *Ägyptisches Vereinswesen zur Zeit der Ptolemäer und Römer, vol. 2: Vereinswesen und Vereinsrecht* (Munich: Beck, 1915).
San Nicolò, M. 'Zur Vereinsgerichtsbarkeit im hellenistischen Ägypten', in *ΕΠΙΤΥΜΒΙΟΝ. Heinrich Swoboda dargebracht* (Reichenberg: Stiepel, 1927), 255–300.
San Nicolò, M. and Ungnad, A. *Neubabylonische Rechts- und Verwaltungsurkunden, vol. 1: Rechts- und Verwaltungsurkunden der Berliner Museen I* (Leipzig: Hinrichs, 1935).
Sänger, P. 'The *politeuma* in the Hellenistic world (third to first century B.C.). A form of organization to integrate minorities' in J. Dahlvik, Ch. Reinprecht and W. Sievers (eds.), *Migration und Integration – wissenschaftliche Perspektiven aus Österreich. Jahrbuch 2/2013* (Göttingen: V&R Unipress, 2014), 51–68.
Sänger, P. 'Considerations on the administrative organisation of the Jewish military colony in Leontopolis. A case of generosity and calculation' in J. Tolan (ed.), *Expulsion and Diaspora Formation. Religious and Ethnic Identities in Flux from Antiquity to the Seventeenth Century* (Turnhout: Brepols, 2015a), 171–94.
Sänger, P. 'Adnotationes Epiraphicae VI. Zu Datierung und Herkunft von SB IV 7270', *Tyche*, 30 (2015b), 258–60.
Sänger, P. 'Military immigration and the emergence of cultural or ethnic identities. The case of Ptolemaic Egypt', *JJurP*, 45 (2015c), 229–53.
Sänger, P. 'Migration, Ethnizität, Identität, Vereinigung und Gemeinde. Überlegungen zur sozio-politischen Einordnung der ethnischen *politeumata*' in R. Lafer and K. Strobel (eds.), *Antike Lebenswelten. Althistorische und papyrologische Studien* (Berlin: de Gruyter, 2015d), 223–37.
Sänger, P. 'Das politeuma in der hellenistischen Staatenwelt. Eine Organisationsform zur Systemintegration von Minderheiten' in P. Sänger (ed.), *Minderheiten und Migration in der griechisch-römischen Welt. Politische, rechtliche, religiöse und kulturelle Aspekte* (Paderborn: Schöningh, 2016a), 25–45.
Sänger, P. 'Heracleopolis, Jewish politeuma' in S. Goldberg (ed.), *The Oxford Classical Dictionary* (Oxford University Press, 2016b), http://classics.oxfordre.com/view/10.1093/acrefore/9780199381135.001.0001/acrefore-9780199381135-e-8036.
Sänger, P. 'Die Jurisdiktion der jüdischen Gemeinde von Herakleopolis. Normaloder Sonderfall im hellenistischen Ägypten?' in D. F. Leão and G. Thür (eds.), *Symposion 2015. Vorträge zur griechischen und hellenistischen Rechtsgeschichte*

(Coimbra, 1.–4. September 2015) (Vienna: Verlag der Österreichischen Akademie der Wissenschaften, 2016c), 213–32.

Sänger, P. 'The meaning of the word πολίτευμα in the light of the Judaeo-Hellenistic literature' in T. Derda, A. Lajtar and J. Urbanik (eds.), *Proceedings of the 27th International Congress of Papyrology, Warsaw, 29 July – 3 August 2013, vol. 3: Studying Papyri* (Warsaw: Rafala Taubenschlaga, 2016d), 1679–93.

Sänger, P. *Die ptolemäische Organisationsform politeuma. Ein Herrschaftsinstrument zugunsten jüdischer und anderer hellenischer Gemeinschaften* (Tübingen: Mohr Siebeck, 2019).

Sarkisjan, G. 'Hellenismus in Babylonien', *Altorientalische Forschungen*, 24.2 (1997), 242–50.

Sartre, M. 'Histoire et mémoire(s) des Maccabées' in M.-F. Baslez and O. Munnich (eds.), *La Mémoire des persecutions. Autour des livres des Maccabées* (Leuven: Peeters, 2014), 1–20.

Savalli-Lestrade, I. 'Remarques sur les élites dans les poleis hellénistiques', in M. Cébeillac-Gervasoni and L. Lamoine (eds.), *Les élites et leurs facettes. Les élites locales dans le monde hellénistique et romain* (Rome: École Française de Rome, 2003), 51–64.

Savalli-Lestrade, I. 'Antioche du Pyrame, Mallos et Tarse/Antioche du Knydos à la lumière de SEG XII, 511. Histoire, géographie, épigraphie, société', *Studi Ellenistici*, 19 (2006), 119–247.

Savvopoulos, K. '*Alexandria in Aegypto*. The use and meaning of Egyptian elements in Hellenistic and Roman Alexandria' in L. Bricault and J. Versluys (eds.), *Isis on the Nile. Egyptian Gods in Hellenistic and Roman Egypt. Proceedings of the IVth International Conference of Isis Studies, Liège, November 27–29, 2008* (Leiden: Brill, 2010), 75–88.

Sawaya, Z. 'Les tétradrachmes séleucides à l'aigle de Bérytos', *NC*, 165 (2005), 99–124.

Schäfer, C. 'Inspiration and impact of Seleucid royal representation' in R. Rollinger and E. v. Dongen (eds.), *Mesopotamia in the Ancient World. Impact, Continuities, Parallels. Proceedings of the Seventh Symposium of the Melammu Project Held in Obergurgl, Austria, November 4–8, 2013* (Münster: Ugarit, 2015), 631–41.

Schäfer, D. *Makedonische Pharaonen und hieroglyphische Stelen. Historische Untersuchungen zur Satrapenstele und verwandten Denkmälern* (Leuven: Peeters, 2011).

Scharrer, U. 'Seleukos I. und das babylonische Königtum' in K. Brodersen (ed.), *Zwischen Ost und West. Studien zur Geschichte des Seleukidenreiches* (Hamburg: Kovač, 1999), 95–128.

Schaudig, H. 'The restauration of temples in the neo- and late-Babylonian periods. A royal prerogative as the setting for political argument' in M. J. Boda and J. Novotny (eds.), *From the Foundations to the Crenellations. Essays on Temple Building in the Ancient Near East and Hebrew Bible* (Münster: Ugarit, 2010), 141–64.

Scheidel, W. 'Creating a metropolis. A comparative demographic perspective', in W. Harris and G. Ruffini (eds.), *Ancient Alexandria between Egypt and Greece* (Leiden: Brill, 2004) 1–31.
Scheidel, W. 'Studying the State' in P. F. Bang and W. Scheidel (eds.), *The Oxford Handbook of the State in the Ancient Near East and Mediterranean* (Oxford University Press, 2013), 5–60.
Scheuble, S. 'Bemerkungen zu den μισθοφόροι und τακτόμισθοι im ptolemäischen Ägypten' in R. Eberhard, H. Kockelmann, S. Pfeiffer, and M. Schentuleit (eds.) '... *vor dem Papyrus sind alle gleich!' Papyrologische Beiträge zu Ehren von Bärbel Kramer* (Berlin: de Gruyter, 2009), 213–22.
Scheuble-Reiter, S. *Die Katökenreiter im ptolemäischen Ägypten* (Munich: Beck, 2012).
Schieder, T. 'Die mittleren Staaten im System der großen Mächte', *HZ*, 232 (1981), 583–604.
Schiffman, Z. *The Birth of the Past* (Baltimore, MD: Johns Hopkins University Press, 2011).
Schmidt, S. 'Fashion and meaning. Beardless portraits of artists and literati in the early Hellenistic period' in R. von den Hoff and P. Schultz (eds.), *Early Hellenistic Portraiture. Image, Style, Context* (Cambridge University Press, 2007), 99–112.
Schmitt, H. H. *Untersuchungen zur Geschichte Antiochos' des Großen und seiner Zeit* (Wiesbaden: Steiner, 1964).
Schneider, T. 'History as festival? A reassessment of the use of the past and the place of historiography in ancient Egyptian thought' in K. A. Raaflaub (ed.), *Thinking, Recording, and Writing History in the Ancient World* (Malden, MA: Wiley Blackwell, 2014), 117–43.
Schreiber, G. 'The final acts of embalming. An archaeological note on some rare objects in Theban elite burials of the early Ptolemaic period' in K. Endreffy and A. Gulyás (eds.), *Proceedings of the Fourth Central European Conference of Young Egyptologists, 31 August – 2 September 2009, Budapest* (Budapest: ELTE Régészeti Tanszék, 2007), 337–56.
Schuler, C. 'Kolonisten und Einheimische in einer attalidischen Polisgründung', *ZPE*, 128 (1999), 124–32.
Schwei, D. 'The reactions of mint workers to the tumultuous second reign of Demetrius II Nicator', *AJN*, 28 (2016), 65–104.
Sciandra, R. 'The Babylonian correspondence of the Seleucid and Arsacid dynasties. New insights into the relations between court and city during the late Babylonian period' in G. Wilhelm (ed.), *Organization, Representation, and Symbols of Power in the Ancient Near East. Proceedings of the 54th Rencontre Assyriologique Internationale at Würzburg, 20–25 July 2008* (Winona Lake, IN: Eisenbrauns, 2012), 225–48.
Sekunda, N. 'Military forces. A. land forces' in P. Sabin, H. van Wees, and M. Whitby (eds.), *The Cambridge History of Greek and Roman Warfare, vol. 1: Greece, the Hellenistic World and the Rise of Rome* (Cambridge University Press, 2007), 325–57.
Selden, D. L. 'Alibis', *ClAnt*, 17 (1998), 289–412.
Seyrig, H. 'Antiquités syriennes. Seleucus I et la fondation de la monarchie syrienne', *Syria*, 47 (1970), 290–311.

Shahin, M. 'A Ptolemaic bronze and silver hoard from Kom Trouga' in F. Duyrat and O. Picard (eds.), *L'exception égyptienne? Production et échanges monétaires en Égypte hellénistique et romaine. Actes du colloque d'Alexandrie, 13–15 avril 2002* (Cairo: IFAO, 2005), 91–116.

Shaw, I. *The Oxford History of Ancient Egypt*, 2nd ed. (Oxford University Press, 2003).

Sheedy, K. A. *Alexander and the Hellenistic Kingdoms. Coins, Images and the Creation of Identity* (Sydney: Australian Centre for Ancient Numismatic Studies, 2007).

Sherwin-White, S. M. 'Aristeas Ardibelteios. Some aspects of the use of double names in Seleucid Babylonia', *ZPE*, 50 (1983a), 209–21.

Sherwin-White, S. M. 'Babylonian chronicle fragments as a source for Seleucid history', *JNES*, 42.4 (1983b), 265–70.

Sherwin-White, S. M. 'Ritual for a Seleucid king at Babylon?', *JHS*, 102 (1983c), 156–9.

Sherwin-White, S. M. 'Seleucid Babylonia. A case-study for the installation and development of Greek rule' in A. Kuhrt and S. M. Sherwin-White (eds.), *Hellenism in the East. The Interaction of Greek and Non-Greek Civilisations from Syria to Central Asia after Alexander* (Berkeley, CA: University of California Press, 1987), 1–31.

Sherwin-White, S. M. and Kuhrt, A. *From Samarkhand to Sardis. A New Approach to the Seleucid Empire* (London: Duckworth, 1993).

Shirun-Grumach, I. 'Lehre des Amenemope' in W. Helck and E. Otto (eds.), *Lexikon der Ägyptologie*, vol. 3 (Wiesbaden: Harrassowitz, 1980), 971–4.

Sidebotham, S. *Berenike and the Ancient Maritime Spice Route* (Berkeley, CA: University of California Press, 2011).

Sidebotham, S. 'Religion and burial at the Ptolemaic-Roman Red Sea emporium of Berenike, Egypt', *African Archaeological Review*, 31 (2014), 599–635.

Sidebotham, S. and Gates-Foster, J. *The Archaeological Survey of the Desert Roads between Berenike and the Nile Valley. Expeditions by the University of Michigan and the University of Delaware to the Eastern Desert of Egypt, 1987–2015* (Boston, MA: American School of Oriental Research, 2019).

Smail, D. 'In the grip of sacred history', *AHR* 110 (2005), 1337–61.

Smith, A. D. *The Ethnic Origins of Nations* (Oxford: Blackwell, 1986).

Smith, J. *Imagining Religion. From Babylon to Jonestown* (University of Chicago Press, 1982).

Smith, M. 'Networks, territories, and the cartography of ancient states', *Annals of the Association of American Geographers*, 95.4 (2005), 832–49.

Smith, R. R. R. *Hellenistic royal portraits* (Oxford: Clarendon, 1988).

Smith, R. R. R. *Hellenistic Sculpture. A Handbook* (London: Thames and Hudson, 1991).

Smith, R. R. R. 'Ptolemaic portraits. Alexandrian types, Egyptian versions' in *Alexandria and Alexandrianism* (Malibu, CA: J. Paul Getty Museum, 1996), 203–13.

Sosin, J. D. 'P. Duk. inv. 677. Aetos, from Arsinoite *strategos* to eponymous priest', *ZPE*, 116 (1997), 141–6.

Spiegelberg, W. *Beiträge zur Erklärung des neuen dreisprachigen Priesterdekretes zu Ehren des Ptolemaios Philopator* (Munich: Bayerische Akademie der Wissenschaften, 1925).

Stanwick, P. E. *Portraits of the Ptolemies. Greek Kings as Egyptian Pharaohs* (Austin, TX: University of Texas Press, 2002).
Stefanakis, M. I. 'Looking towards the north. The circulation of Cyrenaic coins on Crete' in M. Asolati (ed.), *Le monete di Cirene e della Cirenaica nel Mediterraneo. Problemi e prospettive. Atti del V Congresso Internazionale di Numismatica e di Storia Monetaria, Padova, 17–19 marzo 2016* (Padua: Esedra Editrice, 2016), 65–81.
Stefanou, M. 'Waterborne recruits. The military settlers of Ptolemaic Egypt' in K. Buraselis, M. Stefanou and D. J. Thompson (eds.), *The Ptolemies, the Sea and the Nile. Studies in Waterborne Power* (Cambridge University Press, 2013), 108–31.
Stephens, S. A. *Seeing Double. Intercultural Poetics in Ptolemaic Alexandria* (Berkeley, CA: University of California Press, 2003).
Stephens, S. A. *Callimachus. The Hymns* (Oxford University Press, 2015).
Stevens, K. 'The Antiochus Cylinder, Babylonian scholarship and Seleucid imperial ideology', *JHS*, 134 (2014), 66–88.
Stevens, K. 'Empire begins at home. Local elites and imperial ideologies in Hellenistic Greece and Babylonia' in M. Lavan, R. E. Payne and J. Weisweiler (eds.), *Cosmopolitanism and Empire. Universal Rulers, Local Elites, and Cultural Integration in the Ancient Near East and Mediterranean* (Oxford University Press, 2016), 65–88.
Stewart, A. F. *Faces of Power. Alexander's Image and Hellenistic Politics* (Berkeley, CA: University of California Press, 1993).
Stökl Ben Ezra, D. 'A Jewish "archontesse". Remarks on an epitaph from Byblos', *ZPE*, 169 (2009), 287–93.
Stoneman, R. *The Greek Alexander Romance*. Translated with an Introduction and Notes (London: Penguin Books, 1991).
Strathmann, H. 'πόλις κτλ.' in G. Friedrich (ed.), *Theologisches Wörterbuch zum Neuen Testament: Begründet von Gerhard Kittel* (Stuttgart: Kohlhammer, 1990), 516–35.
Strootman, R. 'The Hellenistic royal courts. Court culture, ceremonial and ideology in Greece, Egypt and the Near East, 336–30 BCE', unpublished PhD dissertation, University of Utrecht 2007 (available online at uu.academia.edu/RolfStrootman).
Strootman, R. 'Seleucid era' in: E. Yarshater et al. (eds.), *Encyclopaedia Iranica Online* (2008, available online at www.iranicaonline.org/articles/seleucid-era).
Strootman, R. 'Queen of kings. Cleopatra VII and the donations of Alexandria' in M. Facella and T. Kaizer (eds.), *Kingdoms and Principalities in the Roman Near East* (Stuttgart: Steiner, 2010), 139–58.
Strootman, R. 'The Seleukid empire between Orientalism and Hellenocentrism. Writing the history of Iran in the third and second centuries BCE', *Nāme-ye Irān-e Bāstān. The International Journal of Ancient Iranian Studies*, 11.1–2 (2011), 17–35.
Strootman, R. *Courts and Elites in the Hellenistic Empires. The Near East after the Achaemenids, 330–30 BCE* (Edinburgh University Press, 2014a).
Strootman, R. '"Men to whose rapacity neither sea nor mountain sets a limit". The aims of the Diadochs' in H. Hauben and A. Meeus (eds.), *The Age of the*

Successors and the Creation of the Hellenistic Kingdoms (323–276 B.C) (Leuven: Peeters, 2014b), 307–22.

Strootman, R. 'The dawning of a golden age. Images of peace and abundance in Alexandrian court poetry in the context of Ptolemaic imperial ideology' in M. A. Harder, R. F. Regtuit and G. C. Wakker (eds.), *Hellenistic Poetry in Context. Tenth International Workshop on Hellenistic Poetry, Groningen 25th–27th August 2010* (Leuven: Peeters, 2014c), 325–41.

Strootman, R. 'Hellenistic imperialism and the idea of world unity' in C. Rapp and H. Drake (eds.), *The City in the Classical and Post-Classical World. Changing Contexts of Power and Identity* (Cambridge University Press, 2014d), 38–61.

Strootman, R. *The Birdcage of the Muses. Patronage of the Arts and Sciences at the Ptolemaic Imperial Court, 305–222 BCE* (Leuven: Peeters, 2017).

Strootman, R. 'Antiochos IV and Rome. The festival at Daphne (Syria), the Treaty of Apameia and the revival of Seleukid expansionism in the West' in A. Coşkun and D. Engels (eds.), *Rome and the Seleukid East. Select Papers from Seleukid Study Day V, Université Libre de Bruxelles, 21–23 Aug. 2015* (Brussels: Éditions Latomus, 2019a), 173–216.

Strootman, R. 'Regalità e vita di corte in età ellenistica' in M. Mari (ed.), *L'età ellenistica. Società, politica, cultura* (Rome: Carocci, 2019b), 133–44.

Strootman, R. '"To be magnanimous and grateful". The entanglement of cities and empires in the Hellenistic Aegean' in M. Domingo-Gygax and A. Zuiderhoek (eds.), *Benefactors and the Polis. Origins and Development of the Public Gift in the Greek Cities. From the Homeric World to Late Antiquity* (Cambridge University Press, in press).

Strootman, R. 'The introduction of Hellenic cults in Seleukid Syria. Colonial appropriation and transcultural exchange in the creation of an imperial landscape' in H. Bru and A. Dumitru (eds.), *Colonial Geopolitics and Local Cultures in the Hellenistic and Roman East (IIIrd Century B.C.–IIIrd century A.D.)* (forthcoming).

Svenson, D. *Darstellungen hellenistischer Könige mit Götterattributen* (Frankfurt a. M.: Lang, 1995).

Svoronos, I. N. Τα νομίσματα του κράτους των Πτολεμαίων (Athens: Sakellarios, 1904).

Swinnen, W. 'Sur la politique religieuse de Ptolémée Ier' in *Les Syncrétismes dans les religions grecque et romaine* (Paris: Presses Universitaires de France, 1973), 115–33.

Syon, D. *Small Change in Hellenistic-Roman Galilee. The Evidence from Numismatic Site Finds as a Tool for Historical Reconstruction* (Jerusalem: Israel Numismatic Society, 2015).

Syon, D. *Gamla III: The Smnarya Gutmann Excavations 1976–1989. Finds and Studies Part 2* (Jerusalem: Israel Antiquities Authority, 2016).

Szelényi-Graziotto, K. 'Der Kult in Babylon in seleukidischer Zeit – Tradition oder Wandel?' in B. Funck (ed.), *Hellenismus. Beiträge zur Erforschung von Akkulturation und politischer Ordnung in den Staaten des hellenistischen Zeitalters. Akten des Internationalen Hellenismus-Kolloquiums, 9.–14. März 1994 in Berlin* (Tübingen: Mohr, 1996), 171–92.

Tarn, W. W. *The Greeks in Bactria and India* (Cambridge University Press, 1938 [2nd ed., 1938]).
Taylor, J. E. 'A second temple in Egypt: The evidence for the Zadokite temple of Onias', *Journal for the Study of Judaism, 29*.3 (1998), 297–321.
Thiers, C. *Ptolémée Philadelphe et les prêtres d'Atoum de Tjékou. Nouvelle édition commentée de la "Stèle de Pithom" (CGC 22183)* (Montpellier: Université Paul-Valéry Montpellier III, 2007).
Thiers, C. *La stèle de Ptolémée VIII Évergète II à Héracléion* (Oxford: OCMA, 2009).
Thissen, H. J. *Studien zum Raphiadekret* (Meisenheim a. Glan: A. Hain, 1966).
Thomas, R. *Eine postume Statuette Ptolemaios' IV. und ihr historischer Kontext. Zur Götterangleichung hellenistischer Herrscher* (Mainz: von Zabern, 2002).
Thomas, R. 'Herrscher und Gott. Zur Götterangleichung in hellenistischen Herrscherdarstellungen' in M. Fano Santi (ed.), *Studi in archeologia in onore di Gustavo Traversari, Archaeologica, 141* (Rome: Bretschneider, 2004), 829–48.
Thompson (Crawford), D. J. 'The Idumaeans of Memphis and the Ptolemaic *politeumata*' in International Congress of Papyrologists (ed.) *Atti del XVII Congresso Internazionale di Papirologia (Napoli, 19–26 maggio 1983)* (Napoli: Centro Internazionale per lo Studio dei Papiri Ercolanesi, 1984), 1069–75.
Thompson, D. J. *Memphis under the Ptolemies* (Princeton University Press, 1988 [2nd ed., 2012]).
Thompson, D. J. 'The high priests of Memphis under Ptolemaic rule' in M. Beard and J. North (eds.), *Pagan Priests. Religion and Power in the Ancient World* (Ithaca, NY: Cornell University Press, 1990), 95–116.
Thompson, D. J. 'Hellenistic Hellenes. The case of Ptolemaic Egypt' in I. Malkin (ed.), *Ancient Perceptions of Greek Ethnicity* (Washington, DC: Center for Hellenic Studies, Trustees for Harvard University, 2001), 301–22.
Thompson, D. J. 'Ethnic minorities in Hellenistic Egypt' in O. M. van Nijf and R. Alston (eds.), *Political Culture in the Greek City after the Classical Age* (Leuven: Peeters, 2011a), 101–17.
Thompson, D. J. 'The sons of Ptolemy V in a post-secession world' in A. Jördens and J. F. Quack (eds.), *Ägypten zwischen innerem Zwist und äußerem Druck. Die Zeit Ptolemaios' VI. bis VIII. Internationales Symposion Heidelberg 16.–19.9. 2007* (Wiesbaden: Harrassowitz, 2011b), 10–23.
Thompson, D. J. and Buraselis, K. 'Introduction' in K. Buraselis, M. Stefanou, and D. J. Thompson (eds.) *The Ptolemies, the Sea and the Nile. Studies in Waterborne Power* (Cambridge University Press, 2013), 1–18.
Thonemann, P. *Attalid Asia Minor: Money, International Relations, and the State* (Oxford; New York, 2013).
Thonemann, P. *The Hellenistic World. Using Coins as Sources* (Cambridge University Press, 2015).
Tilly, C. *Coercion, Capital, and European States, AD 990–1992* (Malden, MA: Blackwell, 1992).
Tober, D. 'Greek local historiography and its audiences', *CQ, 67*.2 (2017), 460–84.

Tolini, G. 'Le discours de domination de Cyrus, de Darius Ier et d'Alexandre le Grand sur la Babylonie (539–323)' in C. Feyel et al. (eds.), *Communautés locales et pouvoir central dans l'Orient hellénistique et romain* (Nancy: ADRA, 2012), 259–96.

Tondriau, J. 'Dionysos, dieu royale. Du Bacchos tauromorphe primitif aux souverains hellénistiques Neoi Dionysoi', *Pagkarpeia. Mélanges H. Grégoire*, vol. 4 (Brussels: Secrétariat des Éditions de l'Institut, 1953), 441–66.

Török, L. *Between Two Worlds: The Frontier Region between Ancient Nubia and Egypt, 3700 BC–AD 500* (Leiden: Brill, 2009).

Trümpy, C. *Untersuchungen zu den altgriechischen Monatsnamen und Monatsfolgen* (Heidelberg: Winter, 1997).

Tschopp, S. S. and Weber, W. E. J. (eds.), *Macht und Kommunikation. Augsburger Studien zur europäischen Kulturgeschichte* (Berlin: Akademie-Verlag, 2012).

Tuplin, C. 'The Seleucids and their Achaemenid predecessors. A Persian inheritance?' in S. M. R. Darbandi and A. Zournatzi (eds.), *Ancient Greece and Ancient Iran. Cross-Cultural Encounters* (Athens: National Hellenistic Research Foundation, 2009), 109–36.

Tuplin, C. 'Berossos and Greek historiography' in J. Haubold, G. B. Lanfranchi, R. Rollinger, and J. M. Steele (eds.), *The World of Berossos. Proceedings of the 4th International Colloquium on "The Ancient Near East between Classical and Ancient Oriental Traditions", Hatfield College, Durham 7th–9th July 2010* (Wiesbaden: Harrassowitz, 2013), 177–97.

van de Mieroop, M. *A History of Ancient Egypt* (Malden, MA: Wiley-Blackwell, 2011).

van de Mieroop, M. *Philosophy before the Greeks. The Pursuit of Truth in Ancient Babylonia* (Princeton University Press, 2016).

van der Horst, P. W. 'Antediluvian knowledge. Jewish speculations about wisdom from before the flood in their ancient context' in H. Lichtenberger and G. S. Oegema (eds.), *Jüdische Schriften in ihrem antik-jüdischen und urchristlichen Kontext* (Gütersloh: Gütersloher Verlag, 2002), 163–81.

van der Spek, R. J. 'The Babylonian Temple during the Macedonian and Parthian domination', *Bibliotheca Orientalis*, 42 (1985), 541–62.

van der Spek, R. J. 'The Babylonian city' in A. Kuhrt and S. M. Sherwin-White (eds.), *Hellenism in the East. The Interaction of Greek and Non-Greek Civilisations from Syria to Central Asia after Alexander* (Berkeley, CA: University of California Press, 1987), 57–74.

van der Spek, R. J. 'The Šatammus of Esagila in the Seleucid and Arsacid periods' in J. Marzahn and H. Neumann (eds.), *Assyriologica et Semitica. Festschrift für Joachim Oelsner anläßlich seines 65. Geburtstages am 18. Februar 1997* (Münster: Ugarit 2000), 437–46.

van der Spek, R. J. 'The theatre of Babylon in cuneiform' in W. H. van Soldt et al. (eds.), *Veenhof Anniversary Volume. Studies Presented to Klaas. R. Veenhof on the Occasion of His Sixty-Fifth Birthday* (Leiden: Nederlands Instituut voor het Nabije Oosten, 2001), 445–56.

van der Spek, R. J. 'Ethnic segregation in Hellenistic Babylon' in W. H. van Soldt (ed.), *Ethnicity in Ancient Mesopotamia. Papers Read at the 48th Rencontre*

Assyriologique Internationale, Leiden, 1–4 July 2002 (Leiden: Nederlands Instituut voor het Nabije Oosten, 2005), 393–408.

van der Spek, R. J. 'The size and significance of the Babylonian temples during the Successors' in P. Briant and F. Joannès (eds.), *La transition entre l'empire achéménide et les royaumes hellénistiques (vers 350–300 av. J.-C.)* (Paris: de Boccard, 2006), 261–307.

van Dijk, J. 'Die Inschriftenfunde' in H. J. Lenzen (ed.), *XVIII. vorläufiger Bericht über die von dem Deutschen Archäologischen Institut und der Deutschen Orient-Gesellschaft aus Mitteln der Deutschen Forschungsgemeinschaft unternommenen Ausgrabungen in Uruk-Warka* (Berlin: Mann, 1962), 39–62.

van Dijk, J. 'Die Tontafelfunde der Kampagne 1959/60', *AfO*, 20 (1963), 217–8.

Van't Dack, E. 'Sur l'évolution des institutions militaires lagides' in *Armée et fiscalité dans le monde antique. Actes du colloque, Paris 14–16 Octobre 1976* (Paris: CNRS, 1977), 77–105.

Van't Dack, E. 'Notice au sujet de *SB* I 1106' in International Congress of Papyrologists (ed.) *Atti del XVII Congresso Internazionale di Papirologia (Napoli, 19–26 maggio 1983)*, vol. 3 (Napoli: Centro Internazionale per lo Studio dei Papiri Ercolanesi, 1984), 1325–33.

Van't Dack, E. *Ptolemaica Selecta. Études sur l'armée et l'administration lagides* (Leuven: Peeters, 1988).

Van't Dack, E., Clarysse, W., Cohen, G., Quaegebeur, J. and Winnicki, J. K. *The Judean-Syrian-Egyptian Conflict of 103–101 B.C. A multilingual Dossier Concerning a "War of Sceptres"* (Brussels: Verhandelingen van de Koninklijke Academie van Wetenschappen, Letteren en Schone Kunsten van België, 1989).

Vandorpe, K. 'City of many a gate, harbour for many a rebel. Historical and topographical outline of Greco-Roman Thebes' in S. P. Vleeming (ed.), *Hundred-Gated Thebes. Acts of a Colloquium on Thebes and the Theban Area in the Graeco-Roman Period* (Leiden: Brill, 1995), 203–39.

Vandorpe, K. 'Paying taxes to the *thesauroi* of the Pathyrites in a century of rebellion (186–88 BC)' in L. Mooren (ed.), *Politics, Administration and Society in the Hellenistic and Roman World. Proceedings of the International Colloquium, Bertinoro 19–24 July 1997* (Leuven: Peeters, 2000a), 405–35.

Vandorpe, K. 'The Ptolemaic epigraphe or harvest tax (*shemu*)', *ArchPF*, 46.2 (2000b), 169–232.

Vandorpe, K. 'Agriculture, temples and tax law in Ptolemaic Egypt', *Cahier de recherche de l'Institut de Papyrologie et d'Égyptologie de Lille*, 25 (2005), 165–71.

Vandorpe, K. 'Persian soldiers and Persians of the Epigone. Social mobility of soldiers-herdsmen in Upper Egypt', *ArchPF*, 54.1 (2008), 87–108.

Vandorpe, K. 'The Ptolemaic period' in A. B. Lloyd (ed.), *A Companion to Ancient Egypt*, vol. 1 (Malden, MA: Wiley-Blackwell, 2010) 159–79.

Vandorpe, K. 'A successful, but fragile biculturalism. The Hellenization process in the Upper-Egyptian town of Pathyris under Ptolemy VI and VIII' in A. Jördens and J. F. Quack (eds.), *Ägypten zwischen innerem Zwist und äußerem Druck. Die Zeit Ptolemaios' VI. bis VIII. Internationales Symposion Heidelberg 16.–19.9. 2007* (Wiesbaden: Harrassowitz, 2011), 292–308.

Vandorpe, K. 'The Ptolemaic army in Upper Egypt (2nd–1st centuries B.C.)' in A.-E. Veïsse and S. Wackenier (eds.), *L'Armée en Égypte aux époques perse, ptolémaïque et romaine* (Geneva: Droz, 2014), 105–35.

Vandorpe, K. and Waebens, S. *Reconstructing Pathyris' Archives. A Multicultural Community in Hellenistic Egypt* (Brussels: Koninklijke Vlaamse Academie van België voor Wetenschappen en Kunsten, 2009).

Varoucha-Christodoulopoulou, E. 'Symbolê eis ton Chreimonideion Polemon', *ArchEph* (1953–4), 321–49.

Vasunia, P. *The Gift of the Nile. Hellenizing Egypt from Aeschylos to Alexander* (Berkeley, CA: University of California Press, 2001).

Veïsse, A.-E. *Les "révoltes égyptiennes". Recherches sur les troubles intérieurs en Égypte du règne de Ptolémée III Évergète à la conquête romaine* (Leuven: Peeters, 2004).

Veïsse, A.-E. 'L'"ennemi des dieux" Harsièsis', in A. Jördens and J. F. Quack (eds.), *Ägypten zwischen innerem Zwist und äußerem Druck. Die Zeit Ptolemaios' VI. bis VIII. Internationales Symposion Heidelberg 16.–19.9. 2007* (Wiesbaden: Harrassowitz, 2011), 92–102.

Veïsse, A.-E. 'Retour sur les révoltes égyptiennes' in G. Charpentier and V. Puech (eds.), *Villes et campagnes aux rives de la Méditerranée ancienne. Hommages à Georges Tate* (Lyon: Maison de l'Orient et de la Méditerranée, 2013), 507–16.

Veïsse, A.-E. 'The Great Theban Revolt, 206–186 BC' in I. Moyer and P. Kosmin (eds.), *Cultures of Resistance in the Hellenistic East* (Oxford University Press, forthcoming a).

Veïsse, A.-E. 'De la « Grande Révolte de la Thébaïde » aux événements de 88 : un siécle d'insurrection thébaine ?' in R. Birk and L. Coulon (eds.), *The Thebaid in Times of Crisis* (Le Caire: IFAO, forthcoming b).

Verbrugghe, G. P. and Wickersham, J. M. *Berossos and Manetho, introduced and translated. Native Traditions in Ancient Mesopotamia and Egypt* (Ann Arbor, MI: University of Michigan Press, 1996).

Verhoogt, A. M. F. W. *Regaling Ptolemaic Officials. A Dramatic Reading of Official Accounts from the Menches Papers* (Leiden: Brill, 2005).

Versnel, H. S. *Triumphus. An Inquiry into the Origin, Development and Meaning of the Roman Triumph* (Leiden: Brill, 1970).

Vittmann, G. '"Feinde" in den ptolemäischen Synodaldekreten. Mit einem Anhang: Demotische Termini für "Feind", "Rebell", "rebellieren"' in H. Felber (ed.), *Feinde und Aufrührer. Konzepte von Gegnerschaft in ägyptischen Texten besonders des Mittleren Reiches* (Leipzig: Verlag der Sächsischen Akademie der Wissenschaften zu Leipzig, 2005), 198–219.

Vleeming, S. P. *Some Coins of Artaxerxes and Other Short Texts in the Demotic Script Found on Various Objects Gathered from Many Publications* (Leuven: Peeters, 2001).

von den Hoff, R. *Philosophenporträts des Früh- und Hochhellenismus* (Munich: Biering und Brinkmann, 1994).

von den Hoff, R. 'Naturalism and classicism. Style and perception of early Hellenistic portraits' in R. von den Hoff and P. Schultz (eds.), *Early*

Hellenistic portraiture. Image, Style, Context (Cambridge University Press, 2007), 49–62.
von den Hoff, R. 'Alexanderporträts und Bildnisse frühhellenistischer Herrscher' in S. Hansen, A. Wieczorek, M. Tellenbach (eds.), *Alexander der Grosse und die Öffnung der Welt. Asiens Kulturen im Wandel* (Regensburg: Schnell & Steiner, 2009), 47–53.
von den Hoff, R. 'Bildniskopf des Antiochos IV. von Syrien (1975.5)' in Antikensammlung Berlin (ed.), *Gesamtkatalog der Skulpturen* (Köln: online 2013a) http://arachne.uni-koeln.de/item/objekt/104179.
von den Hoff, R. 'Alexanderbildnisse und imitatio Alexandri in Baktrien' in G. Lindström, S. Hansen, A. Wieczorek and M. Tellenbach (eds.), *Zwischen Ost und West. Neue Forschungen zum antiken Zentralasien*. Wissenschaftliches Kolloquium 30.9–2.10.2009 in Mannheim (Darmstadt: von Zabern, 2013b), 83–98.
von den Hoff, R. 'König, Tyrann, Bürger, Heros, Gott. Bilder von Monarchen in der visuellen Kultur des antiken Griechenland' in S. Rebenich (ed.), *Monarchische Herrschaft im Altertum* (Berlin: de Gruyter, 2017), 263–304.
von den Hoff, R. and Azoulay, V. 'Dissémination. Statues-portraits multiples et diffusion sur d'autres médias' in F. Queyrel and R. von den Hoff (eds.), *Eikones. La vie des portraits grecs. Ve– Ier siècles av. J.-C.* (Paris: Hermann, 2017), 151–94.
von den Hoff, R. and Schultz, P. (eds.) *Early Hellenistic portraiture. Image, Style, Context* (Cambridge University Press, 2007).
von Recklinghausen, D. *Die Philensis Dekrete. Untersuchungen über zwei Synodaldekrete aus der Zeit Ptolemaios' V. und ihre geschichtliche und religiöse Bedeutung* (Wiesbaden: Harrassowitz, 2018).
von Reden, S. 'The politics of monetization in third-century BC Egypt' in A. R. Meadows and K. Shipton (eds.), *Money and Its Uses in the Ancient Greek World* (Oxford University Press 2001), 65–76.
von Reden, S. *Money in Ptolemaic Egypt. From the Macedonian Conquest to the End of the Third Century BC* (Cambridge University Press, 2007).
von Reden, S. *Money in Classical Antiquity* (Cambridge University Press, 2010).
von Reden, S. 'The Hellenistic empires' in dies', M. Dwivedi, L. Fabian, L. Morris and E. J. S. Weaverdyck (eds.) *Handbook of Ancient Afro-Eurasian Economies. Vol. 1: Contexts* (Berlin: de Gruyter, 2019), 15–51.
Vorster, C. 'Das Porträt im vorhellenistischen Griechenland – eine Standortbestimmung' in D. Boschung and F. Queyrel (eds.), *Bilder der Macht. Das griechische Porträt und seine Verwendung in der antiken Welt* (Paderborn: Wilhelm Fink, 2017), 15–48.
Voulgaridis, G. 'Les ateliers monétaires de Ptolémaïs-'Akko et d'Ascalon sous la domination séleucide', unpublished Ph.D. diss., Université Marc Bloch, Strasbourg (2000).
Waage, D. B. *Antioch-on-the-Orontes, Vol. 4.2: Greek, Roman, Byzantine and Crusaders' Coins* (Princeton University Press, 1952).
Waerzeggers, C. 'The Babylonian revolts against Xerxes and the "end of archives"', *AfO*, 50 (2003–2004), 150–73.

Wallerstein, I. *The Modern World System, vol. 1: Capitalist Agriculture and the Origins of the European World-Economy in the Sixteenth Century* (Cambridge University Press, 1974).

Wallerstein, I. *World-Systems Analysis. An Introduction* (Durham, NC: Duke University Press, 2004).

Wardle, D. *Cicero on Divination. De Divinatione Book 1 Translated with Introduction and Historical Commentary* (Oxford University Press, 2006).

Weber, G. 'Die neuen Zentralen. Hauptstädte, Residenzen, Paläste und Höfe' in id. (ed.), *Kulturgeschichte des Hellenismus. Von Alexander dem Großen bis Kleopatra* (Stuttgart: Klett-Cotta, 2007), 99–118.

Weber, G. 'Der ptolemäische Herrscher- und Dynastiekult. Ein Experimentierfeld für Makedonen, Griechen und Ägypter' in L.-M. Günther and S. Plischke (eds.), *Studien zum vorhellenistischen und hellenistischen Herrscherkult* (Berlin: Verlag Antike, 2011), 77–97.

Weber, G. 'Mächtige Könige und mächtige Priester? Kommunikation und Legitimation im ptolemäischen Ägypten' in S. S. Tschopp and W. E. J. Weber (eds.), *Macht und Kommunikation. Augsburger Studien zur europäischen Kulturgeschichte* (Berlin: Akademie Verlag, 2012), 13–37.

Weitzman, S. 'Plotting Antiochus's persecution', *JBL*, 123.2 (2004), 219–34.

Wells, R. *Sigmund Freud and Art. His Personal Collection of Antiquities* (London: Freud Museum, 1989).

Wells, R. and Ueno, Y. *Freud as Collector. A Loan Exhibition from the Freud Museum* (London: Gallery Mikazuki, 1996).

Westermark, U. *Das Bildnis des Philetairos von Pergamon. Corpus der Münzprägung* (Stockholm: Almqvist & Wiksell, 1961).

Whitehouse, D. 'Excavations at Kandahar, 1974: First Interim Report,' *Afghan Studies* 1 (1978), 9–39.

Whitehouse, J. 'Women's Work in Theocritus, *Idyll 15*' *Hermes*, 123 (1995), 63–75.

Wildung, D. and Grimm, G. *Götter, Pharaonen* (Mainz: von Zabern, 1979).

Will, E. 'La capitale des Séleucides' in *Akten des XIII. Internationalen Kongresses für klassische Archäologie, Berlin 1988* (Mainz: von Zabern, 1990), 259–65.

Will, E. *Histoire politique du monde hellénistique, 323–30 av. J.-C*, 2 vols. (Paris: Seuil, 2003).

Will, E., Mossé, C. and Goukowski, P. *Le monde grec et l'Orient, vol. 2: Le IVe siècle et l'époque hellénistique* (Paris: Presses Universitaire de France, 1993).

Winnicki, J. K. 'Petisis, Sohn des Pachnumis, Offizier und Priester an der Südgrenze Ägyptens im 2. Jh. v. Chr.', *JJurP*, 26 (1996), 127–34.

Winnicki, J. K. 'Zur Deutung des demotischen Papyrus Erbach' in K. Geus and K. Zimmermann (eds.), *Punica, Libyca, Ptolemaica. Festschrift für Werner Huß zum 65. Geburtstag dargebracht von Schülern, Freunden und Kollegen* (Leuven: Peeters, 2001), 311–21.

Winter, E. 'Der Herrscherkult in den ägyptischen Ptolemäertempeln' in H. Maehler and V. M. Strocka (eds.), *Das ptolemäische Ägypten. Akten des internationalen Symposions 27.–29. September 1976 in Berlin* (Mainz: von Zabern, 1978), 147–60.

Winter, E. 'Formen ptolemäischer Präsenz in der Ägäis zwischen schriftlicher Überlieferung und archäologischem Befund' in F. Daubner (ed.), *Militärsiedlungen und Territorialherrschaft in der Antike* (Berlin: de Gruyter, 2011), 65–77.
Wolf, D. 'A metrological survey of Ptolemaic bronze coins', *AJN*, 25 (2013), 49–118.
Wolf, D. and Lorber, C. 'The "Galatian shield without Σ" series of Ptolemaic bronze coins', *NC*, 171 (2011), 7–53.
Woods, C. 'Sons of the sun. The mythological foundations of the first dynasty of Uruk', *JANER*, 12 (2012), 78–96.
Wörrle, M. 'Eine hellenistische Inschrift aus Gadara', *Archäologischer Anzeiger*, no. 2 (2000), 265–71.
Worthington, I. *Ptolemy I. King and Pharaoh of Egypt* (Oxford University Press, 2016).
Woźniak, M. and Rądkowska, J. K. 'In search of Berenike of the Ptolemies. The Hellenistic fort of Berenike Trogodytika, its localization, form and development (part one)', *Polish Archaeology in the Mediterranean*, 23.1 (2014), 505–26.
Yap, J. P. *Wars with the Xiongnu. A Translation from Zizhi Tongjian* (Bloomington, IN: AuthorHouse, 2009).
Zanker, P. *Die Maske des Sokrates. Das Bild des Intellektuellen in der antiken Kunst* (Munich: Beck, 1995).
Zauzich, K.-T. 'Das Lamm des Bokchoris' in H. Loebenstein (ed.), *Papyrus Erzherzog Rainer (P. Rainer. Cent.). Festschrift zum 100-jährigen Bestehen der Papyrussammlung der Österreichischen Nationalbibliothek* (Vienna: Hollinek, 1983), 165–74.
Zavyalov, V. A. 'The fortifications of the city of Gyaur Kala, Merv' in J. Cribb and G. Herrmann (eds.), *After Alexander: Central Asia before Islam* (Oxford University Press, 2007), 313–32.
Zhou, R., An, L., Wang, X., Shao, W., Lin, G., Yu, W., Yi, L., Xu, S., Xu, J., Xie, X. 'Testing the hypothesis of an ancient Roman soldier origin of the Liqian people in northwest China. A Y-chromosome perspective', *Journal of Human Genetics*, 52 (2007), 584–91.
Zimmermann, K. 'Eratosthenes' chlamys-shaped world. A misunderstood metaphor' in D. Ogden (ed.) *The Hellenistic World. New Perspectives* (London: Duckworth, 2002), 23–40.
Zuckerman, C. 'Hellenistic *politeumata* and the Jews. A reconsideration (review article)', *Scripta Classica Israelica*, 8–9 (1985–8), 171–85.
Zych, I., Sidebotham, S. E., Hense, M., Rądkowska, J. K., and Woźniak, M. 'Archaeological fieldwork in Berenike in 2014 and 2015. From Hellenistic rock-cut installations to abandoned temple ruins', *Polish Archaeology in the Mediterranean*, 25 (2016), 315–48.

Index

Achaios, 53, 62, 287, 288
administration, 1, 6, 86
  local, 97, 103
  nome, 119, 120
  of temples, 9, 92, 93, 95, 96, 97, 101, 103
  politeuma, 110, 111
  Ptolemaic, 71, 83, 118, 123, 124
  religious, 94, 258
  royal, 92, 93, 94, 95, 96, 101, 103, 104, 193, 210, 263
  urban, 289
Aetos, 68, 274
Agathocles, 271, 274–5
agora, 20, 27, 66, 70, 77
Ai Khanoum, 36, 53, 58–9, 62
  mint, 193, 194
akitu-festival, 252–3, 258, 261
Alexander I Balas
  and the Maccabees, 305, 319
  coin portraits of, 185
  coinage, 201, 203, 225
Alexander II Zabinas
  coin portraits of, 186
  coinage, 204
Alexander III (the Great), 1, 2, 4, 20, 21, 29, 159, 161
  administration, 57
  anastole, 168, 178, 183–7
  and Babylon, 86, 89, 90, 95, 247, 253–5
  birth of, 28
  coin portraits of, 168
  coinage, 185, 191, 206, 214
  cult of, 150
  death, 129
  divinity, 28
  foundation of Alexandria, 19, 25, 29, 67
  king in Babylon, 256
  legacy of, 162
  portraits of, 168, 188
  priesthood of, 268
  religion, 12

settlement policy, 9
settlements, 49, 51, 54, 56, 57–8, 60, 84
Alexander IV, 4, 150, 159
Alexandria, 8, 17, 18–33, 64, 119, 123, 124, 149, 152
  architecture, 43
  capital, 34
  coinage, 203, 214, 215, 217, 219, 222, 226
  court, 273, 274
  decree, 97
  development under Ptolemy I, 34, 67
  foundation, 49
  mint, 208–9, 213, 221
  politeuma, 106, 110, 123
  settlers, 62
  synods, 89, 245
  taxation, 226
  tomb of Alexander, 36
Alexandria (in Arachosia), 53, 55
Alexandria (in Margiana), 53, 54
Alexandria (in Sakastene), 53
Alexandria (in the Caucasus), 53, 57, 60
Alexandria (Oxeiana), 53, 59
Alexandria Eschate, 60
Anaxikles, 278
Andronomos, son of Sotades, 100
Antigonids, 254, 258
Antigonus Monophthalmus, 4, 61
Antioch, 24, 35, 37, 39, 40, 41, 43, 44
  coinage, 198, 203–5
  foundation, 6, 38, 49
  mint, 11, 192, 196, 197, 206, 208–9
  political center, 8, 18, 35, 37
  Ptolemaic conquest, 266
Antiochia-Kydnos. *See* Tarsos
Antiochia-Pyramos, 281–3
Antiochus I, 53, 59
  portraits, 187
Antiochus I Soter, 23, 58, 62, 132, 135, 144, 256
  as co-regent, 61, 63
  as crown prince, 257, 261
  city foundations, 6, 38, 54

coin portraits of, 170
coinage, 170, 193, 202
cylinder, 248–52
ideology, 36
king of Babylon, 249
Antiochus II Theos, 94, 135, 144
and Babylon, 95, 252
coin portraits of, 170
coinage, 193, 195
Antiochus III the Great, 37, 89, 92, 278
and Asia Minor, 292
and Babylon, 252, 259
and Jerusalem, 280
and local elites, 280, 284
and Rome, 13
and the Jews, 133
city foundations, 38, 281
coinage, 198, 203, 225, 228
conquest of Syria and Phoenicia, 265, 272, 277
court, 132
in Asia Minor, 281
portraits of, 175, 188
Roman defeat of, 285, 287, 300
royal cult, 131
taxation, 198
wars, 5, 13
Antiochus IV Epiphanes, 8, 37, 44, 46, 89, 133, 142
and Babylon, 260
and Jerusalem, 305
and the Jews, 134, 306, 317
city foundations, 38, 280
coin portraits of, 178, 183, 184
coinage, 193, 196, 198, 199, 200, 201, 203, 208, 226
Daphne festival, 42, 44, 45
invasion of Egypt, 5, 75
portraits of, 178, 180
reforms, 97, 99
reign, 37, 262
settlements, 83
taxation, 200
Antiochus IX Cyzicenus
coinage, 201, 207
Antiochus V Eupator
and the Jews, 305, 314, 318
coinage, 196, 200
portraits of, 180
Antiochus VII Sidetes, 133
coinage, 201, 203, 204, 205, 209, 327
siege of Jerusalem, 133, 327
Antiochus VIII Grypus
coinage, 201, 207
Apamea, 24
coinage, 203
foundation, 6, 38, 75, 77
peace of, 287, 288, 294, 309, 311
Apis, 41, 99
Apollo, 38, 42, 43
and Daphne, 39, 42
of Didyma, 61, 63
on coinage, 193
apomoira, 94, 98
Arsinoe II, 72, 153, 322
coin portraits of, 171
coinage, 215, 217, 223
Arsinoe III
portraits of, 181
Arsinoite nome, 106, 118, 121, 212
Asia Minor, 5, 12, 114, 285
and Rome, 292
coinage, 171, 196, 206, 207, 218–19
Greek cities of, 280
mints, 193
Seleucid loss of, 199
Seleucid rule of, 119, 288

Babylon, 6, 9, 35, 88, 94, 99, 144, 247
administration, 93
as *polis*, 89, 95, 96, 99, 281
conquest, 89
palace, 37
political reforms, 97
population, 101
reforms, 99
temples, 86
Babylonians
assembly of, 90
Bactria, 23, 49, 60, 61, 62, 63
mint, 193
baths, 65, 66, 70, 71, 74, 81
Begram, 53, 57–8
Berenice Troglodytica, 64, 72, 73
Berossus, 10, 134–43, 144, 145, 147
Boeotians, 106, 108, 110, 111
Boethos, 75–8, 82, 84, 119
Borsippa, 86, 88, 257, 259
cylinder, 248–52, 256
bronze standard, 224, 227

Canopus decree, 12, 79, 149, 239, 240, 246, 250
Chaonnophris, 302, 304, 315, 317
chora, 149, 211, 271
Cilicia, 68, 73
Cleopatra I, 198
dowry, 225
Cleopatra II, 77, 97, 153, 323
Cleopatra III, 77, 97
coinage, 222
cleruchs, 66, 69, 113, 114, 117, 120, 121, 122, 126
cleruchy, 10, 114, 121

Index

closed monetary zone, 191, 197, 198, 199, 200, 201, 211, 214, 217, 225
coinage, 3, 7, 11
  bronze, 191, 227
    Ptolemaic, 205, 211–13, 215, 217–25, 227–30, 307
    Seleucid, 45, 58, 192–5, 198–9, 203–5, 279
  civic, 196
  coin policy, 11
  gold, 64
  hoards, 195, 198, 205, 206, 207, 208, 212, 218, 220, 222, 225, 226
  minting, 192–5, 214, 216
  Ptolemaic, 168, 217
  quasi-municipal, 193, 199, 200, 201, 203, 209
  Seleucid 'eagles', 169, 201, 209, 227, 229
  silver, 197, 198, 200, 211, 217
  Yehud, 213, 214
colonization, 48, 52, 55
communication, 1, 2, 3, 4, 7, 10, 11, 13, 233, 247, 248, 262, 263, 265, 268, 275, 277
comparison, 1, 2, 8, 9, 327
core-periphery, 3, 6, 7, 13
Crocodilopolis, 71, 75, 118, 323 *See* Ptolemais Euergetis (Arsinoite)
Cyprus, 5, 12, 23, 174, 322
  coinage, 217–18, 222, 223
Cyrenaica, 5, 9, 12, 67, 114, 116, 119, 290, 322
  coinage, 219–20, 229

Daphne festival, 43–6
Demetrius I Soter
  and the Jews,
  coin portraits of, 183
  coinage, 196, 203, 204, 205, 206, 229
Demetrius II Nicator
  and the Jews, 318
  coinage, 201, 202, 203
double (jugate) portraits, 172, 184, 185, 189
dynastic cult, 76, 89, 92, 94, 150, 152, 153, 155, 220

Elephantine, 64, 65, 72, 76, 77, 78–80, 239
elites, 91
  civic, 44, 46, 284
  indigenous, 147, 148, 149, 150, 152, 153, 157, 160, 161, 162, 163
  local, 1, 2, 4, 6, 7, 9, 10, 12, 20, 65, 81, 82, 83, 84, 85, 90–1, 95, 97, 101, 103, 132, 152, 201, 229, 233, 262, 284
  Phoenician, 269
  political, 13, 91, 101, 263, 298
  religious, 7, 9, 72, 87, 89, 91, 95, 102, 103, 104, 233, 248, 251
empires, multi-ethnic, 1, 4
entanglement, 1, 7, 11, 18, 33, 46

Esagil temple, 87, 90, 92, 94, 95, 97, 98, 135, 248–52, 256, 259, 281
Euergetis (Heracleopolite), 75, 76–8, 83, 119–20

Fayyum, 23, 69, 70, 71, 75, 307
foundation myths, 17, 20, 25, 29, 32, 38–43
founder *(ktistes)*, 67, 76, 77, 119, 150, 153

Grand Procession, 21, 44, 45
Great Revolt, 5, 13, 75, 81, 120, 213, 301, 303, 307–9, 315–16, 317, 320–6
gymnasium, 71, 81, 84

Haronnophris, 303, 309, 315, 317, 321, 323, 328
Hasmoneans. *See* Maccabees
Heracleopolis, 157, 158, 159, 160
Heracleopolite *nome*, 77, 107, 116, 118, 120
Hermopolis, 70, 71, 102
Hermopolite *nome*, 100, 118

Jason, high priest of Jerusalem, 304, 309, 310, 311, 313
Jerusalem, 133
  mint, 327
  siege of, 133
John Hyrcanus, 115, 304, 305, 313, 320, 327
  coinage, 327
Jonathan Maccabee, 305, 311, 313
Judas Maccabee, 305, 314, 317
  refoundation of the Jewish temple, 304

Kandahar, 53, 55–6, 57

Maccabean revolt, 5, 13, 115, 200, 227, 229, 301, 309–11, 312–15, 318–20, 327
Manetho, 10, 151, 154–6
Margiana, 50, 52, 54, 55
Memphis, 6, 8, 17, 21, 25, 27, 32, 46, 91, 244, 247, 261
  decree, 250
  polis, 72
  politeuma, 106
  population, 26
  priests, 12
Menelaus, high priest of Jerusalem, 304, 309, 311, 313, 317
Merv, 35, 53–5, 59
metropolis, 17, 21, 25, 29, 33, 67, 72, 84

Nectanebids, 10, 88, 94, 95, 154
nome, 79, 122, 237, 243
nome capitals *(metropoleis)*, 65, 66, 67, 71, 75, 79, 80, 81, 84, 112, 118, 119, 121, 123

Onias III, high priest of Jerusalem, 304, 311, 313, 317

Philae, 72, 79, 102, 240
Pithom stele, 72, 73, 84, 246, 259
poliadisation, 83, 89, 95, 97, 99, 100, 102, 103, 104, 310
polis
  Babylon/Babylonia, 49, 89, 95
  citizens, 96, 109, 124
  Greco-Egyptian, 67, 74, 81, 83, 84
  Greek, 10, 199, 284
  of Jerusalem, 13, 304, 310, 312, 327
  political, 65, 67, 68, 69, 73, 74, 75, 76, 77, 82, 83, 85
  Ptolemaic, 64, 65, 66, 67–9, 71, 75–8, 82, 119–26, 152
  Seleucid, 83, 200, 230
  symbolic, 78–80, 82
  of Thebes, 80, 81
politeuma, 7, 9, 49, 82, 106–26
polity, 2, 3, 4, 5, 33, 43, 44, 106, 213
priests/priesthoods, 233
  Babylonian, 92, 246–61
  Egyptian, 30, 31, 73, 76, 78, 79, 82, 91, 102, 124, 154, 159, 160, 235–46, 302, 304, 308, 326
  eponymous, 150, 151, 155, 161
  in politeumata, 111
  indigenous, 233, 236, 246, 256
  of Amun, 99
  of Jerusalem, 304, 310, 311, 314, 317, 318, 320
  of Memphis, 245, 246
  of Ptah, 98, 99, 261
  of royal cult, 283
  Seleucid, 131
Ptolemaios son of Thraseas, 274, 279, 280
Ptolemais Euergetis (Arsinoite), 73, 75, 79
Ptolemais (Hermiou), 6, 64, 65, 67, 119, 124, 152
Ptolemais Theron, 72, 73
Ptolemy I Soter, 12, 21, 31, 32, 41, 159, 235
  and Serapis, 29–33
  as satrap, 4
  coin portraits of, 169, 189
  coinage, 205, 210
  dating, 150
  portraits of, 165, 166–9
  religious policy, 235
  settlements, 69, 121
  temple (re)foundation, 70
Ptolemy II Philadelphus, 21, 69, 150, 153
  coin portraits of, 171 *See* Grand Procession
  coinage, 201, 205, 211, 212
  conquests, 23
  court, 41
  development of Alexandria, 142, 143
  portraits of, 174, 175
  reforms, 98, 151, 211, 216, 311
  religion, 94, 98, 99
  settlements, 49, 67, 72, 121
Ptolemy III Euergetes, 89, 99, 113, 266–70 *See* Syrian Wars, Third, Caopus decree
  coin portraits of, 173, 180
  coinage, 201, 212, 215, 218, 219, 220
  conquests, 32
  Euergetes gate, 99, 241
  'gate of Euergetes', 241
  settlements, 49, 67, 68
  temple construction, 102
  temple dedication, 70
  uprising against, 238
Ptolemy IV Philopator, 270–2
  coin portraits of, 180
  coinage, 212, 219
  court, 275
  dating, 149
  iconography, 242
  losses, 264
  portraits of, 181, 183, 188
  settlements, 75
  victory at Raphia, 5
Ptolemy V Epiphanes, 13 *See also* Great Revolt
  coin portraits of, 180
  coinage, 213, 227
  coronation, 244
  losses, 116, 264
  marriage, 198, 225
  rebellion against, 242
  settlements, 75
  taxation, 200
Ptolemy VI Philometor, 76, 79, 80, 114, 116, 118, 153
  and the Jews, 115
  civil war, 116
  coin portraits of, 182
  coinage, 203, 208, 222, 224, 226, 227, 228
  conquests, 76
  dating, 149
  portraits of, 175
  settlements, 49, 75, 76, 119
  temple construction, 80
Ptolemy VIII Euergetes II, 76, 77, 78, 79, 80
  amnesty decree, 97
  civil war, 116, 323–6
  coinage, 209, 222, 227
  Cyrenaica, 322
  iconography, 153
  portraits of, 183
  settlements, 49, 75, 119
  temple construction, 80
Ptolemy IX Soter II, 49, 78, 79, 80, 224, 228, 321

Ptolemy X Alexander I, 187, 222, 224, 322
Ptolemy the Son, 150, 151

Raphia, 5
  battle of, 89, 264, 270, 271, 272, 273, 307
  Decree, 260, 265, 277, 279
royal (ruler) cult, 10, 76, 98, 131, 178, 263, 267, 270, 289, 298

Second Philae Decree, 302, 304, 317
Seleucia-in-Pieria, 8, 32, 36, 71, 131, 273
  coinage, 203, 204
  foundation, 6, 38
Seleucia-on-the-Tigris, 11, 18, 24, 35, 36
  coinage, 205
  mint, 192
  political center, 35
  royal city, 37
Seleucid Era, 144, 146, 149, 150, 151, 157, 161, 162, 203, 228
Seleucus I Nicator, 10, 35, 36, 40, 53
  and Babylonian priests, 260
  as satrap, 4
  city foundations, 6
  coin portraits of, 170
  coinage, 194
  conquests, 61
  dating, 130
  divine parentage, 131
  in Central Asia, 61
  king of Babylon, 249
  portraits of, 166–9
  return to Babylon, 130, 147, 257
  settlements, 38, 43
  treaty with Chandragupta Maurya, 56
Seleucus II Callinicus
  coin portraits of, 170
  coinage, 195
Seleucus IV Philopator, 89, 131, 196
  and Asia Minor, 286
  coinage, 45, 198
  portraits of, 176
  reforms, 309

settlements, 83
Serapis, 21, 25, 27, 29–33, 38, 99, 181
settlement policy, 64, 65, 69, 85
  Ptolemaic, 68, 73, 75, 80, 83, 125
settlements, 7, 8, 9, 39, 48, 49, 52, 53, 59, 65, 68, 72, 74, 84
  cleruchic, 117
  Egyptian, 80
  Far East, 52, 63, 83
  Greek, 60
  Ptolemaic, 52, 64, 65, 66, 67, 69, 70, 83
  Red Sea basin, 72
synodal decrees, 12, 89, 97, 103, 234, 246, 248, 250
  See also individual decrees
syntaxis, 94, 200, 267, 308
Syrian Wars, 34
  First, 217
  Second, 214, 273
  Third, 215, 218, 220, 266, 268
  Fourth, 5, 273, 278, 279, 307, 309, 311, 327
  Fifth, 5, 75, 212, 216, 223, 273, 274, 278
  Sixth, 5, 133, 199, 200, 226

Tarsos, 175, 282
taxation, 1, 13, 92, 198, 211, 226, 267, 310
temples, 9, 70, 76, 99
  administration, 87, 88, 91, 96, 308
  (re)building, 12, 79, 255
  Egyptian, 73, 74, 79, 88, 91, 102, 150, 264
  (re)foundation, 70
Thebaid, 6, 13, 14, 76, 116, 118, 120, 301, 303, 311
  See Great Revolt
Thebes, 65, 72, 80–2, 99, 161
Thraseas (son of Aetos), 68, 268

Uruk, 87, 88, 96, 142, 247
  administration, 87, 89, 90, 93, 96, 144
  as *polis*, 96, 99
  Eanna temple, 87, 101, 256
  population, 101
  reforms, 99
  temple administration, 260

Made in the USA
Columbia, SC
03 July 2025